Middle School 3-2

학교시험 완벽대비

2학기 전과정

적중 100 plus

영어 기출문제집

중3

비상 | 김진완

Best Collection

KB087414

구성과 특징

교과서의 주요 학습 내용을 중심으로 학습 영역별 특성에 맞춰 단계별로 다양한 학습 기회를 제공하여
단원별 학습능력 평가는 물론 중간 및 기말고사 시험 등에 완벽하게 대비할 수 있도록 내용을 구성

Words & Expressions

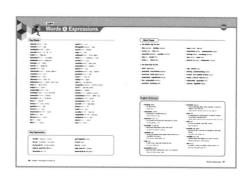

Step1   Key Words 단원별 핵심 단어 설명 및 풀이
        Key Expression 단원별 핵심 숙어 및 관용어 설명
        Word Power 반대 또는 비슷한 뜻 단어 배우기
        English Dictionary 영어로 배우는 영어 단어

Step2   실력평가 단원별 수시평가 대비 주관식, 객관식 문제풀이

Step3   서술형 대비 학업성취도 및 수행능력평가 대비 서술형 문제풀이

Conversation

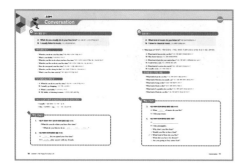

Step1   핵심 의사소통 소통에 필요한 주요 표현 방법 요약
        핵심 Check 기본적인 표현 방법 및 활용능력 확인

Step2   대화문 익히기 교과서 대화문 심층 분석 및 확인

Step3   교과서 확인학습 빈칸 채우기를 통한 문장 완성 능력 확인

Step4   기본평가 시험대비 기초 학습 능력 평가

Step5   실력평가 단원별 수시평가 대비 주관식, 객관식 문제풀이

Step6   서술형 대비 학업성취도 및 수행능력평가 대비 서술형 문제풀이

Grammar

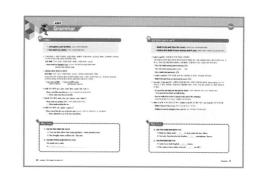

Step1   주요 문법 단원별 주요 문법 사항과 예문을 알기 쉽게 설명
        핵심 Check 기본 문법사항에 대한 이해 여부 확인

Step2   기본평가 시험대비 기초 학습 능력 평가

Step3   실력평가 단원별 수시평가 대비 주관식, 객관식 문제풀이

Step4   서술형 대비 학업성취도 및 수행능력평가 대비 서술형 문제풀이

Reading

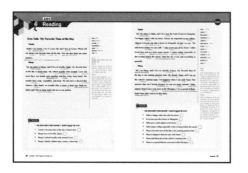

Step1   구문 분석 단원별로 제시된 문장에 대한 구문별 분석과 내용 설명
        확인문제 문장에 대한 기본적인 이해와 인지능력 확인

Step2   확인학습A 빈칸 채우기를 통한 문장 완성 능력 확인

Step3   확인학습B 제시된 우리말을 영어로 완성하여 작문 능력 키우기

Step4   실력평가 단원별 수시평가 대비 주관식, 객관식 문제풀이

Step5   서술형 대비 학업성취도 및 수행능력평가 대비 서술형 문제풀이
        교과서 구석구석 교과서에 나오는 기타 문장까지 완벽 학습

Composition

|영역별 핵심문제|

단어 및 어휘, 대화문, 문법, 독해 등 각 영역별 기출문제의 출제 유형을 분석하여 실전에 대비하고 연습할 수 있도록 문제를 배열

|단원별 예상문제|

기출문제를 분석한 후 새로운 시험 출제 경향을 더하여 새롭게 출제될 수 있는 문제를 포함하여 시험에 완벽하게 대비할 수 있도록 준비

|서술형 실전 및 창의사고력 문제|

학교 시험에서 점차 늘어나는 서술형 시험에 집중 대비하고 고득점을 취득하는데 만전을 기하기 위한 학습 코너

|단원별 모의고사|

영역별, 단계별 학습을 모두 마친 후 실전 연습을 위한 모의고사

교과서 파헤치기

- **단어Test1~3** 영어 단어 우리말 쓰기, 우리말을 영어 단어로 쓰기, 영영풀이에 해당하는 단어와 우리말 쓰기
- **대화문Test1~2** 대화문 빈칸 완성 및 전체 대화문 쓰기
- **본문Test1~5** 빈칸 완성, 우리말 쓰기, 문장 배열연습, 영어 작문하기 복습 등 단계별 반복 학습을 통해 교과서 지문에 대한 완벽한 습득
- **구석구석지문Test1~2** 지문 빈칸 완성 및 전문 영어로 쓰기

Contents

Lesson 5

Critical Minds

 의사소통 기능

- 자세한 설명 요청하기

  A: Did you know that bats aren't blind?

  B: No. **Can you tell me more about** it?

  A: Some bats can see three times better than humans.

- 의견에 대한 이유 묻기

  A: Books of riddles are really useful for adults.

  B: **Why do you say so?**

  A: They help us think more creatively.

 언어 형식

- 분사구문

  Let's look into some articles **thinking about the hidden motives**.

- so that ~ can ...

  They made up this fake article **so that** they **could** draw the readers' attention.

Words & Expressions

Key Words

- **admit**[ədmít] 동 인정하다, 자백하다
- **adult**[ədʌ́lt] 명 성인, 어른
- **argument**[ɑ́ːrgjumənt] 명 논쟁, 언쟁
- **awful**[ɔ́ːfəl] 형 끔찍한, 지독한
- **chemical**[kémikəl] 명 화학 물질
- **chest**[ʧest] 명 가슴, 흉부
- **citizen**[sítəzən] 명 시민
- **competitor**[kəmpétətər] 명 경쟁자, 경쟁 상대
- **condition**[kəndíʃən] 명 상태, 상황
- **confess**[kənfés] 동 고백하다, 인정하다
- **critical**[krítikəl] 형 위험한, 위독한
- **critically**[krítikəli] 부 비판적으로
- **criticize**[krítəsàiz] 동 비난하다
- **current**[kə́ːrənt] 형 현재의, 지금의
- **describe**[diskráib] 동 기술하다
- **disaster**[dizǽstər] 명 참사, 재난
- **escape**[iskéip] 동 달아나다, 탈출하다, 벗어나다
- **extremely**[ikstríːmli] 부 극도로, 극히
- **fake**[feik] 형 가짜의, 거짓의
- **formation**[fɔːrméiʃən] 명 형성
- **goldfish**[góuldfiʃ] 명 금붕어
- **harmful**[hɑ́ːrmfəl] 형 해로운, 유해한
- **height**[hait] 명 키, 신장
- **incident**[ínsədənt] 명 사건
- **injure**[índʒər] 동 부상을 입히다
- **judge**[dʒʌdʒ] 동 판단하다

- **loose**[luːs] 형 풀린, 헐거운
- **measure**[méʒər] 동 측정하다, 재다
- **mine**[main] 명 광산 동 채굴하다
- **mislead**[mìslíːd] 동 잘못 이끌다, 오해하게 하다
- **motive**[móutiv] 명 동기, 이유
- **muscle**[mʌ́sl] 명 근육
- **nevertheless**[nèvərðəlés] 부 그럼에도 불구하고
- **panic**[pǽnik] 동 겁에 질려 어쩔 줄 모르다
- **poem**[póuəm] 명 시, 운문
- **prove**[pruːv] 동 입증하다, 증명하다
- **public**[pʌ́blik] 명 대중, 일반 사람들
- **publish**[pʌ́bliʃ] 동 발행하다, 출판하다, 게재하다
- **recognize**[rékəgnàiz] 동 알아보다
- **reliable**[riláiəbl] 형 믿을 만한, 신뢰할 만한
- **riddle**[rídl] 부 수수께끼
- **seriously**[síəriəsli] 부 진지하게, 심각하게
- **shoot**[ʃuːt] 동 (총 등을) 쏘다
- **Slav**[slɑːv] 명 슬라브인
- **source**[sɔːrs] 명 출처, 자료
- **spell**[spel] 동 철자를 말하다[쓰다]
- **spot**[spɑt] 동 발견하다, 찾아내다
- **strengthen**[stréŋkθən] 동 강하게 하다, 더 튼튼하게 하다
- **support**[səpɔ́ːrt] 동 (사실임을) 입증하다, 뒷받침하다
- **temperature**[témpərətʃər] 명 온도, 기온, 체온
- **trust**[trʌst] 동 신뢰하다
- **wound**[wuːnd] 동 상처를 입히다

Key Expressions

- **according to** ~에 따르면
- **be related to** ~와 연관되다
- **be useful for** ~에게 유용하다
- **break down** ~을 부수다, ~을 무너뜨리다
- **catch a cold** 감기에 걸리다
- **draw one's attention to** ~의 관심을 …로 끌다
- **fall asleep** 잠들다
- **get caught -ing** ~하다가 걸리다
- **in that** ~라는 점에서, ~이기 때문에

- **look into** 조사하다, 들여다보다
- **lose weight** 몸무게를 줄이다
- **make up** 지어내다, 만들어 내다
- **on the loose** 잡히지 않은, 탈주 중인
- **search for** ~을 찾다
- **spend time -ing** ~하면서 시간을 보내다
- **think outside the box** 고정관념에서 벗어나다
- **What if** ~? 만약 ~라면 어떨까?

Word Power

※ 서로 비슷한 뜻을 가진 어휘

- □ **adult** 성인, 어른 – **grownup** 성인
- □ **awful** 끔찍한, 지독한 – **horrible** 끔찍한
- □ **current** 현재의, 지금의 – **present** 현재의
- □ **injure** 부상을 입히다 – **wound** 부상을 입히다

- □ **argument** 논쟁, 언쟁 – **debate** 토론
- □ **criticize** 비난하다 – **blame** 비난하다
- □ **describe** 기술하다 – **illustrate** 설명하다
- □ **spot** 발견하다, 찾아내다 – **detect** 찾아내다

※ 서로 반대의 뜻을 가진 어휘

- □ **competitor** 경쟁자 ↔ **helper** 조력자
- □ **fake** 가짜의, 거짓의 ↔ **true** 진실한
- □ **reliable** 믿을 만한 ↔ **unreliable** 믿을 수 없는
- □ **trust** 신뢰하다 ↔ **distrust** 불신하다

- □ **criticize** 비난하다 ↔ **compliment** 칭찬하다
- □ **harmful** 해로운, 유해한 ↔ **harmless** 무해한
- □ **strengthen** 강하게 하다 ↔ **weaken** 약하게 하다

※ 접두사 mis- [mis+어근]: 잘못된, 나쁜, 나쁘게

- □ **mis-**+**lead** = **mislead** (잘못 이끌다)
- □ **mis-**+**fortune** = **misfortune** (불행, 불운)
- □ **mis-**+**read** = **misread** (잘못 해석하다)
- □ **mis-**+**use** = **misuse** (오용, 오용하다)

- □ **mis-**+**take** = **mistake** (실수, 실수하다)
- □ **mis-**+**behavior** = **misbehavior** (나쁜 행실)
- □ **mis-**+**trust** = **mistrust** (불신하다)
- □ **mis-**+**understand** = **misunderstand** (오해하다)

※ 접미사 –ize [명사/형용사+ize = 동사]: ～으로 되다, ～이 되게 만들다, ～와 같아지게 하다

- □ **critic**+**-ize** = **criticize** (비판하다)
- □ **regular**+**-ize** = **regularize** (합법화하다)
- □ **fossil**+**-ize** = **fossilize** (화석화하다)
- □ **harmony**+**-ize** = **harmonize** (조화를 이루다)
- □ **moisture**+**-ize** = **moisturize** (촉촉하게 하다)

- □ **real**+**-ize** = **realize** (실현하다)
- □ **private**+**-ize** = **privatize** (민영화하다)
- □ **theory**+**-ize** = **theorize** (이론을 세우다)
- □ **memory**+**-ize** = **memorize** (암기하다)

English Dictionary

- □ **disaster** 참사, 재난
  → an event causing great harm, damage, or suffering
  해, 손상, 또는 고통을 초래하는 사건

- □ **citizen** 시민
  → a person who lives in a particular city
  특정 시에 살고 있는 사람

- □ **describe** 기술하다
  → to say or write what someone or something is like
  누군가 또는 무언가가 어떠한지 말하거나 쓰다

- □ **panic** 겁에 질려 어쩔 줄 모르다
  → to suddenly feel so worried that you cannot be reasonable
  너무 걱정이 되어서 이성적일 수 없다고 갑자기 느끼다

- □ **shoot** (총 등을) 쏘다
  → to fire a weapon
  무기를 발사하다

- □ **chest** 가슴, 흉부
  → the upper front part of the body of humans
  인간 신체의 상체 앞부분

- □ **spell** 철자를 말하다, 쓰다
  → to form words with the letters in the correct order
  글자를 가지고 알맞은 순서로 단어를 형성하다

- □ **source** 출처, 자료
  → a place, person, or thing from which something comes
  그것으로부터 무언가가 나오는 장소, 사람 또는 사물

서답형

01 다음 짝지어진 단어의 관계가 같도록 빈칸에 알맞은 말을 쓰시오.

harmless : harmful = trust : _____

02 다음 영영풀이가 가리키는 것을 고르시오.

an event causing great harm, damage, or suffering

① riddle　② formation　③ source
④ disaster　⑤ temperature

중요

03 다음 문장의 빈칸에 공통으로 들어갈 말을 고르시오.

• You can _____ me all the time.
• Don't _____ what people are saying about me.
• If you put your _____ in me, I'll do my best.
• I have complete _____ in John.

① trust　　② judge　　③ spot
④ chest　　⑤ disaster

중요

04 다음 중 밑줄 친 부분의 뜻풀이가 바르지 않은 것은?

① They were caught at the airport because they had fake passports. (가짜의, 거짓의)
② Do you know geese fly in a V formation? (대형)
③ She wants to keep goldfish at home as pets. (금붕어)
④ He injured his back and legs on the mountain. (부상을 입히다)
⑤ My uncle found gold in a mine and became rich. (나의 것)

05 다음 주어진 문장의 밑줄 친 judge와 다른 의미로 쓰인 것은?

Judging by her last letter, they are having a wonderful time.

① As far as I can judge, all of them are to blame.
② To judge from what he said, he was very disappointed.
③ Schools should not be judged only on exam results.
④ Their concert was judged to have been a great success.
⑤ Considering the results, I think the judge was too generous.

서답형

06 다음 우리말과 일치하도록 주어진 단어를 모두 배열하여 완성하시오.

(1) 그는 팔에 상처를 입었었다.
(wounded / in / had / been / the / he / arm)
➡ _____

(2) 그녀가 또 거짓말을 했으므로 나는 그녀를 더 이상 신뢰할 수 없다.
(trust / I / she / her / anymore / again / lied / can't / because)
➡ _____

(3) 기온이 오늘 40도까지 올랐다.
(to / the / today / went / temperature / forty / up)
➡ _____

01 다음 짝지어진 단어의 관계가 같도록 빈칸에 알맞은 말을 쓰시오.

> regular : regularize = real : _____

02 다음 우리말에 맞게 빈칸에 알맞은 말을 쓰시오.

(1) 나는 2,000명의 경쟁자들과 마라톤을 했다.

➡ I ran a marathon with 2,000 _____.

(2) 그 환자는 심각한 상태였다.

➡ The patient was in serious _____.

(3) 마침내, 그들은 경찰에게 모든 것을 고백했다.

➡ Finally, they _____ everything to the police.

(4) 그의 아버지는 위독한 상태이다.

➡ His father is in a _____ condition.

03 다음 문장의 빈칸에 들어갈 말을 〈보기〉에서 골라 쓰시오.

> — 보기 —
> catch a cold / got caught / on the loose /
> search for / think outside the box

(1) The prisoner escaped from jail, and he is still _____.

(2) We started to _____ to make something new.

(3) You can _____ a good hotel on this website.

(4) Be careful not to _____.

(5) One of my classmates _____ cheating.

04 다음 우리말에 맞게 주어진 단어를 사용하여 영작하시오.

(1) 너는 그 식당이 극도로 시끄럽다고 생각하지 않니? (loud, don't)

➡ _____

(2) 설탕을 너무 많이 먹는 것은 너의 치아에 해롭다. (too, for)

➡ _____

(3) 그는 내 여동생과 거의 같은 키이다. (as, the same)

➡ _____

05 다음 주어진 우리말과 일치하도록 주어진 단어를 모두 배열하여 완성하시오.

(1) 그녀는 그녀가 실수했다는 것을 인정했다.
(that / she / had / she / admitted / mistakes / made)

➡ _____

(2) 나는 어제 내 남자 친구와 논쟁을 했다.
(my boyfriend / I / with / yesterday / an argument / had)

➡ _____

(3) 어른들은 입장료를 내야 하지만, 아이들은 무료로 입장한다.
(should / adults / fee / but / an / in / children / get / pay / entrance / free)

➡ _____
_____

Conversation

1 자세한 설명 요청하기

> **A:** Did you know that bats aren't blind? 박쥐가 눈이 안 보이는 것이 아니라는 걸 알고 있었니?
>
> **B:** No. Can you tell me more about it? 아니. 그걸 더 설명해 줄래?
>
> **A:** Some bats can see three times better than humans. 어떤 박쥐는 인간보다 3배 더 잘 볼 수 있어.

■ 상대방이 말하는 내용을 잘 모르거나 상대방이 사용한 단어의 뜻을 몰라서 추가적인 설명을 요청할 때는 'Can you tell me more about it?(그걸 좀 더 설명해 줄래?)'이라고 하거나, 'What does that mean?(그것이 무슨 뜻입니까?)', 'What do you mean by that?(그것이 무슨 뜻이니?)'이라고 한다.

■ 상대방에게 설명을 요청할 때는 '설명하다, 말하다'의 의미를 가지는 동사 explain, tell이나 give information, be specific 등의 표현을 사용하여 'Could you explain the meaning of it?', 'Could you tell me more about them?' 등의 표현을 사용하기도 한다. Could 대신 Would, Can, Will 등을 사용할 수 있고, 'Do you mind if I ask you to explain ~?'이라고 말할 수도 있다.

■ 상대방의 말을 알아듣지 못했을 때는 'I'm not following you.(잘 못 알아듣겠습니다.)', 'I don't get it.(제대로 이해를 못하겠어요.)' 등의 표현을 사용하여 상대방이 다시 설명을 하도록 요청할 수도 있다.

자세한 설명 요청하기

- Can you tell me more about it? 그걸 좀 더 설명해 줄래?
- Could you give me more information? 좀 더 정보를 주시겠습니까?
- Can you explain more in detail? 좀 더 자세히 설명해 주시겠습니까?
- Could you be more specific? 좀 더 구체적으로 말해 주시겠습니까?
- What do you mean by that? 그게 무슨 말이야?
- Could you explain what it means? 그게 무엇을 의미하는지 설명해 주시겠습니까?

핵심 Check

1. 주어진 문장에 이어지도록 적절한 순서로 배열하시오.

> **W:** I think I caught a cold because I didn't dress warmly yesterday.
>
> (A) Really? Can you tell me more about it?
>
> (B) The article said that people catch colds because of viruses.
>
> (C) Well, I've read an article saying that you don't catch a cold because your body temperature is low.

➡ _____

2 의견에 대한 이유 묻기

> **A: Books of riddles are really useful for adults.** 수수께끼 책이 어른들에게는 매우 유용해.
>
> **B: Why do you say so?** 왜 그렇게 말하니?
>
> **A: They help us think more creatively.** 그것들이 더 창의적으로 생각하게 도와주니까.

■ 상대방이 왜 그렇게 말하는지, 혹은 왜 그렇게 생각하는지 등에 대해 이유를 물을 때는 의문사 why를 써서 'Why do you say so?(왜 그렇게 말하니?)' 또는 'Why do you think so?(왜 그렇게 생각하니?)'처럼 물어본다.

■ why 대신 의문사 what을 사용해서 '무엇이 ~하도록 만들었느냐?'의 의미로 'What makes you+동사원형 ~?'의 형태를 사용할 수 있다. 'What makes you say that?(무엇 때문에 그렇게 말하니?)' 또는 'What makes you think so?(무엇 때문에 그렇게 생각하니?)'처럼 'What makes you ~?'로 이유를 물어볼 때 'what'은 '무엇'이라고 해석할 수도 있지만 '왜'라고 해석하기도 한다.

■ 의문사로 시작하는 이유를 묻는 말 앞에 'Can you tell me'나 'I'd like to know', 'I wonder' 등을 붙여, 간접의문문의 형식으로 좀 더 격식을 갖춰 물어볼 수도 있다. 이유를 말할 때에는 문장 앞에 'I think'나 'In my opinion' 등을 덧붙일 수도 있다.

이유 묻기

- Why do you say/think so? 왜 그렇게 말하니/생각하니?
- What makes you say so? 왜 그렇게 말하니?
- What makes you think so? 무엇 때문에 그렇게 생각하니?
- Why is that? 왜 그렇지?
- Can you tell me (the reason) why ~? ~ 한 이유를 설명해 주겠니?

이유 말하기

- I did it because ~. ~ 때문에 그렇게 했어요.
- (Because) ~. 왜냐하면 ~ 때문이야.
- That's because ~. 그것은 ~ 때문입니다.
- Because of ~. ~ 때문이야.

핵심 Check

2. 다음 대화의 밑줄 친 문장과 같은 의미의 문장을 주어진 단어로 시작하여 쓰시오.

> **W:** I think children write better poems than adults.
>
> **M:** <u>Why do you say so?</u>
>
> **W:** They're really honest about their feelings and much more creative than adults.

➡ What _____?

Listen and Talk 1 B

W: I read an article ❶saying ❷that Napoleon was actually ❸fairly tall.

M: Oh, really? ❹Can you tell me more about it?

W: ❺According to the article, a French doctor wrote down Napoleon's height according to the French measuring system, not the English one.

M: What was the difference?

W: At that time, an inch in France was longer than an inch in England. So, Napoleon was actually about 168 cm tall, ❻which was not that short in those times.

W: 나폴레옹이 실제로 키가 꽤 컸다고 하는 기사를 읽었어.

M: 오, 정말? 그것에 대해 더 말해 줄 수 있니?

W: 기사에 따르면 한 프랑스 의사가 영국식이 아닌 프랑스식 측정법으로 나폴레옹의 키를 기록했다는 거야.

M: 차이가 뭐였니?

W: 그 당시에 프랑스에서의 1인치가 영국에서의 1인치보다 더 길었어. 그래서 나폴레옹은 사실 168cm 정도였는데, 그것이 그 시대에는 그렇게 작은 키가 아니었어.

❶ 현재분사로 an article을 수식한다. ❷ 접속사 that으로 명사절을 이끈다. ❸ fairly: 꽤
❹ 상대방이 말하는 내용을 잘 모르거나 상대방이 사용한 단어의 뜻을 몰라서 추가적인 설명을 요청할 때 사용하는 표현으로 'What does that mean?'이나 'What do you mean by that?'으로 바꾸어 표현할 수 있다.
❺ according to: ~에 따르면
❻ 관계대명사의 계속적인 용법으로 that으로 바꾸어 쓸 수 없다.

Check(√) True or False

(1) An inch in England was shorter than the one in France.　　T ☐ F ☐

(2) Napoleon was actually not that short in those times.　　T ☐ F ☐

Listen and Talk 2 B

M: Hey, Sandy. Do you think I should buy this drink? It is said that it can help me ❶lose weight.

W: Let me read the label more closely. Hmm, it looks ❷a bit strange to me, David.

M: ❸Why do you say so?

W: There ❹isn't enough information about what's in the drink.

M: Oh, you're right.

W: Also, it doesn't tell you how much you have to drink to lose weight.

M: 안녕, Sandy. 너는 내가 이 음료를 사야 한다고 생각해? 내가 살을 빼는 것을 도와줄 수 있다고 적혀 있어.

W: 라벨을 더 자세히 읽어 볼게. 음, 내가 보기에 좀 이상해, David.

M: 왜 그렇게 생각해?

W: 음료 안에 무엇이 들었는지에 대한 충분한 정보가 없어.

M: 오, 네 말이 맞아.

W: 게다가, 체중을 감량하려면 얼마나 마셔야 하는지도 나와 있지 않아.

❶ lose weight: 살이 빠지다 ❷ a bit: 약간, 조금
❸ 상대방이 왜 그렇게 말하는지, 혹은 왜 그렇게 생각하는지 등에 대해 이유를 물을 때 쓰는 표현으로 'Why do you think so?' 등으로 바꾸어 표현할 수 있다.
❹ 'there is+단수 명사', 'there are+복수 명사': ~가 있다

Check(√) True or False

(3) David is wondering whether he should buy the drink or not.　　T ☐ F ☐

(4) Sandy advised David to buy the drink to lose weight.　　T ☐ F ☐

Listen and Talk 1 A-1

W: I think I ❶caught a cold ❷because I didn't dress warmly yesterday.

M: Well, I've read an article saying that you don't catch a cold because your body ❸ temperature is low.

W: Really? Can you tell me more about it?

M: The article said that people catch colds ❷ because of viruses.

❶ catch a cold: 감기에 걸리다 ❷ 'because+주어+동사', 'because of+명사(구)' ❸ temperature: 온도

 Listen and Talk 1 A-2

W: I usually drink ❶a glass of warm milk before I go to bed, but it doesn't ❷help me fall asleep.

M: I saw a show on TV, and a doctor said that a glass of warm milk doesn't actually help you fall asleep.

W: Oh, it doesn't? Can you tell me more about it?

M: Milk has special ❸chemicals ❹that make people sleepy. But the amount in a glass is ❺too small to have any effect.

❶ a glass of ~: 한 잔의 ~ ❷ help는 준사역동사로 목적격보어로 to부정사나 원형부정사(fall)가 이어진다. ❸ chemical: 화학물질 ❹ 관계대명사로 'which'로 바꾸어 쓸 수 있다. ❺ too ~ to ...: 너무 ~해서 …할 수 없다

 Listen and Talk 2 A-1

W: What are you reading, John?

M: I'm reading a book of ❶riddles.

W: Riddles? Aren't ❷they for children?

M: Actually, no. Books of riddles are really useful for adults.

W: Really? ❸Why do you say so?

M: ❷They help us think more creatively. We need to ❹think outside the box to find the answers.

❶ riddle: 수수께끼 ❷ they는 riddles를 가리킨다. ❸ 'What makes you think so?' 또는 'Why is that?' 등으로 바꾸어 표현할 수 있다. ❹ think outside the box: 고정관념에서 벗어나다

 Communication

W: There are so many pieces of information we call "facts" that are ❶completely wrong.

M: Why do you say so?

W: I read a book, and there were a lot of examples of these facts ❷that are wrong.

M: Like what?

W: Well, most people think ❸goldfish are not smart. But, goldfish are actually smart.

M: Really? Can you tell me more about ❹that?

W: They can ❺recognize their owners.

M: Oh, I didn't know that.

❶ completely: 완전히 ❷ 관계대명사로 which로 바꾸어 쓸 수 있다. ❸ goldfish: 금붕어 ❹ that은 금붕어가 실제로는 똑똑하다는 것을 가리킨다. ❺ recognize: 알아보다, 인식하다

 Wrap Up 1

M: Jane, do you usually get news online or from the newspaper?

W: Well, I usually watch TV news.

M: TV news? Is there any special reason?

W: I think ❶TV is the most useful way to get news.

M: Why do you say so?

W: I have to ❷spend too much time reading all the news online or in the newspaper. So, I just watch the main news on TV.

M: ❸I see your point.

❶ 접속사 that이 생략되어 있다. ❷ spend time ~ing: ~하는 데 시간을 보내다 ❸ I see your point.: 무슨 말인지 알겠다.

• 다음 우리말과 일치하도록 빈칸에 알맞은 말을 쓰시오.

Listen & Talk 1 A-1

W: I think I _____ _____ _____ because I didn't dress _____ yesterday.

M: Well, I've read an _____ saying that you don't catch a cold because your _____ _____ is low.

W: Really? Can you tell me _____ _____ _____?

M: The article said that people catch colds _____ _____.

해석
W: 어제 옷을 따뜻하게 입지 않아서 감기에 걸린 것 같아.
M: 글쎄, 체온이 낮다고 해서 감기에 걸리지는 않는다고 쓰여 있는 기사를 읽었어.
W: 정말? 그것에 대해 더 말해 줄 수 있니?
M: 기사에서는 사람들이 바이러스 때문에 감기에 걸린다고 했어.

Listen & Talk 1 A-2

W: I usually drink _____ _____ _____ _____ _____ before I go to bed, but it doesn't help me _____ _____.

M: I saw a show on TV, and a doctor said that a glass of warm milk doesn't actually _____ you _____ asleep.

W: Oh, it doesn't? Can you _____ _____ _____ _____?

M: Milk has special _____ that make people sleepy. But the _____ in a glass is _____ small _____ have any _____.

W: 나는 보통 잠자리에 들기 전에 따뜻한 우유 한 잔을 마시는데, 그것이 잠드는 데 도움이 되지 않아.
M: 내가 텔레비전 프로그램에서 봤는데, 어떤 의사가 따뜻한 우유 한 잔이 실제로 잠드는 데 도움을 주는 건 아니라고 말했어.
W: 오, 그래? 그것에 대해 더 말해 줄 수 있니?
M: 우유에는 사람들을 졸리게 만드는 특별한 성분이 있어. 하지만 한 잔에 있는 양이 너무 적어서 효과가 없어.

Listen & Talk 2 A-1

W: _____ _____ _____ _____, John?

M: I'm reading a book of _____.

W: Riddles? Aren't they _____ children?

M: _____, no. Books of riddles are really _____ _____ _____.

W: Really? Why do you _____ _____?

M: They help us think more _____. We need to _____ _____ _____ _____ to find the answers.

W: 무엇을 읽고 있니, John?
M: 나는 수수께끼 책을 읽고 있어.
W: 수수께끼? 그거 아이들용 아니니?
M: 사실은, 그렇지 않아. 수수께끼 책은 어른들에게 굉장히 유용해.
W: 정말? 왜 그렇게 생각해?
M: 그 책들은 우리가 더 창의적으로 생각하도록 도와. 우리는 답을 찾기 위해 고정관념에서 벗어나야 하거든.

Listen & Talk 2 A-2

M: Are these all _____ _____?

W: Yeah. These are all poems _____ by children.

M: By children?

W: Yeah. I think children _____ _____ poems than adults.

M: Why do you _____ _____?

W: They're really _____ about their _____ and much _____ _____ than adults.

M: 이거 전부 시집이니?
W: 응. 이것들은 모두 아이들이 쓴 시야.
M: 아이들이?
W: 응. 내 생각에 아이들이 어른들보다 더 좋은 시를 쓰는 것 같아.
M: 왜 그렇게 생각해?
W: 아이들은 그들의 감정에 아주 솔직하고 어른들보다 훨씬 더 창의적이거든.

Listen & Talk 2 B

M: Hey, Sandy. Do you think _____ _____ _____ _____
_____? It is said that it can help me _____ _____.

W: Let me read the _____ more _____. Hmm, it looks a bit
_____ to me, David.

M: Why do _____ _____ _____?

W: There isn't _____ _____ about _____ in the _____.

M: Oh, you're _____.

W: Also, it doesn't tell you _____ _____ _____ _____
_____ _____ to lose weight.

Communication

W: There are so many pieces of _____ we call "_____" that are
_____ _____.

M: Why do you say so?

W: I read a book, and there were a lot of _____ of these _____
_____ _____ _____.

M: Like _____?

W: Well, most people think _____ are not smart. But, _____ are
actually smart.

M: Really? Can you tell me more about that?

W: They can _____ _____ _____.

M: Oh, I didn't _____ _____.

Wrap Up 2

W: I read an _____ _____ about the Black Sea. Do you know
_____ _____ _____?

M: Yes. It's _____ Eastern Europe _____ Western Asia, right?

W: Right. _____ _____ do you think it is?

M: Well, black, I _____.

M: No, it isn't. It's blue.

M: Really? Then why is it _____ the Black Sea? Can you tell me more
about it?

W: People call it the Black Sea because it is very _____.

해석

M: 안녕, Sandy. 너는 내가 이 음료를 사야 한다고 생각해? 내가 살을 빼는 것을 도와줄 수 있다고 적혀 있어.

W: 라벨을 더 자세히 읽어 볼게. 음, 내가 보기에 좀 이상해, David.

M: 왜 그렇게 생각해?

W: 음료 안에 무엇이 들었는지에 대한 충분한 정보가 없어.

M: 오, 네 말이 맞아.

W: 게다가, 체중을 감량하려면 얼마나 마셔야 하는지도 나와 있지 않아.

W: 우리가 '사실'이라고 말하는 정보 중에 완전히 틀린 것들이 너무 많아.

M: 왜 그렇게 생각해?

W: 내가 책을 읽었는데, 거기에는 이러한 틀린 '사실'의 예시가 많이 있었어.

M: 예를 들면 어떤 것?

W: 음, 대부분의 사람들은 금붕어가 똑똑하지 않다고 생각해. 하지만 금붕어는 사실 똑똑해.

M: 정말? 그것에 대해 더 말해 줄 수 있니?

W: 그들은 그들의 주인을 알아 볼 수 있어.

M: 오, 그건 몰랐어.

W: 나는 흑해에 관한 흥미로운 기사를 읽었어. 너 그게 어디에 있는지 아니?

M: 응. 그것은 동유럽과 서아시아 사이에 있어, 그렇지?

W: 맞아. 그게 무슨 색일 거라고 생각해?

M: 글쎄, 검은색일 것 같아.

W: 아니야, 그렇지 않아. 그것은 파란색이야.

M: 정말? 그럼 왜 흑해라고 불리는 거야? 그것에 대해 더 말해 줄 수 있니?

W: 사람들이 흑해라고 부르는 이유는 그곳이 매우 위험하기 때문이야.

[01~02] 다음 대화를 읽고 물음에 답하시오.

Suji: I usually drink a glass of warm milk ⓐbefore I go to bed, but it doesn't help me fall asleep.

Minsu: I saw a show on TV, and a doctor said ⓑthat a glass of warm milk doesn't actually help you fall asleep.

Suji: Oh, it doesn't? Can you tell me ⓒmore about it?

Minsu: Milk has special chemicals that ⓓmakes people sleepy. But the amount in a glass is too ⓔsmall to have any effect.

01 위 대화의 밑줄 친 ⓐ~ⓔ 중 어법상 틀린 것을 찾아 바르게 고치시오.

➡ _____

02 위 대화의 내용과 일치하지 <u>않는</u> 것은?

① 수지는 자기 전에 따뜻한 우유 한 잔을 마신다.
② 자기 전에 따뜻한 우유 한 잔은 수지가 잠드는 데 도움이 되지 않았다.
③ 민수는 TV에서 어떤 의사가 따뜻한 우유 한 잔이 실제로 잠드는 데 도움을 주는 건 아니라고 말하는 것을 들었다.
④ 우유에는 사람들을 졸리게 만드는 특별한 성분이 있다.
⑤ 우유 한 잔에 있는 특별한 성분의 양으로 숙면을 취할 수 있다.

[03~04] 다음 대화를 읽고 물음에 답하시오.

W: I think I caught a cold because I didn't dress ⓐwarmly yesterday.

M: Well, I've read an article ⓑsaying that you don't catch a cold because your body temperature is low.

W: Really? Can you tell me more ⓒabout it?

M: The article said that people catch colds ⓓbecause viruses.

03 위 대화에서 밑줄 친 ⓐ~ⓓ 중 어법상 틀린 것을 찾아 바르게 고치시오

➡ _____

04 위 대화의 내용과 일치하도록 빈칸을 완성하시오.

According to the article, people catch colds not because of (A)_____ but because of (B)_____ .

[01~02] 다음 대화를 읽고 물음에 답하시오.

Jane: I read an article ⓐsaying that Napoleon was actually fairly tall.

Tom: Oh, really? Can you tell me more about it?

Jane: According to the article, a French doctor ⓑwrote down Napoleon's height according to the French measuring system, not the English ⓒone.

Tom: What was the difference?

Jane: At that time, an inch in France was ⓓlonger than an inch in England. So, Napoleon was actually about 168 cm tall, ⓔthat was not that short in those times.

서답형

01 위 대화의 밑줄 친 ⓐ~ⓔ 중 어법상 틀린 것을 찾아 바르게 고치시오.

➡ _____

중요

02 위 대화의 내용과 일치하지 않는 것은?

① Jane은 나폴레옹이 실제로 꽤 키가 컸다는 기사를 읽었다.

② 기사에 따르면 프랑스 의사는 나폴레옹의 키를 프랑스 측정 체계에 따라 기록했다.

③ 나폴레옹 시대에 프랑스의 1인치는 영국의 1인치보다 더 길었다.

④ 나폴레옹은 실제로 약 168 cm로 그 당시에는 작은 편이 아니었다.

⑤ 프랑스 측정 체계와 영국의 측정 체계는 다르지 않았다.

[03~05] 다음 대화를 읽고 물음에 답하시오.

Suji: I usually drink a glass of warm milk before I go to bed, but it doesn't help me fall asleep.

Minsu: I saw a show on TV, and a doctor said that a glass of warm milk doesn't actually help you fall asleep.

Suji: Oh, it doesn't? Can you tell me more about it?

Minsu: Milk has special chemicals that make people sleepy. But the amount in a glass is too small to have any effect.

서답형

03 What does Suji do before going to bed?

➡ _____

서답형

04 What is the effect of special chemicals in milk?

➡ _____

서답형

05 Why are the chemicals in a glass of warm milk not helpful for falling asleep?

➡ _____

_____

서답형

06 다음 대화가 자연스럽게 이어지도록 순서대로 배열하시오.

M: Are these all poetry books?

(A) By children?

(B) Why do you say so?

(C) Yeah. These are all poems written by children.

(D) Yeah. I think children write better poems than adults.

(E) They're really honest about their feelings and much more creative than adults.

➡ _____

07 다음 짝지어진 대화가 <u>어색한</u> 것은?

① A: Did you know that bats aren't blind?

   B: No. Can you tell me more about it?

② A: Books of riddles are really useful for adults.

   B: Why do you say so?

③ A: Actually, frozen fruits are as good as fresh ones.

   B: Really? Can you give me more information about it?

④ A: You know what? I'm planning to visit Canada this summer vacation.

   B: I'm wondering if you could tell me more about your vacation plan.

⑤ A: Did you know that Bill's birthday is on May 4th?

   B: I see your point.

[08~09] 다음 대화를 읽고 물음에 답하시오.

Susan: What are you reading, John?

John: I'm reading a book of riddles.

Susan: Riddles? Aren't they for children?

John: Actually, no. Books of riddles are really useful for adults.

Susan: Really? (A)_____

John: They help us think more creatively.

   (B)_____

08 위 대화의 빈칸 (A)에 들어갈 말로 나머지와 의도가 <u>다른</u> 것은?

① Why do you say so?

② What makes you say so?

③ What makes you think so?

④ Can you tell me the reason why?

⑤ What do you think about it?

---

09 위 대화의 빈칸 (B)에 들어갈 말을 보기에 주어진 단어들을 모두 배열하여 완성하시오.

┌─ 보기 ─┐

need / we / to / find / to / the answers / outside / think / the box

➡ _____

_____

[10~12] 다음 대화를 읽고 물음에 답하시오.

Mike: Are these all poetry books?

Sue: Yeah. These are all poems (A)_____ (write) by children.

Mike: By children?

Sue: Yeah. I think children write better poems than adults.

Mike: (B)<u>Why do you say so</u>?

Sue: (C)<u>They</u>'re really honest about their feelings and much more creative than adults.

10 위 대화의 빈칸 (A)에 주어진 단어를 알맞은 형태로 쓰시오.

➡ _____

11 위 대화의 밑줄 친 (B)와 바꾸어 쓰기에 <u>어색한</u> 것은?

① Why do you think so?

② What makes you say so?

③ What makes you think so?

④ Can you tell me why?

⑤ How do you feel about that?

12 위 대화의 밑줄 친 (C)가 가리키는 것을 찾아 쓰시오.

➡ _____

[01~02] 다음 대화를 읽고 물음에 답하시오.

W: I think I caught a cold because I didn't dress warmly yesterday.

M: Well, I've read an article saying that you don't catch a cold because your body temperature is low.

W: Really? (A)_____?

M: The article said that people catch colds because of viruses.

01
위 대화의 빈칸 (A)에 들어갈 말을 <보기>에 주어진 단어들을 배열하여 완성하시오.

┌── 보기 ──┐
you / more / it / can / about / tell / me

➡ _____?

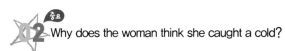 02
Why does the woman think she caught a cold?

➡ _____

_____

03
다음 대화의 내용과 일치하도록 기사를 완성하시오.

Jane: I read an article saying that Napoleon was actually fairly tall.

Tom: Oh, really? Can you tell me more about it?

Jane: According to the article, a French doctor wrote down Napoleon's height according to the French measuring system, not the English one.

Tom: What was the difference?

Jane: At that time, an inch in France was longer than an inch in England. So, Napoleon was actually about 168 cm tall, which was not that short in those times.

↓

Daily News, May 7th 2020

Was (A)_____Really Short?

We have been wrong about Napoleon's (B)_____. The misunderstanding came from the difference between (C)_____ _____ and (D)_____ _____. He was actually about 168 cm tall!

[04~06] 다음 대화를 읽고 물음에 답하시오.

Mike: Are these all poetry books?

Sue: Yeah. These are all poems written by children.

Mike: By children?

Sue: Yeah. I think children write better poems than adults.

Mike: (A)왜 그렇게 생각해? (say)

Sue: They're really honest about their feelings and much more creative than adults.

04
위 대화의 밑줄 친 (A)의 우리말을 주어진 단어를 사용하여 5 단어로 영작하시오.

➡ _____

05
By whom were all the poems in the poetry books written?

➡ _____

06
Why does Sue think that children write better poems than adults?

➡ _____

_____

Grammar

① 분사구문

> • Let's look into some articles **thinking about the hidden motives.** 숨겨진 동기를 생
> 각하면서 몇 가지 뉴스 기사를 살펴보자.

■ 분사가 이끄는 구를 분사구문이라고 하며, 이유, 조건, 시간, 동시동작, 양보 등의 뜻을 나타낸다. 분사
구문은 '접속사+주어+동사'로 이루어진 부사절의 주어가 주절의 주어와 일치할 때 접속사와 주어를 생
략하고 동사를 분사(동사원형+-ing)로 만든 구문이다. 이때 생략되는 접속사에 따라 뜻이 달라진다.

- When I arrived at the party, it began to rain. → **Arriving at the party**, it began to rain. (시간) (파티에
도착했을 때 비가 내리기 시작했다.)

■ 부사절과 주절의 주어가 다를 때는 부사절의 주어를 생략하지 않고 사용하며 이것을 독립분사구문이라
고 한다. 일반인이 주어일 경우에는 생략한다. (비인칭 독립분사구문)

- As it was raining, we couldn't go out. → **It being raining**, we couldn't go out. (우리는 비가 오고 있었
기 때문에 나갈 수가 없었다.)

■ 분사구문의 부정은 분사 앞에 'not'이나 'never'를 쓴다.

- As he didn't feel well, he took the last Wednesday off. → **Not feeling well**, he took the last
Wednesday off. (그는 지난 수요일 몸이 불편하여 쉬었다.)

■ 분사구문의 뜻을 명확히 하기 위해 접속사를 생략하지 않기도 한다. 이 경우는 부사절에서 '주어+be동
사'를 생략한 것과 같은 형태가 된다.

- I mailed a letter **while taking a walk**. (나는 산책을 하면서 편지를 부쳤다.)

■ 부사절의 시제가 주절보다 앞선 경우에는 완료분사구문(having+과거분사)으로 쓴다.

- As he had done it before, he was going to do it.
  = **Having done it before**, he was going to do it.

■ 과거분사로 시작되는 분사구문은 being이 생략된 것으로 수동의 의미를 갖는다.

- **Written in English**, the book is not easy to read. (영어로 쓰여졌기 때문에, 그 책은 읽기에 쉽지 않다.)

핵심 Check

1. 다음 괄호 안에서 알맞은 말을 고르시오.

   (1) (Live / Living) next door, I often see Billy.

   (2) (Listening / Listened) to the music, she stayed up late.

② so that ~ can ...

> • They made up this fake article **so that** they **could** draw the readers' attention.
> 그들은 독자들의 주의를 끌기 위해 이 가짜 기사를 지어냈다.

■ so that은 '~하기 위해', '~하고자', '~하도록'의 의미로 '목적'이나 '의도'를 나타낸다. 일반적으로 '주절+so that+주어+can/will+동사원형 ~'의 형태로 쓰인다.
  • He tried to make friends with him **so that** he **could** get help from the wolf. (그는 늑대로부터 도움을 받을 수 있도록 그와 친구가 되려고 하였다.)
  • She worked hard **so that** everything **would** be ready in time. (그녀는 모든 것이 제시간에 준비될 수 있도록 열심히 일을 했다.)

■ 'so that ~ can ...'은 'in order that ~ can ...'으로 바꿔 쓸 수 있으며, 주절과 종속절의 주어가 같은 경우 '(in order[so as]) to부정사'로 바꿔 쓸 수 있다.
  • I borrowed a book **so that** I **could** read during weekends. (나는 주말 동안 읽으려고 책을 한 권 빌렸다.)
  = I borrowed a book **in order that** I **could** read during weekends.
  = I borrowed a book **to read** during weekends. 〈to부정사의 부사적 용법 – 목적〉
  = I borrowed a book **in order to read** during weekends.
  = I borrowed a book **so as to read** during weekends.

■ so that을 기준으로 앞과 뒤의 동사의 시제를 일치시킨다.
  • He takes a taxi **so that** he **won't** be late. (그는 지각하지 않기 위해 택시를 탄다.)
  • He took a taxi **so that** he **wouldn't** be late. (그는 지각하지 않기 위해 택시를 탔다.)

■ 'so that'은 '결과'의 부사절을 이끌어 '그래서, 그러므로'의 의미를 갖는 접속사로 쓰이기도 하는데, 대개 앞에 쉼표(,)가 온다.
  • He always breaks his promises, **so that** he has no friends. (그는 항상 약속을 어긴다. 그래서 그는 친구가 없다.)

■ so와 that 사이에 수식어가 오면, '너무 ~해서 결국 …하다'라는 뜻이 되며, 'so+형용사[부사]+that+주어+can ...(매우 ~해서 …할 수 있는)'은 '형용사+enough to ...(…할 정도로 충분히 ~한)'로 바꿔 쓸 수 있으며, 'so+형용사[부사]+that+주어+can't ...(너무 ~해서 …할 수 없는)'은 'too+형용사[부사]+to부정사(…하기에 너무 ~한)'로 바꿔 쓸 수 있다.
  • I got **so** excited **that** I was at a loss for words. (나는 너무 흥분한 나머지 말문이 막혔다.)
  • He was **so** happy **that** he could dance. (그는 뛸 듯이 기뻐했다.)
  = He was happy **enough to** dance.

핵심 Check

2. 다음 괄호 안에서 알맞은 말을 고르시오.

(1) She hurried up so (that / which) she could get there on time.

(2) Use a hand signal (in that / so that) drivers can see you.

01 다음 우리말에 맞게 빈칸에 알맞은 것은?

> 당신이 그곳에 제시간에 도착할 수 있게 빨리 몰겠습니다.
> = I'll drive fast so _____ you can get there in time.

① this   ② that   ③ what
④ which   ⑤ it

02 다음 괄호 안에서 알맞은 말을 고르시오.

(1) (Have / Having) no money, I couldn't buy a new bike.

(2) (Knowing not / Not knowing) what to do, I was at my wits' end.

(3) I went to the zoo (though / so that) my sister could see wild animals.

(4) I was very excited, (because / so that) I couldn't get to sleep.

03 다음 빈칸에 들어갈 말로 알맞은 것은?

> _____ me, the man ran off.

① Seeing   ② Seen   ③ Sees
④ Saw   ⑤ See

04 다음 우리말에 맞게 주어진 어휘를 바르게 배열하시오.

(1) 성적표를 보면서, 엄마의 얼굴이 어두워졌다.

(mom's face, the report card, looking, darkened, at)

➡ _____

(2) 우리는 책을 빌릴 수 있도록 도서관에 갈 것이다.

(we, we, can, are, borrow, going, so, books, the library, that, to)

➡ _____

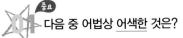
01 다음 중 어법상 어색한 것은?

① Feeling happy, she sang a song.
② Working in the hospital, my aunt helped many people.
③ Aaron danced on the stage listened to the music.
④ He uses his cellphone while walking on the street.
⑤ Turning left, you can find the bus stop.

02 다음 중 어법상 바르지 않은 것은?

① Speak clearly so that we can understand you.
② I had to save much money to buy a new car.
③ The bird practiced flying hard so to fly up high.
④ I took a taxi in order that I could be there on time.
⑤ She arrived early in order to get a good seat.

03 다음 빈칸에 알맞은 말이 바르게 짝지어진 것은?

> • He is eating his favorite egg sandwich _____ a newspaper.
> • Put on a helmet _____ that you can protect your head.

① reading – so
② reading – for
③ reads – so
④ reads – for
⑤ read – in

서답형

04 다음 괄호 안에서 알맞은 말을 고르시오.

(1) Save electricity so (that / as) we can save polar bears.
(2) He noted every detail so (as / that) to fix the scene in his mind.
(3) Come early in (order / condition) that you can see him.
(4) (Neglected / Neglecting) his duty, he was fired.
(5) When (process / processing) your request, an error occurred.
(6) (Knowing not / Not knowing) what to do, I asked for my mom's advice.

05 주어진 두 문장을 한 문장으로 바꿀 때 옳지 않은 것은?

> • I arrived home late at night.
> • I saw some fruits and ate them.

① When I arrived home late at night, I saw some fruits and ate them.
② As I arrived home late at night, I saw some fruits and ate them.
③ Arriving home late at night, I saw some fruits and ate them.
④ When arriving home late at night, I saw some fruits and ate them.
⑤ When arrived home late at night, I saw some fruits and ate them.

06 빈칸 (A)와 (B)에 알맞은 것으로 바르게 짝지어진 것은?

> • Get up early ___(A)___ as to be in time for the first train.
> • He is ___(B)___ rich that he can buy the sports car.

	(A)	(B)
①	too	so
②	too	too
③	so	so
④	so	too
⑤	enough	as

07 다음 문장의 밑줄 친 부분 중 어법상 어색한 것은?

> David, ⓐthought ⓑthat ⓒit ⓓwould soon pass, ⓔignored his headache.

① ⓐ   ② ⓑ   ③ ⓒ
④ ⓓ   ⑤ ⓔ

08 다음 밑줄 친 부분과 바꿔 쓸 수 있는 것은?

> Jim sold his watch so that he could buy the coat.

① in that   ② so as to   ③ to
④ in order   ⑤ in order that

서답형
09 다음 두 문장을 한 문장으로 바꿔 쓸 때 빈칸에 들어갈 한 단어를 쓰시오.

> • You cross the street.
> • You should be careful.
> = _____ the street, you should be careful.

10 다음 우리말을 바르게 영작한 것을 고르시오.

> 네가 건강해질 수 있도록 채소를 더 많이 먹어야 한다.

① You should eat more vegetables so what you can be healthy.
② You should eat more vegetables so that you can be healthy.
③ You should eat more vegetables in that you can be healthy.
④ You should eat more vegetables so as you can be healthy.
⑤ You should eat more vegetables so to you can be healthy.

11 분사구문의 의미가 밑줄 친 부분과 같은 것은?

> Being small, the kitchen is well designed.

① Having nothing to do, I went for a walk to the park.
② The sun being shining, it wasn't very warm.
③ We need luck when taking tests.
④ He told me a shocking story while having lunch together.
⑤ Not paying the rent, you'll be thrown out.

서답형
12 다음 문장에서 생략할 수 있는 것을 찾아 쓰시오.

(1) Though he was young, he had much gray hair.
➡ _____

(2) She had her picture taken when she was in Italy.
➡ _____

13 다음 문장과 뜻이 같은 것을 고르시오.

> The girl is too shy to speak in front of others.

① The girl is shy so that she can't speak in front of others.

② The girl is so that shy she can't speak in front of others.

③ The girl is so shy that can't speak in front of others.

④ The girl is so shy that she can't speak in front of others.

⑤ The girl is too shy to she can't speak in front of others.

서답형

14 다음 문장에서 어법상 어색한 것을 바르게 고쳐 다시 쓰시오.

(1) Don't throw trash in the sea in order for animals can live safely.

➡ _____

_____

(2) Look for hidden ideas so as that you can see what the writer really means.

➡ _____

_____

(3) Swum in the pond, she was wearing her swimming cap.

➡ _____

_____

(4) Being fine, we went for a walk to the beach.

➡ _____

(5) Seeing from high above, the cars looked tiny.

➡ _____

15 다음 우리말을 바르게 영작한 것을 고르시오.

> Kathryn은 그들의 이름을 들었지만, 그들을 구별하지 못했다.

① Although she hearing their names, Kathryn couldn't recognize them.

② She having heard their names, Kathryn couldn't recognize them.

③ Having heard their names, Kathryn not recognizing them.

④ Kathryn having heard their names, she couldn't recognize them.

⑤ Having heard their names, Kathryn couldn't recognize them.

16 다음 중 어법상 어색한 것을 모두 고르시오. (2개)

① She became too weak to move her own body easily.

② I was enough stupid to believe him.

③ Come early so as that you can have plenty of time.

④ Don't use smartphones so that others can study in a quiet place.

⑤ They made up this fake article so that they could draw the readers' attention.

서답형

17 다음 두 문장을 'so that'을 이용하여 한 문장으로 바꿔 쓰시오.

> • They confessed that they made it up.
> • They could draw the readers' attention to the unsafe conditions at the zoo.

➡ _____

_____

_____

01 다음 문장을 분사구문으로 바꿔 쓰시오.

(1) Because my mom caught a bad cold, she couldn't get to work.

➡ _____

_____

(2) After I finished breakfast, I took a taxi to school.

➡ _____

(3) If you mix blue and yellow, you get green.

➡ _____

(4) Although she was nervous, she said it was a good experience.

➡ _____

_____

(5) Because I didn't know what happened, I called my friend, Sam.

➡ _____

(6) If it is fine tomorrow, I will go hiking.

➡ _____

02 'so that'을 이용하여 다음 두 문장을 한 문장으로 바꿔 쓰시오.

(1) • Read the book carefully.
   • You can find hidden ideas.

➡ _____

_____

(2) • Sally bought a camera.
   • She could take great pictures.

➡ _____

_____

03 다음 우리말에 맞게 주어진 단어를 바르게 배열하시오.

(1) 그 뉴스가 거짓이라는 것을 알지 못했기 때문에 많은 사람이 겁에 질려 어쩔 줄 몰랐다. (people, the news, was, knowing, panicked, many, not, false)

➡ _____

_____

(2) 일찍 떠났지만, 그는 회의에 늦었다. (he, the meeting, was, leaving, early, late, for)

➡ _____

(3) 그는 매우 열심히 공부해서 마침내 변호사가 되었다. (he, he, a lawyer, that, worked, became, hard, finally, so)

➡ _____

(4) 그는 일찍 일어나서 첫 버스를 탈 수 있었다. (he, he, bus, catch, could, got, that, the, early, first, so, up)

➡ _____

_____

04 다음 문장에서 어법상 <u>어색한</u> 부분을 바르게 고치시오.

(1) Exhausting from the work, he lay down on the sofa.

➡ _____

(2) Failing twice, Jaden didn't want to try again.

➡ _____

05 그림을 보고 주어진 어휘를 이용하여 빈칸을 알맞게 채우시오.

(1) Mina reads newspapers every day
_____ keep up with
current affairs. (can, so)

(2) Mina reads newspapers every day
_____ keep up with
current affairs. (to, in)

(3) Mina reads newspapers every day
_____ keep up with
current affairs. (to, so)

06 그림을 보고 접속사 없이 주어진 어휘를 이용하여 빈칸을 알맞게 채우시오.

(1) _____ rainy, they cannot go for a
walk. (be)

(2) _____ the rain, they are talking
about whether to go shopping. (watch)

07 다음 우리말을 괄호 안의 지시대로 영작하시오.

(1) 왼쪽으로 돌면, 그 집을 찾을 겁니다.

➡ _____

(분사구문을 써서)

➡ _____

(접속사를 써서)

(2) 그녀는 아파서 학교에 결석했다.

➡ _____

(분사구문을 써서)

➡ _____

_____

(접속사를 써서)

(3) Lisa는 그녀의 엄마가 오렌지 주스를 만들 수
있도록 오렌지를 좀 샀다.

➡ _____

_____

(that을 써서)

08 다음 문장에서 <u>잘못된</u> 것을 알맞게 고쳐 다시 쓰시오.

(1) Judy practices playing the piano in
order to that she can win the top prize.

➡ _____

_____

(2) I got up early so as to I could go
jogging.

➡ _____

_____

(3) Arrived late at the station, I saw the
train leaving.

➡ _____

_____

Can You Spot Fake News?

Every day we watch, hear, or read interesting news. However, have you ever seriously considered whether an article is really true? Everyone likes an interesting news story but what if it is completely made up?

Fake news can be very harmful in that it can make people less informed or even misled. Nevertheless, there have been various fake news reports throughout history. Why have some people written such false information? Let's look into some articles thinking about the hidden motives behind them.

AWFUL DISASTER

Last night, an angry group of rhinoceroses broke down the walls of the cage at the zoo and escaped. They also broke down the walls of the other wild animals' cages. These animals ran down the streets and injured hundreds of people. Twelve of the animals are still on the loose. Citizens should stay indoors until further notice.

* Not a single act or incident described above has taken place.

spot 발견하다, 찾아내다
fake 가짜의, 거짓의
seriously 진지하게, 심각하게
harmful 해로운, 유해한
mislead 잘못 이끌다, 오해하게 하다
nevertheless 그럼에도 불구하고
motive 동기, 이유
make up 지어내다, 만들어 내다
awful 끔찍한, 지독한
disaster 참사, 재난
escape 달아나다, 탈출하다, 벗어나다
injure 부상을 입히다
citizen 시민
incident 사건
describe 기술하다
rhinoceros 코뿔소
break down ~을 부수다, ~을 무너뜨리다
on the loose 잡히지 않은, 탈주 중인
single 단 하나의
act 행동

 확인문제

● 다음 문장이 본문의 내용과 일치하면 T, 일치하지 않으면 F를 쓰시오.

1 Each day we watch, hear, or read interesting news. ☐

2 Fake news can make people well-informed. ☐

3 There have been various fake news reports throughout history. ☐

4 All the acts or incidents described in the article above actually took place. ☐

At that time, those who read the article carefully laughed out loud.
= the people 크게 웃었다

Those who didn't read it to the end got really worried. Not knowing
주격 관계대명사절 who didn't read it to the end가 선행사 Those를 수식　　이유를 나타내는 분사구문의 부정

the news was false, many people panicked. Some tried to escape the
Because they didn't know the news was false.

city while others went into the parks with guns to hunt the animals.
= other people

So why did *The Herald* make up such news? Later, they confessed
(남을 속이거나 즐겁게 하기 위해 이야기 등을) 지어내다, 만들어 내다　　　= The Herald

that they made it up so that they could draw the readers' attention to
= such news　　(in order) to draw

the unsafe conditions at the zoo.

SLAV SHOOTS A FRIEND IN ARGUMENT

Mejk Swenekafew, a Slav worker at the Columbia Coal Mine, was
Mejk Swenekafew와 a Slav worker at the Columbia Coal Mine은 동격

shot and seriously wounded by John Pecitello near the mining camp

Thursday evening.

The two men had an argument during a meeting. The argument led
언쟁을 벌였다, 말다툼을 했다　during+기간을 나타내는 명사

to a fight, and Pecitello shot Swenekafew twice, in the chest and leg.

He is now at the hospital in critical condition. Pecitello ran away after
be in critical condition: 위독한 상태에 있다

the shooting. The police are searching for him now and are warning
복수 취급　　　search for: ~을 찾다　　are searching and are warning: 접속사 and에 의해 병렬 구조로 연결되어 있음.

citizens that he is extremely dangerous.

panic 겁에 질려 어쩔 줄 모르다
confess 고백하다, 인정하다
unsafe 안전하지 않은
condition 상태
Slav 슬라브인
shoot (총 등을) 쏘다
argument 논쟁, 언쟁
mine 광산, 채굴하다
lead to ~을 이끌다
twice 두 번
wound 상처를 입히다
chest 가슴, 흉부
critical 위험한, 위독한
extremely 극도로, 극히
run away 도망치다

확인문제

● 다음 문장이 본문의 내용과 일치하면 T, 일치하지 <u>않으면</u> F를 쓰시오.

1　At that time, those who read the article carefully laughed out loud. ☐

2　Those who read the article to the end got really worried. ☐

3　As they didn't know the news was false, many people panicked. ☐

4　John Pecitello was shot and seriously wounded by Mejk Swenekafew Thursday evening. ☐

5　Swenekafew is now at the hospital in critical condition. ☐

6　The police are warning citizens that Swenekafew is extremely dangerous. ☐

Is there anything strange about the article? Read the Slav's name backwards; it spells, "we-fake-news." Who wrote this and why?

the Slav's name. 즉 'Swenekafew'를 가리킨다.　fake: '위조하다, 조작하다'

The Daily Telegram published this fake article so that they could

= in order to prove

prove if *The Daily News*, their competitor, was stealing their articles.

if(= whether): '~인지 아닌지'라는 의미의 명사절을 이끄는 접속사.

The Daily News published the same article about "Swenekafew" the next day and thus got caught stealing. The people at *The Daily News*

잡혔다, 포착되었다

had to admit their act and were harshly criticized by the public.

그동안 몰래 데일리 텔레그램 사의 기사를 훔쳤던 행위
The people at The Daily News를 주어로 하는 수동태 문장. "The public harshly criticized the people at The Daily News ."(능동태)

The two articles were special cases, but there are many "fake" news

there+be동사: '~이 있다'는 의미, 주어는 many "fake" news articles

articles published every day. As readers, we need to read critically

과거분사로 앞에 나온 명사 articles를 수식

and judge whether the news is real or fake.

'~인지 아닌지'라는 의미의 접속사 = if

How to spot fake news!

how+to부정사: ~하는 방법

Consider the Source

기사의 출처인 원본 자료나 뉴스의 정보원 혹은 소식통을 의미

Is it from a reliable source?
Can we trust the writer?

Check the Date

Is it a new or an old story?
Is it related to current events?

be related to: ~와 관련이 있다

Read Beyond the Headlines

단순히 기사 제목만 읽고 뉴스의 내용을 짐작하여 판단하지 말고, 그 기사의 내용까지 모두 읽으라는 의미

Does the headline match the content?

Find Supporting Sources

Do other related stories provide similar content?

---

spell 철자를 말하다(쓰다)
publish 발행하다, 출판하다, 게재하다
competitor 경쟁자, 경쟁 상대
admit 인정하다, 자백하다
criticize 비난하다
public 대중, 일반 사람들
critically 비판적으로
judge 판단하다
source 출처, 자료
reliable 믿을 만한, 신뢰할 만한
current 현재의, 지금의
support 뒷받침하다

📎 **확인문제**

- 다음 문장이 본문의 내용과 일치하면 T, 일치하지 <u>않으면</u> F를 쓰시오.

1 *The Daily Telegram* published this fake article so that they could prove that *The Daily News* was stealing their articles. ☐

2 *The Daily News* published a little bit different article about "Swenekafew" the next day. ☐

3 The people at *The Daily News* were harshly criticized by the public. ☐

4 To spot fake news, we need not check many sources. ☐

5 To spot fake news, it is necessary to check the date. ☐

6 To spot fake news, we shouldn't read beyond the headlines. ☐

● 우리말을 참고하여 빈칸에 알맞은 말을 쓰시오.

1 Can You _____ _____ _____?

2 Every day we watch, hear, or read _____ _____.

3 However, have you ever seriously considered _____ an article is really true?

4 Everyone likes an interesting news story but _____ _____ it is completely _____ _____?

5 Fake news can be very harmful _____ _____ it can make people _____ _____ or even _____.

6 _____, there have been various fake news reports _____ _____.

7 Why have some people written _____ _____ _____?

8 Let's look into some articles _____ about _____ _____ behind them.

9 _____ DISASTER

10 Last night, an angry group of rhinoceroses _____ _____ the walls of the cage at the zoo and escaped.

11 They also broke down the walls of _____ _____ wild animals' cages.

12 These animals ran down the streets and injured _____ _____ people.

13 Twelve of the animals are still _____ _____ _____.

14 Citizens should stay indoors _____ _____ _____.

15 Not a single act or incident _____ _____ has taken place.

16 At that time, those who read the article carefully _____ _____ _____.

---

1 당신은 가짜 뉴스임을 알아챌 수 있는가?

2 매일 우리는 흥미로운 뉴스를 보고, 듣고, 읽는다.

3 그러나 당신은 뉴스 기사가 정말로 진실인지 심각하게 고려해 본 적이 있는가?

4 모든 사람이 흥미로운 뉴스 기사를 좋아하지만, 만약 그것이 완전히 지어낸 것이라면 어떻게 할 것인가?

5 가짜 뉴스는 사람들에게 정보를 부족하게 제공하거나 사람들을 잘못 이끌 수 있다는 점에서 매우 해로울 수 있다.

6 그럼에도 불구하고, 역사를 통틀어 다양한 가짜 뉴스 보도들이 존재해 왔다.

7 왜 어떤 사람들은 그러한 거짓 정보를 써 왔던 것일까?

8 그 뒤에 숨겨진 동기를 생각하면서 몇 가지 뉴스 기사를 살펴보자.

9 끔찍한 참사

10 어젯밤, 화가 난 코뿔소 떼가 동물원 우리의 벽을 부수고 도망쳤다.

11 그들은 또한 다른 야생 동물 우리의 벽도 부수었다.

12 이 동물들은 거리를 뛰어다니며 수백 명의 사람들에게 부상을 입혔다.

13 그중 열두 마리의 동물들이 아직 잡히지 않았다.

14 시민들은 추후 안내가 있을 때까지 집 안에 머물러야 한다.

15 위에 기술된 어떤 행동이나 사건도 일어나지 않았다.

16 그 당시 이 기사를 주의 깊게 읽었던 사람들은 크게 웃었다.

17 Those who didn't read it to the end _____ _____ _____ .

18 _____ _____ the news was false, many people _____ .

19 _____ tried to escape the city while _____ went into the parks with guns to hunt the animals.

20 So why did *The Herald* _____ _____ _____ _____ ?

21 Later, they confessed that they _____ _____ _____ _____ _____ they _____ draw the readers' attention to the unsafe conditions at the zoo.

22 SLAV SHOOTS A FRIEND _____ _____

23 Mejk Swenekafew, a Slav worker at the Columbia Coal Mine, _____ _____ and seriously _____ by John Pecitello near the mining camp Thursday evening.

24 The two men _____ _____ during a meeting.

25 The argument _____ _____ a fight, and Pecitello shot Swenekafew twice, _____ _____ _____ and leg.

26 He is now at the hospital _____ _____ _____ .

27 Pecitello ran away _____ _____ _____ .

28 The police _____ _____ _____ him now and _____ _____ citizens that he is extremely dangerous.

29 Is there _____ _____ about the article?

30 Read the Slav's name _____ ; it spells, "we-fake-news."

31 Who wrote this and _____ ?

17 그것을 끝까지 읽지 않은 사람들은 정말로 걱정하였다.

18 그 기사가 거짓이라는 것을 알지 못했기 때문에 많은 사람이 겁에 질려 어쩔 줄 몰랐다.

19 어떤 사람들은 도시를 빠져나가려고 했고 다른 사람들은 그 동물들을 사냥하기 위해 총을 들고 공원으로 나갔다.

20 그렇다면 왜 헤럴드 사는 이러한 뉴스를 만들어 냈을까?

21 나중에 그들은 동물원의 안전하지 않은 상태에 대해 독자들의 주의를 끌기 위해 그 기사를 지어냈다고 고백했다.

22 슬라브인이 언쟁 중에 친구에게 총을 쏘다

23 목요일 저녁 채굴 야영지 근처에서, 컬럼비아 광산 소속의 슬라브인 노동자 Mejk Swenekafew가 John Pecitello에 의해 총상을 입어 심각하게 다쳤다.

24 그 두 사람은 회의 중에 언쟁을 벌였다.

25 언쟁이 싸움으로 번졌고, Pecitello가 Swenekafew의 가슴과 다리에 두 번 총을 쏘았다.

26 현재 그는 위독한 상태로 입원 중이다.

27 Pecitello는 총격 이후 도주했다.

28 경찰이 지금 그를 찾고 있으며, 그가 극히 위험하다고 시민들에게 경고하고 있다.

29 이 기사에 뭔가 이상한 점이 있는가?

30 그 슬라브인의 이름을 거꾸로 읽어 보아라. 그것의 철자는 "우리는 뉴스를 조작한다."가 된다.

31 누가 이것을 썼고 왜 그랬을까?

32 *The Daily Telegram* published this fake article _____ _____ they _____ prove _____ *The Daily News*, their competitor, was stealing their articles.

33 *The Daily News* published the same article about "Swenekafew" the next day and thus _____ _____ _____.

34 The people at *The Daily News* had to _____ their act and _____ _____ _____ by the public.

35 The two articles were special cases, but there are many "fake" news articles _____ every day.

36 _____ readers, we need to read critically and judge _____ the news is real _____ fake.

37 _____ _____ _____ fake news!

38 Consider the _____

39 Is it from a _____ source?

40 Can we _____ the writer?

41 _____ the Date

42 Is it a _____ or an _____ story?

43 _____ it _____ _____ _____ events?

44 Read _____ _____ _____

45 Does the headline _____ _____ _____ ?

46 Find _____ Sources

47 Do other _____ stories provide _____ content?

---

32 데일리 텔레그램 사는 그들의 경쟁자인 데일리 뉴스 사가 그들의 기사를 훔치는지를 증명하기 위해서 이 거짓 기사를 발행했다.

33 데일리 뉴스 사는 그 다음 날 'Swenekafew'에 대한 동일한 기사를 발행했고 그래서 훔친 것이 발각되었다.

34 데일리 뉴스 사의 사람들은 그들의 행동을 인정해야만 했고 대중들로부터 혹독한 비난을 받았다.

35 이 두 기사는 특별한 경우였지만, 매일 발행되는 '가짜' 뉴스 기사는 많이 있다.

36 독자로서, 우리는 비판적으로 읽고 그 뉴스가 진짜인지 가짜인지 판단할 필요가 있다.

37 가짜 뉴스 판별 방법!

38 출처를 고려하라

39 그것은 믿을 만한 출처에서 온 것인가?

40 우리는 그 필자를 신뢰할 수 있는가?

41 날짜를 확인하라

42 그것은 새로운 이야기인가 혹은 오래된 이야기인가?

43 그것은 현재의 사건들과 관련된 것인가?

44 기사 제목 그 이상을 읽어라

45 기사 제목이 기사 내용과 일치하는가?

46 뒷받침하는 자료를 찾아라

47 다른 관련된 이야기도 비슷한 내용을 제공하는가?

• 우리말을 참고하여 본문을 영작하시오.

1 당신은 가짜 뉴스임을 알아챌 수 있는가?

➡ _____

2 매일 우리는 흥미로운 뉴스를 보고, 듣고, 읽는다.

➡ _____

3 그러나 당신은 뉴스 기사가 정말로 진실인지 심각하게 고려해 본 적이 있는가?

➡ _____

4 모든 사람이 흥미로운 뉴스 기사를 좋아하지만, 만약 그것이 완전히 지어낸 것이라면 어떻게 할 것인가?

➡ _____

5 가짜 뉴스는 사람들에게 정보를 부족하게 제공하거나 사람들을 잘못 이끌 수 있다는 점에서 매우 해로울 수 있다.

➡ _____

6 그럼에도 불구하고, 역사를 통틀어 다양한 가짜 뉴스 보도들이 존재해 왔다.

➡ _____

7 왜 어떤 사람들은 그러한 거짓 정보를 써 왔던 것일까?

➡ _____

8 그 뒤에 숨겨진 동기를 생각하면서 몇 가지 뉴스 기사를 살펴보자.

➡ _____

9 끔찍한 참사

➡ _____

10 어젯밤, 화가 난 코뿔소 떼가 동물원 우리의 벽을 부수고 도망쳤다.

➡ _____

11 그들은 또한 다른 야생 동물 우리의 벽도 부수었다.

➡ _____

12 이 동물들은 거리를 뛰어다니며 수백 명의 사람들에게 부상을 입혔다.

➡ _____

13 그중 열두 마리의 동물들이 아직 잡히지 않았다.

➡ _____

14 시민들은 추후 안내가 있을 때까지 집 안에 머물러야 한다.

➡ _____

15 위에 기술된 어떤 행동이나 사건도 일어나지 않았다.

➡ _____

16 그 당시 이 기사를 주의 깊게 읽었던 사람들은 크게 웃었다.

➡ _____

17 그것을 끝까지 읽지 않은 사람들은 정말로 걱정하였다.

　➡ _____

18 그 기사가 거짓이라는 것을 알지 못했기 때문에 많은 사람이 겁에 질려 어쩔 줄 몰랐다.

　➡ _____

19 어떤 사람들은 도시를 빠져나가려고 했고 다른 사람들은 그 동물들을 사냥하기 위해 총을 들고 공원으로 나갔다.

　➡ _____

20 그렇다면 왜 헤럴드 사는 이러한 뉴스를 만들어 냈을까?

　➡ _____

21 나중에 그들은 동물원의 안전하지 않은 상태에 대해 독자들의 주의를 끌기 위해 그 기사를 지어냈다고 고백했다.

　➡ _____

22 슬라브인이 언쟁 중에 친구에게 총을 쏘다

　➡ _____

23 목요일 저녁 채굴 야영지 근처에서, 컬럼비아 광산 소속의 슬라브인 노동자 Mejk Swenekafew가 John Pecitello에 의해 총상을 입어 심각하게 다쳤다.

　➡ _____

24 그 두 사람은 회의 중에 언쟁을 벌였다.

　➡ _____

25 언쟁이 싸움으로 번졌고, Pecitello가 Swenekafew의 가슴과 다리에 두 번 총을 쏘았다.

　➡ _____

26 현재 그는 위독한 상태로 입원 중이다.

　➡ _____

27 Pecitello는 총격 이후 도주했다.

　➡ _____

28 경찰이 지금 그를 찾고 있으며, 그가 극히 위험하다고 시민들에게 경고하고 있다.

　➡ _____

29 이 기사에 뭔가 이상한 점이 있는가?

　➡ _____

30 그 슬라브인의 이름을 거꾸로 읽어 보아라. 그것의 철자는 "우리는 뉴스를 조작한다."가 된다.

　➡ _____

31 누가 이것을 썼고 왜 그랬을까?

　➡ _____

32 데일리 텔레그램 사는 그들의 경쟁자인 데일리 뉴스 사가 그들의 기사를 훔치는지를 증명하기 위해서 이 거짓 기사를 발행했다.

➡ _____

_____

33 데일리 뉴스 사는 그 다음 날 'Swenekafew'에 대한 동일한 기사를 발행했고 그래서 훔친 것이 발각되었다.

➡ _____

34 데일리 뉴스 사의 사람들은 그들의 행동을 인정해야만 했고 대중들로부터 혹독한 비난을 받았다.

➡ _____

34 이 두 기사는 특별한 경우였지만, 매일 발행되는 '가짜' 뉴스 기사는 많이 있다.

➡ _____

36 독자로서, 우리는 비판적으로 읽고 그 뉴스가 진짜인지 가짜인지 판단할 필요가 있다.

➡ _____

37 가짜 뉴스 판별 방법!

➡ _____

38 출처를 고려하라

➡ _____

39 그것은 믿을 만한 출처에서 온 것인가?

➡ _____

40 우리는 그 필자를 신뢰할 수 있는가?

➡ _____

41 날짜를 확인하라

➡ _____

42 그것은 새로운 이야기인가 혹은 오래된 이야기인가?

➡ _____

43 그것은 현재의 사건들과 관련된 것인가?

➡ _____

44 기사 제목 그 이상을 읽어라

➡ _____

45 기사 제목이 기사 내용과 일치하는가?

➡ _____

46 뒷받침하는 자료를 찾아라

➡ _____

47 다른 관련된 이야기도 비슷한 내용을 제공하는가?

➡ _____

[01~04] 다음 글을 읽고 물음에 답하시오.

Every day we watch, hear, or read interesting news. ___ⓐ___, have you ever seriously considered whether an article is really true? (①) Everyone likes an interesting news story but what if it is completely made up? (②)

ⓑFake news can be very harmful in that they can make people less informed or even misled. (③) Why have some people written such false information? (④) Let's look into some articles thinking about the hidden motives behind them. (⑤)

01 위 글의 빈칸 ⓐ에 들어갈 알맞은 말을 고르시오.

① In addition　　② In other words
③ Therefore　　④ However
⑤ For example

02 위 글의 흐름으로 보아, 주어진 문장이 들어가기에 가장 적절한 곳은?

> Nevertheless, there have been various fake news reports throughout history.

①　　②　　③　　④　　⑤

03 According to the passage, which is NOT true?

① Day after day we watch, hear, or read interesting news.
② There is no one that doesn't like an interesting news story.
③ Fake news can be very damaging.
④ People may be well-informed because of fake news.
⑤ Fake news can mislead people.

04 위 글의 밑줄 친 ⓑ에서 어법상 틀린 부분을 찾아 고치시오.

➡ _____

[05~07] 다음 글을 읽고 물음에 답하시오.

AWFUL DISASTER

Last night, an angry group of rhinoceroses broke down the walls of the cage at the zoo and escaped. They also broke down the walls of the other wild animals' cages. These animals ran down the streets and injured hundreds of people. Twelve of the animals are still ___ⓐ___ the loose. Citizens should stay indoors ___ⓑ___ further notice.

*Not ⓒa single act or incident described above has ⓓtaken place.

05 위 글의 빈칸 ⓐ와 ⓑ에 들어갈 전치사가 바르게 짝지어진 것은?

　　ⓐ　ⓑ　　　　　　　ⓐ　ⓑ
① at – by　　　　② on – until
③ in – until　　　④ at – for
⑤ on – with

06 다음 중 위 글의 밑줄 친 ⓒ에 해당하지 않는 것을 고르시오.

① 어젯밤, 화가 난 코뿔소 떼가 동물원 우리의 벽을 부수고 도망쳤다.
② 코뿔소 떼가 다른 야생 동물 우리의 벽도 부수었다.
③ 이 동물들이 거리를 뛰어다녔다.
④ 수백 명의 사람들이 부상을 입었다.
⑤ 그 중 열두 마리의 동물들이 잡혔다.

07 위 글의 밑줄 친 ⓐtaken place와 바꿔 쓸 수 있는 말을 모두 고르시오.

① been held   ② happened
③ occurred   ④ been hosted
⑤ arisen

[08~10] 다음 글을 읽고 물음에 답하시오.

At that time, those who read the article carefully laughed out loud. Those who didn't read it to the end got really worried. ⓐNot knowing the news was false, many people panicked. Some tried to escape the city while others went into the parks with guns to hunt the animals.

So why did *The Herald* ⓑmake up such news? Later, they confessed that they made it up so that they could draw the readers' attention to the unsafe conditions at the zoo.

08 아래 〈보기〉에서 위 글의 밑줄 친 ⓐ와 분사구문의 용법이 다른 것의 개수를 고르시오.

┌─ 보기 ─────────────────────┐
① Not having much money, he acted like a rich man.
② Having nothing to do, I went to bed earlier than usual.
③ Finding my son in the mall, please let me know.
④ Not failing the test, she still looked miserable.
⑤ Being sick, she decided not to go to school.
└──────────────────────────┘

① 1개   ② 2개   ③ 3개   ④ 4개   ⑤ 5개

09 위 글의 밑줄 친 ⓑmake up과 같은 의미로 쓰인 것을 고르시오.

① He likes to make up fun songs.
② Can I leave early this afternoon and make up the time tomorrow?
③ They fight and make up quite often.
④ Eleven players make up a team.
⑤ I make up my face to look like a clown.

10 위 글의 주제로 알맞은 것을 고르시오.

① the laughter of the readers who read the article carefully
② the worry of the readers who didn't read the article to the end
③ the reason why many people panicked
④ the false news to draw the readers' attention
⑤ the unsafe conditions at the zoo

[11~13] 다음 글을 읽고 물음에 답하시오.

SLAV SHOOTS A FRIEND IN ARGUMENT
Mejk Swenekafew, a Slav worker at the Columbia Coal Mine, was (A)[shot / shut] and seriously wounded by John Pecitello near the mining camp Thursday evening.

The two men had an argument during a meeting. The argument led to a fight, and Pecitello shot Swenekafew twice, in the chest and leg. ⓐHe is now at the hospital in critical condition. Pecitello ran away after the shooting. The police (B)[is / are] searching for him now and (C)[is / are] warning citizens that he is extremely dangerous.

서답형

11 위 글의 괄호 (A)~(C)에서 문맥이나 어법상 알맞은 낱말을 골라 쓰시오.

➡ (A)_____ (B)_____ (C)_____

서답형

12 위 글의 밑줄 친 ⓐHe가 가리키는 것을 본문에서 찾아 쓰시오.

➡ _____

13 위 글을 읽고 Mejk Swenekafew에 대해 알 수 없는 것을 고르시오.

① Where did he work?
② Why did he have an argument with John Pecitello?
③ When was he shot?
④ How many times was he shot?
⑤ Where is he now?

[14~16] 다음 글을 읽고 물음에 답하시오.

Every day we watch, hear, or read interesting news. However, ⓐhave you ever seriously considered whether an article is really true? Everyone likes an interesting news story but what if it is completely made up?

Fake news can be very harmful (A)[in that / in which] it can make people less informed or even (B)[misleading / misled]. Nevertheless, there have been various fake news reports throughout history. Why have some people written (C)[so / such] false information? Let's look into some articles thinking about the hidden motives behind them.

서답형

14 위 글의 괄호 (A)~(C)에서 어법상 알맞은 낱말을 골라 쓰시오.

➡ (A)_____ (B)_____ (C)_____

15 위 글의 밑줄 친 문장 ⓐ의 현재완료 have considered와 용법이 같은 것을 모두 고르시오.

① How many times have you done it?
② He has gone to New York.
③ He has been ill for two weeks.
④ She has seen my brother before.
⑤ I have just finished my homework.

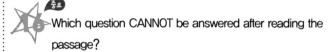

Which question CANNOT be answered after reading the passage?

① How many interesting news do we watch, hear, or read each day?
② What kind of news story does everyone like?
③ Can fake news make people less informed?
④ Can fake news mislead people?
⑤ Have there been various fake news reports throughout history?

[17~19] 다음 글을 읽고 물음에 답하시오.

The two articles were special cases, but there are many "fake" news articles ⓐ_____ every day. As readers, we need to read critically and judge whether the news is real or fake.

How to spot fake news!
Consider the Source
Is it from a reliable source?
Can we trust the writer?

Check the Date
Is it a new or an old story?
Is it related to ⓑcurrent events?

Read Beyond the Headlines
Does the headline match the content?

Find Supporting Sources
Do other related stories provide similar content?

17 위 글의 빈칸 ⓐ에 publish를 알맞은 형태로 쓰시오.

➡ _____

18 위 글의 밑줄 친 ⓑcurrent와 같은 의미로 쓰인 것을 고르시오.

① These words are no longer current.
② He swam to the shore against a strong current.
③ The direct current flows in one direction.
④ Do you know the budget for the current year?
⑤ He doesn't want to swim against the current.

19 위 글을 읽고 가짜 뉴스 판별 방법에 해당하지 않는 것을 고르시오.

① to consider the source
② to guess the content by the headlines
③ to check the date
④ to read beyond the headlines
⑤ to find supporting sources

[20~23] 다음 글을 읽고 물음에 답하시오.

Is there anything strange about the article? ⓐ Read the Slav's name forward; it spells, "we-fake-news." Who wrote this and why?

The Daily Telegram published this fake article so that they could prove ⓑif *The Daily News*, their competitor, was stealing their articles. *The Daily News* published the same article about "Swenekafew" the next day and thus got caught stealing. The people at *The Daily News* had to admit their act and were harshly criticized by the public.

20 위 글의 밑줄 친 ⓐ에서 흐름상 어색한 부분을 찾아 고치시오.

➡ _____

21 위 글의 밑줄 친 ⓑif와 문법적 쓰임이 같은 것을 모두 고르시오.

① I can come at once if necessary.
② You can stay for the weekend if you like.
③ Do you know if he's married?
④ She will forgive you if you apologize to her.
⑤ I wonder if I should wear a coat.

22 According to the passage, which is NOT true?

① *The Daily Telegram* published this fake article.
② *The Daily News* was the competitor of *The Daily Telegram*.
③ *The Daily Telegram* published the same article about "Swenekafew" the next day.
④ *The Daily News* got caught stealing.
⑤ *The Daily News* were harshly criticized by the public.

23 다음 주어진 영영풀이에 해당하는 단어를 본문에서 찾아 쓰시오.

not genuine or real

➡ _____

[24~26] 다음 글을 읽고 물음에 답하시오.

Every day we watch, hear, or read interesting news. However, have you ever seriously considered whether an article is really true? Everyone likes an interesting news story but what if it is completely made up?

Fake news can be very harmful in that it can make people less informed or even misled. ⓐ Nevertheless, there have been various fake news reports throughout history. Why have some people written such false information? Let's look into some articles thinking about the hidden motives behind ⓑthem.

[27~29] 다음 글을 읽고 물음에 답하시오.

At that time, those who read the article carefully laughed out loud. (A)그것을 끝까지 읽지 않은 사람들은 정말로 걱정하였다. Not knowing the news was false, many people panicked. __ⓐ__ tried to escape the city while __ⓑ__ went into the parks with guns to hunt the animals.

So why did The Herald make up such news? (B)Later, they confessed that they made up it so that they could draw the readers' attention to the unsafe conditions at the zoo.

24 위 글의 밑줄 친 ⓐNevertheless와 바꿔 쓸 수 있는 말을 모두 고르시오.

① Despite ② Therefore
③ Still ④ Otherwise
⑤ Nonetheless

27 위 글의 빈칸 ⓐ와 ⓑ에 들어갈 알맞은 말을 고르시오.

① One – the other
② Some – the others
③ Another – the other
④ The first – the second
⑤ Some – others

25 위 글의 밑줄 친 ⓑthem이 가리키는 것을 본문에서 찾아 쓰시오.

➡ _____

28 위 글의 밑줄 친 (A)의 우리말에 맞게 주어진 어휘를 알맞게 배열하시오.

worried / end / who / to / didn't / got / it / those / really / the / read

➡ _____

 위 글의 제목으로 알맞은 것을 고르시오.

① Do You Want to Spot Fake News?
② Have You Considered If the News Is True?
③ Who Doesn't Like an Interesting News Story?
④ Harmful but Continuous Fake News Reports
⑤ Let's Write Faithful News Reports from Now on.

29 위 글의 밑줄 친 (B)에서 어법상 틀린 부분을 찾아 고치시오.

➡ _____

[01~03] 다음 글을 읽고 물음에 답하시오.

Every day we watch, hear, or read interesting news. However, have you ever seriously considered whether an article is really true? Everyone likes an interesting news story but what (A)[if / whether] it is completely made up?

Fake news can be very (B)[harmful / harmless] in that it can make people less (C)[informing / informed] or even misled. Nevertheless, there have been various fake news reports throughout history. ⓐ왜 어떤 사람들은 그러한 거짓 정보를 써 왔던 것일까? Let's look into some articles ⓑthinking about the hidden motives behind them.

01 위 글의 괄호 (A)~(C)에서 문맥이나 어법상 알맞은 낱말을 골라 쓰시오.

➡ (A) _____ (B) _____ (C) _____

02 위 글의 밑줄 친 ⓐ의 우리말에 맞게 주어진 어휘를 알맞게 배열하시오.

people / false / written / some / information / why / such / have / ?

➡ _____

_____

03 위 글의 밑줄 친 ⓑ를 부사절로 고치시오.

➡ _____

_____

[04~06] 다음 글을 읽고 물음에 답하시오.

AWFUL DISASTER

Last night, an angry group of rhinoceroses broke down the walls of the cage at the zoo and escaped. They also broke down the walls of the other wild animals' cages. These animals ran down the streets and injured hundreds of people. Twelve of the animals are still ⓐ_____ _____ _____. Citizens should stay indoors until further notice.

*ⓑNot a single act or incident described above has been taken place.

04 주어진 영영풀이를 참고하여 빈칸 ⓐ에 철자 o로 시작하는 어구를 쓰시오.

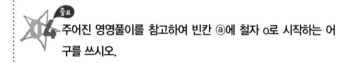

having escaped; not under control

➡ _____

05 위 글의 밑줄 친 ⓑ에서 어법상 틀린 부분을 찾아 고치시오.

➡ _____

06 Actually how many people were injured by the escaped animals from the zoo last night? Fill in the blanks (A) and (B) with suitable words.

(A)_____ one was injured by the escaped animals from the zoo because the animals didn't (B)_____ from the zoo last night in reality.

[07~08] 다음 글을 읽고 물음에 답하시오.

At that time, those who read the article carefully laughed out loud. Those who didn't read it to the end got really worried. Not knowing the news was false, many people panicked. Some tried to escape the city while ⓐothers went into the parks with guns to hunt the animals.

So why did *The Herald* make up such news? Later, they confessed that they made ⓑit up so that they could draw the readers' attention to the unsafe conditions at the zoo.

07 위 글의 밑줄 친 ⓐ를 다음과 같이 바꿔 쓸 때 빈칸에 들어갈 알맞은 말을 쓰시오.

➡ others went into the parks with guns _____ they _____ hunt the animals

08 위 글의 밑줄 친 ⓑit이 가리키는 것을 본문에서 찾아 쓰시오.

➡ _____

[09~10] 다음 글을 읽고 물음에 답하시오.

SLAV SHOOTS A FRIEND IN ARGUMENT
Mejk Swenekafew, a Slav worker at the Columbia Coal Mine, was shot and seriously wounded ①by John Pecitello ②near from the mining camp Thursday evening.

The two men had an argument during a meeting. The argument led to a fight, and Pecitello shot Swenekafew twice, ③in the chest and leg. He is now at the hospital ④in critical condition. Pecitello ran away after the shooting. The police are searching ⑤for him now and are warning citizens that he is extremely dangerous.

09 위 글의 밑줄 친 ①~⑤에서 어법상 어색한 것을 찾아 알맞게 고치시오.

➡ _____

10 본문의 내용과 일치하도록 다음 빈칸 (A)와 (B)에 알맞은 단어를 쓰시오.

Mejk Swenekafew (A)_____ _____ _____ with John Pecitello during a meeting and Pecitello shot him. Swenekafew is now at the hospital and his condition is (B)_____.

[11~12] 다음 글을 읽고 물음에 답하시오.

Is there anything strange about the article? Read the Slav's name backwards; it spells, "we-fake-news." Who wrote this and why?
The Daily Telegram published this fake article so that they could prove ⓐif *The Daily News*, their competitor, was stealing their articles. *The Daily News* published the same article about "Swenekafew" the next day and thus got caught stealing. The people at *The Daily News* had to admit ⓑtheir act and were harshly criticized by the public.

11 위 글의 밑줄 친 ⓐif와 바꿔 쓸 수 있는 말을 쓰시오.

➡ _____

12 위 글의 밑줄 친 ⓑtheir act가 가리키는 것을 본문에서 찾아 쓰시오.

➡ _____
_____

Wrap Up 3

A: Wow! The news title says "Longer Vacation for Students." Hey, we're going

to have a longer vacation!

B: Wait! We should check first if it is true.
　　　　　　　　　　　　　 = whether

A: Why do you say so?

B: Some news uses a shocking title but its content may tell a different story.
　　　　　　　　　　　 단수 동사　　　　　　　　　　　　　　 추측의 조동사

A: Oh, I see. I should read beyond the news title.

구문해설　• shocking: 충격적인　• content: 내용

해석

A: 와! 뉴스 제목이 "학생들을 위한 더 긴 방학"이야. 이봐, 우리 더 긴 방학을 갖나봐!

B: 기다려! 우리는 먼저 이게 사실인지를 확인해야 해.

A: 왜 그렇게 생각해?

B: 어떤 뉴스는 충격적인 제목을 사용하지만 그 내용은 다른 이야기를 할지도 몰라.

A: 오, 알았다. 뉴스 제목 너머를 읽어야 하는구나.

Read & Think After You Read B

Reporter: Why did *The Herald* write the "Awful Disaster" story, Mr. Right?

Mr. Right: They just wanted to draw the readers' attention to the unsafe
　　　　　　　　　　　　　　　 draw one's attention to ~: ~에 …의 주의를 끌다
　　　　conditions at the zoo.

Reporter: Actually, readers were very upset to find that it was false. How
　　　　　　 = In fact/As a matter of fact: 사실,　　　　　　 to부정사의 부사적 용법(원인)
　　　　about "Slav Shoots a Friend in Argument?" What was the motive?
　　　　 = What about ~?: ~은 어떤가?

Mr. Right: *The Daily Telegram* wanted to prove that *The Daily News* was
　　　　　　　　　　　　　　　　　　 명사절(목적어)을 이끄는 접속사(생략 가능)
　　　　stealing their articles.
　　　　 = The Daily Telegram's

구문해설　• awful: 끔찍한　• disaster: 참사, 재난　• unsafe: 안전하지 않은　• upset: 속상한, 마음이 상한
　　　　• motive: 동기　• article: 기사

기자: 왜 헤럴드 사는 〈끔찍한 참사〉 이야기를 썼을까요, Right 씨?

Mr. Right: 그들은 단지 동물원의 안전하지 않은 상태에 대해 독자들의 주의를 끌고 싶었답니다.

기자: 사실, 독자들은 그것이 거짓이라는 것을 알고 매우 화가 났어요. 〈슬라브인이 언쟁 중에 친구에게 총을 쏘다〉는 어떤가요? 동기가 무엇이었나요?

Mr. Right: 데일리 텔레그램 사는 데일리 뉴스 사가 그들의 기사를 훔치고 있다는 것을 증명하기를 원했어요.

Read & Think After You Read C

A: Among the four tips, which do you think is the most important, and why?
간접의문문(= Do you think? + Which is the most important?)이며 think 동사가 있어서 의문사 which가 문두로 이동 뒤에 do you think it is
　　　　　　　　　　　　　　　　　　　　　　　　　　 the most important 생략
B: I think finding supporting sources is the most important because I can
　　　　　 동명사 주어　현재분사로 sources 수식　동명사 주어는 단수 취급　　 간접의문문으로 명사절을 이끄는 접속사(~인지 아닌지)

check if the information is correct.

구문해설　• tip: 조언　• support: (진술 따위를) 입증하다, 뒷받침하다　• source: 자료

A: 네 가지 조언 중에서 너는 어떤 것이 가장 중요하다고 생각하며, 그 이유는 무엇이니?

B: 나는 뒷받침하는 자료들을 찾는 것이 가장 중요하다고 생각하는데, 그 정보가 올바른지 확인할 수 있기 때문이야.

영역별 핵심문제

01 다음 짝지어진 단어의 관계가 같도록 빈칸에 알맞은 말을 쓰시오.

> lead : mislead = understand : _____

02 다음 중 밑줄 친 부분의 뜻풀이가 바르지 않은 것은?

① People panicked and screamed when the hotel caught on fire. (겁에 질렸다)
② Nevertheless, many people came to the festival. (더욱이, 게다가)
③ These exercises help keep your muscles strong. (근육)
④ The motive for the fight between them was unknown. (동기)
⑤ News often misleads us with wrong information. (잘못 이끌다)

03 다음 문장의 빈칸에 들어갈 말을 〈보기〉에서 골라 쓰시오.

> ┤ 보기 ├
> riddle / seriously / reliable / source / shoot

(1) We are looking for someone who is honest and _____.
(2) Solve this _____, or you can't open the door.
(3) He can't talk now because he is _____ hurt.
(4) They will _____ arrows at bottles.
(5) He couldn't find the _____ of the story.

04 다음 영영풀이가 가리키는 것을 고르시오.

> to suddenly feel so worried that you cannot be reasonable

① panic   ② reliable
③ current   ④ critical
⑤ private

05 다음 주어진 문장의 밑줄 친 current와 다른 의미로 쓰인 것은?

> Did you have any idea about the current issue?

① I'll interview the current Olympic title-holder soon.
② Corona 19 seems so serious that the current situation will continue.
③ We got together here to find the solution to the current crisis.
④ You can check the current price by visiting our website.
⑤ Mike swam to the shore against a strong current.

06 다음 우리말에 맞게 빈칸에 알맞은 말을 쓰시오.

(1) 소방관들은 집으로 들어가기 위해 문을 부숴야 했다.
⇒ The firefighters had to _____ _____ the door to get into the house.
(2) 계획에 따르면, 그들은 목요일까지 그것을 끝내야 한다.
⇒ _____ _____ the plan, they should finish it by Thursday.
(3) 그녀는 잠잘 때 보는 무서운 동화를 만들어 냈다.
⇒ She _____ _____ a scary bedtime story.

07 다음 우리말을 주어진 단어를 이용하여 영작하시오.

(1) 그녀는 지난밤에 있었던 일을 기술했다. (happened) (6 words)

➡ _____

(2) 이것은 최악의 자연 재난 중의 하나이다. (worst) (8 words)

➡ _____

(3) 사자가 한 시간 전에 동물원에서 탈출했다. (ago, a lion) (9 words)

➡ _____

Conversation

08 다음 대화가 자연스럽게 이어지도록 순서대로 배열하시오.

> Chris: Jane, do you usually get news online or from the newspaper?
> Jane: Well, I usually watch TV news.
> (A) I see your point.
> (B) Why do you say so?
> (C) TV news? Is there any special reason?
> (D) I think TV is the most useful way to get news.
> (E) I have to spend too much time reading all the news online or in the newspaper. So, I just watch the main news on TV.

➡ _____

[09~10] 다음 대화를 읽고 물음에 답하시오.

> David: Hey, Sandy. Do you think I should buy this drink? It is said that it can help me lose weight.
> Sandy: Let me read the label more closely. Hmm, it looks a bit strange to me, David.
> David: Why do you say so?
> Sandy: There isn't enough information about what's in the drink.

> David: Oh, you're right.
> Sandy: Also, it doesn't tell you how much you have to drink to lose weight.

09 위 대화에서 나타난 Sandy의 성격으로 적절한 것은?

① careful   ② diligent
③ creative   ④ adventurous
⑤ hardworking

10 위 대화의 내용과 일치하지 않는 것은?

① David is wondering if he should buy the drink.
② It is said that the drink can be helpful to lose weight.
③ Sandy finds out something strange about the drink.
④ There isn't enough information about how much David should drink to lose weight.
⑤ There's some information about what the drink is made of.

[11~12] 다음 대화를 읽고 물음에 답하시오.

> Susan: What are you reading, John?
> John: I'm reading a book of riddles.
> Susan: Riddles? Aren't they for children?
> John: Actually, no. Books of riddles are really useful for adults.
> Susan: Really? Why do you say so?
> John: They help us think more creatively. We need to think outside the box to find the answers.

11 Why does John think books of riddles are useful for adults?

➡ _____

12 What do we need to do to find the answers to riddles?

➡ _____

[13~14] 다음 대화를 읽고 물음에 답하시오.

> W: I think I caught a cold because I didn't dress warmly yesterday.
> M: Well, I've read an article saying that you don't catch a cold because your body temperature is low.
> W: Really? _____
> M: The article said that people catch colds because of viruses.

13 위 대화의 빈칸에 들어갈 말로 나머지와 의도가 다른 것은?

① Can you tell me more about it?
② Could you give me more information?
③ Can you explain more in detail?
④ Could you be more specific?
⑤ Can you give me your hand?

14 위 대화의 내용과 일치하지 않는 것은?

① The woman was not feeling well.
② The man read the article related to catching a cold.
③ The woman didn't dress warmly yesterday.
④ The article explained that people catch colds due to viruses.
⑤ The woman caught a cold because her body temperature was low.

Grammar

15 다음 두 문장을 괄호 안의 단어를 이용하여 한 문장으로 바꾸시오.

(1) • Linda was stupid.
　　• She made a big mistake. (enough)

　　➡ _____

(2) • Bill is very poor.
　　• So he can't buy the house. (too)

　　➡ _____

16 다음 밑줄 친 부분과 바꿔 쓸 수 있는 것은?

> Slow down so that children can cross the street safely.

① in order that
② in order to
③ so as to
④ such that
⑤ so which

17 다음 문장 중에서 어법상 어색한 문장을 고르시오.

① Not knowing the language, we had to use sign language.
② Working in a hospital, John is always busy.
③ Things getting more difficult, we should draw on our wisdom.
④ Arriving at the store, I found it closed.
⑤ Not handing out the report, she is responsible for the result.

18 다음 문장을 바꿔 썼을 때 빈칸에 알맞은 말을 쓰시오.

(1) The two articles having been special cases, there are many "fake" news articles published every day.

　　➡ _____,
　　there are many "fake" news articles published every day.

(2) In the morning Harold greeted her smiling brightly.

　　➡ In the morning Harold greeted her
　　_____.

(3) Being tired from the work, I fell asleep.

　　➡ _____,
　　I fell asleep.

19 다음 문장의 빈칸에 공통으로 알맞은 것은?

> • He sat smiling, _____ his legs crossed.
> • Don't speak _____ your mouth full.

① in   ② with
③ of   ④ from
⑤ along

Reading

[20~23] 다음 글을 읽고 물음에 답하시오.

①Every day we watch, hear, or read interesting news. However, have you ever seriously considered ②whether an article is really true? Everyone likes an interesting news story but ③what if it is completely made up?

Fake news can be very harmful ④in that it can make people less informed or even misled. _____ⓐ_____ , there have been various fake news reports throughout history. Why have some people written such false information? Let's look _____ⓑ_____ some articles thinking about the hidden ⑤motives behind them.

20 위 글의 빈칸 ⓐ에 알맞은 것을 고르시오.

① Furthermore   ② Nevertheless
③ Likewise   ④ That is
⑤ Thus

21 다음 중 위 글의 밑줄 친 ①~⑤와 바꿔 쓸 수 있는 말로 옳지 않은 것을 고르시오.

① Each day
② if
③ what would happen if
④ in the sense that
⑤ themes

22 위 글의 빈칸 ⓑ에 알맞은 것을 고르시오.

① for   ② at
③ on   ④ with
⑤ into

23 위 글의 뒤에 올 내용으로 가장 알맞은 것을 고르시오.

① the way we can spot fake news
② various kinds of interesting news we watch, hear, or read every day
③ some fake news articles through which we can think about the hidden motives behind them
④ people who are less informed or even misled by fake news
⑤ the harmful effects of fake news

[24~26] 다음 글을 읽고 물음에 답하시오.

AWFUL DISASTER

Last night, an angry group of rhinoceroses ⓐ broke down the walls of the cage at the zoo and escaped. They also broke down the walls of (A)[another / the other] wild animals' cages. These animals ran down the streets and injured hundreds of people. ⓑ그중 열두 마리의 동물들이 아직 잡히지 않았다. Citizens should stay indoors until (B)[farther / further] notice.
*Not a single act or incident (C)[describing / described] above has taken place.

24 위 글의 밑줄 친 ⓐbroke down과 같은 의미로 쓰인 것을 고르시오.

① The peace talks between them broke down.
② Our car broke down on the freeway.
③ His health broke down under the pressure of work.
④ In the stomach, acids broke down food into bits.
⑤ The telephone system broke down.

25 위 글의 괄호 (A)~(C)에서 문맥이나 어법상 알맞은 낱말을 골라 쓰시오.

➡ (A)_____ (B)_____ (C)_____

26 위 글의 밑줄 친 ⓑ의 우리말에 맞게 주어진 어휘를 이용하여 9 단어로 영작하시오.

> loose, of

➡ _____

[27~28] 다음 글을 읽고 물음에 답하시오.

SLAV SHOOTS A FRIEND IN ARGUMENT
  Mejk Swenekafew, a Slav worker at the Columbia Coal Mine, was shot and seriously wounded by John Pecitello near the mining camp Thursday evening. (①)
  The two men had an argument during a meeting. (②) He is now at the hospital in critical condition. (③) Pecitello ran away after the shooting. (④) The police are searching for him now and are warning citizens that ⓐhe is extremely dangerous. (⑤)

27 위 글의 밑줄 친 ⓐhe가 가리키는 것을 본문에서 찾아 쓰시오.

➡ _____

28 위 글의 흐름으로 보아, 주어진 문장이 들어가기에 가장 적절한 곳은?

> The argument led to a fight, and Pecitello shot Swenekafew twice, in the chest and leg.

①   ②   ③   ④   ⑤

[29~30] 다음 글을 읽고 물음에 답하시오.

Reporter: Why did *The Herald* write ⓐthe "Awful Disaster" story, Mr. Right?
Mr. Right: They just wanted to draw the readers' attention to the unsafe conditions at the zoo.
Reporter: Actually, readers were very upset to find that it was false. How about "ⓑSlav Shoots a Friend in Argument?" What was the motive?
Mr. Right: *The Daily Telegram* wanted to prove that *The Daily News* was stealing their articles.

29 위 글의 종류로 알맞은 것을 고르시오.
① article   ② essay
③ review   ④ interview
⑤ summary

30 위 글을 읽고 The Herald가 가짜 기사인 ⓐthe "Awful Disaster" story를 지어낸 동기와, The Daily Telegram이 가짜 기사인 ⓑSlav Shoots a Friend in Argument를 지어낸 동기를 각각 본문에서 찾아, to부정사로 시작하여 쓰시오.

➡ ⓐ _____
    _____
    ⓑ _____
    _____

✏ 출제율 90%

01 다음 영영풀이가 가리키는 것을 고르시오.

> to form words with the letters in the correct order

① shoot   ② spot
③ support   ④ strengthen
⑤ spell

[02~03] 다음 대화를 읽고 물음에 답하시오.

Suji: I usually drink a glass of warm milk before I go to bed, but it doesn't help me fall asleep.

Minsu: I saw a show on TV, and a doctor said that a glass of warm milk doesn't actually help you fall asleep.

Suji: Oh, it doesn't? (A)Can you tell me more about it? (information)

Minsu: Milk has special chemicals that make people sleepy. But the amount in a glass is too small to have any effect.

✏ 출제율 90%

02 위 대화의 밑줄 친 (A)와 의도가 같도록 주어진 어휘를 사용하여 다시 쓰시오.

➡ _____

✏ 출제율 100%

03 위 대화를 읽고 대답할 수 <u>없는</u> 것은?

① What's the matter with Suji?
② What does Suji do before going to bed?
③ What is the effect of special chemicals in milk?
④ Why are the chemicals in a glass of warm milk not helpful for falling asleep?
⑤ How many glasses of milk should Suji drink to sleep better?

[04~05] 다음 대화를 읽고 물음에 답하시오.

Jane: I read an article saying that Napoleon was actually fairly tall. (A)

Tom: Oh, really? (B)

Jane: According to the article, a French doctor wrote down Napoleon's height according to the French measuring system, not the English one. (C)

Tom: What was the difference? (D)

Jane: At that time, an inch in France was longer than an inch in England. So, Napoleon was actually about 168 cm tall, which was not that short in those times. (E)

✏ 출제율 90%

04 위 대화의 (A)~(E) 중 주어진 문장이 들어가기에 적절한 곳은?

> Can you tell me more about it?

① (A)   ② (B)   ③ (C)   ④ (D)   ⑤ (E)

✏ 출제율 100%

05 위 대화를 읽고 대답할 수 <u>없는</u> 것은?

① What is the article about?
② Who wrote down Napoleon's height?
③ In what way was Napoleon's height written down?
④ Why was an inch in France different from an inch in England?
⑤ What was the difference between French and English measuring systems?

[06~07] 다음 대화를 읽고 물음에 답하시오.

Susan: What are you reading, John?

John: I'm reading a book of riddles.

Susan: Riddles? Aren't they for children?

John: Actually, no. Books of riddles are really useful for adults.

Susan: Really? Why do you say so?

John: They help us think more creatively. We need to think outside the box to find the answers.

06 위 대화에서 다음 영영풀이가 가리키는 말을 찾아 쓰시오.

> a question that is difficult to understand, and that has a surprising answer, that you ask somebody as a game

➡ _____

07 위 대화의 내용과 일치하지 않는 것은?

① John은 수수께끼 책을 읽고 있다.

② 수수께끼 책은 어른들에게 유용하다.

③ 수수께끼 책은 좀 더 창의적으로 생각하도록 돕는다.

④ 수수께끼 답을 찾기 위해 고정관념에서 벗어날 필요가 있다.

⑤ 수수께끼 답을 찾기 위해 상자를 밖으로 꺼내야 한다.

[08~09] 다음 대화를 읽고 물음에 답하시오.

W: I read an interesting article about the Black Sea. Do you know ⓐwhere is it?

M: Yes. It's ⓑbetween Eastern Europe and Western Asia, right?

W: Right. ⓒWhat color do you think it is?

M: Well, black, I guess.

W: No, it isn't. It's blue.

M: Really? Then why is it ⓓcalled the Black Sea? Can you tell me more about it?

W: People call it the Black Sea ⓔbecause it is very dangerous.

08 위 대화의 밑줄 친 ⓐ~ⓔ 중 어법상 틀린 것을 찾아 바르게 고치시오.

➡ _____

09 위 대화의 내용과 일치하지 않는 것은?

① 여자는 흑해에 관한 흥미로운 기사를 읽었다.

② 흑해는 동유럽과 서아시아 사이에 있다.

③ 흑해는 검은색이 아니라 파란색이다.

④ 사람들이 흑해라고 부르는 이유는 그곳이 매우 위험하기 때문이다.

⑤ 남자는 사람들이 흑해하고 부르는 이유에 대해 알고 있었다.

10 다음 중 어법상 어색한 문장을 고르시오.

① He didn't want to be late, so that he took a taxi.

② Put it down gently so that it doesn't break.

③ She was so tired to think straight.

④ Is she healthy enough to travel?

⑤ I studied Italian so that I would be able to read Dante in the original.

11 다음 분사구문을 접속사를 이용한 문장으로 바꿔 쓰시오.

(1) Driving my car, I couldn't reply to your text message.

➡ _____

_____

(2) Walking down the street, I met my friend.

➡ _____

_____

(3) There being no work to do, he remained at his office until late.

➡ _____

_____

12 다음 그림을 보고 주어진 어휘를 이용하여 빈칸을 알맞게 채우시오.

Mary was sitting on the sofa, _____

_____. (play, the guitar)

13 다음 중 의미가 <u>다른</u> 문장을 고르시오.

① Don't waste water so that we can prevent water shortages.

② Don't waste water in order that we can prevent water shortages.

③ Don't waste water so as to prevent water shortages.

④ Don't waste water in order can prevent water shortages.

⑤ Don't waste water to prevent water shortages.

[14~16] 다음 글을 읽고 물음에 답하시오.

Every day we watch, hear, or read interesting news. However, have you ever seriously considered whether an ⓐarticle is really true? Everyone likes an interesting news story but what if it is completely made up?

Fake news can be very harmful in that it can make people less informed or even misled. Nevertheless, there have been various fake news reports throughout history. Why have some people written such false information? Let's look into some articles ⓑthinking about the hidden motives behind them.

14 위 글의 밑줄 친 ⓐarticle과 같은 의미로 쓰인 것을 <u>모두</u> 고르시오.

① Bread is an article of food.

② He contributed an article to a journal.

③ That word has to have a definite article before it.

④ I read every last article in the newspaper.

⑤ I'm looking for an article of clothing.

15 위 글의 밑줄 친 ⓑthinking과 문법적 쓰임이 같은 것을 <u>모두</u> 고르시오.

① My hobby is reading books.

② Who is the girl playing the piano?

③ I saw the boy eating an apple.

④ Taking a walk every day is very good for you.

⑤ He is collecting stamps.

16 위 글의 주제로 알맞은 것을 고르시오.

① We are living in a flood of information.

② Everyone likes an interesting news story.

③ It is difficult to spot fake news.

④ There are many ways to write news reports faithfully.

⑤ Despite their harmful effects, there have been various fake news reports.

[17~19] 다음 글을 읽고 물음에 답하시오.

At that time, those who read the article carefully laughed out loud. Those who didn't read it to the end got really worried. (A)Not knowing the news was false, many people ⓐ_____ . Some tried to escape the city while others went into the parks with guns to hunt the animals.

So why did *The Herald* make up such news? Later, they confessed that they made it up so that they could draw the readers' attention to the unsafe conditions at the zoo.

> 출제율 95%

17 위 글의 빈칸 ⓐ에 panic을 알맞은 형태로 쓰시오. (one word)

➡ _____

> 출제율 90%

18 위 글의 밑줄 친 (A)를 부사절로 고치시오.

➡ _____

> 출제율 95%

19 According to the passage, which is NOT true?

① The readers who read the article carefully laughed out loud.

② Some of the readers who didn't read the article to the end tried to escape the city.

③ Some of the readers who didn't read the article to the end went into the parks with guns to hunt the animals.

④ *The Herald* made up such false news to scare people.

⑤ The conditions of the zoo were unsafe.

[20~22] 다음 글을 읽고 물음에 답하시오.

Is there anything strange about the article? Read the Slav's name backwards; it spells, "we-fake-news." Who wrote this and why?

The Daily Telegram published this fake article so that they could prove if *The Daily News*, their competitor, was stealing (A)their articles. *The Daily News* published the same article about "Swenekafew" the next day and ⓐ_____ got caught stealing. The people at *The Daily News* had to admit (B)their act and (C) were harshly criticized by the public.

> 출제율 90%

20 위 글의 빈칸 ⓐ에 들어갈 알맞은 말을 고르시오.

① additionally ② alternatively
③ on the other hand ④ moreover
⑤ thus

> 출제율 95%

21 위 글의 밑줄 친 (A)their와 (B)their가 가리키는 것을 각각 본문에서 찾아 쓰시오.

➡ (A) _____
(B) _____

> 출제율 100%

22 위 글의 밑줄 친 (C)를 능동태로 고치시오.

➡ _____
_____

[01~03] 다음 대화를 읽고 물음에 답하시오.

Jane: I read an article saying that Napoleon was actually fairly tall.

Tom: Oh, really? Can you tell me more about it?

Jane: According to the article, a French doctor wrote down Napoleon's height according to the French measuring system, not the English one.

Tom: What was the difference?

Jane: At that time, an inch in France was longer than an inch in England. So, Napoleon was actually about 168 cm tall, which was not that short in those times.

01 What does the article say about Napoleon's height?

➡ _____

02 Who wrote down Napoleon's height and in what way was it written down?

➡ _____

_____

03 What was the difference between French and English measuring systems?

➡ _____

04 분사구문은 부사절로, 부사절은 분사구문으로 바꿔 쓰시오.

(1) Winning the first prize, Jenny was so happy.

➡ _____

_____

(2) Walking with Wing Walker, you burn more calories and get slimmer.

➡ _____

_____

(3) Because they use the hidden board technology, they strengthen leg muscles.

➡ _____

_____

(4) She studied very hard and passed the exam.

➡ _____

05 다음 문장을 같은 뜻을 갖는 문장으로 바꿔 쓰려고 한다. 빈칸을 알맞게 채우시오.

(1) I want to have Harry Potter's magic cloak so that I could become invisible.

= I want to have Harry Potter's magic cloak _____ _____ _____ I could become invisible.

(2) Take a rest every hour so that you can keep warm.

= Take a rest every hour _____ _____ _____ keep warm.

(3) Be so humble that you can learn from your mistakes.

= Be humble _____ _____ learn from your mistakes.

(4) It was so hot that we couldn't go out.

= It was _____ _____ for us _____ go out.

Every day we watch, hear, or read interesting news. ⓐHowever, have you ever seriously considered that an article is really true? Everyone likes an interesting news story but ⓑ 만약 그것이 완전히 지어낸 것이라면 어떻게 할 것인가?

Fake news can be very harmful in that it can make people less informed or even misled. Nevertheless, there have been various fake news reports throughout history. Why have some people written such false information? Let's look into some articles thinking about the hidden motives behind them.

06 위 글의 밑줄 친 ⓐ에서 어법상 **틀린** 부분을 찾아 고치시오.

➡ _____

07 위 글의 밑줄 친 ⓑ의 우리말에 맞게 주어진 어휘를 이용하여 7 단어로 영작하시오.

> what, made, completely

➡ _____

08 본문의 내용과 일치하도록 다음 빈칸 (A)와 (B)에 공통으로 들어갈 알맞은 단어를 쓰시오.

> Though people can be less informed or even misled because of (A)_____ _____, there have been various (B)_____ _____ reports throughout history.

At that time, those who read the article carefully laughed out loud. Those who didn't read ⓐit to the end got really worried. Not knowing the news was false, many people panicked. Some tried to escape the city while others went into the parks with guns to hunt the animals.

So why did *The Herald* make up such news? Later, they confessed that they made it up ⓑ so that they could draw the readers' attention to the unsafe conditions at the zoo.

09 위 글의 밑줄 친 ⓐit이 가리키는 것을 본문에서 찾아 쓰시오.

➡ _____

10 위 글의 밑줄 친 ⓑ를 to부정사를 사용하여 고치시오.

➡ _____

_____

11 How did the readers who didn't know the news was false react? Fill in the blanks (A) and (B) with suitable words.

> Some tried to (A)_____ _____ _____ while others (B)_____ _____ _____ _____ with guns to hunt the animals.

01 다음 대화를 읽고 Suji의 일기를 완성하시오.

> **Suji:** I usually drink a glass of warm milk before I go to bed, but it doesn't help me fall asleep.
>
> **Minsu:** I saw a show on TV, and a doctor said that a glass of warm milk doesn't actually help you fall asleep.
>
> **Suji:** Oh, it doesn't? Can you tell me more about it?
>
> **Minsu:** Milk has special chemicals that make people sleepy. But the amount in a glass is too small to have any effect.

> Recently, I couldn't sleep well, so (A)_____ before I went to bed. However, it didn't work at all. I talked about it to Minsu. He explained that (B)_____ _____. According to the doctor, there are special chemicals in milk that (C)_____, but the (D)_____ in a glass is too small. I think I should find another way to get a sound sleep.

02 다음 내용을 바탕으로 제품의 광고 내용에 대해 문의하는 게시 글을 쓰시오.

> Q1 What product are they advertising?
>
> A1 They are advertising the walking shoes, Wing Walker.
>
> Q2 What are the strong points of the product?
>
> A2 Walking with Wing Walker, people burn more calories and get slimmer. They also strengthen leg muscles because they use the hidden board technology.
>
> Q3 What information is not shown in the ad?
>
> A3 First, is it scientifically proven that walking with Wing Walker, people burn more calories? Second, what materials are used for the hidden board?

> I saw the ad about (A)_____. It says that walking with Wing Walker, people (B)_____. They also strengthen leg muscles because they use (C)_____. But here are some questions. First, is it (D)_____ that walking with Wing Walker, people burn more calories? Second, (E)_____ are used for the hidden board? It would be great if you could answer my questions.

단원별 모의고사

01 다음 대화가 자연스럽게 이어지도록 순서대로 배열하시오.

> (A) Really? Can you tell me more about it?
>
> (B) The article said that people catch colds because of viruses.
>
> (C) Well, I've read an article saying that you don't catch a cold because your body temperature is low.
>
> (D) I think I caught a cold because I didn't dress warmly yesterday.

➡ _____

02 다음 우리말에 맞게 빈칸에 알맞은 말을 쓰시오.

(1) 저 치즈의 냄새는 지독하다.
➡ The smell of that cheese is _____.

(2) 너는 이 화학 물질을 다룰 때 장갑을 껴야만 한다.
➡ You must wear gloves when you handle these _____.

(3) 그는 가슴 위로 팔짱을 꼈다.
➡ He crossed his arms over his _____.

(4) 그는 한국인 여인과 결혼해서 한국 시민이 되었다.
➡ He married a Korean woman and became a Korean _____.

03 다음 문장의 빈칸에 들어갈 말을 〈보기〉에서 골라 알맞은 형태로 쓰시오.

> ┌ 보기 ┐
> public / recognize / publish / prove / poems

(1) He enjoys writing _____ in his free time.

(2) She should _____ they are wrong.

(3) The museum will be open to the _____ next month.

(4) He has _____ several novels, and I have read them all.

(5) I was able to _____ my old friend by her voice.

04 다음 문장에 공통으로 들어갈 말을 고르시오.

> • My grandfather used to work in the gold _____.
> • The _____ was closed because of the safety problem.
> • People _____ for coal in this area.
> • Half of the money was _____.

① panic　　　② condition
③ mine　　　④ strengthen
⑤ support

[05~06] 다음 대화를 읽고 물음에 답하시오.

> Suji: There are so many pieces of information we call "facts" that are completely wrong.
> Jack: (A) Why do you say so?
> Suji: (B) I read a book, and there were a lot of examples of these facts that are wrong.
> Jack: (C) Like what?
> Suji: (D) But goldfish are actually smart.
> Jack: (E) Really? Can you tell me more about that?
> Suji: They can recognize their owners.
> Jack: Oh, I didn't know that.

05 위 대화의 (A)~(E) 중 주어진 문장이 들어가기에 적절한 곳은?

> Well, most people think goldfish are not smart.

① (A)　② (B)　③ (C)　④ (D)　⑤ (E)

06 위 대화를 읽고 대답할 수 없는 것은?

① What did Suji read about?
② What do most people think about goldfish?
③ What can goldfish actually do?
④ Why does Suji think that goldfish are smart?
⑤ How can goldfish recognize their owners?

[07~09] 다음 대화를 읽고 물음에 답하시오.

David: Hey, Sandy. Do you think I should buy this drink? It is said that it can help me lose weight.
Sandy: Let me read the label more closely. Hmm, it looks a bit strange to me, David.
David: Why do you say so?
Sandy: There isn't enough information about what's in the drink.
David: Oh, you're right.
Sandy: Also, it doesn't tell you how much you have to drink to lose weight.

07 What does Sandy read closely?

➡ _____

08 Why does Sandy think that David shouldn't buy the drink?

➡ _____

_____

09 What are the two things that are not shown on the label?

➡ _____

_____

[10~11] 다음 대화를 읽고 물음에 답하시오.

Susan: What are you reading, John?
John: I'm reading a book of riddles.
Susan: Riddles? Aren't they for children?
John: Actually, no. Books of riddles are really (A)[useful / useless] for adults.
Susan: Really? Why do you say so?
John: They help us think more (B)[ordinarily / creatively]. We need to think (C)[inside / outside] the box to find the answers.

10 위 대화의 (A)~(C)에 들어갈 말로 바르게 짝지어진 것은?

	(A)	(B)	(C)
①	useful	ordinarily	inside
②	useful	creatively	outside
③	useful	creatively	inside
④	useless	creatively	outside
⑤	useless	ordinarily	inside

11 위 대화를 읽고 대답할 수 없는 것은?

① What is John reading now?
② Are the books of riddles for children?
③ Why are the books of riddles useful for adults?
④ What should people do to find the answers to the riddles?
⑤ What is there outside John's box?

12 다음 우리말을 주어진 단어를 이용하여 영작하시오.

(1) 비판적으로 생각하고 그들이 너에게 말하는 모든 것을 믿지는 마라. (critically)

➡ _____

_____

(2) 너의 학급 친구들을 비난하거나 놀리지 마라.
(of, fun)

➡ _____

(3) 이것이 너의 현재 주소니? (current)

➡ _____

(4) 그것이 맞는지 아닌지는 판단하기가 어렵다.
(whether, difficult, judge)

➡ _____

13 다음 문장에서 어법상 <u>어색한</u> 것을 바르게 고쳐 다시 쓰시오.

(1) Sam saved some money so as to he could buy a new backpack.

➡ _____

_____

(2) You must follow the rules in order to everyone enjoy the experience.

➡ _____

_____

_____

_____

(3) She saw Thomas entered the classroom.

➡ _____

(4) Very embarrassing, she didn't tell us that news.

➡ _____

_____

14 다음 우리말을 주어진 어휘를 이용하여 영작하시오.

(1) 할 일이 없을 때, 그는 낚시하러 간다. (have, work, do, 8 단어)

➡ _____

(2) Susan은 다른 사람들이 그녀의 목소리를 들을 수 없도록 조용히 얘기했다. (other people, voice, that, speak, hear, quietly, 11 단어)

➡ _____

_____

15 Which is grammatically wrong?

① Getting up late, I brought some bread to school for breakfast.

② Never use your phone in order to look in front of you.

③ Wear a swimming cap in order to the pool be kept clean.

④ Wear bright-colored clothes in order that people can see you at night.

⑤ Let's plant many trees so that they can help provide fresh air.

16 다음 중 어법상 옳은 문장을 <u>모두</u> 고르시오.

① Starting a class, my teacher plays a pop song.

② Pass the exam, I felt really happy.

③ After taking a walk in the park, I went to bed.

④ He plays computer games with his friends having some snacks.

⑤ Feeling not hungry, I concentrated on reading.

⑥ Meeting her several times, he noticed her immediately.

17 다음 두 문장을 해석하고 그 차이를 설명하시오.

(1) Jinho studied English hard so that he could talk with foreigners in English.

➡ 해석 _____

차이 _____

(2) Jinho studied English so hard that he could talk with foreigners in English.

➡ 해석 _____

차이 _____

[18~19] 다음 글을 읽고 물음에 답하시오.

Every day we watch, hear, or read interesting news. However, have you ever seriously considered whether an article is really true? Everyone likes an interesting news story but what if ⓐit is completely made up?

Fake news can be very harmful in that it can make people less informed or even misled. Nevertheless, there ⓑhave been various fake news reports throughout history. Why have some people written such false information? Let's look into some articles thinking about the hidden motives behind them.

18 아래 〈보기〉에서 위 글의 밑줄 친 ⓑhave been과 현재완료의 용법이 같은 것의 개수를 고르시오.

┌─── 보기 ───┐
① I have lost my cellphone.
② Have you finished reading the book yet?
③ I have studied English since the third grade of elementary school.
④ He has now completed the project.
⑤ She has been to Japan twice.
└──────────┘

① 1개　② 2개　③ 3개　④ 4개　⑤ 5개

19 위 글의 밑줄 친 ⓐit이 가리키는 것을 본문에서 찾아 쓰시오.

➡ _____

[20~22] 다음 글을 읽고 물음에 답하시오.

At that time, those who read the article carefully laughed out loud. (①) Those who didn't read it ___ⓐ___ the end got really worried. (②) Not knowing the news was false, many people panicked. (③) Some tried to escape the city (A)while others went into the parks with guns to hunt the animals.

(④) Later, they confessed that they made it up so that they could draw the readers' attention ___ⓑ___ the unsafe conditions at the zoo. (⑤)

20 위 글의 빈칸 ⓐ와 ⓑ에 공통으로 들어갈 알맞은 전치사를 고르시오.

① of　　　　② from
③ to　　　　④ at
⑤ for

21 위 글의 밑줄 친 (A)while과 의미와 문법적 쓰임이 같지 않은 것을 고르시오.

① I've read fifty pages, while he's read only twenty.
② Some are rich, while others are poor.
③ They chatted for a while.
④ Tom's very good at science, while his brother is absolutely hopeless.
⑤ The walls are green, while the ceiling is white.

22 위 글의 흐름으로 보아, 주어진 문장이 들어가기에 가장 적절한 곳은?

> So why did *The Herald* make up such news?

① ② ③ ④ ⑤

24 위 글의 밑줄 친 ⓑ의 우리말에 맞게 주어진 어휘를 알맞게 배열하시오.

> during / men / a / argument / two / had / an / meeting / the

➡ _____

_____

[23~26] 다음 글을 읽고 물음에 답하시오.

ⓐ_____

Mejk Swenekafew, a Slav worker at the Columbia Coal Mine, was shot and seriously wounded by John Pecitello near the mining camp Thursday evening. ⓑ그 두 사람은 회의 중에 언쟁을 벌였다. The argument led to a fight, and Pecitello shot Swenekafew twice, in the chest and leg. He is now at the hospital in critical condition. Pecitello ran ⓒ_____ after the shooting. The police are searching for him now and are warning citizens that he is extremely dangerous.

25 위 글의 빈칸 ⓒ에 알맞은 것은?

① in ② to
③ away ④ from
⑤ along

26 According to the passage, which is NOT true?

① Mejk Swenekafew was a Slav worker at the Columbia Coal Mine.
② Mejk Swenekafew was seriously wounded by John Pecitello.
③ Swenekafew was shot in the chest and leg.
④ The police are searching for Swenekafew.
⑤ The police are warning citizens that Pecitello is extremely dangerous.

23 위 글의 빈칸 ⓐ에 들어갈 제목으로 알맞은 것을 고르시오.

① A Slav Worker at the Columbia Coal Mine
② Argument Near the Mining Camp
③ Swenekafew Is in Critical Condition
④ Extremely Dangerous Criminal
⑤ Slav Shoots a Friend in Argument

MEMO

Lesson 6

Words of Wisdom

 의사소통 기능

- 상대방을 안심시키기
  A: I keep making mistakes. I'm so worried.
  B: **Don't worry about** making mistakes.
- 상상한 내용 묻기
  A: **What would you do if** you had a magic carpet?
  B: I would fly to wherever I want.

 언어 형식

- 'It ~ that ...' 강조 구문
  It was this wisdom **that** our father tried to explain.
- have+목적어+과거분사
  I **had** my bed **designed** by experts.

Words & Expressions

Key Words

- **captain** [kǽptin] 명 선장
- **carpet** [kɑ́:rpit] 명 카펫, 양탄자
- **castle** [kǽsl] 명 성
- **character** [kǽriktər] 명 등장인물
- **chat** [tʃæt] 동 한가롭게 이야기하다, 담소하다
- **chef** [ʃef] 명 요리사
- **comfortably** [kʌ́mfərtəbli] 부 편안하게
- **confusing** [kʌnfjú:ziŋ] 형 혼란스러운, 헷갈리는
- **continue** [kʌntínju:] 동 계속하다
- **deadline** [dédlain] 명 기한, 마감 일자
- **death** [deθ] 명 죽음
- **design** [dizáin] 동 설계하다
- **dragon** [drǽgən] 명 용
- **dwarf** [dwɔ:rf] 명 난장이
- **exhibit** [igzíbit] 동 전시하다
- **expensive** [ikspénsiv] 형 비싼, 돈이 많이 드는
- **expert** [ékspə:rt] 명 전문가
- **explain** [ikspléin] 동 설명하다
- **express** [iksprés] 동 표현하다
- **failure** [féiljər] 명 실패
- **far-away** [fɑ́rəwei] 형 멀리 떨어진

- **foolish** [fú:liʃ] 형 어리석은, 바보 같은
- **forest** [fɔ́:rist] 명 숲, 삼림, 산림
- **forever** [fərévər] 부 영원히
- **freedom** [frí:dəm] 명 자유
- **hire** [haiər] 동 고용하다
- **lastly** [lǽstli] 부 마지막으로, 끝으로
- **luxurious** [lʌgʒúəriəs] 형 사치스러운, 호화로운
- **magical** [mǽdʒikəl] 형 마술의, 마력이 있는
- **matter** [mǽtər] 동 중요하다
- **motto** [mɑ́tou] 명 좌우명
- **past** [pæst] 명 과거
- **pot** [pɑt] 명 항아리, 단지, 독
- **priceless** [práislis] 형 대단히 귀중한, 값을 매길 수 없는
- **puzzled** [pʌ́zld] 형 당혹스러운, 어리둥절한
- **reward** [riwɔ́:rd] 명 보상
- **situation** [sìtʃuéiʃən] 명 상황, 환경
- **stardom** [stɑ́:rdəm] 명 스타덤, 스타의 반열
- **suppose** [səpóuz] 동 추측하다, 추정하다
- **twin** [twin] 형 쌍둥이의
- **wisdom** [wízdəm] 명 지혜, 현명함

Key Expressions

- **after a hard day's work** 하루 종일 열심히 일하고 나서
- **be stuck on** ~에 갇히다
- **bring back** 돌려주다
- **come true** 이루어지다, 실현되다
- **deserted island** 무인도
- **explain oneself** 심중을 털어놓다
- **fill up** 채우다
- **from head to toe** 머리에서 발끝까지
- **get lost** 길을 잃다
- **go wrong** 잘못하다, 실수를 하다

- **live by** (신조, 원칙 등)에 따라 살다
- **lock up** 투옥시키다
- **look after** ~을 살피다, ~을 돌보다
- **make friends** 친구를 사귀다
- **pass away** 세상을 떠나다, 돌아가시다
- **run out of** ~이 없어지다, ~이 다 떨어지다
- **settle in** ~에 자리 잡다, ~에 정착하다
- **take one's share** 자기 몫을 차지하다[취하다]
- **throughout one's life** 일생을 통해
- **with open arms** 두 팔을 벌리고

Word Power

※ 서로 비슷한 뜻을 가진 어휘

- □ **bring back** 돌려주다 – **return** 돌려주다, 반납하다
- □ **expensive** 비싼 – **costly** 값비싼
- □ **far-away** 멀리 떨어진 – **distant** 먼, 떨어져 있는
- □ **hire** 고용하다 – **employ** 고용하다
- □ **puzzled** 당혹스러운, 어리둥절한 – **confused** 혼란스러운
- □ **priceless** 대단히 귀중한, 값을 매길 수 없는 – **invaluable** 값을 헤아릴 수 없는

- □ **exhibit** 전시하다 – **show** 보여주다
- □ **explain** 설명하다 – **describe** 묘사하다
- □ **forever** 영원히 – **perpetually** 영원히
- □ **look after** 돌보다 – **take care of** 돌보다
- □ **return** 돌려주다 – **bring back** 돌려주다

※ 서로 반대의 뜻을 가진 어휘

- □ **comfortably** 편안하게 ↔ **uncomfortably** 불편하게
- □ **continue** 계속하다 ↔ **stop** 멈추다, 그만두다
- □ **expensive** 비싼, 돈이 많이 드는 ↔ **inexpensive** 비싸지 않은
- □ **hire** 고용하다 ↔ **fire** 해고하다
- □ **priceless** 대단히 귀중한, 값을 매길 수 없는 ↔ **worthless** 가치 없는, 보잘 것 없는

- □ **confusing** 혼란스러운 ↔ **clear** 명료한
- □ **death** 죽음 ↔ **life** 삶, 인생, 생명
- □ **failure** 실패 ↔ **success** 성공
- □ **lastly** 마지막으로, 끝으로 ↔ **firstly** 첫째로

※ 접두사 ex- (밖으로)

- □ **ex-** + **ceed** → **exceed** 능가하다, 초과하다
- □ **ex-** + **clude** → **exclude** 배제하다, 제외하다
- □ **ex-** + **plain** → **explain** 설명하다
- □ **ex-** + **press** → **express** 표현하다

- □ **ex-** + **change** → **exchange** 교환하다
- □ **ex-** + **hibit** → **exhibit** 전시하다
- □ **ex-** + **port** → **export** 수출하다
- □ **ex-** + **tend** → **extend** 확장시키다

※ 접미사 –dom (영역, 상태)

- □ **bore** + -**dom** → **boredom** 지루함, 따분함
- □ **free** + -**dom** → **freedom** 자유
- □ **star** + -**dom** → **stardom** 스타덤

- □ **fan** + -**dom** → **fandom** 팬덤, 팬층
- □ **king** + -**dom** → **kingdom** 왕국
- □ **wis** + -**dom** → **wisdom** 지혜

English Dictionary

- □ **character** 등장인물
  → a person represented in a film, play, or story
  영화나 연극 혹은 이야기 속에 나오는 사람

- □ **expert** 전문가
  → a person with a high level of knowledge or skill relating to a particular subject or activity
  특정한 주제나 활동에 관련된 높은 수준의 지식이나 기술을 가진 사람

- □ **explain** 설명하다
  → to make something clear or easy to understand by describing or giving information about it
  어떤 것에 대한 정보를 묘사하거나 제공함으로써 분명하거나 이해하기 쉽게 만들다

- □ **express** 표현하다
  → to show what you think or feel
  당신이 생각하거나 느끼는 것을 보여주다

- □ **failure** 실패
  → a lack of success in doing or achieving something, especially in relation to a particular activity
  특히 특정 활동과 관련해서 어떤 일을 하거나 성취하는 데 있어서 성공의 결여

- □ **hire** 고용하다
  → to employ a person or pay him to do a particular job for you
  당신을 위해 특정한 일을 하도록 어떤 사람에게 일을 주거나 그에게 돈을 지불하다

- □ **luxurious** 사치스러운, 호화로운
  → very comfortable and expensive
  매우 편안하고 비용이 많이 드는

- □ **priceless** 대단히 귀중한, 값을 매길 수 없는
  → worth a large amount of money
  많은 양의 돈의 가치가 있는

- □ **reward** 보상
  → something given in exchange for good behavior or good work, etc.
  좋은 행동이나 업적 등의 대가로 주어지는 어떤 것

- □ **wisdom** 지혜, 현명함
  → the ability to use your knowledge and experience to make good decisions and judgments
  좋은 결정이나 판단을 할 수 있는 지식과 경험을 사용하는 능력

01 접미사 -dom을 붙여 명사로 만들 수 <u>없는</u> 것을 고르시오.

① wise ② free ③ bore
④ novel ⑤ fan

02 다음 밑줄 친 부분과 의미가 가장 가까운 것을 고르시오.

> He is a person with a <u>priceless</u> ability to make people feel comfortable around him.

① valueless ② worthless
③ precious ④ economic
⑤ expensive

03 다음 빈칸 (A)와 (B)에 들어갈 말이 바르게 짝지어진 것을 고르시오.

> • After he had traveled for years, he settled (A)_____ New York.
> • If you get stuck (B)_____ a difficult word, just ask for help.

① for – in ② in – on
③ for – on ④ in – to
⑤ for - to

서답형

04 다음 괄호 안의 단어를 문맥에 맞게 변형하여 빈칸을 채우시오.

> His new film was a complete _____.
> (fail)

05 다음 밑줄 친 부분의 의미로 알맞지 <u>않은</u> 것은?

① He is the funniest <u>character</u> in this film. (등장인물)
② I would like to <u>express</u> my thanks to my friend, Jina. (설명하다)
③ They gave him a <u>reward</u> for his hard work. (보상)
④ It's a difficult <u>situation</u> and I don't know what to do. (상황)
⑤ My grandmother lived on a <u>far-away</u> mountain. (멀리 떨어진)

06 다음 영영풀이가 나타내는 단어를 고르시오.

> to employ someone or pay him to do a particular job for you

① hire ② afford
③ demand ④ require
⑤ encourage

07 다음 빈칸에 공통으로 들어갈 말을 고르시오.

> • I _____ many friends at the summer camp.
> • As they watched the shooting star, they _____ a wish.

① found ② went ③ put
④ took ⑤ made

01 다음 짝지어진 단어의 관계가 같도록 빈칸에 알맞은 말을 쓰시오.

> hire : employ = return : b_____

02 다음 우리말에 맞게 주어진 단어를 이용하여 빈칸을 채우시오.

(1) 하루 종일 열심히 일하고 나서, 나는 매우 피곤했다. (after, day)

➡ _____, I was very tired.

(2) 나는 그 사건에 대해서 내 심중을 털어놓고 싶지 않았다. (explain)

➡ I didn't want to _____ about the incident.

03 다음 밑줄 친 부분과 바꿔 쓸 수 있는 말을 주어진 철자로 시작하여 쓰시오.

> Who's going to <u>look after</u> the children while you're away?

➡ t_____ (3 단어)

04 다음 빈칸에 공통으로 들어갈 단어를 쓰시오.

> • I didn't finish the test – I _____ out of time.
> • I _____ to school as fast as possible.

05 다음 우리말에 맞게 주어진 단어를 바르게 배열하시오.

(1) 너는 일생을 통해 배울 것이 매우 많다.
(your, to, so, you, throughout, have, learn, much, life)

➡ _____

(2) 가격은 이번 주에 내려갈 것으로 추측된다.
(this, to, is, the, go, week, price, supposed, down)

➡ _____

(3) 모든 학생들은 그 질문에 어리둥절했다.
(question, were, all, by, the, puzzled, students, the)

➡ _____

(4) 이 상황이 아주 중요하다.
(situation, a, matters, lot, this)

➡ _____

(5) 그건 내가 삶에서 신조로 삼을 만한 철학이다.
(that's, I, live, could, philosophy, a, by)

➡ _____

06 다음 그림에 맞게 빈칸에 알맞은 말을 쓰시오.

➡ My aunt welcomed me _____ _____ _____.

Conversation

① 상대방을 안심시키기

> **A:** I'm so worried about going to high school. 고등학교 올라가는 게 너무 걱정돼.
>
> **B:** Don't worry about it. It'll be a great chance to get to know new people.
> 걱정하지 마. 새로운 사람들을 알게 되는 좋은 기회가 될 거야.

■ 상대방을 안심시키는 표현으로는 'Don't worry about ~.'이라는 말을 쓸 수 있다. 이와 같은 표현으로는 'Don't let ~ bother you.(~에 대해 너무 신경 쓰지 마.)', 'Don't sweat over ~.(~에 대해 너무 걱정하지 마.)' 등이 있다.

■ 'Don't worry about ~.'은 뭔가에 대하여 걱정을 하는 상대방을 안심시킬 때 사용하고, 이와 유사한 표현으로 'Never mind.'를 사용하기도 한다. 'Never mind.'는 '걱정하지 마.'의 의미 이외에도 '괜찮아.' 혹은 '신경 쓰지 마.' 등 다양한 의미로도 쓰인다.

상대방을 안심시키기

- Don't worry about ~.
- Don't let ~ bother you.
- Don't think twice about ~.
- Don't sweat it.

핵심 Check

1. 다음 대화의 빈칸에 들어갈 말로 적절하지 <u>않은</u> 것은?

> **A:** I don't have anything to wear to the party. I can't afford it.
>
> **B:** _____, Cinderella. The fairy Godmother will make a dress for you.

① Don't forget about it

② Don't let it bother you

③ Don't think twice about it

④ Don't sweat it

⑤ Don't worry about it

2 상상한 내용 묻기

A: What would you do if you could time travel? 만약 네가 시간 여행을 할 수 있다면 무엇을 하겠니?

B: I would travel to the 1940s and prevent World War Ⅱ. How about you? 나는 1940년대로 가서 제2차 세계 대전을 막고 싶어, 너는 어때?

A: I would go to the Joseon Dynasty and meet King Sejong. 나는 조선 시대로 가서 세종 대왕을 만나고 싶어.

■ 상상한 내용을 묻는 표현으로는 'What would you do if ~?(~라면 무엇을 할 거니?)'가 있다. 이와 같은 표현으로는 'Imagine that ~. What would you do?', 'If you were ~, what would you do?', 'Let's say that you ~. What would you do?' 등이 있다.

■ 가정법 과거 – if +주어+동사의 과거형, 주어+조동사의 과거형+동사원형 ~.(~라면 …할 텐데)
현재 사실과 반대되는 상황이나 일에 대해 가정하거나 현재 사실에 대한 후회나 아쉬움을 강조할 때, 가정법 과거를 쓴다. 즉, 현재 사실과 반대이므로, 과거 시제를 쓴다. 조건절은 'if+주어+동사의 과거형'으로, 주절은 '주어+would/should/could/might+동사원형 ~'을 쓴다. 이때 해석은 '~라면 …할 텐데.'라고 해석한다.

■ 'What would you do if ~?'는 거의 일어날 가능성이 없는 상황에서 무엇을 할 것인가에 대한 질문인 반면, 'What will you do if ~?'는 미래의 계획이나 가능성을 묻는 질문이다.

상상한 내용 묻기

- What would you do if you ~?
- Imagine that ~. What would you do?
- If you were ~, what would you do?
- Let's say that you ~. What would you do?

핵심 Check

2. 다음 대화의 빈칸에 들어갈 말이 바르게 짝지어진 것은?

> **A:** What would you do if you __(A)__ a million dollars?
> **B:** I __(B)__ buy a car. How about you?
> **A:** I __(C)__ donate the half of it for the poor.

	(A)	(B)	(C)		(A)	(B)	(C)
①	have	– would	– could	②	have	– will	– can
③	had	– would	– can	④	had	– will	– can
⑤	had	– would	– would				

Listen & Talk 1 A-1

W: James, why are you still ❶up? It's 11 o'clock!

M: I can't sleep ❷because ❸I'm worried about the Bookworm Competition tomorrow.

W: You've read all of the books on the list. What do you ❹have to worry about?

M: Some of the writers' names are ❺confusing, so ❻I'm worried that I might not remember them.

W: ❼Don't worry about something ❽that hasn't happened yet. You'll do fine.

M: Thanks. I'll try ❾not to worry so much.

W: James, 왜 아직 깨어 있니? 11시야!

M: 내일 있을 책벌레 경연 대회가 걱정되어서 저는 잠을 잘 수가 없어요.

W: 너는 목록에 있는 책들을 다 읽었잖아. 뭐가 걱정이니?

M: 몇몇 작가들의 이름이 헷갈려서 그들을 기억하지 못할까봐 걱정이 돼요.

W: 아직 일어나지 않은 일을 걱정하지 마. 너는 잘할 거야.

M: 고마워요. 너무 걱정하지 않도록 해 볼게요.

❶ up은 부사로 '기상하여, 잠이 깨어'의 의미로 사용되었다.

❷ 자지 못하는 이유를 설명하기 위해 접속사 because를 사용하였다. because 대신에 접속사 since, as를 사용할 수도 있다.

❸ 'I'm worried about ~.'은 '나는 ~에 대해 걱정한다.'의 의미로 걱정을 나타낼 때 사용하는 표현이다. 같은 의미의 표현으로 'I'm anxious about ~.', 'I'm concerned about ~.' 등이 있다.

❹ have to 동사원형: ~해야 한다

❺ confusing: 혼란스러운

❻ 'I'm worried (that)+주어+동사.'는 '나는 (주어)가 ~인 것이 걱정돼.'라는 의미로 that절 이하에 걱정하는 내용이 온다.

❼ 상대방을 안심시키는 표현으로는 'Don't worry about ~.'이라는 말을 쓸 수 있다. 이와 같은 표현으론 'Don't let ~ bother you.(~에 대해 너무 신경 쓰지 마.)', 'Don't sweat over ~.(~에 대해 너무 걱정하지 마.)' 등이 있다.

❽ that은 something을 수식하는 주격 관계대명사이다.

❾ to worry는 try의 목적어이다. to부정사를 부정하기 위해서 앞에 not을 썼다. 'try to 동사원형'은 '~하도록 노력하다'라는 의미이므로, 'try not to 동사원형'은 '~하지 않도록 노력하다'로 해석할 수 있다.

Check(√) True or False

(1) James read all of the books on the list for the Bookworm Competition.　　T ☐ F ☐

(2) James needs to worry about something that hasn't happened yet.　　T ☐ F ☐

Listen & Talk 2 C

A: What would you do ❶if you had a magic carpet?

B: ❷I would never walk, and always fly to ❸wherever I want.

A: 마법 양탄자를 갖는다면 무엇을 하겠니?

B: 나는 절대 걷지 않고 항상 내가 원하는 어디든지 날아다닐 거야.

❶ 실제로는 일어나기 어려운 상황을 가정하거나 상상하여 물을 때 가정법 과거를 사용하여 'If you+동사의 과거형 ~, what would you+동사원형 ~?'으로 묻는다.

❷ 'If you+동사의 과거형 ~, what would you+동사원형 ~?'에 답을 할 때는 'I would+동사원형 ~.'을 쓴다.

❸ whenever는 '~할 때는 언제든지'의 의미를 가지며 부사절을 이끈다.

Check(√) True or False

(3) B had a magic carpet.　　T ☐ F ☐

(4) B would never walk if she or he had a magic carpet.　　T ☐ F ☐

Listen and Speak 2 A-2

W: Jason, what are you reading?

M: I'm reading a book ❶called *Three Wishes*.

W: Oh, ❷I've heard about it. A genie ❸makes a boy's wishes ❹ come true, right?

M: Yeah. ❺What would you do if you could make one wish?

W: I ❻would make the genie stay with me forever. Then, I could make all my wishes come true.

M: That's smart!

W: Jason, 무엇을 읽고 있니?
M: 나는 〈세 가지 소원〉이라는 책을 읽고 있어.
W: 오, 그것에 대해 들어 본 적 있어. 요정이 어떤 남자아이의 소원을 들어주는 거지, 그렇지?
M: 맞아. 만약 소원 하나를 빌 수 있다면 너는 무엇을 할 거니?
W: 나는 요정을 영원히 내 옆에 있도록 만들 거야. 그러면, 나는 나의 모든 소원들을 이룰 수 있어.
M: 그거 똑똑한데!

❶ called는 과거분사로 '~라는 이름의, ~라고 불려지는'의 의미로 앞에 있는 명사 a book을 수식하고 있다.
❷ have heard는 현재완료의 '경험' 용법으로 '들어본 적이 있다'로 해석한다.
❸ make는 '…에게 ~하게 하다'라는 의미를 가지는 사역동사로, 목적격보어로 동사원형을 쓴다. 여기서 목적어는 a boy's wishes이며 목적격보어는 come true이다.
❹ come true: 이루어지다, 실현되다
❺ 실제로는 일어나기 어려운 상황을 가정하거나 상상하여 물을 때 'If you+동사의 과거형 ~, what would you+동사원형 ~?'의 형태인 가정법 과거를 사용하여 현재 사실과 반대되는 것을 말할 수 있다.
❻ 'If you+동사의 과거형 ~, what would you+동사원형 ~?'에 대한 응답은 'I would ~.'가 주로 사용되는데 would는 조동사이므로 뒤에 동사원형이 와야 한다.

Check(√) True or False

(5) W never heard about the book, *Three Wishes*.　　　T ☐ F ☐

(6) In the book, a genie makes a boy's wishes come true.　　　T ☐ F ☐

Wrap Up 1

M: ❶I've heard that you're going to be in the writing contest next week.

W: Yeah, it's already next week.

M: You ❷look worried. What's wrong?

W: ❸I'm worried that the topic would be too difficult for me.

M: Don't worry about something ❹you can't change. Just ❺ believe in yourself.

W: Thanks. I'll try.

M: 네가 다음 주에 글쓰기 대회에 나간다고 들었어.
W: 맞아, 그게 벌써 다음 주야.
M: 너 걱정스러워 보인다. 무슨 일이니?
W: 주제가 나에게 너무 어려울까봐 걱정이야.
M: 네가 바꿀 수 없는 것에 대해 걱정하지 마. 그저 자신을 믿어봐.
W: 고마워. 그렇게 해 볼게.

❶ 'I've heard (that) 주어+동사 ~.'는 '나는 ~하다는 것을 들었어.'라는 뜻으로 알고 있음을 표현하는 말이다.
❷ look+형용사: ~하게 보이다
❸ 'be worried (that) 주어+동사'는 '(주어)가 ~인 것이 걱정이다.'라는 의미로 걱정을 표현할 때 사용하는 표현이다.
❹ something과 you can't change 사이에 목적격 관계대명사 that이 생략되어 있다.
❺ believe in 사람: ~을[~의 능력을] 믿다

Check(√) True or False

(7) W will participate in the writing contest next week.　　　T ☐ F ☐

(8) W is concerned about the writing contest.　　　T ☐ F ☐

Listen & Talk 1 A-2

M: Sujin, what are you doing this weekend?

W: Nothing special, why?

M: I ❶have to go to Busan for a family trip tomorrow but I can't find anyone ❷to feed my dog, Lucy.

W: Don't worry about Lucy. I'll take care of her.

M: Oh, thank you so much. I was so worried.

W: I'll ❸take her for a walk in the park, too. The weather's ❹supposed to be nice tomorrow.

❶ have to 동사원형: ～해야 한다
❷ to feed 이하는 앞의 명사 anyone을 수식하는 형용사적 용법이다.
❸ take ～ for a walk: ～를 산책하러 데리고 가다
❹ suppose: 추측하다, 추정하다

Listen & Talk 1 B

M: Jane, you look worried. What's the matter?

W: I got a big part in the school musical.

M: I heard you singing. You sound great!

W: It's just that I ❶keep ❷making mistakes. I'm so worried.

M: Oh, you just need a little more practice. Don't ❸worry about making mistakes. You can actually learn from them.

W: Thanks, Dad. ❹I hope I do a good job.

M: You'll do great.

❶ keep은 동명사를 목적어로 받는다. ❷ make a mistake: 실수하다
❸ worry about (동)명사: ～에 대해 걱정하다
❹ 'I hope (that) 주어+동사 ～.'나 'I hope to 동사원형'을 사용해 희망이나 바람을 나타낼 수 있다.

Listen & Talk 2 A-1

M: Caroline, have you read the book, *Tuck Everlasting*?

W: Yeah, it is about a family that drank magical water and lived forever, right?

M: Right. ❶What would you do if you could live forever?

W: Well, ❷I would live in different cities all around the world.

M: Really? I would collect interesting items and make a museum.

W: Cool.

❶ '만약 ～라면 어떻게 하겠니?'라고 실제가 아닌 상황이나 사실을 가정하여 물어볼 때는 가정법 과거를 이용하여 'What would you do if you+과거시제 ～?'로 표현한다.
❷ 'What would you do if you+과거시제 ～?'에 대한 대답으로 '나는 ～할 거야.'라는 의미로 'I would 동사원형 ～.' 형태의 가정법 과거를 사용하여 대답한다.

Listen & Talk 2 B

W: What are you doing, Jinho?

M: I'm writing a review of the movie, *The Time Traveler's Wife*.

W: I saw that movie, too. It's ❶one of my favorite romantic movies.

M: I loved it, too. Emily, ❷what would you do if you could time travel?

W: I would travel to the 1940s and prevent World War II. How about you?

M: I would go to the Joseon Dynasty and meet King Sejong. I'm a big fan of him.

❶ one of 복수명사: ～중의 하나
❷ 현재 사실과 반대되는 상황이나 일에 대해 가정하거나 현재 사실에 대한 후회나 아쉬움을 강조할 때, 가정법 과거를 쓴다.

Communication Step A

M: How's your online story going, Amy?

W: Not well. The deadline is this weekend but I ❶ran out of ideas.

M: Don't worry about it. I can help you.

W: That would be great. My main character has special powers. What would you do if you were able to read people's minds?

M: Well, I would find out ❷if the girl I like likes me.

W: That's a good idea. Thanks.

❶ run out of: ～이 없어지다, 다 떨어지다
❷ 여기서 if의 의미는 '～인지 아닌지'로 whether로 바꿔 쓸 수 있다.

● 다음 우리말과 일치하도록 빈칸에 알맞은 말을 쓰시오.

Listen & Talk 1 A

1. W: James, why are _____ _____? It's 11 o'clock!

   M: I can't sleep _____ _____ _____ _____ the Bookworm Competition tomorrow.

   W: _____ _____ all of the books on the list. What do you _____ _____ _____ _____?

   M: Some of the writers' names are _____, so I'm _____ I might not remember them.

   W: Don't worry about something _____ _____ _____ yet. You'll do fine.

   M: Thanks. I'll _____ _____ _____ _____ so much.

2. M: Sujin, what are you doing this weekend?

   W: _____ _____, why?

   M: I _____ _____ _____ _____ Busan for a family trip tomorrow but I _____ _____ _____ to feed my dog, Lucy.

   W: Don't _____ _____ Lucy. I'll take care of her.

   M: Oh, thank you so much. I was so _____.

   W: I'll take her for a walk in the park, too. The weather's _____ _____ _____ nice tomorrow.

Listen & Talk 1 B

M: Jane, you look _____. What's the matter?

W: I _____ _____ _____ _____ _____ the school musical.

M: I heard you singing. You sound great!

W: It's just that I _____ _____ _____. I'm so worried.

M: Oh, you just need a little more _____. Don't worry about _____ _____. You can actually learn from them.

W: Thanks, Dad. I hope I do a good job.

M: You'll do great.

Listen & Talk 2 A

1. **M:** Caroline, have you read the book, *Tuck Everlasting*?

   W: Yeah, it is about a family that drank magical water and _____ _____, right?

   M: Right. _____ _____ _____ _____ _____ you could live forever?

   W: Well, I _____ live in different cities all around the world.

   M: Really? I would collect _____ items and make a museum.

   W: Cool.

2. **W:** Jason, what are you reading?

   M: I'm reading a book _____ *Three Wishes*.

   W: Oh, I've _____ about it. A genie makes a boy's wishes _____ _____, right?

   M: Yeah. What would you do _____ _____ _____ _____ _____?

   W: I _____ _____ the genies _____ with me forever. Then, I could _____ _____ _____ _____ _____ _____.

   M: That's smart!

Listen & Talk 2 B

W: What are you doing, Jinho?

M: I'm writing a review of the movie, *The Time Traveler's Wife*.

W: I saw that movie, too. It's _____ _____ my favorite romantic _____.

M: I loved it, too. Emily, _____ _____ _____ _____ _____ _____ _____ time travel?

W: I would travel to the 1940s and _____ World War II. How about you?

M: I _____ _____ _____ the Joseon Dynasty and _____ King Sejong. I'm a big fan of him.

해석

1. **M:** Caroline, 너 트리갭의 샘물(Tuck Everlasting)이라는 책을 읽어 봤니?

   W: 응, 그것은 마법의 물을 마시고 영원히 살게 된 한 가족에 대한 이야기잖아, 맞지?

   M: 맞아. 만약 네가 영원히 살게 된다면 너는 뭘 할 거야?

   W: 글쎄, 나는 전 세계의 다양한 도시에서 살고 싶어.

   M: 정말? 나는 흥미로운 물건들을 모아서 박물관을 만들 거야.

   W: 멋지다.

2. **W:** Jason, 무엇을 읽고 있니?

   M: 나는 〈세 가지 소원〉이라는 책을 읽고 있어.

   W: 오, 그것에 대해 들어 본 적 있어. 요정이 어떤 남자아이의 소원을 들어주는 거지, 그렇지?

   M: 맞아. 만약 소원 하나를 빌 수 있다면 너는 무엇을 할 거니?

   W: 나는 요정을 영원히 내 옆에 있도록 만들 거야. 그러면, 나는 나의 모든 소원들을 이룰 수 있어.

   M: 그거 똑똑한데!

W: 진호야, 무엇을 하고 있니?

M: 나는 〈시간 여행자의 아내〉라는 영화의 후기를 쓰고 있어.

W: 나도 그 영화 봤어. 그건 내가 가장 좋아하는 로맨스 영화 중 하나야.

M: 나도 너무 좋았어. Emily, 만약 네가 시간 여행을 할 수 있다면 무엇을 하겠니?

W: 나는 1940년대로 가서 제2차 세계 대전을 막고 싶어. 너는 어때?

M: 나는 조선 시대로 가서 세종대왕을 만나고 싶어. 나는 그의 엄청난 팬이야.

Communication Step A

M: _____ your online story going, Amy?

W: Not well. The deadline is this weekend but I _____ _____ of ideas.

M: _____ _____ _____ it. I can help you.

W: That would be great. My main _____ has special powers. _____ _____ _____ _____ _____ _____ _____ able to read people's minds?

M: Well, I would _____ _____ _____ the girl I like likes me.

W: That's a good idea. Thanks.

M: 네 온라인 이야기는 어떻게 되어 가고 있니, Amy?

W: 별로야. 마감이 이번 주말인데 아이디어가 다 떨어졌어.

M: 그건 걱정하지 마. 내가 도와줄게.

W: 그럼 정말 좋겠다. 내 주인공은 특별한 능력을 가지고 있어. 만약 네가 사람들의 생각을 읽을 수 있다면 무엇을 하겠니?

M: 음, 나는 내가 좋아하는 여자아이가 나를 좋아하는지 알아보고 싶어.

W: 그거 좋은 생각이다. 고마워.

Wrap Up

1. M: _____ _____ _____ you're going to be in the writing contest next week.

   W: Yeah, it's already next week.

   M: You look _____. What's wrong?

   W: _____ _____ _____ the topic would be _____ _____ for me.

   M: _____ _____ _____ something you can't change. Just _____ _____ _____.

   W: Thanks. I'll try.

1. M: 네가 다음 주에 글쓰기 대회에 나간다고 들었어.

   W: 맞아, 그게 벌써 다음 주야.

   M: 너 걱정스러워 보인다. 무슨 일이니?

   W: 주제가 나에게 너무 어려울까봐 걱정이야.

   M: 네가 바꿀 수 없는 것에 대해 걱정하지 마. 그저 자신을 믿어봐.

   W: 고마워. 그렇게 해 볼게.

2. M: Lisa, have you _____ the movie, *Cast Away*?

   W: No, I haven't. What is it about?

   M: It's about _____ _____ _____ _____ _____ _____ a deserted island for 4 years.

   W: It sounds interesting.

   M: Yeah, the man _____ everything to stay alive. What _____ you do _____ _____ _____ _____?

   W: To stay _____? Well, I would build a tree house and hunt for food.

   M: Yeah, me too. And _____ _____ _____ _____ _____ in the movie.

2. M: Lisa, 영화 〈캐스트 어웨이〉 본 적 있니?

   W: 아니, 없어. 무슨 내용이야?

   M: 4년 동안 외딴섬에 갇힌 어떤 남자에 관한 영화야.

   W: 재미있게 들린다.

   M: 응, 그 남자는 살기 위해 모든 것을 시도해. 만약 네가 그 남자라면 무엇을 하겠니?

   W: 살기 위해서? 글쎄, 나는 나무로 집을 만들고 먹을 것을 사냥할 거야.

   M: 응, 나도. 그리고 그게 그 남자가 영화에서 했던 거야.

[01~02] 다음 대화의 빈칸에 알맞은 것을 고르시오.

01

M: Caroline, have you read the book, *Tuck Everlasting*?

W: Yeah, it is about a family that drank magical water and lived forever, right?

M: Right. What would you do if you could live forever?

W: Well, I would live in different cities all around the world.

M: Really? _____

W: Cool.

① I would like to read many books.

② I want to make all my wishes come true.

③ I will buy every game in the world.

④ I would collect interesting items and make a museum.

⑤ I have become rich.

02

W: James, why are you still up? It's 11 o'clock!

M: I can't sleep because I'm worried about the Bookworm Competition tomorrow.

W: You've read all of the books on the list. What do you have to worry about?

M: Some of the writers' names are confusing, so I'm worried that I might not remember them.

W: _____ You'll do fine.

M: Thanks. I'll try not to worry so much.

① Don't worry about something that hasn't happened yet.

② I'm concerned about the competition, too.

③ You have to remember all of the writers' names.

④ You are supposed to win the competition.

⑤ I've never heard about the tomorrow's competition.

[01~03] 다음 대화를 읽고 물음에 답하시오.

M: How's your online story going, Amy?
W: (①) Not well. The deadline is this weekend (A)_____ I ran out of ideas.
M: (②) I can help you.
W: That would be great. (③) My main character has special powers. What would you do if you (B)_____ able to read people's minds? (④)
M: Well, I would find out if the girl I like likes me. (⑤)
W: That's a good idea. Thanks.

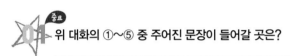

01 위 대화의 ①~⑤ 중 주어진 문장이 들어갈 곳은?

> Don't worry about it.

①   ②   ③   ④   ⑤

02 빈칸 (A)에 알맞은 말을 고르시오.

① because   ② so
③ but   ④ therefore
⑤ since

03 빈칸 (B)에 알맞은 말을 고르시오.

① were   ② was
③ be   ④ will be
⑤ being

04 다음 중 짝지어진 대화가 어색한 것은?

① A: I'm concerned about the final test.
   B: Don't worry about it. You will do well.
② A: Don't go too far. And you're supposed to be back before dark.
   B: Don't worry. We'll be back soon.
③ A: What would you do if you were free now?
   B: I would go to the amusement park with my friends.
④ A: What would you do if you were a fashion model?
   B: I could be very tall.
⑤ A: What would you do if you were a university student now?
   B: I would go backpacking all around the world.

[05~06] 다음 대화를 읽고 물음에 답하시오.

M: Caroline, have you read the book, *Tuck Everlasting*?
W: Yeah, it is about a family that drank magical water and lived forever, right?
M: Right. What would you do if (A)_____ _____?
W: Well, I would live in different cities all around the world.
M: Really? I would collect interesting items and make a museum.
W: Cool.

05 빈칸 (A)에 알맞은 말을 고르시오.

① you can time travel
② you could live forever
③ you make all your wishes come true
④ you will have a million dollars
⑤ you may become rich

06 위 대화의 내용과 일치하지 <u>않는</u> 것을 고르시오.

① 영원히 살게 된다면 남자는 흥미로운 물건들을 모아서 박물관을 만들 것이다.

② Caroline은 *Tuck Everlasting*을 읽어본 적이 있다.

③ 영원히 살게 된다면 Caroline은 한 도시에서 오래 살 것이다.

④ *Tuck Everlasting*은 마법의 물을 마시고 영원히 살게 된 한 가족에 대한 이야기이다.

⑤ 남자는 *Tuck Everlasting*을 읽어봤다.

09 빈칸 (A)에 알맞은 말을 고르시오.

① I'm worried about taking care of them.

② I'm so worried about going to high school.

③ I'm worried that I can't find anyone to read them.

④ I'm worried that I might not remember them.

⑤ I'm concerned about knowing new people.

[07~09] 다음 대화를 읽고 물음에 답하시오.

W: (①) James, why are you still up? It's 11 o'clock!

M: I can't sleep because I'm worried about the Bookworm Competition tomorrow. (②)

W: You've read all of the books on the list. (③)

M: Some of the writers' names are confusing, so (A)_____ (④)

W: Don't worry about something that hasn't happened yet. You'll do fine. (⑤)

M: Thanks. 너무 걱정하지 않도록 해 볼게요.(so, to, try, much, I'll, worry, not)

[10~11] 다음 대화를 읽고 물음에 답하시오.

M: Jane, you look worried. (①) What's the matter?

W: I got a big part in the school musical. (②)

M: I heard you singing. (③) You sound great!

W: It's just that I keep (A)_____. (④) I'm so worried.

M: Oh, you just need a little more practice. Don't worry about making mistakes. (⑤)

W: Thanks, Dad. I hope I do a good job.

M: You'll do great.

07 위 대화의 ①~⑤ 중 주어진 문장이 들어갈 곳은?

| What do you have to worry about? |

① ② ③ ④ ⑤

10 위 대화의 ①~⑤ 중 주어진 문장이 들어갈 곳은?

| You can actually learn from them. |

① ② ③ ④ ⑤

08 밑줄 친 우리말에 맞게 주어진 단어를 알맞게 배열하시오.

➡ _____

11 빈칸 (A)에 알맞은 말을 고르시오.

① avoiding it　　② making mistakes

③ realizing it　　④ wanting to sing

⑤ playing a main character

[01~02] 다음 대화를 읽고 물음에 답하시오.

W: Jason, what are you reading?
M: I'm reading a book _____(call) *Three Wishes*.
W: Oh, I've heard about it. A genie (A)_____ s a boy's wishes come true, right?
M: Yeah. What would you do if you could (B)_____ one wish?
W: I would (C)_____ the genie stay with me forever. Then, I could (D)_____ all my wishes come true.
M: That's smart!

01 괄호 안의 단어를 활용하여 빈칸에 알맞은 말을 쓰시오.

➡ _____

02 빈칸 (A)~(D)에 공통으로 들어갈 말을 쓰시오.

➡ _____

[03~04] 다음 대화를 읽고 물음에 답하시오.

W: James, why are you still up? It's 11 o'clock!
M: I can't sleep because I'm worried (A)_____ the Bookworm Competition tomorrow.
W: You've read all of the books on the list. What do you have to worry about?
M: Some of the writers' names are (B)_____ (confuse), so I'm worried that I might not remember them.
W: Don't worry about something that hasn't happened yet. You'll do fine.
M: Thanks. I'll try not to worry so much.

빈칸 (A)에 알맞은 말을 쓰시오.

➡ _____

04 괄호 안의 단어를 활용하여 빈칸 (B)에 알맞은 말을 쓰시오.

➡ _____

[05~06] 다음 대화를 읽고 물음에 답하시오.

M: Caroline, have you read the book, *Tuck Everlasting*?
W: Yeah, it is about a family that drank magical water and lived forever, right?
M: Right. (A)만약 네가 영원히 살게 된다면 너는 뭘 할 거야?
W: Well, I would live in different cities all around the world.
M: Really? (B)I would collect interesting items and made a museum.
W: Cool.

05 밑줄 친 우리말 (A)를 주어진 단어와 대화의 단어를 이용해 영작하시오.

➡ _____

(would, could, if)

06 밑줄 친 문장 (B)에서 흐름상 또는 어법상 어색한 것을 바르게 고치시오.

➡ _____

Grammar

---

1 'It ~ that ...' 강조 구문

> • **It was** this wisdom **that** our father tried to explain. 우리의 아버지가 설명하려고 하셨던 것은 바로 이 지혜였다.

■ 'It+is/was+강조어(구)+that ...'의 형태로 주어나 목적어, 부사(구/절) 등을 강조하기 위해서 쓰이며, 강조하고자 하는 부분을 'it is/was'와 'that' 사이에 쓰고, 나머지 부분을 that 뒤에 그대로 쓴다. 'be'동사는 문장의 시제에 맞춰 'is'나 'was'를 사용하며 이때, 해석은 '~한 것은 바로 …이다'라고 한다.

   • I washed my pet dog from head to toe. 나는 내 애완견을 머리부터 발끝까지 씻겼다.
   → **It was** I **that** washed my pet dog from head to toe. (주어 강조)
   → **It was** my pet dog **that** I washed from head to toe. (목적어 강조)

■ 'It ~ that ...' 강조 구문에서 강조하는 대상이 사람일 때는 that 대신에 who[whom], 사물이나 동물일 때는 which로 바꿔 쓸 수 있으며, 시간이나 장소의 부사(구/절)일 경우에는 when(시간) 또는 where(장소)로 바꿔 쓸 수 있다.

   • I bought a book at the bookstore yesterday. 나는 어제 그 서점에서 책을 한 권 샀다.
   → **It was** I **that[who]** bought a book at the bookstore yesterday.
   → **It was** a book **that[which]** I bought at the bookstore yesterday.
   → **It was** at the bookstore **that[where]** I bought a book yesterday.
   → **It was** yesterday **that[when]** I bought a book at the bookstore.

■ 'It ~ that ...' 강조 구문에서 강조하는 대상이 부사(구/절)일 경우 that 다음에 완전한 절이 나오지만, 그 외의 경우에는 불완전한 절이 나오는 것에 유의한다. 또한 강조되는 부분에 형용사나 동사는 올 수 없다. 동사를 강조할 때는 동사 앞에 조동사 do/does/did를 쓴다.

   • **It was** the meeting **that** changed my life. 내 삶을 바꿔 놓은 것은 바로 그 만남이었다. (that 다음에 불완전한 절)

   • **It was** at this point **that** her acting career really took off. 그녀의 연기가 인기를 얻기 시작한 것은 바로 이 시점이었다. (that 다음에 완전한 절)

   • It was beautiful that she was when young.(X) (형용사 강조 X)

   • It was cleaned that I my room last night.(X) (동사 강조 X)

   cf. 강조 구문에서는 'it is/was'와 that을 지우면 완전한 문장이 남지만, 'It(가주어) ~ that(진주어)' 구문에서는 'It is/was'와 that을 지우면 불완전한 문장이 남는다.

핵심 Check ┅┅┅┅┅┅┅┅┅┅┅┅┅┅┅┅┅┅

1. 다음 괄호 안에서 알맞은 말을 고르시오.

   (1) (It / That) was in the morning that I drank a cup of coffee.
   (2) It was Nathalie (that / what) came from Russia.

---

② have+목적어+과거분사

• I **had** my bed **designed** by experts.
나는 내 침대를 전문가들에 의해 설계되게 했다.

■ 'have/has/had+목적어+목적격보어'의 형태로 목적어의 '능동/수동' 여부에 따라 목적격보어 자리에 원형동사 또는 과거분사가 온다. 즉, 목적어가 목적격보어의 동작을 당하는 대상(주로 사물)이면 과거분사를 사용하고, 목적어가 목적격보어의 동작을 하는 주체(주로 사람)면 동사원형을 사용한다. have는 '~하게 시키다, 만들다'라는 의미의 사역동사로 '~이 되도록 누군가를 시키다'라는 의미를 가진다. 해석은 직역보다는 '~가 …되게 했다'라는 뜻으로 의역하면 자연스럽다.

※ have+목적어+동사원형: 목적어가 그 행위를 하는 주체

• I **had** him **wash** my car.

※ have+목적어+과거분사: 목적어는 그 동작을 당하는 대상

• I **had** my car **washed** by him.

■ 'have+목적어+과거분사' 유형은 어떤 일을 간접적으로 행할 때 쓰는 표현이다. 행위의 주체를 밝힐 때에는 'by+사람'의 형태로 쓴다.

• I **had** him **do** the work. 나는 그로 하여금 그 일을 하게 했다. (능동: 동사원형)

• I **had** the work **done** by him. 나는 그 일이 그에 의해 해지도록 했다. (수동: 과거분사)

■ cf. have와 get
get이 'get+목적어+to부정사'나 'get+목적어+과거분사'의 형태로 쓰여 have와 같은 의미를 갖는다.

• She **had** him **fix** the bike. 그녀는 그가 자전거를 고치도록 시켰다.
= She **got** him **to fix** the bike.
= She **had**[**got**] the bike **fixed** by him.

• She **had** the letter **written** by him. 그녀는 편지가 그에 의해 쓰여지게 했다.
= She **got** the letter **written** by him.

■ 'have+목적어+과거분사'에는 '~당하다'라는 피동의 뜻도 있다.

• She **had** her purse **stolen** in the subway. 그녀는 지하철에서 지갑을 도난당했다.

핵심 Check

2. 다음 괄호 안에서 알맞은 말을 고르시오.

(1) She had the students (finish / finishing) their homework.

(2) Jake had his leg (break / broken) in the accident.

(3) The teacher got him (sing / to sing) on the stage.

Grammar 시험대비 기본평가

01 다음 빈칸에 알맞은 것은?

> It was Tom _____ studied math in the library yesterday.

① where   ② when   ③ which
④ that   ⑤ what

다음 빈칸에 들어갈 말로 알맞은 것은?

> Sam had the chair _____.

① fixes   ② to fix   ③ fixing
④ fix   ⑤ fixed

03 다음 괄호 안에서 알맞은 말을 고르시오.

(1) I had him (repair / repaired) my watch.

(2) I had my money (steal / stolen) yesterday.

(3) (It / That) was several hours later that he went to the garden.

(4) It was Romeo (which / who) first met Juliet at the party.

04 다음 우리말에 맞게 주어진 어휘를 바르게 배열하시오.

(1) 그 피자를 먹은 사람은 바로 민지였다.

(the pizza, Minji, it, ate, was, that)

➡ _____

(2) 그곳은 윌리엄 왕자가 다녔던 바로 그 학교에요.

(Prince William, it, the school, is, went, that, to)

➡ _____

(3) Della는 Jim의 다리가 부러졌다는 것에 놀랐다.

(Jim, Della, his leg, broken, surprised, had, was, that)

➡ _____

중요
01 다음 중 어법상 <u>어색한</u> 것은?

① It was this wisdom that our father tried to explain.
② It was Lisa who played soccer in the park.
③ It was ended that World War Ⅱ in 1945.
④ It was his advice which prevented me from believing her.
⑤ It was yesterday that I met Jane.

02 다음 중 어법상 <u>어색한</u> 것은?

① I hired people and had the house looked after.
② How did you have him posed for this picture?
③ Lucy had her dog cleaned.
④ She had me help her with her math homework.
⑤ Why don't you have your furniture recycled?

중요
03 다음 빈칸에 알맞은 말이 바르게 짝지어진 것은?

> • It was the necklace _____ the princess bought.
> • My grandfather had his eyes _____.

① that – checked
② what – checked
③ that – checking
④ what – checking
⑤ which – to check

서답형
04 다음 괄호 안에서 알맞은 말을 고르시오.

(1) She had her face (paint / painted) red and blue.
(2) I had him (wash / washed) the dishes after dinner.
(3) Millar got her husband (to bring / bringing) the box.
(4) It was the princess (which / who) killed the dragon.
(5) It was last night (which / when) I sent you the message.
(6) It was at the festival (which / where) Mary went to a face painting booth.

중요
05 주어진 문장의 <u>틀린</u> 부분을 찾아, 올바르게 고친 것을 고르시오.

> Do you need to have the computer fixes? Call the Computer Doctor.

① Do you need to have the computer to fix? Call the Computer Doctor.
② Do you need to have the computer fixing? Call the Computer Doctor.
③ Do you need to have the computer to fixing? Call the Computer Doctor.
④ Do you need to have the computer fixed? Call the Computer Doctor.
⑤ Do you need to have the computer fix? Call the Computer Doctor.

06 빈칸 (A)와 (B)에 알맞은 것으로 바르게 짝지어진 것은?

> It was milk ___(A)___ I ___(B)___ every morning.

	(A)	(B)
①	that	deliver
②	that	delivered
③	what	deliver
④	what	delivering
⑤	what	delivered

07 다음 〈보기〉의 밑줄 친 that과 쓰임이 같은 것은?

┌─── 보기 ───

> It was in 1888 <u>that</u> Vincent Gogh painted *Sunflowers*.

① The poison of the cobra is more deadly than <u>that</u> of the rattlesnake.

② Are you sure she's <u>that</u> young?

③ It was the question <u>that</u> aimed at the heart of the matter.

④ We argued it this way and we argued it <u>that</u> way.

⑤ Are you mad <u>that</u> you should do such a thing?

08 다음 문장의 밑줄 친 ⓐ~ⓔ 중 어법상 어색한 것은?

> Your shoes ⓐ<u>look</u> ⓑ<u>dirty</u>. Why ⓒ<u>don't</u> you have ⓓ<u>them</u> ⓔ<u>clean</u>?

① ⓐ ② ⓑ ③ ⓒ
④ ⓓ ⑤ ⓔ

[09~10] 다음 문장의 빈칸에 알맞은 말을 고르시오.

09

> It was Jean Valjean _____ stole the bread from the bakery.

① that ② what ③ when
④ which ⑤ where

10

> Anna got the bike _____ by the neighbour.

① to repair ② repairing
③ had repaired ④ repaired
⑤ repair

11 다음 우리말을 바르게 영작한 것을 고르시오.

> Gogh가 Arles에서 만난 사람은 바로 Gauguin이었다.

① It was Gogh that Gauguin met in Arles.

② It was Gauguin whom Gogh met in Arles.

③ It was Gauguin what Gogh met in Arles.

④ It was Gauguin when Gogh met in Arles.

⑤ It was Gauguin which Gogh met in Arles.

서답형

12 다음 문장에서 어법상 어색한 것을 바르게 고쳐 다시 쓰시오.

> Mary had her table make by her brother.

➡ _____

13 다음 중 It ~ that의 쓰임이 나머지와 <u>다른</u> 하나는?

① It is very important that students develop an awareness of how the Internet can be used.

② It was in August that we went hiking together.

③ It was soccer that I played with him yesterday.

④ It was with Jane that I had *gimbap* in the restaurant yesterday.

⑤ It was she that asked me to study math together yesterday.

서답형
14 다음 두 문장을 한 문장으로 바꿔 쓰고자 한다. 빈칸에 들어갈 알맞은 말을 쓰시오.

> • Mary asked Simon to buy a used computer.
> • She asked him to repair the computer yesterday.
> = Mary had Simon _____ a used computer and got it _____ by him yesterday.

15 다음 밑줄 친 어휘의 쓰임이 〈보기〉와 <u>다른</u> 것은?

> ┤ 보기 ├
> I had the vegetables and fruit <u>mixed</u> well.

① I had my car <u>washed</u> by my son.

② I had my hair <u>cut</u> yesterday.

③ Her little baby had just <u>woken</u> from a deep sleep.

④ I had what I bought at the store <u>delivered</u> yesterday.

⑤ We had our house <u>decorated</u> with flowers last Christmas.

서답형
16 다음 문장에서 어법상 어색한 것을 바르게 고쳐 다시 쓰시오.

(1) The writer had his book print at his own expense.

➡ _____

(2) How can I get him dress better?

➡ _____

(3) I found out that it was the price who frightened me.

➡ _____

(4) It was when they are heated which metals expand.

➡ _____

(5) It was the theater that I met Jack last weekend.

➡ _____

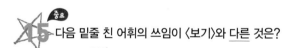
17 다음 우리말을 알맞게 영작한 것을 고르시오.

> Jenny가 어제 공원에서 본 것은 바로 별똥별이었다.

① It was a shooting star when Jenny saw at the park yesterday.

② It was at the park that Jenny saw a shooting star yesterday.

③ It was Jenny that saw a shooting star at the park yesterday.

④ It was yesterday that Jenny saw a shooting star at the park.

⑤ It was a shooting star which Jenny saw at the park yesterday.

01 〈보기〉와 같이 두 문장이 비슷한 의미가 되도록 주어진 단어를 활용하여 빈칸을 알맞게 채우시오. (어형 변화 가능.)

> ┌ 보기 ┐
> Allow the students to play soccer on the playground.
> → Let the students play soccer on the playground. (let)

(1) You'd better ask a catering service to prepare the food.

➡ Why don't you _____ by a catering service? (have)

(2) The teacher had Harry hand in his report by May 10.

➡ The teacher _____ _____ by May 10. (get)

(3) She made Nick repair her computer.

➡ She _____ her computer. (force)

02 다음 우리말에 맞게 주어진 어구를 바르게 배열하시오.

(1) Romeo가 Juliet을 처음 만난 건 바로 파티에서였어. (Romeo, Juliet, the party, that, it, was, first, met, at)

➡ _____

_____

(2) 내가 빌린 것은 바로 그의 공책이었다. (I, notebook, it, borrowed, was, his, which)

➡ _____

(3) Jim은 Della가 그녀의 머리카락을 자른 것에 놀랐다. (Jim, Della, hair, surprised, had, was, her, cut, that)

➡ _____

_____

(4) 그녀는 차를 세차시킬 필요가 있다. (she, the car, have, needs, washed, to)

➡ _____

03 다음 문장에서 어법상 어색한 부분을 바르게 고쳐 다시 쓰시오.

(1) Tom made his son have his eyes check.

➡ _____

(2) He got his brother do his homework for him.

➡ _____

_____

(3) It was pizza who Jake ate at a cafe.

➡ _____

(4) It is the restaurant that I'll have dinner with you this evening.

➡ _____

(5) It was more carefully that he read the letter again.

➡ _____

04 그림을 보고, 주어진 어휘를 이용하여 빈칸을 알맞게 채우시오.

(1) The princess _____ her to the castle yesterday. (have, take, the dragon)

(2) _____ made the first PC in 1976. (Steve Jobs, who)

05 다음 문장을 have를 이용하여 바꾸어 쓸 때 빈칸에 알맞은 말을 쓰시오.

(1) They asked Zaha Hadid to design Dongdaemun Design Plaza.

➡ They had Dongdaemun Design Plaza _____ .

(2) In Korea, some people order groceries through the Internet and the sellers deliver them to their homes.

➡ In Korea, some people order groceries through the Internet and _____ _____ by the sellers.

다음 문장을 주어진 단어를 강조하는 문장으로 고쳐 쓰시오. (that은 사용하지 말 것.)

| Matthew met Jake at the park last weekend. |

(1) Matthew

➡ _____

_____

(2) met

➡ _____

(3) Jake

➡ _____

_____

(4) at the park

➡ _____

_____

(5) last weekend

➡ _____

_____

07 다음 문장의 밑줄 친 부분을 강조하는 문장으로 바꿔 쓰시오.

(1) They started a swimming class last week.

➡ _____

_____

(2) Mary and Mike danced hard to be a mascot.

➡ _____

_____

(3) Robin broke the vase yesterday.

➡ _____

_____

(4) Did his sister teach him how to play the guitar?

➡ _____

_____

Reading

A Father's Wisdom

A rich and wise father had two sons, Puru and Puneet. Before he
two sons와 Puru and Puneet은 동격
passed away, he called his two sons to give them some last words of
to부정사의 부사적 용법 중 목적(~하기 위해서)
advice.

"Listen carefully, my dear sons. Live by these words throughout your
life, and you will be happy," he said.
명령문, ~and … : ~해라, 그러면 …

"Build a house in every city. Sleep comfortably. Enjoy your food.
Lastly, spend money like a rich man... ."
전치사(~처럼)

Before he could explain himself, he passed away.
재귀대명사의 재귀적 용법(주어와 목적어가 같을 때 목적어로 재귀대명사 사용)

After his death, the two sons took their share of the father's wealth
and settled in different cities. Five years passed. Puru, who had been
took과 병렬 연결　　　　　　　　　　　　　　과거완료진행형
following his father's words carefully, had no money left.

But his brother was richer than ever. Puru was puzzled about where
he had gone wrong, so he visited Puneet to find out.
간접의문문(의문사+주어+동사): 전치사 about의 목적어　　　　　부사적 용법(목적)

Puneet welcomed Puru with open arms. That night, when the brothers
sat down to chat after dinner, Puru asked the question that had been on
주격 관계대명사(선행사: the question)
his mind for days.

"It was our father's advice that I followed, but I am not happy.
It ~ that 강조 구문(I followed our father's advice. but I am not happy.)
I built a house in every city. But because I could not always stay
every+단수명사　　　이유를 이끄는 접속사(~이기 때문에)
there, I hired people and had the house looked after.
사역동사+목적어+p.p.(목적어와 목적격보어의 관계가 수동일 때)

---

wisdom: 지혜, 현명함
comfortably: 편안하게
lastly: 마지막으로
pass away: 세상을 떠나다
live by: (신조, 원칙 등)에 따라 살다
throughout one's life: 일생을 통해
explain oneself: 심중을 털어놓다
death: 죽음
puzzled: 당혹스러운, 어리둥절한
take one's share: 자기 몫을 차지하다
settle in: ~에 자리 잡다
go wrong: 잘못하다, 실수를 하다
with open arms: 두 팔을 벌리고
chat: 한가롭게 이야기하다
hire: 고용하다

📎 확인문제

● 다음 문장이 본문의 내용과 일치하면 T, 일치하지 않으면 F를 쓰시오.

1　The father died before he explained his words of advice. ☐

2　Puru, who had been following his father's words carefully, was richer than ever. ☐

3　Puru's houses were looked after by his wife. ☐

4　Puru lived near his brother after his father passed away. ☐

Father said we should sleep comfortably and enjoy our food, so I had my bed designed by experts and my meals prepared by a great
사역동사(had)의 목적어와 목적격보어의 관계가 수동   사역동사 had의 목적어 my bed와 병렬 연결
chef. He told us to spend like a rich man, so I bought what I wanted
　　　　　tell+목적어+to부정사　　　　　　　　　　관계대명사(the thing which): ~하는 것
without worrying about money. But look at me now! I am empty-
동명사(전치사 without의 목적어)
handed. Did you not follow our father's wisdom? Tell me, brother, how did you get so rich?"

Puneet smiled and said, "My dear brother, I also followed our father's wisdom. But I understood it a bit differently. When he said
　　　　　　　　　　　　　　　　　　　our father's wisdom 지칭
'build a house in every city,' I took it as having a place to stay all
　　　　　　　　　　　take A as B: A를 B로 여기다　　　　　　　형용사적 용법
around the world. So I made friends in every city and I stayed at their houses when I visited those cities. Also, I slept comfortably each night because I would be tired after a hard day's work, and it did not
　　　　이유를 이끄는 접속사(~ 때문에)
matter if I was sleeping on a bed or on the hard floor. I ate only when
　　　　명사절 접속사(~인지 아닌지)
I was hungry, so even a simple meal tasted great."
　　　　　　　　　　　　　　　　　　　2형식 동사(taste+형용사 보어)

"Spend money like a rich man?" continued Puneet.
　　　　　　　　　　~처럼
"A rich man knows how to make money grow. So, I tried to spend
　　　　　　　　　　의문사+to부정사(~하는 방법) 사역동사+목적어+동사원형
money on something that would bring me back more money rather
spend 시간/돈+on ~: 시간이나 돈을 ~에 쓰다
than on luxurious things. For me, it was this wisdom that our father
A rather than B: B하느니 차라리 A　　　　　　　It was ~ that 강조 구문
tried to explain."

Now Puru realized how foolish he had been. With this wisdom in
　　　　　　　　　　간접의문문(의문사+주어+동사): realized의 목적어
mind, Puru started a new life.

design: 설계하다; 디자인
expert: 전문가
chef: 요리사
matter: 중요하다
a bit 조금
make friends: 친구를 사귀다
after a hard day's work: 하루 종일 열심히 일하고 나서
continue: 말을 계속하다
luxurious: 사치스러운, 호화로운
foolish: 어리석은
bring back: 돌려주다

📎 **확인문제**

● 다음 문장이 본문의 내용과 일치하면 T, 일치하지 않으면 F를 쓰시오.

1 For Puneet, sleeping on a bed or on the floor didn't matter because he would be tired after a hard day's work. ☐

2 Puneet ate only the delicious food. ☐

3 Puneet tried to spend money on something that would bring him back more money. ☐

4 Puru made his brother realize his foolishness. ☐

5 What Puneet understood about their father's wisdom was different from what Puru understood. ☐

• 우리말을 참고하여 빈칸에 알맞은 말을 쓰시오.

1 A rich and wise father _____ _____ _____, Puru and Puneet.

2 Before he _____ _____, he _____ his two sons _____ _____ _____ some _____ _____ _____ _____.

3 "_____ _____, my dear sons. _____ _____ these words _____ _____ _____, and you will be happy," he said.

4 "_____ a house in _____ _____. Sleep _____. _____ your food. _____, spend money _____ a rich man... ."

5 Before he could _____ _____, he _____ _____.

6 After _____ _____, the two sons took _____ _____ _____ the father's _____ and _____ _____ different cities.

7 Five years passed. Puru, _____ _____ _____ _____ his father's words carefully, had _____ _____ _____.

8 But his brother _____ _____ _____ _____ _____.

9 Puru _____ _____ _____ _____ he _____ _____ _____, so he visited Puneet _____ _____ _____.

10 Puneet _____ Puru _____ _____ _____.

11 That night, when the brothers _____ _____ _____ _____ after dinner, Puru asked the question _____ _____ _____ _____ for days.

12 "_____ _____ our father's advice _____ I followed, but I am not happy. I built a house _____ _____ _____.

13 But because I could not _____ _____ _____, I hired people and _____ the house _____ _____.

---

1 부유하고 지혜로운 아버지에게 두 아들, Puru와 Puneet이 있었다.

2 아버지는 돌아가시기 전에, 마지막 충고의 말을 하기 위해 그의 두 아들을 불렀다.

3 "주의 깊게 듣거라, 사랑하는 아들들아. 너희의 일생 동안 이 말대로 살면, 행복해질 것이다." 그는 말했다.

4 "모든 도시에 집을 지어라. 편하게 자거라. 음식을 즐기거라. 마지막으로, 돈을 부자처럼 쓰거라…."

5 아버지는 그 말을 설명하기도 전에 돌아가셨다.

6 그의 죽음 후에, 두 아들은 아버지의 재산 중 자신들의 몫을 가지고 다른 도시에 정착했다.

7 5년이 지났다. 아버지의 말을 신중히 따라온 Puru는 남은 돈이 없었다.

8 그러나 그의 동생은 그 어느 때보다 더 부자가 되었다.

9 Puru는 그가 어디서부터 잘못했는지 어리둥절했고, 그래서 그는 (그것을) 알아내기 위해 Puneet을 방문했다.

10 Puneet은 Puru를 두 팔 벌려 환영했다.

11 그날 밤, 형제가 저녁식사 후 이야기를 하려고 앉았을 때, Puru는 며칠간 자신의 마음에 있었던 그 질문을 했다.

12 "내가 따른 건 바로 우리 아버지의 조언이었지만, 나는 행복하지 않아. 나는 모든 도시에 집을 지었어.

13 그러나 나는 그곳에 항상 머물 수 없었으므로 사람들을 고용하여 집을 돌보게 했지.

14 Father said we should _____ _____ and _____ our food, so I _____ my bed _____ by experts and _____ _____ _____ _____ a great chef.

15 He _____ us _____ _____ _____ a rich man, so I bought _____ _____ _____ _____ without _____ about money.

16 But _____ _____ _____ now! I am _____.

17 Did you _____ _____ our _____ _____?

18 Tell me, brother, _____ _____ you _____ so _____?"

19 Puneet _____ and said, "My dear brother, I _____ _____ our _____ _____.

20 But I understood _____ _____ _____ _____.

21 When he said '_____ a house in every city,' I _____ _____ _____ _____ all around the world.

22 So I _____ _____ in every city and I _____ their houses when I visited _____ _____.

23 Also, I slept _____ each night _____ I would be tired after a hard day's work, and it did not matter _____ _____ _____ on a bed _____ on the hard floor.

24 I ate _____ _____ _____ _____ _____, so even a simple meal _____ _____."

25 "Spend money _____ _____ _____ _____?" _____ Puneet.

26 "A rich man knows _____ _____ _____ _____.

27 So, I tried to spend money _____ something _____ would _____ _____ _____ more money _____ _____ luxurious things.

28 For me, _____ _____ this wisdom _____ our father _____ _____ _____."

29 Now Puru realized _____ _____ _____ _____.

30 _____ this wisdom _____ _____, Puru started a new life.

---

14 아버지께서 우리는 편하게 자고 음식을 즐겨야 한다고 말씀하셔서 나는 내 침대를 전문가들에 의해 설계되게 했고, 내 식사는 훌륭한 요리사에 의해 준비되도록 했단다.

15 아버지는 우리에게 부자처럼 돈을 쓰라고 하셨으므로, 나는 돈 걱정을 하지 않고 내가 원하는 것을 샀지.

16 그렇지만 지금 나를 봐! 나는 빈털터리야.

17 너는 우리 아버지의 지혜를 따르지 않았니?

18 나에게 말해 보렴, 동생아, 너는 어떻게 그렇게 부유해졌니?"

19 Puneet은 웃으며 말했다. "친애하는 형님, 저 또한 우리 아버지의 지혜를 따랐습니다.

20 하지만 저는 조금 다르게 이해했지요.

21 아버지가 '모든 도시에 집을 지어라'라고 말하셨을 때, 저는 그것을 전 세계에 머물 수 있는 장소를 가지는 것으로 여겼지요.

22 그래서 저는 모든 도시에서 친구를 사귀었고 그 도시들을 방문했을 때 그들의 집에 머물렀어요.

23 또한, 저는 하루 종일 열심히 일하고 나서 피곤해지곤 했기 때문에 침대에서 자든 딱딱한 바닥에서 자든 상관없이 매일 밤 편안하게 잠을 잤지요.

24 저는 배고플 때만 먹었기 때문에 간단한 식사마저도 훌륭한 맛이 났습니다."

25 "부자처럼 돈을 쓰라고요?" Puneet은 계속했다.

26 "부자는 돈을 불리는 방법을 알고 있어요.

27 그래서 저는 사치스러운 물건에 돈을 쓰는 것보다는 저에게 더 많은 돈을 돌려줄 수 있는 것에 돈을 쓰려고 노력했지요.

28 저에게는 이게 우리의 아버지가 설명하려고 하셨던 바로 그 지혜입니다."

29 이제 Puru는 그가 얼마나 어리석었었는지를 깨달았다.

30 이 지혜를 마음에 새기고, Puru는 새로운 삶을 시작했다.

● 우리말을 참고하여 본문을 영작하시오.

1 부유하고 지혜로운 아버지에게 두 아들, Puru와 Puneet이 있었다.

➡ _____

2 아버지는 돌아가시기 전에, 마지막 충고의 말을 하기 위해 그의 두 아들을 불렀다.

➡ _____

3 "주의 깊게 듣거라, 사랑하는 아들들아. 너희의 일생 동안 이 말대로 살면, 행복해질 것이다." 그는 말했다.

➡ _____

4 "모든 도시에 집을 지어라. 편하게 자거라. 음식을 즐기거라. 마지막으로, 돈을 부자처럼 쓰거라…."

➡ _____

5 아버지는 그 말을 설명하기도 전에 돌아가셨다.

➡ _____

6 그의 죽음 후에, 두 아들은 아버지의 재산 중 자신들의 몫을 가지고 다른 도시에 정착했다.

➡ _____

7 5년이 지났다. 아버지의 말을 신중히 따라온 Puru는 남은 돈이 없었다.

➡ _____

8 그러나 그의 동생은 그 어느 때보다 더 부자가 되었다.

➡ _____

9 Puru는 그가 어디서부터 잘못했는지 어리둥절했고, 그래서 그는 (그것을) 알아내기 위해 Puneet을 방문했다.

➡ _____

10 Puneet은 Puru를 두 팔 벌려 환영했다.

➡ _____

11 그날 밤, 형제가 저녁식사 후 이야기를 하려고 앉았을 때, Puru는 며칠간 자신의 마음에 있었던 그 질문을 했다.

➡ _____

12 "내가 따른 건 바로 우리 아버지의 조언이었지만, 나는 행복하지 않아. 나는 모든 도시에 집을 지었어.

➡ _____

13 그러나 나는 그곳에 항상 머물 수 없었으므로 사람들을 고용하여 집을 돌보게 했지.

➡ _____

14 아버지께서 우리는 편하게 자고 음식을 즐겨야 한다고 말씀하셔서 나는 내 침대를 전문가들에 의해 설계되게 했고, 내 식사는 훌륭한 요리사에 의해 준비되도록 했단다.

➡ _____

15 아버지는 우리에게 부자처럼 돈을 쓰라고 하셨으므로, 나는 돈 걱정을 하지 않고 내가 원하는 것을 샀지.

➡ _____

16 그렇지만 지금 나를 봐! 나는 빈털터리야.

➡ _____

17 너는 우리 아버지의 지혜를 따르지 않았니?

➡ _____

18 나에게 말해 보렴, 동생아, 너는 어떻게 그렇게 부유해졌니?"

➡ _____

19 Puneet은 웃으며 말했다. "친애하는 형님, 저 또한 우리 아버지의 지혜를 따랐습니다.

➡ _____

20 하지만 저는 조금 다르게 이해했지요.

➡ _____

21 아버지가 '모든 도시에 집을 지어라'라고 말하셨을 때, 저는 그것을 전 세계에 머물 수 있는 장소를 가지는 것으로 여겼지요.

➡ _____

22 그래서 저는 모든 도시에서 친구를 사귀었고 그 도시들을 방문했을 때 그들의 집에 머물렀어요.

➡ _____

23 또한, 저는 하루 종일 열심히 일하고 나서 피곤해지곤 했기 때문에 침대에서 자든 딱딱한 바닥에서 자든 상관없이 매일 밤 편안하게 잠을 잤지요.

➡ _____
_____

24 저는 배고플 때만 먹었기 때문에 간단한 식사마저도 훌륭한 맛이 났습니다."

➡ _____

25 "부자처럼 돈을 쓰라고요?" Puneet은 계속했다.

➡ _____

26 "부자는 돈을 불리는 방법을 알고 있어요.

➡ _____

27 그래서 저는 사치스러운 물건에 돈을 쓰는 것보다는 저에게 더 많은 돈을 돌려줄 수 있는 것에 돈을 쓰려고 노력했지요.

➡ _____
_____

28 저에게는 이게 우리의 아버지가 설명하려고 하셨던 바로 그 지혜입니다."

➡ _____

29 이제 Puru는 그가 얼마나 어리석었었는지를 깨달았다.

➡ _____

30 이 지혜를 마음에 새기고, Puru는 새로운 삶을 시작했다.

➡ _____

[01~04] 다음 글을 읽고 물음에 답하시오.

A rich and wise father had two sons, Puru and Puneet. Before he passed away, he called his two sons to give them some last words of advice.

"Listen carefully, my dear sons. Live (A)_____ these words throughout your life, and you will be happy," he said.

"Build a house in every city. Sleep comfortably. Enjoy your food. Lastly, spend money like a rich man... ."

Before he could explain himself, he passed away. After his death, the two sons took their share of the father's wealth and settled in different cities. Five years passed. Puru, who had been following his father's words carefully, had no money left. But his brother was richer than ever. Puru was puzzled about where he had gone wrong, so he visited Puneet to find out.

01 다음 중 빈칸 (A)에 들어갈 말과 같은 말이 들어가는 것은?

① He took part _____ the contest.
② Breakfast consisted _____ bread with butter.
③ As time goes _____, I miss her more and more.
④ We are different _____ each other in many ways.
⑤ Their house is very similar _____ ours, but ours is more beautiful.

02 다음과 같이 풀이되는 말을 위 글에서 찾아 쓰시오.

the end of life

➡ _____

03 What were the names of the two sons? Answer in English with a full sentence.

➡ _____

04 다음 중 위 글을 읽고 답할 수 있는 것은?

① How rich was the father?
② What made the father rich?
③ How old was the rich man when he died?
④ Where were two sons before their father called them?
⑤ What did the rich man say to his sons when he was dying?

[05~08] 다음 글을 읽고 물음에 답하시오.

Puneet welcomed Puru with open arms. That night, when the brothers sat down ①to chat after dinner, Puru asked the question ②that had been on his mind for days.

"It was our father's advice that I followed, but I am not happy. I built a house in every city. But ③because I could not always stay there, I hired people and had the house ④look after. Father said we should sleep comfortably and enjoy our food, so I had my bed designed by experts and my meals prepared by a great chef. He told us ⑤to spend like a rich man, so I bought what I wanted without worrying about money. But look at me now! I am empty-handed. Did you not follow (A)our father's wisdom? Tell me, brother, how did you get so rich?"

05 What did Puru follow? Answer in English.

➡ _____

06 다음 중 밑줄 친 (A)에 해당하는 것은?

① Be curious about everything.

② Be proud of yourself.

③ Don't spend much money.

④ Take pleasure in eating food.

⑤ Build your house in your hometown.

07 밑줄 친 ①~⑤ 중 어법상 바르지 않은 것은?

①   ②   ③   ④   ⑤

08 Choose one that is TRUE.

① Puneet didn't like his brother's visit.

② Puru regrets not following his father's advice.

③ Puru had his house designed by experts.

④ Puru was employed by a chef to prepare a meal.

⑤ Puru bought everything he wanted without worrying about money.

[09~12] 다음 글을 읽고 물음에 답하시오.

 Puneet smiled and said, "My dear brother, I also followed our father's wisdom. But I understood it a bit differently. When he said 'build a house in every city,' I took it as having a place to stay all around the world. So I made friends in every city and I stayed at their houses when I visited those cities. (A) Also, I slept comfortably each night because I would be tired after a hard day's work, and it did not matter if I was sleeping on a bed or on the hard floor. I ate only when I was hungry, so even a simple meal tasted great."
"Spend money like a rich man?" continued Puneet.

"A rich man knows how to make money grow. So, I tried to spend money on something that would bring ⓐ_____ rather than on luxurious things. For me, it was this wisdom that our father tried to explain."
Now Puru realized how foolish he had been. With this wisdom in mind, Puru started a new life.

09 위 글의 흐름상 빈칸 ⓐ에 들어갈 말로 가장 적절한 것은?

① you a big fortune

② us happy lives

③ me back more money

④ up my children comfortably

⑤ about a change

10 다음 중 밑줄 친 (A)를 대신하여 쓸 수 있는 것은?

① Therefore   ② For instance

③ In addition   ④ However

⑤ On the other hand

11 서답형 Write the reason why Puneet could be satisfied with only a simple meal. Answer in English with a full sentence.

➡ _____

12 서답형 Where did Puneet stay when he visited cities all around the world? Answer in English.

➡ _____
_____

[13~16] 다음 글을 읽고 물음에 답하시오.

A rich and wise father had two sons, Puru and Puneet. Before he passed away, he called his two sons to give them some last words of advice.

"Listen carefully, my dear sons. Live by these words throughout your life, and you will be happy," he said.

"Build a house in every city. Sleep comfortably. Enjoy your food. Lastly, spend money like a rich man... ." Before he could explain (A)himself, he passed away.

(①) After his death, the two sons took their share of the father's wealth and settled in different cities. (②) Five years passed. (③) Puru, who had been following his father's words carefully, had no money left. (④) Puru was puzzled about where he had gone wrong, so he visited Puneet to find out. (⑤)

13 (①)~(⑤) 중 주어진 문장이 들어가기에 가장 적절한 곳은?

> But his brother was richer than ever.

① ② ③ ④ ⑤

중요

14 위 글에 이어질 내용으로 가장 적절한 것은?

① Puneet leaving for making more money
② Puneet wanting to help his brother
③ The way Puneet became richer than ever
④ The reason why Puru visited his brother
⑤ Two brothers visiting their father's grave

서답형

15 What happened to Puru five years after his father's death? Answer in English with five words.

➡ _____

16 다음 중 밑줄 친 (A)와 쓰임이 다른 것은?

① They enjoyed themselves a lot.
② He spoke to the principal himself.
③ He cut himself on a knife yesterday.
④ Please help yourself to the salad.
⑤ She couldn't make herself understood.

[17~20] 다음 글을 읽고 물음에 답하시오.

(A)Puneet welcomed Puru with open arms. That night, when the brothers sat down to chat after dinner, Puru asked the question that had been on his mind for days.

"It was our father's advice that I followed, but I am not happy. I built a house in every city. But because I could not always stay there, I hired people and had the house looked after. Father said we should sleep comfortably and enjoy our food, so I had my bed designed by experts and my meals ⓐ_____ by a great chef. He told us to spend like a rich man, so I bought what I wanted without worrying about money. But look at me now! I am empty-handed. Did you not follow our father's wisdom? Tell me, brother, how did you get so rich?"

서답형

17 주어진 단어를 어법에 맞게 빈칸 ⓐ에 쓰시오.

> (prepare)

➡ _____

18 밑줄 친 (A)의 의미로 가장 적절한 것은?

① Puru was rejected by Puneet.
② Puru held Puneet by the arm.
③ Puneet welcomed Puru reluctantly.
④ Puneet wanted Puru to go away.
⑤ Puneet gave Puru a warm welcome.

서답형
19 What did Puru do in every city? Answer in English.

➡ _____

20 위 글에 이어질 내용으로 가장 적절한 것은?

① what Puneet did to help his brother

② how Puru became rich again

③ how Puneet became richer

④ what Puru did to follow the advice

⑤ what happened to Puru before he came back

[21~25] 다음 글을 읽고 물음에 답하시오.

Puneet smiled and said, "My dear brother, I also followed our father's wisdom. But I understood it a bit differently. When he said 'build a house in every city,' I took it as having a place to stay all around the world. So I made friends in every city and I stayed at their houses when I visited those cities. ⓐAlso, I slept comfortably each night because I would be tired after a hard day's work, and it did not matter if I was sleeping on a bed or on the hard floor. I ate only when I was hungry, so even a simple meal tasted great."

"Spend money like a rich man?" continued Puneet.

"A rich man knows how to make money grow. So, I tried to spend money on something that would bring me back more money rather than (A)_____ luxurious things. For me, it was this wisdom that our father tried to explain."

Now Puru realized how foolish he had been. With this wisdom in mind, Puru started a new life.

21 빈칸 (A)에 들어갈 말로 적절한 것은?

① at ② on ③ about ④ to ⑤ by

22 According to the underlined ⓐ, what was their father's last word?

① Get a good rest.

② Sleep comfortably.

③ Work like a bee.

④ Make money as I did.

⑤ Always sleep at home.

23 What did Puru do after hearing what his brother said?

① He went home with anger.

② He made his brother start a new life.

③ He went back to his old habit.

④ He made a fresh start.

⑤ He realized his brother's foolishness.

서답형
24 위 글의 내용에 맞게 빈칸에 알맞은 말을 쓰시오.

Both brothers understood their father's wisdom _____.

25 다음 중 위 글의 내용과 일치하지 않는 것은?

① Puru followed his father's advice.

② Their father told them to build a house in every city.

③ Puneet built houses as his father told him to.

④ Puru finally understood what his father tried to say.

⑤ Puneet made his money grow like a rich man does.

[01~05] 다음 글을 읽고 물음에 답하시오.

A rich and wise father had two sons, Puru and Puneet. Before he passed away, he called his two sons to give them some last words of advice.

"Listen carefully, my dear sons. (A)Live by these words throughout your life, and you will be happy," he said.

"Build a house in every city. Sleep comfortably. Enjoy your food. Lastly, spend money like a rich man... ." Before he could explain himself, he passed away.

After his death, the two sons took their share of the father's wealth and settled in different cities. Five years passed. Puru, who had been following his father's words carefully, had no money left. But his brother was richer than ever. Puru was puzzled about where he had gone wrong, so he visited Puneet to find out.

01 Write the reason why the father called his two sons before he passed away. Use the phrase 'It was because.'

➡ _____

_____

02 What had Puru been doing since his father passed away? Answer in English.

➡ _____

03 접속사 lf를 사용하여 밑줄 친 (A)와 같은 의미의 문장을 쓰시오.

➡ _____

_____

04 위 글의 내용과 일치하도록 빈칸에 알맞은 말을 쓰시오.

Unlike _____, _____ became richer than ever.

05 What did the two sons do after their father died? Answer in English with a full sentence.

➡ _____

_____

[06~11] 다음 글을 읽고 물음에 답하시오.

Puneet smiled and said, "My dear brother, I also followed our father's wisdom. But I understood it a bit differently. When he said 'build a house in every city,' I took it as having a place to stay all around the world. So I made friends in every city and I stayed at their houses when I visited those cities. Also, I slept comfortably each night because I would be tired after a hard day's work, and it did not matter if I was sleeping on a bed or on the hard floor. I ate only when I was hungry, so even a simple meal tasted great."

"Spend money like a rich man?" continued Puneet.

"A rich man (A)_____. So, I tried to spend money on something that would bring me back more money rather than on luxurious things. For me, it was this wisdom that our father tried to explain."

Now Puru realized how foolish he had been. With this wisdom in mind, Puru started a new life.

06 주어진 단어를 바르게 나열하여 빈칸 (A)에 들어갈 말을 완성하시오.

(grow / knows / make / to / money / how)

➡ _____

07 Why did a simple meal taste great to Puneet? Answer in English and use the word 'because.'

➡ _____

_____

08 What did Puneet do to spend money like a rich man? Answer in English with a full sentence.

➡ _____

_____

_____

09 다음 중 위 글의 내용과 일치하지 <u>않는</u> 곳을 두 군데 찾아 바르게 고쳐 쓰시오.

> Puneet understood what his brother had said differently from Puru. Thanks to his own deep understanding, Puneet became poor and happy.

➡ _____

10 Write the reason why Puneet could sleep anywhere comfortably. Use the phrase 'It was because.'

➡ _____

11 What did Puru realize? Answer in English.

➡ _____

[12~15] 다음 글을 읽고 물음에 답하시오.

Puneet welcomed Puru with open arms. That night, when the brothers sat down to chat after dinner, Puru asked the question that had been on his mind for days.

"It was our father's advice that I followed, but I am not happy. I built a house in every city. But because I could not always stay (A)<u>there</u>, I hired people and (B)집을 돌보게 했지. Father said we should sleep comfortably and enjoy our food, so I had my bed designed by experts and my meals prepared by a great chef. He told us to spend like a rich man, so I bought what I wanted without worrying about money. But look at me now! I am empty-handed. Did you not follow our father's wisdom? Tell me, brother, how did you get so rich?"

12 밑줄 친 (A)there가 의미하는 것을 우리말로 쓰시오.

➡ _____

13 주어진 단어를 활용하여 밑줄 친 우리말 (B)를 5 단어의 영어로 쓰시오.

> (have / look)

➡ _____

14 What did their father tell them to do? Answer in English with a full sentence.

➡ _____

15 위 글의 내용에 맞게 괄호 (A)～(C)에서 적절한 말을 고르시오.

> (A)[Although / Unless] Puru followed his father's advice, he lived an (B)[easy / unhappy] life and became (C)[wealthy / broke].

➡ (A) _____ (B) _____ (C) _____

Language in Use

• Everyone has <u>freedom</u> of speech and expression.
형용사에 '-dom'을 붙이면 명사가 되어 '영역, 상태'라는 의미가 더해진다.

• Can you <u>explain</u> the rules of the game before we start playing it?
특정 어근 앞에 'ex-'를 붙이면 '밖으로'라는 의미를 더한다.

구문해설 • **freedom**: 자유 • **explain**: 설명하다

• 모든 사람들은 언론과 표현의 자유가 있다.

• 우리가 경기를 시작하기 전에 규칙을 설명해 줄래?

Grammar in Real Life B Look and Write

1. Do you need to have the computer <u>fixed</u>? Call the Computer Doctor.
have+목적어+과거분사: 목적어가 목적격 보어의 동작을 당하는 대상(주로 사물)

2. Why don't you <u>have your hair cut</u> at Susie's Hair Studio?
~하는 게 어때?   과거분사(머리카락이 잘리는 것)

3. <u>How about</u> having your pet <u>cleaned</u> from head to toe? Come to Happy Pet.
~하는 게 어때?   과거분사(애완동물이 깨끗하게 되는 것)

4. Do you want to have your party room <u>decorated</u> with flowers?
과거분사(파티 룸이 장식되는 것)

Look for Mary's Flowers.

구문해설 • **fix**: 수리하다, 고치다 • **toe**: 발가락, 발끝 • **decorate**: 장식하다

1. 컴퓨터를 고쳐야 하나요? '컴퓨터 닥터'에게 전화하세요.

2. '수지의 헤어 스튜디오'에서 머리카락을 자르는 게 어때요?

3. 당신의 애완동물을 머리부터 발끝까지 깨끗하게 하는 것은 어떨까요? '해피 펫'으로 오세요.

4. 당신의 파티 룸을 꽃으로 장식하고 싶은가요? '메리의 꽃들'을 찾아 주세요.

Think & Write C

Let me introduce my motto.
사역동사+목적어+동사원형
It is "Go for it!"

It means "Go and do things without fear <u>because</u> failure is also a good
이유를 이끄는 접속사
experience." I made it my motto when I was a kicker in the school soccer
team. From the motto, I learned <u>that</u> even the bad kicks made me a better
kicker at the end. <u>It is this motto that changed my life!</u>

구문해설 • **introduce**: 소개하다 • **motto**: 좌우명 • **failure**: 실패

나의 좌우명을 소개하게 해 줘.

그것은 "어서 해!"야.

그것은 "실패 또한 좋은 경험이기 때문에 두려움 없이 무언가를 해'라는 의미야. 나는 학교 축구팀에서 키커였을 때, 그것을 나의 좌우명으로 삼았어. 그 좌우명에서 나는 나쁜 킥들조차 결국엔 나를 더 좋은 키커로 만들어 준다는 것을 배웠지. 나의 삶을 바꾼 것은 바로 이 좌우명이야!

Words & Expressions

01 다음 밑줄 친 부분의 의미로 알맞지 않은 것은?

① It was really priceless information. (가치 없는)

② My brother is an expert at computer programming. (전문가)

③ She laughed and chatted happily with her family. (담소하다)

④ The princess lived in this old castle for her entire life. (성)

⑤ The chef is famous in Korea for Chinese food. (요리사)

02 다음 괄호 안의 단어를 문맥에 맞게 고쳐 쓰시오.

> He has lived on this _____ island alone for 10 years. (desert)

03 다음 빈칸에 알맞은 단어를 고르시오.

> We've nearly _____ out of paper. Do you think there's enough for today?

① made   ② taken   ③ run
④ got   ⑤ put

04 다음 밑줄 친 부분과 바꿔 쓸 수 있는 말을 고르시오.

> He died at the age of eighty-four.

① passed out   ② passed up
③ got through   ④ passed away
⑤ took back

Conversation

[05~08] 다음 대화를 읽고 물음에 답하시오.

W: What are you doing, Jinho?

M: (①) I'm writing a (A)_____ of the movie, *The Time Traveler's Wife*. (②)

W: I saw that movie, too. It's one of my favorite romantic movies. (③)

M: (④) Emily, (B)만약 네가 시간 여행을 할 수 있다면 무엇을 하겠니?

W: I would travel to the 1940s and prevent World War II. How about you?

M: I would go to the Joseon Dynasty and meet King Sejong. (⑤) I'm a big fan of him.

05 위 대화의 (①)~(⑤) 중 주어진 문장이 들어갈 곳은?

> I loved it, too.

①   ②   ③   ④   ⑤

06 빈칸 (A)에 알맞은 것을 고르시오.

① reward   ② review   ③ wisdom
④ paper   ⑤ motto

07 위 대화를 읽고 답할 수 없는 질문을 고르시오.

① Emily는 시간 여행을 할 수 있다면, 1940년대 로 가서 무엇을 하고 싶어 하는가?

② Emily는 <시간 여행자의 아내>라는 영화를 보 았는가?

③ 진호는 왜 세종대왕을 만나고 싶어 하는가?

④ 진호는 지금 무엇을 하고 있는가?

⑤ Emily는 어떤 종류의 영화를 좋아하는가?

08 밑줄 친 우리말 (B)를 주어진 단어를 이용하여 영작하시오.

➡ _____

    (time travel, will)

[09~11] 다음 대화를 읽고 물음에 답하시오.

M: ⓐ_____'s your online story going, Amy?

W: Not well. The deadline is this weekend but I ⓑ_____ out of ideas.

M: Don't worry about it. I can help you.

W: That would be great. My main character has special powers. What would you do if you ⓒ_____ able to ⓓ_____ people's minds?

M: Well, I would find out ⓔ_____ the girl I like likes me.

W: That's a good idea. Thanks.

09 빈칸 ⓐ~ⓔ에 들어가지 <u>않는</u> 것을 고르시오. (대·소문자 무시)

① read   ② that   ③ ran
④ how   ⑤ were

10 위 대화에서 다음 영영풀이에 해당하는 단어를 찾아 쓰시오.

a person represented in a film, play, or story

➡ _____

11 위 대화를 읽고 답할 수 <u>없는</u> 질문을 고르시오.

① What power does the main character of her story have?
② What is Amy worried about?
③ Does the man help Amy who worried about the online story?
④ When is the deadline of the online story?
⑤ What would Amy do if she could read people's mind?

12 다음 대화의 빈칸에 들어갈 말을 〈보기〉에서 골라 순서대로 옳게 배열한 것은?

M: _____
W: _____
M: _____
W: _____
M: Really? I would collect interesting items and make a museum.
W: Cool.

┤ 보기 ├

(A) Right. What would you do if you could live forever?
(B) Caroline, have you read the book, *Tuck Everlasting*?
(C) Yeah, it is about a family that drank magical water and lived forever, right?
(D) Well, I would live in different cities all around the world.

① (B) – (A) – (C) – (D)
② (B) – (C) – (A) – (D)
③ (B) – (D) – (A) – (C)
④ (C) – (B) – (A) – (D)
⑤ (C) – (D) – (B) – (A)

Grammar

13 다음 밑줄 친 부분과 바꿔 쓸 수 있는 것은?

It was on the subway <u>that</u> I lost my bag.

① what   ② which   ③ who
④ when   ⑤ where

14 다음 문장 중에서 어법상 <u>어색한</u> 문장을 고르시오.

① David had the TV turned on after dinner.

② I know that my mom had the dishes done by Jake.

③ The government had the markets closed because of the Covid-19.

④ Dad had me returned home as it was very late at night.

⑤ Dad had my elder brother wash the pet dog.

15 다음 주어진 문장과 뜻이 같도록 빈칸을 알맞게 채우시오. (that 사용 금지.)

> The cafe is the place at which Jane is reading a comic book.
>
> ➡ It is ＿＿＿＿＿＿＿＿＿＿＿＿ a comic book.

16 다음 ⓐ～ⓖ 중 어법상 옳은 것을 <u>모두</u> 고르시오.

> ⓐ Do you want to have your party room decorated with flowers?
>
> ⓑ Dad had the tree plant in the yard last Saturday.
>
> ⓒ Lisa got her daughter come back home by 10 p.m.
>
> ⓓ It is Mina and Junha that are waiting in line for the roller coaster.
>
> ⓔ I think it was on the bus when Mina got her wallet steal.
>
> ⓕ It is in her room which Linda is taking a selfie.
>
> ⓖ It was the cat that ate the sandwiches on your desk.

➡ ＿＿＿＿＿＿＿＿＿＿＿＿＿＿

17 다음 우리말을 괄호 안의 조건에 맞게 영작하시오.

> Tom은 Rene에게 자기 대신 공항에서 그의 엄마를 모셔오게 했다.
>
> (the airport, had, pick up, for 이용, 총 12 단어)

➡ ＿＿＿＿＿＿＿＿＿＿＿＿＿＿

＿＿＿＿＿＿＿＿＿＿＿＿＿＿

18 다음 중 어법상 <u>어색한</u> 것을 고르시오. (2개)

① I had my bed design by experts and my meals prepared by a great chef.

② It was the stage that BTS performed their first show.

③ I must have the broken car fixed tomorrow.

④ It was in the morning that the dragon took the princess.

⑤ It was in 1893 that Edvard Munch painted *The Scream*.

19 다음 우리말에 맞게 영작한 것은?

> 아빠가 TV에서 보고 계시던 것은 바로 축구 경기였다.

① It was a soccer game that Dad was watching on TV.

② It was Dad that was watching a soccer game on TV.

③ It was on TV that Dad was watching a soccer game.

④ It was watching on TV that Dad a soccer game.

⑤ Dad watched a soccer game on TV.

20 다음 그림을 보고, 주어진 어휘를 이용하여 빈칸을 알맞게 채우시오.

> They will _____ next week. (the writing contest, have, hold)

Reading

[21~24] 다음 글을 읽고 물음에 답하시오.

Puneet smiled and said, "My dear brother, I also followed our father's wisdom. But I understood it a bit ①differently. When he said 'build a house in every city,' I took it as ② having a place to stay all around the world. So I made friends in every city and I stayed at their houses when I visited ③those cities. Also, I slept comfortably each night because I would be tired after a hard day's work, and it did not matter if I was sleeping on a bed or on the hard floor. I ate only when I was hungry, so even a simple meal tasted ④great."

"Spend money like a rich man?" continued Puneet.

"A rich man knows how to make money ⑤to grow. So, I tried to spend money on something that would bring me back more money rather than on luxurious things. For me, it was this wisdom that our father tried to explain."

Now Puru realized how foolish he had been. With this wisdom ___(A)___ mind, Puru started a new life.

---

21 ①~⑤ 중 어법상 바르지 않은 것은?

①   ②   ③   ④   ⑤

22 위 글의 빈칸 (A)에 알맞은 것은?

① in   ② to
③ at   ④ with
⑤ from

23 다음과 같이 풀이되는 말을 위 글에서 찾아 쓰시오.

> extremely comfortable or elegant, especially when involving great expense

➡ _____

24 According to what Puneet said, what didn't matter to him after a hard day's work? Answer in English.

➡ _____
_____

[25~26] 다음 글을 읽고 물음에 답하시오.

Let me introduce my motto
It is "Go for it!"
It means "Go and do things without fear because failure is also a good experience." I made it my motto when I was a kicker in the school soccer team. From the motto, I learned that even the bad kicks made me a better kicker at the end. It is this motto that changed my life!

25 Write the reason why the writer tries to go and do things without fear. Use the phrase 'It is because.'

➡ _____

26 Choose one that is TRUE.

① The writer doesn't have her or his own motto yet.

② One of the kickers gave the motto to the writer.

③ The writer thinks she or he can be a better kicker with bad kicks.

④ The writer's life was changed by the school soccer team.

⑤ The writer was not a good kicker.

[27~30] 다음 글을 읽고 물음에 답하시오.

Puneet welcomed Puru with open arms. That night, when the brothers sat down to chat after dinner, Puru asked ⓐthe question that had been on his mind for days.

"(A) He told us to spend like a rich man, so I bought what I wanted without ⓑworrying about money. But look at me now! I am empty-handed. Did you not follow our father's wisdom? Tell me, brother, how did you get so rich?

(B) But because I could not always stay there, I hired people and had the house looked after. Father said we should sleep comfortably and enjoy our food, so I had my bed designed by experts and my meals prepared by a great chef.

(C) It was our father's advice that I followed, but I am not happy. I built a house in every city."

27 자연스러운 글이 되도록 (A)~(C)를 바르게 나열하시오.

➡ _____

28 What does the underlined ⓐ mean?

① how Puru became so wealthy

② how his brother got so rich

③ what made Puru become miserable

④ what made Puneet become unhappy

⑤ why Puru wasn't welcomed by his brother

29 Choose one that is TRUE.

① Puru welcomed his brother heartily.

② Puru hired experts to build houses in every city.

③ Puru took care of all the houses for himself.

④ Puru's houses could be found in every city.

⑤ Puneet didn't offer dinner to his brother, Puru.

30 다음 중 밑줄 친 ⓑ와 쓰임이 다른 하나는?

① Did you enjoy making dinner with her?

② David finished doing his homework already.

③ June was waiting for you at the bus stop.

④ My job is protecting you from dangerous things.

⑤ Tom was fond of listening to music.

01 다음 빈칸에 공통으로 들어갈 접두어를 쓰시오. (출제율 90%)

> • She _____plained how the machine worked.
> • His paintings have been _____hibited in China.
> • He _____pressed an interest in meeting her.

02 빈칸을 다음 영영풀이에 해당하는 말을 이용하여 채우시오. (주어진 철자로 시작할 것.) (출제율 90%)

> something given in exchange for good behavior or good work, etc.

> They gave him a _____ for his hard work.

➡ r_____

03 빈칸 (A)와 (B)에 들어갈 말이 바르게 짝지어진 것을 고르시오. (출제율 95%)

> • It was cold, so I slept with a blanket covering me (A)_____ head to toe.
> • It's hard work to (B)_____ after three children all day.

	(A)	(B)
①	on	look
②	on	take
③	from	look
④	from	take
⑤	from	care

04 밑줄 친 부분과 바꿔 쓸 수 있는 말을 고르시오. (출제율 90%)

> Lastly, I would like to ask about your future plans.

① In addition
② Therefore
③ Later
④ Finally
⑤ Eventually

[05~06] 다음 대화를 읽고 물음에 답하시오.

> M: Caroline, have you ⓐread the book, *Tuck Everlasting*?
> W: Yeah, it is about a family ⓑthat drank magical water and ⓒlives forever, right?
> M: Right. What (A)_____ you do if you could live forever?
> W: Well, I (B)_____ live in different cities all around the world.
> M: Really? I (C)_____ collect ⓓinteresting items and ⓔmake a museum.
> W: Cool.

05 ⓐ~ⓔ 중 흐름상 또는 어법상 어색한 것을 고르시오. (출제율 100%)

① ⓐ   ② ⓑ   ③ ⓒ   ④ ⓓ   ⑤ ⓔ

06 빈칸 (A)~(C)에 공통으로 들어갈 말을 쓰시오. (출제율 90%)

➡ _____

[07~09] 다음 대화를 읽고 물음에 답하시오.

> W: What are you doing, Jinho?
> M: I'm writing a review of the movie, *The Time Traveler's Wife*.

W: I saw that movie, too. It's one of my favorite romantic movies.

M: I loved it, too. Emily, (A)_____?

W: I would travel to the 1940s and (B)_____ World War II. How about you?

M: 나는 조선 시대로 가서 세종대왕을 만날 거야. I'm a big fan of him.

출제율 100%

07 빈칸 (A)에 알맞은 말을 고르시오.

① what will you do if you can time travel
② what would you do if you have time machine
③ what will you do if you have a magic suit
④ what would you do if you could time travel
⑤ what could you do if you make time machine

출제율 95%

08 빈칸 (B)에 알맞은 말을 고르시오.

① prevent ② express ③ allow
④ obtain ⑤ exhibit

출제율 90%

09 밑줄 친 우리말과 일치하도록 주어진 단어를 이용해 영작하시오.

➡ I _____
_____. (the Joseon Dynasty, King Sejong)

[10~11] 다음 대화를 읽고 물음에 답하시오.

M: I've heard that you're going to be in the writing contest next week.

W: Yeah, it's already next week.

M: You look worried. What's wrong?

W: I'm worried that the topic would be too difficult for me.

M: 네가 바꿀 수 없는 것에 대해 걱정하지 마. Just believe (A)_____ yourself.

W: Thanks. I'll try.

출제율 90%

10 빈칸 (A)에 알맞은 전치사를 쓰시오.

➡ _____

출제율 90%

11 밑줄 친 우리말과 일치하도록 주어진 단어를 이용해 영작하시오.

➡ _____

(something, change, about, 7 단어)

출제율 95%

12 다음 우리말에 맞게 영작한 것은?

나는 그가 내 시계를 수리하게 했다.

① I had my watch repair him.
② I got my watch repaired him.
③ I had him repaired my watch.
④ I had him repair my watch.
⑤ I got him repair my watch.

출제율 100%

13 다음 중 어법상 어색한 문장은?

① Ted needs to have the plants watered.
② It was my mom that named my pet dog Lucky.
③ My grandma had me fix her computer last week.
④ It was the amusement park that Minsu rode the roller coaster.
⑤ It was the movie *Parasite* that I watched last Sunday.

14 다음 빈칸에 들어갈 말을 순서대로 바르게 묶은 것은? 출제율 95%

> • Mom had the dinner _____ before everyone came.
>
> • It was yesterday _____ I played tennis with Mike.

① prepared – where

② prepared – when

③ prepare – where

④ prepare – what

⑤ prepares – that

15 밑줄 친 부분을 바르게 고쳐 문장을 다시 쓰시오. 출제율 95%

(1) My dad <u>has his car to wash</u> once a month.

➡ _____

(2) Mom <u>had a robot vacuum cleaner to clean</u> the floor.

➡ _____
_____

(3) Jane <u>got Richard guessing</u> her age when she first met him.

➡ _____
_____

(4) <u>It was the restaurant which</u> Angelina had dinner with her friends.

➡ _____
_____

(5) <u>It was a knife where</u> I forgot to bring to the cooking class.

➡ _____
_____

16 그림을 보고, 주어진 어휘를 이용하여 빈칸을 알맞게 채우시오. (변형 가능) 출제율 90%

It was the princess _____

_____ with flowers. (the table, have, decorate)

[17~20] 다음 글을 읽고 물음에 답하시오.

> A rich and wise father had two sons, Puru and Puneet. Before he ①passed away, he called his two sons to give them some last words of advice.
>
> "Listen carefully, my dear sons. ②Live on these words throughout your life, and you will be ③happy," he said.
>
> "Build a house in every city. Sleep comfortably. Enjoy your food. Lastly, spend money like a rich man... ." Before he could ④explain himself, he passed away.
>
> After his death, the two sons took their share of the father's wealth and settled in different cities. Five years passed. Puru, who had been following his father's words carefully, had no money ⑤left. But his brother was richer than ever. Puru was puzzled about where he had gone wrong, so he visited Puneet to find out.

17 ①~⑤ 중 글의 흐름상 어색한 것은? 출제율 95%

① 　　② 　　③　　④ 　　⑤

출제율 90%

18 Who was richer after five years, Puru or Puneet? Answer in English with a full sentence.

➡ _____

출제율 100%

19 Choose one that is TRUE.

① The father passed away without saying a word.
② Two sons couldn't watch their father pass away.
③ The father left nothing for his two sons.
④ Two sons settled in the same city where they grew up together.
⑤ Puru stuck to what his father had said.

출제율 95%

20 How did Puru feel about his brother's news? Answer in English with three words.

➡ _____

[21~24] 다음 글을 읽고 물음에 답하시오.

Puneet smiled and said, "My dear brother, I also followed our father's wisdom. (①) But I understood (A)it a bit differently. (②) When he said 'build a house in every city,' I took it as having a place (B)to stay all around the world. (③) Also, I slept comfortably each night because I would be tired after a hard day's work, and it did not matter if I was sleeping on a bed or on the hard floor. I ate only when I was hungry, so even a simple meal tasted great." (④)

"Spend money like a rich man?" continued Puneet. (⑤)

"A rich man knows how to make money grow. So, I tried to spend money on something that would bring me back more money rather than on luxurious things. For me, it was this

wisdom that our father tried to explain."

Now Puru realized how foolish he had been. (C)With this wisdom in mind, Puru started a new life.

출제율 100%

21 (①)~(⑤) 중 주어진 문장이 들어가기에 가장 적절한 곳은?

So I made friends in every city and I stayed at their houses when I visited those cities.

①　　②　　③　　④　　⑤

출제율 95%

22 밑줄 친 (A)it이 가리키는 것을 위 글에서 찾아 쓰시오.

➡ _____

출제율 95%

23 다음 중 밑줄 친 (B)와 쓰임이 같은 것은?

① He went out to find some food.
② Did they want you to do it?
③ It was interesting to see the movie.
④ That is the simple way to do it.
⑤ She was very sad to hear the news.

출제율 90%

24 What does underlined (C) mean?

① He didn't bother to remember the wisdom.
② He tried to bear the wisdom in mind.
③ He didn't understand what his brother said.
④ He often forgot keeping the wisdom in mind.
⑤ He wondered how his brother made money.

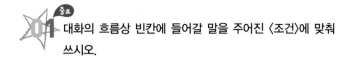

01 대화의 흐름상 빈칸에 들어갈 말을 주어진 〈조건〉에 맞춰 쓰시오.

> M: Lisa, have you watched the movie, *Cast Away*?
>
> W: No, I haven't. What is it about?
>
> M: It's about a man who was stuck on a deserted island for 4 years.
>
> W: It sounds interesting.
>
> M: Yeah, the man tries everything to stay alive. _____
>
> W: To stay alive? Well, I would build a tree house and hunt for food.
>
> M: Yeah, me too. And that's what the man did in the movie.

┤ 조건 ├
- 상상한 내용을 묻기
- will, be, do, him을 이용할 것 (형태 변화 가능)
- 총 8 단어

➡ _____

02 다음 대화에서 흐름상 어색한 것을 찾아 바르게 고치시오.

> M: ①I've heard that you're going to be in the writing contest next week.
>
> W: Yeah, it's already next week.
>
> M: ②You look worried. What's wrong?
>
> W: ③I'm worried that the topic would be too easy for me.
>
> M: ④Don't worry about something you can't change. ⑤Just believe in yourself.
>
> W: Thanks. I'll try.

➡ _____

03 다음 대화의 밑줄 친 부분과 같은 뜻이 되도록 빈칸에 알맞은 말을 쓰시오.

> M: Sujin, what are you doing this weekend?
>
> W: Nothing special, why?
>
> M: I have to go to Busan for a family trip tomorrow but I can't find anyone to feed my dog, Lucy.
>
> W: Don't worry about Lucy. <u>I'll take care of her.</u>

➡ I'll _____ after her.

04 다음 문장에서 틀린 것을 고쳐 다시 쓰시오.

(1) Why don't you have the groceries to deliver to your home?

➡ _____
_____

(2) The students got their classroom paint.

➡ _____

(3) It was Matt which had coffee at the office this morning.

➡ _____
_____

[05~08] 다음 글을 읽고 물음에 답하시오.

> Puneet welcomed Puru with open arms. That night, when the brothers sat down to chat after dinner, Puru asked the question that had been on his mind for days.
>
> "It was our father's advice that I followed, but I am not happy. I built a house in every city. But because I could not always stay there, I hired people and had the house looked after. Father said we should sleep comfortably and enjoy

our food, so I had my bed designed by experts and my meals prepared by a great chef. (A)그는 우리에게 부자처럼 돈을 쓰라고 했어, so I bought what I wanted without worrying about money. But look at me now! I am empty-handed. Did you not follow our father's wisdom? Tell me, brother, how did you get so rich?"

Puneet smiled and said, "My dear brother, I also followed our father's wisdom. But I understood it a bit differently. When he said 'build a house in every city,' I took it as having a place to stay all around the world. So I made friends in every city and I stayed at their houses when I visited those cities. Also, I slept comfortably each night because I would be tired after a hard day's work, and it did not matter if I was sleeping on a bed or on the hard floor. I ate only when I was hungry, so even a simple meal tasted great."

05 What did they do after dinner? Answer in English with a full sentence.

➡ _____

06 How did Puneet take his father's advice of building a house in every city? Answer in English with eleven words including 'making', 'living', 'different.'

➡ _____

_____

07 빈칸에 알맞은 말을 넣어, 아버지의 유언을 형제가 어떻게 해석했는지 정리하시오.

(1) Build a house in every city.

  Puru: I _____ _____ _____ in every city.

  Puneet: I _____ _____ in every city.

(2) Sleep comfortably.

  Puru: I had _____ _____

  _____ _____ experts.

  Puneet: I slept comfortably because I would be _____ after

  _____ _____ _____

  _____.

(3) Enjoy your food.

  Puru: I had _____ _____ _____

  by a great chef.

  Puneet: I ate only when _____

  _____ _____.

08 주어진 단어를 활용하여 밑줄 친 우리말 (A)를 영어로 쓰시오.

| (tell / like / man) |

➡ _____

[09~10] 다음 글을 읽고 물음에 답하시오.

Let me (A)_____ my motto.
It is "Go for it!"
It means "Go and do things without fear because failure is also a good experience." I made it my motto when I was a kicker in the school soccer team. From the motto, I learned that even the bad kicks made me a better kicker at the end. It is this motto that changed my life!

09 빈칸 (A)에 introduce를 알맞게 쓰시오.

➡ _____

10 What does "Go for it" mean? Answer in English with a full sentence.

➡ _____

_____

01 다음 질문에 자유롭게 대답하시오.

> Q: What would you do if you were invisible for a day?

> A: _____
>
> _____

02 다음 문장을 'have+목적어+목적격보어' 유형을 사용하여 비슷한 뜻으로 바꾸어 쓰시오.

> (1) She checked her ears.
>
> ➡ _____
>
> (2) They asked Jørn Utzon to design the Opera House in Sydney.
>
> ➡ _____
>
> ➡ _____
>
> (3) Mom allowed me to play a computer game after dinner.
>
> ➡ _____
>
> ➡ _____

03 다음 내용을 바탕으로 제품의 광고 내용에 대해 문의하는 게시 글을 쓰시오.

> Q: What is your motto?
> A: It's "No Pain, No Gain."
> Q: What does it mean?
> A: It means "Without hard work, you can get nothing as a reward."
> Q: When did you make it your motto?
> A: I made it my motto when I was a kicker in the school soccer team.
> Q: What did the motto help you learn?
> A: I learned that even the bad kicks made me a better kicker at the end.

> Let me introduce my motto.
> It is "_____"
> It means "_____" I made it my motto when
> _____. From the motto, I learned that _____
> _____. It is this motto that changed my life!

단원별 모의고사

01 다음 짝지어진 단어의 관계가 <u>다른</u> 하나를 고르시오.

① puzzled – confused
② hire – fire
③ priceless – worthless
④ death – life
⑤ lastly – firstly

02 다음 빈칸에 가장 알맞은 말을 고르시오.

> A: I will have a soccer game tomorrow.
> I'm so nervous.
> B: _____ yourself. You're a good
> soccer player.

① Live by
② Explain
③ Look after
④ Believe in
⑤ Worry about

03 다음 빈칸에 공통으로 들어갈 말을 쓰시오.

> • I'm going to _____ the dog for a
> walk.
> • He's old enough to _____ care of
> himself.
> • He only wanted to _____ his
> share.

04 다음 영영풀이에 해당하는 말을 주어진 철자로 시작하여 쓰시오.

> very comfortable and expensive

➡ l_____

[05~06] 다음 대화를 읽고 물음에 답하시오.

> M: Jane, you look ⓐ_____. What's the matter?
> W: I ⓑ_____ a big part in the school musical.
> M: I heard you ⓒ_____. You sound great!
> W: It's just that I keep ⓓ_____ mistakes. I'm
> so worried.
> M: Oh, you just need a little more practice. <u>실수하
> 는 것에 대해서는 걱정하지 마</u>. You can actually ⓔ
> _____ from them.
> W: Thanks, Dad. I hope I do a good job.
> M: You'll do great.

05 빈칸 ⓐ~ⓔ에 들어가지 <u>않는</u> 말을 고르시오.

① singing
② worried
③ learn
④ got
⑤ to make

06 밑줄 친 우리말과 일치하도록 주어진 단어를 이용하여 영작
하시오.

➡ _____

(about, mistakes, 5 단어)

07 다음 대화의 흐름상 빈칸에 들어갈 말을 주어진 단어를 이용해
문장을 완성하시오.

> A: _____
> (have, will, if, a magic carpet, 형태변형
> 가능)
> B: I would never walk, and always fly to
> wherever I want.

[08~09] 다음 대화를 읽고 물음에 답하시오.

A: I'm worried (A)[that / what / about] I can't finish my online story by the deadline.
B: 그건 걱정하지 마. I can help you.
A: That would be great. My main (B)[character / director / letter] has special powers. What would you do (C)[when / whether / if] you could change (D)[you / yours / yourself] into anyone every day?
B: Well, I would change myself into famous people and live different lives.

08 위 대화의 괄호 (A)~(D)에서 적절한 것을 골라 쓰시오.

➡ (A) _____ (B) _____
   (C) _____ (D) _____

09 밑줄 친 우리말과 일치하도록 주어진 단어를 이용해 영작하시오.

➡ (1) _____ (it, worry)
   (2) _____ (it, bother)

[10~13] 다음 대화를 읽고 물음에 답하시오.

M: Sujin, what are you doing this weekend?
W: (①) Nothing special, why?
M: (②) I have to go to Busan for a family trip tomorrow (A)_____ I can't find anyone to feed my dog, Lucy.
W: (③) I'll (B)_____ of her.
M: Oh, thank you so much. (④) I was so worried. (⑤)
W: I'll take her for a walk in the park, too. The weather's (C)_____ to be nice tomorrow.

10 ①~⑤ 중 주어진 문장이 들어갈 곳은?

Don't worry about Lucy.

①   ②   ③   ④   ⑤

11 빈칸 (A)에 들어갈 말을 고르시오.

① but   ② since   ③ if
④ because   ⑤ when

12 위 대화의 흐름상 빈칸 (B)에 들어갈 말을 쓰시오. (2 단어)

➡ _____

13 빈칸 (C)에 들어갈 말을 고르시오.

① worried   ② explained
③ expressed   ④ taken
⑤ supposed

14 다음 중 어법상 옳은 문장을 모두 고르시오.

① Why don't we have it brought to our hotel room?
② How about having your pet to clean from head to toe?
③ Why don't you go to see a dentist and have the tooth pulled out?
④ It was a book that Jack bought for his sister.
⑤ It was in the street which I saw Jane this morning.
⑥ It was our father's advice that I followed.
⑦ It was a cat what went to save the princess.

15 다음 문장에서 어법상 어색한 것을 바르게 고쳐 다시 쓰시오.

(1) It was many bugs where were in the bottle.

➡ _____

(2) It was at the concert I saw her.

➡ _____

(3) This morning I had my watch that I had bought last month repair.

➡ _____
_____

(4) I'll help you so that you can have your homework finish before the movie starts.

➡ _____
_____

16 괄호 안의 단어를 이용하여 다음 대화의 빈칸을 완성하시오.

> A: I have to return the book I borrowed from the library but I feel sick.
> B: Don't worry. I'll _____ for sure. (return, have)

17 Which is grammatically WRONG?

① It was not until then that I learned Hangeul.

② The princess had her dress designed by a famous designer.

③ It was at the park which I met Tim last Sunday.

④ It was pasta that I made for Lucy the other day.

⑤ It wouldn't be a good idea to have your dream job fixed now.

[18~21] 다음 글을 읽고 물음에 답하시오.

Puneet welcomed Puru with open arms. That night, when the brothers sat down to chat after dinner, Puru asked the question that had been on his mind for days.

"It was our father's advice that I followed, but I am ①not happy. I built a house in every city. But because I could not always stay there, I hired people and had the house ②looked after. Father said we should ③sleep comfortably and enjoy our food, so I had my bed designed by experts and my meals prepared by a great chef. He told us to spend like a rich man, so I bought (A)_____ I wanted ④with worrying about money. But look at me now! I am ⑤ empty-handed. Did you not follow our father's wisdom? Tell me, brother, how did you get so rich?"

18 다음 중 빈칸 (A)에 들어갈 말과 같은 말이 들어가는 것은?

① I don't believe _____ he made a mistake.

② There is one problem _____ you need to be aware of.

③ The news _____ he was alive made people shocked.

④ Kevin said _____ we had to accept his apology.

⑤ So, did you give him _____ he wanted from you?

19 ①~⑤ 중 글의 흐름상 어색한 것은?

①   ②   ③   ④   ⑤

20 Write the reason why Puru had his meals prepared by a great chef. Use the phrase 'in order to.'

➡ _____

_____

21 다음 중 위 글을 읽고 답할 수 있는 것은?

① How many people did Puru hire to look after his houses?
② How big were the houses that Puru built?
③ Why did Puru employ experts?
④ When did Puru visit his brother Puneet?
⑤ How did Puneet become so rich?

[22~26] 다음 글을 읽고 물음에 답하시오.

A rich and wise father had two sons, Puru and Puneet. Before ①he passed away, he called his two sons to give them some last words of advice.

"Listen carefully, my dear sons. Live by these words throughout your life, and you will be happy," ②he said.

"Build a house in every city. Sleep comfortably. Enjoy your food. Lastly, spend money like a rich man... ." Before (A)he could explain himself, ③he passed away. After ④his death, the two sons took their share of the father's wealth and settled in different cities. Five years passed. Puru, who had been following his father's words carefully, had no money left. But his brother was richer than ever. Puru was puzzled about where ⑤he had gone wrong, so he visited Puneet to find out.

22 What does the underlined (A) mean?

① wanting to hear some explanation
② telling what he meant by those words
③ putting his sons in a difficult situation
④ letting the sons explain what the words meant
⑤ making the situation worse than before

23 위 글의 내용에 맞게 빈칸에 알맞은 말을 바르게 짝지은 것은?

A wise and rich man gave his two sons some last words of advice, which would be ⓐ_____ for them to live a happy life. However, two sons lived a ⓑ_____ life.

① harmful – similar
② helpful – similar
③ harmful – contrasting
④ helpful – contrasting
⑤ beneficial – various

24 Write the reason why Puru visited Puneet. Use the word 'because.'

➡ _____

_____

25 What did the two brothers do after their father's death? Answer in English.

➡ _____

_____

26 위 글의 밑줄 친 ①~⑤에서 가리키는 대상이 다른 하나는?

①   ②   ③   ④   ⑤

Lesson **7**

Spend Wisely

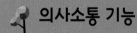 **의사소통 기능**

- 어떤 것에 만족하거나 불만이 있는지 묻기
  A: How do you like this dress?
  B: The design is cool and interesting.
- 후회하는 일 말하기
  A: What's wrong with your laptop?
  B: It makes too much noise and gets overheated.
    I should have read more reviews.

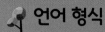 **언어 형식**

- 접속사 as
  As more and more people get on the bandwagon, others are more likely to get on it.

- 수의 일치
  Half of the boys on his soccer team **wear** those shoes.

Words & Expressions

교과서

Key Words

- **aboard** [əbɔ́:rd] 분 ~에 탑승하고, ~에 타서
- **above** [əbʌ́v] 전 ~ 위에
- **affect** [əfékt] 동 ~에 영향을 주다
- **allowance** [əláuəns] 명 용돈
- **although** [ɔ:lðóu] 접 비록 ~이지만
- **anchor** [ǽŋkər] 명 닻 동 닻을 내리다
- **behavior** [bihéivjər] 명 행동, 행위
- **billion** [bíljən] 명 10억
- **combine** [kəmbáin] 동 결합하다
- **compare** [kəmpɛ́ər] 동 비교하다
- **compete** [kəmpí:t] 동 경쟁하다
- **complete** [kəmplí:t] 동 완성하다
- **concept** [kánsept] 명 개념
- **consume** [kənsú:m] 동 소비하다, 소모하다
- **convenient** [kənví:njənt] 형 편리한, 간편한
- **deal** [di:l] 명 거래
- **difference** [dífərəns] 명 차이, 차이점
- **disappear** [dìsəpíər] 동 사라지다
- **discount** [dískaunt] 명 할인 동 할인하다
- **effect** [ifékt] 명 효과
- **encourage** [inkɔ́:ridʒ] 동 부추기다, 조장하다
- **endanger** [indéindʒər] 동 위험에 빠뜨리다
- **even though** 비록 ~이지만
- **fix** [fiks] 동 고정하다
- **furniture** [fɔ́:rnitʃər] 명 가구

- **immediately** [imí:diətli] 분 즉시, 바로
- **influence** [ínfluəns] 동 ~에 영향을 주다
- **lack** [læk] 명 부족, 결핍
- **laptop** [lǽptɑp] 명 휴대용 노트북 컴퓨터
- **last** [læst] 동 오래가다, (기능이) 지속되다
- **match** [mætʃ] 동 어울리다
- **mention** [ménʃən] 동 언급하다, 말하다
- **miss** [mis] 동 놓치다
- **overheated** [ouvərhítid] 형 지나치게 뜨거운, 과열된
- **parade** [pəréid] 명 행렬, 퍼레이드
- **purchase** [pɔ́:rtʃəs] 동 구매하다, 구입하다
- **quality** [kwáləti] 명 질, 품질, 특성, 자질
- **quarter** [kwɔ́:rtər] 명 4분의 1
- **raise** [reiz] 동 기르다, 키우다
- **refund** [rifʌ́nd] 명 환불
- **release** [rilí:s] 동 출시하다, 발매하다
- **replace** [ripléis] 동 바꾸다, 교체하다
- **spending** [spéndiŋ] 명 지출
- **striped** [straipt] 형 줄무늬가 있는
- **suit** [su:t] 동 어울리다
- **tight** [tait] 형 꽉 조이는, 딱 붙는
- **unplanned** [ənplǽnd] 형 미리 계획하지 않은
- **wagon** [wǽgən] 명 사륜 마차, 짐마차
- **waste** [weist] 동 낭비하다, 소모하다

Key Expressions

- **as such** 그러한 결과로
- **at a glance** 한눈에, 즉시
- **a pair of** ~ 한 짝의 ~
- **be likely to** ~할 가능성이 있다, ~하기 쉽다
- **end up –ing** 결국 ~하게 되다
- **for a moment** 잠깐
- **go well with** ~와 잘 어울리다
- **go window shopping** 진열된 상품을 구경하고 다니다
- **in comparison** 비교해 보면
- **in this way** 이런 방식으로

- **just because** 단지 ~라는 이유로
- **keep track of** ~을 기록하다
- **lead to** ~로 이어지다
- **more and more** 점점 더 많은
- **more than half** 반 이상의
- **on display** 진열된, 전시된
- **soon after** 직후
- **spend A on 동사ing** A를 ~하는 데 쓰다
- **the next time 주어+동사** 다음번에 ~할 때에
- **when it comes to** ~에 관해서, ~에 대해 말하자면

Word Power

※ 서로 비슷한 뜻을 가진 어휘

- □ **affect** ~에 영향을 주다 – **influence** ~에 영향을 주다
- □ **effect** 결과, 효과 – **result** 결과, 성과
- □ **lack** 부족, 결핍 – **shortage** 결핍, 부족
- □ **purchase** 구매하다, 구입하다 – **buy** 사다
- □ **replace** 바꾸다, 교체하다 – **substitute** 대신하다

- □ **complete** 완성하다 – **perfect** 완벽하게 하다
- □ **immediately** 즉시, 바로 – **at once** 즉시
- □ **mention** 언급하다, 말하다 – **refer to** 언급하다
- □ **quality** 질, 품질 – **characteristic** 특질, 특징
- □ **suit** 어울리다 – **match** 어울리다

※ 서로 반대의 뜻을 가진 어휘

- □ **above** ~ 위에 ↔ **under** ~ 아래에
- □ **difference** 차이(점) ↔ **similarity** 유사(성)
- □ **encourage** 부추기다, 조장하다 ↔ **discourage** 낙담시키다
- □ **purchase** 구매하다, 구입하다 ↔ **sell** 팔다
- □ **unplanned** 미리 계획하지 않은 ↔ **planned** 미리 계획된

- □ **convenient** 편리한, 간편한 ↔ **inconvenient** 불편한, 곤란한
- □ **disappear** 사라지다 ↔ **appear** 나타나다
- □ **endanger** 위험에 빠뜨리다 ↔ **save** 구하다
- □ **tight** 꽉 조이는, 딱 붙는 ↔ **loose** 헐거운, 느슨한
- □ **waste** 낭비하다, 소모하다 ↔ **save** 절약하다

※ 접두사 en-: en-+특정 어근: 동사로 만들어 '~하게 하다', '어떤 상태가 되게 하다', '안에'라는 의미를 더함.

- □ **en-** + **able** → **enable** 가능케 하다
- □ **en-** + **courage** → **encourage** 조장하다, 권유하다
- □ **en-** + **hance** → **enhance** 향상시키다, 높이다
- □ **en-** + **rich** → **enrich** 풍부하게 하다

- □ **en-** + **close** → **enclose** 에워싸다, 둘러싸다
- □ **en-** + **force** → **enforce** 집행하다, 강요하다
- □ **en-** + **large** → **enlarge** 확대하다, 확장하다
- □ **en-** + **danger** → **endanger** 위험에 빠뜨리다

※ 접두사 com-: com-+특정 어근: '함께'라는 의미를 더함.

- □ **com-** + **bine** → **combine** 결합하다
- □ **com-** + **pare** → **compare** 비교하다
- □ **com-** + **pile** → **compile** 편찬하다
- □ **com-** + **pound** → **compound** 합성의

- □ **com-** + **pany** → **company** 회사, 동료
- □ **com-** + **pete** → **compete** 경쟁하다
- □ **com-** + **pose** → **compose** 구성하다
- □ **com-** + **promise** → **compromise** 타협하다

English Dictionary

- □ **affect** ~에 영향을 주다
  → to have an influence on someone or something, or to cause a change in someone or something
  어떤 사람이나 사물에 영향을 미치다, 혹은 어떤 사람이나 사물에 변화를 야기하다

- □ **combine** 결합하다
  → to join together to make a single thing or group
  하나의 물건 혹은 하나의 집단으로 만들기 위해 합치다

- □ **concept** 개념
  → a principle or idea
  어떤 원리나 생각

- □ **consume** 소비하다, 소모하다
  → to use fuel, energy, or time, especially in large amounts or to eat or drink, especially a lot of something
  연료, 에너지, 혹은 시간을 특히 많은 양으로 쓰다. 또는 특히 어떤 것을 많이 먹고 마시다

- □ **convenient** 편리한, 간편한
  → suitable for your purposes and needs and causing the least difficulty
  목적이나 필요에 맞고 어려움을 최소한으로 야기하는

- □ **encourage** 부추기다, 조장하다
  → to support an activity or make it more likely
  어떤 활동을 지원하거나 더 쉽게 만들다

- □ **endanger** 위험에 빠뜨리다
  → to put someone or something at risk or in danger of being harmed, damaged, or destroyed
  어떤 사람이나 사물을 해를 입고 망가지고 파괴되는 위험에 처하게 하다

- □ **lack** 부족, 결핍
  → a condition of not having any or enough of something, especially something necessary or wanted
  특히 필요하거나 원하는 어떤 것이 조금도 없거나 충분하지 않은 상태

- □ **suit** 어울리다
  → to be right for a particular person, situation, or occasion
  어떤 특정한 사람이나 상황, 또는 경우에 알맞다

- □ **tight** 꽉 조이는, 딱 붙는
  → rather small and fit closely to your body
  다소 작거나 몸에 밀착되게 맞는

01 접두사 en-을 붙여 동사를 만들 때, en이 '~하게 하다'의 의미를 가지지 <u>않는</u> 단어를 고르시오.

① enlarge ② enclose ③ enable
④ enforce ⑤ enrich

02 다음 밑줄 친 부분과 의미가 가장 가까운 것을 고르시오.

> We have to <u>change</u> this carpet soon.

① replace ② repair ③ remove
④ impact ⑤ preserve

서답형

03 다음 주어진 단어를 이용하여 우리말에 맞도록 빈칸에 알맞은 말을 쓰시오.

> 축구에 관해서라면, Mark가 최고의 선수이다.
> ➡ _____ soccer, Mark is the best player. (when, come)

04 다음 영영풀이에 해당하는 단어로 알맞은 것은?

> to use fuel, energy, or time, especially in large amounts or to eat or drink, especially a lot of something

① contain   ② require
③ maintain   ④ assume
⑤ consume

05 다음 짝지어진 단어의 관계가 〈보기〉와 같은 것끼리 짝지어진 것을 고르시오.

> ┤ 보기 ├
>
> quality – characteristic

> ⓐ tight – loose
> ⓑ endanger – save
> ⓒ effect – result
> ⓓ replace – substitute
> ⓔ encourage – discourage

① ⓐ, ⓑ ② ⓐ, ⓔ ③ ⓑ, ⓒ
④ ⓒ, ⓓ ⑤ ⓓ, ⓔ

06 다음 밑줄 친 부분의 의미로 알맞지 <u>않은</u> 것은?

① His words had a soothing <u>effect</u>. (효과)
② It is difficult to define the <u>concept</u> of beauty. (개념)
③ Your opinion will <u>affect</u> many people. (영향을 주다)
④ I receive an <u>allowance</u> from my parents. (허락)
⑤ The bus was nearly empty as she stepped <u>aboard</u>. (탄, 탑승한)

07 다음 빈칸에 알맞은 단어를 고르시오.

> The shirt is beautiful. _____, it is cheap.

① Thus   ② Although
③ Furthermore ④ Therefore
⑤ Likewise

01 다음 빈칸에 공통으로 들어갈 접두사를 쓰시오.

> • I made the two plans for _____ parison.
> • We finally reached a _____ promise.
> • Three judges _____ pose the committee.

02 다음 주어진 우리말에 맞게 빈칸을 채우시오.

(1) 그 학생들 중 3분의 1이 그들의 지출을 기록한다.
➡ One third of the students record their _____. (one word)

(2) 다음번에 우리가 만날 때, 나는 더 건강해질 것이다.
➡ The _____ we meet, I will be healthier. (two words)

(3) 날씨가 좋지 않았음에도 불구하고 우리는 하이킹을 갔다.
➡ We went hiking _____ the weather was not good. (two words)

(4) 너는 보통 진열된 상품을 구경하고 다니는 것을 좋아하니?
➡ Do you usually like to _____ _____? (three words)

03 다음 빈칸에 공통으로 들어갈 말을 쓰시오.

> • The painting is currently _____ display in New York.
> • Tickets are _____ sale from the booking office.

04 다음 빈칸에 들어갈 전치사를 〈보기〉에서 골라 쓰시오.

> ┤ 보기 ├
> at   for   in   with   as

(1) I think this blouse goes well _____ the skirt you are wearing.

(2) _____ comparison to her problems, mine seems small.

(3) You should hold your breath _____ a moment.

(4) I noticed what had happened _____ a glace.

(5) _____ such, he was a man with persistence.

05 다음 빈칸에 알맞은 말을 〈보기〉에서 골라 쓰시오. (한 단어는 한 번만 사용할 것, 형태 변화 가능.)

> ┤ 보기 ├
> combine   compare   endanger   mention

(1) Did I _____ that I will move to Canada next month?

(2) You should _____ prices before you buy things.

(3) He wants to _____ his job with pleasure.

(4) The fire _____ animals in the forest.

Conversation

1 어떤 것에 만족하거나 불만이 있는지 묻기

> **A:** Can I try on that cap with stars over there? 저기 별들이 그려진 모자를 써 볼 수 있나요?
>
> **B:** Sure. How do you like it? 그럼요. 어떠세요?
>
> **A:** The design is nice, but I don't think the color suits me. Do you have it in black? 디자인은 좋은데, 색이 제게 안 어울리는 것 같아요. 이거 검은색으로 있나요?

■ 어떤 것에 만족하거나 불만이 있는지 물어보는 표현으로 'How do you like it?(마음에 드니?)'을 쓸 수 있다. 이외에도 'Are you satisfied with ~?(~에 만족하십니까?)', 'How is ~?(~는 어떠십니까?)', 'Are you enjoying ~?(~이 마음에 드십니까?)' 등이 있다.

어떤 것에 만족하거나 불만이 있는지 묻기

- How do you like ~?
- Are you satisfied[happy] with ~?
- How is ~?
- Are you enjoying ~?
- Do you like ~?

■ 'How do you like ~?'는 상대방의 의견 혹은 만족 여부를 물을 때 사용한다. 이미 지난 일에 대한 만족 여부를 물을 때는 'How did you like ~?'를 쓸 수 있다. 'Do you like ~?'는 상대방의 구체적인 의견보다는 단순히 만족 여부에 초점을 둘 때 사용한다.

■ 'How do you like ~?'는 상대방의 만족이나 불만족을 묻는 표현이고, 'What do you like?'은 '무엇을 좋아하니?'라는 의미로 상대방이 좋아하는 것을 묻는 표현이다.

핵심 Check

1. 다음 대화의 빈칸에 들어갈 말로 가장 적절한 것은?

> **A:** Hi, I'm looking for a backpack for hiking.
>
> **B:** These two are popular among hikers. _____
>
> **A:** The green one is lighter than the blue one. I'll take the lighter one.

① How were the backpacks?

② How do you like them?

③ Did you enjoy the backpacks?

④ What do you like?

⑤ What is your favorite?

2 후회하는 일 말하기

> **A:** What's wrong with your laptop? 노트북에 무슨 문제가 있어?
>
> **B:** It makes too much noises and gets overheated. I should have read more reviews. 소음이 너무 심하고 과열이 돼. 난 후기를 더 많이 읽어 봤어야 했어.

■ 'I should have p.p. ~.'는 어떤 일을 했어야 했다고, 또는 하지 말았어야 했다고 후회할 때 사용한다. 예를 들어, 공부를 열심히 하지 않은 것을 후회하며 더 열심히 공부했어야 했다고 말할 때는 'I should have studied harder!'라고 말할 수 있다.

■ 과거 사실에 대해 후회나 유감을 나타낼 때 '~했어야 했다'는 의미로 'should have p.p. ~'를 쓴다. 이 때 조동사 should 뒤에는 과거의 일을 의미하므로 동사원형 대신 'have+p.p.'를 써야 한다. 이외에도 'I regret -ing ~.', 'I wish I had p.p. ~.', 'If I could, I would+동사원형 ~.' 등으로 쓸 수 있다.

■ 'should have p.p.'는 '~했어야 했는데 (못했다)'라는 후회의 의미이고, 'could have p.p.'는 '~할 뻔 했다'라는 가능성의 의미이고, 'must have p.p.'는 '~이었음이 틀림없다'라는 추측의 의미를 갖는다.

후회하는 일 말하기

• I should have checked the size before buying it.
  = I regret not checking the size before buying it.
  = I wish I had checked the size before buying it.

핵심 Check

2. 괄호 안에 주어진 단어를 이용하여 밑줄 친 우리말을 영작하시오.

> **A:** Are you okay? You look tired today.
> **B:** Yeah, I missed the school bus again. <u>내가 더 일찍 일어났어야 했는데.</u> (get up earlier)

➡

Listen & Talk 1 A-2

M: Good morning. Welcome to Kelly's Sporting Goods Store.

W: Hi, I'm ❶looking for a backpack for hiking.

M: These two are ❷popular among hikers. ❸How do you like them?

W: The green one is ❹lighter than the blue one. I'll take the lighter one.

M: Great choice.

M: 안녕하세요. Kelly의 스포츠 용품 가게에 오신 것을 환영합니다.

W: 안녕하세요, 저는 하이킹할 때 쓸 배낭을 찾고 있어요.

M: 이 두 개가 하이킹하시는 분들 사이에서 인기가 있어요. 어떠세요?

W: 초록색 배낭이 파란색 배낭보다 더 가볍네요. 더 가벼운 걸로 할게요.

M: 탁월한 선택입니다.

❶ look for: ~을 찾다
❷ popular: 인기 있는 among: ~ 중에, ~ 사이에
❸ 'How do you like ~?'는 어떤 사물이나 사건 등에 관해 상대방의 만족이나 불만족을 묻고자 할 때 사용한다.
❹ lighter는 light(가벼운)의 비교급이다.

Check(√) True or False

(1) The woman will buy the green backpack.   T ☐ F ☐

(2) The woman wants to buy a backpack for books.   T ☐ F ☐

Listen & Talk 2 A-1

M: Oh, this coat is ❶too uncomfortable.

W: Why? ❷What's wrong with it?

M: It's too ❸tight.

W: Didn't you ❹try it on before buying it?

M: No. It was my size, so I just bought it. I ❺should have tried it on.

M: 오, 이 코트는 너무 불편해.
W: 왜? 무슨 문제가 있니?
M: 너무 꽉 껴.
W: 사기 전에 입어 보지 않았어?
M: 아니. 내 사이즈여서 그냥 사 버렸어. 난 그것을 입어 봤어야 했어.

❶ too: 너무 uncomfortable: 불편한
❷ 'What's wrong with you?'는 '무슨 문제가 있니?'라는 의미로 불만족의 원인이나 걱정을 물을 때 사용하는 표현이다.
❸ tight: 꽉 조이는, 딱 붙는
❹ try on: (옷 등을 시험 삼아) 입어 보다
❺ 'I should have p.p. ~.'는 어떤 일을 했어야 했다고, 했다고 후회할 때 사용한다.

Check(√) True or False

(3) The man tried on the coat before he bought it.   T ☐ F ☐

(4) The coat is comfortable but tight.   T ☐ F ☐

Listen & Talk 2 A-2

W: Hey, Eric. Camilla and I ❶are going to watch a movie. Do you want to join us?

M: I'd love to, but I can't. ❷I've spent all of my ❸allowance for this week.

W: Didn't you just get ❹it a few days ago? How did you spend it all?

M: I'm not sure. I ❺should have kept track of my ❻spending.

W: 안녕, Eric. Camilla랑 나는 영화를 보러 갈 거야. 우리랑 같이 갈래?
M: 그러고 싶지만, 안 돼. 이번 주 용돈을 전부 써 버렸거든.
W: 너 고작 며칠 전에 받지 않았어? 어떻게 다 써 버렸어?
M: 잘 모르겠어. 내 지출을 기록했어야 했어.

❶ be going to 동사원형: ～할 것이다
❷ have spent는 현재완료형으로 여기에서는 '완료' 용법으로 사용하였다.
❸ allowance: 용돈
❹ it은 allowance를 가리킨다.
❺ 과거 사실에 대해 후회나 유감을 나타낼 때 '～했어야 했다'는 의미로 'should have p.p. ～'를 쓴다. '주어 should have p.p. ～'와 같은 의미로 '주어+regret not+동명사 ～.', '주어+wish+주어+had p.p. ～.', 'If+주어+could, 주어+would+동사원형 ～.' 등이 있다. keep track of: ～을 기록하다
❻ spending: 지출

Check(√) True or False

(5) Eric received an allowance a few days ago. T ☐ F ☐

(6) Camilla and Eric are going to watch a movie. T ☐ F ☐

Wrap Up 1

M: Good morning. May I help you?

W: ❶I'd like to buy a T-shirt for my sister. She's eleven years old.

M: ❷How do you like this red one? This character is ❸quite popular among children.

W: Well, she doesn't like animation characters that much. Can I see the blue one?

M: You mean this blue striped T-shirt? Its design is simple and cool.

W: Yes, ❹I think my sister will like it. I'll take it.

M: 안녕하세요. 도와 드릴까요?
W: 저는 여동생에게 티셔츠를 사 주고 싶어요. 그 애는 11살이에요.
M: 이 빨간색 티셔츠는 어떠세요? 이 캐릭터는 아이들 사이에서 꽤 인기가 있어요.
W: 글쎄요, 그 애는 만화 캐릭터를 그다지 좋아하지 않아요. 파란색 티셔츠 좀 볼 수 있을까요?
M: 파란색 줄무늬 티셔츠 말씀이시죠? 그건 디자인이 단순하고 멋있어요.
W: 네, 제 여동생이 좋아할 것 같아요. 그걸로 할게요.

❶ would like to 동사원형: ～하고 싶다(= want to 동사원형)
❷ 'How do you like ～?'는 '～는 어떠니?'라는 뜻으로 어떤 것에 대한 의견을 물을 때 쓰인다. 비슷한 표현인 'Are you satisfied[happy] with ～?'는 직접적으로 만족이나 불만족 여부를 물을 때 쓸 수 있다.
❸ quite는 부사로 '꽤, 상당히'의 의미이다.
❹ think의 목적어는 that my sister will like it이다. 접속사 that은 생략했다

Check(√) True or False

(7) The woman wants to buy a T-shirt with animation characters for her sister. T ☐ F ☐

(8) What the woman will choose is the blue striped T-shirt. T ☐ F ☐

Listen & Talk 1 A-1

M: Hi, can I help you with anything?

W: Yes, can I ❶try on that cap with stars ❷ over there?

M: Sure. ❸How do you like it?

W: The design is nice, but I don't think the color ❹suits me. Do you have it in black?

M: Yes. I'll get one from the back. *(pause)* Here it is.

W: Great. I'll take it.

❶ try on: (옷 등을 시험 삼아) 입어 보다

❷ over there: 저기에, 저쪽에

❸ 'How do you like ~?'는 '~는 어때?'라는 의미로 상대방에게 어떤 것에 대한 만족 또는 불만족을 묻는 표현이다.

❹ suit: 어울리다

Listen & Talk 1 B

W: Hi, Luke. Is that a new speaker?

M: Yes, I ❶bought it a few weeks ago.

W: It looks cool. ❷How do you like it?

M: It's ❸convenient. I can take it anywhere and listen to music. The sound ❹quality is good, too.

W: Great. How long does the battery ❺last?

M: About 2 hours. The battery doesn't last long.

W: That's too bad.

M: Yeah, but I'm ❻pretty happy with it, anyway.

❶ bought는 buy(사다)의 과거형이다.

❷ 'How do you like ~?'는 '너는 ~이 어떠니?'라는 뜻으로 어떤 것에 대한 만족이나 불만족을 묻는 표현이다. 바꿔 쓸 수 있는 표현으로 'Are you satisfied [happy] with ~?', 'How is ~?', 'Are you enjoying ~?', 'Do you like ~?' 등이 있다.

❸ convenient: 편리한, 간편한 ❹ quality: 질, 품질

❺ last: 오래가다, (기능이) 지속되다 ❻ pretty: 아주, 매우

Listen & Talk 2 B

M: Did you get a new phone, Jamie? It's just like mine.

W: Yeah, I got it last weekend ❶on sale.

M: It was on sale? But it ❷has just been ❸ released, hasn't it?

W: Right, but the store on Green Street is having ❹a year-end sale.

M: Oh, I bought mine ❺at full price!

W: Really? That's too bad. They're selling them at a 40 percent discount.

M: I ❻should have checked the sales before buying mine.

❶ on sale: 할인 중인

❷ 현재완료형인 have+p.p.와 부사 just를 사용하면 '방금 ~하다'로 해석된다. (완료 용법)

❸ release: 출시하다, 발매하다 ❹ a year-end sale: 연말 세일

❺ at full price: 정가에, 제값에

❻ 'should have p.p. ~'는 '~했어야 했는데 (사실은 하지 않았다)'의 뜻으로 과거 사실에 대한 유감을 나타내는 표현이다. '주어+regret not+동명사 ~.', '주어+wish+주어+had p.p ~.', 'If+주어+could, 주어+would+동사원형 ~.' 등으로 바꿔 쓸 수 있다.

Communication Step A

M: Hi, Riley. ❶I heard that you bought a laptop online. ❷How do you like it?

W: Oh, ❸I'm not happy with it.

M: Why? What's wrong?

W: It makes too much noise and ❹gets overheated. ❺I should have read more reviews.

M: Oh, then you should ❻ask for your money back.

W: The online store won't ❼give me back my money because I've used it for a week.

M: ❽How about calling the online shop and explaining your problem?

W: Yeah, I think I should ❾do that.

❶ 어떤 내용을 들어서 알고 있음을 표현할 때 'I heard that+주어+동사'의 형태로 말할 수 있다.

❷ 'How do you like ~?'는 어떤 물건이나 사건 등에 관해 상대방의 만족이나 불만족을 묻고자 할 때 사용한다.

❸ 어떤 것에 대해 만족이나 불평을 표현할 때 '나는 ~이 만족스럽다/그다지 만족스럽지 않다'라는 의미의 'I'm (not) really[so] happy[satisfied] with ~.'로 말할 수 있다. 만족스럽지 않는 경우에 'I want to complain about ~.'으로도 바꿔 말할 수 있다.

❹ makes와 gets는 문장의 동사로, 접속사 and로 연결되어 있다. get 다음에 형용사가 오면, '(~의 상태가) 되다, (~하기에) 이르다'의 의미이다.

❺ 'I should have p.p. ~.'는 어떤 일을 했어야 했다고 후회할 때 사용한다.

❻ ask for: 요청하다 ❼ give back: 돌려주다

❽ 'How about ~?'은 '~하는 게 어때?'라는 뜻으로 상대방에게 권유할 때 사용하는 표현이고, about은 전치사이기 때문에 뒤에 명사나 동명사가 올 수 있다. explaining은 calling과 접속사 and로 연결되어 있다.

❾ do that은 'call the online shop and explain my problem'을 의미한다.

● 다음 우리말과 일치하도록 빈칸에 알맞은 말을 쓰시오.

Listen & Talk 1 A

1. **M:** Hi, can I _____ you with anything?

   W: Yes, can I _____ _____ that cap with stars over there?

   M: Sure. _____ _____ _____ _____ it?

   W: The design is nice, _____ I don't think the color _____ me. Do you _____ it in black?

   M: Yes. I'll get _____ from the back. *(pause)* Here it is.

   W: Great. I'll take it.

2. **M:** Good morning. Welcome _____ Kelly's Sporting Goods Store.

   W: Hi, _____ _____ _____ a backpack for hiking.

   M: These two are _____ _____ hikers. _____ _____ _____ _____ them?

   W: The _____ _____ _____ _____ _____ the blue _____. I'll take the lighter one.

   M: Great choice.

Listen & Talk 1 B

W: Hi, Luke. Is that a new speaker?

M: Yes, I _____ it a few weeks _____.

W: It _____ cool. _____ _____ _____ _____ it?

M: It's _____. I can take it _____ and listen to music. The sound _____ is good, too.

W: Great. _____ _____ does the battery _____?

M: About 2 hours. The battery _____ _____ long.

W: That's _____ _____ .

M: Yeah, but I'm _____ _____ with it, anyway.

해석

1. **M:** 안녕하세요, 무엇을 도와 드릴까요?

   W: 네, 저기 별들이 그려진 모자를 써 볼 수 있나요?

   M: 그럼요. 어떠세요?

   W: 디자인은 좋은데, 색이 제게 안 어울리는 것 같아요. 이거 검은색으로 있나요?

   M: 네. 제가 안쪽에서 가져다 드릴게요. (잠시 후) 여기 있어요.

   W: 좋아요. 그걸로 할게요.

2. **M:** 안녕하세요. Kelly의 스포츠 용품 가게에 오신 것을 환영합니다.

   W: 안녕하세요, 저는 하이킹할 때 쓸 배낭을 찾고 있어요.

   M: 이 두 개가 하이킹하시는 분들 사이에서 인기가 있어요, 어떠세요?

   W: 초록색 배낭이 파란색 배낭보다 더 가볍네요. 더 가벼운 걸로 할게요.

   M: 탁월한 선택입니다.

W: 안녕, Luke. 그거 새 스피커니?

M: 응, 몇 주 전에 샀어.

W: 멋져 보인다. 그거 어때?

M: 편리해. 나는 그것을 어디든지 가져가서 음악을 들을 수 있어. 음질도 좋아.

W: 좋다. 배터리가 얼마나 오래가니?

M: 2시간 정도야. 배터리가 그렇게 오래 가지 않아.

W: 그거 안타깝구나.

M: 응, 하지만 어쨌든 나는 꽤 만족해.

Listen & Talk 2 A

1. M: Oh, this coat is _____ _____.

 W: Why? _____ _____ _____ _____?

 M: It's too _____.

 W: Didn't _____ _____ _____ _____ _____ it?

 M: No. It was my size, _____ I just bought it. I _____ _____ _____ it _____.

2. W: Hey, Eric. Camilla and I _____ _____ _____ _____ a movie. Do you want to join us?

 M: I'd love to, but I can't. _____ _____ all of my _____ for this week.

 W: Didn't you just _____ _____ a few days ago? How did you spend it all?

 M: I'm not sure. I _____ _____ _____ _____ _____ _____ _____.

Listen & Talk 2 B

M: Did you get a new phone, Jamie? It's just like mine.

W: Yeah, I got it last weekend _____ _____.

M: It was _____ _____? But it _____ _____ _____ _____, hasn't it?

W: Right, but the store on Green Street _____ _____ a year-end sale.

M: Oh, I bought mine _____ _____ _____!

W: Really? That's too bad. They're selling them _____ a 40 percent _____.

M: I _____ _____ _____ _____ _____ _____ buying mine.

해석

1. M: 오, 이 코트는 너무 불편해.
 W: 왜? 무슨 문제가 있니?
 M: 너무 꽉 껴.
 W: 사기 전에 입어 보지 않았어?
 M: 아니. 내 사이즈여서 그냥 사 버렸어. 난 그것을 입어 봤어야 했어.

2. W: 안녕, Eric. Camilla랑 나는 영화를 보러 갈 거야. 우리랑 같이 갈래?
 M: 그러고 싶지만, 안 돼. 이번 주 용돈을 전부 써 버렸거든.
 W: 너 고작 며칠 전에 받지 않았어? 어떻게 다 써 버렸어?
 M: 잘 모르겠어. 내 지출을 기록했어야 했어.

M: 새 전화기를 샀니, Jamie? 내 것과 똑같다.
W: 응, 나는 이것을 지난주 할인할 때 샀어.
M: 그거 할인 중이었어? 하지만 그것은 막 출시되었잖아, 그렇지 않아?
W: 맞아, 하지만 Green가에 있는 가게에서 연말 할인 판매를 하더라.
M: 오, 나는 내 것을 정가를 주고 샀는데!
W: 정말? 그것 참 안됐다. 40퍼센트 할인하여 팔고 있어.
M: 내 것을 사기 전에 할인 판매를 확인했어야 했어.

Communication Step A

M: Hi, Riley. I _____ _____ _____ _____ a laptop online. How do you like it?

W: Oh, I'm _____ _____ with _____.

M: _____? _____ wrong?

W: It makes too much noise and _____ _____. I should _____ _____ more reviews.

M: Oh, then you should ask _____ your money back.

W: The online store _____ _____ _____ _____ my money because _____ _____ it for a week.

M: How about _____ the online shop and _____ your problem?

W: Yeah, I think I should _____ that.

Wrap Up

1. M: Good morning. May I help you?

   W: _____ _____ _____ buy a T-shirt for my sister. She's eleven years old.

   M: _____ _____ _____ _____ _____ _____? This character is quite popular among children.

   W: Well, she doesn't like animation characters _____ much. Can I see the blue _____?

   M: You mean this blue _____ T-shirt? _____ design is simple and cool.

   W: Yes, I think my sister will like it. I'll _____ it.

2. W: Jake, here's a package for you.

   M: It's my helmet. I bought it at an _____ _____ _____ a few days ago.

   W: Oh, open it and _____ _____ _____ it.

   M: Okay. *(pause)* Oh, this outer part _____ _____ _____ _____. The seller _____ _____ it's perfectly fine though.

   W: Didn't you check the pictures of the helmet _____ you bought it?

   M: No, _____ _____ _____ the seller. I _____ _____ _____ _____ _____.

   W: You _____ _____ the seller and _____ _____ _____ _____.

01 다음 대화의 빈칸에 알맞은 것을 고르시오.

> M: Hi, can I help you with anything?
> W: Yes, can I try on that cap with stars over there?
> M: Sure. _____
> W: The design is nice, but I don't think the color suits me. Do you have it in black?
> M: Yes. I'll get one from the back. *(pause)* Here it is.
> W: Great. I'll take it.

① What do you think of this black hat?

② How do you like it?

③ What do you like?

④ Which cap do you like better, the one with stars or black one?

⑤ Please tell me where to buy it.

[02~03] 다음 대화를 읽고 물음에 답하시오.

> M: _____
> W: _____
> M: _____
> W: _____
> M: No. It was my size, so I just bought it. I ⓐ_____.

02 위 대화의 빈칸에 들어갈 말을 〈보기〉에서 골라 순서대로 바르게 배열한 것은?

> ┤ 보기 ├
> (A) Didn't you try it on before buying it?
> (B) It's too tight.
> (C) Oh, this coat is too uncomfortable.
> (D) Why? What's wrong with it?

① (B) – (A) – (C) – (D)　　② (B) – (C) – (A) – (D)

③ (C) – (A) – (B) – (D)　　④ (C) – (B) – (A) – (D)

⑤ (C) – (D) – (B) – (A)

03 위 대화의 빈칸 ⓐ에 알맞은 것을 고르시오.

① should have tried it on　② should not have tried it on

③ cannot have tried it on　④ must have tried it on

⑤ may have tried it on

01 다음 대화의 빈칸에 들어갈 알맞은 것을 모두 고르면?

> A: _____
> B: I love them. They are very comfortable.

① What do you like in your new pants?
② How do you like your new pants?
③ Are you concerned about your new pants?
④ Are you enjoying your new pants?
⑤ Are you satisfied with your new pants?

[02~03] 다음 대화를 읽고 물음에 답하시오.

> M: Oh, this coat is too uncomfortable.
> W: Why? (A)_____
> M: It's too tight.
> W: (B)_____
> M: No. It was my size, so I just bought it. 난 그것을 입어 봤어야 했어.

02 위 대화의 빈칸 (A)와 (B)에 들어갈 말을 〈보기〉에서 골라 기호를 쓰시오.

> ─┤ 보기 ├─
> ⓐ What do you think of this coat?
> ⓑ Didn't you try it on before buying it?
> ⓒ How about trying it on?
> ⓓ Can I help you with anything?
> ⓔ What's wrong with it?
> ⓕ Can I see the loose one?

➡ (A) _____ (B) _____

03 밑줄 친 우리말에 맞게 주어진 단어를 알맞게 배열하시오.

➡ _____ (it, have, on, should, tried, I)

04 다음 빈칸에 가장 알맞은 말을 고르시오.

> A: I heard that you bought some iced tea online. How do you like it?
> B: Oh, I'm not happy with it.
> A: Why? What's wrong?
> B: There is too much sugar in it.
> _____

① I should not have read more reviews.
② I should bring more food with less sugar.
③ I should have checked the nutrition facts first.
④ I should buy it at online used store a few days ago.
⑤ I should have kept track of my spending.

05 다음 중 짝지어진 대화가 어색한 것은?

① A: I bought a new cell phone last week.
　B: How do you like it?
　A: I like it a lot. It's very light.
② A: Are you happy with your new books?
　B: Yes, I am. They are interesting.
③ A: How did you like it?
　B: I liked it a lot. It was delicious.
④ A: How do you like the weather there?
　B: I love it. It's sunny and warm.
⑤ A: I watched a new movie last Sunday.
　B: It looks really interesting. How did you like it?
　A: No, I'm not. It's boring.

[06~07] 다음 대화를 읽고 물음에 답하시오.

M: Did you get a new phone, Jamie? It's just like mine. (①)

W: Yeah, I got it last weekend on sale.

M: It was on sale? (②) But it (A)_____, hasn't it?

W: Right, but the store on Green Street is having a year-end sale. (③)

M: Oh, I bought mine at full price!

W: Really? (④) They're selling them at a 40 percent discount.

M: I (B)_____ the sales before buying mine. (⑤)

06 위 대화의 ①~⑤ 중 주어진 문장이 들어갈 곳은?

> That's too bad.

①　　　②　　　③　　　④　　　⑤

07 다음 빈칸 (A)와 (B)에 들어갈 말로 알맞게 짝지어진 것은?

　　　　(A)　　　　　　　(B)

① has just released – should check

② has just released – should not have checked

③ has just been released – should check

④ has just been released – should have checked

⑤ has just been released – should not have checked

[08~09] 다음 대화를 읽고 물음에 답하시오.

W: Hi, Luke. Is that a new speaker?

M: Yes, I bought it a few weeks ago.

W: It looks cool. (A)_____

M: It's convenient. I can take it anywhere and listen to music. The sound quality is good, too.

W: Great. How long does the battery last?

M: About 2 hours. The battery doesn't last long.

W: That's too bad.

M: Yeah, but I'm pretty happy with it, anyway.

08 위 대화의 빈칸 (A)에 알맞은 말을 고르시오.

① When did you buy it?

② How long can you use it?

③ How do you like it?

④ What's wrong with it?

⑤ How do you get it?

09 위 대화를 읽고 답할 수 <u>없는</u> 질문을 고르시오.

① How is the sound quality of the new speaker?

② What will Luke use the new speaker for?

③ When did Luke buy the new speaker?

④ Are Luke satisfied with the new speaker?

⑤ How long does the battery last?

01 그림을 보고, should have와 주어진 단어를 이용해 빈칸을 채우시오.

Alison

A: What's the problem?
B: Alison _____.
    (warm, wear, jacket)

[02~04] 다음 대화를 읽고 물음에 답하시오.

M: Hi, Riley. I heard that you bought a laptop online. (A)_____
W: Oh, I'm not happy with it.
M: Why? What's wrong?
W: It makes too much noise and gets overheated. (a)난 후기를 더 많이 읽어 봤어야 했어.
M: Oh, then you should ask for your money back.
W: The online store won't give me back my money because I've used it for a week.
M: How about calling the online shop and (B)_____(explain) your problem?
W: Yeah, I think I should do that.

02 대화의 흐름상 빈칸 (A)에 들어갈 말을 주어진 단어를 이용해 문장을 완성하시오.

➡ _____ (like, it)

03 빈칸 (B)에 괄호 안의 단어를 문맥에 맞게 고쳐 채우시오.

➡ _____

04 밑줄 친 우리말 (a)를 주어진 단어를 이용해 영작하시오.

➡ _____
    (reviews, read, more)

[05~06] 다음 대화를 읽고 물음에 답하시오.

M: Did you get a new phone, Jamie? It's just like mine.
W: Yeah, I got it last weekend (A)_____ sale.
M: It was (A)_____ sale? But it has just been released, hasn't it?
W: Right, but the store on Green Street is having a year-end sale.
M: Oh, I bought mine (B)_____ full price!
W: Really? That's too bad. They're selling them at a 40 percent discount.
M: (C)_____ (buying, sales, checked, mine, before, should, I, have, the)

05 빈칸 (A)와 (B)에 알맞은 전치사를 쓰시오.

➡ (A) _____ (B) _____

06 빈칸 (C)를 괄호 안에 주어진 단어를 알맞게 배열하여 채우시오.

➡ _____
_____

Grammar

① 접속사 as

> • **As** more and more people get on the bandwagon, others are more likely to get on it. 더 많은 사람들이 밴드왜건에 올라탈수록 다른 사람들이 더욱 그것에 올라타려고 한다.

■ 접속사 as는 보통 'as+주어+동사 ~, 주어+동사 ….'의 형태로 사용하며, 종속절을 문장의 주절에 연결하는 종속접속사로서 부사절을 이끈다.

  • **As** I entered the room, they applauded. 내가 방안에 들어서자 그들은 박수를 쳤다.

■ 접속사 **as**의 역할

  (1) 비례, 추이: ~함에 따라서, ~에 비례하여

  • **As** it grew darker, it became colder. 어두워짐에 따라 더욱 추워졌다.

  (2) 시간: ~할 때, ~하는 동안, ~하면서

  • He came up **as** she was speaking. 그녀가 이야기하고 있을 때 그가 왔다.

  (3) 이유: ~해서, ~이므로, ~ 때문에

  • **As** I am ill, I will not go. 몸이 아파서 나는 안 가겠다.

  (4) 방식(양태): ~하듯이, ~하는 것처럼, ~ 같이, ~하는 대로, ~와 마찬가지로

  • **As** food nourishes our body, so books nourish our mind. 음식이 몸의 영양이 되는 것처럼 책은 마음의 영양이 된다.

  (5) 비교: ~와 같이, ~와 같은 정도로, ~만큼

  • She can walk as quickly **as** I can. 그녀는 나만큼 빨리 걸을 수 있다.

  (6) 양보: 비록 ~할지라도, ~이지만, ~이긴 하나

  • Rich **as** she is, she is not happy. 그녀는 부자이긴 하지만 행복하지는 않다.

■ **전치사 as**: ~ 같이, ~로서(자격)

전치사 as 뒤에는 명사나 명사구가 오지만 접속사 as 뒤에는 '주어+동사'가 오는 것에 유의한다.

  • It can be used **as** a knife. (전치사) 그건 나이프 대용으로 쓸 수가 있다.

  • We didn't go, **as** it rained hard. (접속사) 비가 몹시 쏟아져서 우리는 가지 않았다.

핵심 Check

1. 다음 빈칸에 공통으로 들어갈 알맞은 단어를 고르시오. (대 · 소문자 구분 안 함)

> • _____ she grew older, she became weaker.
> • Do _____ I tell you.

① that   ② what   ③ since   ④ as   ⑤ for

❷ 수의 일치

> • **Half of the boys** on his soccer team **wear** those shoes. 그의 축구팀에 있는 소년들의 반이 그
> 축구화를 신는다.

■ '부분을 나타내는 명사+of' 다음에 명사가 올 때 동사의 수를 명사의 수에 일치시킨다.
   ※ 부분을 나타내는 말+단수 명사: 단수 동사
   　 부분을 나타내는 말+복수 명사: 복수 동사
   • **Some of the music was** weird. 그 음악의 일부는 기묘했다.
   • **Some of the studies show** positive results. 그 연구들 중 일부는 긍정적인 결과를 보여준다.

■ 부분을 나타내는 명사에는 most, all, some, half, percent, rest, part, 분수(one-third, two-thirds) 등이 있다.
   • **Most of the rooms face** the sea. 그 방들의 대부분은 바다를 향하고 있다.

cf. 1. many of/(a) few of/a number of+복수 명사+복수 동사
   　　much of/(a) little of/+단수 명사, the number of+단수(복수) 명사+단수 동사

   • **Many of the pictures show** violence. 많은 장면들이 폭력을 보여줍니다.
   • **Much of the region is** lowland. 그 지역은 많은 부분이 저지대이다.

cf. 2. one of+복수 명사+단수 동사

   • **One** of the screws **is** loose. 그 나사들 중 하나가 헐겁다.

cf. 3. none of+단수 명사+단수 동사
   　　none of+복수 명사+단수 동사[복수 동사]

   • **None** of these computers **works[work]**. 이 컴퓨터들이 하나도 작동이 안 된다.

cf. 4. every, each, -thing, -one, -body, 시간, 거리, 금액, 무게, 학문 이름+단수 명사+단수 동사

   • **Every** move **was** painful. 몸을 움직일 때마다 아팠다.

※ 시제의 일치
   주어와 종속절의 시제를 일치시켜야 한다.
   주절의 동사가 현재시제인 경우 종속절에는 모든 시제를 쓸 수 있지만, 주절의 동사가 과거시제인 경우 종속절의 시제는 과거나 과거완료가 온다.
   주절의 시제가 과거일지라도 종속절이 불변의 진리, 격언, 현재의 습관, 과학적 사실 등을 나타내면 현재시제를 쓴다.
   • She **said** that knowledge **is** power.(진리) 그녀는 지식은 힘이라고 말했다.

핵심 Check

2. 괄호 안에 주어진 어휘를 빈칸에 현재형으로 알맞게 쓰시오.
   (1) The rest of the paper _____ on the table. (be)
   (2) Quite a few of the members _____ present. (be)
   (3) More than one third of wage earners _____ concerned about reduced wages. (be)

01 다음 각 문장의 빈칸에 as를 넣을 때 어색한 것은?

① Leave the papers _____ they are.
② My mother was crying _____ I waved her goodbye.
③ _____ he aged, his memory got worse.
④ The trouble is _____ we are short of money.
⑤ Her voice lowered _____ she spoke.

02 다음 빈칸에 알맞은 것을 고르시오.

> Half of the money _____ mine.

① being   ② to be   ③ was
④ were   ⑤ are

03 다음 문장의 빈칸에 가장 알맞은 말은?

> _____ he grows older, Ted gets more popular.

① As   ② Because   ③ What
④ Whether   ⑤ That

04 다음 빈칸에 들어갈 수 있는 말이 다른 하나는?

① The orchestra was tuning up _____ we entered the hall.
② _____ she gave no sign, I was sure she had seen me.
③ The new rules could mean the end of football _____ we know it.
④ _____ we get older, our bodies become less efficient at burning up calories.
⑤ I like him _____ he is honest.

05 다음 우리말을 괄호 안에 주어진 어휘를 이용하여 영작하시오.

> 시간이 지날수록 나는 너를 사랑한다. (as, go by, 7 단어)

➡ _____

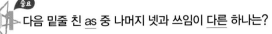

01 다음 밑줄 친 as 중 나머지 넷과 쓰임이 다른 하나는?

① As the prices of the tickets increase, people are less likely to go to concerts.
② As I was tired, I fell asleep early.
③ You don't need to be unconfident, as you are perfect the way you are.
④ We are, as you know, a leading company in the industry of benchmarking.
⑤ He is widely acknowledged as the best player in the world.

02 다음 밑줄 친 as 중 나머지 넷과 그 뜻이 다른 하나는?

① As you grow older, you will become wiser.
② The game was called off as it rained cats and dogs.
③ As she practiced the piano, she enjoyed it more and more.
④ As the movie progresses, the tension builds.
⑤ As she got older, offers of modelling work began to dry up.

03 다음 두 문장을 한 문장으로 바꾸어 쓸 때 알맞게 표현한 것을 고르시오.

> • The graph shows.
> • People are spending more and more money on food.

① Although the graph shows, people are spending more and more money on food.
② If the graph shows, people are spending more and more money on food.

③ As the graph shows, people are spending more and more money on food.
④ Since the graph shows, people are spending more and more money on food.
⑤ After the graph shows, people are spending more and more money on food.

04 다음 빈칸에 공통으로 들어갈 알맞은 말을 고르시오.

> (1) All of my songs _____ written by myself.
> (2) A quarter of all the people surveyed _____ don't-knows.
> (3) Only half of the rooms _____ occupied at that time.

① to be   ② being   ③ be
④ was   ⑤ were

05 다음 중 어법상 어색한 것은?

① Most of the students listen to music while studying.
② Some of the pie is missing.
③ Thirty percent of the country is plains.
④ About one third of all the students in our school wears glasses.
⑤ One of the most important things in a partner is a sense of humor.

서답형
06 다음 문장에서 어법상 어색한 단어 한 개를 찾아서 고치시오.

> One fourth of the students likes to go on a picnic, but the others don't.

➡ _____

중요
07 다음 빈칸에 공통으로 들어갈 알맞은 말을 고르시오. (대 · 소문자 무시)

> (1) _____ you spend more time giving thanks, you will be happier.
> (2) More people want to buy them _____ the price of apples falls.
> (3) They were all dressed _____ clowns.

① because   ② as   ③ while
④ when   ⑤ what

[08~09] 다음 우리말을 어법상 알맞게 영작한 것을 고르시오.

08

> 햄버거를 더 많이 먹음에 따라, 우리는 더 많은 소를 키워야 한다.

① As we eat more hamburgers, we need to raise more cows.
② Because we eat more hamburgers, we need to raise more cows.
③ Even though we eat more hamburgers, we need to raise more cows.
④ Since we eat more hamburgers, we need to raise more cows.
⑤ If we eat more hamburgers, we need to raise many cows.

09

> 그 문제를 축소하기 위해 많은 조치가 취해졌다.

① The number of measures was taken to reduce the problem.
② The number of measures were taken to reduce the problem.
③ A number of measures was taken to reduce the problem.
④ A number of measures were taken to reduce the problem.
⑤ A great deal of measures were taken to reduce the problem.

중요
10 다음 밑줄 친 as가 어법상 문장 속에서 바르게 쓰인 것을 고르시오.

① <u>As</u> every product sells well, being tested before being sold.
② Do you think <u>as</u> these latest changes will do any good?
③ Ann got a lot of experience <u>as</u> she traveled a lot.
④ Now she's caught up in a love triangle and doesn't know <u>as</u> to do.
⑤ In addition, <u>as</u> they were unable to mobilize the resources they needed.

11 다음 빈칸에 들어갈 말이 나머지와 다른 하나는?

① Half of the money _____ mine.
② Seventy percent of the participants _____ Asian.
③ Some of the teachers _____ criticized for poor performance.
④ The old part of the cities _____ destroyed during the war.
⑤ Most of the houses _____ built of stone.

12 다음 주어진 문장의 밑줄 친 as와 가장 가까운 뜻의 as가 쓰인 것을 고르시오.

> As more and more people get on the bandwagon, others are more likely to get on or follow it.

① Famous as she is, she is still quite modest.
② As it was raining heavily, we couldn't go out.
③ As she was advised, she practiced speaking constantly.
④ The audience fell silent as the curtain rose.
⑤ Picasso became more and more famous as he painted with more freedom.

13 다음 두 문장을 한 문장으로 연결할 때 가장 적절한 것은?

> • Nick tried many Korean dishes while he was in Seoul.
> • Nick tried *samgyupsal*.

① Nick tried many Korean dishes while he was in Seoul *samgyupsal* was one of the dishes.
② Nick tried *samgyupsal* that he tried Korean dishes while he was in Seoul.
③ Nick tried many Korean dishes while he was in Seoul that *samgyupsal* was.
④ One of the Korean dishes Nick tried in Seoul was *samgyupsal*.
⑤ One of the Korean dishes which Nick tried were *samgyupsal*.

14 다음 중 밑줄 친 as의 쓰임이 적절하지 <u>않은</u> 것을 고르시오.

① As you exercise harder, your heart rate will increase.
② A monkey is a monkey as he wears a gold ring.
③ As time went by, we became more confident and happy to meet them.
④ You'll experience more things as you grow up.
⑤ As you read more, you will be able to read faster.

15 다음 우리말을 바르게 영작한 것을 고르시오.

> 그녀는 그녀의 남편이 매일 아침 커피 한 잔을 마신다고 말했다.

① She said that her husband drinks a cup of coffee every morning.
② She says that her husband drinks a cup of coffee every morning.
③ She said that her husband has drunk a cup of coffee every morning.
④ She said that her husband had drunk a cup of coffee every morning.
⑤ She says that her husband drank a cup of coffee every morning.

서답형

16 우리말과 일치하도록 괄호 안에 주어진 어휘를 바르게 배열하시오.

> 비록 이상해 보일지 모르지만, 그것들은 실제 사람들이 일상생활에서 마주하고 있는 공포다.
> → (it, as, seem, strange, may), they are actually real fears that people confront every day.

➡ _____

01 다음 우리말과 일치하도록 괄호 안에 주어진 어구를 바르게 배열하여 영작하시오.

(1) 로마에 가면 로마인 방식대로 해라. (Rome, the Romans, you, are, do, do, as, when, in)

➡ _____

(2) 그 노래가 더 유명해질수록, 그는 더 많은 사람들에게 알려졌다. (he, people, the song, known, was, became, popular, more, more, as, to)

➡ _____
_____

(3) 그 물의 절반 가량이 미국에서 동물을 키우기 위해 사용된다. (half, animals, the water, about, is, raise, used, the U.S., to, in, of)

➡ _____
_____

(4) 전체 인구의 약 14퍼센트는 교육의 부족으로 읽는 법을 알지 못한다. (all people, 14 percent, education, lack, know, don't, read, due, how, about, to, to, of, of)

➡ _____
_____

02 다음 문장에서 어법상 어색한 것을 바르게 고쳐 다시 쓰시오.

(1) I caught him just though he was leaving the building.

➡ _____
_____

(2) As brave he was, he could not help weeping at the sight.

➡ _____
_____

(3) Each blind student were paired with a sighted student.

➡ _____
_____

(4) Jeff buys soccer shoes because more than half of the boys on his team wears them.

➡ _____
_____

(5) Most of the allowance are spent on clothes and one fourth of the allowance are spent on snacks.

➡ _____
_____

03 다음 문장을 as를 이용하여 같은 뜻의 문장으로 바꿔 쓰시오.

(1) The more love you give, the more love you will receive.

➡ _____
_____

(2) The harder you exercise, the healthier you become.

➡ _____
_____

04 그림을 보고, 주어진 어휘를 이용하여 빈칸을 알맞게 채우시오.

Only one of them at the party _____ on the sofa. (sit)

05 그림을 보고, 주어진 어휘를 이용하여 빈칸을 알맞게 채우시오.

_____ at night, you will get fatter. (eat more)

06 괄호 안에 주어진 동사를 어법에 맞게 빈칸에 쓰시오.

(1) Most of the boys _____ to eat hamburgers. (like)

(2) All of the stars seen in the sky _____ part of our Milky Way Galaxy. (be)

(3) None of the audience really _____ me. (know)

(4) The teacher told us that the Moon _____ around the earth once in 30 days. (go)

(5) The number of students _____ day by day. (decrease)

(6) I knew that World War II _____ in 1945. (end)

07 주어진 두 문장을 〈보기〉처럼 하나의 문장으로 쓰시오.

┌─── 보기 ───
• Julie gave Edan some money.
• Edan bought a new backpack with only half of the money.
→ Only half of the money that Julie gave to Edan was used to buy a new backpack by him.
└────────────

(1) • Sophie wrote many books.
  • Steve read about two thirds of them.
  ➡ _____
  _____

(2) • Mom made the food.
  • Mike threw away some of the food.
  ➡ _____
  _____

(3) • Dominic has a few hobbies.
  • Basketball is his hobby.
  ➡ _____

Reading
교과서

Why We Buy What We Buy

Have you ever wondered why you've bought things that you don't
간접의문문(의문사+주어+동사)   목적격 관계대명사
even want or need? Let's consider what affects us when it comes to
간접의문문(의문사(주어)+동사+목적어)
buying things.
동명사(to의 목적어)

Why do I want to buy what my friends bought?

Jeff goes to the shopping center and sees a pair of soccer shoes on
display. He recognizes the shoes at a glance because more than half of
이유를 이끄는 접속사(~ 때문에)
the boys on his soccer team wear them. Although he already has many
half of+명사: 명사에 수의 일치 (the boys에 수의 일치를 하여 복수동사 wear)   양보의 부사절을 이끄는 접속사
pairs of soccer shoes, he ends up buying another new pair.

We can use the "bandwagon effect" to explain Jeff's behavior. A
to부정사의 부사적 용법 중 목적(~하기 위해서)
bandwagon is a wagon in a parade that encourages people to jump
encourage+목적어+to부정사
aboard and enjoy the music. As more and more people get on the
접속사(~함에 따라)
bandwagon, others are more likely to get on or follow it. In this way,
people tend to buy something just because other people have bought it.
단지 ~이기 때문에

Why do I buy a pair of pants and a bag after I have bought a new coat?

Lisa buys a coat that she really loves. Immediately, she realizes that
목적격 관계대명사(+불완전한 절)   명사절 접속사(+완전한 절)
her pants do not match her new coat. So, she buys new pants that go
perfectly with her new coat. But she sees that none of her bags match
none of+명사: 명사에 수의 일치
her new clothes. So, she buys a new bag. Most of her money is spent
Most of+명사: 명사에 수의 일치(단수동사 is)
on buying the new items to complete her new look.
= in order to complete

affect: ~에 영향을 주다
when it comes to: ~에 관해서, ~에 대해 말하자면
effect: 효과
behavior: 행동, 행위
wagon: 사륜마차, 짐마차
parade: 행렬, 퍼레이드
encourage: 부추기다
aboard: 탑승하고
on display: 진열된, 전시된
at a glance: 한눈에, 즉시
be likely to: ~하기 쉽다
immediately: 즉시
match: 어울리다

 확인문제

● 다음 문장이 본문의 내용과 일치하면 T, 일치하지 않으면 F를 쓰시오.

1   Jeff sees a pair of soccer shoes on display in the shopping center. ☐

2   As more and more people get on the bandwagon, others are more likely to avoid it. ☐

What made Lisa search for new items immediately after buying
_{사역동사+목적어+동사원형}
a new coat? The "Diderot effect" may explain it. Denis Diderot, a
French writer, received a new gown as a gift. Soon after receiving
_{Denis Diderot와 동격}   = After he received the gift.
the gift, he noticed that all of his furniture did not go well with his
new gown. So, he ended up replacing most of it. The Diderot effect,
_{end up Ving: 결국 V하게 되다}
therefore, is the concept that purchasing a new item often leads to
_{the concept를 설명하는 동격의 명사절을 이끎}
more unplanned purchases.

Why do I buy things just because they are on sale?
Nathan goes window shopping and sees a pair of headphones. He
checks the price and finds out that they are $200. He thinks that the
_{checks와 병렬 연결   finds out의 목적어를 이끄는 명사절 접속사}
headphones are too expensive. The sales person approaches him and
says, "You can get a 20 percent discount on those headphones." Even
though the discounted price is still not very low, Nathan decides to
_{양보절 접속사(비록 ~일지라도)}
buy the headphones.

The situation described above is an example of the "anchoring
_{(which is) described}
effect."

The price mentioned first affects our opinion of prices mentioned
_{The price를 수식하는 과거분사}
afterwards. For example, if we start with $200, then $160 will seem
cheap in comparison. Furthermore, as the difference of the two prices
_{접속사(~함에 따라, ~할수록)}
becomes bigger, the effect will be more powerful. As such, the price
mentioned first acts as an "anchor" that fixes our thoughts about the
price of an item.
Just like Jeff and his friends, we tend to buy things without seriously
considering why we are buying them. As these effects have shown,
_{간접의문문(의문사+주어+동사)   접속사(~하듯이)}
many things influence our purchases. The next time you decide to buy
_{접속사구(다음번에 ~할 때에)}
something, think for a moment about why you are buying it.
_{간접의문문(의문사+주어+동사)}

furniture: 가구
replace: 바꾸다
concept: 개념
purchase: 구입, 구매
go well with: ~와 잘 어울리다
lead to: ~로 이어지다
discount: 할인; 할인하다
mention: 언급하다, 말하다
furthermore: 더욱이
anchor: 닻; 닻을 내리다
fix: 고정하다
go window shopping: 진열된 상품
을 구경하며 다니다
in comparison: 비교해 보면
influence: ~에 영향을 주다
for a moment: 잠깐

확인문제

● 다음 문장이 본문의 내용과 일치하면 T, 일치하지 <u>않으면</u> F를 쓰시오.

1   Most of Lisa's money is spent on repairing the new items. ☐

2   A French writer, Denis Diderot, received a new gown as a gift. ☐

3   Nathan decides to buy the headphones because the discounted price is low. ☐

● 우리말을 참고하여 빈칸에 알맞은 말을 쓰시오.

1 Have you ever wondered _____ _____ _____ _____ you don't even want or need?

2 Let's consider _____ _____ _____ when it comes to _____ things.

3 Why do I want to buy _____ _____ _____?

4 Jeff _____ to the shopping center and _____ _____ _____ soccer shoes _____ _____.

5 He _____ the shoes at a glance _____ more than _____ _____ _____ on his soccer team _____ them.

6 _____ he already has _____ _____ _____ soccer shoes, he _____ _____ _____ another new pair.

7 We can use the "_____ _____" _____ Jeff's behavior.

8 A bandwagon is a wagon in a parade _____ _____ people _____ _____ _____ and enjoy the music.

9 As _____ _____ _____ _____ get on the bandwagon, _____ _____ more _____ _____ _____ or follow it.

10 In this way, people tend _____ something _____ _____ other people _____ _____.

11 Why do I _____ _____ _____ _____ pants and a bag _____ I _____ _____ a new coat?

12 Lisa buys a coat _____ she really loves. Immediately, she _____ _____ her pants do not _____ her new coat.

13 So, she buys new pants _____ _____ perfectly _____ her new coat.

14 But she sees _____ _____ _____ _____ her new clothes.

15 So, she _____ a new bag. _____ _____ _____ _____ _____ spent _____ buying the new items _____ _____ her new look.

16 What _____ Lisa _____ _____ new items immediately _____ _____ a new coat?

1 여러분은 원하거나 필요로 하지도 않는 것들을 자신이 왜 구입했는지 궁금해 한 적이 있는가?

2 물건들을 구입하는 것에 관하여 무엇이 우리에게 영향을 주는지 생각해 보자.

3 나는 왜 친구들이 산 것을 사고 싶은 걸까?

4 Jeff는 쇼핑센터에 가서 진열되어 있는 축구화 한 켤레를 보게 된다.

5 그의 축구팀에 있는 소년들의 반 이상이 그 축구화를 신기 때문에 그는 그 신발을 한눈에 알아챈다.

6 이미 그에게는 축구화가 많이 있지만 결국 그는 또 다른 새 축구화를 사 버리고 만다.

7 우리는 Jeff의 행동을 설명하기 위해 '밴드왜건 효과'를 이용할 수 있다.

8 밴드왜건(악대차)은 사람들이 올라타서 음악을 즐기게끔 부추기는 퍼레이드에 있는 사륜마차이다.

9 더 많은 사람들이 밴드왜건에 올라탈수록 다른 사람들이 더욱 그것에 올라타거나 그것을 따라가려 한다.

10 이런 식으로, 사람들은 단지 다른 사람들이 어떤 것을 샀다는 이유로 그것을 구매하는 경향이 있다.

11 나는 왜 새 코트를 구입한 후에 바지와 가방을 사는 걸까?

12 Lisa는 정말 마음에 드는 코트를 산다. 그녀는 그녀의 바지가 새 코트와 어울리지 않는다는 것을 즉시 알아차린다.

13 그래서 그녀는 새 코트와 완벽하게 어울리는 새 바지를 구입한다.

14 하지만 그녀는 자신의 가방 중 어느 것도 새로운 옷들과 어울리지 않는다는 것을 알게 된다.

15 그래서 그녀는 새 가방을 산다. 그녀의 돈 대부분이 그녀의 새로운 모습을 완성하기 위하여 새로운 물품을 사는 데 쓰인다.

16 무엇이 Lisa로 하여금 새 코트를 산 후 즉시 새로운 물품을 찾게 했을까?

17 The "Diderot effect" may _____ _____. Denis Diderot, a French writer, _____ a new gown _____ a gift.

18 Soon _____ _____ the gift, he _____ _____ all of his _____ did not _____ _____ with his new gown. So, he ended up _____ _____ _____ _____ _____.

19 The Diderot effect, _____, is the concept _____ _____ _____ _____ often _____ _____ more _____ purchases.

20 Why do I buy things just because _____ _____ _____?

21 Nathan _____ _____ _____ _____ and _____ a pair of headphones.

22 He _____ the price and _____ _____ _____ they are $200. He thinks _____ the headphones are _____ _____.

23 The sales person _____ _____ and says, "You can get a 20 percent _____ _____ those headphones."

24 _____ _____ the discounted price _____ _____ not very _____, Nathan decides _____ _____ the headphones.

25 The situation _____ _____ is an example of the "_____ _____."

26 The price _____ first _____ our _____ _____ _____ mentioned afterwards.

27 _____ _____, if we start with $200, then $160 will _____ _____ _____ _____.

28 _____, as the difference of the two prices _____ _____, the effect will _____ _____ _____.

29 _____ _____, the price _____ _____ acts as an "_____" that _____ _____ _____ _____ about the price of an item.

30 _____ _____ Jeff and his friends, we tend _____ things without seriously _____ _____ _____ them.

31 _____ these effects _____ _____, many things _____ our purchases.

32 _____ _____ _____ you decide to buy something, _____ for a moment _____ _____ _____ _____ _____ it.

---

17 '디드로 효과'가 그것을 설명해 줄지도 모른다. 프랑스 작가인 Denis Diderot는 선물로 새 가운을 받았다.

18 그 선물을 받은 후에 곧 그는 그의 모든 가구가 새로운 가운과 어울리지 않는다는 것을 알아챘다. 그래서 그는 결국 대부분의 가구를 바꾸고 말았다.

19 그러므로 디드로 효과는 새로운 물품을 구입하는 것이 흔히 계획에 없던 더 많은 구매로 이어진다는 개념이다.

20 나는 왜 단지 할인 중이라는 이유로 물건을 구입하는 걸까?

21 Nathan은 진열된 상품을 구경하러 가서 헤드폰을 하나 본다.

22 그는 가격을 확인하고 그것이 200달러임을 알게 된다. 그는 그 헤드폰이 너무 비싸다고 생각한다.

23 점원이 그에게 다가와 "이 헤드폰에 20퍼센트 할인을 받을 수 있어요."라고 말한다.

24 비록 할인된 가격이 여전히 별로 저렴하지는 않지만 Nathan은 그 헤드폰을 사기로 결심한다.

25 위에 기술된 상황은 '앵커링 효과'의 한 예이다.

26 처음에 언급된 가격이 이후에 언급되는 가격에 대한 우리의 의견에 영향을 미친다.

27 예를 들어, 만약 우리가 200달러로 시작한다면, 비교해 볼 때 160달러는 저렴해 보일 것이다.

28 그뿐만 아니라, 두 가격의 차이가 커질수록 그 효과는 더욱 강력해질 것이다.

29 이와 같이 처음에 언급된 가격이 물건의 가격에 대한 우리의 생각을 고정하는 '닻'으로서 작동한다.

30 Jeff와 그의 친구들처럼, 우리는 우리가 왜 물건들을 사는지 진지하게 고려하지 않고 그것들을 구입하는 경향이 있다.

31 이러한 효과들이 보여 주듯이, 많은 것들이 우리의 구매에 영향을 미친다.

32 다음번에 여러분이 어떤 것을 구매하려고 결정할 때에는, 자신이 그것을 왜 사려는지 잠시 동안 생각해 보아라.

● 우리말을 참고하여 본문을 영작하시오.

1 여러분은 원하거나 필요로 하지도 않는 것들을 자신이 왜 구입했는지 궁금해 한 적이 있는가?
➡ _____

2 물건들을 구입하는 것에 관하여 무엇이 우리에게 영향을 주는지 생각해 보자.
➡ _____

3 나는 왜 친구들이 산 것을 사고 싶은 걸까?
➡ _____

4 Jeff는 쇼핑센터에 가서 진열되어 있는 축구화 한 켤레를 보게 된다.
➡ _____

5 그의 축구팀에 있는 소년들의 반 이상이 그 축구화를 신기 때문에 그는 그 신발을 한눈에 알아챈다.
➡ _____
_____

6 이미 그에게는 축구화가 많이 있지만 결국 그는 또 다른 새 축구화를 사 버리고 만다.
➡ _____

7 우리는 Jeff의 행동을 설명하기 위해 '밴드왜건 효과'를 이용할 수 있다.
➡ _____

8 밴드왜건(악대차)은 사람들이 올라타서 음악을 즐기게끔 부추기는 퍼레이드에 있는 사륜마차이다.
➡ _____
_____

9 더 많은 사람들이 밴드왜건에 올라탈수록 다른 사람들이 더욱 그것에 올라타거나 그것을 따라가려 한다.
➡ _____

10 이런 식으로, 사람들은 단지 다른 사람들이 어떤 것을 샀다는 이유로 그것을 구매하는 경향이 있다.
➡ _____

11 나는 왜 새 코트를 구입한 후에 바지와 가방을 사는 걸까?
➡ _____

12 Lisa는 정말 마음에 드는 코트를 산다. 그녀는 그녀의 바지가 새 코트와 어울리지 않는다는 것을 즉시 알아차린다.
➡ _____
_____

13 그래서 그녀는 새 코트와 완벽하게 어울리는 새 바지를 구입한다.
➡ _____

14 하지만 그녀는 자신의 가방 중 어느 것도 새로운 옷들과 어울리지 않는다는 것을 알게 된다.
➡ _____

15 그래서 그녀는 새 가방을 산다. 그녀의 돈 대부분이 그녀의 새로운 모습을 완성하기 위하여 새로운 물품을 사는 데 쓰인다.
➡ _____

16 무엇이 Lisa로 하여금 새 코트를 산 후 즉시 새로운 물품을 찾게 했을까?
➡ _____

17 '디드로 효과'가 그것을 설명해 줄지도 모른다. 프랑스 작가인 Denis Diderot는 선물로 새 가운을 받았다.

➡ _____

18 그 선물을 받은 후에 곧 그는 그의 모든 가구가 새로운 가운과 어울리지 않는다는 것을 알아챘다. 그래서 그는 결국 대부분의 가구를 바꾸고 말았다.

➡ _____

19 그러므로 디드로 효과는 새로운 물품을 구입하는 것이 흔히 계획에 없던 더 많은 구매로 이어진다는 개념이다.

➡ _____

_____

20 나는 왜 단지 할인 중이라는 이유로 물건을 구입하는 걸까?

➡ _____

21 Nathan은 진열된 상품을 구경하러 가서 헤드폰을 하나 본다.

➡ _____

22 그는 가격을 확인하고 그것이 200달러임을 알게 된다. 그는 그 헤드폰이 너무 비싸다고 생각한다.

➡ _____

23 점원이 그에게 다가와 "이 헤드폰에 20퍼센트 할인을 받을 수 있어요."라고 말한다.

➡ _____

24 비록 할인된 가격이 여전히 별로 저렴하지는 않지만 Nathan은 그 헤드폰을 사기로 결심한다.

➡ _____

25 위에 기술된 상황은 '앵커링 효과'의 한 예이다.

➡ _____

26 처음에 언급된 가격이 이후에 언급되는 가격에 대한 우리의 의견에 영향을 미친다.

➡ _____

27 예를 들어, 만약 우리가 200달러로 시작한다면, 비교해 볼 때 160달러는 저렴해 보일 것이다.

➡ _____

28 그뿐만 아니라, 두 가격의 차이가 커질수록 그 효과는 더욱 강력해질 것이다.

➡ _____

29 이와 같이 처음에 언급된 가격이 물건의 가격에 대한 우리의 생각을 고정하는 '닻'으로서 작동한다.

➡ _____

30 Jeff와 그의 친구들처럼, 우리는 우리가 왜 물건들을 사는지 진지하게 고려하지 않고 그것들을 구입하는 경향이 있다.

➡ _____

31 이러한 효과들이 보여 주듯이, 많은 것들이 우리의 구매에 영향을 미친다.

➡ _____

32 다음번에 여러분이 어떤 것을 구매하려고 결정할 때에는, 자신이 그것을 왜 사려는지 잠시 동안 생각해 보아라.

➡ _____

[01~04] 다음 글을 읽고 물음에 답하시오.

Have you ever wondered why you've bought things that you don't even want or need? Let's consider what affects us when it comes to buying things.

Why do I want to buy (A)_____?

Jeff goes to the shopping center and sees a pair of soccer shoes on display. He recognizes the shoes at a glance because more than half of the boys on his soccer team wear them. Although he already has many pairs of soccer shoes, he ends up buying another new pair.

We can use the "bandwagon effect" to explain Jeff's behavior. A bandwagon is a wagon in a parade that encourages people to jump aboard and enjoy the music. As more and more people get on the bandwagon, others are more likely to get on or follow it. In this way, people tend to buy something just because other people have bought it.

01 다음 중 빈칸 (A)에 들어갈 말로 가장 적절한 것은?

① luxurious things
② what my friends bought
③ what my friends want me to buy
④ things that is not good for me
⑤ what I need most

서답형

02 Where does Jeff go? Answer in English with a full sentence.

➡ _____

서답형

03 다음과 같이 풀이되는 말을 위 글에서 찾아 쓰시오.

> the things that a person or an animal does

➡ _____

04 다음 중 위 글을 읽고 답할 수 있는 것은?

① What did Jeff want to buy at the shopping center?
② How many pairs of soccer shoes does Jeff have?
③ When Jeff sees the shoes on display, what does he do?
④ How many members are there on Jeff's soccer team?
⑤ When did people start to use a bandwagon?

[05~08] 다음 글을 읽고 물음에 답하시오.

Why do I buy a pair of pants and a bag after I have bought a new coat?

Lisa buys a coat that she really loves. Immediately, she realizes that her pants do not match her new coat. So, she buys new pants that go perfectly with her new coat. (①) But she sees that none of her bags match her new clothes. (②) So, she buys a new bag. Most of her money is spent on buying the new items to complete her new look. (③)

What made Lisa search for new items immediately after buying a new coat? (④) Denis Diderot, a French writer, received a new gown as a gift. Soon after receiving the gift, he noticed that all of his furniture did not go well with his new gown. (⑤) So, he ended up replacing most of it. The Diderot effect, therefore, is the concept that purchasing a new item often leads to more unplanned purchases.

05 (①)~(⑤) 중 주어진 문장이 들어가기에 적절한 곳은?

> The "Diderot effect" may explain it.

①   ②   ③   ④   ⑤

06 Choose two things that Lisa didn't buy.

① a hat   ② a coat   ③ pants
④ shoes   ⑤ a bag

07 다음 중 글의 내용과 일치하는 것은?

① Lisa bought two pairs of pants.
② Denis Didreot is one of Lisa's friends.
③ Denis gave someone a new gown as a gift.
④ Lisa spent money on what she planned to buy.
⑤ What Lisa wanted was to complete her new look.

08 서답형 What did Lisa do after buying her new clothes? Answer in English.

➡ _____

[09~13] 다음 글을 읽고 물음에 답하시오.

Why do I buy things just because they are ①on sale?

Nathan goes window shopping and sees a pair of headphones. He checks the price and finds out that they are $200. He thinks that the headphones are ②too expensive. The sales person approaches him and says, "You can get a 20 percent discount on those headphones." Even though the discounted price is still not very ③low, Nathan decides to buy the headphones.

The situation described above is an example of the "anchoring effect." The price mentioned first affects our opinion of prices mentioned ④before. (A)_____, if we start with $200, then $160 will seem cheap in comparison. Furthermore, as the difference of the two prices

becomes ⑤bigger, the effect will be more powerful. As such, the price mentioned first acts as an "anchor" that fixes our thoughts about the price of an item.

09 밑줄 친 ①~⑤ 중 글의 흐름상 어색한 것은?

①   ②   ③   ④   ⑤

10 빈칸 (A)에 들어갈 말로 가장 적절한 것은?

① Nevertheless   ② Therefore
③ For example   ④ However
⑤ On the other hand

11 What is the passage mainly talking about?

① What makes people buy things they don't need?
② The reason we buy something only because it is on sale.
③ The reason some products are constantly on sale while others are not.
④ Who determines a price of a product on sale?
⑤ What kind of products attract people most?

12 서답형 According to the passage, what is the price of the headphones which fixes Nathan's thought about the price of them? Answer in English.

➡ _____

13 서답형 What does the sales person say when he approaches Nathan? Answer in English.

➡ _____
_____

[14~18] 다음 글을 읽고 물음에 답하시오.

Have you ever wondered why you've bought things ①that you don't even want or need? Let's consider what affects us when it comes to ②buy things.

Why do I want to buy ③what my friends bought?

(A) Although he already has many pairs of soccer shoes, he ends up buying another new pair.

(B) As more and more people get on the bandwagon, others are more likely to get on or follow it. In this way, people tend to buy something just because ④other people have bought it.

(C) Jeff goes to the shopping center and sees a pair of soccer shoes on display. He recognizes the shoes at a glance because more than half of the boys on his soccer team wear them.

(D) We can use the "bandwagon effect" ⑤to explain Jeff's behavior. A bandwagon is a wagon in a parade that encourages people to jump aboard and enjoy the music.

14 자연스러운 글이 되도록 (A)~(D)를 바르게 나열한 것은?

① (B)–(A)–(C)–(D) ② (B)–(D)–(A)–(C)
③ (C)–(A)–(D)–(B) ④ (C)–(B)–(A)–(D)
⑤ (D)–(A)–(B)–(C)

15 밑줄 친 ①~⑤ 중 어법상 바르지 않은 것은?

① ② ③ ④ ⑤

16 서답형 What does Jeff see at the shopping center? Answer in English.

➡ _____

17 위 글의 제목으로 가장 적절한 것은?

① What Makes You Survive?
② What Makes You Feel Happy?
③ Things That Money Can't Buy
④ What Makes Us Spend Money?
⑤ Ways To Be a Good Consumer: Follow Your Friends

18 서답형 What can we use to explain Jeff's behavior?

➡ _____

[19~22] 다음 글을 읽고 물음에 답하시오.

Why do I buy a pair of pants and a bag (A)_____?

Lisa buys a coat that she really loves. Immediately, she realizes that her pants do not match her new coat. So, she buys new pants that go perfectly with her new coat. But she sees that none of her bags match her new clothes. So, she buys a new bag. Most of her money is spent (B)_____ buying the new items to complete her new look.

What made Lisa search for new items immediately after buying a new coat? The "Diderot effect" may explain it. Denis Diderot, a French writer, received a new gown as a gift. Soon after receiving the gift, he noticed that all of his furniture did not go well with his new gown. So, he ended up replacing most of (C)it. The Diderot effect, therefore, is the concept (D)that purchasing a new item often leads to more unplanned purchases.

19 서답형 주어진 단어를 활용하여 빈칸 (A)에 들어갈 말을 완성하시오.

(after / have bought)

➡ _____

20 빈칸 (B)에 들어갈 말과 같은 말이 들어가는 것은?

① The refrigerator broke _____.
② What does the T.C. stand _____?
③ Jina was brought _____ by her sister.
④ Don't put _____ what you have to do today.
⑤ What does the insect mainly live _____?

21 밑줄 친 (C)가 가리키는 것을 위 글에서 찾아 쓰시오.

➡ _____

22 밑줄 친 (D)와 쓰임이 다른 것은?

① The fact that she betrayed us is true.
② They thought that you lied to them.
③ The name that he mentioned is yours.
④ It is true that the earth is round.
⑤ The news that he won first prize is true.

[23~25] 다음 글을 읽고 물음에 답하시오.

Why do I buy things just ①because they are on sale?

Nathan goes window shopping and sees a pair of headphones. He checks the price and finds out ②that they are $200. He thinks that the headphones are too expensive. The sales person ③approaches to him and says, "You can get a 20 percent discount on those headphones." Even though the discounted price is still not very low, Nathan decides ④to buy the headphones.

The situation described above is an example of the "anchoring effect." The price mentioned first affects our opinion of prices mentioned afterwards. For example, if we start with $200, then $160 will seem cheap in comparison. Furthermore, as the difference of the two prices ⑤becomes bigger, the effect will be more powerful. As such, the price mentioned first acts as an "anchor" that fixes our thoughts about the price of an item.

Just like Jeff and his friends, we tend to buy things without seriously considering why we are buying them. As (a)these effects have shown, many things influence our purchases. The next time you decide to buy something, think for a moment about (A)_____.

23 밑줄 친 ①~⑤ 중 어법상 바르지 않은 것은?

①   ②   ③   ④   ⑤

24 빈칸 (A)에 들어갈 말로 가장 적절한 것은?

① who made you spend money
② why you are buying it
③ when you started to think
④ what influences your life style
⑤ how you spend money wisely

25 What have the underlined (a)these effects shown?

➡ _____
_____

[01~05] 다음 글을 읽고 물음에 답하시오.

Have you ever wondered why you've bought things that you don't even want or need? Let's consider (A)물건을 구매하는 것에 관하여 무엇이 우리에게 영향을 주는지.

Why do I want to buy what my friends bought?

Jeff goes to the shopping center and sees a pair of soccer shoes on display. He recognizes the shoes at a glance because more than half of the boys on his soccer team ⓐwear them. Although he already has many pairs of soccer shoes, he ends up buying another new pair.

We can use the "bandwagon effect" to explain Jeff's behavior. A bandwagon is a wagon in a parade that encourages people to jump aboard and enjoy the music. As more and more people get on the bandwagon, others are more likely to get on or follow ⓑit. In this way, people tend to buy something just because other people have bought it.

01 주어진 단어를 활용하여 밑줄 친 우리말 (A)를 영어로 쓰시오.

(affect / when / come)

➡ _____

02 밑줄 친 ⓐ를 어법에 맞게 쓰시오.

➡ _____

03 밑줄 친 ⓑ가 가리키는 것을 위 글에서 찾아 쓰시오.

➡ _____

04 What is likely to happen when more and more people get on the bandwagon? Answer in English.

➡ _____

_____

05 According to the "bandwagon effect," why do people tend to buy something?

➡ _____

[06~09] 다음 글을 읽고 물음에 답하시오.

Why do I buy a pair of pants and a bag after I have bought a new coat?

Lisa buys a coat that she really loves. Immediately, she realizes that her pants do not match her new coat. So, she buys new pants that go perfectly with her new coat. But she sees that none of her bags match her new clothes. So, she buys a new bag. Most of her money is spent on buying the new items to complete her new look.

What made Lisa search for new items immediately after buying a new coat? The "Diderot effect" may explain it. Denis Diderot, a French writer, received a new gown as a gift. Soon after receiving the gift, he noticed that all of his furniture did not go well with his new gown. So, he ended up replacing most of it. The Diderot effect, therefore, is the concept that purchasing a new item often leads to more unplanned purchases.

06 What does Lisa buy at first?

➡ _____

07 What does Lisa realize after buying a new coat? Answer in English.

➡ _____

_____

08 Write the reason why Diderot replaced most of his furniture after receiving a new gown as a gift. Use the phrase 'It was because.'

➡ _____

_____

09 다음 중 위 글의 내용과 일치하지 <u>않는</u> 곳을 한 군데 찾아 바르게 고쳐 쓰시오.

> Lisa buys a series of new items because, according to the "Diderot effect," one new item leads to a series of planned purchases.

➡ _____

[10~13] 다음 글을 읽고 물음에 답하시오.

Why do I buy things just because they are on sale?

Nathan goes window shopping and sees a pair of headphones. He checks the price and finds out that they are $200. He thinks that the headphones are too expensive. The sales person approaches him and says, "You can get a 20 percent discount on those headphones." Even though the discounted price is still not very low, Nathan decides to buy the headphones.

The situation described above is an example of the "anchoring effect." The price mentioned first affects our opinion of prices mentioned afterwards. For example, if we start with $200, then $160 will seem cheap in comparison.

Furthermore, as the difference of the two prices becomes bigger, the effect will be more powerful. As such, the price mentioned first acts as an "anchor" that fixes our thoughts about the price of an item.

Just like Jeff and his friends, we tend to buy things without seriously considering why we are buying them. As these effects have shown, many things influence our purchases. The next time you decide to buy something, think for a moment about why you are buying it.

10 What does Nathan see when he goes window shopping? Answer in English.

➡ _____

11 What does Nathan find out when he checks the price of the headphone?

➡ _____

12 다음과 같이 풀이되는 말을 위 글에서 찾아 쓰시오.

> a heavy object that is dropped into the water to prevent a boat from moving

➡ _____

13 What does the writer suggest we should do the next time we decide to buy something? Answer in English.

➡ _____

_____

구석구석

Language in Use

- It is difficult to compare the results in detail.
  특정 어근 앞에 com-을 붙이면 '함께'라는 의미를 더한다. com+pare(가지런히 놓다) → compare(비교하다)
- We encourage children to think for themselves.

구문해설 · in detail: 상세히 · for oneself: 스스로

해석

- 결과를 상세히 비교하는 것은 어렵다.
- 우리는 아이들이 스스로 생각하도록 장려한다.

Grammar in Real Life B Look and Write

1. About half of the water is used to raise animals in the U.S.
   부분을 나타내는 말은 뒤에 오는 명사의 수에 따라 그 수가 결정된다.(the water/is)
2. One third of the world's food is wasted —1.3 billion tons every year.
   the world's food에 맞춰 is
3. In Somalia, only ten percent of the children go to school.
   the children에 맞춰 go
4. About fourteen percent of all people don't know how to read due to lack of
   약   all people에 맞춰 don't know   의문사+to부정사(= how they should read)
   education.

구문해설 · raise: 키우다 · waste: 낭비하다 · billion: 10억 · due to: ~ 때문에 · lack: 부족, 결핍
· education: 교육

1. 그 물의 절반 가량이 미국에서 동물을 키우기 위해 사용된다.
2. 세계 식량의 삼분의 일, 즉 매년 13억 톤이 낭비된다.
3. 소말리아에서는 단지 10퍼센트의 아이들이 학교에 다닌다.
4. 전체 인구의 약 14퍼센트는 교육의 부족으로 읽는 법을 알지 못한다.

Think & Write C

I did a survey about allowance. First, I asked 10 students how often they get
                                                      간접의문문(의문사+주어+동사) ask의 직접목적어
an allowance. Twenty percent of the students get an allowance every week and
                                            the students에 수의 일치
seventy percent of the students get an allowance every month. Second, I asked

them what they spend most of their allowance on. Most of the allowance is
    asked와 on의 목적어 역할을 함.   the allowance에 수의 일치
spent on clothes and one fourth of the allowance is spent on snacks.
                    4분의 1(분자는 기수, 분모는 서수)
Lastly, I asked them whether they think that they should get a higher
                        ask의 직접목적어(명사절 접속사: ~인지 아닌지)
allowance. Ninety percent of the students think that they should get a higher

allowance.

구문해설 · survey: 설문 조사 · allowance: 용돈 · spend+시간/돈+on ~: ~에 시간이나 돈을 쓰다
· whether: ~인지 아닌지

저는 용돈에 관하여 설문 조사를 했습니다. 우선, 저는 10명의 학생들에게 그들이 얼마나 자주 용돈을 받는지 물었습니다. 20퍼센트의 학생들은 매주 용돈을 받고, 70퍼센트의 학생들은 매달 용돈을 받습니다. 두 번째로, 저는 학생들에게 어디에 용돈의 대부분을 쓰는지 물었습니다. 대부분의 용돈은 옷에 쓰이고, 용돈의 4분의 1은 간식에 쓰입니다. 마지막으로, 저는 학생들에게 그들이 더 많은 용돈을 받아야 한다고 생각하는지 물었습니다. 학생들의 90퍼센트는 그들이 더 많은 용돈을 받아야 한다고 생각합니다.

영역별 핵심문제

01 다음 밑줄 친 부분과 의미가 가장 가까운 것을 고르시오.

> Young people tend to be greatly affected by their peer group.

① invented   ② controlled

③ improved   ④ generated

⑤ influenced

02 다음 빈칸에 들어갈 알맞은 말을 고르시오.

> That jacket _____ your skirt perfectly.

① matches   ② consumes   ③ lasts

④ replaces   ⑤ adapts

03 다음 괄호 안의 단어를 문맥에 맞게 고쳐 문장을 완성하시오.

> The new teacher _____ students to think creatively. (courage)

04 다음 빈칸에 공통으로 들어갈 말을 쓰시오.

> • _____ and more people are using the Internet.
> • The roads were closed for _____ than half an hour.

[05~06] 다음 대화를 읽고 물음에 답하시오.

W: Hey, Eric. Camilla and I are going to watch a movie. (①) Do you want to join us?

M: I'd love to, but I can't. (②) I've spent all of my allowance for this week. (③)

W: Didn't you just get it a few days ago? (④)

M: I'm not sure. (⑤) (A)내 지출을 기록했어야 했어. (keep, spending, track)

05 ①~⑤ 중 주어진 문장이 들어갈 곳은?

> How did you spend it all?

①   ②   ③   ④   ⑤

06 밑줄 친 (A)의 우리말과 일치하도록 주어진 단어를 이용하여 영작하시오.

➡ _____

[07~08] 다음 대화를 읽고 물음에 답하시오.

A: I heard (A)_____ you bought some iced tea online. (a)How do you like it?

B: Oh, I'm (B)_____ with it.

A: Why? What's wrong?

B: There is too much sugar in it. I (C)_____ the nutrition facts first.

07 다음 빈칸 (A)~(C)에 들어갈 말이 알맞게 짝지어진 것은?

① what – not happy – should check

② what – satisfied – should have checked

③ that – satisfied – should check

④ that – satisfied – should have checked

⑤ that – not happy – should have checked

08 밑줄 친 (a)와 바꿔 쓸 수 없는 것을 고르시오.

① Are you satisfied with it?

② Are you enjoying it?

③ Do you like it?

④ Why do you like it?

⑤ Are you happy with it?

[09~10] 다음 대화를 읽고 물음에 답하시오.

M: Good morning. May I help you?

W: I'd like to buy a T-shirt for my sister. She's eleven years old. (①)

M: How do you (A)_____ this red one? (②) This character is quite popular among children. (③)

W: Well, she doesn't (B)_____ animation characters that much. (④)

M: You mean this blue striped T-shirt? Its design is simple and cool. (⑤)

W: Yes, I think my sister will like it. I'll take it.

09 ①~⑤ 중 주어진 문장이 들어갈 곳은?

Can I see the blue one?

①　　②　　③　　④　　⑤

10 빈칸 (A)와 (B)에 공통으로 들어갈 말을 쓰시오.

➡ _____

[11~12] 다음 대화를 읽고 물음에 답하시오.

M: Good morning. Welcome to Kelly's Sporting Goods Store.

W: Hi, I'm looking for a backpack for hiking.

M: These two are popular among hikers.

W: The green one is lighter than the blue one. I'll take the lighter one.

M: Great choice.

11 대화의 흐름상 빈칸에 들어갈 말을 주어진 단어를 이용해 문장을 완성하시오.

➡ (1) _____ (how, like)

(2) _____ (satisfied)

12 〈보기〉의 ⓐ~ⓓ 중 대화를 읽고 답할 수 있는 것을 모두 고른 것은?

┌─── 보기 ───┐

ⓐ Which backpack does the woman take, the green one or the blue one?

ⓑ Which backpack is lighter, the green one or the blue one?

ⓒ What will the woman use a backpack for?

ⓓ Which backpack is more popular, the green one or the blue one?

① ⓐ, ⓑ　　　　② ⓐ, ⓑ, ⓒ

③ ⓐ, ⓑ, ⓒ, ⓓ　　④ ⓑ, ⓒ

⑤ ⓑ, ⓒ, ⓓ

Grammar

13 다음 중 어법상 옳지 않은 것은?

① As you learn more, you can achieve more.

② As the price goes up, the demand goes down.

③ As you were reborn as an animal, which animal would you be?

④ You have to show your ticket as you go in.

⑤ I couldn't borrow the book from him as James was not at home.

14 다음 중 어법상 옳은 문장을 <u>모두</u> 고르시오.

① One of the highlights were seeing the Taj Mahal.

② 10 percent of the students work to earn money.

③ The number of employees were reduced from 40 to 25.

④ The rest of the money are used to run other government programs.

⑤ Two hours is enough for me to take a walk.

15 다음 밑줄 친 부분이 어법상 옳지 <u>않은</u> 것을 고르시오.

① <u>As she entered the room</u>, she turned the TV on.

② Furthermore, <u>as the difference of the two prices becomes bigger</u>, the effect will be more powerful.

③ <u>As the study shows</u>, those who drink diet sodas tend to get fatter.

④ She earns her living <u>as a freelance journalist</u>.

⑤ Jane met him <u>so as he was leaving the building</u>.

16 다음 문장의 빈칸에 들어갈 말로 알맞은 말은?

> Last weekend, a few of his friends _____ at the party.

① is   ② are   ③ was

④ were   ⑤ has been

17 다음 문장의 밑줄 친 <u>as</u>와 의미상 쓰임이 같은 것을 고르시오.

> <u>As</u> you make more money, you'll want to spend more.

① <u>As</u> the weather gets hotter, more people go to the beach.

② <u>As</u> she was sick, he cared for his wife day and night.

③ <u>As</u> I would not be a slave, so I would not be a master.

④ I wish I could speak English as easily <u>as</u> Korean.

⑤ She was liked by many people <u>as</u> she was honest.

18 다음 문장에서 어법상 <u>어색한</u> 것을 바르게 고쳐 다시 쓰시오.

(1) One third of the students is here.

  ➡ _____

(2) Much of the house were ruined by the heavy rain.

  ➡ _____

(3) Ten percent of the girls wants to learn Spanish.

  ➡ _____

(4) None of the furniture in our house are made of wood.

  ➡ _____

_____

(5) Last night she said that she took a shower every day.

  ➡ _____

_____

19 다음 문장에서 잘못된 것을 내용에 맞게 한 단어만 고치시오.

(1) She never took a taxi, as she could afford to.

➡ _____

(2) I usually sleep with the window open as it's really cold.

➡ _____

(3) Korea is regarded like the Mecca of cosmetic surgery.

➡ _____

20 다음 문장에서 어법상 틀린 부분을 찾아 바르게 쓰시오.

Only 20 percent of students in my school enjoys outdoor activities.

➡ _____

Reading

[21~24] 다음 글을 읽고 물음에 답하시오.

Have you ever wondered why you've bought things that you don't even want or need? Let's consider ①what affects us when it comes to buying things.

Why do I want to buy what my friends bought?

Jeff goes to the shopping center and ② sees a pair of soccer shoes ③on display. He recognizes the shoes at a glance because more than half of the boys on his soccer team wear them. Although he already has many pairs of soccer shoes, he ends up (A) _____ .

We can use the "bandwagon effect" to explain Jeff's behavior. A bandwagon is a wagon in a parade that encourages people to jump aboard and ④enjoys the music. As more and more people get on the bandwagon, others are more likely to get on or follow it. In this way, people tend to buy something just because other people have bought ⑤it.

21 글의 흐름상 빈칸 (A)에 들어갈 말로 가장 적절한 것은?

① throwing them away
② passing by them in the end
③ buying his friends new soccer shoes
④ focusing on playing games
⑤ buying another new pair

22 ①~⑤ 중 어법상 바르지 않은 것을 찾아 바르게 쓰시오.

➡ _____

23 다음 중 글의 내용과 일치하지 않는 곳을 한 군데 찾아 바르게 고쳐 쓰시오.

As people jump on the bandwagon in a parade, people tend to buy things just because no other people have bought them.

➡ _____

24 다음 중 위 글을 읽고 답할 수 있는 것은?

① How often does Jeff go to the shopping center?
② What does Jeff recognize as soon as he sees the shoes?
③ What makes Jeff go to the shopping center?
④ Who invented the term "bandwagon effect" first?
⑤ Who made a bandwagon first in the world?

[25~28] 다음 글을 읽고 물음에 답하시오.

Why do I buy a pair of pants and a bag after I have bought a new coat?

Lisa buys a coat that she really loves. Immediately, she realizes that her pants do not match her new coat. So, she buys new pants that go perfectly with her new coat. But she sees that none of her bags match her new clothes. So, she buys a new bag. Most of her money is spent on buying the new items to complete her new look.

What made Lisa search for new items immediately after buying a new coat? The "Diderot effect" may explain it. Denis Diderot, a French writer, received a new gown as a gift. Soon after receiving the gift, he noticed that all of his furniture did not go well with his new gown. So, he ended up replacing most of it. The Diderot effect, (A)_____, is the concept that purchasing a new item often leads to more unplanned purchases.

25 빈칸 (A)에 들어갈 말로 가장 적절한 것은?

① on the other hand   ② however

③ therefore   ④ for instance

⑤ furthermore

26 What does Lisa buy after buying a new coat?

➡ _____

27 What did Diderot do when he noticed all of his furniture didn't go well with his new gown? Answer in English.

➡ _____

28 Choose one that is TRUE.

① Lisa receives a coat as a gift.

② Lisa keeps buying new items because she needs them.

③ Lisa already had a pair of pants perfectly matching her new coat.

④ What Lisa planned to buy was just a coat.

⑤ Diderot was not satisfied with the new gown, so he replaced it with a new one.

[29~30] 다음 글을 읽고 물음에 답하시오.

I did a survey about allowance. First, I asked 10 students (A)_____. Twenty percent of the students get an allowance every week and seventy percent of the students get an allowance every month. Second, I asked them what they spend most of their allowance on. Most of the allowance is spent on clothes and one fourth of the allowance is spent on snacks. Lastly, I asked them whether they think that they should get a higher allowance. Ninety percent of the students think that they should get a higher allowance.

29 빈칸 (A)에 들어갈 말로 가장 적절한 것은?

① how they usually spend their allowance

② how much allowance they save

③ how often they buy things with their allowance

④ how much allowance they get

⑤ how often they get an allowance

30 On what is most of the allowance spent? Answer in English.

➡ _____

출제율 90%

01 다음 짝지어진 단어의 관계가 같도록 빈칸에 알맞은 단어를 주어진 철자로 시작하여 쓰시오.

(1) immediately : at once = buy : p_____
(2) waste : save = loose : t_____

출제율 95%

02 다음 괄호 안의 단어를 문맥에 맞게 고쳐 빈칸에 쓰시오.

What's the _____ between these two computers? (differ)

출제율 100%

03 빈칸 (A)~(C)에 들어갈 말이 바르게 짝지어진 것을 고르시오.

- We're spending a lot more (A)____ food than we used to.
- We need a system to (B)____ track of all our expenses.
- There is no doubt that stress can (C)____ to physical illness.

	(A)	(B)	(C)
①	on	have	result
②	on	make	lead
③	on	keep	lead
④	in	keep	lead
⑤	in	make	result

출제율 90%

04 다음 영영풀이가 해당하는 단어를 주어진 철자로 시작하여 빈칸에 쓰고, 알맞은 것을 골라 문장을 완성하시오.

- a_____ : to have an influence on someone or something, or to cause a change in someone or something
- c_____ : to join together to make a single thing or group
- c_____ : a principle or idea

(1) We need to come up with a new _____ now.
(2) Every choice you make _____ your life.
(3) He wants to _____ his job with pleasure.

출제율 95%

05 다음 대화의 빈칸에 들어갈 말을 <보기>에서 골라 순서대로 배열하시오.

W: Hi, Luke. Is that a new speaker?
M: _____
W: _____
M: _____
W: _____
M: About 2 hours. The battery doesn't last long.
W: That's too bad.
M: Yeah, but I'm pretty happy with it, anyway.

(A) Great. How long does the battery last?
(B) It looks cool. How do you like it?
(C) It's convenient. I can take it anywhere and listen to music. The sound quality is good, too.
(D) Yes, I bought it a few weeks ago.

➡ _____

[06~07] 다음 대화를 읽고 물음에 답하시오.

M: Hi. (A)_____

W: Yes, can I try on that cap with stars over there?

M: Sure. (B)_____

W: The design is nice, but I don't think the color suits me. (C)_____

M: Yes. I'll get one from the back. *(pause)* Here it is.

W: Great. I'll take it.

출제율 95%

06 위 대화의 빈칸 (A)~(C)에 들어갈 말을 〈보기〉에서 골라 기호를 쓰시오.

┌─── 보기 ───┐

ⓐ Are you enjoying your new cap?

ⓑ How do you like it?

ⓒ What's wrong?

ⓓ Can I help you with anything?

ⓔ Do you have it in black?

ⓕ Didn't you check the picture of it?

ⓖ How about trying on that cap?

└──────────────┘

➡ (A) _____ (B) _____ (C) _____

출제율 90%

07 위 대화에서 다음 영영풀이에 해당하는 단어를 찾아 쓰시오.

┌──────────────────────────────┐
to be right for a particular person, situation, or occasion
└──────────────────────────────┘

➡ _____

[08~11] 다음 대화를 읽고 물음에 답하시오.

M: Hi, Riley. (①) I heard that you bought a laptop online. How do you like it?

W: Oh, I'm not happy with it.

M: Why? What's wrong?

W: (②) I should have read more reviews.

M: (③) Oh, then you should ask (A)_____ your money back.

W: (④) The online store won't give me back my money (B)_____ I've used it for a week.

M: (⑤) How about calling the online shop and explaining your problem?

W: Yeah, I think I should (a)do that.

출제율 100%

08 ①~⑤ 중 주어진 문장이 들어갈 곳은?

┌──────────────────────────────┐
It makes too much noise and gets overheated.
└──────────────────────────────┘

① ② ③ ④ ⑤

출제율 90%

09 빈칸 (A)에 알맞은 전치사를 쓰시오.

➡ _____

출제율 95%

10 빈칸 (B)에 알맞은 말을 고르시오.

① therefore   ② because

③ but   ④ before

⑤ until

출제율 90%

11 밑줄 친 (a)do that이 가리키는 것을 쓰시오.

➡ _____

12 다음 빈칸에 알맞은 말을 고르시오.

> A: Clara, what's the matter?
> B: I missed the school bus again.
> _____

① I should have gotten up earlier.
② I should have stayed home in bed.
③ I should not have the alarm.
④ I must have told it earlier.
⑤ I must have taken the subway.

13 다음 밑줄 친 as의 쓰임이 다른 하나를 고르시오.

① As he grew up, he got more interested in history.
② As we need more land to raise cows on, we cut more trees to make land.
③ We soon went back as it was getting darker.
④ As a joke to please her, Jake told a story that he made up.
⑤ As he ran faster and faster, his heart pounded loudly.

14 다음 문장에서 어법상 틀린 부분을 찾아 바르게 고쳐 쓰시오.

> The greater part of the expenses was collected from the members.

➡ _____

15 다음 두 문장을 접속사 as를 이용하여 한 문장으로 고치시오.

> • People eat more junk food.
> • They may gain more weight.

➡ _____
_____

16 다음 빈칸에 들어갈 말이 나머지와 다른 하나는?

① Most of the kids _____ wearing caps.
② Some of the pie _____ missing.
③ There _____ several reasons why I can't come.
④ None of the books _____ worth reading.
⑤ A number of new homes _____ being built in this area.

17 다음 문장을 접속사 as를 이용하여 바꿔 쓰시오.

> The more you run, the stronger you become.

➡ _____

[18~21] 다음 글을 읽고 물음에 답하시오.

Why do I buy things just because they are (A) [for sale / on sale]?

Nathan goes window shopping and sees a pair of headphones. He checks the price and finds out that they are $200. He thinks that the headphones are too expensive. The sales person approaches him and says, "You can get a 20 percent discount on those headphones." (B)[Even though / Because] the discounted price is still not very low, Nathan decides to buy the headphones.

The situation described above is an example of the "anchoring effect." The price mentioned first affects our opinion of prices mentioned afterwards. For example, if we start with $200, then $160 will seem cheap in comparison. Furthermore, as the difference of the two prices becomes bigger, the effect will be ⓐ_____. As such, the price mentioned first acts as an "anchor" that (C)[fixes / releases] our thoughts about the price of an item.

Just like Jeff and his friends, we tend to buy things without seriously considering why we are buying them. As these effects have shown, many things influence our purchases. The next time you decide to buy something, think for a moment about why you are buying it.

18 (A)~(C)에서 글의 흐름상 옳은 것끼리 바르게 짝지어진 것은?

① for sale – Even though – fixes
② for sale – Even though – releases
③ on sale – Even though – fixes
④ on sale – Because – releases
⑤ on sale – Because - fixes

19 위 글의 내용에 맞게 빈칸에 알맞은 말을 쓰시오.

> The price mentioned first works like an
> _____. If the price mentioned later
> is _____ than the first, you will think
> that the item is cheap.

20 Choose one that is TRUE.

① Our purchases are influenced by only one thing.
② Nathan finds out on his own that the headphone is on sale.
③ Nathan thinks the price of the headphones is reasonable.
④ The headphone is on Nathan's shopping list.
⑤ Nathan buys the headphone because he is affected by the anchoring effect.

21 According to the "anchoring effect," what affects our opinion of prices mentioned afterwards? Answer in English.

➡ _____
_____

[22~24] 다음 글을 읽고 물음에 답하시오.

I did a survey about allowance. First, I asked 10 students how often they get an allowance. Twenty percent of the students ①get an allowance every week and seventy percent of the students get an allowance every month. Second, I asked them ②what they spend most of their allowance on. Most of the allowance ③is spent on clothes and one fourth of the allowance is spent ④on snacks. Lastly, I asked them ⑤ that they think that they should get a higher allowance. Ninety percent of the students think that they should get a higher allowance.

22 밑줄 친 ①~⑤ 중 어법상 바르지 않은 것은?

①   ②   ③   ④   ⑤

23 What do nine students think about their allowance? Answer in English.

➡ _____

24 위 글을 읽고 답할 수 있는 것은?

① When was the survey conducted?
② How many students were asked for the survey?
③ How often do they buy clothes?
④ How much allowance do they want to get?
⑤ How long does it take them to spend all of their allowance?

01 그림을 보고 괄호 안에 주어진 어휘를 이용하여 과거 사실에 대해 유감을 나타내는 말로 빈칸을 채우시오.

A: What's the problem?
B: Sam and Ted _____
_____. (an umbrella, bring, should)

02 밑줄 친 문장과 비슷한 뜻을 가진 문장을 주어진 단어를 이용하여 쓰시오.

A: How do you like this dress?
B: The design is cool and interesting.

➡ (1) (enjoy) _____
(2) (satisfied) _____
(3) (happy) _____

03 대화의 흐름상 빈칸에 들어갈 말을 주어진 〈조건〉에 맞춰 쓰시오.

┤ 조건 ├
• 6 단어로 후회하는 일 말하기
• 대화에 나와 있는 어휘 이용하기

M: Oh, this coat is too uncomfortable.
W: Why? What's wrong with it?
M: It's too tight.
W: Didn't you try it on before buying it?
M: No. It was my size, so I just bought it.
_____

➡ _____

04 〈보기〉에 주어진 단어를 활용하여 빈칸을 알맞게 채우시오.

┤ 보기 ├
be   die   have   spend

(1) Half of the money _____ for children in need last month.
(2) Economics _____ not the subject which I'm good at.
(3) I knew that Frida Kahlo _____ in 1954.
(4) The number of homeless people _____ increased dramatically.

05 다음 우리말에 맞도록 괄호 안에 주어진 어휘를 알맞게 배열하시오.

(1) 내가 말하고 있을 때, Jason이 내게 다가왔다.
(Jason, I, me, speaking, came, was, to, as, up)
➡ _____

(2) 그는 젊지만 아주 현명했다. (he, he, young, wise, was, was, very, as)
➡ _____

(3) 이러한 효과들이 보여 주듯이, 많은 것들이 우리의 구매에 영향을 미친다. (effects, things, influence, purchases, these, many, shown, our, have, as)
➡ _____

(4) 세계 식량의 삼분의 일이 낭비된다. (one, third, of, the world's food, is, wasted)
➡ _____

Have you ever wondered why you've bought things that you don't even want or need? Let's consider what affects us when it comes to buying things.

Why do I want to buy what my friends bought?

Jeff goes to the shopping center and sees a pair of soccer shoes on display. He recognizes the shoes at a glance because more than half of the boys on his soccer team wear them. Although he already has many pairs of soccer shoes, he ends up buying another new pair.

We can use the "bandwagon effect" to explain Jeff's behavior. A bandwagon is a wagon in a parade that encourages people to jump aboard and enjoy the music. As more and more people get on the bandwagon, others are more likely to get on or follow it. In this way, people tend to buy something just because other people have bought it.

06 According to the passage, why does Jeff buy a pair of soccer shoes on display? Answer in English with a full sentence.

➡ _____

_____

07 What kind of wagon is a bandwagon? Answer in English with a full sentence.

➡ _____

_____

Why do I buy a pair of pants and a bag after I have bought a new coat?

Lisa buys a coat that she really loves. Immediately, she realizes that her pants do not match her new coat. So, she buys new pants that go perfectly with her new coat. But she sees that none of her bags match her new clothes. So, she buys a new bag. Most of her money is spent on buying the new items to complete her new look.

What made Lisa search for new items immediately after buying a new coat? The "Diderot effect" may explain it. Denis Diderot, a French writer, received a new gown as a gift. Soon after receiving the gift, he noticed that all of his furniture did not go well with his new gown. So, he ended up replacing most of it. The Diderot effect, therefore, is the concept that purchasing a new item often leads to more unplanned purchases.

08 Why does Lisa spend most of her money on buying new items? Answer in English with a full sentence.

➡ _____

09 What may explain Lisa's spending? Answer in English.

➡ _____

10 What concept is the "Diderot effect?" Answer in English.

➡ _____

01 다음 문장의 빈칸에 알맞은 말을 〈조건〉에 맞춰 쓰시오.

┌── 조건 ──┐
- 후회하는 일 말하기
- should 이용하기
└──┘

I went to school yesterday, even though I felt sick. Today I feel even worse. I _____
_____ .

02 〈보기〉와 같이, 주어진 문장의 빈칸을 채워 본인만의 문장을 쓰시오.

┌── 보기 ──┐
As the night becomes darker, the stars become brighter.
└──┘

(1) As I understood her better, _____ .
(2) As I didn't eat anything, _____ .
(3) As I spend more money, _____ .
(4) As the boy grows older, _____ .

03 10명의 학생을 대상으로 한 설문 조사의 응답을 읽고 그 결과를 설명하는 글을 완성하시오.

Q: How often do you get an allowance?
  □ every week (2명)   □ every month (7명)
Q: What do you spend most of your allowance on?
  □ clothes (용돈의 대부분) □ snacks (용돈의 4분의 1)
Q: Do you think you should get a higher allowance?
  □ Yes (9명)   □ No (1명)

I did a survey about allowance. First, I asked 10 students _____ .
_____ percent of the students get an allowance _____ and _____
_____ . Second, I asked them what they
spend most of their allowance on. Most of the allowance is _____ and
_____ is spent on snacks. Lastly, I asked them _____
_____ . _____
_____ .

단원별 모의고사

01 다음 빈칸에 공통으로 들어갈 말을 쓰시오.

> • Which shoes _____ best with this dress?
>
> • I will _____ window shopping with my friend next weekend.

02 다음 우리말에 맞도록 빈칸에 알맞은 말을 쓰시오. (주어진 단어를 이용하고, 철자가 주어진 경우 주어진 철자로 시작할 것.)

(1) 나는 다음 해에 티켓이 더 비싸질 가능성이 있다고 생각한다. (likely)

➡ I think tickets _____ more expensive next year.

(2) 나는 이 딱 붙는 바지가 편하지 않다.

➡ I am not _____ in these tight pants.

(3) 나는 내가 한 말을 곧 후회했다.

➡ I regretted my words s_____ a_____.

(4) 나는 무슨 일이 일어났었는지 한눈에 알아챘다.

➡ I noticed what had happened _____ _____. (at)

03 다음 빈칸에 알맞은 단어를 〈보기〉에서 골라 쓰시오

> ┌─ 보기 ─┐
>
> although   because   when

(1) _____ it comes to cooking, he is better than me.

(2) Just _____ I don't complain, people think I'm satisfied.

(3) _____ the sun was shining, it wasn't very warm.

04 다음 괄호 안의 단어를 문맥에 맞게 고쳐 빈칸에 쓰시오.

> In _____ there are those living in wealth and luxury. (compare)

[05~06] 다음 대화를 읽고 물음에 답하시오.

> M: Good morning. ⓐMay I help you?
>
> W: ⓑI'd like to buy a T-shirt for my sister. She's eleven years old.
>
> M: (A)이 빨간색 티셔츠는 어떠세요? This character is quite popular among children.
>
> W: Well, ⓒshe likes animation characters that much. Can I see the blue one?
>
> M: You mean this blue striped T-shirt? ⓓIts design is simple and cool.
>
> W: ⓔYes, I think my sister will like it. I'll take it.

05 밑줄 친 ⓐ~ⓔ 중 흐름상 또는 어법상 어색한 것을 고르시오.

① ⓐ   ② ⓑ   ③ ⓒ   ④ ⓓ   ⑤ ⓔ

06 밑줄 친 (A)의 우리말과 일치하도록 주어진 단어를 이용하여 영작하시오. (like, how)

➡ _____

[07~08] 다음 대화를 읽고 물음에 답하시오.

> M: Did you get a new phone, Jamie? It's just like mine.
>
> W: Yeah, I got it last weekend on sale.
>
> M: It was on sale? But it has just been released, hasn't it?

W: Right, but the store on Green Street is having a year-end sale.

M: Oh, I bought mine at full price!

W: Really? That's too bad. They're selling them at a 40 percent discount.

M: (A)I should have checked the sales before buying mine.

07 밑줄 친 (A)의 문장과 바꿔 쓸 수 있는 문장을 주어진 단어를 이용하여 쓰시오.

➡ _____

_____ (regret)

➡ _____

_____ (wish)

08 위 대화의 내용과 일치하지 <u>않는</u> 것을 고르시오.

① 남자는 정가에 전화기를 샀다.
② 여자는 지난 주말에 새 전화기를 샀다.
③ 남자는 할인 판매를 확인했었다.
④ 여자는 남자와 같은 전화기를 샀다.
⑤ 전화기는 출시된 지 얼마 되지 않았다.

[09~10] 다음 대화를 읽고 물음에 답하시오.

M: Hi, Riley. I heard that you bought a laptop online. How do you like it?

W: Oh, I'm not happy with it.

M: Why? What's wrong?

W: It makes too much noise and gets overheated. I (A)_____ have read more reviews.

M: Oh, then you (B)_____ ask for your money back.

W: The online store (C)_____ give me back my money because I've used it for a week.

M: How about calling the online shop and explaining your problem?

W: Yeah, I think I (D)_____ do that.

09 빈칸 (A)~(D)에 들어갈 말을 〈보기〉에서 골라 쓰시오. (중복 사용가능)

┌── 보기 ──┐
should   shouldn't   will   won't
└─────────────┘

➡ (A) _____   (B) _____
(C) _____   (D) _____

10 위 대화의 내용과 일치하지 <u>않는</u> 것을 고르시오.

① Riley가 산 노트북은 소음이 심하고 과열이 된다.
② Riley는 새로 산 노트북이 문제가 있어 마음에 들어 하지 않는다.
③ 남자는 전화해서 문제를 설명하라고 Riley에게 조언해 주었다.
④ Riley는 온라인으로 노트북을 샀다.
⑤ Riley는 환불을 받을 수 있을 것이다.

[11~12] 다음 대화를 읽고 물음에 답하시오.

W: ⓐJake, here's a package for you.

M: It's my helmet. I bought it at an online (A)_____ (use) store a few days ago.

W: Oh, open it and let me (B)_____ (see) it.

M: Okay. (pause) Oh, this outer part is a little (C)_____ (break). ⓑThe seller said that it's perfectly fine though.

W: ⓒDidn't you check the pictures of the helmet before you bought it?

M: No, I just trusted the seller. ⓓI must have checked a bit more.

W: ⓔYou should call the seller and ask for a refund.

11 빈칸 (A)~(C)에 괄호 안의 단어를 문맥에 맞게 고쳐 빈칸을 채우시오.

➡ (A) _____ (B) _____ (C) _____

12 밑줄 친 ⓐ~ⓔ 중 흐름상 또는 어법상 어색한 것을 고르시오.

① ⓐ ② ⓑ ③ ⓒ ④ ⓓ ⑤ ⓔ

13 다음 문장에 공통으로 들어갈 알맞은 말을 고르시오. (대·소문자 구분 안 함.)

• _____ you go up a mountain, it gets cooler.
• Treat me _____ a friend.
• Leave the documents _____ they are.

① when ② since ③ as
④ that ⑤ if

[14~15] 다음 우리말에 맞게 주어진 어휘를 활용하여 영작하시오.

14

우리가 땅을 만들기 위해서 더 많은 나무를 베어 냄에 따라, 더 많은 숲들이 지구에서 사라진다. (forests, trees, land, make, disappear, cut, on Earth, to)

➡ _____

_____

15

여러분의 몸이 소비하는 힘의 3분의 1은 여러분이 먹는 음식으로부터 나옵니다. (the power, food, consume, come, from, eat)

➡ _____

_____

[16~19] 다음 글을 읽고 물음에 답하시오.

Why do I buy things just because they are on sale?

Nathan goes window shopping and sees a pair of headphones. He checks the price and finds out that they are $200. He thinks that the headphones are too (A)_____. The sales person approaches him and says, "You can get a 20 percent discount on those headphones." Even though the discounted price is still not very low, Nathan decides to buy the headphones.

The situation described above is an example of the "anchoring effect." The price mentioned first affects our opinion of prices mentioned afterwards. For example, if we start with $200, then $160 will seem cheap in comparison. Furthermore, as the difference of the two prices becomes bigger, the effect will be more powerful. As such, the price mentioned first acts as an "anchor" that fixes our thoughts about the price of an item.

16 빈칸 (A)에 들어갈 말로 적절한 것을 모두 고르시오.

① costly ② pricy ③ low
④ bargain ⑤ expensive

17 How much is the discounted price of the headphones?

➡ _____

18 What acts as an anchor that fixes our thoughts about the price of an item?

➡ _____

19 위 글의 내용을 바르게 이해한 사람은?

① Ann: Like Nathan, I buy things just because they are famous among friends.

② Kirl: Nathan will buy the headphones whether or not they are on sale.

③ Lisa: The price acting as an anchor here is the discounted price.

④ Paul: The price mentioned later makes the price mentioned first seem more expensive.

⑤ Jake: The effect will be more influential if Nathan gets a 10 percent discount on the headphones.

[20~21] 다음 글을 읽고 물음에 답하시오.

Why do I want to buy what my friends bought?

Jeff goes to the shopping center and sees a pair of soccer shoes on display. He recognizes the shoes at a glance because more than half of the boys on his soccer team wear them. Although he already has many pairs of soccer shoes, he ends up buying another new pair.

We can use the "bandwagon effect" to explain Jeff's behavior. A bandwagon is a wagon in a parade that encourages people to jump aboard and enjoy the music. As more and more people get on the bandwagon, others are more likely to (A)_____. In this way, people tend to buy something just because other people have bought it.

20 위 글의 흐름상 빈칸 (A)에 들어갈 말로 가장 적절한 것은?

① get off or take off from it

② jump on or fight off each other

③ get on or follow it

④ move on and find other wagons

⑤ come along and get ahead of it

21 다음 중 밴드왜건 효과의 영향을 받은 사람은?

① Andrea: I bought another new sweater to complete my new look.

② Paul: I bought a yellow shirt to look fancier than other friends.

③ Chris: I bought a bike because it was on sale.

④ Dave: I bought several notes because I needed them.

⑤ Ethan: I bought a laptop computer because most of my friends have one.

[22~23] 다음 글을 읽고 물음에 답하시오.

What made Lisa search for new items immediately after buying a new coat?

(A) Soon after receiving the gift, he noticed that all of his furniture did not go well with his new gown.

(B) The "Diderot effect" may explain it. Denis Diderot, a French writer, received a new gown as a gift.

(C) So, he ended up replacing most of it. The Diderot effect, therefore, is the concept that purchasing a new item often leads to more unplanned purchases.

22 자연스러운 글이 되도록 (A)~(C)를 바르게 나열하시오.

➡ _____

23 위 글의 내용에 맞게 빈칸에 들어갈 말이 바르게 짝지어진 것은?

The "Diderot effect"explains that there can be _____ because of _____.

① planned purchases – their expectancy

② unexpected expenditures – one new item

③ unplanned purchases – their greed

④ careful expenditures – their carefulness

⑤ unplanned explorations – one new item

Lesson

8

Wonders of Space Travel

 의사소통 기능

- 어떤 일이 실제로 가능한지 묻기
  A: Is it possible to lie down to sleep in space?
  B: Yes, it is.
- 이루어지기를 바라는 일 표현하기
  A: I wish I could have a pet robot.
  B: Me, too.

 언어 형식

- 가정법 과거
  If such wormholes **existed** in space, we **could get** to somewhere!

- 'with + 명사 + 분사'
  Wormholes may contain two mouths, **with a throat connecting** the two.

교과서

Words & Expressions

Key Words

- **achieve** [ətʃíːv] 동 달성하다, 성취하다
- **apply** [əplái] 동 적용하다, 응용하다
- **as** [əz] 접 ~(이)듯이, ~(이)다시피
- **astronaut** [ǽstrənɔ̀ːt] 명 우주 비행사
- **attach** [ətǽtʃ] 동 붙이다
- **bend** [bend] 동 굽히다, 구부리다
- **bottom** [bátəm] 명 맨 아랫부분, 바닥
- **celebrate** [séləbrèit] 동 축하하다
- **changeable** [tʃéindʒəbl] 형 바뀔 수 있는, 변덕스러운
- **connect** [kənékt] 동 연결되다, 이어지다
- **contain** [kəntéin] 동 ~이 들어 있다, 포함하다
- **cotton candy** 솜사탕
- **crush** [krʌʃ] 동 눌러 부수다, 찌부러뜨리다
- **detect** [ditékt] 동 감지하다, 발견하다
- **distance** [dístəns] 명 거리
- **dot** [dɑt] 명 점
- **eatable** [íːtəbl] 형 먹을 수 있는
- **eventually** [ivéntʃuəli] 부 결국
- **exist** [igzíst] 동 존재하다
- **exploration** [èkspləréiʃən] 명 탐사, 탐구
- **extend** [iksténd] 동 (팔, 다리를) 뻗다
- **gravity** [grǽvəti] 명 중력
- **impossible** [impásəbl] 형 불가능한
- **incorrect** [ìnkərékt] 형 부정확한, 사실이 아닌
- **infinite** [ínfənət] 형 무한한
- **instantly** [ínstəntli] 부 즉시
- **layer** [léiər] 명 층
- **lean** [liːn] 동 몸을 숙이다, 굽히다
- **lower** [lóuər] 동 낮추다
- **Mars** [mɑːrz] 명 화성
- **measure** [méʒər] 동 측정하다
- **ongoing** [ɔngóuiŋ] 형 계속 진행 중인
- **passenger** [pǽsəndʒər] 명 승객, 탑승객
- **persistent** [pərsístənt] 형 끈질긴, 집요한, 지속적인
- **physics** [fíziks] 명 물리학
- **planet** [plǽnit] 명 행성
- **punch** [pʌntʃ] 동 구멍을 뚫다
- **researcher** [risə́ːrtʃər] 명 연구자, 조사자
- **root** [ruːt] 명 뿌리
- **shortcut** [ʃɔ́ːrtkət] 명 지름길
- **spaceship** [speisʃip] 명 우주선
- **sunrise** [sʌ́nraiz] 명 일출
- **surface** [sə́ːrfis] 명 표면
- **telescope** [téləskòup] 명 망원경
- **theory** [θíːəri] 명 이론, 학설
- **throat** [θrout] 명 목구멍
- **tough** [tʌf] 형 힘든, 어려운
- **unstable** [ənstéibəl] 형 불안정한
- **vast** [væst] 형 거대한, 광대한
- **waterless** [wɔ́ːtərlis] 형 물기 없는
- **weigh** [wei] 동 무게가 나가다
- **wipe** [waip] 동 닦다
- **worm** [wəːrm] 명 벌레
- **wormhole** [wə́ːrmhoul] 명 벌레 먹은 구멍, (우주의) 웜홀

Key Expressions

- **according to~** ~에 따르면
- **at first** 처음에는
- **at the bottom of ~** ~의 아래에
- **at the speed of ~** ~의 속도로
- **balance on ~** 위에서 균형을 잡다
- **be expected to+동사원형** ~가 …할 것으로 예상되다
- **billions of** 수십억의
- **different from** ~와 다른
- **far away from** ~에서 멀리 떨어져
- **figure out** ~을 알아내다, 생각해 내다
- **float around** 떠다니다
- **for a second** 잠시
- **in theory** 이론상으로는, 원칙상으로는
- **in the blink of an eye** 눈 깜박할 사이에
- **lie down** 눕다, 누워 있다
- **look back on** ~을 되돌아보다
- **match up** 맞추다
- **natural resources** 천연 자원
- **print out** (프린터로) 출력하다
- **such+a[an]+형용사+명사** 그렇게 ~한
- **too ~ to+동사원형** 너무 ~해서 …할 수 없다
- **Who knows**? 혹시 모르지, 어쩌면.

Word Power

※ 서로 비슷한 뜻을 가진 어휘
- □ **achieve** 달성하다, 성취하다 – **accomplish** 이루다, 성취하다
- □ **celebrate** 축하하다 – **commemorate** 기념하다, 축하하다
- □ **detect** 감지하다, 발견하다 – **discover** 발견하다, 알아채다
- □ **extend** (팔, 다리를) 뻗다 – **expand** 확대하다, 팽창하다
- □ **unstable** 불안정한 – **changeable** 변덕스러운
- □ **attach** 붙이다 – **stick** 붙이다
- □ **contain** 포함하다 – **include** 포함하다, 포함시키다
- □ **eatable** 먹을 수 있는 – **edible** 먹을 수 있는
- □ **persistent** 끈질긴, 지속적인 – **continuous** 끊임없는, 연속적인
- □ **vast** 거대한, 광대한 – **huge** 막대한, 거대한

※ 서로 반대의 뜻을 가진 어휘
- □ **attach** 붙이다 ↔ **detach** 떼다, 분리하다
- □ **connect** 연결되다, 이어지다 ↔ **disconnect** 연결을 끊다
- □ **impossible** 불가능한 ↔ **possible** 가능한
- □ **infinite** 무한한 ↔ **finite** 한정의, 유한의
- □ **unstable** 불안정한 ↔ **stable** 안정된
- □ **bottom** 맨 아랫부분, 바닥 ↔ **top** 꼭대기, 정상
- □ **eatable** 먹을 수 있는 ↔ **inedible** 먹을 수 없는
- □ **incorrect** 부정확한, 사실이 아닌 ↔ **correct** 맞는, 정확한
- □ **tough** 힘든, 어려운 ↔ **easy** 쉬운, 수월한
- □ **vast** 거대한, 광대한 ↔ **tiny** 아주 조그마한, 작은

※ 접두사 im-[in-]
- □ im- + partial → **impartial** 공정한
- □ im- + possible → **impossible** 불가능한
- □ im- + patient → **impatient** 안달하는
- □ in- + active → **inactive** 활발하지 않은, 소극적인

※ 접미사 -able
- □ comfort + -able → **comfortable** 편안한
- □ account + -able → **accountable** 셀 수 있는
- □ desire + -able → **desirable** 바람직한, 가치 있는
- □ compare + -able → **comparable** 비슷한, 비교할 만한
- □ avail + -able → **available** 사용가능한
- □ reason + -able → **reasonable** 합리적인
- □ rely + -able → **reliable** 신뢰할 만한

English Dictionary

□ **achieve** 달성하다, 성취하다
→ to succeed in finishing something or reaching an aim, especially after a lot of work or effort
특히 어떤 일이나 노력 후에 일을 끝내거나 목적을 달성하는 데 성공하다

□ **connect** 연결되다, 이어지다
→ to join or be joined with something else
다른 어떤 것과 합치거나 합쳐지다

□ **detect** 감지하다, 발견하다
→ to notice something that is partly hidden or not clear, or to discover something, especially using a special method
부분적으로 숨겨져 있거나 명확하지 않은 것을 알게 되거나 혹은 특히 특별한 방법을 통해 무언가를 발견하다

□ **distance** 거리
→ the amount of space between two places
두 장소 사이의 공간의 총계

□ **exploration** 탐사, 탐구
→ the activity of searching and finding out about something
어떤 것에 대하여 탐색하고 알아내는 활동

□ **gravity** 중력
→ the force that attracts objects towards one another, especially the force that makes things fall to the ground
물체를 서로 당기는 힘으로, 특히 사물을 땅으로 떨어지게 하는 힘

□ **ongoing** 계속 진행 중인
→ continuing to exist or develop, or happening at the present moment
현재 계속 존재하거나 전개되고 있는 혹은 일어나고 있는

□ **planet** 행성
→ an extremely large, round mass of rock and metal, such as Earth, or of gas, such as Jupiter, that moves in a circular path around the sun or another star
태양이나 다른 별 주위를 순환하는, 지구 같은 바위와 금속으로 이루어진 혹은 목성 같은 가스로 이루어진 광장히 크고 둥근 것

□ **unstable** 불안정한
→ not solid and firm and therefore not strong, safe, or likely to last
단단하거나 견고하지 않아서 강하거나 안전하거나 오래 지속될 것 같지 않는

□ **vast** 거대한, 광대한
→ extremely big 굉장히 큰

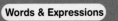

01 다음 중 접두사 -in의 의미가 <u>다른</u> 하나를 고르시오.

① infinite   ② incorrect

③ insecure   ④ insight

⑤ inexpensive

02 다음 짝지어진 단어의 관계가 〈보기〉와 같은 것끼리 짝지어진 것을 고르시오.

┌─── 보기 ───┐
vast – huge
└───────────┘

ⓐ achieve – accomplish
ⓑ persistent – occasional
ⓒ tough – easy
ⓓ bottom – top
ⓔ attach – stick

① ⓐ, ⓑ   ② ⓑ, ⓒ   ③ ⓒ, ⓓ
④ ⓓ, ⓔ   ⑤ ⓐ, ⓔ

03 다음 밑줄 친 부분의 의미로 알맞지 <u>않은</u> 것은?

① A <u>wormhole</u> can connect two different universes. ((우주의) 웜홀)

② There are many <u>theories</u> about why the dinosaurs went extinct. (이론, 학설)

③ They <u>stick</u> a tube into a water pack, and drink it. (막대기)

④ Every <u>passenger</u> must wear a seatbelt. (승객)

⑤ Earth is the third closest <u>planet</u> to the sun. (행성)

04 빈칸 (A)~(C)에 들어갈 말이 바르게 짝지어진 것을 고르시오.

┌─────────────────────────────────────┐
│ • How is life in space different (A)_____ │
│   that on Earth? │
│ • (B)_____ theory, wormholes exist. │
│ • What did Einstein figure (C)_____ │
│   about space and time? │
└─────────────────────────────────────┘

    (A)   (B)   (C)
① in   In   of
② in   About   out
③ from   In   out
④ from   About   of
⑤ from   On   of

05 다음 문장의 빈칸을 〈보기〉에 있는 어휘로 채울 수 <u>없는</u> 것을 고르시오.

┌─── 보기 ───┐
bend   connect   detect   punch
└───────────┘

① Beetles _____ their way by the stars.

② The point of SNS is to _____ with other people.

③ You should _____ your back to stretch your muscles.

④ This belt is too big, so I'll _____ an extra hole in it.

⑤ Instant noodles _____ a lot of salt.

01 다음 빈칸에 공통으로 들어갈 접미사를 쓰시오.

> • The food is eat_____ but not good.
> • The rules are very change_____.

02 다음 〈보기〉에서 알맞은 단어를 골라 빈칸에 쓰시오. (형태 변화 가능, 한 단어는 한 번만 사용 가능.)

┌─ 보기 ─┐
bottom   dot   layer   surface
└──────┘

(1) You can see a small black dot on the sun's _____.

(2) Mom removed the outer _____ of the onion.

(3) Thanks to their beaks, dolphins can hunt for fish at the _____ of the sea.

(4) My new skirt was blue with white _____.

03 다음 주어진 우리말에 맞게 빈칸을 채우시오. (철자가 주어진 경우 주어진 철자로 시작할 것.)

(1) 일기예보에 따르면 오늘 밤에는 기온이 영하로 내려간다고 한다.

➡ _____ the weather forecast, it'll freeze tonight.

(2) 우리 집은 공항에서 멀리 떨어져 있다.

➡ My home is f_____ a_____ f_____ an airport.

(3) 이 열기구를 타면, 너는 이 도시 전체를 떠다닐 수 있다.

➡ If you take this hot-air balloon, you can _____ the whole city.

(4) 유성은 눈 깜박할 사이에 떨어진다.

➡ Shooting stars fall _____.

(5) 그녀는 곧 그녀의 유럽 순회공연을 되돌아볼 필요가 있다.

➡ She needs to _____ her European tour soon.

04 다음 빈칸에 공통으로 들어갈 말을 쓰시오.

> • Even _____ the Hunminjeongum was mentioned in many books, no one knows where it really was.
> • _____ we eat the food before he comes back, he will be mad.

05 다음 빈칸에 들어갈 말을 〈보기〉에서 찾아 쓰시오.

┌─ 보기 ─┐
changeable   eatable   impossible incorrect
└──────┘

(1) The food at that restaurant isn't _____.

(2) You can't pass the test with so many _____ answers.

(3) It is _____ to live without water.

(4) The weather in London is very _____.

Conversation

① **어떤 일이 실제로 가능한지 묻기**

> **A:** Is it possible to lie down to sleep in space? 우주에서 누워 자는 게 가능할까요?
>
> **B:** Yes, it is. Astronauts attach their sleeping bag to a wall. 그럼요. 우주비행사들은 침낭을 벽에 붙여요.

■ 어떤 일이 실제로 가능한지 묻는 표현으로 'Is it possible to ~?'를 쓸 수 있다. 같은 표현으로 'Are we able to ~?', 'Can we actually ~?', 'Is there a possibility that 주어+동사 ~?', 'Would it be possible ~?' 등이 있다.

■ Is it possible for the astronauts to lie down to sleep in space?
  = Are the astronauts able to lie down to sleep in space?
  = Can the astronauts actually lie down to sleep in space?
  = Is there a possibility that the astronauts lie down to sleep in space?
  = Would it be possible for the astronauts to lie down to sleep in space?

어떤 일이 실제로 가능한지 묻기

- Is it possible to 동사원형 ~?
- Are 주어 able to 동사원형 ~?
- Can 주어 (actually) 동사 ~?
- Is there a possibility that 주어+동사 ~?
- Would it be possible ~?

핵심 Check

1. 다음 대화의 밑줄 친 부분과 바꿔 쓸 수 <u>없는</u> 것은?

> **A:** <u>Is it possible to drink water in space?</u>
> **B:** Yes, it is. Astronauts stick a tube into a water pack and drink it.

① Are astronauts able to drink water in space?

② Can astronauts actually drink water in space?

③ Is there a possibility that astronauts drink water in space?

④ Would it be possible for astronauts to drink water in space?

⑤ Could astronauts drink water in space?

② 이루어지기를 바라는 일 표현하기

A: I wish I could have a pet robot. 애완 로봇이 있으면 참 좋겠다.

B: Me, too. I'm sure that's every teenager's wish. 나도 그래. 그건 모든 10대들의 꿈일 거야.

■ 어떤 일이 이루어지기를 바라는 표현으로 'I wish I could ~.'를 쓸 수 있다. 이는 가능성이 낮거나 이루어지기 힘든 일에 대해 '할 수 있으면 좋겠다'라는 바람의 의미로 쓰인다. 같은 표현으로 '~ would be a dream come true.', 'How I wish I could ~!', 'It would be great if I could ~.' 등이 있다.

■ I wish I could have a pet robot.
  = Having a pet robot would be a dream come true.
  = It would be great if I could have a pet robot.
  = How I wish I could have a pet robot!

이루어지기를 바라는 일 표현하기

  • I wish I could ~.
  • ~ would be a dream come true.
  • It would be great if 주어 could ~.

■ I wish I could ~. vs. I hope I can ~.
  두 표현은 바라는 일을 나타내는 비슷한 의미로 이해할 수 있지만 'I wish I could ~.'는 가정법, 즉 실제로는 일어날 수 없는 일에 대한 바람과 소망을 나타내는 반면에, 'I hope I can ~.'은 실제로 일어날 가능성이 있는 일에 대한 바람과 소망을 나타낸다는 차이가 있다.

  • I wish I could live up to 200 years old.
  • I hope I will be able to buy that house some day.

핵심 Check

2. 다음 대화의 밑줄 친 부분을 영작한 문장으로 적절하지 <u>않은</u> 것은?

> A: 난 수학 천재가 되었으면 좋겠어.
> B: Me, too. I'm sure you could if you study hard.

① Being a math genius would be a dream come true.

② It would be great if I could be a math genius.

③ I thought I could be a math genius.

④ I wish I could be a math genius.

⑤ How I wish I could be a math genius!

 Listen & Talk 1 A-1

M: Welcome back to Earth, Irene. What was your favorite part about ❶ being in the space station?

W: I could see a beautiful ❷sunrise 16 times a day. It was great.

M: ❸Is it possible to see the sunrise several times a day in space?

W: Yes, ❹it's possible because we moved around Earth every 90 minutes in the station.

M: Wow, that's amazing!

M: 지구에 돌아오신 것을 환영합니다. Irene 씨. 우주 정거장에서 보낸 시간 중 최고의 기억이 무엇인가요?

W: 저는 하루에 16번씩 아름다운 일출을 볼 수 있었어요. 그것은 굉장했죠.

M: 우주에서는 하루에 일출을 여러 번 보는 게 가능한가요?

W: 네, 가능해요. 왜냐하면 우주 정거장이 지구 주위를 90분마다 돌았거든요.

M: 와, 놀랍네요!

---

❶ 전치사 about 다음에는 명사나 동명사가 올 수 있다. be동사 다음에 장소를 나타내는 부사구가 오면 '있다, 존재하다'의 의미로 해석한다.

❷ sunrise: 일출(↔ sunset: 일몰)

❸ 'Is it possible to 동사원형 ~?'은 '~하는 것이 가능한가요?'의 의미로 상대방에게 가능성을 묻는 표현이다. possible 대신에 likely, probable을 사용할 수 있다. 같은 의미로 'Are 주어 able to 동사원형 ~?', 'Can 주어 (actually) 동사 ~?', 'Is there a possibility that 주어+동사 ~?', 'Would it be possible ~?' 등이 있다.

❹ 'It is possible[likely/probably] ~.' 등을 사용해 가능성 정도를 표현할 수 있다.

Check(√) True or False

(1) Irene has been to the space station. T ☐ F ☐

(2) At the space station, Irene could see a sunrise only twice a day. T ☐ F ☐

Listen & Talk 2 A-1

M: Look at these colorful pictures of the universe.

W: Oh, ❶they're beautiful. ❷I wish I could see Earth from space with my own eyes.

M: Actually, you can ❸do that at the National Youth Space Center.

W: Really?

M: Yeah, you can use the VR glasses. ❹I heard that you ❺feel like you are actually in space!

M: 이 다채로운 색깔의 우주 사진들을 좀 봐.

W: 오, 그것들은 아름다워. 내가 지구를 우주에서 직접 내 눈으로 볼 수 있으면 좋을 텐데.

M: 사실 넌 국립 청소년 우주 센터에서 그걸 해 볼 수 있어.

W: 정말?

M: 응, 가상 현실(VR) 안경을 써 볼 수 있거든. 실제로 우주에 있는 것 같은 기분이 든다고 들었어!

---

❶ they는 앞 문장의 'these colorful pictures of the universe(다채로운 색깔의 우주 사진들)'을 의미한다.

❷ 'I wish I could ~.'는 '내가 ~할 수 있으면 좋겠다.'의 뜻으로 현재 사실과 반대되거나 현재 이룰 수 없는 소망을 말할 때 사용한다. '~ would be a dream come true.', 'It would be great if 주어 could ~.'등으로 바꿔 쓸 수 있다.

❸ do that은 앞 문장의 'see Earth from space with your own eyes'를 받는다.

❹ 'I heard that 주어+동사 ~.'는 '~에 대해 들었다'의 뜻으로 알고 있거나 들은 것에 대해 말할 때 쓰는 표현이다.

❺ feel like 다음에는 동명사나 절이 올 수 있다. 여기서는 주어와 동사가 있는 절의 형식이 like 다음에 왔다. '~ 같이 느끼다, ~ 같은 기분이 든다'의 의미이다.

Check(√) True or False

(3) They are looking at the pictures of the universe. T ☐ F ☐

(4) People can see Earth from space by using the VR glasses at the National Youth Space Center. T ☐ F ☐

Listen & Talk 1 A-2

M: Irene, what was the best food ❶you ate in the space station?

W: Hmm... . ❷We grew some vegetables and ate them every day. They were ❸pretty fresh and tasty!

M: Wow, ❹is it possible to grow vegetables in the space station?

W: Yes. ❺Since there's no gravity in space, we had to grow them in special bags. The bags ❻helped the roots to grow.

M: How interesting!

M: Irene 씨, 우주 정거장에서 드셨던 것 중 최고의 음식은 무엇이었나요?

W: 음… . 우리는 채소를 키워서 매일 그걸 먹었어요. 그것은 매우 신선하고 맛있었어요!

M: 와, 우주 정거장에서 채소를 키우는 것이 가능한가요?

W: 네. 우주에는 중력이 없기 때문에, 우리는 그것을 특수한 봉지 안에서 키워야 했어요. 그 봉지는 뿌리가 자라는 데 도움을 줬어요.

M: 참 흥미롭네요!

❶ the best food와 you ate 사이에 목적격 관계대명사 which나 that이 생략되어 있다.

❷ grew와 ate는 접속사 and로 연결되어 있다. them은 vegetables를 의미한다.

❸ pretty는 부사로 '매우'의 의미이며 형용사인 fresh(신선한)와 tasty(맛있는)를 수식하고 있다.

❹ 'Is it possible to 동사원형 ~?'은 무언가가 가능한지 여부를 묻는 표현으로 'Is it possible that 주어+동사 ~?'로 바꿔 쓸 수 있다.

❺ since는 이유의 접속사로 '~ 때문에'라고 해석하며 because나 as로 바꿔 쓸 수 있다.

❻ 'help+목적어+목적격보어'는 '~에게 …하도록 도움을 주다'이며 목적어와 목적격보어의 관계가 능동일 때 목적격보어에는 동사원형이나 to부정사가 올 수 있다.

Check(√) True or False

(5) In the space staion, Irene couldn't eat vegetables at all.　　T ☐ F ☐

(6) It was possible that Irene grow vegetables in the space station.　　T ☐ F ☐

 Listen & Talk 2 C

A: ❶I wish I could have a pet robot.

B: Me, too. ❷I'm sure that's every teenager's wish.

A: 난 애완 로봇을 가질 수 있으면 좋을 텐데.

B: 나도. 나는 그것이 모든 십대들의 바람이라고 확신해.

❶ 현재 사실과 반대되는 일에 대한 소망이나 유감을 나타낼 때 'I wish+주어+could+동사원형 ~.'으로 쓰며 '~라면 좋을 텐데'라고 해석한다. 'I wish+주어+동사의 과거형 ~.'으로도 나타내며 be동사는 보통 were를 쓴다. 바꿔 쓸 수 있는 표현으로 '~ would be a dream come true.', 'It would be great if 주어 could ~.' 등이 있다.

❷ '나는 ~라고 확신해.'라는 뜻으로 어떤 일에 대한 확신을 표현할 때, 'I'm sure (that) ~.' 또는 'I'm sure about ~.'라고 한다. 접속사 that 다음에는 절이, 전치사 about 다음에는 명사(구)가 오고, that은 생략할 수 있다.

Check(√) True or False

(7) A wants to have a pet robot.　　T ☐ F ☐

(8) B isn't interested in a pet robot.　　T ☐ F ☐

Listen & Talk 1 B

M: ❶Have you heard that NASA is going to send a 3D printer into space?

W: They're going to send a 3D printer into space? Why?

M: ❷I've heard that the 3D printer will ❸be used to print out food for astronauts.

W: ❹Is it possible to print out food using a 3D printer?

M: Yes, it's possible. It can print out a fresh pizza in ❺less than five minutes.

W: Really? ❻I wonder what it would taste like.

❶ 'Have you heard that 주어+동사 ~?'는 '~를 들어 본 적 있니?'의 의미로 알고 있는지 묻는 표현이다.

❷ 'I've heard that ~.'은 '~에 대해 들었다.'의 뜻으로 알고 있거나 들은 것에 대해 말할 때 쓰는 표현이다.

❸ be used to+동사원형: ~하기 위해 사용되다 print out: (프린터로) 출력하다 astronaut: 우주 비행사

❹ 'Is it possible to+동사원형 ~?'은 '~하는 것이 가능한가요?'라는 의미로 가능 여부를 물을 때 사용하는 표현이다.

❺ less than: ~보다 적은

❻ 궁금증을 표현할 때 '~를 궁금해 하다'라는 의미를 가진 동사 wonder를 이용하여 'I wonder ~.'라고 말한다. I wonder 뒤에는 간접의문문의 어순인 '의문사+주어+동사'를 사용한다.

Listen & Talk 1 C

A: ❶Is it possible to lie down to sleep in space?

B: Yes, astronauts ❷attach their sleeping bag to a wall.

A: Sounds interesting. Life in space is so ❸different from ❹that on Earth.

❶ 'Is it possible to+동사원형 ~?'은 무언가가 가능한지 여부를 묻는 표현이다. lie down: 눕다, 누워 있다

❷ attach A to B: A를 B에 붙이다

❸ different from: ~와 다른

❹ that은 life를 받는 지시대명사이다.

Listen & Talk 2 B

W: Look at this man, Jake. He lived in space for one year.

M: It ❶must have been tough for him.

W: Right, but you know what's interesting? He grew 2 inches ❷while in space.

M: Really? How is that possible?

W: I'm not sure, but maybe it's because there's no gravity in space.

M: That's so cool. ❸I wish I could live in space. That way, I could become taller.

W: ❹I'm sure there are other ways ❺to become taller than going to space.

❶ 'must have+과거분사'는 과거 사실에 대한 강한 추측을 나타내는 표현으로 '~이었음에 틀림이 없다'라는 의미를 가진다.

❷ while (he was) in space로 접속사 while 다음에 '주어와 be동사'가 생략되어 있다.

❸ 'I wish I could ~.'는 소망이나 바람을 나타낼 때 사용하는 표현으로 '내가 ~할 수 있다면 좋을 텐데.'라는 뜻이다. 'I wish+가정법 과거'의 형태로 현재 사실과 반대되는 소망을 나타낸다.

❹ 어떤 일에 대해 확실한 의견이 있을 때 'I'm sure (that) 주어+동사 ~.'로 말할 수 있다.

❺ to become은 other ways를 수식하고 있으므로 '키가 더 커지는 다른 방법들'로 해석한다. (to부정사의 형용사적 용법)

Communication Step A

W: Hello, everyone, welcome to *All about Movies*! Today, we're going to talk about the top three things from movies ❶that we wish were real.

M: Let's start with number three, the flying skateboard from *Back to the Future*.

W: It's a cool item. ❷I wish I could have a flying skateboard.

M: Actually, ❸I read somewhere that this is not entirely impossible.

W: Really? ❹Is it actually possible to fly on a skateboard?

M: Yes. Some companies have ❺applied physics to create flying skateboards.

❶ that은 주격 관계대명사로 선행사는 the top three things from movies이다.

❷ 현재 사실과 반대되는 일에 대한 소망이나 유감을 나타낼 때 'I wish+주어+could+동사원형 ~.'으로 쓰며 '~라면 좋을 텐데'라고 해석한다. 'I wish+주어+동사의 과거형 ~.'으로도 나타내며 be동사는 보통 were를 쓴다.

❸ somewhere는 부사로 '어딘가에서'의 의미이며, read의 목적어로 that절이 사용되었다.

❹ 'Is it possible to+동사원형 ~?'은 '~하는 것은 가능한가요?'라는 의미로 가능 여부를 물을 때 사용하는 표현이다.

❺ apply: 적용하다, 응용하다

● 다음 우리말과 일치하도록 빈칸에 알맞은 말을 쓰시오.

Listen & Talk 1 A

1. **M:** Welcome back _____ Earth, Irene. _____ was your favorite part about _____ in the space station?

   W: I _____ _____ a beautiful sunrise 16 _____ _____ _____. It was great.

   M: _____ _____ _____ _____ _____ the sunrise several times _____ _____ in space?

   W: Yes, it's _____ _____ we moved around Earth every 90 minutes in the station.

   M: Wow, that's _____!

2. **M:** Irene, what was _____ _____ in the space station?

   W: Hmm… . We _____ some vegetables and _____ them every day. They were pretty _____ _____ _____!

   M: Wow, _____ _____ _____ _____ _____ vegetables in the space station?

   W: Yes. _____ there's no gravity in space, we _____ _____ grow them in special bags. The bags _____ _____ _____ grow.

   M: How interesting!

Listen & Talk 1 B

M: _____ _____ _____ _____ NASA is going to _____ a 3D printer into space?

W: They're going to send a 3D printer _____ _____? Why?

M: _____ _____ the 3D printer _____ _____ _____ _____ _____ _____ food for astronauts.

W: Is it _____ _____ _____ _____ food using a 3D printer?

M: Yes, it's possible. It can print out a fresh pizza _____ _____ _____ five minutes.

W: Really? I wonder _____ _____ _____ _____ _____.

해석

1. **M:** 지구에 돌아오신 것을 환영합니다, Irene 씨. 우주 정거장에서 보낸 시간 중 최고의 기억이 무엇인가요?
   W: 저는 하루에 16번씩 아름다운 일출을 볼 수 있었어요. 그것은 굉장했죠.
   M: 우주에서는 하루에 일출을 여러 번 보는 게 가능한가요?
   W: 네, 가능해요. 왜냐하면 우주 정거장이 지구 주위를 90분마다 돌았거든요.
   M: 와, 놀랍네요!

2. **M:** Irene 씨, 우주 정거장에서 드셨던 것 중 최고의 음식은 무엇이었나요?
   W: 음… . 우리는 채소를 키워서 매일 그걸 먹었어요. 그것은 매우 신선하고 맛있었어요!
   M: 와, 우주 정거장에서 채소를 키우는 것이 가능한가요?
   W: 네. 우주에는 중력이 없기 때문에, 우리는 그것을 특수한 봉지 안에서 키워야 했어요. 그 봉지는 뿌리가 자라는 데 도움을 줬어요.
   M: 참 흥미롭네요!

M: 나사(NASA)가 3D 프린터를 우주로 보낼 거라는 이야기 들어 봤니?
W: 그들이 3D 프린터를 우주로 보낸다고? 왜?
M: 우주 비행사들이 먹을 음식을 출력하는 데 3D 프린터가 쓰일 거라고 들었어.
W: 3D 프린터를 이용해 음식을 출력하는 게 가능해?
M: 응, 가능해. 그것은 신선한 피자를 5분도 안 되서 출력해 낼 수 있어.
W: 정말? 그게 어떤 맛일지 궁금하다.

해석

Listen & Talk 2 A

1. **M:** Look at these colorful pictures of the universe.

   W: Oh, they're beautiful. _____ _____ _____ _____ _____ Earth _____ space _____ _____ _____ _____.

   M: Actually, you can _____ _____ at the National Youth Space Center.

   W: Really?

   M: Yeah, you can use the VR glasses. I heard _____ you feel like you are actually _____ _____!

2. **W:** What are you watching?

   M: It's a documentary about life in space. Everything _____ so _____.

   W: Yes, _____ _____ there's _____ _____ in space.

   M: Right. _____ _____ _____ _____ float around like an _____!

   W: Really? I don't. It _____ _____.

1. **M:** 이 다채로운 색깔의 우주 사진들을 좀 봐.
   W: 오, 그것들은 아름다워. 내가 지구를 우주에서 직접 내 눈으로 볼 수 있으면 좋을 텐데.
   M: 사실 넌 국립 청소년 우주 센터에서 그걸 해 볼 수 있어.
   W: 정말?
   M: 응, 가상 현실(VR) 안경을 써 볼 수 있거든. 실제로 우주에 있는 것 같은 기분이 든다고 들었어!

2. **W:** 너는 무엇을 보고 있니?
   M: 우주에서의 삶에 관한 다큐멘터리야. 모든 것이 너무 달라 보여.
   W: 응, 왜냐하면 우주에는 중력이 없기 때문이지.
   M: 맞아. 나도 우주 비행사처럼 떠다닐 수 있다면 좋을 텐데!
   W: 정말이니? 나는 아니야. 그건 불편해 보여.

Listen & Talk 2 B

W: Look at this man, Jake. He _____ _____ space for one year.

M: It _____ _____ _____ _____ for him.

W: Right, but you know what's interesting? He grew 2 inches _____ _____ _____.

M: Really? How is that _____?

W: I'm not sure, but maybe _____ _____ there's no _____ in space.

M: That's so cool. _____ _____ _____ _____ _____ _____ space. That way, I could _____ _____.

W: _____ _____ _____ are other _____ _____ _____ than going to space.

W: 이 남자 좀 봐, Jake. 그는 우주에서 1년 동안 살았어.
M: 그는 분명히 힘들었을 거야.
W: 맞아, 하지만 흥미로운 게 뭔 줄 아니? 그가 우주에 있는 동안 키가 2인치 자랐어.
M: 정말? 어떻게 그게 가능해?
W: 확실하진 않지만, 아마 우주에 중력이 없기 때문일 거야.
M: 정말 멋지다. 내가 우주에서 살 수 있으면 좋을 텐데. 그러면 난 키가 더 커질 수 있을 텐데.
W: 우주에 가는 것 말고 키가 더 커지는 다른 방법들이 있을 거라고 확신해.

Communication Step A

W: Hello, everyone, welcome to *All about Movies*! Today, we're going _____ _____ _____ the top three things from movies _____ _____ _____ _____ _____.

M: Let's _____ _____ number three, the flying skateboard from *Back to the Future*.

W: It's a cool item. _____ _____ _____ _____ _____ a flying skateboard.

M: Actually, I read _____ _____ this is not entirely impossible.

W: Really? _____ _____ _____ _____ _____ _____ on a skateboard?

M: Yes. Some companies _____ _____ physics to create flying skateboards.

W: 안녕하세요, 여러분, '영화에 대한 모든 것(All about Movies)'에 오신 것을 환영합니다! 오늘 우리는 실제로 가능하기를 바라는 영화 속 물건들 중에서 상위 세 개에 관해 이야기해 보려고 합니다.
M: 우선 3위부터 시작하자면, '백 투 더 퓨처'에 나온, 날아다니는 스케이트보드입니다.
W: 멋진 물건이에요. 제가 날아다니는 스케이트보드를 가질 수 있다면 좋을 텐데요.
M: 사실, 전 그것이 전혀 불가능한 일은 아니라고 어딘가에서 읽었어요.
W: 정말요? 스케이트보드를 타고 날아다니는 것이 실제로 가능해요?
M: 네. 몇몇 회사들이 날아다니는 스케이트보드를 만들기 위해 물리학을 적용했어요.

Wrap Up

1. W: Mr. Scott, did you _____ your trip to space?

   M: Yes, it was _____ _____ _____ of my life.

   W: Can you tell us _____ _____ _____ _____ during your trip?

   M: I flew in space _____ _____ and saw our blue planet, Earth.

   W: _____ _____ _____ _____ _____ in space _____ _____?

   M: Yes, I _____ _____ to a special line, so it was safe.

   W: Sounds fantastic!

2. M: Hey, Cindy. I _____ _____ you went to the National Space Center last weekend. _____ was it?

   W: It was great, Chris. I experienced _____ _____ and astronauts' space life.

   M: Sounds fun. Did you meet _____ _____ in person?

   W: Yes, and I heard about their _____ stories.

   M: Oh, I wish I could become an _____ like them and _____ _____.

1. W: Scott 씨, 우주로의 여행은 즐거우셨나요?
   M: 네, 그것은 제 인생 최고의 경험이었어요.
   W: 여행 중 어떤 부분이 최고였는지 말씀해 주실 수 있나요?
   M: 혼자 우주를 날아서 우리의 푸른 행성인 지구를 보았어요.
   W: 우주에서 혼자 나는 것이 가능한가요?
   M: 네, 제 자신을 특수한 선에 연결해서 그건 안전했어요.
   W: 환상적이네요!

2. M: 안녕, Cindy. 지난 주말에 네가 국립 우주 센터에 갔다고 들었어. 어땠어?
   W: 굉장히 좋았어, Chris. 난 무중력 상태와 우주 비행사들의 우주 생활을 경험했어.
   M: 재미있었겠다. 너는 직접 진짜 우주인을 만났어?
   W: 응, 그리고 나는 그들의 모험 이야기를 들었어.
   M: 오, 나는 그들처럼 우주인이 돼서 화성을 탐험하고 싶어.

01 다음 중 의도하는 바가 나머지 넷과 <u>다른</u> 하나를 고르시오.

① I wish I could go to the same high school as my friends.

② If I go to the high school, I will be able to go to the same high school as my friends.

③ Going to the same high school as my friends would be a dream come true.

④ How I wish I could go to the same high school as my friends!

⑤ It would be great if I could go to the same high school as my friends.

[02~03] 다음 대화를 읽고 물음에 답하시오.

M: Welcome back to Earth, Irene. What was your favorite part about being in the space station?

W: I could see a beautiful sunrise 16 times a day. It was great.

M: (A)＿＿＿＿＿＿＿＿＿ see the sunrise several times a day in space?

W: Yes. (B)＿＿＿＿＿＿＿＿＿＿＿＿＿＿＿＿

M: Wow, that's amazing!

02 빈칸 (A)에 알맞은 말을 고르시오.

① Is it possible that　　② Is it necessary to

③ Is it possible to　　④ Is it probably that

⑤ Is it okay if

03 빈칸 (B)에 알맞은 말을 고르시오..

① Astronauts use special toothpaste, and drink it after brushing their teeth.

② Since there's no gravity in space, it's possible.

③ It's possible. It can print out a fresh pizza in less than five minutes.

④ It's possible because we grow vegetables in the space station.

⑤ It's possible because we moved around Earth every 90 minutes in the station.

Conversation 시험대비 실력평가

[01~02] 다음 대화를 읽고 물음에 답하시오.

M: Look at these colorful pictures of the universe.
W: Oh, they're beautiful. I wish (A)_____ _____.
M: Actually, you can do that at the National Youth Space Center.
W: Really?
M: Yeah, you can use the VR glasses. I heard that you feel like you are actually in space!

01 빈칸 (A)에 알맞은 말을 고르시오.

① I can see other pictures of space
② you could use the VR glasses
③ I could see Earth from space with my own eyes
④ you could live in space
⑤ I can be good at all kinds of sports

02 위 대화를 읽고 답할 수 <u>없는</u> 질문을 <u>모두</u> 고르시오.

① Where is the National Youth Space Center?
② What does the woman wish to do?
③ When are they going to the National Youth Space Center?
④ What are they looking at?
⑤ Where can the woman feel like she is actually in the space?

03 다음 중 짝지어진 대화가 <u>어색한</u> 것은?

① A: I wish I had a map of the area.
   B: Don't worry. There is an information desk over there.
② A: I wish I could have the robotic taxi from the movie *Total Recall*.
   B: Actually, I read somewhere that this is not entirely impossible.
③ A: I'm going to visit the museum this Saturday.
   B: I wish I could go there with you.
④ A: What would you do if you made a lot of money?
   B: It is not possible to make a lot of money.
⑤ A: I wish I could see the launch of satellite in person.
   B: So do I.

[04~05] 다음 대화를 읽고 물음에 답하시오.

A: (A)_____? (possible, space, wash, in, it, body, is, their, to)
B: Yes, astronauts use waterless soap, and wipe their body with a wet towel.
A: Sounds interesting. Life in space is so different (B)_____ that on Earth.

서답형
04 빈칸 (A)를 괄호 안에 주어진 단어를 알맞게 배열하여 채우시오.

➡ _____

서답형
05 빈칸 (B)에 알맞은 전치사를 쓰시오.

➡ _____

06 밑줄 친 ⓐ~ⓔ 중 흐름상 <u>어색한</u> 것을 고르시오.

> W: What are you watching?
> M: ⓐIt's a documentary about life in space. ⓑEverything seems so different.
> W: ⓒYes, it's because there's no gravity in space.
> M: Right. ⓓI wish I could float around like an astronaut!
> W: Really? I don't. ⓔIt looks comfortable.

① ⓐ 　② ⓑ 　③ ⓒ 　④ ⓓ 　⑤ ⓔ

[07~09] 다음 대화를 읽고 물음에 답하시오.

> W: Look at this man, Jake. He lived in space for one year.
> M: It (A)_____ tough for him.
> W: Right, but you know what's interesting? He grew 2 inches while in space.
> M: Really? How is that possible?
> W: I'm not sure, but maybe it's because there's no gravity in space.
> M: That's so cool. I wish I could live in space. That way, I could become taller.
> W: I'm sure there are other ways (B)_____ _____.

07 빈칸 (A)에 알맞은 말을 고르시오.

① must have been　② must be
③ should have been　④ should be
⑤ might be

08 빈칸 (B)에 알맞은 말을 고르시오.

① to live in space alone
② to become a famous star
③ to make a spacecraft
④ to become taller than going to space
⑤ to do space exploration

09 대화의 내용과 일치하지 <u>않는</u> 것을 고르시오.

① 남자와 여자가 보고 있는 남자는 우주에서 1년 동안 살았다.
② 남자는 키가 2인치 이상 더 크고 싶어한다.
③ 우주에서 1년 동안 산 남자는 키가 더 커졌다.
④ 남자는 키가 더 커지고 싶어서 우주에서 살기를 바라고 있다.
⑤ 여자는 우주에 있는 동안 키가 커졌던 이유를 중력이 없기 때문이라고 생각하고 있다.

[10~11] 다음 대화를 읽고 물음에 답하시오.

> W: Mr. Scott, did you enjoy your trip to space?
> M: Yes, it was the best experience of my life.
> W: Can you tell us what was the best part during your trip?
> M: I flew in space by myself and (A)_____ (see) our blue planet, Earth.
> W: (B) 우주에서 혼자 나는 것이 가능한가요? (possible, yourself, fly, by, it, space, is, in, to)
> M: Yes, I attached myself to a special line, so it was safe.
> W: Sounds fantastic!

> 서답형

10 다음 괄호 안의 단어를 문맥에 맞게 고쳐 빈칸 (A)를 채우시오.

➡ _____

> 서답형

11 밑줄 친 (B)의 우리말과 일치하도록 괄호 안에 주어진 단어를 알맞게 배열하시오.

➡ _____

Conversation 서술형 시험대비

[01~04] 다음 대화를 읽고 물음에 답하시오.

M: Irene, (A)_____? (우주 정거장에서 드셨던 것 중 최고의 음식은 무엇이었나요? was, ate, the, the, station, what, space, food, in, you, best)

W: Hmm... . We grew some vegetables and ate them every day. They were pretty fresh and tasty!

M: Wow, is it (B)_____ to grow vegetables in the space station?

W: Yes. Since there's no gravity in space, we had to grow (a)them in special bags. The bags helped the roots (C)_____ (grow).

M: How interesting!

01 빈칸 (A)를 우리말에 맞춰 괄호 안에 주어진 단어를 알맞게 배열하시오.

➡ _____

_____

02 위 대화의 내용에 맞게 빈칸 (B)에 알맞은 말을 주어진 철자로 시작하여 쓰시오.

➡ p_____

03 빈칸 (C)를 괄호 안의 단어를 활용하여 채우시오.

➡ _____

04 밑줄 친 (a)them이 가리키는 것을 찾아 쓰시오.

➡ _____

05 밑줄 친 우리말을 주어진 단어를 이용해 영작하시오.

M: Look at these colorful pictures of the universe.

W: Oh, they're beautiful. 내가 지구를 우주에서 직접 내 눈으로 볼 수 있으면 좋을 텐데. (own, could, wish, I, with)

M: Actually, you can do that at the National Youth Space Center.

W: Really?

M: Yeah, you can use the VR glasses. I heard that you feel like you are actually in space!

➡ _____

_____

[06~07] 다음 대화를 읽고 물음에 답하시오.

M: Have you heard that NASA is going to send a 3D printer into space?

W: They're going to send a 3D printer into space? Why?

M: I've heard that the 3D printer will be used (A)_____ out food for astronauts.

W: (B) 3D 프린터를 이용해 음식을 출력하는 게 가능해? (print, using, possible, is, to)

M: Yes, it's possible. It can print out a fresh pizza in less than five minutes.

W: Really? I wonder what it would taste like.

06 빈칸 (A)를 print를 활용하여 채우시오.

➡ _____

07 밑줄 친 (B)의 우리말을 주어진 단어를 이용해 영작하시오.

➡ _____

Grammar

1 가정법 과거

> **If** such wormholes **existed** in space, we **could get** to somewhere! 그런 웜홀들이 우주에 존재한다면, 우리는 어딘가에 빠르게 도달할 수 있을 텐데!

■ '만약 ~한다면 …할 텐데'라는 의미로, 현재 사실을 반대로 가정하거나 실현 가능성이 없는 일에 대해서 가정할 때 쓰며, 'If+주어+were/동사의 과거형 ~, 주어+조동사의 과거형(would/should/could/might)+동사원형 …'의 형태로 쓴다. 가정법이라는 표시로 if절에 과거 동사를 사용할 뿐이며, 가정법 '과거'라고 해서 과거의 일에 반대되는 가정이 아님을 유의한다.

■ 가정법 과거 문장은 현재시제의 직설법으로 바꿔 쓸 수 있다.

- If I **knew** Susan's phone number, I **could** call her. 내가 Susan의 전화번호를 안다면 그녀에게 전화할 텐데. (가정법 과거, 현재 사실의 반대 가정)
  = As I **don't** know Susan's phone number, I **can't** call her. 내가 Susan의 전화번호를 모르기 때문에 그녀에게 전화를 걸 수 없다.
  cf. If I **know** Susan's phone number, I **can** call her. 내가 Susan의 전화번호를 안다면, 그녀에게 전화를 걸 수 있다. (조건문, 사실)

■ 'be' 동사는 주어의 인칭 및 수와 무관하게 'were'를 쓰지만, 구어체에서는 주어가 'I' 또는 3인칭 단수인 경우 'was'를 쓰기도 한다.

- If I **were[was]** a bird, I'**d** fly to you. 내가 새라면 너한테 날아가련만.

■ 가정법의 다양한 표현

- If there **were** no air, we **could** not live even a single day. 공기가 없다면, 우리는 단 하루도 살 수 없을 텐데. (가정법)
  = If it **were** not for air, we **could** not live even a single day.
  = **Were** it not for air, we **could** not live even a single day. (If 생략 후 도치)
  = **But for** air, we **could** not live even a single day. (but for = if it were not for)
  = **Without** air, we **could** not live even a single day. (without = if it were not for)

※ if절의 동사가 'were' 또는 'had'일 때 생략하여 쓸 수 있으며, 이때 주어와 동사가 도치된다.

핵심 Check

1. 다음 괄호 안의 단어를 가정법 문장으로 바르게 배열하시오.

(you, I, I, if, would, looking, were, start, another job, for)

➡ _____

② with + 명사 + 분사

> Wormholes may contain two mouths, **with** a throat **connecting** the two. 웜홀은 두 개의
> 입과 그 둘을 연결하는 목구멍을 지니고 있을 지도 모른다.

■ 의미: '~이 …한 채, ~이 …하면서'라는 뜻으로 동시 동작이나 부가적인 상황을 생생하게 표현할 때 사용한다.
  • The girl ran **with** her hair **blowing** in the wind. (그 소녀는 바람에 머리가 날리면서 뛰어갔다.)
  • Jason thought about the days **with** his eyes **closed**. (Jason은 눈을 감은 채로 그 날들에 대해 생각했다.)
■ 쓰임: 'with+명사+분사'에서, 명사가 분사의 의미상 주어 역할을 한다.
  • Jenny counted the stars **with** her finger **pointing** at each of them. (Jenny는 손가락으로 별들을 하나하나 가리키며 세었다.)
  • She sat **with** her legs **crossed**. (그녀는 다리를 꼬고 앉았습니다.)
■ 명사와 분사가 능동 관계이면 현재 분사를, 수동 관계이면 과거 분사를 쓴다. (명사를 분사의 주어처럼 생각하여 능동과 수동의 관계를 파악한다.)
  • A dog came into the classroom **with** everyone **staring** at him. (개 한 마리가 모두가 쳐다보는 가운데 교실로 들어왔다.) → 모두가 쳐다보고 있으므로 능동 관계
  • Sit comfortably **with** your eyes **closed**. (눈을 감은 채, 편안하게 앉으세요.) → 눈이 감긴 상태이므로 수동 관계
■ 명사와 분사 관계가 수동일 때 쓰이는 과거 분사는 본래 'with+명사+(being+)과거 분사'에서 being이 생략된 형태로 볼 수 있다.
  • He was sitting **with** his arms **(being) folded**. (그는 팔짱을 끼고 앉아 있었다.)

핵심 Check

2. 다음 괄호 안에 주어진 어휘를 빈칸에 알맞게 쓰시오.
  (1) He fell asleep with the TV _____ on. (turn)
  (2) She tried to do the dishes with the baby _____. (cry)

01 다음 각 가정법 문장에서 어법상 <u>어색한</u> 단어를 한 개씩만 찾아 고치시오.

(1) If Paul has money, he could buy a new computer.

_____ ➡ _____

(2) If such wormholes existed in space, we can get to places billions of light-years away quickly!

_____ ➡ _____

(3) If I know her phone number, I would call her.

_____ ➡ _____

(4) I will have nothing to do with him, if I were you.

_____ ➡ _____

02 다음 빈칸에 알맞은 것은?

Julie went to work, _____ her legs broken.

① to   ② at   ③ with

④ during   ⑤ while

03 다음 빈칸에 들어갈 말로 알맞은 것은?

If I _____ you, I would go to bed earlier.

① be   ② am   ③ are

④ were   ⑤ have been

04 괄호 안에 주어진 단어를 활용하여 우리말을 영작할 때 빈칸에 알맞은 말을 쓰시오.

(1) Rachel은 다리를 꼬고 앉았다. (cross)

➡ Rachel sat _____.

(2) Paul은 시원한 바람을 얼굴에 맞으며 자전거를 타고 있다. (the cool wind, blow)

➡ Paul is riding a bike, _____ on his face.

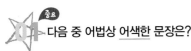

01 다음 중 어법상 어색한 문장은?

① If it were not for the knee injury, he would play.
② If I had wings, I could fly wherever I want.
③ If the weather were nice, I would go hiking.
④ If Lisa studied math a little harder, she will get a good grade.
⑤ If it didn't rain, I would go out to play basketball.

02 다음 중 빈칸에 알맞은 것은?

> Ella is playing the piano with her eyes _____.

① closing   ② closed   ③ close
④ to close   ⑤ are closed

03 다음 문장의 밑줄 친 ①~⑤ 중 어법상 어색한 것은?

> If a spaceship ①fly into a wormhole, it ②might be ③crushed or ④broken into ⑤pieces.

04 다음 중 어법상 어색한 것은?

① Brian was leaning against the wall with his arms folded.
② Julie is riding her bike with her hair blowing in the wind.
③ John spoke with his mouth full.
④ Last night Maryanne fell asleep with the window open.
⑤ John slept with the TV turning on.

05 다음 중 같은 뜻의 문장으로 바르게 바꿔 쓴 것은?

① If I could travel abroad alone, I would take a trip to Africa.
= I can travel abroad alone, so I take a trip to Africa.
② If Emma knew Eric's address, she would send him a letter.
= As Emma didn't know Eric's address, she wouldn't send him a letter.
③ If I had much money, I could help people in need.
= I don't have much money, so I can't help people in need.
④ I would be glad if Chad visited me.
= Chad doesn't visit me, so I will be glad.
⑤ Sumi doesn't have a computer, so she wants to have one.
= Sumi wants to have a computer if she had one.

서답형

06 다음 괄호 안에서 어법상 바른 것을 고르시오.

(1) If I (win / won) the lottery, I would buy the most expensive car.
(2) If he (has / had) a key, he could open the door.
(3) Ellie left the office, with her work (finishing / finished).
(4) The woman was running, with her hair (flying / flown) in the wind.

[07~08] 다음 우리말을 바르게 영작한 것을 고르시오.

07

> 만약 Sam이 일찍 일어나지 않는다면, 커피를 마실 수 없을 텐데.

① If Sam doesn't wake up early, he cannot drink coffee.
② If Sam doesn't wake up early, he could not drink coffee.
③ If Sam didn't wake up early, he could not drink coffee.
④ If Sam didn't wake up early, he cannot drink coffee.
⑤ If Sam hadn't woken up early, he could not have drunk coffee.

08

> Tom은 셔츠를 밖으로 드러낸 채 걸어다니고 있었다.

① Tom was walking around by his shirt hanging out with.
② Tom was walking around with his shirt hanging out.
③ Tom was walking around his shirt with hanging out.
④ Tom was walking around hanging out with his shirt.
⑤ Tom was walking around with his shirt hung out.

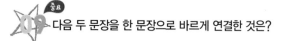 다음 두 문장을 한 문장으로 바르게 연결한 것은?

> • Emma is crying.
> • Tears are running down her face.

① Emma is crying with tears running down her face.
② Emma is crying with tears run down her face.
③ Emma is crying with tears ran down her face.
④ Emma is crying with tears to run down her face.
⑤ Emma is crying with tears runs down her face.

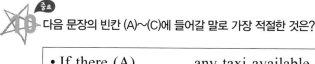 다음 문장의 빈칸 (A)~(C)에 들어갈 말로 가장 적절한 것은?

> • If there (A)＿＿＿＿ any taxi available now, I could take it.
> • Were it not for computers, our lives (B)＿＿＿＿ be very inconvenient.
> • If Harry (C)＿＿＿＿ enough money, he could buy a new bike.

	(A)	(B)	(C)
①	is	could	had
②	is	will	has
③	will be	could	had had
④	were	would	had
⑤	were	will	has

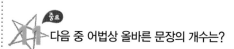 다음 중 어법상 올바른 문장의 개수는?

> ⓐ If I am a famous singer, I would meet my favorite stars.
> ⓑ If Lily had some more money, she can buy a new computer.
> ⓒ If I became a doctor, I could help many people.
> ⓓ If you have super powers, what would you do?
> ⓔ Do not speak with your mouth full.
> ⓕ Mark remembered those days with his eyes closing.
> ⓖ He sat alone, with his arms folding.

① 1개   ② 2개   ③ 3개   ④ 4개   ⑤ 5개

12 다음 문장과 같은 의미의 문장을 고르시오.

> If there were no laws of physics, the world would be crazy.

① The world will be crazy so there are laws of physics.
② There are no laws of physics, so the world won't be crazy.
③ Though there are laws of physics, the world will be crazy.
④ As there are no laws of physics, the world won't be crazy.
⑤ As there are laws of physics, the world won't be crazy.

13 다음 빈칸에 적절하지 <u>않은</u> 것을 고르시오.

> Jake is sitting on the sofa _____.

① with the TV on
② with his eyes closed
③ with his legs crossed
④ with the alarm rung
⑤ with a book in his hand

14 다음 우리말을 영작할 때, 어색한 문장을 고르시오.

> 만일 옥수수가 없다면, 냉동 피자도 없을 텐데.

① But for corn, there would be no frozen pizza.
② If it were not for corn, there would be no frozen pizza.
③ If there are no corn, there would be no frozen pizza.
④ Were it not for corn, there would be no frozen pizza.
⑤ Without corn, there would be no frozen pizza.

서답형
15 with를 이용하여 두 문장을 한 문장으로 고쳐 쓸 때 빈칸에 알맞은 말을 쓰시오.

(1) • My sister was standing in the rain.
  • She folded her umbrella.
  = My sister was standing in the rain
  _____ _____ _____ _____.

(2) • The student entered the library.
  • She was holding a book in her hand.
  = The student entered the library
  _____ _____ _____
  _____ _____.

(3) • Taylor is waiting for a bus.
  • Her hair is blowing in the wind.
  = Taylor is waiting for a bus _____
  _____ _____ _____ in the
  wind.

서답형
16 다음 문장에서 어법상 어색한 부분을 찾아서 한 단어만 고쳐 다시 쓰시오.

(1) If I can travel into the past, I would bring back all the latest technology.
  ➡ _____
  _____

(2) If your coach were here, he will be proud of you.
  ➡ _____
  _____

(3) Andy slept with the door closing.
  ➡ _____

[01~02] 다음 우리말과 일치하도록 괄호 안에 주어진 어구를 바르게 배열하시오.

01

내가 우주에 간다면, 셀피를 찍을 텐데.
(I, I, space, selfie, take, went, would, a, if, to)

➡ _____

02

Chris는 한 쪽 눈을 감은 채 망원경으로 별을 바라보았다.
(Chris, the stars, a telescope, eye, one, looked, closed, through, at, with)

➡ _____
_____

03 다음 문장과 같은 뜻이 되도록 괄호 안에 주어진 어휘를 활용하여 단어 수에 맞게 빈칸을 채우시오.

Without his idleness, he would be a good man.

(1) _____ his idleness, he would be a good man. (it, be, 5 단어)
(2) _____ his idleness, he would be a good man. (it, be, 4 단어)
(3) _____ his idleness, he would be a good man. (there, 4 단어)
(4) _____ his idleness, he would be a good man. (but, 2 단어)
(5) _____ his idleness, he won't be a good man. (as, 3 단어, 직설법으로 쓸 것.)

04 다음 그림을 보고, 주어진 어휘를 이용하여 빈칸을 알맞게 채우시오.

An astronaut is standing on a board with a pizza _____. (hand)

05 다음 그림을 보고, 괄호 안에 주어진 단어를 빈칸에 알맞게 채우시오.

If Sean _____(come) to the party, he could enjoy himself with us.

06 우리말에 맞게 빈칸에 알맞은 말을 쓰시오.

TV를 켠 채로 공부하는 것은 좋지 않다.
= It is not good to study with the TV _____ _____. (2 단어)

07 다음 주어진 문장과 뜻이 같도록 빈칸을 알맞게 채우시오.

> We can't live on a new planet, so we won't live on Dream Planet.
>
> → If we _____ _____ on a new planet, we _____ _____ on Dream Planet.

08 다음 우리말을 괄호 안에 주어진 어구들을 활용하여 영작하시오.

(1) 우리가 달에 산다면, 몸무게가 더 적게 나갈 텐데. (less, live, weigh)

　➡ _____

(2) 만약 우리가 시간이 더 있다면, 너를 도와줄 수 있을 텐데. (have, more time)

　➡ _____

(3) 팔을 뻗은 채, 고개를 바닥으로 숙이세요. (your arms, your head, the ground, lower, stretch, to)

　➡ _____

　_____

(4) Alice는 뺨에 눈물을 흘리며 서 있었다. (her cheeks, was standing, run down)

　➡ _____

　_____

09 다음 글에서 어법상 잘못 쓰인 것을 찾아 알맞게 고치시오. (3곳)

> If we can make a planet for future generations to live on, we will like to make a planet calling Zetopia. It would be a perfect planet for future generations.

➡ _____

10 다음 직설법 문장을 가정법 문장으로 고쳐 쓰시오.

(1) As I am not an architect, I can't build my own house.

　➡ _____

　_____

(2) Since Mom doesn't have an apple, she won't make me apple pie.

　➡ _____

　_____

(3) It doesn't rain, so we will go on a picnic.

　➡ _____

(4) Because she didn't have enough time, she couldn't spend time with us.

　➡ _____

　_____

11 다음 문장에서 어법상 어색한 것을 찾아 바르게 고치시오.

(1) If there is a time machine in real life, I would go to the future.

　➡ _____

(2) If people moved to it, they can communicate with animals on the planet.

　➡ _____

(3) My sister smelled the flower, with her closed eyes.

　➡ _____

(4) Cathy was singing, with the guitar played.

　➡ _____

Wormholes: Fact or Theory?

Sci Teen: Hi, science fans. Today, we're going to talk about space travel. As we all know, there is nothing faster than light in the universe. So, 접속사(~이듯이, ~이다시피) if we travel at the speed of light, we should be able to get to another 조건의 부사절을 이끄는 접속사(~라면) planet in the blink of an eye, right?

Dr. Sci: That would be nice, but space is so vast that it is not possible. In so ~ that …: 너무 ~해서 …하다 the movie, *Passengers*, a spaceship headed to a different planet travels a spaceship에 수의 일치 at one-half the speed of light. So it should get to another planet very quickly, right? But, the passengers sleep for 120 years because it is expected to take that much time to get to a different planet. It takes+시간+to V: V하는 데 ~만큼의 시간이 걸리다

Sci Teen: 120 years? Wow, that's a long time! Is there a faster way to travel through space? to부정사의 형용사적 용법(way 수식)

Dr. Sci: Well, in order to answer that question, I'd like you to think = so as to would like+목적어+to부정사 about this apple for a second. Imagine a worm is on this apple. It detects something sweet at the bottom and wants to move from the -thing으로 끝나는 부정대명사는 형용사의 수식을 뒤에서 받음 top to the bottom. For the worm, the apple's surface is as vast as our universe. Now the worm can either move around the outer layer or either A or B: A 혹은 B 둘 중 하나 down a wormhole. Which do you think it will choose? Well, it would think로 인해 의문사가 문두로 나간 간접의문문 choose the wormhole because it is a shortcut.

Sci Teen: Is there such a shortcut in the universe?

Dr. Sci: According to some researchers, yes. Einstein figured out that 명사절 접속사(figure out의 목적어를 이끎) space and time are connected, and he called it space-time. He thought that space-time could actually be bent. When it is bent, parts that are 주격 관계대명사 far away from each other are suddenly closer.

---

wormhole: 벌레 먹은 구멍
theory: 이론, 학설
passenger: 승객, 탑승객
in the blink of an eye: 눈 깜박할 사이에
detect: 발견하다, 감지하다
bottom: 맨 아랫부분, 바닥
vast: 광대한, 거대한
layer: 층
shortcut: 지름길
researcher: 연구자
connect: 이어지다
bend: 굽히다, 구부리다
figure out: ~을 생각해 내다

📎 확인문제

● 다음 문장이 본문의 내용과 일치하면 T, 일치하지 <u>않으면</u> F를 쓰시오.

1 The apple is as enormous as our space to the worm. ☐

2 Einstein thought that space-time could actually be broken. ☐

3 A wormhole is not helpful for us to travel through space as fast as possible. ☐

To understand this, take a sheet of paper and make a small dot at the
부사적 용법 중 목적(= in order to = so as to)
top of the paper and another at the bottom of the paper. On a flat sheet
of paper, the dots are far away from one another. Now, take the paper
and fold it with the dots matched up. Punch a hole in the paper and
with+목적어+과거분사(목적어가 ~된 채로)
the dots will be instantly connected. Like this, wormholes in space
may contain two mouths, with a throat connecting the two.
with+목적어+현재분사(목적어가 ~하는 채로)

Sci Teen: Just like a wormhole in the apple, right? If such wormholes
existed in space, we could get to places billions of light-years away
가정법 과거(If+주어+동사의 과거형, 주어+조동사의 과거형+동사원형): 현재 사실과 반대되는 일에 대한 가정
quickly!

Dr. Sci: Yes, but it's too early to celebrate. Wormholes exist in theory
only.

Sci Teen: So all we need to do is find one, right?
주어부에 do동사가 있을 때 be동사의 보어로 to를 생략한 원형부정사 사용 가능
Dr. Sci: Even if we find one, there are many things to consider before
to부정사의 형용사적 용법(things 수식)
actually going through one. A wormhole would be very unstable. If a
spaceship flew into one, it might be crushed or broken into pieces.
우주선이 웜홀로 날아 들어가는 것이 당장 현실적으로 불가능하므로 가정법 과거로 표현

Sci Teen: Ouch! That's not a pretty picture. So, are we hopeless? Is
traveling in space through a wormhole simply an idea that only exists
in theory?
주격 관계대명사
Dr. Sci: I wouldn't say so. The debate about wormholes is still ongoing,
토론이 지금도 계속되고 있음
but with persistent exploration and research, I believe we will
eventually find one and learn how to travel through it. Look back at
a wormhole 지칭
our history. We've achieved so many things that seemed impossible at
= which(관계대명사)
first. Who knows? Maybe you can be the one to find the answer!
to부정사의 형용사적 용법(the one 수식) 웜홀을 통해 우주여행을 하는 방법에 대한 해답

---

dot: 점
punch: 구멍을 뚫다
instantly: 즉시
contain: 포함하다
throat: 목구멍
far away from: ~에서 멀리 떨어져
match up: 맞추다
exist: 존재하다
celebrate: 축하하다
unstable: 불안정한
crush: 눌러 부수다, 찌부러뜨리다
billions of: 수십억의
ongoing: 계속 진행 중인
persistent: 끈질긴, 집요한
exploration: 탐사, 탐구
eventually: 결국
achieve: 달성하다, 성취하다
impossible: 불가능한
look back: 되돌아보다

🖇 **확인문제**

● 다음 문장이 본문의 내용과 일치하면 T, 일치하지 않으면 F를 쓰시오.

1 A wormhole in the universe is a shortcut that connects two places. ☐

2 Researchers have found a few wormholes in space. ☐

3 A wormhole is very stable, so we can travel through it safely. ☐

4 The debate about wormholes is in progress. ☐

● 우리말을 참고하여 빈칸에 알맞은 말을 쓰시오.

1 Sci Teen: Hi, science fans. Today, we're _____ _____ _____ _____ space travel.

2 _____ _____ _____ _____, there is _____ _____ light in the universe.

3 So, if we _____ _____ the speed of light, we should _____ _____ _____ _____ _____ another planet _____ _____ _____ _____ an eye, right?

4 Dr. Sci: That would be nice, but space _____ _____ _____ it is not possible.

5 In the movie, *Passengers*, a spaceship _____ _____ a different planet _____ at _____ the speed of light.

6 So it should _____ _____ _____ planet very quickly, right?

7 But, the passengers sleep _____ _____ _____ because it _____ _____ _____ _____ that much time to get to a different planet.

8 Sci Teen: 120 years? Wow, that's a long time! Is there _____ _____ _____ _____ _____ through space?

9 Dr. Sci: Well, _____ _____ _____ answer that question, I'd like _____ _____ _____ about this apple for a second.

10 Imagine a worm is _____ _____ _____. It detects _____ _____ at the bottom and _____ _____ _____ from the top to the bottom.

11 For the worm, the apple's surface is _____ _____ _____ our universe.

12 Now the worm can _____ _____ _____ the outer layer _____ _____ a wormhole.

13 _____ _____ _____ _____ it will choose? Well, it would choose the wormhole _____ _____ _____.

14 Sci Teen: Is there _____ _____ _____ in the universe?

15 Dr. Sci: According to some researchers, yes. Einstein _____ _____ that space and time _____ _____, and he called it _____.

1 Sci Teen: 안녕하세요, 과학 팬 여러분. 오늘 우리는 우주여행에 대해 이야기할 것입니다.

2 우리가 모두 알다시피, 우주에서 빛보다 더 빠른 것은 없습니다.

3 그래서 만약 우리가 빛의 속도로 여행을 한다면, 우리는 다른 행성에 눈 깜박할 사이에 도달할 수 있어야 해요, 그렇죠?

4 Dr. Sci: 그렇다면 좋겠지만, 우주는 너무 광활해서 그건 불가능하답니다.

5 영화 〈Passengers〉에서 다른 행성으로 향하는 우주선이 빛의 속도의 절반으로 이동합니다.

6 그러면 그들은 다른 행성에 매우 빨리 도달해야겠지요, 그렇죠?

7 하지만 승객들은 120년 동안 잠을 자게 되는데, 왜냐하면 다른 행성에 도달하는 데 그만큼 많은 시간이 걸릴 것으로 예상되기 때문입니다.

8 Sci Teen: 120년이요? 우아, 그건 정말 긴 시간이네요! 우주를 여행하는 더 빠른 방법이 있나요?

9 Dr. Sci: 글쎄요, 그 질문에 답하기 위해서 여러분들이 이 사과에 대해 잠깐 생각해 보기 바랍니다.

10 한 마리 벌레가 이 사과 위에 있다고 상상해 보세요. 그것은 맨 아래에 있는 달콤한 무언가를 감지하고 맨 위에서 아래로 이동하기를 원합니다.

11 그 벌레에게 사과의 표면은 우리의 우주만큼이나 광대합니다.

12 이제 그 벌레는 바깥 표면의 껍질을 돌아서 이동하거나 벌레 구멍 아래로 이동할 수 있습니다.

13 그것이 어떤 것을 선택할 거라고 생각하십니까? 음, 그것은 벌레 구멍을 선택할 것인데 왜냐하면 그것이 지름길이기 때문입니다.

14 Sci Teen: 우주에 그런 지름길이 있나요?

15 Dr. Sci: 몇몇 연구자들에 따르면, 그렇습니다. 아인슈타인은 공간과 시간이 연결되어 있다는 것을 생각해 냈고, 그것을 시공간이라고 불렀습니다.

16 He thought that _____ _____ _____ _____.
When it is bent, parts _____ _____ _____ _____
from each other _____ suddenly closer.

17 _____ _____ this, _____ a sheet of paper and _____
a small dot _____ _____ _____ _____ the paper and
_____ at the _____ of the paper.

18 _____ _____ _____ _____ of paper, the dots are
_____ _____ from one another.

19 Now, take the paper and _____ it _____ the dots _____
_____. _____ a hole in the paper and _____ _____
will _____ instantly _____.

20 Like this, wormholes in space may _____ _____ _____,
with a throat _____ the two.

21 Sci Teen: _____ _____ a wormhole in the apple, right?
If such wormholes _____ in space, we could _____
_____ _____ billions of light-years _____ quickly!

22 Dr. Sci: Yes, but it's _____ _____ _____.
Wormholes _____ in theory only.

23 Sci Teen: So _____ we need _____ _____ is _____
_____, right?

24 Dr. Sci: _____ _____ we find one, there are many things
_____ _____ before actually _____ _____ _____.

25 A wormhole _____ _____ very _____. If a spaceship
_____ _____ one, it might _____ _____ or _____
into pieces.

26 Sci Teen: Ouch! That's not _____ _____ _____. So, are
we _____?

27 Is traveling in space _____ a wormhole simply an idea
_____ only _____ in theory?

28 Dr. Sci: I _____ _____ so. The debate about wormholes
_____ still _____, but _____ _____ _____
and _____, I believe we will eventually find _____ and
_____ _____ _____ _____ through it.

29 _____ _____ _____ our history. We've achieved
_____ _____ _____ _____ seemed impossible at
first.

30 Who _____? Maybe you can be the one _____ _____
_____ _____!

16 '그는 시공간이 실제로 구부러질 수 있다고 생각했습니다. 그것이 구부러질 때 서로 멀리 떨어져 있는 부분들이 갑자기 더 가까워질 수 있습니다.

17 이것을 이해하기 위해서, 종이를 한 장 갖고 와서 그 종이의 윗부분에 작은 점을 찍고 또 다른 점을 그 종이의 아랫부분에 찍어 보세요.

18 펼쳐 놓은 종이에서 그 점들은 서로 멀리 떨어져 있습니다.

19 이제 그 종이를 들고 점들이 맞춰지도록 그것을 접으세요. 종이에 구멍을 뚫으면 그 점들이 즉시 연결될 것입니다.

20 이와 마찬가지로 우주의 웜홀은 두 개의 입과 그 둘을 연결하는 목구멍을 지니고 있을 겁니다.

21 Sci Teen: 사과에 있는 벌레 구멍처럼요, 그렇죠? 그런 웜홀이 우주에 존재한다면 우리는 수십억 광년 떨어져 있는 곳에 빠르게 도달할 수 있을 텐데요!

22 Dr. Sci: 그렇죠, 하지만 축하하기에는 너무 이릅니다. 웜홀은 이론상에서만 존재합니다.

23 Sci Teen: 그러면 우리가 해야 할 것이라고는 그것을 찾는 거네요, 그렇죠?

24 Dr. Sci: 우리가 그것을 찾는다고 하더라도 실제로 그걸 통과하여 가기 전에 고려해야 할 것들이 많이 있습니다.

25 웜홀은 매우 불안정할 것입니다. 만약 우주선이 그 안으로 날아가게 되면, 그것은 부서지거나 산산조각이 날 수도 있습니다.

26 Sci Teen: 어이쿠! 그건 좋은 광경이 아니네요. 그럼 우리는 가망이 없는 건가요?

27 우주에서 웜홀을 통하여 여행을 하는 것은 단지 이론상으로만 존재하는 아이디어인가요?

28 Dr. Sci: 그렇게 말하지는 않겠어요. 웜홀에 대한 논쟁은 여전히 진행 중이긴 하지만, 끊임없는 탐구와 연구로 우리가 결국 하나를 찾아 그것을 통해 여행하는 법을 배울 수 있을 거라고 믿습니다.

29 우리의 역사를 돌아보세요. 우리는 처음에는 불가능해 보였던 아주 많은 것들을 달성해 왔습니다.

30 누가 알겠어요? 아마도 여러분이 그 답을 찾아내는 그 사람이 될 수 있을지도요!

● 우리말을 참고하여 본문을 영작하시오.

1 Sci Teen: 안녕하세요, 과학 팬 여러분. 오늘 우리는 우주여행에 대해 이야기할 것입니다.

➡ _____

2 우리가 모두 알다시피, 우주에서 빛보다 더 빠른 것은 없습니다.

➡ _____

3 그래서 만약 우리가 빛의 속도로 여행을 한다면, 우리는 다른 행성에 눈 깜박할 사이에 도달할 수 있어야 해요, 그렇죠?

➡ _____
_____

4 Dr. Sci: 그렇다면 좋겠지만, 우주는 너무 광활해서 그건 불가능하답니다.

➡ _____

5 영화 〈Passengers〉에서 다른 행성으로 향하는 우주선이 빛의 속도의 절반으로 이동합니다.

➡ _____

6 그러면 그들은 다른 행성에 매우 빨리 도달해야겠지요, 그렇죠?

➡ _____

7 하지만 승객들은 120년 동안 잠을 자게 되는데, 왜냐하면 다른 행성에 도달하는 데 그만큼 많은 시간이 걸릴 것으로 예상되기 때문입니다.

➡ _____
_____

8 Sci Teen: 120년이요? 우아, 그건 정말 긴 시간이네요! 우주를 여행하는 더 빠른 방법이 있나요?

➡ _____

9 Dr. Sci: 글쎄요, 그 질문에 답하기 위해서 여러분들이 이 사과에 대해 잠깐 생각해 보기 바랍니다.

➡ _____

10 한 마리 벌레가 이 사과 위에 있다고 상상해 보세요. 그것은 맨 아래에 있는 달콤한 무언가를 감지하고 맨 위에서 아래로 이동하기를 원합니다.

➡ _____
_____

11 그 벌레에게 사과의 표면은 우리의 우주만큼이나 광대합니다.

➡ _____

12 이제 그 벌레는 바깥 표면의 껍질을 돌아서 이동하거나 벌레 구멍 아래로 이동할 수 있습니다.

➡ _____

13 그것이 어떤 것을 선택할 거라고 생각하십니까? 음, 그것은 벌레 구멍을 선택할 것인데 왜냐하면 그것이 지름길이기 때문입니다.

➡ _____

14 Sci Teen: 우주에 그런 지름길이 있나요?

➡ _____

15 Dr. Sci: 몇몇 연구자들에 따르면, 그렇습니다. 아인슈타인은 공간과 시간이 연결되어 있다는 것을 생각해 냈고, 그것을 시공간이라고 불렀습니다.

➡ _____
_____

16 그는 시공간이 실제로 구부러질 수 있다고 생각했습니다. 그것이 구부러질 때 서로 멀리 떨어져 있는 부분들이 갑자기 더 가까워질 수 있습니다.

➡ _____

_____

17 이것을 이해하기 위해서, 종이를 한 장 갖고 와서 그 종이의 윗부분에 작은 점을 찍고 또 다른 점을 그 종이의 아랫부분에 찍어 보세요.

➡ _____

_____

18 펼쳐 놓은 종이에서 그 점들은 서로 멀리 떨어져 있습니다.

➡ _____

19 이제 그 종이를 들고 점들이 맞춰지도록 그것을 접으세요. 종이에 구멍을 뚫으면 그 점들이 즉시 연결될 것입니다.

➡ _____

_____

20 이와 마찬가지로 우주의 웜홀은 두 개의 입과 그 둘을 연결하는 목구멍을 지니고 있을 겁니다.

➡ _____

21 Sci Teen: 사과에 있는 벌레 구멍처럼요, 그렇죠? 그런 웜홀이 우주에 존재한다면 우리는 수십억 광년 떨어져 있는 곳에 빠르게 도달할 수 있을 텐데요!

➡ _____

22 Dr. Sci: 그렇죠, 하지만 축하하기에는 너무 이릅니다. 웜홀은 이론상에서만 존재합니다.

➡ _____

23 Sci Teen: 그러면 우리가 해야 할 것이라고는 그것을 찾는 거네요, 그렇죠?

➡ _____

24 Dr. Sci: 우리가 그것을 찾는다고 하더라도 실제로 그걸 통과하여 가기 전에 고려해야 할 것들이 많이 있습니다.

➡ _____

25 웜홀은 매우 불안정할 것입니다. 만약 우주선이 그 안으로 날아가게 되면, 그것은 부서지거나 산산조각이 날 수도 있습니다.

➡ _____

_____

26 Sci Teen: 어이쿠! 그건 좋은 광경이 아니네요. 그럼 우리는 가망이 없는 건가요?

➡ _____

27 우주에서 웜홀을 통하여 여행을 하는 것은 단지 이론상으로만 존재하는 아이디어인가요?

➡ _____

28 Dr. Sci: 그렇게 말하지는 않겠어요. 웜홀에 대한 논쟁은 여전히 진행 중이긴 하지만, 끊임없는 탐구와 연구로 우리가 결국 하나를 찾아 그것을 통해 여행하는 법을 배울 수 있을 거라고 믿습니다.

➡ _____

_____

29 우리의 역사를 돌아보세요. 우리는 처음에는 불가능해 보였던 아주 많은 것들을 달성해 왔습니다.

➡ _____

30 누가 알겠어요? 아마도 여러분이 그 답을 찾아내는 그 사람이 될 수 있을지도요!

➡ _____

[01~03] 다음 글을 읽고 물음에 답하시오.

Sci Teen: Hi, science fans. Today, we're going to talk about space travel. As we all know, there is nothing faster than light in the universe. So, if we travel at the speed of light, we should be able to get to another planet in the blink of an eye, right?

Dr. Sci: (A)That would be nice, but space is so ⓐ_____ that it is not possible. In the movie, *Passengers*, a spaceship headed to a different planet travels at one-half the speed of light. So it should get to another planet very quickly, right? But, the passengers sleep for 120 years because it is expected to take that much time to get to a different planet.

01 위 글의 흐름상 빈칸 ⓐ에 들어갈 말로 가장 적절한 것은?

① empty   ② small   ③ vast
④ dangerous   ⑤ dark

02 밑줄 친 (A)의 의미로 가장 적절한 것은?

① making space travel possible
② arriving at another planet in a blink
③ getting to another planet in the future
④ traveling the universe without any help
⑤ moving from one place to another whenever we want

서답형

03 What are they going to talk about today? Answer in English with a full sentence.

➡ _____

[04~06] 다음 글을 읽고 물음에 답하시오.

Sci Teen: 120 years? Wow, that's a long time!
(A)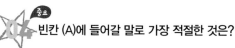

Dr. Sci: Well, in order to answer that question, I'd like you to think about this apple for a second. Imagine a worm is on this apple. ⓐIt detects something sweet at the bottom and wants to move from the top to the bottom. For the worm, the apple's surface is as vast as our universe. Now the worm can either move around the outer layer or down a wormhole. Which do you think ⓑit will choose? Well, ⓒit would choose the wormhole because ⓓit is a shortcut.

04 빈칸 (A)에 들어갈 말로 가장 적절한 것은?

① Did someone find a wormhole?
② Do you know how to get to another planet?
③ Is there a safe way to travel through space?
④ How can we find a shortcut in our universe?
⑤ Is there a faster way to travel through space?

05 ⓐ~ⓓ에서 가리키는 것이 같은 것을 바르게 묶은 것은?

① ⓑ-ⓒ, ⓐ-ⓓ   ② ⓐ, ⓑ-ⓒ-ⓓ
③ ⓒ, ⓐ-ⓑ-ⓓ   ④ ⓐ-ⓑ-ⓒ, ⓓ
⑤ ⓑ-ⓓ, ⓐ-ⓒ

서답형

06 How big is the apple's surface for the worm? Answer in English.

➡ _____

[07~08] 다음 글을 읽고 물음에 답하시오.

Sci Teen: Is there such a shortcut in the universe?

Dr. Sci: According to some researchers, yes. Einstein figured out that space and time are connected, and he called it space-time. (①) He thought that space-time could actually be bent. (②) When it is bent, parts that are far away from each other are suddenly closer. (③) On a flat sheet of paper, the dots are far away from one another. (④) Now, take the paper and fold it with the dots matched up. Punch a hole in the paper and the dots will be instantly connected. (⑤) Like this, wormholes in space may contain two mouths, with a throat connecting the two.

07 (①)~(⑤) 중 주어진 문장이 들어가기에 가장 적절한 곳은?

> To understand this, take a sheet of paper and make a small dot at the top of the paper and another at the bottom of the paper.

①   ②   ③   ④   ⑤

08 Choose one that is TRUE.

① A short cut can't be found in the universe.

② There is no mouth in a wormhole.

③ Nothing can connect those mouths in wormholes.

④ Einstein thought bending space-time could be impossible.

⑤ Einstein thought space and time are connected.

[09~10] 다음 글을 읽고 물음에 답하시오.

Sci Teen: Just like a wormhole in the apple, right? If such wormholes existed in space, we could get to places billions of light-years away quickly!

Dr. Sci: Yes, but it's too early to celebrate. Wormholes exist in theory only.

Sci Teen: So all we need to do is find (A)one, right?

Dr. Sci: Even if we find one, there are many things to consider before actually going through one. A wormhole would be very unstable. If a spaceship flew into one, it might be crushed or broken into pieces.

Sci Teen: Ouch! That's not a pretty picture. So, are we hopeless? Is traveling in space through a wormhole simply an idea that only exists in theory?

Dr. Sci: I wouldn't say so. The debate about wormholes is still ongoing, but with persistent exploration and research, I believe we will eventually find one and learn how to travel through it. Look back at our history. We've achieved so many things that seemed impossible at first.

서답형

09 밑줄 친 (A)가 가리키는 것을 위 글에서 찾아 쓰시오.

➡ _____

서답형

10 What have we achieved? Answer in English.

➡ _____

_____

[11~13] 다음 글을 읽고 물음에 답하시오.

Sci Teen: Hi, science fans. Today, we're going to talk about space travel. As we all know, there is nothing faster than light in the universe. So, ⓐ만약 우리가 빛의 속도로 여행을 한다면, we should be able to get to another planet in the blink of an eye, right?

Dr. Sci: That would be nice, but space is so vast that it is not possible.

(A) But, the passengers sleep for 120 years because it is expected to take that much time to get to a different planet.

(B) So it should get to another planet very quickly, right?

(C) In the movie, *Passengers*, a spaceship headed to a different planet travels at one-half the speed of light.

서답형

11 주어진 단어를 바르게 나열하여 밑줄 친 우리말 ⓐ를 영어로 쓰시오.

(light / the / travel / if / of / speed / at / we)

➡ _____

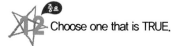

12 Choose one that is TRUE.

① They are talking about a spaceship.

② The conversation is for science fans.

③ Many things can travel as fast as light in the universe.

④ We can travel from a planet to another planet in the blink of an eye.

⑤ In the movie, *Passengers*, a spaceship travel at the speed of light.

서답형

13 자연스러운 글이 되도록 (A)~(C)를 바르게 나열하시오.

➡ _____

[14~15] 다음 글을 읽고 물음에 답하시오.

Sci Teen: 120 years? Wow, that's a long time! Is there a faster way (A)to travel through space?

Dr. Sci: Well, in order to answer that question, I'd like you to think about this apple for a second. Imagine a worm is on this apple. It detects something sweet at the bottom and wants to move from the top to the bottom. For the worm, the apple's surface is as vast as our universe. Now the worm can either move around the outer layer or down a wormhole. Which do you think it will choose? Well, it would choose the wormhole because it is a shortcut.

14 다음 중 밑줄 친 (A)와 쓰임이 같은 것은?

① It was kind of you to say so.

② He came in to find his wallet.

③ You must be upset to hear the news.

④ Is there any chance to meet her?

⑤ We'd like you to think about it.

15 On the apple, what does the worm detect? Answer in English.

➡ _____

_____

[16~18] 다음 글을 읽고 물음에 답하시오.

Sci Teen: Is there such a shortcut in the universe?

Dr. Sci: According to some researchers, yes. Einstein figured out that space and time are connected, and he called it space-time. He thought that space-time could actually be ①bent. When it is bent, parts that are far away from each other are suddenly ②closer. To understand this, take a sheet of paper and make a small dot at the top of the paper and another at the bottom of the paper. On a ③flat sheet of paper, the dots are ④far away from one another. Now, take the paper and ⑤hold it with the dots matched up. Punch a hole in the paper and the dots will be instantly connected. Like this, wormholes in space may contain two mouths, with a throat connecting the two.

 다음 중 위 글의 제목으로 가장 적절한 것은?

① A Wormhole: a Secret Way to the Mars
② Wormholes Disconnecting Universe
③ A Wormhole: a Shortcut of Universe
④ How to Find a Shortcut of Universe
⑤ What You Should Do to Find Wormholes

17 ①~⑤ 중 글의 흐름상 어색한 단어는?

①   ②   ③   ④   ⑤

18 If you punch a hole in the paper, what will happen? Answer in English.

➡ _____

_____

[19~21] 다음 글을 읽고 물음에 답하시오.

Sci Teen: Just like a wormhole in the apple, right? If ①such wormholes existed in space, we could get to places billions of light-years away quickly!

Dr. Sci: Yes, but it's too early ②to celebrate. Wormholes exist in theory only.

Sci Teen: So all we need to do is ③find one, right?

Dr. Sci: Even if we find one, there are many things to consider before actually going through one. A wormhole would be very (A)unstable. If a spaceship flew into one, it might be crushed or broken into pieces.

Sci Teen: Ouch! That's not a pretty picture. So, are we hopeless? Is traveling in space through a wormhole simply an idea that only ④exists in theory?

Dr. Sci: I wouldn't say so. The debate about wormholes ⑤are still ongoing, but with persistent exploration and research, I believe we will eventually find one and learn how to travel through it. Look back at our history. We've achieved so many things that seemed impossible at first. Who knows? Maybe you can be the one to find the answer!

19 밑줄 친 (A)를 대신하여 쓸 수 있는 것은?

① constant   ② insecure   ③ vast
④ instant   ⑤ exclusive

20 ①~⑤ 중 어법상 바르지 않은 것은?

①   ②   ③   ④   ⑤

21 빈칸에 공통으로 들어갈 말을 쓰시오.

> **Q:** Then, traveling in space through a wormhole is _____, isn't it?
> **Dr. Sci:** I wouldn't say so. We've achieved so many things that seemed _____ at first. We will eventually find one and learn how to travel through it.

[01~03] 다음 글을 읽고 물음에 답하시오.

Sci Teen: Hi, science fans. Today, we're going to talk about space travel. As we all know, there is nothing faster than light in the universe. So, if we travel at the speed of light, we should be able to get to another planet in the blink of an eye, right?

Dr. Sci: That would be nice, but space is so vast that it is not possible. In the movie, *Passengers*, a spaceship headed to a different planet travels at one-half the speed of light. So it should get to another planet very quickly, right? But, the passengers sleep for 120 years because it is expected to take that much time to get to a different planet.

01 How fast does the spaceship in the movie, *Passengers*, travel?

➡ _____

02 Why do the passengers in the movie, *Passengers*, sleep so long? Answer in English.

➡ _____

_____

03 위 글의 내용과 일치하도록 빈칸에 알맞은 말을 쓰시오. (한 칸에 하나의 단어만 쓰시오.)

Space is too vast for us to _____ _____ _____ _____ _____ _____ _____ _____ although we travel at the speed of light.

[04~05] 다음 글을 읽고 물음에 답하시오.

Sci Teen: 120 years? Wow, that's a long time! Is there a faster way to travel through space?

Dr. Sci: Well, in order to answer that question, (A)여러분들이 이 사과에 대해 잠깐 생각해 보기 바랍니다. Imagine a worm is on this apple. It detects something sweet at the bottom and wants to move from the top to the bottom. For the worm, the apple's surface is as vast as our universe. Now the worm can either move around the outer layer or down a wormhole. Which do you think it will choose? Well, it would choose the ⓐ _____ because it is a shortcut.

04 위 글의 흐름상 빈칸 ⓐ에 들어갈 알맞은 말을 쓰시오.

➡ _____

05 주어진 어구를 활용하여 밑줄 친 우리말 (A)를 영어로 쓰시오.

(would like / for a second)

➡ _____

[06~08] 다음 글을 읽고 물음에 답하시오.

Sci Teen: Is there such a shortcut in the universe?

Dr. Sci: According to some researchers, yes. Einstein figured out that space and time are connected, and he called it space-time. He thought that space-time could actually be bent. When it is bent, parts that are far away from each other are suddenly closer. To understand (A)this, take a sheet of paper and make a small dot at the top of the paper and another at the bottom of the paper. On a flat sheet of paper, the dots are far away from one another. Now, take the paper and fold it with the dots matched up. Punch a hole in the paper and the dots will be instantly connected. Like this, wormholes in space may contain two mouths, with a throat connecting the two.

06 밑줄 친 (A)this가 의미하는 것을 우리말로 쓰시오.

➡ _____

_____

07 What do we need to do after making dots on a sheet of paper? Answer in English.

➡ _____

_____

08 위 글의 내용에 맞게 과학 노트를 완성하시오.

> _____ in space
> Einstein thought space and time are _____ and space-time can be _____.
> When it is _____, parts far away from each other can become _____.

[09~12] 다음 글을 읽고 물음에 답하시오.

Sci Teen: Just like a wormhole in the apple, right? If such wormholes existed in space, we could get to places billions of light-years away quickly!

Dr. Sci: Yes, but (A)it's too early to celebrate. Wormholes exist in theory only.

Sci Teen: So all we need to do is find one, right?

Dr. Sci: Even if we find one, there are many things to consider before actually going through one. A wormhole would be very unstable. If a spaceship flew into one, it might be crushed or broken into pieces.

Sci Teen: Ouch! That's not a pretty picture. So, are we hopeless? Is traveling in space through a wormhole simply an idea that only exists in theory?

Dr. Sci: I wouldn't say so. The debate about wormholes is still ongoing, but with persistent exploration and research, I believe we will eventually find one and learn how to travel through it. Look back at our history. We've achieved so many things that seemed impossible at first. Who knows? Maybe you can be the one to find the answer!

09 Write the reason why Dr. Sci says like the underlined (A). Use the phrase 'It is because.'

➡ _____

10 According to Dr. Sci, what will we do if we eventually find a wormhole? Answer in English.

➡ _____

11 If a spaceship flew into a wormhole, what would happen to it? Answer in English.

➡ _____

12 Is the debate about wormholes over?

➡ _____

After You Read A

 해석

A faster way to travel through space

① Idea from an apple

A wormhole is a shortcut for a worm to move from the top to the bottom.
　　　　　　　　　　　　　　의미상의 주어　　형용사적 용법(shortcut 수식)

② Wormholes in space

Einstein thought space and time are connected and space-time can be bent.
　　　　　　　　　　　　　　　　　과학적 사실이므로 현재 시제 사용

When it is bent, parts far away from each other can become closer.

Do wormholes really exist?

③ In theory, wormholes exist.

Wormholes would be unstable. A spaceship could be crushed or broken into
　　　　　　추측　　　　　　　　　　　'가정에 대한 결과의 상상'
pieces.

Still I believe with persistent exploration and research we will find a
그럼에도, 하지만, 그러나(접속사처럼 쓰여 but. however보다 센 뜻을 나타냄.)
wormhole!

 구문해설　• shortcut: 지름길　• worm: 벌레　• connect: 연결하다　• bend: 굽히다, 구부리다　• theory: 이론
　　　　　　• exist: 존재하다　• unstable: 불안정한　• spaceship: 우주선　• crush: 눌러 부수다, 찌부러뜨리다
　　　　　　• persistent: 끈질긴, 집요한, 지속적인　• exploration: 탐구

우주로 여행을 떠나는 더 빠른 방법
① 사과에서 얻은 아이디어
• 벌레 구멍은 벌레가 맨 위에서 아래로 이동하는 지름길이다.
② 우주에서의 웜홀
• 아인슈타인은 공간과 시간은 연결되어 있고 시공간은 구부러질 수 있다고 생각했다. 그것이 구부러질 때, 서로 멀리 떨어져 있는 부분들이 더 가까워질 수 있다.
웜홀이 실제로 존재할까?
③ 이론상, 웜홀은 존재한다.
• 웜홀은 불안정할 것이다. 우주선이 부서지거나 산산조각이 날 수도 있다.
하지만 나는 끊임없는 탐구와 연구로 우리가 결국 웜홀을 찾아낼 거라고 믿는다!

Language in Use

• Is the universe finite or infinite?
특정 어근에 im-[in-]을 붙이면 부정의 의미를 더한다. im-은 뒤에 오는 어근의 철자가 m. p. b로 시작할 때 붙일 수 있다.(in→finite = infinite)

• Luckily, the driver is in a stable condition after the accident.
동사 뒤에 –able을 붙이면 '~할 수 있는'이라는 의미의 형용사가 된다. (stay+–able = stable)

• 우주는 유한할까 아니면 무한할까?
• 운 좋게도, 그 운전자는 사고 이후에 안정적인 상태이다.

Think & Write C

If I could make a planet for us to live on in the future, I would like to make
　　　　　　　　　　　to부정사의 의미상 주어　a planet 수식

a planet called Atlas. It would be a beautiful green planet. Its size would be
　　　　　　과거분사(~라고 불리는)

bigger than the moon, but smaller than Earth. The temperature of it would be
　　　　　　　　　　　　　　　　　　　　　　　　　　　　　　Atlas 지칭

about 30℃. It would have beautiful nature. Interestingly, if people moved to it,
　　　대략

they could communicate with animals on this planet.

 구문해설　• would like to V: V하고 싶다　• temperature: 온도　• nature: 자연　• communicate: 의사소통하다

만약 제가 미래에 우리가 살 행성을 만든다면, 나는 아틀라스라고 불리는 행성을 만들고 싶습니다. 그것은 아름다운 푸른 행성일 것입니다. 그것의 크기는 달보다 더 크지만 지구보다 더 작을 것입니다. 그것의 온도는 약 섭씨 30도일 것입니다. 그것은 아름다운 자연을 가지고 있을 것입니다. 흥미롭게도, 만약 사람들이 그곳으로 간다면, 그들은 이 행성에서 동물들과 의사소통할 수 있을 것입니다.

01 다음 중 반의어의 연결이 <u>어색한</u> 것은?

① sensitive – insensitive
② active – inactive
③ stable – unstable
④ correct – imcorrect
⑤ possible – impossible

02 다음 괄호 안의 단어를 우리말에 맞게 변형하여 빈칸에 쓰시오.

> 그 인형은 움직일 수 있는 팔과 다리를 가지고 있다.
> → The doll has _____ arms and legs.
> (move)

03 다음 괄호 안의 단어를 문맥에 맞게 고쳐 쓰시오.

> Space _____ seems exciting to me. (explore)

04 다음 빈칸 (A)와 (B)에 들어갈 말이 알맞게 짝지어진 것은?

> • This puzzle is (A)_____ complicated for me to put together.
> • I've never seen (B)_____ a thrilling game.

　　(A)　(B)　　　　　(A)　(B)
① so – so　　　　② so – such
③ too – so　　　　④ too – such
⑤ too – too

05 다음 빈칸에 공통으로 들어갈 말을 쓰시오.

> • They are quite different (A)_____ each other in many ways.
> • My house is not far away (B)_____ here.

06 자연스러운 대화가 되도록 (A)~(D)를 배열한 것을 고르시오.

> (A) Yes, it's possible because we moved around Earth every 90 minutes in the station.
> (C) I could see a beautiful sunrise 16 times a day. It was great.
> (B) What was your favorite part about being in the space station?
> (D) Is it possible to see the sunrise several times a day in space?

① (B) – (A) – (C) – (D)
② (B) – (C) – (A) – (D)
③ (B) – (C) – (D) – (A)
④ (C) – (B) – (A) – (D)
⑤ (C) – (D) – (B) – (A)

[07~09] 다음 대화를 읽고 물음에 답하시오.

> W: What are you watching? (①)
> M: It's a documentary about life in space. (②)
> W: Yes, it's because there's no gravity in space. (③)
> M: Right. (④) 나도 우주 비행사처럼 떠다닐 수 있다면 좋을 텐데! (⑤)
> W: Really? I don't. It looks uncomfortable.

07 ①~⑤ 중 주어진 문장이 들어갈 곳은?

> Everything seems so different.

①   ②   ③   ④   ⑤

08 위 대화에서 다음 영영풀이에 해당하는 단어를 찾아 쓰시오.

> the force that attracts objects towards one another, especially the force that makes things fall to the ground

➡ _____

09 밑줄 친 우리말과 일치하도록 주어진 어구를 이용하여 영작하시오.

> like, float around, wish, could

➡ _____

[10~12] 다음 대화를 읽고 물음에 답하시오.

W: Hello, everyone, welcome to *All about Movies*! Today, we're going to talk about the top three things from movies that we wish were real.

M: Let's start with number three, the flying skateboard from *Back to the Future*.

W: It's a cool item. I wish I could have a flying skateboard.

M: Actually, I read somewhere that this is not entirely (A)_____.

W: Really? Is it actually possible to fly on a skateboard?

M: Yes. Some companies have (B)_____ physics to create flying skateboards.

10 대화의 흐름상 빈칸 (A)에 들어갈 말을 대화의 단어를 이용해 쓰시오.

➡ _____

11 빈칸 (B)에 알맞은 말을 고르시오.

① worked   ② applied   ③ made
④ showed   ⑤ required

12 위 대화의 내용과 일치하지 <u>않는</u> 것을 고르시오

① 실제로 가능하기를 바라는 영화 속 물건들에 대해서 말하고 있다.
② 남자는 날아다니는 스케이트보드를 만들 수 있다는 것을 어딘가에서 읽었다.
③ 남자는 날아다니는 스케이트보드를 가지기를 원한다.
④ 날아다니는 스케이트보드가 실제로 가능하기를 바라는 영화 속 물건들 중 3위이다.
⑤ 몇몇 회사들이 날아다니는 스케이트보드를 만들기 위해 노력 중이다.

Grammar

13 다음 중 밑줄 친 if의 쓰임이 나머지와 <u>다른</u> 하나를 고르시오.

① If I were you, I would call her.
② I would live in London if I could live anywhere I wanted.
③ I don't know if there is anything else I can do.
④ What would you do if you became an adult now?
⑤ If I were not sick, I could go to the meeting.

14 다음 중 어법상 <u>어색한</u> 문장은?

① Mike was standing by the door with his arms folded.

② Mozart was playing the piano with his eyes closed.

③ Jenny counted the stars with her finger pointing at each of them.

④ Alice was waiting for him with her legs crossing.

⑤ The little poor girl spoke with tears in her eyes.

15 다음 주어진 문장을 가정법으로 바르게 고친 것은?

> As I don't become an adult now, I won't get a driver's license.

① If I became an adult now, I won't get a driver's license.

② If I became an adult now, I would get a driver's license.

③ If I became an adult now, I wouldn't get a driver's license.

④ If I had become an adult now, I would get a driver's license.

⑤ If I hadn't become an adult now, I wouldn't get a driver's license.

[16~17] 우리말에 맞게 주어진 어휘를 이용하여 빈칸에 알맞은 말을 쓰시오.

16

> 웜홀은 두 개의 입과 그 둘을 연결하는 목구멍을 지니고 있을 것이다.
> = Wormholes may contain two mouths, _____ the two. (connect)

17

> 만약 Joe가 거짓말하지 않는다면, 선생님은 화내지 않을 텐데.
> = If Joe _____, the teacher _____ angry. (be, lie)

18 다음 괄호 안에 주어진 단어를 어법에 맞게 빈칸에 쓰시오.

(1) The woman was sitting on the chair with her legs _____. (cross)

(2) The girl ran with her hair _____ in the wind. (blow)

(3) Henry sat on the sofa with his eyes _____. (close)

(4) I ran out of the house with my dog _____ me. (follow)

(5) Listen to me carefully with your book _____. (close)

19 다음 그림을 보고, 괄호 안에 주어진 단어를 빈칸에 알맞게 채우시오.

> If I _____ an astronaut, I _____ _____ space travel. (become, enjoy)

20 다음 주어진 문장과 의미가 같은 것은?

> The children listened to their teacher with their eyes shining.

① Their teacher listened to the children and their eyes were shining.

② Their eyes shining made the children listen to their teacher.

③ The children listened to their teacher and their teacher shone her eyes.

④ The children listened to their teacher and their eyes were shining.

⑤ The children listened to their teacher and their eyes shine.

21 다음 중 어법상 어색한 것을 고르시오.

① Jean and Tom are listening to music with their eyes closing.

② We slept in the room, with the door closed.

③ Don't go out with the gas on.

④ The girls walked along, singing merrily.

⑤ Let the patient sit down on a chair with her injured arm raised higher than her heart.

Reading

[22~26] 다음 글을 읽고 물음에 답하시오.

Wormholes: Fact or Theory?

Sci Teen: Hi, science fans. Today, we're going to talk about space travel. As we all know, there is nothing faster than light in the universe. So, if we travel at the speed of light, we should be able to get to another planet in the blink of an eye, right?

Dr. Sci: That would be nice, but space is so vast that it is not possible. In the movie, *Passengers*, a spaceship headed to a different planet travels at one-half the speed of light. So it should get to another planet very quickly, right? But, the passengers sleep for 120 years because it is expected to take that much time to get to a different planet.

Sci Teen: 120 years? Wow, that's a long time! Is there a faster way to travel through space?

Dr. Sci: Well, in order to answer that question, I'd like you to think about this apple for a second. Imagine a worm is on this apple. It detects something sweet at the bottom and wants to move from the top to the bottom. For the worm, the apple's surface is as vast as our universe. Now the worm can either move around the outer layer or down a wormhole. (A) 그것이 어떤 것을 선택할 거라고 생각하십니까? Well, it would choose the wormhole ⓐ＿＿＿＿ it is a shortcut.

22 빈칸 ⓐ에 들어갈 말로 가장 적절한 것은?

① although   ② because   ③ if

④ unless   ⑤ as if

23 주어진 단어를 바르게 나열하여 밑줄 친 우리말 (A)를 영어로 쓸 때 네 번째로 오는 단어는?

> (choose / which / will / think / it / do / you)?

① it   ② which   ③ you

④ think   ⑤ do

24 What is the fastest thing in the universe? Answer in English with a full sentence.

➡ ＿＿＿＿＿＿＿＿＿＿＿＿＿＿＿＿

25 If we travel at the speed of light, what does Sci Teen think should happen? Answer in English.

➡ _____

_____

_____

26 Choose one that is NOT true.

① What they are going to talk about is space travel.

② Dr. Sci explains what a wormhole is with an example.

③ Passengers in the movie, *Passengers*, travel to another planet while waking up.

④ A wormhole is considered to be a shortcut existing in the universe.

⑤ It is expected to take 120 years to move from one planet to another planet in the movie, *Passengers*.

[27~28] 다음 글을 읽고 물음에 답하시오.

Sci Teen: Ouch! That's not a pretty picture. So, are we hopeless? Is traveling in space through a wormhole simply an idea that only exists in theory?

Dr. Sci: I wouldn't say so. The debate about wormholes is still (A)ongoing, but with persistent exploration and research, I believe we will eventually find one and learn how to travel through it. Look back at our history. We've achieved so many things that seemed impossible at first. Who knows? Maybe you can be the one to find the answer!

27 밑줄 친 (A)를 대신하여 쓰일 수 있는 것은?

① upcoming ② promising

③ continuing ④ following

⑤ underlying

28 What is Dr. Sci's attitude toward the existence of a wormhole?

① critical ② pessimistic

③ encouraging ④ desperate

⑤ regretful

[29~31] 다음 글을 읽고 물음에 답하시오.

If I could make a planet ①for us ②to live in the future, I would like to make a planet called Atlas. It would be a beautiful green planet. Its size would be bigger ③than the moon, but smaller than Earth. The temperature of it would be ④about 30℃. It would have beautiful nature. Interestingly, if people moved to it, they could communicate with animals ⑤on this planet.

29 ①~⑤ 중 어법상 바르지 않은 것은?

① ② ③ ④ ⑤

30 글쓴이가 만들 행성에 관하여 알 수 없는 것을 모두 고르시오.

① its name ② its size

③ its temperature ④ its location

⑤ how to get there

31 With what could people communicate on the planet 'Atlas'? Answer in English.

➡ _____

_____

01 밑줄 친 부분과 바꿔 쓸 수 있는 말을 접미사 -able을 이용하여 쓰시오. (출제율 90%)

> The political situation is still very <u>unstable</u>.

➡ _____

02 다음 빈칸에 들어갈 말을 〈보기〉에서 찾아 쓰시오. (출제율 100%)

┌── 보기 ──┐
ongoing   persistent   tough   unstable
└──────────┘

(1) It was a _____ decision to move to Busan.

(2) What do you think about this _____ issue?

(3) That chair looks _____ to me.

(4) I have a _____ headache and neck pain.

03 다음 영영풀이가 나타내는 말을 고르시오. (출제율 90%)

> to succeed in finishing something or reaching an aim, especially after a lot of work or effort

① achieve
② acquire
③ improve
④ perform
⑤ obtain

04 다음 빈칸에 들어갈 말을 고르시오. (출제율 95%)

> The rules don't _____ to children.

① apply   ② weigh   ③ lower
④ lean   ⑤ attach

[05~06] 다음 대화를 읽고 물음에 답하시오.

M: Irene, what was the best food you ate in the space station?

W: Hmm... . We grew some vegetables and ate them every day. They were pretty fresh and tasty!

M: Wow, (a)is it possible to grow vegetables in the space station?

W: Yes. (A)_____ there's no gravity in space, we had to grow them in special bags. The bags helped the roots to grow.

M: How interesting!

05 빈칸 (A)에 알맞은 말을 고르시오. (출제율 90%)

① Since
② Therefore
③ Although
④ But
⑤ However

06 밑줄 친 문장 (a)와 같은 의미가 <u>아닌</u> 것을 고르시오. (출제율 95%)

① are you able to grow vegetables in the space station?

② can you grow vegetables in the space station?

③ maybe should you grow vegetables in the space station?

④ would it be possible to grow vegetables in the space station?

⑤ is there a possibility that you grow vegetables in the space station?

M: Have you heard ⓐwhat NASA is going to send a 3D printer ⓑinto space?

W: They're going to send a 3D printer into space? Why?

M: I've heard that the 3D printer will be used ⓒprinting (A)_____ food for astronauts.

W: (B)_____ food using a 3D printer?

M: Yes, it's ⓓimpossible. It can print (C)_____ a fresh pizza in less than five minutes.

W: Really? I wonder ⓔthat it would taste like.

출제율 90%

07 빈칸 (A)와 (C)에 공통으로 들어갈 말을 쓰시오.

➡ _____

출제율 90%

08 빈칸 (B)에 알맞은 말을 고르시오.

① Is it a possibility that print out

② Is it possible to print out

③ Is that possible to printing out

④ Do you find it possible print out

⑤ Do you make possible to print out

출제율 95%

09 ⓐ~ⓔ 중 흐름상 또는 어법상 알맞은 것을 고르시오.

① ⓐ ② ⓑ ③ ⓒ ④ ⓓ ⑤ ⓔ

[10~11] 다음 대화를 읽고 물음에 답하시오.

M: Look at these colorful pictures of the universe.

W: Oh, they're beautiful. (①)

M: (②) Actually, you can do that at the National Youth Space Center. (③)

W: Really? (④)

M: Yeah, you can use the VR glasses. (⑤) I heard that (A)_____!

출제율 100%

10 ①~⑤ 중 주어진 문장이 들어갈 곳은?

I wish I could see Earth from space with my own eyes.

① ② ③ ④ ⑤

출제율 95%

11 빈칸 (A)에 알맞은 말을 고르시오.

① I wish to see the shooting star

② you grow vegetables in the space station

③ you see the beautiful sunrise several times a day

④ I lie down to sleep in space

⑤ you feel like you are actually in space

출제율 95%

12 주어진 문장 이후에 올 대화의 순서를 바르게 배열하시오.

What are you watching?

(A) Yes, it's because there's no gravity in space.

(B) Right. I wish I could float around like an astronaut!

(C) It's a documentary about life in space. Everything seems so different.

(D) Really? I don't. It looks uncomfortable.

➡ _____

13 다음 중 어법상 올바른 문장은?

① If I were the principal of my school, I will let students have PE class every day.

② If there were no cold air and warm air, a wind can not be made.

③ Without your help, I could not get along well enough.

④ If were it not for water, no living things could survive.

⑤ But for your advice, I will ruin my reputation.

14 다음 문장에서 어법상 어색한 부분을 찾아 고치시오.

(1) If Drake has a lot of money, he can start a business right now. But he's poor.

➡ _____

(2) Sit with your legs extending and lean forward.

➡ _____

15 다음 우리말을 괄호 안에 주어진 조건대로 영작하시오.

(1) 만약 Carrie가 시험에 통과한다면, 변호사가 될 텐데. (if로 시작) (같은 뜻을 as로 시작)

➡ _____
_____

(2) 우리가 빛의 속도로 여행한다면, 화성에 13분 안에 도착할 수 있을 텐데. (if로 시작) (같은 뜻을 since로 시작)

➡ _____
_____
_____

(3) 그 종이를 들고 점들이 맞춰지도록 그것을 접으세요. (with 이용)

➡ _____
_____

16 다음 중 〈보기〉의 밑줄 친 부분과 바꿔 쓸 수 없는 것은?

┌─── 보기 ───┐
The world would be a better place if there were no more wars.
└─────────────┘

① if it were not for more wars
② were it not for more wars
③ but for more wars
④ had there no more wars
⑤ without more wars

[17~21] 다음 글을 읽고 물음에 답하시오.

Sci Teen: Is there ⓐ_____ in the universe?

Dr. Sci: According to some researchers, yes. Einstein figured out ⓑthat space and time are connected, and he called it space-time. He thought that space-time could actually be bent. When it is bent, parts that are far away from each other are suddenly closer.

(A) On a flat sheet of paper, the dots are far away from one another. Now, take the paper and fold it with the dots matched up.

(B) To understand this, take a sheet of paper and make a small dot at the top of the paper and another at the bottom of the paper.

(C) Punch a hole in the paper and the dots will be instantly connected. Like this, wormholes in space may contain two mouths, with a throat connecting the two.

Sci Teen: Just like a wormhole in the apple, right? If such wormholes existed in space, we could get to places billions of light-years away quickly!

Dr. Sci: Yes, but it's too early to celebrate. Wormholes exist in theory only.

출제율 90%

17 글의 흐름상 빈칸 ⓐ에 들어갈 말로 가장 적절한 것은?

① such a planet   ② a room to rest

③ so much noise   ④ such a big hole

⑤ such a shortcut

출제율 95%

18 자연스러운 글이 되도록 (A)~(C)를 바르게 나열하시오.

➡ _____

출제율 100%

19 밑줄 친 ⓑ와 쓰임이 다른 하나는?

① Did you just say that he had left for London?

② The news that he came back surprised me.

③ It was regretful that I didn't visit him more often.

④ The idea that he came up with is brilliant for us to use.

⑤ Have you heard about the rumor that Jane and Tom broke up?

출제율 90%

20 다음과 같이 풀이되는 말을 위 글에서 찾아 쓰시오.

> a formal statement of the rules on which a subject of study is based

➡ _____

출제율 100%

21 Choose one that is NOT true.

① It was thought that space-time could be bent.

② Einstein was the one who figured out space and time are connected.

③ A wormhole makes it possible to get to another planet safely.

④ Parts far away from each other can be closer if space-time is bent.

⑤ It is assumed that wormholes contain two mouths with a throat.

[22~23] 다음 글을 읽고 물음에 답하시오.

If I could make a planet for us to live (A)_____ in the future, I would like to make a planet called Atlas. It would be a beautiful green planet. Its size would be bigger than the moon, but smaller than Earth. The temperature of it would be about 30℃. It would have beautiful nature. Interestingly, if people moved to it, they could communicate with animals (B)_____ this planet.

출제율 95%

22 빈칸 (A)와 (B)에 들어갈 말이 바르게 짝지어진 것은?

① in – at   ② on – on

③ about – at   ④ to – on

⑤ by – by

출제율 90%

23 What is the name of the planet the writer wants to make?

➡ _____

01 밑줄 친 우리말과 일치하도록 주어진 단어를 이용하여 영작하시오. (단어 변형 가능)

> **A:** <u>내가 우주 여행을 가면 좋을 텐데.</u>
> **B:** Me, too. I'm sure that's every teenager's wish.

➡ (1) _____
     (take, wish, could)
  (2) _____
     (come true, would, take)
  (3) _____
     (if, take, would, great)

02 다음 그림을 보고 〈보기〉의 단어를 이용하여 이루어지기를 바라는 일을 표현하는 문장 2개를 완성하시오.

Tony

> ┤ 보기 ├
> cooking show, wish, could, open,
> appear, own, also, restaurant

➡ (1) _____
  (2) _____
     _____

03 다음 그림을 보고 주어진 단어를 이용해 대화의 빈칸을 완성하시오.

> **A:** _____ to sleep in space?
>   (possible, down, 6 단어)
> **B:** Yes, astronauts attach _____ a wall. (attach, sleeping bag)
> **A:** Sounds interesting. Life in space is so different from that on Earth.

04 다음 문장을 주어진 조건대로 바꿔 쓰시오.

(1) If Mary heard the news, she would be happy. (as 이용)
➡ _____.

(2) If my father knew the fact, he would not let me go there. (so 이용)
➡ _____
   _____

(3) As the man can't speak English, I won't employ him. (if 이용)
➡ _____
   _____

(4) Since the weather is not fine, Jini won't go on a picnic. (were 이용, if를 쓰지 말 것.)
➡ _____
   _____

(5) Half the pleasure of our daily lives could be lost if there were no television. (without을 문두에 쓸 것.)
➡ _____
   _____

05 다음 두 문장을 with를 이용해서 한 문장으로 바꿔 쓰시오.

(1) • Mr. Jones is sitting on a chair.
  • He crossed his legs.

  ➡ _____

(2) • Bella laughed out loud.
  • She pointed her finger at me.

  ➡ _____

  _____

(3) • It was a beautiful morning.
  • Little wind blows.

  ➡ _____

  _____

[06~08] 다음 글을 읽고 물음에 답하시오.

> **Sci Teen:** Is there such a shortcut in the universe?
>
> **Dr. Sci:** According to some researchers, yes. Einstein figured out that space and time are connected, and he called it space-time. He thought that space-time could actually be bent. When it is bent, parts that are far away from each other are suddenly closer. To understand this, take a sheet of paper and make a small dot at the top of the paper and another at the bottom of the paper. On a flat sheet of paper, the dots are far away from one another. Now, take the paper and fold it with the dots (A)_____ up. Punch a hole in the paper and the dots will be instantly connected. Like this, wormholes in space may contain two mouths, with a throat connecting the two.

06 빈칸 (A)에 동사 match를 어법에 맞게 쓰시오.

  ➡ _____

07 What did Einstein figure out about space and time? Answer in English.

  ➡ _____

08 What connects two mouths of a wormhole? Answer in English with a full sentence.

  ➡ _____

[09~10] 다음 글을 읽고 물음에 답하시오.

> **Sci Teen:** Hi, science fans. Today, we're going to talk about space travel. As we all know, there is nothing faster than (A)_____ in the universe. So, if we travel at the speed of light, we should be able to get to another planet in the blink of an eye, right?
>
> **Dr. Sci:** That would be nice, but space is so vast that it is not possible. In the movie, *Passengers*, a spaceship (B)_____ to a different planet (C)_____ at one-half the speed of light. So it should get to another planet very quickly, right? But, the passengers sleep for 120 years because it is (D)_____ to take that much time to get to a different planet.

09 문맥상 빈칸 (A)에 알맞은 말을 위 글에서 찾아 쓰시오.

  ➡ _____

10 주어진 단어를 문맥과 어법에 맞게 빈칸 (B)~(D)에 쓰시오.

(travel / expect / head)

  ➡ (B)_____ (C)_____ (D)_____

창의사고력 서술형 문제

01 I wish를 사용해 자신만의 소원 3가지 이상을 쓰시오.

(1) _____

(2) _____

(3) _____

02 다음 우리말을 가정법을 사용하여 영작하시오.

(1) 지구에 공기가 없다면, 하늘은 언제나 깜깜할 텐데.

➡ _____

(2) 중력이 없다면, 공기는 우주로 가 버릴 텐데. (주어진 조건에 맞춰 영작할 것.)

(a) there를 이용할 것. (b) if를 이용할 것. (c) if를 쓰지 말고 were를 이용할 것. (d) but을 이용할 것. (e) without을 이용할 것.

➡ _____

_____

_____

_____

03 다음 질의응답을 참고하여 Jane이 구상한 행성에 대한 글을 완성하시오.

Q: What is the name of the planet? / And what color is it?

A: It's called Minas. It is a beautiful pink planet.

Q: How big is the planet? And what is the temperature of it?

A: Its size is bigger than the moon, but smaller than Earth. The temperature is about 20℃.

Q: What is special about the planet? If people moved to it, what would be good for them?

A: It has cotton candy mountains. If people moved to it, they could feel time pass slowly on this planet.

If I could make a planet for us to live on in the future, I would like to make a planet called _____. It would be a beautiful _____ planet. Its size would be _____ _____. The temperature of it would be about _____. It would have _____. Interestingly, if people moved to it, they could _____.

단원별 모의고사

01 빈칸에 전치사 in이 들어가지 <u>않는</u> 것을 <u>모두</u> 고르시오. (대·소문자 무시)

① _____ theory, it takes only 2 days to climb the mountain, but in practice it is impossible.
② Will you print _____ your report?
③ It disappeared _____ the blink of an eye.
④ I studied hard _____ order to pass the exam.
⑤ Lie _____ here and take a rest.

02 접두사 im-이나 in-을 붙여서 반의어를 만들 수 <u>없는</u> 것을 고르시오.

① partial   ② patient   ③ usual
④ credible   ⑤ sensitive

03 다음 빈칸을 〈보기〉에 있는 어휘를 이용하여 채우시오. (형태 변화 가능)

┌─ 보기 ─────────────────────
│   attach   crush   exist   extend
└─────────────────────────────

(1) Lie down on the floor and _____ your legs.
(2) You should _____ your photograph to the form.
(3) These cars were _____ in the accident.
(4) Do you believe life _____ on other planets?

04 다음 우리말에 맞도록 빈칸에 알맞은 말을 쓰시오. (철자가 주어진 경우 주어진 철자로 시작할 것.)

(1) 그 회사는 1주일에 수십억 달러를 쓴다.
➡ The company spends _____ _____ dollars a week.
(2) 그의 생일을 축하하기 위한 파티를 여는 게 어떠니?
➡ How about having a party to c_____ his birthday?
(3) 이 기계는 물 사용을 감지하는 센서가 있다.
➡ This machine has sensors to d_____ water use.
(4) 한참을 찾은 후에, 나는 잃어버렸던 우산을 결국 찾았다.
➡ After a long search, I e_____ the missing umbrella.

[05~06] 다음 대화를 읽고 물음에 답하시오.

A: Look at this movie. People are walking in the spaceship, just like on Earth.
B: That's because they can make "gravity" in the spaceship.
A: Is it possible to create gravity in space? If so, the space trip would be more (A) [comfortable / uncomfortable].
B: I heard it's not entirely (B)[possible / impossible]. Scientists are developing the technology.
A: Really? I wish I could travel long distance in a spaceship someday.

05 위 대화의 괄호 (A)와 (B)에서 적절한 것을 골라 쓰시오.

➡ (A) _____   (B) _____

06 위 대화에서 다음 영영풀이에 해당하는 단어를 찾아 쓰시오.

> the amount of space between two places

➡ _____

[07~09] 다음 대화를 읽고 물음에 답하시오.

> W: Look at this man, Jake. (①) He lived in space for one year.
> M: It must have been tough for him. (②)
> W: Right, but you know what's interesting? He grew 2 inches (A)_____ in space. (③)
> M: Really? How is that possible?
> W: I'm not sure, but maybe it's (B)_____ there's no gravity in space. (④)
> M: That's so cool. (a)내가 우주에서 살 수 있으면 좋을 텐데. (wish, could) (⑤)
> W: I'm sure there are other ways to become taller than going to space.

07 ①~⑤ 중 주어진 문장이 들어갈 곳은?

> That way, I could become taller.

① ② ③ ④ ⑤

08 빈칸 (A)와 (B)에 들어갈 말이 알맞게 짝지어진 것은?

	(A)	(B)
①	while	why
②	while	so
③	while	because
④	for	why
⑤	for	because

09 밑줄 친 (a)의 우리말과 일치하도록 주어진 단어를 이용해 영작하시오.

➡ _____

[10~12] 다음 대화를 읽고 물음에 답하시오.

> M: Hey, Cindy. (①) I heard that you went to the National Space Center last weekend. How was it?
> W: It was great, Chris. (②) I experienced zero gravity and astronauts' space life. (③)
> M: Sounds fun. (④)
> W: Yes, and I heard about their adventure stories. (⑤)
> M: Oh, (a)나는 그들처럼 우주인이 돼서 화성을 탐험하고 싶어. (could, Mars, I, I, an astronaut, explore, become, and, like, them, wish)

10 ①~⑤ 중 주어진 문장이 들어갈 곳은?

> Did you meet real astronauts in person?

① ② ③ ④ ⑤

11 밑줄 친 (a)의 우리말과 일치하도록 괄호 안에 주어진 단어를 알맞게 배열하시오.

➡ _____

_____

12 ⓐ~ⓓ 중 위 대화를 읽고 답할 수 있는 질문을 모두 고르시오.

> ⓐ What did Cindy do at the National Space Center?
> ⓑ Is it possible for Cindy to become an astronaut?
> ⓒ When did Cindy go to the National Space Center?
> ⓓ Did Cindy meet the astronauts?

➡ _____

13 다음 중 문장의 뜻이 나머지 넷과 다른 것은?

① If I had a magic lamp, I could wish for happiness and health.
② Had I a magic lamp, I could wish for happiness and health.
③ Since I have a magic lamp, I can wish for happiness and health.
④ As I don't have a magic lamp, I can't wish for happiness and health.
⑤ I don't have a magic lamp, so I can't wish for happiness and health.

14 다음 빈칸에 공통으로 알맞은 것은?

- My little brother was crying _____ tears running down his face.
- Brian looked at the children, _____ his arms folded.

① when　　② since　　③ if
④ with　　⑤ as

15 다음 중 밑줄 친 부분의 쓰임이 나머지 넷과 다른 것은?

① She said if she had a million dollars, she would buy a fancy house and a car.
② He had no idea if the students would like his gifts.
③ If Mike spoke English, he could make many foreign friends.
④ If I were the president, I would make more holidays.
⑤ We could go to a movie if my mom were not tired.

16 다음 문장에서 틀린 것을 고쳐 다시 쓰시오.

(1) They jogged with their dog followed them.
　➡ _____

(2) Drake walked for a long time with his eyes fixing upon the floor.
　➡ _____

(3) The prince entered the hall with the people cheered.
　➡ _____
　_____

17 괄호 안에 주어진 어휘를 활용하여 우리말과 일치하도록 영작하시오.

(1) 내가 우주 비행사라면, 난 우주를 걸어다닐 텐데. (an astronaut, walk in space)
　➡ _____

(2) 만약 비가 멈춘다면 우리는 야구를 할 수 있을 텐데. (stop, rain)
　➡ _____

(3) 어머니를 다시 살아 돌아오시게 할 수 있으면 좋겠어요. (wish, bring back to, life)
　➡ _____

(4) 윗팔에 무릎을 둔 채, 팔로 균형을 유지하세요. (balance, rest, the upper arms, on)
　➡ _____
　_____

(5) 나의 선생님은 하루 종일 문을 닫은 채 일하셨다. (work, all day, close)
　➡ _____
　_____

[18~21] 다음 글을 읽고 물음에 답하시오.

Sci Teen: Is there a faster way to travel through space?

Dr. Sci: Well, in order to answer that question, I'd like you to think about this apple for a second. Imagine a worm is on this apple. It detects something sweet at the bottom and wants to move from the top to the bottom. For the worm, the apple's surface is as vast as our universe. Now the worm can either move around the outer layer or down a wormhole. Which do you think it will choose? Well, it would choose the wormhole because it is a shortcut.

Sci Teen: Is there such a shortcut in the universe?

Dr. Sci: According to some researchers, yes. Einstein figured out that space and time are connected, and he called it space-time. He thought that space-time could actually be bent. (①) When it is bent, parts that are far away from each other are suddenly closer. (②) To understand this, take a sheet of paper and make a small dot at the top of the paper and another at the bottom of the paper. (③) Now, take the paper and fold it with the dots matched up. (④) Punch a hole in the paper and the dots will be instantly connected. (⑤) Like this, wormholes in space may contain two mouths, (A)_____.

18 주어진 단어를 바르게 나열하여 빈칸 (A)에 들어갈 말을 완성하시오. 필요할 경우 어형을 바꾸시오.

> (the two / a throat / connect / with)

➡ _____

19 (①)~(⑤) 중 주어진 문장이 들어가기에 가장 적절한 곳은?

> On a flat sheet of paper, the dots are far away from one another.

①   ②   ③   ④   ⑤

20 What are the two ways for the worm to move from the top to the bottom of an apple? Answer in English.

➡ _____
_____

21 위 글을 읽고 답할 수 <u>없는</u> 것은?

① Why does the worm want to move to the bottom of the apple?

② Which way is better for the worm to choose to move to the bottom of the apple?

③ Who figured out that space and time are connected?

④ What happens to the dots if we punch a hole in the paper?

⑤ How did Einstein find out space and time are connected?

[22~25] 다음 글을 읽고 물음에 답하시오.

Sci Teen: Just like a wormhole in the apple, right? If such wormholes existed in space, we could get to places billions of light-years away quickly!

Dr. Sci: Yes, but it's too early to celebrate. Wormholes exist in theory only.

Sci Teen: So all we need to do is find one, right?

Dr. Sci: Even if we find one, there are many things to consider before actually going through one. A wormhole would be very unstable. If a spaceship flew into one, it might be crushed or broken into pieces.

Sci Teen: Ouch! That's not a pretty picture. So, are we hopeless? Is traveling in space through a wormhole simply an idea that only exists in theory?

Dr. Sci: I wouldn't say so. The debate about wormholes is still ongoing, but with persistent exploration and research, I believe we will eventually find one and learn how to travel through it. Look back at our history. We've achieved so many things that seemed impossible at first. Who knows? Maybe you can be the one to find (A)the answer!

22 빈칸에 들어갈 말로 가장 적절한 것은?

> Q: Why do we need to consider many things before going through a wormhole?
>
> A: It is because _____.

① there are too many wormholes
② lots of people want to go there
③ there is no place like a wormhole
④ a wormhole would be very unstable
⑤ a wormhole makes people comfortable

23 밑줄 친 (A)의 의미로 가장 적절한 것은?

① 웜홀의 기원을 연구하는 방법에 대한 답
② 웜홀을 통해 우주여행을 하는 방법에 대한 해답
③ 불가능한 것을 가능하게 만드는 것에 대한 해답
④ 웜홀을 증명하는 이론을 찾는 방법에 대한 답
⑤ 이론상에만 존재하는 웜홀의 존재를 증명하는 답

24 How will we find a wormhole and learn how to travel through it according to Dr. Sci? Answer in English.

➡ _____

_____

25 What could we do if wormholes existed in space? Answer in English.

➡ _____

_____

MEMO

MEMO

중간 + 기말

적중100 plus

영어 기출문제집

영어 중 3

비상 | 김진완

Best Collection

내용문의 중등영어발전소 적중100 편집부 TEL 070-7707-0457

INSIGHT
on the textbook

교과서 파헤치기

영어 기출 문제집

적중 100 plus
2학기 전과정

영어 중 **3**

비상 | 김진완

INSIGHT
on the textbook

교과서 파헤치기

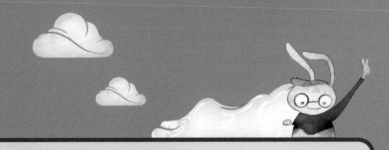

※ 다음 영어를 우리말로 쓰시오.

01 seriously	22 disaster
02 admit	23 escape
03 critically	24 judge
04 awful	25 describe
05 extremely	26 nevertheless
06 fake	27 reliable
07 confess	28 wound
08 critical	29 muscle
09 harmful	30 support
10 citizen	31 mine
11 mislead	32 measure
12 height	33 source
13 strengthen	34 chest
14 adult	35 be related to
15 argument	36 look into
16 publish	37 make up
17 recognize	38 break down
18 incident	39 according to
19 criticize	40 draw one's attention to
20 prove	41 think outside the box
21 current	42 be useful for
	43 on the loose

※ 다음 우리말을 영어로 쓰시오.

01 인정하다, 자백하다

02 근육

03 그럼에도 불구하고

04 경쟁자, 경쟁 상대

05 진지하게, 심각하게

06 성인, 어른

07 잘못 이끌다, 오해하게 하다

08 광산; 채굴하다

09 비난하다

10 입증하다, 증명하다

11 비판적으로

12 참사, 재난

13 달아나다, 탈출하다

14 대중, 일반 사람들

15 강하게 하다, 더 튼튼하게 하다

16 가짜의, 거짓의

17 고백하다, 인정하다

18 극도로, 극히

19 해로운, 유해한

20 사건

21 논쟁, 언쟁

22 믿을 만한, 신뢰할 만한

23 끔찍한, 지독한

24 시민

25 판단하다

26 측정하다, 재다

27 현재의, 지금의

28 발행하다, 출판하다

29 위험한, 위독한

30 알아보다

31 출처, 자료

32 기술하다

33 (사실임을) 입증하다, 뒷받침하다

34 상처를 입히다

35 조사하다, 들여다보다

36 ~을 찾다

37 ~와 연관되다

38 ~의 관심을 ...로 끌다

39 잠들다

40 ~을 부수다, ~을 무너뜨리다

41 ~에 따르면

42 ~에게 유용하다

43 지어내다, 만들어 내다

※ 다음 영영풀이에 알맞은 단어를 <보기>에서 골라 쓴 후, 우리말 뜻을 쓰시오.

1 _____ : to fire a weapon: _____

2 _____ : not genuine; appearing to be something it is not: _____

3 _____ : a person who lives in a particular city: _____

4 _____ : an event causing great harm, damage, or suffering: _____

5 _____ : to say or write what someone or something is like: _____

6 _____ : to suddenly feel so worried that you cannot be reasonable:

    _____

7 _____ : the upper front part of the body of humans: _____

8 _____ : to form words with the letters in the correct order: _____

9 _____ : to express disapproval of someone or something: _____

10 _____ : a place, person, or thing from which something comes: _____

11 _____ : to injure someone or something by cutting or breaking the skin:

    _____

12 _____ : an unexpected and usually unpleasant thing that happens: _____

13 _____ : to prepare and produce a book, magazine, etc. for sale: _____

14 _____ : to believe that someone is honest or will not do anything bad or wrong:

    _____

15 _____ : to show the existence, truth, or correctness of something by using

    evidence, logic, etc.: _____

16 _____ : a conversation or discussion in which two or more people disagree, often

    angrily: _____

보기			
trust	publish	fake	citizen
incident	criticize	source	panic
prove	wound	spell	disaster
shoot	argument	chest	describe

※ 다음 우리말과 일치하도록 빈칸에 알맞은 말을 쓰시오.

 해석

Listen & Talk 1 A-1

W: I think I _____ _____ _____ _____ I didn't _____
_____ yesterday.

M. Well, I've read an _____ saying that you don't catch a _____
because your _____ _____ is _____.

W: Really? Can you tell me _____ _____ _____?

M: The article said that people catch colds _____ _____.

Listen & Talk 1 A-2

W: I usually drink _____ _____ _____ _____ _____ before
I go to bed, but it doesn't help me _____ _____.

M: I saw a show on TV, and a doctor said that a glass of warm milk
doesn't actually _____ you _____ _____.

W: Oh, it doesn't? Can you _____ _____ _____ _____ _____?

M: Milk has special _____ that _____ people _____. But the
_____ in a glass is _____ small _____ have any _____.

Listen & Talk 2 A-1

W: _____ _____ _____ _____, John?

M: I'm reading a book of _____.

W: Riddles? Aren't they _____ children?

M: _____, no. Books of riddles are really _____ _____ _____.

W: Really? Why do you _____ _____?

M: They _____ us _____ more _____. We need to _____
_____ _____ _____ _____ _____ the answers.

Listen & Talk 2 A-2

M: Are these all _____ _____?

W: Yeah. These are all poems _____ _____ children.

M: By children?

W: Yeah. I think children _____ _____ _____ than adults.

M: Why do you _____ _____?

W: They're really _____ about their _____ and much _____
_____ _____ _____.

W: 어제 옷을 따뜻하게 입지 않아서 감기에 걸린 것 같아.
M: 글쎄, 체온이 낮다고 해서 감기에 걸리지는 않는다고 쓰여 있는 기사를 읽었어.
W: 정말? 그것에 대해 더 말해 줄 수 있니?
M: 기사에서는 사람들이 바이러스 때문에 감기에 걸린다고 했어.

W: 나는 보통 잠자리에 들기 전에 따뜻한 우유 한 잔을 마시는데, 그것이 잠드는 데 도움이 되지 않아.
M: 내가 텔레비전 프로그램에서 봤는데, 어떤 의사가 따뜻한 우유 한 잔이 실제로 잠드는 데 도움을 주는 건 아니라고 말했어.
W: 오, 그래? 그것에 대해 더 말해 줄 수 있니?
M: 우유에는 사람들을 졸리게 만드는 특별한 성분이 있어. 하지만 한 잔에 있는 양이 너무 적어서 효과가 없어.

W: 무엇을 읽고 있니, John?
M: 나는 수수께끼 책을 읽고 있어.
W: 수수께끼? 그거 아이들용 아니니?
M: 사실은, 그렇지 않아. 수수께끼 책은 어른들에게 굉장히 유용해.
W: 정말? 왜 그렇게 생각해?
M: 그 책들은 우리가 더 창의적으로 생각하도록 도와. 우리는 답을 찾기 위해 고정관념에서 벗어나야 하거든.

M: 이거 전부 시집이니?
W: 응. 이것들은 모두 아이들이 쓴 시야.
M: 아이들이?
W: 응. 내 생각에 아이들이 어른들보다 더 좋은 시를 쓰는 것 같아.
M: 왜 그렇게 생각해?
W: 아이들은 그들의 감정에 아주 솔직하고 어른들보다 훨씬 더 창의적이거든.

Listen & Talk 2 B

M: Hey, Sandy. Do you think _____ _____ _____ _____ _____? It is said that it can _____ me _____ _____.

W: _____ _____ _____ the _____ more _____. Hmm, it looks a bit _____ to me, David.

M: Why do _____ _____ _____?

W: There isn't _____ _____ about _____ in the _____.

M: Oh, you're _____.

W: Also, it doesn't tell you _____ _____ _____ _____ _____ _____ _____ _____ _____.

M: 안녕, Sandy. 너는 내가 이 음료를 사야 한다고 생각해? 내가 살을 빼는 것을 도와줄 수 있다고 적혀 있어.
W: 라벨을 더 자세히 읽어 볼게. 음, 내가 보기에 좀 이상해, David.
M: 왜 그렇게 생각해?
W: 음료 안에 무엇이 들었는지에 대한 충분한 정보가 없어.
M: 오, 네 말이 맞아.
W: 게다가, 체중을 감량하려면 얼마나 마셔야 하는지도 나와 있지 않아.

Communication

W: There are so many _____ _____ _____ we call "_____" that are _____ _____.

M: Why do you say so?

W: I read a book, and _____ _____ a lot of _____ of these _____ _____ _____ _____.

M: Like _____?

W: Well, most people think _____ are not smart. But, _____ are _____ _____.

M: Really? Can you _____ me _____ about that?

W: They can _____ _____ _____.

M: Oh, I didn't _____ _____.

W: 우리가 '사실'이라고 말하는 정보 중에 완전히 틀린 것들이 너무 많아.
M: 왜 그렇게 생각해?
W: 내가 책을 읽었는데, 거기에는 이러한 틀린 '사실'의 예시가 많이 있었어.
M: 예를 들면 어떤 것?
W: 음, 대부분의 사람들은 금붕어가 똑똑하지 않다고 생각해. 하지만 금붕어는 사실 똑똑해.
M: 정말? 그것에 대해 더 말해 줄 수 있니?
W: 그들은 그들의 주인을 알아 볼 수 있어.
M: 오, 그건 몰랐어.

Wrap Up 2

W: I read an _____ _____ about the Black Sea. Do you know _____ _____ _____?

M: Yes. It's _____ Eastern Europe _____ Western Asia, _____?

W: Right. _____ _____ do you think _____ _____?

M: Well, black, I _____.

M: No, it isn't. It's blue.

M: Really? Then why is it _____ the Black Sea? Can you _____ _____ _____ about it?

W: People call it the Black Sea _____ it is very _____.

W: 나는 흑해에 관한 흥미로운 기사를 읽었어. 너 그게 어디에 있는지 아니?
M: 응. 그것은 동유럽과 서아시아 사이에 있어, 그렇지?
W: 맞아. 그게 무슨 색일 거라고 생각해?
M: 글쎄, 검은색일 것 같아.
W: 아니야, 그렇지 않아. 그것은 파란색이야.
M: 정말? 그럼 왜 흑해라고 불리는 거야? 그것에 대해 더 말해 줄 수 있니?
W: 사람들이 흑해라고 부르는 이유는 그곳이 매우 위험하기 때문이야.

※ 다음 우리말에 맞도록 대화를 영어로 쓰시오.

Listen & Talk 1 A-1

W: _____

M: _____

_____

W: _____

M: _____

해석

W: 어제 옷을 따뜻하게 입지 않아서 감기에 걸린 것 같아.

M: 글쎄, 체온이 낮다고 해서 감기에 걸리지는 않는다고 쓰여 있는 기사를 읽었어.

W: 정말? 그것에 대해 더 말해 줄 수 있니?

M: 기사에서는 사람들이 바이러스 때문에 감기에 걸린다고 했어.

Listen & Talk 1 A-2

W: _____

M: _____

_____

W: _____

M: _____

_____

W: 나는 보통 잠자리에 들기 전에 따뜻한 우유 한 잔을 마시는데, 그것이 잠드는 데 도움이 되지 않아.

M: 내가 텔레비전 프로그램에서 봤는데, 어떤 의사가 따뜻한 우유 한 잔이 실제로 잠드는 데 도움을 주는 건 아니라고 말했어.

W: 오, 그래? 그것에 대해 더 말해 줄 수 있니?

M: 우유에는 사람들을 졸리게 만드는 특별한 성분이 있어. 하지만 한 잔에 있는 양이 너무 적어서 효과가 없어.

Listen & Talk 2 A-1

W: _____

M: _____

W: _____

M: _____

W: _____

M: _____

_____

W: 무엇을 읽고 있니, John?

M: 나는 수수께끼 책을 읽고 있어.

W: 수수께끼? 그거 아이들용 아니니?

M: 사실은, 그렇지 않아. 수수께끼 책은 어른들에게 굉장히 유용해.

W: 정말? 왜 그렇게 생각해?

M: 그 책들은 우리가 더 창의적으로 생각하도록 도와. 우리는 답을 찾기 위해 고정관념에서 벗어나야 하거든.

Listen & Talk 2 A-2

M: _____

W: _____

M: _____

W: _____

M: _____

W: _____

M: 이거 전부 시집이니?

W: 응. 이것들은 모두 아이들이 쓴 시야.

M: 아이들이?

W: 응. 내 생각에 아이들이 어른들보다 더 좋은 시를 쓰는 것 같아.

M: 왜 그렇게 생각해?

W: 아이들은 그들의 감정에 아주 솔직하고 어른들보다 훨씬 더 창의적이거든.

Listen & Talk 2 B

M: _____

_____

W: _____

M: _____

W: _____

M: _____

W: _____

Communication

W: _____

_____

M: _____

W: _____

M: _____

W: _____

M: _____

W: _____

M: _____

Wrap Up 2

W: _____

M: _____

W: _____

M: _____

W: _____

M: _____

W: _____

M: 안녕, Sandy. 너는 내가 이 음료를 사야 한다고 생각해? 내가 살을 빼는 것을 도와줄 수 있다고 적혀 있어.
W: 라벨을 더 자세히 읽어 볼게. 음, 내가 보기에 좀 이상해, David.
M: 왜 그렇게 생각해?
W: 음료 안에 무엇이 들었는지에 대한 충분한 정보가 없어.
M: 오, 네 말이 맞아.
W: 게다가, 체중을 감량하려면 얼마나 마셔야 하는지도 나와 있지 않아.

W: 우리가 '사실'이라고 말하는 정보 중에 완전히 틀린 것들이 너무 많아.
M: 왜 그렇게 생각해?
W: 내가 책을 읽었는데, 거기에는 이러한 틀린 '사실'의 예시가 많이 있었어.
M: 예를 들면 어떤 것?
W: 음, 대부분의 사람들은 금붕어가 똑똑하지 않다고 생각해. 하지만 금붕어는 사실 똑똑해.
M: 정말? 그것에 대해 더 말해 줄 수 있니?
W: 그들은 그들의 주인을 알아 볼 수 있어.
M: 오, 그건 몰랐어.

W: 나는 흑해에 관한 흥미로운 기사를 읽었어. 너 그게 어디에 있는지 아니?
M: 응. 그것은 동유럽과 서아시아 사이에 있어, 그렇지?
W: 맞아. 그게 무슨 색일 거라고 생각해?
M: 글쎄, 검은색일 것 같아.
W: 아니야, 그렇지 않아. 그것은 파란색이야.
M: 정말? 그럼 왜 흑해라고 불리는 거야? 그것에 대해 더 말해 줄 수 있니?
W: 사람들이 흑해라고 부르는 이유는 그곳이 매우 위험하기 때문이야.

Step1

※ 다음 우리말과 일치하도록 빈칸에 알맞은 것을 골라 쓰시오.

1 Can You _____ _____ _____ ?
A. News   B. Spot   C. Fake

2 Every day we _____ , _____ , or read _____ _____ .
A. news   B. hear   C. watch   D. interesting

3 However, have you ever _____ _____ an _____
is really true?
A. article   B. considered   C. seriously   D. whether

4 Everyone likes an interesting news story but _____ _____ it is
completely _____ _____ ?
A. if   B. up   C. what   D. made

5 Fake news can be very _____ in that it can make people
_____ _____ or even _____ .
A. misled   B. less   C. harmful   D. informed

6 _____ , there have been _____ fake news reports _____
_____ .
A. various   B. throughout   C. nevertheless   D. history

7 Why have some people _____ _____ _____ _____ ?
A. written   B. false   C. such   D. information

8 Let's look into some articles _____ about the _____
_____ _____ them.
A. hidden   B. thinking   C. behind   D. motives

9 _____ _____
A. DISATER   B. AWFUL

10 Last night, an angry group of rhinoceroses _____ _____
the walls of the _____ at the zoo and _____ .
A. down   B. escaped   C. broke   D. cage

11 They also _____ _____ the walls of the _____ wild
animals' _____ .
A. other   B. broke   C. cages   D. down

12 These animals _____ _____ the streets and _____
_____ of people.
A. hundreds   B. ran   C. injured   D. down

13 Twelve of the animals are _____ _____ _____ _____ .
A. the   B. on   C. still   D. loose

14 Citizens should _____ indoors _____ _____ _____ _____ .
A. further   B. stay   C. notice   D. until

15 Not a single act or _____ _____ above has _____ .
A. described   B. place   C. incident   D. taken

16 At that time, those who read the _____ carefully _____
_____ .
A. out   B. article   C. loud   D. laughed

---

1 당신은 가짜 뉴스임을 알아챌 수 있는가?

2 매일 우리는 흥미로운 뉴스를 보고, 듣고, 읽는다.

3 그러나 당신은 뉴스 기사가 정말로 진실인지 심각하게 고려해 본 적이 있는가?

4 모든 사람이 흥미로운 뉴스 기사를 좋아하지만, 만약 그것이 완전히 지어낸 것이라면 어떻게 할 것인가?

5 가짜 뉴스는 사람들에게 정보를 부족하게 제공하거나 사람들을 잘못 이끌 수 있다는 점에서 매우 해로울 수 있다.

6 그럼에도 불구하고, 역사를 통틀어 다양한 가짜 뉴스 보도들이 존재해 왔다.

7 왜 어떤 사람들은 그러한 거짓 정보를 써 왔던 것일까?

8 그 뒤에 숨겨진 동기를 생각하면서 몇 가지 뉴스 기사를 살펴보자.

9 끔찍한 참사

10 어젯밤, 화가 난 코뿔소 떼가 동물원 우리의 벽을 부수고 도망쳤다.

11 그들은 또한 다른 야생 동물 우리의 벽도 부수었다.

12 이 동물들은 거리를 뛰어다니며 수백 명의 사람에게 부상을 입혔다.

13 그중 열두 마리의 동물들이 아직 잡히지 않았다.

14 시민들은 추후 안내가 있을 때까지 집 안에 머물러야 한다.

15 위에 기술된 어떤 행동이나 사건도 일어나지 않았다.

16 그 당시 이 기사를 주의 깊게 읽었던 사람들은 크게 웃었다.

17 _____ who didn't read it to the end _____ _____ _____.

    A. worried   B. those   C. got   D. really

18 _____ the news was _____, many people _____.

    A. false   B. knowing   C. panicked   D. not

19 _____ tried to _____ the city while _____ went into the parks with guns to _____ the animals.

    A. others   B. hunt   C. escape   D. some

20 So why did *The Herald* _____ _____ _____ _____?

    A. such   B. make   C. news   D. up

21 Later, they _____ that they made it _____ so that they could draw the readers' _____ to the _____ conditions at the zoo.

    A. attention   B. confessed   C. unsafe   D. up

22 _____ _____ A FRIEND _____ _____

    A. IN   B. SLAV   C. ARGUMENT   D. SHOOTS

23 Mejk Swenekafew, a Slav worker at the Columbia Coal Mine, was _____ and seriously _____ by John Pecitello _____ the _____ camp Thursday evening.

    A. shot   B. near   C. wounded   D. mining

24 The two men _____ an _____ _____ a meeting.

    A. argument   B. had   C. during

25 The argument _____ to a fight, and Pecitello _____ Swenekafew _____, in the _____ and leg.

    A. twice   B. led   C. chest   D. shot

26 He is now at the hospital _____ _____ _____.

    A. critical   B. in   C. condition

27 Pecitello _____ _____ _____ the _____.

    A. away   B. shooting   C. after   D. ran

28 The police are _____ for him now and are _____ _____ that he is extremely _____.

    A. warning   B. searching   C. dangerous   D. citizens

29 Is _____ _____ _____ about the _____?

    A. article   B. strange   C. anything   D. there

30 _____ the Slav's name _____; it _____, "we-fake-news."

    A. backwards   B. read   C. spells

31 _____ _____ this and _____?

    A. wrote   B. why   C. who

17 그것을 끝까지 읽지 않은 사람들은 정말로 걱정하였다.

18 그 기사가 거짓이라는 것을 알지 못했기 때문에 많은 사람이 겁에 질려 어쩔 줄 몰랐다.

19 어떤 사람들은 도시를 빠져나가려고 했고 다른 사람들은 그 동물들을 사냥하기 위해 총을 들고 공원으로 나갔다.

20 그렇다면 왜 헤럴드 사는 이러한 뉴스를 만들어 냈을까?

21 나중에 그들은 동물원의 안전하지 않은 상태에 대해 독자들의 주의를 끌기 위해 그 기사를 지어냈다고 고백했다.

22 슬라브인이 언쟁 중에 친구에게 총을 쏘다

23 목요일 저녁 채굴 야영지 근처에서, 컬럼비아 광산 소속의 슬라브인 노동자 Mejk Swenekafew가 John Pecitello에 의해 총상을 입어 심각하게 다쳤다.

24 그 두 사람은 회의 중에 언쟁을 벌였다.

25 언쟁이 싸움으로 번졌고, Pecitello가 Swenekafew의 가슴과 다리에 두 번 총을 쏘았다.

26 현재 그는 위독한 상태로 입원 중이다.

27 Pecitello는 총격 이후 도주했다.

28 경찰이 지금 그를 찾고 있으며, 그가 극히 위험하다고 시민들에게 경고하고 있다.

29 이 기사에 뭔가 이상한 점이 있는가?

30 그 슬라브인의 이름을 거꾸로 읽어 보아라. 그것의 철자는 "우리는 뉴스를 조작한다."가 된다.

31 누가 이것을 썼고 왜 그랬을까?

32 *The Daily Telegram* published this fake article _____ _____ they could prove if *The Daily News*, their _____, was _____ their articles.

    A. stealing   B. that   C. competitor   D. so

33 *The Daily News* _____ the same _____ about "Swenekafew" the next day and thus got _____ _____.

    A. caught   B. published   C. stealing   D. article

34 The people at *The Daily News* had to _____ their act and were _____ _____ by the _____.

    A. criticized   B. admit   C. harshly   D. public

35 The two articles were _____ _____, but there are many "fake" news _____ _____ every day.

    A. cases   B. published   C. articles   D. special

36 As readers, we need to read _____ and _____ _____ the news is real or _____.

    A. whether   B. fake   C. critically   D. judge

37 _____ _____ _____ fake news!

    A. to   B. how   C. spot

38 _____ the _____

    A. Source   B. Consider

39 Is it _____ a _____ _____?

    A. sources   B. from   C. reliable

40 _____ we _____ the _____?

    A. trust   B. can   C. writer

41 _____ the _____

    A. Date   B. Check

42 Is it a _____ or an _____ _____?

    A. old   B. new   C. story

43 _____ it _____ _____ _____ events?

    A. to   B. is   C. current   D. related

44 Read _____ _____ _____

    A. Headlines   B. the   C. Beyong

45 Does the _____ _____ the _____?

    A. content   B. match   C. headline

46 Find _____ _____

    A. Sources   B. Supporting

47 Do other _____ stories _____ _____ _____?

    A. content   B. related   C. similar   D. provide

---

32 데일리 텔레그램 사는 그들의 경쟁자인 데일리 뉴스 사가 그들의 기사를 훔치는지를 증명하기 위해서 이 거짓 기사를 발행했다.

33 데일리 뉴스 사는 그 다음 날 'Swenekafew'에 대한 동일한 기사를 발행했고 그래서 훔친 것이 발각되었다.

34 데일리 뉴스 사의 사람들은 그들의 행동을 인정해야만 했고 대중들로부터 혹독한 비난을 받았다.

35 이 두 기사는 특별한 경우였지만, 매일 발행되는 '가짜' 뉴스 기사는 많이 있다.

36 독자로서, 우리는 비판적으로 읽고 그 뉴스가 진짜인지 가짜인지 판단할 필요가 있다.

37 가짜 뉴스 판별 방법!

38 출처를 고려하라

39 그것은 믿을 만한 출처에서 온 것인가?

40 우리는 그 필자를 신뢰할 수 있는가?

41 날짜를 확인하라

42 그것은 새로운 이야기인가 혹은 오래된 이야기인가?

43 그것은 현재의 사건들과 관련된 것인가?

44 기사 제목 그 이상을 읽어라

45 기사 제목이 기사 내용과 일치하는가?

46 뒷받침하는 자료를 찾아라

47 다른 관련된 이야기도 비슷한 내용을 제공하는가?

※ 다음 우리말과 일치하도록 빈칸에 알맞은 것을 골라 쓰시오.

1 Can You _____ _____ _____?

2 Every day we watch, hear, or read _____ _____.

3 However, _____ you ever seriously _____ _____ an article is really true?

4 Everyone likes an interesting news story but _____ _____ it is _____ _____ _____?

5 Fake news can be very _____ _____ _____ it can make people _____ _____ or even _____.

6 _____, there have been _____ _____ news reports _____ _____.

7 Why have some people _____ _____ _____ _____?

8 _____ _____ _____ some articles _____ about _____ _____ _____ _____ them.

9 _____ DISASTER

10 Last night, an angry group of rhinoceroses _____ _____ the walls of the cage at the zoo and _____.

11 They also _____ _____ the walls of _____ _____ wild animals' cages.

12 These animals _____ _____ the streets and _____ _____ _____ people.

13 Twelve of the animals are still _____ _____ _____.

14 _____ should stay indoors _____ _____ _____.

15 Not a single act or incident _____ _____ has _____ _____.

16 At that time, those who read the article carefully _____ _____ _____.

1 당신은 가짜 뉴스임을 알아챌 수 있는가?

2 매일 우리는 흥미로운 뉴스를 보고, 듣고, 읽는다.

3 그러나 당신은 뉴스 기사가 정말로 진실인지 심각하게 고려해 본 적이 있는가?

4 모든 사람이 흥미로운 뉴스 기사를 좋아하지만, 만약 그것이 완전히 지어낸 것이라면 어떻게 할 것인가?

5 가짜 뉴스는 사람들에게 정보를 부족하게 제공하거나 사람들을 잘못 이끌 수 있다는 점에서 매우 해로울 수 있다.

6 그럼에도 불구하고, 역사를 통틀어 다양한 가짜 뉴스 보도들이 존재해 왔다.

7 왜 어떤 사람들은 그러한 거짓 정보를 써 왔던 것일까?

8 그 뒤에 숨겨진 동기를 생각하면서 몇 가지 뉴스 기사를 살펴보자.

9 끔찍한 참사

10 어젯밤, 화가 난 코뿔소 떼가 동물원 우리의 벽을 부수고 도망쳤다.

11 그들은 또한 다른 야생 동물 우리의 벽도 부수었다.

12 이 동물들은 거리를 뛰어다니며 수백 명의 사람들에게 부상을 입혔다.

13 그중 열두 마리의 동물들이 아직 잡히지 않았다.

14 시민들은 추후 안내가 있을 때까지 집 안에 머물러야 한다.

15 위에 기술된 어떤 행동이나 사건도 일어나지 않았다.

16 그 당시 이 기사를 주의 깊게 읽었던 사람들은 크게 웃었다.

17 Those who didn't read it to the end _____ _____ _____ .

18 _____ _____ the news was _____ , many people _____ .

19 _____ tried _____ _____ the city while _____ went into the parks with guns _____ _____ the animals.

20 So why did *The Herald* _____ _____ _____ _____ ?

21 Later, they confessed that they _____ _____ _____ _____ _____ they _____ draw the _____ _____ _____ the unsafe conditions at the zoo.

22 SLAV _____ A FRIEND _____ _____

23 Mejk Swenekafew, a Slav worker at the Columbia Coal Mine, _____ _____ and _____ _____ _____ John Pecitello near the mining camp Thursday evening.

24 The two men _____ _____ _____ _____ a meeting.

25 The argument _____ _____ a fight, and Pecitello shot Swenekafew _____ , _____ _____ _____ and leg.

26 He is now at the hospital _____ _____ _____ .

27 Pecitello _____ _____ _____ _____ _____ .

28 The police _____ _____ _____ him now and _____ _____ citizens that he is _____ _____ .

29 Is there _____ _____ about the _____ ?

30 Read the Slav's name _____ ; it spells, "we-fake-news."

31 Who _____ this and _____ ?

17 그것을 끝까지 읽지 않은 사람들은 정말로 걱정하였다.

18 그 기사가 거짓이라는 것을 알지 못했기 때문에 많은 사람이 겁에 질려 어쩔 줄 몰랐다.

19 어떤 사람들은 도시를 빠져나가려고 했고 다른 사람들은 그 동물들을 사냥하기 위해 총을 들고 공원으로 나갔다.

20 그렇다면 왜 헤럴드 사는 이러한 뉴스를 만들어 냈을까?

21 나중에 그들은 동물원의 안전하지 않은 상태에 대해 독자들의 주의를 끌기 위해 그 기사를 지어냈다고 고백했다.

22 슬라브인이 언쟁 중에 친구에게 총을 쏘다

23 목요일 저녁 채굴 야영지 근처에서, 컬럼비아 광산 소속의 슬라브인 노동자 Mejk Swenekafew가 John Pecitello에 의해 총상을 입어 심각하게 다쳤다.

24 그 두 사람은 회의 중에 언쟁을 벌였다.

25 언쟁이 싸움으로 번졌고, Pecitello가 Swenekafew의 가슴과 다리에 두 번 총을 쏘았다.

26 현재 그는 위독한 상태로 입원 중이다.

27 Pecitello는 총격 이후 도주했다.

28 경찰이 지금 그를 찾고 있으며, 그가 극히 위험하다고 시민들에게 경고하고 있다.

29 이 기사에 뭔가 이상한 점이 있는가?

30 그 슬라브인의 이름을 거꾸로 읽어 보아라. 그것의 철자는 "우리는 뉴스를 조작한다."가 된다.

31 누가 이것을 썼고 왜 그랬을까?

32 *The Daily Telegram* _____ this fake article _____ _____ they _____ prove _____ *The Daily News*, their competitor, was stealing _____ _____.

33 *The Daily News* published the same article about "Swenekafew" the next day and thus _____ _____ _____.

34 The people at *The Daily News* _____ _____ _____ their act and _____ _____ _____ by the public.

35 The two articles were _____ _____, but there are many "fake" news articles _____ every day.

36 _____ readers, we need to read _____ and _____ _____ the news is real _____ fake.

37 _____ _____ _____ fake news!

38 _____ the _____

39 Is it from a _____ _____?

40 Can we _____ the _____?

41 _____ the Date

42 Is it a _____ or an _____ _____?

43 _____ it _____ _____ _____ events?

44 Read _____ _____ _____

45 Does the headline _____ _____ _____?

46 Find _____ _____

47 Do other _____ stories provide _____ _____?

32 데일리 텔레그램 사는 그들의 경쟁자인 데일리 뉴스 사가 그들의 기사를 훔치는지를 증명하기 위해서 이 거짓 기사를 발행했다.

33 데일리 뉴스 사는 그 다음 날 'Swenekafew'에 대한 동일한 기사를 발행했고 그래서 훔친 것이 발각되었다.

34 데일리 뉴스 사의 사람들은 그들의 행동을 인정해야만 했고 대중들로부터 혹독한 비난을 받았다.

35 이 두 기사는 특별한 경우였지만, 매일 발행되는 '가짜' 뉴스 기사는 많이 있다.

36 독자로서, 우리는 비판적으로 읽고 그 뉴스가 진짜인지 가짜인지 판단할 필요가 있다.

37 가짜 뉴스 판별 방법!

38 출처를 고려하라

39 그것은 믿을 만한 출처에서 온 것인가?

40 우리는 그 필자를 신뢰할 수 있는가?

41 날짜를 확인하라

42 그것은 새로운 이야기인가 혹은 오래된 이야기인가?

43 그것은 현재의 사건들과 관련된 것인가?

44 기사 제목 그 이상을 읽어라

45 기사 제목이 기사 내용과 일치하는가?

46 뒷받침하는 자료를 찾아라

47 다른 관련된 이야기도 비슷한 내용을 제공하는가?

※ 다음 문장을 우리말로 쓰시오.

1 Can You Spot Fake News?

➡ _____

2 Every day we watch, hear, or read interesting news.

➡ _____

3 However, have you ever seriously considered whether an article is really true?

➡ _____

4 Everyone likes an interesting news story but what if it is completely made up?

➡ _____

5 Fake news can be very harmful in that it can make people less informed or even misled.

➡ _____

6 Nevertheless, there have been various fake news reports throughout history.

➡ _____

7 Why have some people written such false information?

➡ _____

8 Let's look into some articles thinking about the hidden motives behind them.

➡ _____

9 AWFUL DISASTER

➡ _____

10 Last night, an angry group of rhinoceroses broke down the walls of the cage at the zoo and escaped.

➡ _____

11 They also broke down the walls of the other wild animals' cages.

➡ _____

12 These animals ran down the streets and injured hundreds of people.

➡ _____

13 Twelve of the animals are still on the loose.

➡ _____

14 Citizens should stay indoors until further notice.

➡ _____

15 Not a single act or incident described above has taken place.

➡ _____

16 At that time, those who read the article carefully laughed out loud.

➡ _____

17 Those who didn't read it to the end got really worried.

➡ _____

18 Not knowing the news was false, many people panicked.

➡ _____

19 Some tried to escape the city while others went into the parks with guns to hunt the animals.

➡ _____

20 So why did *The Herald* make up such news?

➡ _____

21 Later, they confessed that they made it up so that they could draw the readers' attention to the unsafe conditions at the zoo.

➡ _____

22 SLAV SHOOTS A FRIEND IN ARGUMENT

➡ _____

23 Mejk Swenekafew, a Slav worker at the Columbia Coal Mine, was shot and seriously wounded by John Pecitello near the mining camp Thursday evening.

➡ _____

➡ _____

24 The two men had an argument during a meeting.

➡ _____

25 The argument led to a fight, and Pecitello shot Swenekafew twice, in the chest and leg.

➡ _____

26 He is now at the hospital in critical condition.

➡ _____

27 Pecitello ran away after the shooting.

➡ _____

28 The police are searching for him now and are warning citizens that he is extremely dangerous.

➡ _____

29 Is there anything strange about the article?

➡ _____

30 Read the Slav's name backwards; it spells, "we-fake-news."

➡ _____

31 Who wrote this and why?

➡ _____

32 *The Daily Telegram* published this fake article so that they could prove if *The Daily News*, their competitor, was stealing their articles.

➡ _____

_____

33 *The Daily News* published the same article about "Swenekafew" the next day and thus got caught stealing.

➡ _____

34 The people at *The Daily News* had to admit their act and were harshly criticized by the public.

➡ _____

35 The two articles were special cases, but there are many "fake" news articles published every day.

➡ _____

36 As readers, we need to read critically and judge whether the news is real or fake.

➡ _____

37 How to spot fake news!

➡ _____

38 Consider the Source

➡ _____

39 Is it from a reliable source?

➡ _____

40 Can we trust the writer?

➡ _____

41 Check the Date

➡ _____

42 Is it a new or an old story?

➡ _____

43 Is it related to current events?

➡ _____

44 Read Beyond the Headlines

➡ _____

45 Does the headline match the content?

➡ _____

46 Find Supporting Sources

➡ _____

47 Do other related stories provide similar content?

➡ _____

※ 다음 괄호 안의 단어들을 우리말에 맞도록 바르게 배열하시오.

1 (You / Can / Fake / Spot / News?)
➡ _____

2 (day / every / watch, / we / or / hear, / read / news. / interesting)
➡ _____

3 (have / however, / ever / you / considered / seriously / an / whether / is / article / true? / really)
➡ _____

4 (likes / everyone / an / news / interesting / but / story / if / what / is / it / made / completely / up?)
➡ _____

5 (news / fake / be / can / harmful / very / that / in / can / it / people / make / less / or / informed / misled. / even)
➡ _____

6 (there / nevertheless, / been / have / fake / various / reports / news / history. / throughout)
➡ _____

7 (have / why / people / some / such / written / information? / false)
➡ _____

8 (look / let's / some / into / thinking / articles / the / about / motives / hidden / them. / behind)
➡ _____

9 (DISASTER / AWFUL)
➡ _____

10 (night, / last / angry / an / group / rhinoceroses / of / down / broke / walls / the / the / of / cage / the / at / zoo / escaped. / and)
➡ _____

11 (also / they / down / broke / walls / the / the / of / other / animals' / wild / cages.)
➡ _____

12 (animals / these / down / ran / streets / the / and / hundreds / injured / people. / of)
➡ _____

13 (of / twelve / animals / the / still / are / on / loose. / the)
➡ _____

14 (should / citizens / indoors / stay / further / until / notice.)
➡ _____

15 (a / not / act / single / or / described / incident / has / above / place. / taken)
➡ _____

16 (that / at / time, / who / those / the / read / carefully / article / out / laughed / loud.)
➡ _____

1 당신은 가짜 뉴스임을 알아챌 수 있는가?

2 매일 우리는 흥미로운 뉴스를 보고, 듣고, 읽는다.

3 그러나 당신은 뉴스 기사가 정말로 진실인지 심각하게 고려해 본 적이 있는가?

4 모든 사람이 흥미로운 뉴스 기사를 좋아하지만, 만약 그것이 완전히 지어낸 것이라면 어떻게 할 것인가?

5 가짜 뉴스는 사람들에게 정보를 부족하게 제공하거나 사람들을 잘못 이끌 수 있다는 점에서 매우 해로울 수 있다.

6 그럼에도 불구하고, 역사를 통틀어 다양한 가짜 뉴스 보도들이 존재해 왔다.

7 왜 어떤 사람들은 그러한 거짓 정보를 써 왔던 것일까?

8 그 뒤에 숨겨진 동기를 생각하면서 몇 가지 뉴스 기사를 살펴보자.

9 끔찍한 참사

10 어젯밤, 화가 난 코뿔소 떼가 동물원 우리의 벽을 부수고 도망쳤다.

11 그들은 또한 다른 야생 동물 우리의 벽도 부수었다.

12 이 동물들은 거리를 뛰어다니며 수백 명의 사람들에게 부상을 입혔다.

13 그중 열두 마리의 동물들이 아직 잡히지 않았다.

14 시민들은 추후 안내가 있을 때까지 집 안에 머물러야 한다.

15 위에 기술된 어떤 행동이나 사건도 일어나지 않았다.

16 그 당시 이 기사를 주의 깊게 읽었던 사람들은 크게 웃었다.

17 (who / those / read / didn't / to / it / end / the / got / worried. / really)

➡ _____

18 (knowing / not / news / the / false, / was / people / many / panicked.)

➡ _____

19 (tried / some / escape / to / city / the / others / while / into / went / parks / the / guns / with / hunt / to / animals. / the)

➡ _____

20 (why / so / *The* / did / make / *Herald* / up / news? / such)

➡ _____

21 (they / later, / that / confessed / made / they / up / it / that / so / could / they / the / draw / readers' / the / to / attention / conditions / unsafe / at / zoo. / the)

➡ _____

22 (SHOOTS / SLAV / FRIEND / A / ARGUMENT / IN)

➡ _____

23 (Swenekafew, / Mejk / Slave / a / worker / the / at / Columbia / Mine, / Coal / shot / was / and / wounded / seriously / by / Pecitello / John / near / mining / the / camp / evening. / Thursday)

➡ _____

24 (two / the / had / men / an / during / argument / meeting. / a)

➡ _____

25 (argument / the / to / led / fight, / a / and / shot / Pecitello / Swenekafew / twice, / the / in / chest / leg. / and)

➡ _____

26 (is / he / at / now / the / in / hospital / condition. / critical)

➡ _____

27 (Pecitello / away / ran / the / after / shooting.)

➡ _____

28 (police / the / searching / are / him / for / now / are / and / warning / that / citizens / is / he / dangerous. / extremely)

➡ _____

29 (there / is / strange / anything / about / article? / the)

➡ _____

30 (the / read / name / Slav's / backwards; / it / "we-fake-news." / spells,)

➡ _____

31 (wrote / who / why? / and / this)

➡ _____

---

17 그것을 끝까지 읽지 않은 사람들은 정말로 걱정하였다.

18 그 기사가 거짓이라는 것을 알지 못했기 때문에 많은 사람이 겁에 질려 어쩔 줄 몰랐다.

19 어떤 사람들은 도시를 빠져나가려고 했고 다른 사람들은 그 동물들을 사냥하기 위해 총을 들고 공원으로 나갔다.

20 그렇다면 왜 헤럴드 사는 이러한 뉴스를 만들어 냈을까?

21 나중에 그들은 동물원의 안전하지 않은 상태에 대해 독자들의 주의를 끌기 위해 그 기사를 지어냈다고 고백했다.

22 슬라브인이 언쟁 중에 친구에게 총을 쏘다

23 목요일 저녁 채굴 야영지 근처에서, 컬럼비아 광산 소속의 슬라브인 노동자 Mejk Swenekafew가 John Pecitello에 의해 총상을 입어 심각하게 다쳤다.

24 그 두 사람은 회의 중에 언쟁을 벌였다.

25 언쟁이 싸움으로 번졌고, Pecitello가 Swenekafew의 가슴과 다리에 두 번 총을 쏘았다.

26 현재 그는 위독한 상태로 입원 중이다.

27 Pecitello는 총격 이후 도주했다.

28 경찰이 지금 그를 찾고 있으며, 그가 극히 위험하다고 시민들에게 경고하고 있다.

29 이 기사에 뭔가 이상한 점이 있는가?

30 그 슬라브인의 이름을 거꾸로 읽어 보아라. 그것의 철자는 "우리는 뉴스를 조작한다."가 된다.

31 누가 이것을 썼고 왜 그랬을까?

32 (*Daily* / *The* / *Telegram* / this / published / fake / so / article / that / could / they / if / prove *Daily* / *The* / *News,* / competitor, / their / stealing / was / articles. / their)

➡ _____

33 (*Daily* / *The* / *News* / the / published / article / same / "Swenekafew" / about / next / the / day / thus / and / caught / got / stealing.)

➡ _____

34 (people / the / at / *News* / *The* / *Daily* / to / had / admit / act / their / and / harshly / were / criticized / the / by / public.)

➡ _____
_____

35 (two / the / were / articles / cases, / special / there / but / many / are / news / "fake" / articles / every / published / day.)

➡ _____

36 (readers, / as / need / we / read / to / and / critically / whether / judge / news / the / real / is / fake. / or)

➡ _____
_____

37 (to / how / fake / spot / news!)

➡ _____

38 (the / consider / Source)

➡ _____

39 (it / is / a / from / source? / reliable)

➡ _____

40 (we / can / the / trust / writer?)

➡ _____

41 (the / check / Date)

➡ _____

42 (it / is / new / a / or / old / an / story?)

➡ _____

43 (is / related / it / current / to / events?)

➡ _____

44 (Beyond / Read / Headlines / the)

➡ _____

45 (the / does / match / headline / content? / the)

➡ _____

46 (Supporting / Find / Sources)

➡ _____

47 (other / do / stories / related / similar / provide / content?)

➡ _____

32 데일리 텔레그램 사는 그들의 경쟁자인 데일리 뉴스 사가 그들의 기사를 훔치는지를 증명하기 위해서 이 거짓 기사를 발행했다.

33 데일리 뉴스 사는 그 다음 날 'Swenekafew'에 대한 동일한 기사를 발행했고 그래서 훔친 것이 발각되었다.

34 데일리 뉴스 사의 사람들은 그들의 행동을 인정해야만 했고 대중들로부터 혹독한 비난을 받았다.

35 이 두 기사는 특별한 경우였지만, 매일 발행되는 '가짜' 뉴스 기사는 많이 있다.

36 독자로서, 우리는 비판적으로 읽고 그 뉴스가 진짜인지 가짜인지 판단할 필요가 있다.

37 가짜 뉴스 판별 방법!

38 출처를 고려하라

39 그것은 믿을 만한 출처에서 온 것인가?

40 우리는 그 필자를 신뢰할 수 있는가?

41 날짜를 확인하라

42 그것은 새로운 이야기인가 혹은 오래된 이야기인가?

43 그것은 현재의 사건들과 관련된 것인가?

44 기사 제목 그 이상을 읽어라

45 기사 제목이 기사 내용과 일치하는가?

46 뒷받침하는 자료를 찾아라

47 다른 관련된 이야기도 비슷한 내용을 제공하는가?

※ **다음 우리말을 영어로 쓰시오.**

1 당신은 가짜 뉴스임을 알아챌 수 있는가?

➡ _____

2 매일 우리는 흥미로운 뉴스를 보고, 듣고, 읽는다.

➡ _____

3 그러나 당신은 뉴스 기사가 정말로 진실인지 심각하게 고려해 본 적이 있는가?

➡ _____

4 모든 사람이 흥미로운 뉴스 기사를 좋아하지만, 만약 그것이 완전히 지어낸 것이라면 어떻게 할 것인가?

➡ _____

5 가짜 뉴스는 사람들에게 정보를 부족하게 제공하거나 사람들을 잘못 이끌 수 있다는 점에서 매우 해로울 수 있다.

➡ _____

6 그럼에도 불구하고, 역사를 통틀어 다양한 가짜 뉴스 보도들이 존재해 왔다.

➡ _____

7 왜 어떤 사람들은 그러한 거짓 정보를 써 왔던 것일까?

➡ _____

8 그 뒤에 숨겨진 동기를 생각하면서 몇 가지 뉴스 기사를 살펴보자.

➡ _____

9 끔찍한 참사

➡ _____

10 어젯밤, 화가 난 코뿔소 떼가 동물원 우리의 벽을 부수고 도망쳤다.

➡ _____

11 그들은 또한 다른 야생 동물 우리의 벽도 부수었다.

➡ _____

12 이 동물들은 거리를 뛰어다니며 수백 명의 사람들에게 부상을 입혔다.

➡ _____

13 그중 열두 마리의 동물들이 아직 잡히지 않았다.

➡ _____

14 시민들은 추후 안내가 있을 때까지 집 안에 머물러야 한다.

➡ _____

15 위에 기술된 어떤 행동이나 사건도 일어나지 않았다.

➡ _____

16 그 당시 이 기사를 주의 깊게 읽었던 사람들은 크게 웃었다.

➡ _____

17 그것을 끝까지 읽지 않은 사람들은 정말로 걱정하였다.

➡ _____

18 그 기사가 거짓이라는 것을 알지 못했기 때문에 많은 사람이 겁에 질려 어쩔 줄 몰랐다.

➡ _____

19 어떤 사람들은 도시를 빠져나가려고 했고 다른 사람들은 그 동물들을 사냥하기 위해 총을 들고 공원으로 나갔다.

➡ _____

20 그렇다면 왜 헤럴드 사는 이러한 뉴스를 만들어 냈을까?

➡ _____

21 나중에 그들은 동물원의 안전하지 않은 상태에 대해 독자들의 주의를 끌기 위해 그 기사를 지어냈다고 고백했다.

➡ _____

_____

22 슬라브인이 언쟁 중에 친구에게 총을 쏘다

➡ _____

23 목요일 저녁 채굴 야영지 근처에서, 컬럼비아 광산 소속의 슬라브인 노동자 Mejk Swenekafew가 John Pecitello에 의해 총상을 입어 심각하게 다쳤다.

➡ _____

_____

24 그 두 사람은 회의 중에 언쟁을 벌였다.

➡ _____

25 언쟁이 싸움으로 번졌고, Pecitello가 Swenekafew의 가슴과 다리에 두 번 총을 쏘았다.

➡ _____

26 현재 그는 위독한 상태로 입원 중이다.

➡ _____

27 Pecitello는 총격 이후 도주했다.

➡ _____

28 경찰이 지금 그를 찾고 있으며, 그가 극히 위험하다고 시민들에게 경고하고 있다.

➡ _____

29 이 기사에 뭔가 이상한 점이 있는가?

➡ _____

30 그 슬라브인의 이름을 거꾸로 읽어 보아라. 그것의 철자는 "우리는 뉴스를 조작한다."가 된다.

➡ _____

31 누가 이것을 썼고 왜 그랬을까?

➡ _____

32 데일리 텔레그램 사는 그들의 경쟁자인 데일리 뉴스 사가 그들의 기사를 훔치는지를 증명하기 위해서 이 거짓 기사를 발행했다.

➡ _____

_____

33 데일리 뉴스 사는 그 다음 날 'Swenekafew'에 대한 동일한 기사를 발행했고 그래서 훔친 것이 발각되었다.

➡ _____

34 데일리 뉴스 사의 사람들은 그들의 행동을 인정해야만 했고 대중들로부터 혹독한 비난을 받았다.

➡ _____

35 이 두 기사는 특별한 경우였지만, 매일 발행되는 '가짜' 뉴스 기사는 많이 있다.

➡ _____

36 독자로서, 우리는 비판적으로 읽고 그 뉴스가 진짜인지 가짜인지 판단할 필요가 있다.

➡ _____

37 가짜 뉴스 판별 방법!

➡ _____

38 출처를 고려하라

➡ _____

39 그것은 믿을 만한 출처에서 온 것인가?

➡ _____

40 우리는 그 필자를 신뢰할 수 있는가?

➡ _____

41 날짜를 확인하라

➡ _____

42 그것은 새로운 이야기인가 혹은 오래된 이야기인가?

➡ _____

43 그것은 현재의 사건들과 관련된 것인가?

➡ _____

44 기사 제목 그 이상을 읽어라

➡ _____

45 기사 제목이 기사 내용과 일치하는가?

➡ _____

46 뒷받침하는 자료를 찾아라

➡ _____

47 다른 관련된 이야기도 비슷한 내용을 제공하는가?

➡ _____

※ 다음 우리말과 일치하도록 빈칸에 알맞은 말을 쓰시오.

Wrap Up 3

1. A: Wow! The news _____ _____ "Longer Vacation for Students." Hey, we're _____ _____ _____ _____ _____ _____!

2. B: Wait! We _____ _____ first _____ _____ _____ _____.

3. A: _____ do you _____ _____?

4. B: Some news _____ _____ _____ _____ but _____ _____ _____ _____ a different story.

5. A: Oh, I see. I _____ _____ _____ the news title.

Read & Think After You Read B

1. Reporter: Why did *The Herald* _____ the "_____ _____" story, Mr. Right?

2. Mr. Right: They just wanted to _____ _____ _____ _____ to the _____ _____ at the zoo.

3. Reporter: _____, readers _____ _____ _____ _____ _____ that it was _____. _____ _____ "Slav Shoots a Friend in Argument?" What was the _____?

4. Mr. Right: *The Daily Telegram* _____ _____ _____ _____ *The Daily News* _____ _____ _____ _____.

Read & Think After You Read C

1. A: _____ the four tips, which do you _____ _____ _____ _____, and why?

2. B: I think _____ _____ _____ _____ the most important _____ I can check _____ the _____ _____ _____.

※ **다음 우리말을 영어로 쓰시오.**

Wrap Up 3

1. A: 와! 뉴스 제목이 "학생들을 위한 더 긴 방학"이야. 이봐, 우리 더 긴 방학을 갖나봐!

   ➡ _____

   _____

2. B: 기다려! 우리는 먼저 이게 사실인지를 확인해야 해.

   ➡ _____

3. A: 왜 그렇게 생각해?

   ➡ _____

4. B: 어떤 뉴스는 충격적인 제목을 사용하지만 그 내용은 다른 이야기를 할지도 몰라.

   ➡ _____

5. A: 오, 알았다. 뉴스 제목 너머를 읽어야 하는구나.

   ➡ _____

Read & Think After You Read B

1. 기자: 왜 헤럴드 사는 〈끔찍한 참사〉 이야기를 썼을까요, Right 씨?

   ➡ _____

2. Mr. Right: 그들은 단지 동물원의 안전하지 않은 상태에 대해 독자들의 주의를 끌고 싶었답니다.

   ➡ _____

3. 기자: 사실, 독자들은 그것이 가짜라는 것을 알고 매우 화가 났어요. 〈슬라브인이 언쟁 중에 친구에게 총을 쏘다〉는 어떤가요? 동기가 무엇이었나요?

   ➡ _____

4. Mr. Right: 데일리 텔레그램 사는 데일리 뉴스 사가 그들의 기사를 훔치고 있다는 것을 증명하기를 원했어요.

   ➡ _____

Read & Think After You Read C

1. A: 네 가지 조언 중에서 너는 어떤 것이 가장 중요하다고 생각하며, 그 이유는 무엇이니?

   ➡ _____

2. B: 나는 뒷받침하는 자료들을 찾는 것이 가장 중요하다고 생각하는데, 그 정보가 올바른지 확인할 수 있기 때문이야.

   ➡ _____

※ 다음 영어를 우리말로 쓰시오.

01 forever	22 luxurious
02 suppose	23 dwarf
03 confusing	24 hire
04 design	25 forest
05 exhibit	26 dragon
06 freedom	27 lastly
07 expensive	28 deadline
08 twin	29 magical
09 priceless	30 far-away
10 comfortably	31 reward
11 stardom	32 situation
12 death	33 castle
13 puzzled	34 character
14 wisdom	35 fill up
15 expert	36 bring back
16 matter	37 lock up
17 captain	38 pass away
18 motto	39 run out of
19 failure	40 be stuck on
20 express	41 come true
21 foolish	42 live by
	43 look after

※ 다음 우리말을 영어로 쓰시오.

01 좌우명

02 한가롭게 이야기하다,
   담소하다

03 전시하다

04 죽음

05 스타덤, 스타의 반열

06 사치스러운, 호화로운

07 표현하다

08 기한, 마감 일자

09 자유

10 선장

11 고용하다

12 용

13 상황, 환경

14 마술의, 마력이 있는

15 편안하게

16 영원히

17 난장이

18 어리석은, 바보 같은

19 실패

20 혼란스러운, 헷갈리는

21 대단히 귀중한,
   값을 매길 수 없는

22 비싼, 돈이 많이 드는

23 당혹스러운, 어리둥절한

24 보상

25 멀리 떨어진

26 성

27 숲, 삼림, 산림

28 전문가

29 추측하다, 추정하다

30 마지막으로, 끝으로

31 쌍둥이의

32 지혜, 현명함

33 설명하다

34 설계하다

35 돌려주다

36 (신조, 원칙 등)에 따라 살다

37 투옥시키다

38 세상을 떠나다, 돌아가시다

39 ~이 없어지다,
   ~이 다 떨어지다

40 ~에 자리 잡다,
   ~에 정착하다

41 ~을 살피다, ~을 돌보다

42 잘못하다, 실수를 하다

43 이루어지다, 실현되다

※ 다음 영영풀이에 알맞은 단어를 <보기>에서 골라 쓴 후, 우리말 뜻을 쓰시오.

1 _____ : to show what you think or feel: _____

2 _____ : very comfortable and expensive: _____

3 _____ : worth a large amount of money: _____

4 _____ : a person who is in charge of a ship or an airplane: _____

5 _____ : a person represented in a film, play, or story: _____

6 _____ : to employ them or pay them to do a particular job for you: _____

7 _____ : a professional cook, especially the most senior cook in a restaurant, hotel, etc.: _____

8 _____ : a specific time or date by which you have to do something: _____

9 _____ : a large aggressive animal with wings and a long tail, that can breathe out fire: _____

10 _____ : something given in exchange for good behavior or good work, etc.: _____

11 _____ : to show something in a public place for people to enjoy or to give them information: _____

12 _____ : a person with a high level of knowledge or skill relating to a particular subject or activity: _____

13 _____ : to make something clear or easy to understand by describing or giving information about it: _____

14 _____ : a lack of success in doing or achieving something, especially in relation to a particular activity: _____

15 _____ : the ability to use your knowledge and experience to make good decisions and judgments: _____

16 _____ : a large building usually with high, thick walls and towers that was built in the past to protect against attack: _____

보기			
explain	hire	failure	chef
wisdom	luxurious	reward	express
exhibit	character	castle	deadline
expert	priceless	dragon	captain

※ 다음 우리말과 일치하도록 빈칸에 알맞은 말을 쓰시오.

Listen & Talk 1 A

1. W: James, why are _____ _____ _____? It's 11 o'clock!

   M: I can't sleep _____ _____ _____ _____ the Bookworm Competition tomorrow.

   W: _____ _____ all of the books on the list. What do you _____ _____ _____ _____?

   M: Some of the writers' names are _____, so I'm _____ _____ I _____ _____ _____ them.

   W: _____ _____ about something _____ _____ _____ yet. You'll do fine.

   M: Thanks. I'll _____ _____ _____ _____ so much.

2. M: Sujin, what are you doing this weekend?

   W: _____ _____, why?

   M: I _____ _____ _____ _____ Busan for a family trip tomorrow but I _____ _____ _____ _____ _____ my dog, Lucy.

   W: Don't _____ _____ Lucy. I'll _____ _____ _____ her.

   M: Oh, thank you so much. I was so _____.

   W: I'll take her _____ _____ _____ in the park, too. The weather's _____ _____ _____ nice tomorrow.

Listen & Talk 1 B

M: Jane, you look _____. What's the _____?

W: I _____ _____ _____ _____ _____ the school musical.

M: I _____ you _____. You sound great!

W: It's just that I _____ _____ _____. I'm so _____.

M: Oh, you just need _____ _____ more _____. Don't worry about _____ _____. You can actually learn from them.

W: Thanks, Dad. I hope I do a good job.

M: You'll do great.

해석

1. W: James, 왜 아직 깨어 있니? 11시야!
   M: 내일 있을 책벌레 경연 대회가 걱정되어서 저는 잠을 잘 수가 없어요.
   W: 너는 목록에 있는 책들을 다 읽었잖아. 뭐가 걱정이니?
   M: 몇몇 작가들의 이름이 헷갈려서 그들을 기억하지 못할까봐 걱정이 돼요.
   W: 아직 일어나지 않은 일을 걱정하지 마. 너는 잘할 거야.
   M: 고마워요. 너무 걱정하지 않도록 해 볼게요.

2. M: 수진아, 이번 주말에 뭐 할 거야?
   W: 특별한 일은 없어, 왜?
   M: 내일 부산으로 가족 여행을 가야 하는데 내 개 Lucy에게 먹이를 줄 사람을 아무도 찾을 수가 없어.
   W: Lucy에 대해서는 걱정하지 마. 내가 그 개를 돌봐 줄게.
   M: 오, 정말 고마워. 나 너무 걱정했거든.
   W: 내가 그 개를 데리고 공원에서 산책도 시켜 줄게. 내일 날씨가 좋을 거래.

M: Jane, 너 걱정스러워 보이는구나. 무슨 일 있니?
W: 제가 학교 뮤지컬에서 큰 역할을 맡았어요.
M: 네가 노래하는 것을 들었어. 잘하던데!
W: 그냥 제가 자꾸만 실수하는 거예요. 저는 너무 걱정돼요.
M: 오, 너는 그저 조금만 더 연습하면 돼. 실수하는 것에 대해서는 걱정하지 마. 사실 실수로부터 배울 수 있어.
W: 고마워요, 아빠. 제가 잘하면 좋겠어요.
M: 너는 아주 잘해 낼 거야.

1. **M:** Caroline, _____ you _____ the book, *Tuck Everlasting*?

   W: Yeah, it is about a family that drank _____ _____ and _____ _____, right?

   M: Right. _____ _____ _____ _____ _____ you could live _____?

   W: Well, I _____ live in _____ _____ all around the world.

   M: Really? I would collect _____ items and make a museum.

   W: Cool.

2. **W:** Jason, what are you reading?

   M: I'm reading a book _____ *Three Wishes*.

   W: Oh, I've _____ about it. A genie makes a boy's wishes _____ _____, right?

   M: Yeah. What would you do _____ _____ _____ _____ _____?

   W: I _____ _____ the genies _____ with me _____. Then, I could _____ _____ _____ _____ _____.

   M: That's _____!

W: What are you doing, Jinho?

M: I'm _____ _____ _____ of the movie, *The Time Traveler's Wife*.

W: I saw that movie, too. It's _____ _____ my favorite romantic _____.

M: I loved it, too. Emily, _____ _____ _____ _____ _____ _____ time travel?

W: I _____ _____ to the 1940s and _____ World War II. _____ _____ you?

M: I _____ _____ _____ the Joseon Dynasty and _____ King Sejong. I'm a _____ _____ _____ him.

---

1. **M:** Caroline, 너 트리갭의 샘물(Tuck Everlasting)이라는 책을 읽어 봤니?

   W: 응, 그것은 마법의 물을 마시고 영원히 살게 된 한 가족에 대한 이야기잖아, 맞지?

   M: 맞아. 만약 네가 영원히 살게 된다면 너는 뭘 할 거야?

   W: 글쎄, 나는 전 세계의 다양한 도시에서 살고 싶어.

   M: 정말? 나는 흥미로운 물건들을 모아서 박물관을 만들 거야.

   W: 멋지다.

2. **W:** Jason, 무엇을 읽고 있니?

   M: 나는 〈세 가지 소원〉이라는 책을 읽고 있어.

   W: 오, 그것에 대해 들어 본 적 있어. 요정이 어떤 남자아이의 소원을 들어주는 거지, 그렇지?

   M: 맞아. 만약 소원 하나를 빌 수 있다면 너는 무엇을 할 거니?

   W: 나는 요정을 영원히 내 옆에 있도록 만들 거야. 그러면, 나는 나의 모든 소원들을 이룰 수 있어.

   M: 그거 똑똑한데!

W: 진호야, 무엇을 하고 있니?

M: 나는 〈시간 여행자의 아내〉라는 영화의 후기를 쓰고 있어.

W: 나도 그 영화 봤어. 그건 내가 가장 좋아하는 로맨스 영화 중 하나야.

M: 나도 너무 좋았어. Emily, 만약 네가 시간 여행을 할 수 있다면 무엇을 하겠니?

W: 나는 1940년대로 가서 제2차 세계 대전을 막고 싶어. 너는 어때?

M: 나는 조선 시대로 가서 세종대왕을 만나고 싶어. 나는 그의 엄청난 팬이야.

Communication Step A

M: _____ your online story _____, Amy?

W: Not well. The deadline is this weekend but I _____ _____ of ideas.

M: _____ _____ _____ it. I can help you.

W: That would be great. My main _____ has special powers. _____ _____ _____ _____ _____ _____ able to read people's minds?

M: Well, I would _____ _____ _____ the girl I like _____ me.

W: That's a good idea. Thanks.

Wrap Up

1. M: _____ _____ _____ you're going to be in the _____ _____ next week.

   W: Yeah, it's _____ next week.

   M: You look _____. What's _____?

   W: _____ _____ _____ the topic would be _____ _____ for me.

   M: _____ _____ _____ something you can't change. Just _____ _____ _____.

   W: Thanks. I'll try.

2. M: Lisa, have you _____ the movie, *Cast Away*?

   W: No, I _____. What is it about?

   M: It's about _____ _____ _____ _____ _____ _____ a _____ _____ for 4 years.

   W: It sounds interesting.

   M: Yeah, the man _____ everything to stay alive. What _____ you do _____ _____ _____ _____?

   W: To stay _____? Well, I would _____ a tree house and _____ for food.

   M: Yeah, me too. And _____ _____ _____ _____ _____ in the movie.

M: 네 온라인 이야기는 어떻게 되어 가고 있니, Amy?
W: 별로야. 마감이 이번 주말인데 아이디어가 다 떨어졌어.
M: 그건 걱정하지 마. 내가 도와줄게.
W: 그럼 정말 좋겠다. 내 주인공은 특별한 능력을 가지고 있어. 만약 네가 사람들의 생각을 읽을 수 있다면 무엇을 하겠니?
M: 음, 나는 내가 좋아하는 여자아이가 나를 좋아하는지 알아보고 싶어.
W: 그거 좋은 생각이다. 고마워.

1. M: 네가 다음 주에 글쓰기 대회에 나간다고 들었어.
   W: 맞아, 그게 벌써 다음 주야.
   M: 너 걱정스러워 보인다. 무슨 일이니?
   W: 주제가 나에게 너무 어려울까봐 걱정이야.
   M: 네가 바꿀 수 없는 것에 대해 걱정하지 마. 그저 자신을 믿어봐.
   W: 고마워. 그렇게 해 볼게.

2. M: Lisa, 영화 〈캐스트 어웨이〉 본 적 있니?
   W: 아니, 없어. 무슨 내용이야?
   M: 4년 동안 외딴섬에 갇힌 어떤 남자에 관한 영화야.
   W: 재미있게 들린다.
   M: 응, 그 남자는 살기 위해 모든 것을 시도해. 만약 네가 그 남자라면 무엇을 하겠니?
   W: 살기 위해서? 글쎄, 나는 나무로 집을 만들고 먹을 것을 사냥할 거야.
   M: 응, 나도. 그리고 그게 그 남자가 영화에서 했던 거야.

※ 다음 우리말에 맞도록 대화를 영어로 쓰시오.

Listen & Talk 1 A

1. W: _____

   M: _____

   _____

   W: _____

   M: _____

   _____

   W: _____

   M: _____

2. M: _____

   W: _____

   M: _____

   _____

   W: _____

   M: _____

   W: _____

Listen & Talk 1 B

M: _____

W: _____

M: _____

W: _____

M: _____

_____

W: _____

M: _____

해석

1. W: James, 왜 아직 깨어 있니? 11시야!
   M: 내일 있을 책벌레 경연 대회가 걱정되어서 저는 잠을 잘 수가 없어요.
   W: 너는 목록에 있는 책들을 다 읽었잖아. 뭐가 걱정이니?
   M: 몇몇 작가들의 이름이 헷갈려서 그들을 기억하지 못할까봐 걱정이 돼요.
   W: 아직 일어나지 않은 일을 걱정하지 마. 너는 잘할 거야.
   M: 고마워요. 너무 걱정하지 않도록 해 볼게요.

2. M: 수진아, 이번 주말에 뭐 할 거야?
   W: 특별한 일은 없어, 왜?
   M: 내일 부산으로 가족 여행을 가야 하는데 내 개 Lucy에게 먹이를 줄 사람을 아무도 찾을 수가 없어.
   W: Lucy에 대해서는 걱정하지 마. 내가 그 개를 돌봐 줄게.
   M: 오, 정말 고마워. 나 너무 걱정했거든.
   W: 내가 그 개를 데리고 공원에서 산책도 시켜 줄게. 내일 날씨가 좋을 거래.

M: Jane, 너 걱정스러워 보이는구나. 무슨 일 있니?
W: 제가 학교 뮤지컬에서 큰 역할을 맡았어요.
M: 네가 노래하는 것을 들었어. 잘하던데!
W: 그냥 제가 자꾸만 실수하는 거예요. 저는 너무 걱정돼요.
M: 오, 너는 그저 조금만 더 연습하면 돼. 실수하는 것에 대해서는 걱정하지 마. 사실 실수로부터 배울 수 있어.
W: 고마워요, 아빠. 제가 잘하면 좋겠어요.
M: 너는 아주 잘해 낼 거야.

Listen & Talk 2 A

1. M: _____
   W: _____
   M: _____
   W: _____
   M: _____
   W: _____

2. W: _____
   M: _____
   W: _____
   M: _____
   W: _____
   M: _____

Listen & Talk 2 B

W: _____
M: _____
W: _____
M: _____
W: _____
M: _____

1. M: Caroline, 너 트리갭의 샘물(Tuck Everlasting)이라는 책을 읽어 봤니?
   W: 응, 그것은 마법의 물을 마시고 영원히 살게 된 한 가족에 대한 이야기잖아, 맞지?
   M: 맞아. 만약 네가 영원히 살게 된다면 너는 뭘 할 거야?
   W: 글쎄, 나는 전 세계의 다양한 도시에서 살고 싶어.
   M: 정말? 나는 흥미로운 물건들을 모아서 박물관을 만들 거야.
   W: 멋지다.

2. W: Jason, 무엇을 읽고 있니?
   M: 나는 〈세 가지 소원〉이라는 책을 읽고 있어.
   W: 오, 그것에 대해 들어 본 적 있어. 요정이 어떤 남자아이의 소원을 들어주는 거지, 그렇지?
   M: 맞아. 만약 소원 하나를 빌 수 있다면 너는 무엇을 할 거니?
   W: 나는 요정을 영원히 내 옆에 있도록 만들 거야. 그러면, 나는 나의 모든 소원들을 이룰 수 있어.
   M: 그거 똑똑한데!

W: 진호야, 무엇을 하고 있니?
M: 나는 〈시간 여행자의 아내〉라는 영화의 후기를 쓰고 있어.
W: 나도 그 영화 봤어. 그건 내가 가장 좋아하는 로맨스 영화 중 하나야.
M: 나도 너무 좋았어. Emily, 만약 네가 시간 여행을 할 수 있다면 무엇을 하겠니?
W: 나는 1940년대로 가서 제2차 세계 대전을 막고 싶어. 너는 어때?
M: 나는 조선 시대로 가서 세종대왕을 만나고 싶어. 나는 그의 엄청난 팬이야.

Communication Step A

M: _____

W: _____

M: _____

W: _____

M: _____

W: _____

M: 네 온라인 이야기는 어떻게 되어 가고 있니, Amy?

W: 별로야. 마감이 이번 주말인데 아이디어가 다 떨어졌어.

M: 그건 걱정하지 마. 내가 도와줄게.

W: 그럼 정말 좋겠다. 내 주인공은 특별한 능력을 가지고 있어. 만약 네가 사람들의 생각을 읽을 수 있다면 무엇을 하겠니?

M: 음, 나는 내가 좋아하는 여자아이가 나를 좋아하는지 알아보고 싶어.

W: 그거 좋은 생각이다. 고마워.

Wrap Up

1. M: _____

   W: _____

   M: _____

   W: _____

   M: _____

   W: _____

2. M: _____

   W: _____

   M: _____

   W: _____

   M: _____

   W: _____

   M: _____

1. M: 네가 다음 주에 글쓰기 대회에 나간다고 들었어.

   W: 맞아, 그게 벌써 다음 주야.

   M: 너 걱정스러워 보인다. 무슨 일이니?

   W: 주제가 나에게 너무 어려울까봐 걱정이야.

   M: 네가 바꿀 수 없는 것에 대해 걱정하지 마. 그저 자신을 믿어봐.

   W: 고마워. 그렇게 해 볼게.

2. M: Lisa, 영화 〈캐스트 어웨이〉 본 적 있니?

   W: 아니, 없어. 무슨 내용이야?

   M: 4년 동안 외딴섬에 갇힌 어떤 남자에 관한 영화야.

   W: 재미있게 들린다.

   M: 응, 그 남자는 살기 위해 모든 것을 시도해. 만약 네가 그 남자라면 무엇을 하겠니?

   W: 살기 위해서? 글쎄, 나는 나무로 집을 만들고 먹을 것을 사냥할 거야.

   M: 응, 나도. 그리고 그게 그 남자가 영화에서 했던 거야.

※ 다음 우리말과 일치하도록 빈칸에 알맞은 것을 골라 쓰시오.

1 A _____ and _____ father _____ two _____, Puru and Puneet.

　A. had　　　B. wise　　　C. sons　　　D. rich

2 Before he _____ _____, he called his two sons to give them some last _____ of _____.

　A. away　　　B. words　　　C. passed　　　D. advice

3 "Listen carefully, my dear sons. _____ _____ these words _____ your _____, and you will be happy," he said.

　A. throughout　B. by　　　C. life　　　D. live

4 "_____ a house in every city. Sleep _____. Enjoy your food. _____, spend money _____ a rich man... ."

　A. comfortably　B. like　　　C. lastly　　　D. build

5 Before he could _____ _____, he _____ _____.

　A. passed　　　B. explain　　　C. away　　　D. himself

6 After his _____, the two sons took their _____ of the father's _____ and _____ in different cities.

　A. settled　　　B. death　　　C. share　　　D. wealth

7 Five years _____. Puru, who had been _____ his father's _____ carefully, had no money _____.

　A. words　　　B. following　C. passed　　　D. left

8 But his brother was _____ _____ _____.

　A. than　　　B. richer　　　C. ever

9 Puru was _____ about where he had gone _____, so he visited Puneet to _____ _____.

　A. wrong　　　B. puzzled　　C. out　　　D. find

10 Puneet _____ Puru _____ _____ _____.

　A. open　　　B. welcomed　C. arms　　　D. with

11 That night, when the brothers sat _____ to _____ after dinner, Puru asked the question that had _____ on his _____ for days.

　A. mind　　　B. chat　　　C. been　　　D. down

12 "_____ was our father's advice _____ I followed, but I am not happy. I _____ a house in _____ city.

　A. every　　　B. that　　　C. built　　　D. it

13 But because I could not always _____ there, I hired people and _____ the house _____ _____.

　A. stay　　　B. after　　　C. had　　　D. looked

1 부유하고 지혜로운 아버지에게 두 아들, Puru와 Puneet이 있었다.

2 아버지는 돌아가시기 전에, 마지막 충고의 말을 하기 위해 그의 두 아들을 불렀다.

3 "주의 깊게 들거라, 사랑하는 아들들아. 너희의 일생 동안 이 말대로 살면, 행복해질 것이다." 그는 말했다.

4 "모든 도시에 집을 지어라. 편하게 자거라. 음식을 즐기거라. 마지막으로, 돈을 부자처럼 쓰거라…."

5 아버지는 그 말을 설명하기도 전에 돌아가셨다.

6 그의 죽음 후에, 두 아들은 아버지의 재산 중 자신들의 몫을 가지고 다른 도시에 정착했다.

7 5년이 지났다. 아버지의 말을 신중히 따라온 Puru는 남은 돈이 없었다.

8 그러나 그의 동생은 그 어느 때보다 더 부자가 되었다.

9 Puru는 그가 어디서부터 잘못했는지 어리둥절했고, 그래서 그는 (그것을) 알아내기 위해 Puneet을 방문했다.

10 Puneet은 Puru를 두 팔 벌려 환영했다.

11 그날 밤, 형제가 저녁식사 후 이야기를 하려고 앉았을 때, Puru는 며칠간 자신의 마음에 있었던 그 질문을 했다.

12 "내가 따른 건 바로 우리 아버지의 조언이었지만, 나는 행복하지 않아. 나는 모든 도시에 집을 지었어.

13 그러나 나는 그곳에 항상 머물 수 없었으므로 사람들을 고용하여 집을 돌보게 했지.

14 Father said we should sleep _____ and enjoy our food, so I _____ my bed _____ by experts and my meals _____ by a great chef.

    A. designed   B. prepared   C. comfortably   D. had

15 He told us to _____ _____ a rich man, so I bought _____ I wanted without _____ about money.

    A. worrying   B. like   C. what   D. spend

16 But _____ _____ me now! I am _____.

    A. empty-handed   B. at   C. look

17 Did you _____ _____ our _____ _____?

    A. wisdom   B. follow   C. father's   D. not

18 Tell me, brother, _____ _____ you _____ so _____?"

    A. get   B. how   C. rich   D. did

19 Puneet _____ and said, "My dear brother, I _____ _____ our father's _____.

    A. followed   B. wisdom   C. smiled   D. also

20 But I understood it _____ _____ _____.

    A. bit   B. a   C. differently

21 When he said ' _____ a house in every city,' I _____ it _____ having a place to _____ all around the world.

    A. as   B. took   C. build   D. stay

22 So I _____ in every city and I _____ _____ their houses when I visited those cities.

    A. at   B. stayed   C. made   D. friends

23 Also, I slept _____ each night because I would be _____ after a hard day's _____, and it did not matter if I was sleeping on a bed or on the hard _____.

    A. tired   B. comfortably   C. work   D. floor

24 I ate _____ _____ I was _____, so even a simple meal _____ great."

    A. hungry   B. when   C. tasted   D. only

25 " _____ money _____ a _____ man?" _____ Puneet.

    A. rich   B. like   C. continued   D. spend

26 "A rich man knows _____ _____ _____ money _____.

    A. how   B. grow   C. make   D. to

27 So, I tried to spend money on something that would _____ me _____ more money _____ than on _____ things.

    A. rather   B. luxurious   C. back   D. bring

28 For me, _____ was this wisdom _____ our father _____ uo _____."

    A. explain   B. that   C. it   D. tried

29 Now Puru realized _____ _____ he _____ _____.

    A. foolish   B. had   C. how   D. been

30 _____ this wisdom _____ _____, Puru started a new _____.

    A. mind   B. with   C. in   D. life

---

14 아버지께서 우리는 편하게 자고 음식을 즐겨야 한다고 말씀하셔서 나는 내 침대를 전문가들에 의해 설계되게 했고, 내 식사는 훌륭한 요리사에 의해 준비되도록 했단다.

15 아버지는 우리에게 부자처럼 돈을 쓰라고 하셨으므로, 나는 돈 걱정을 하지 않고 내가 원하는 것을 샀지.

16 그렇지만 지금 나를 봐! 나는 빈털터리야.

17 너는 우리 아버지의 지혜를 따르지 않았니?

18 나에게 말해 보렴, 동생아, 너는 어떻게 그렇게 부유해졌니?"

19 Puneet은 웃으며 말했다. "친애하는 형님, 저 또한 우리 아버지의 지혜를 따랐습니다.

20 하지만 저는 조금 다르게 이해했지요.

21 아버지가 '모든 도시에 집을 지어라'라고 말하셨을 때, 저는 그것을 전 세계에 머물 수 있는 장소를 가지는 것으로 여겼지요.

22 그래서 저는 모든 도시에서 친구를 사귀었고 그 도시들을 방문했을 때 그들의 집에 머물렀어요.

23 또한, 저는 하루 종일 열심히 일하고 나서 피곤해지곤 했기 때문에 침대에서 자든 딱딱한 바닥에서 자든 상관없이 매일 밤 편안하게 잠을 잤지요.

24 저는 배고플 때만 먹었기 때문에 간단한 식사마저도 훌륭한 맛이 났습니다."

25 "부자처럼 돈을 쓰라고요?" Puneet은 계속했다.

26 "부자는 돈을 불리는 방법을 알고 있어요.

27 그래서 저는 사치스러운 물건에 돈을 쓰는 것보다는 저에게 더 많은 돈을 돌려줄 수 있는 것에 돈을 쓰려고 노력했지요.

28 저에게는 이게 우리의 아버지가 설명하려고 하셨던 바로 그 지혜입니다."

29 이제 Puru는 그가 얼마나 어리석었었는지를 깨달았다.

30 이 지혜를 마음에 새기고, Puru는 새로운 삶을 시작했다.

※ 다음 우리말과 일치하도록 빈칸에 알맞은 것을 골라 쓰시오.

1 A _____ and _____ father _____ _____ _____, Puru and Puneet.

2 Before he _____ _____, he _____ his two sons _____ _____ _____ some _____ _____ _____ _____ _____.

3 "_____ _____, my dear sons. _____ _____ these words _____ _____ _____, and you will be happy," he said.

4 "_____ a house in _____ _____. Sleep _____. _____ your food. _____, _____ money _____ a rich man... ."

5 Before he could _____ _____, he _____ _____.

6 After _____ _____, the two sons took _____ _____ the father's _____ and _____ _____ _____ _____.

7 Five years _____. Puru, _____ _____ _____ _____ his father's words carefully, had _____ _____ _____.

8 But his brother _____ _____ _____ _____ _____.

9 Puru _____ _____ _____ _____ _____ he _____ _____ _____, so he visited Puneet _____ _____ _____.

10 Puneet _____ Puru _____ _____ _____.

11 That night, when the brothers _____ _____ _____ after dinner, Puru asked the question _____ _____ _____ _____ _____ _____.

12 "_____ _____ our father's advice _____ I followed, but I am not happy. I built a house _____ _____ _____.

13 But because I could not _____ _____ _____, I _____ people and _____ the house _____ _____.

1 부유하고 지혜로운 아버지에게 두 아들, Puru와 Puneet이 있었다.

2 아버지는 돌아가시기 전에, 마지막 충고의 말을 하기 위해 그의 두 아들을 불렀다.

3 "주의 깊게 듣거라, 사랑하는 아들들아. 너희의 일생 동안 이 말대로 살면, 행복해질 것이다." 그는 말했다.

4 "모든 도시에 집을 지어라. 편하게 자거라. 음식을 즐기거라. 마지막으로, 돈을 부자처럼 쓰거라…."

5 아버지는 그 말을 설명하기도 전에 돌아가셨다.

6 그의 죽음 후에, 두 아들은 아버지의 재산 중 자신들의 몫을 가지고 다른 도시에 정착했다.

7 5년이 지났다. 아버지의 말을 신중히 따라온 Puru는 남은 돈이 없었다.

8 그러나 그의 동생은 그 어느 때보다 더 부자가 되었다.

9 Puru는 그가 어디서부터 잘못했는지 어리둥절했고, 그래서 그는 (그것을) 알아내기 위해 Puneet을 방문했다.

10 Puneet은 Puru를 두 팔 벌려 환영했다.

11 그날 밤, 형제가 저녁식사 후 이야기를 하려고 앉았을 때, Puru는 며칠간 자신의 마음에 있었던 그 질문을 했다.

12 "내가 따른 건 바로 우리 아버지의 조언이었지만, 나는 행복하지 않아. 나는 모든 도시에 집을 지었어.

13 그러나 나는 그곳에 항상 머물 수 없었으므로 사람들을 고용하여 집을 돌보게 했지.

14 Father said we should _____ _____ and _____ our food, so I _____ my bed _____ by experts and _____ _____ _____ _____ a great chef.

15 He _____ us _____ _____ _____ a rich man, so I bought _____ _____ _____ without _____ about money.

16 But _____ _____ _____ now! I am _____.

17 Did you _____ _____ our _____ _____?

18 Tell me, brother, _____ _____ you _____ so _____?"

19 Puneet _____ and said, "My dear brother, I _____ _____ our _____ _____.

20 But I understood _____ _____ _____ _____.

21 When he said '_____ a house in every city,' I _____ _____ _____ _____ _____ _____ _____ _____ _____ all around the world.

22 So I _____ _____ in every city and I _____ _____ their houses when I visited _____ _____.

23 Also, I slept _____ each night _____ I would be tired after a hard day's work, and it did not matter _____ _____ _____ on a bed _____ on the _____ _____.

24 I ate _____ _____ _____ _____ _____, so even a simple meal _____ _____."

25 "Spend money _____ _____ _____ _____?" Puneet.

26 "A rich man knows _____ _____ _____ _____ _____.

27 So, I tried to spend money _____ something _____ would _____ _____ _____ more money _____ _____ _____ _____ _____.

28 For me, _____ _____ this wisdom _____ our father _____ _____."

29 Now Puru realized _____ _____ _____ _____ _____.

30 _____ this wisdom _____ _____, Puru started a new life.

14 아버지께서 우리는 편하게 자고 음식을 즐겨야 한다고 말씀하셔서 나는 내 침대를 전문가들에 의해 설계되게 했고, 내 식사는 훌륭한 요리사에 의해 준비되도록 했단다.

15 아버지는 우리에게 부자처럼 돈을 쓰라고 하셨으므로, 나는 돈 걱정을 하지 않고 내가 원하는 것을 샀지.

16 그렇지만 지금 나를 봐! 나는 빈털터리야.

17 너는 우리 아버지의 지혜를 따르지 않았니?

18 나에게 말해 보렴, 동생아. 너는 어떻게 그렇게 부유해졌니?"

19 Puneet은 웃으며 말했다. "친애하는 형님, 저 또한 우리 아버지의 지혜를 따랐습니다.

20 하지만 저는 조금 다르게 이해했지요.

21 아버지가 '모든 도시에 집을 지어라'라고 말하셨을 때, 저는 그것을 전 세계에 머물 수 있는 장소를 가지는 것으로 여겼지요.

22 그래서 저는 모든 도시에서 친구를 사귀었고 그 도시들을 방문했을 때 그들의 집에 머물렀어요.

23 또한, 저는 하루 종일 열심히 일하고 나서 피곤해지곤 했기 때문에 침대에서 자든 딱딱한 바닥에서 자든 상관없이 매일 밤 편안하게 잠을 잤지요.

24 저는 배고플 때만 먹었기 때문에 간단한 식사마저도 훌륭한 맛이 났습니다."

25 "부자처럼 돈을 쓰라고요?" Puneet은 계속했다.

26 "부자는 돈을 불리는 방법을 알고 있어요.

27 그래서 저는 사치스러운 물건에 돈을 쓰는 것보다는 저에게 더 많은 돈을 돌려줄 수 있는 것에 돈을 쓰려고 노력했지요.

28 저에게는 이게 우리의 아버지가 설명하려고 하셨던 바로 그 지혜입니다."

29 이제 Puru는 그가 얼마나 어리석었었는지를 깨달았다.

30 이 지혜를 마음에 새기고, Puru는 새로운 삶을 시작했다.

※ 다음 문장을 우리말로 쓰시오.

1 A rich and wise father had two sons, Puru and Puneet.

➡ _____

2 Before he passed away, he called his two sons to give them some last words of advice.

➡ _____

3 "Listen carefully, my dear sons. Live by these words throughout your life, and you will be happy," he said.

➡ _____

4 "Build a house in every city. Sleep comfortably. Enjoy your food. Lastly, spend money like a rich man... ."

➡ _____

5 Before he could explain himself, he passed away.

➡ _____

6 After his death, the two sons took their share of the father's wealth and settled in different cities.

➡ _____

7 Five years passed. Puru, who had been following his father's words carefully, had no money left.

➡ _____

8 But his brother was richer than ever.

➡ _____

9 Puru was puzzled about where he had gone wrong, so he visited Puneet to find out.

➡ _____

10 Puneet welcomed Puru with open arms.

➡ _____

11 That night, when the brothers sat down to chat after dinner, Puru asked the question that had been on his mind for days.

➡ _____

12 "It was our father's advice that I followed, but I am not happy. I built a house in every city.

➡ _____

13 But because I could not always stay there, I hired people and had the house looked after.

➡ _____

14 Father said we should sleep comfortably and enjoy our food, so I had my bed designed by experts and my meals prepared by a great chef.

➡ _____

_____

15 He told us to spend like a rich man, so I bought what I wanted without worrying about money.

➡ _____

16 But look at me now! I am empty-handed.

➡ _____

17 Did you not follow our father's wisdom?

➡ _____

18 Tell me, brother, how did you get so rich?"

➡ _____

19 Puneet smiled and said, "My dear brother, I also followed our father's wisdom.

➡ _____

20 But I understood it a bit differently.

➡ _____

21 When he said 'build a house in every city,' I took it as having a place to stay all around the world.

➡ _____

22 So I made friends in every city and I stayed at their houses when I visited those cities.

➡ _____

23 Also, I slept comfortably each night because I would be tired after a hard day's work, and it did not matter if I was sleeping on a bed or on the hard floor.

➡ _____

_____

24 I ate only when I was hungry, so even a simple meal tasted great."

➡ _____

25 "Spend money like a rich man?" continued Puneet.

➡ _____

26 "A rich man knows how to make money grow.

➡ _____

27 So, I tried to spend money on something that would bring me back more money rather than on luxurious things.

➡ _____

28 For me, it was this wisdom that our father tried to explain."

➡ _____

29 Now Puru realized how foolish he had been.

➡ _____

30 With this wisdom in mind, Puru started a new life.

➡ _____

※ 다음 괄호 안의 단어들을 우리말에 맞도록 바르게 배열하시오.

1 (rich / a / and father / wise / two / had / sons, / Puneet. / and / Puru)
➡ _____

2 (he / before / away, / passed / called / he / two / his / give / to / sons / some / them / words / last / advice. / of)
➡ _____

3 (carefully, / "listen / dear / my / sons. // by / live / words / these / throughout / life, / your / and / will / you / happy." / be / said. / he)
➡ _____

4 (a / "build / house / every / in / city. // comfortably. / sleep // food. / enjoy / your // lastly, / money / spend / a / like / man...." / rich)
➡ _____

5 (he / before / explain / could / himself, / passed / he / away.)
➡ _____

6 (his / after / death, / two / the / took / sons / share / their / the / of / wealth / father's / and / in / settled / cities. / different)
➡ _____

7 (years / five / passed. // who / Puru, / been / had / following / father's / his / words / carefully, / no / had / left. / money)
➡ _____

8 (his / but / was / brother / than / richer / ever.)
➡ _____

9 (was / Puru / puzzled / where / about / had / he / wrong, / gone / so / he / Puneet / visited / find / to / out.)
➡ _____

10 (welcomed / Puneet / with / Puru / arms. / open)
➡ _____

11 (night, / that / the / when / sat / brothers / down / chat / to / dinner, / after / asked / Puru / the / question / had / that / on / been / mind / his / days. / for)
➡ _____

12 (was / "it / our / advice / father's / I / that / followed, / I / but / not / am / happy. // built / I / house / a / every / in / city.)
➡ _____

13 (because / but / could / I / always / not / there, / stay / hired / I / people / and / the / had / house / after. / looked)
➡ _____

1 부유하고 지혜로운 아버지에게 두 아들, Puru와 Puneet이 있었다.

2 아버지는 돌아가시기 전에, 마지막 충고의 말을 하기 위해 그의 두 아들을 불렀다.

3 "주의 깊게 듣거라, 사랑하는 아들들아. 너희의 일생 동안 이 말대로 살면, 행복해질 것이다." 그는 말했다.

4 "모든 도시에 집을 지어라. 편하게 자거라. 음식을 즐기거라. 마지막으로, 돈을 부자처럼 쓰거라…."

5 아버지는 그 말을 설명하기도 전에 돌아가셨다.

6 그의 죽음 후에, 두 아들은 아버지의 재산 중 자신들의 몫을 가지고 다른 도시에 정착했다.

7 5년이 지났다. 아버지의 말을 신중히 따라온 Puru는 남은 돈이 없었다.

8 그러나 그의 동생은 그 어느 때보다 더 부자가 되었다.

9 Puru는 그가 어디서부터 잘못했는지 어리둥절했고, 그래서 그는 (그것을) 알아내기 위해 Puneet을 방문했다.

10 Puneet은 Puru를 두 팔 벌려 환영했다.

11 그날 밤, 형제가 저녁식사 후 이야기를 하려고 앉았을 때, Puru는 며칠간 자신의 마음에 있었던 그 질문을 했다.

12 "내가 따른 건 바로 우리 아버지의 조언이었지만, 나는 행복하지 않아. 나는 모든 도시에 집을 지었어.

13 그러나 나는 그곳에 항상 머물 수 없었으므로 사람들을 고용하여 집을 돌보게 했지.

14 (said / father / should / we / comfortably / sleep / enjoy / and / food, / our / I / so / my / had / bed / my / by / designed / experts / and / meals / my / by / prepared / great / a / chef.)
➡ _____

15 (told / he / to / us / like / spend / a / man, / rich / so / bought / I / what / wanted / I / worrying / without / money. / about)
➡ _____

16 (look / but / me / at / now! // am / I / empty-handed.)
➡ _____

17 (you / did / follow / not / father's / our / wisdom?)
➡ _____

18 (me, / tell / how / brother, / did / get / you / rich?" / so)
➡ _____

19 (smiled / Puneet / said, / and / dear / "my / brother, / also / I / our / followed / wisdom. / father's)
➡ _____

20 (I / but / it / understood / bit / a / differently.)
➡ _____

21 (he / when / 'build / said / house / a / every / in / city,' / took / I / as / it / a / having / place / to / stay / around / all / world. / the)
➡ _____

22 (I / so / friends / made / every / in / city / I / and / stayed / their / at / when / houses / I / those / visited / cities.)
➡ _____

23 (I / also, / comfortably / slept / night / each / because / would / I / tired / be / a / after / day's / hard / work, / it / and / did / matter / not / if / was / I / on / sleeping / bed / a / the / on / or / floor. / hard)
➡ _____

24 (ate / I / when / only / was / I / hungry / even / so, / simple / a / tasted / meal / great."
➡ _____

25 (money / "spend / a / like / man?" / rich / Puneet. / continued)
➡ _____

26 (rich / "a / knows / man / to / how / money / make / grow.)
➡ _____

27 (I / so, / to / tried / money / spend / something / on / would / that / me / bring / back / money / more / than / rather / luxurious / on / things.)
➡ _____

28 (me, / for / was / it / wisdom / this / our / that / father / to / tried / explain.")
➡ _____

29 (Puru / now / how / realized / foolish / had / he / been.)
➡ _____

30 (this / with / in / wisdom / mind, / started / Puru / new / a / life.)
➡ _____

14 아버지께서 우리는 편하게 자고 음식을 즐겨야 한다고 말씀하셔서 나는 내 침대를 전문가들에 의해 설계되게 했고, 내 식사는 훌륭한 요리사에 의해 준비되도록 했단다.

15 아버지는 우리에게 부자처럼 돈을 쓰라고 하셨으므로, 나는 돈 걱정을 하지 않고 내가 원하는 것을 샀지.

16 그렇지만 지금 나를 봐! 나는 빈털터리야.

17 너는 우리 아버지의 지혜를 따르지 않았니?

18 나에게 말해 보렴, 동생아, 너는 어떻게 그렇게 부유해졌니?"

19 Puneet은 웃으며 말했다. "친애하는 형님, 저 또한 우리 아버지의 지혜를 따랐습니다.

20 하지만 저는 조금 다르게 이해했지요.

21 아버지가 '모든 도시에 집을 지어라'라고 말하셨을 때, 저는 그것을 전 세계에 머물 수 있는 장소를 가지는 것으로 여겼지요.

22 그래서 저는 모든 도시에서 친구를 사귀었고 그 도시들을 방문했을 때 그들의 집에 머물렀어요.

23 또한, 저는 하루 종일 열심히 일하고 나서 피곤해지곤 했기 때문에 침대에서 자든 딱딱한 바닥에서 자든 상관없이 매일 밤 편안하게 잠을 잤지요.

24 저는 배고플 때만 먹었기 때문에 간단한 식사마저도 훌륭한 맛이 났습니다."

25 "부자처럼 돈을 쓰라고요?" Puneet은 계속했다.

26 "부자는 돈을 불리는 방법을 알고 있어요.

27 그래서 저는 사치스러운 물건에 돈을 쓰는 것보다는 저에게 더 많은 돈을 돌려줄 수 있는 것에 돈을 쓰려고 노력했지요.

28 저에게는 이게 우리의 아버지가 설명하려고 하셨던 바로 그 지혜입니다."

29 이제 Puru는 그가 얼마나 어리석었었는지를 깨달았다.

30 이 지혜를 마음에 새기고, Puru는 새로운 삶을 시작했다.

※ 다음 우리말을 영어로 쓰시오.

1 부유하고 지혜로운 아버지에게 두 아들, Puru와 Puneet이 있었다.

➡ _____

2 아버지는 돌아가시기 전에, 마지막 충고의 말을 하기 위해 그의 두 아들을 불렀다.

➡ _____

3 "주의 깊게 듣거라, 사랑하는 아들들아. 너희의 일생 동안 이 말대로 살면, 행복해질 것이다." 그는 말했다.

➡ _____

4 "모든 도시에 집을 지어라. 편하게 자거라. 음식을 즐기거라. 마지막으로, 돈을 부자처럼 쓰거라…."

➡ _____

5 아버지는 그 말을 설명하기도 전에 돌아가셨다.

➡ _____

6 그의 죽음 후에, 두 아들은 아버지의 재산 중 자신들의 몫을 가지고 다른 도시에 정착했다.

➡ _____

7 5년이 지났다. 아버지의 말을 신중히 따라온 Puru는 남은 돈이 없었다.

➡ _____

8 그러나 그의 동생은 그 어느 때보다 더 부자가 되었다.

➡ _____

9 Puru는 그가 어디서부터 잘못했는지 어리둥절했고, 그래서 그는 (그것을) 알아내기 위해 Puneet을 방문했다.

➡ _____

10 Puneet은 Puru를 두 팔 벌려 환영했다.

➡ _____

11 그날 밤, 형제가 저녁식사 후 이야기를 하려고 앉았을 때, Puru는 며칠간 자신의 마음에 있었던 그 질문을 했다.

➡ _____

_____

12 "내가 따른 건 바로 우리 아버지의 조언이었지만, 나는 행복하지 않아. 나는 모든 도시에 집을 지었어.

➡ _____

13 그러나 나는 그곳에 항상 머물 수 없었으므로 사람들을 고용하여 집을 돌보게 했지.

➡ _____

14 아버지께서 우리는 편하게 자고 음식을 즐겨야 한다고 말씀하셔서 나는 내 침대를 전문가들에 의해 설계되게 했고, 내 식사는 훌륭한 요리사에 의해 준비되도록 했단다.
➡ _____

15 아버지는 우리에게 부자처럼 돈을 쓰라고 하셨으므로, 나는 돈 걱정을 하지 않고 내가 원하는 것을 샀지.
➡ _____

16 그렇지만 지금 나를 봐! 나는 빈털터리야.
➡ _____

17 너는 우리 아버지의 지혜를 따르지 않았니?
➡ _____

18 나에게 말해 보렴, 동생아, 너는 어떻게 그렇게 부유해졌니?"
➡ _____

19 Puneet은 웃으며 말했다, "친애하는 형님, 저 또한 우리 아버지의 지혜를 따랐습니다.
➡ _____

20 하지만 저는 조금 다르게 이해했지요.
➡ _____

21 아버지가 '모든 도시에 집을 지어라'라고 말하셨을 때, 저는 그것을 전 세계에 머물 수 있는 장소를 가지는 것으로 여겼지요.
➡ _____

22 그래서 저는 모든 도시에서 친구를 사귀었고 그 도시들을 방문했을 때 그들의 집에 머물렀어요.
➡ _____

23 또한, 저는 하루 종일 열심히 일하고 나서 피곤해지곤 했기 때문에 침대에서 자든 딱딱한 바닥에서 자든 상관없이 매일 밤 편안하게 잠을 잤지요.
➡ _____
_____

24 저는 배고플 때만 먹었기 때문에 간단한 식사마저도 훌륭한 맛이 났습니다."
➡ _____

25 "부자처럼 돈을 쓰라고요?" Puneet은 계속했다.
➡ _____

26 "부자는 돈을 불리는 방법을 알고 있어요.
➡ _____

27 그래서 저는 사치스러운 물건에 돈을 쓰는 것보다는 저에게 더 많은 돈을 돌려줄 수 있는 것에 돈을 쓰려고 노력했지요.
➡ _____
_____

28 저에게는 이게 우리의 아버지가 설명하려고 하셨던 바로 그 지혜입니다."
➡ _____

29 이제 Puru는 그가 얼마나 어리석었었는지를 깨달았다.
➡ _____

30 이 지혜를 마음에 새기고, Puru는 새로운 삶을 시작했다.
➡ _____

※ 다음 우리말과 일치하도록 빈칸에 알맞은 말을 쓰시오.

Language in Use

1. Everyone has _____ _____ _____ and _____.
2. Can you _____ _____ _____ of the game _____ _____
_____ _____ _____?

1. 모든 사람들은 언론과 표현의 자유가 있다.
2. 우리가 경기를 시작하기 전에 규칙을 설명해 줄래?

Grammar in Real Life B Look and Write

1. Do you _____ _____ _____ the computer _____? Call the Computer Doctor.
2. _____ _____ you _____ _____ _____ _____ at Susie's Hair Studio?
3. _____ _____ _____ your pet cleaned from head to toe? Come to Happy Pet.
4. Do you want to have your party room _____ _____ _____? _____ _____ Mary's Flowers.

1. 컴퓨터를 고쳐야 하나요? '컴퓨터 닥터'에게 전화하세요.
2. '수지의 헤어 스튜디오'에서 머리카락을 자르는 게 어때요?
3. 당신의 애완동물을 머리부터 발끝까지 깨끗하게 하는 것은 어떨까요? '해피 펫'으로 오세요.
4. 당신의 파티 룸을 꽃으로 장식하고 싶은가요? '메리의 꽃들'을 찾아 주세요.

Think & Write C

1. _____ me _____ my motto.
2. It is "Go _____ it!"
3. It _____ "Go and do things _____ _____ because failure is also a _____ _____."
4. I _____ it _____ _____ _____ _____ _____ _____ _____ in the school soccer team.
5. _____ the motto, I learned that _____ the bad kicks _____ me _____ _____ _____ _____ _____ _____ _____.
6. _____ is this motto _____ _____ _____ _____ _____!

1. 나의 좌우명을 소개하게 해 줘.
2. 그것은 "어서 해!"야
3. 그것은 "실패 또한 좋은 경험이기 때문에 두려움 없이 무언가를 해'라는 의미야.
4. 나는 학교 축구팀에서 키커였을 때, 그것을 나의 좌우명으로 삼았어.
5. 그 좌우명에서 나는 나쁜 킥들조차 결국엔 나를 더 좋은 키커로 만들어 준다는 것을 배웠지.
6. 나의 삶을 바꾼 것은 바로 이 좌우명이야!

※ 다음 우리말을 영어로 쓰시오.

Language in Use

1. 모든 사람들은 언론과 표현의 자유가 있다.

➡ _____

2. 우리가 경기를 시작하기 전에 규칙을 설명해 줄래?

➡ _____

Grammar in Real Life B Look and Write

1. 컴퓨터를 고쳐야 하나요? '컴퓨터 닥터'에게 전화하세요.

➡ _____

2. '수지의 헤어 스튜디오'에서 머리카락을 자르는 게 어때요?

➡ _____

3. 당신의 애완동물을 머리부터 발끝까지 깨끗하게 하는 것은 어떨까요? '해피 펫'으로 오세요.

➡ _____

4. 당신의 파티 룸을 꽃으로 장식하고 싶은가요? '메리의 꽃들'을 찾아 주세요.

➡ _____

Think & Write C

1. 나의 좌우명을 소개하게 해 줘.

➡ _____

2. 그것은 "어서 해!"야

➡ _____

3. 그것은 "실패 또한 좋은 경험이기 때문에 두려움 없이 무언가를 해'라는 의미야.

➡ _____

4. 나는 학교 축구팀에서 키커였을 때, 그것을 나의 좌우명으로 삼았어.

➡ _____

5. 그 좌우명에서 나는 나쁜 킥들조차 결국엔 나를 더 좋은 키커로 만들어 준다는 것을 배웠지.

➡ _____

6. 나의 삶을 바꾼 것은 바로 이 좌우명이야!

➡ _____

※ 다음 영어를 우리말로 쓰시오.

01 convenient

02 last

03 match

04 compete

05 allowance

06 purchase

07 release

08 affect

09 disappear

10 behavior

11 combine

12 replace

13 mention

14 aboard

15 discount

16 encourage

17 effect

18 compare

19 refund

20 spending

21 concept

22 endanger

23 complete

24 fix

25 striped

26 difference

27 immediately

28 tight

29 influence

30 lack

31 anchor

32 billion

33 overheated

34 consume

35 on display

36 in comparison

37 go well with

38 just because

39 keep track of

40 when it comes to

41 be likely to

42 more than half

43 at a glance

※ 다음 우리말을 영어로 쓰시오.

01 용돈

02 결합하다

03 즉시, 바로

04 효과

05 편리한, 간편한

06 거래

07 10억

08 완성하다

09 ～에 영향을 주다

10 언급하다, 말하다

11 소비하다, 소모하다

12 닻; 닻을 내리다

13 행동, 행위

14 놓치다

15 차이, 차이점

16 비교하다

17 부추기다, 조장하다

18 경쟁하다

19 위험에 빠뜨리다

20 개념

21 줄무늬가 있는

22 환불

23 출시하다, 발매하다

24 ～에 영향을 주다

25 부족, 결핍

26 사라지다

27 할인; 할인하다

28 어울리다

29 구매하다, 구입하다

30 기르다, 키우다

31 바꾸다, 교체하다

32 지출

33 꽉 조이는, 딱 붙는

34 낭비하다, 소모하다

35 진열된, 전시된

36 한눈에, 즉시

37 비교해 보면

38 ～을 기록하다

39 그러한 결과로

40 단지 ～라는 이유로

41 ～와 잘 어울리다

42 ～에 관해서,
～에 대해 말하자면

43 ～할 가능성이 있다,
～하기 쉽다

※ 다음 영영풀이에 알맞은 단어를 <보기>에서 골라 쓴 후, 우리말 뜻을 쓰시오.

1 _____ : without delay: _____

2 _____ : a principle or idea: _____

3 _____ : to become impossible to see: _____

4 _____ : to buy property, goods, etc.: _____

5 _____ : to make something available to the public: _____

6 _____ : to be right for a particular person, situation, or occasion: _____

7 _____ : rather small and fit closely to your body: _____

8 _____ : to join together to make a single thing or group: _____

9 _____ : to use more of something than is necessary or useful: _____

10 _____ : suitable for your purposes and needs and causing the least difficulty:
    _____

11 _____ : to support an activity or make it more likely: _____

12 _____ : an amount of money that is given to someone regularly or for a particular
    purpose: _____

13 _____ : to use fuel, energy, or time, especially in large amounts or to eat or drink,
    especially a lot of something: _____

14 _____ : to put someone or something at risk or in danger of being harmed,
    damaged, or destroyed: _____

15 _____ : a condition of not having any or enough of something, especially
    something necessary or wanted: _____

16 _____ : to have an influence on someone or something, or to cause a change in
    someone or something: _____

lack	combine	affect	tight
convenient	disappear	encourage	concept
endanger	suit	consume	release
waste	immediately	allowance	purchase

※ 다음 우리말과 일치하도록 빈칸에 알맞은 말을 쓰시오.

Listen & Talk 1 A

1. **M:** Hi, can I _____ you _____ anything?

   W: Yes, can I _____ _____ that cap _____ stars over there?

   M: Sure. _____ _____ _____ _____ it?

   W: The design is nice, _____ I don't think the color _____ me. Do you _____ it in black?

   M: Yes. I'll get _____ from the back. *(pause)* Here it is.

   W: Great. I'll _____ it.

2. **M:** Good morning. _____ _____ Kelly's Sporting Goods Store.

   W: Hi, _____ _____ _____ a backpack for hiking.

   M: These two are _____ _____ hikers. _____ _____ _____ _____ them?

   W: The _____ _____ _____ _____ _____ the blue _____. I'll take the _____ _____.

   M: Great _____.

1. **M:** 안녕하세요, 무엇을 도와 드릴까요?
   W: 네, 저기 별들이 그려진 모자를 써 볼 수 있나요?
   M: 그럼요. 어떠세요?
   W: 디자인은 좋은데, 색이 제게 안 어울리는 것 같아요. 이거 검은색으로 있나요?
   M: 네. 제가 안쪽에서 가져다 드릴게요. (잠시 후) 여기 있어요.
   W: 좋아요. 그걸로 할게요.

2. **M:** 안녕하세요. Kelly의 스포츠 용품 가게에 오신 것을 환영합니다.
   W: 안녕하세요. 저는 하이킹할 때 쓸 배낭을 찾고 있어요.
   M: 이 두 개가 하이킹하시는 분들 사이에서 인기가 있어요. 어떠세요?
   W: 초록색 배낭이 파란색 배낭보다 더 가볍네요. 더 가벼운 걸로 할게요.
   M: 탁월한 선택입니다.

Listen & Talk 1 B

W: Hi, Luke. Is that a new speaker?

M: Yes, I _____ it a _____ _____ _____ _____.

W: It _____ cool. _____ _____ _____ _____ it?

M: It's _____. I can take it _____ and listen to music. The sound _____ is good, _____.

W: Great. _____ _____ does the battery _____?

M: _____ 2 hours. The battery _____ _____ long.

W: That's _____ _____.

M: Yeah, but I'm _____ _____ with it, _____.

W: 안녕, Luke. 그거 새 스피커니?
M: 응, 몇 주 전에 샀어.
W: 멋져 보인다. 그거 어때?
M: 편리해. 나는 그것을 어디든지 가져가서 음악을 들을 수 있어. 음질도 좋아.
W: 좋다. 배터리가 얼마나 오래가니?
M: 2시간 정도야. 배터리가 그렇게 오래 가지 않아.
W: 그거 안타깝구나.
M: 응, 하지만 어쨌든 나는 꽤 만족해.

Listen & Talk 2 A

1. M: Oh, this coat is _____ _____.

   W: Why? _____ _____ _____ _____?

   M: It's too _____.

   W: Didn't _____ _____ _____ _____ _____ _____

   it?

   M: No. It was my size, _____ I just _____ it. I _____ _____

   _____ it _____.

2. W: Hey, Eric. Camilla and I _____ _____ _____ _____ a

   movie. Do you want _____ _____ us?

   M: I'd _____ _____, but I can't. _____ _____ all of my

   _____ for this week.

   W: Didn't you just _____ _____ a few days _____? How

   did you spend it all?

   M: I'm not sure. I _____ _____ _____ _____ _____

   _____ _____.

Listen & Talk 2 B

M: Did you get a new phone, Jamie? It's just _____ _____.

W: Yeah, I got it last weekend _____ _____.

M: It was _____ _____? But it _____ _____ _____

_____, hasn't it?

W: Right, but the store on Green Street _____ _____ a year-end

_____.

M: Oh, I bought mine _____ _____ _____!

W: Really? That's too bad. They're _____ them _____ a 40 percent

_____.

M: I _____ _____ _____ _____ _____ _____ buying

mine.

1. M: 오, 이 코트는 너무 불편해.
   W: 왜? 무슨 문제가 있니?
   M: 너무 꽉 껴.
   W: 사기 전에 입어 보지 않았어?
   M: 아니. 내 사이즈여서 그냥 사 버렸어. 난 그것을 입어 봤어야 했어.

2. W: 안녕, Eric. Camilla랑 나는 영화를 보러 갈 거야. 우리랑 같이 갈래?
   M: 그러고 싶지만, 안 돼. 이번 주 용돈을 전부 써 버렸거든.
   W: 너 고작 며칠 전에 받지 않았어? 어떻게 다 써 버렸어?
   M: 잘 모르겠어. 내 지출을 기록했어야 했어.

M: 새 전화기를 샀니, Jamie? 내 것과 똑같다.
W: 응, 나는 이것을 지난주 할인할 때 샀어.
M: 그거 할인 중이었어? 하지만 그것은 막 출시되었잖아, 그렇지 않아?
W: 맞아, 하지만 Green가에 있는 가게에서 연말 할인 판매를 하더라.
M: 오, 나는 내 것을 정가를 주고 샀는데!
W: 정말? 그것 참 안됐다. 40퍼센트 할인하여 팔고 있어.
M: 내 것을 사기 전에 할인 판매를 확인했어야 했어.

Communication Step A

M: Hi, Riley. I _____ _____ _____ _____ a laptop online. _____ do you _____ it?

W: Oh, I'm _____ _____ with _____.

M: _____? _____ wrong?

W: It makes too much noise and _____ _____. I should _____ _____ more _____.

M: Oh, then you should _____ _____ your money back.

W: The online store _____ _____ _____ _____ my money because _____ _____ it for a week.

M: How about _____ the online shop and _____ your problem?

W: Yeah, I think I should _____ that.

M: 안녕, Riley. 네가 온라인으로 노트북을 샀다고 들었어. 그거 어때?

W: 아, 나는 별로 마음에 들지 않아.

M: 왜? 무슨 문제가 있어?

W: 소음이 너무 심하고 과열이 돼. 난 후기를 더 많이 읽어 봤어야 했어.

M: 오, 그럼 환불을 요청해 봐.

W: 내가 그것을 일주일 동안 사용했기 때문에 온라인 가게는 환불을 해 주지 않을 거야.

M: 온라인 가게에 전화해서 문제를 설명하는 건 어때?

W: 응, 그렇게 해야 할 것 같아.

Wrap Up

1. M: Good morning. May I help you?

W: _____ _____ _____ buy a T-shirt for my sister. She's eleven years old.

M: _____ _____ _____ _____ _____ _____ _____ _____? This character is quite popular _____ children.

W: Well, she doesn't like animation characters _____ much. Can I see the blue _____?

M: You mean this blue _____ T-shirt? _____ design is simple and cool.

W: Yes, I think my sister will like it. I'll _____ it.

2. W: Jake, here's a _____ for you.

M: It's my helmet. I _____ it at an _____ _____ _____ a few days _____.

W: Oh, open it and _____ _____ _____ it.

M: Okay. *(pause)* Oh, this outer part _____ _____ _____ _____. The seller _____ _____ it's perfectly fine though.

W: Didn't you check the pictures of the helmet _____ you bought it?

M: No, _____ _____ _____ the seller. I _____ _____ _____ _____ _____ _____.

W: You _____ _____ the seller and _____ _____ _____ _____.

1. M: 안녕하세요.. 도와 드릴까요?

W: 저는 여동생에게 티셔츠를 사 주고 싶어요. 그 애는 11살이에요.

M: 이 빨간색 티셔츠는 어떠세요? 이 캐릭터는 아이들 사이에서 꽤 인기가 있어요.

W: 글쎄요, 그 애는 만화 캐릭터를 그다지 좋아하지 않아요. 파란색 티셔츠 좀 볼 수 있을까요?

M: 파란색 줄무늬 티셔츠 말씀이시죠? 그건 디자인이 단순하고 멋있어요.

W: 네, 제 여동생이 좋아할 것 같아요. 그걸로 할게요.

2. W: Jake, 여기 네 소포가 있어.

M: 그거 내 헬멧이야. 며칠 전에 온라인 중고 가게에서 샀어.

W: 오, 열어서 보여 줘.

M: 그래. (잠시 후) 아, 이 바깥 부분이 조금 깨졌어. 하지만 판매자는 이것이 완벽하게 괜찮다고 말했어.

W: 사기 전에 헬멧 사진을 확인해 보지 않았니?

M: 아니, 나는 그냥 판매자를 믿었어. 조금 더 확인을 했어야 했어.

W: 너는 판매자에게 전화해서 환불을 요청해야 해.

※ 다음 우리말에 맞도록 대화를 영어로 쓰시오.

Listen & Talk 1 A

1. M: _____
   W: _____
   M: _____
   W: _____
   _____
   M: _____
   W: _____

2. M: _____
   W: _____
   M: _____
   W: _____
   M: _____

Listen & Talk 1 B

W: _____
M: _____
W: _____
M: _____
_____
W: _____
M: _____
W: _____
M: _____

1. M: 안녕하세요, 무엇을 도와 드릴까요?
   W: 네, 저기 별들이 그려진 모자를 써 볼 수 있나요?
   M: 그럼요. 어떠세요?
   W: 디자인은 좋은데, 색이 제게 안 어울리는 것 같아요. 이거 검은색으로 있나요?
   M: 네. 제가 안쪽에서 가져다 드릴게요. (잠시 후) 여기 있어요.
   W: 좋아요. 그걸로 할게요.

2. M: 안녕하세요. Kelly의 스포츠 용품 가게에 오신 것을 환영합니다.
   W: 안녕하세요, 저는 하이킹할 때 쓸 배낭을 찾고 있어요.
   M: 이 두 개가 하이킹하시는 분들 사이에서 인기가 있어요. 어떠세요?
   W: 초록색 배낭이 파란색 배낭보다 더 가볍네요. 더 가벼운 걸로 할게요.
   M: 탁월한 선택입니다.

W: 안녕, Luke. 그거 새 스피커니?
M: 응, 몇 주 전에 샀어.
W: 멋져 보인다. 그거 어때?
M: 편리해. 나는 그것을 어디든지 가져가서 음악을 들을 수 있어. 음질도 좋아.
W: 좋다. 배터리가 얼마나 오래가니?
M: 2시간 정도야. 배터리가 그렇게 오래 가지 않아.
W: 그거 안타깝구나.
M: 응, 하지만 어쨌든 나는 꽤 만족해.

1. M: _____

   W: _____

   M: _____

   W: _____

   M: _____

2. W: _____

   _____

   M: _____

   W: _____

   M: _____

M: _____

W: _____

M: _____

W: _____

M: _____

W: _____

M: _____

1. M: 오, 이 코트는 너무 불편해.
   W: 왜? 무슨 문제가 있니?
   M: 너무 꽉 껴.
   W: 사기 전에 입어 보지 않았어?
   M: 아니. 내 사이즈여서 그냥 사 버
   렸어. 난 그것을 입어 봤어야 했
   어.

2. W: 안녕, Eric. Camilla랑 나는 영화
   를 보러 갈 거야. 우리랑 같이 갈
   래?
   M: 그러고 싶지만, 안 돼. 이번 주 용
   돈을 전부 써 버렸거든.
   W: 너 고작 며칠 전에 받지 않았어?
   어떻게 다 써 버렸어?
   M: 잘 모르겠어. 내 지출을 기록했어
   야 했어.

M: 새 전화기를 샀니, Jamie? 내 것과
   똑같다.
W: 응, 나는 이것을 지난주 할인할 때
   샀어.
M: 그거 할인 중이었어? 하지만 그것은
   막 출시되었잖아, 그렇지 않아?
W: 맞아, 하지만 Green가에 있는 가게
   에서 연말 할인 판매를 하더라.
M: 오, 나는 내 것을 정가를 주고 샀는
   데!
W: 정말? 그것 참 안됐다. 40퍼센트 할
   인하여 팔고 있어.
M: 내 것을 사기 전에 할인 판매를 확인
   했어야 했어.

Communication Step A

M: _____

W: _____

M: _____

W: _____

_____

M: _____

W: _____

M: _____

W: _____

Wrap Up

1. M: _____

W: _____

M: _____

W: _____

_____

M: _____

W: _____

2. W: _____

M: _____

W: _____

M: _____

W: _____

M: _____

W: _____

M: 안녕, Riley. 네가 온라인으로 노트북을 샀다고 들었어. 그거 어때?
W: 아, 나는 별로 마음에 들지 않아.
M: 왜? 무슨 문제가 있어?
W: 소음이 너무 심하고 과열이 돼. 난 후기를 더 많이 읽어 봤어야 했어.
M: 오, 그럼 환불을 요청해 봐.
W: 내가 그것을 일주일 동안 사용했기 때문에 온라인 가게는 환불을 해 주지 않을 거야.
M: 온라인 가게에 전화해서 문제를 설명하는 건 어때?
W: 응, 그렇게 해야 할 것 같아.

1. M: 안녕하세요. 도와 드릴까요?
W: 저는 여동생에게 티셔츠를 사 주고 싶어요. 그 애는 11살이에요.
M: 이 빨간색 티셔츠는 어떠세요? 이 캐릭터는 아이들 사이에서 꽤 인기가 있어요.
W: 글쎄요, 그 애는 만화 캐릭터를 그다지 좋아하지 않아요. 파란색 티셔츠 좀 볼 수 있을까요?
M: 파란색 줄무늬 티셔츠 말씀이시죠? 그건 디자인이 단순하고 멋있어요.
W: 네, 제 여동생이 좋아할 것 같아요. 그걸로 할게요.

2. W: Jake, 여기 네 소포가 있어.
M: 그거 내 헬멧이야. 며칠 전에 온라인 중고 가게에서 샀어.
W: 오, 열어서 보여 줘.
M: 그래. (잠시 후) 아, 이 바깥 부분이 조금 깨졌어. 하지만 판매자는 이것이 완벽하게 괜찮다고 말했어.
W: 사기 전에 헬멧 사진을 확인해 보지 않았니?
M: 아니, 나는 그냥 판매자를 믿었어. 조금 더 확인을 했어야 했어.
W: 너는 판매자에게 전화해서 환불을 요청해야 해.

대화문 Test **55**

※ 다음 우리말과 일치하도록 빈칸에 알맞은 것을 골라 쓰시오.

1 Have you ever _____ _____ you've _____ things that you don't _____ want or need?

    A. bought   B. wondered   C. why   D. even

2 Let's consider _____ _____ us when it _____ to _____ things.

    A. affects   B. buying   C. what   D. comes

3 Why do I want to buy _____ _____ _____ _____ ?

    A. bought   B. my   C. what   D. friends

4 Jeff _____ to the shopping center and sees a _____ of soccer shoes _____ _____ .

    A. display   B. goes   C. pair   D. on

5 He _____ the shoes at a glance _____ more than _____ of the boys on his soccer team _____ them.

    A. half   B. recognizes   C. wear   D. because

6 _____ he already has many pairs of soccer shoes, he _____ _____ buying _____ new pair.

    A. ends   B. although   C. up   D. another

7 We can use the "bandwagon _____ " _____ _____ Jeff's _____ .

    A. behavior   B. effect   C. explain   D. to

8 A bandwagon is a wagon in a _____ that _____ people to _____ _____ and enjoy the music.

    A. encourages   B. aboard   C. parade   D. jump

9 As more and more people get on the bandwagon, _____ are more _____ to _____ on or _____ it.

    A. others   B. get   C. follow   D. likely

10 In this _____ , people _____ to buy something _____ because other people have _____ it.

    A. bought   B. way   C. just   D. tend

11 Why do I _____ a _____ of pants and a bag _____ I have _____ a new coat?

    A. bought   B. pair   C. after   D. buy

---

1 여러분은 원하거나 필요로 하지도 않는 것들을 자신이 왜 구입했는지 궁금해 한 적이 있는가?

2 물건들을 구입하는 것에 관하여 무엇이 우리에게 영향을 주는지 생각해 보자.

3 나는 왜 친구들이 산 것을 사고 싶은 걸까?

4 Jeff는 쇼핑센터에 가서 진열되어 있는 축구화 한 켤레를 보게 된다.

5 그의 축구팀에 있는 소년들의 반 이상이 그 축구화를 신기 때문에 그는 그 신발을 한눈에 알아챈다.

6 이미 그에게는 축구화가 많이 있지만 결국 그는 또 다른 새 축구화를 사 버리고 만다.

7 우리는 Jeff의 행동을 설명하기 위해 '밴드왜건 효과'를 이용할 수 있다.

8 밴드왜건(악대차)은 사람들이 올라타서 음악을 즐기게끔 부추기는 퍼레이드에 있는 사륜마차이다.

9 더 많은 사람들이 밴드왜건에 올라탈수록 다른 사람들이 더욱 그것에 올라타거나 그것을 따라가려 한다.

10 이런 식으로, 사람들은 단지 다른 사람들이 어떤 것을 샀다는 이유로 그것을 구매하는 경향이 있다.

11 나는 왜 새 코트를 구입한 후에 바지와 가방을 사는 걸까?

12 Lisa buys a coat _____ she really loves. _____, she _____ that her pants do not _____ her new coat.

A. realizes　　　B. match　　　C. immediately　　D. that

13 So, she _____ new pants that _____ _____ her new coat.

A. go　　　　　B. buys　　　　C. with　　　　　D. perfectly

14 But she _____ that _____ of her bags _____ her new _____.

A. clothes　　　B. none　　　　C. match　　　　D. sees

15 So, she buys a new bag. _____ of her money is spent _____ buying the new _____ to _____ her new look.

A. most　　　　B. on　　　　　C. complete　　　D. items

16 What _____ Lisa _____ for new items immediately _____ _____ a new coat?

A. search　　　B. buying　　　C. made　　　　D. after

17 The "Diderot effect" may _____ it. Denis Diderot, a French writer, _____ a new gown _____ a _____.

A. received　　　B. explain　　　C. gift　　　　D. as

18 Soon after receiving the gift, he _____ that all of his _____ did not _____ well with his new gown. So, he ended up _____ most of it.

A. noticed　　　B. go　　　　　C. replacing　　　D. furniture

19 The Diderot effect, _____, is the concept that _____ a new item often _____ to more _____ purchases.

A. leads　　　　B. therefore　　C. unplanned　　D. purchasing

20 Why do I buy things _____ _____ they are _____ _____?

A. sale　　　　B. because　　　C. on　　　　　D. just

21 Nathan _____ _____ shopping and _____ a _____ of headphones.

A. goes　　　　B. sees　　　　C. pair　　　　D. window

---

12 Lisa는 정말 마음에 드는 코트를 산다. 그녀는 그녀의 바지가 새 코트와 어울리지 않는다는 것을 즉시 알아차린다.

13 그래서 그녀는 새 코트와 완벽하게 어울리는 새 바지를 구입한다.

14 하지만 그녀는 자신의 가방 중 어느 것도 새로운 옷들과 어울리지 않는다는 것을 알게 된다.

15 그래서 그녀는 새 가방을 산다. 그녀의 돈 대부분이 그녀의 새로운 모습을 완성하기 위하여 새로운 물품을 사는 데 쓰인다.

16 무엇이 Lisa로 하여금 새 코트를 산 후 즉시 새로운 물품을 찾게 했을까?

17 '디드로 효과'가 그것을 설명해 줄지도 모른다. 프랑스 작가인 Denis Diderot는 선물로 새 가운을 받았다.

18 그 선물을 받은 후에 곧 그는 그의 모든 가구가 새로운 가운과 어울리지 않는다는 것을 알아챘다. 그래서 그는 결국 대부분의 가구를 바꾸고 말았다.

19 그러므로 디드로 효과는 새로운 물품을 구입하는 것이 흔히 계획에 없던 더 많은 구매로 이어진다는 개념이다.

20 나는 왜 단지 할인 중이라는 이유로 물건을 구입하는 걸까?

21 Nathan은 진열된 상품을 구경하러 가서 헤드폰을 하나 본다.

22 He _____ the price and_____ _____ that they are $200. He thinks that the headphones are too _____.

    A. out   B. expensive   C. checks   D. finds

23 The _____ person _____ him and says, "You can get a 20 percent _____ _____ those headphones."

    A. discount   B. sales   C. on   D. approaches

24 Even _____ the _____ price is _____ not very _____, Nathan decides to buy the headphones.

    A. low   B. discounted   C. though   D. still

25 The situation _____ _____ is an _____ of the "anchoring _____."

    A. above   B. effect   C. example   D. described

26 The price _____ first _____ our _____ of _____ mentioned afterwards.

    A. prices   B. mentioned   C. opinion   D. affects

27 For example, if we start with $200, then $160 will _____ _____ _____ _____.

    A. comparison   B. seem   C. in   D. cheap

28 _____, as the difference of the two prices _____ _____, the effect will be more _____.

    A. bigger   B. furthermore   C. powerful   D. becomes

29 _____ _____, the price mentioned first acts as an "anchor" that _____ our _____ about the price of an item.

    A. thoughts   B. such   C. fixes   D. as

30 Just _____ Jeff and his friends, we tend to buy _____ without seriously _____ why we are _____ them.

    A. considering   B. buying   C. like   D. things

31 _____ these effects have _____, many things _____ our _____.

    A. shown   B. purchases   C. as   D. influence

32 The next _____ you decide to buy something, _____ for a moment _____ why you are _____ it.

    A. think   B. about   C. time   D. buying

22 그는 가격을 확인하고 그것이 200달러임을 알게 된다. 그는 그 헤드폰이 너무 비싸다고 생각한다.

23 점원이 그에게 다가와 "이 헤드폰에 20퍼센트 할인을 받을 수 있어요."라고 말한다.

24 비록 할인된 가격이 여전히 별로 저렴하지는 않지만 Nathan은 그 헤드폰을 사기로 결심한다.

25 위에 기술된 상황은 '앵커링 효과'의 한 예이다.

26 처음에 언급된 가격이 이후에 언급되는 가격에 대한 우리의 의견에 영향을 미친다.

27 예를 들어, 만약 우리가 200달러로 시작한다면, 비교해 볼 때 160달러는 저렴해 보일 것이다.

28 그뿐만 아니라, 두 가격의 차이가 커질수록 그 효과는 더욱 강력해질 것이다.

29 이와 같이 처음에 언급된 가격이 물건의 가격에 대한 우리의 생각을 고정하는 '닻'으로서 작동한다.

30 Jeff와 그의 친구들처럼, 우리는 우리가 왜 물건들을 사는지 진지하게 고려하지 않고 그것들을 구입하는 경향이 있다.

31 이러한 효과들이 보여 주듯이, 많은 것들이 우리의 구매에 영향을 미친다.

32 다음번에 여러분이 어떤 것을 구매하려고 결정할 때에는, 자신이 그것을 왜 사려는지 잠시 동안 생각해 보아라.

※ 다음 우리말과 일치하도록 빈칸에 알맞은 것을 골라 쓰시오.

1 Have you ever wondered _____ _____ _____ _____ you don't even want or need?

2 Let's consider _____ _____ _____ when it _____ _____ _____ things.

3 Why do I want to buy _____ _____ _____ _____?

4 Jeff _____ to the shopping center and _____ _____ _____ _____ soccer shoes _____ _____.

5 He _____ the shoes at a glance _____ more than _____ _____ _____ _____ on his soccer team _____ them.

6 _____ he already has _____ _____ _____ soccer shoes, he _____ _____ _____ _____ new pair.

7 We can use the "_____ _____" _____ _____ Jeff's _____.

8 A bandwagon is a wagon in a parade _____ _____ people _____ _____ _____ and enjoy the music.

9 As _____ _____ _____ _____ get on the bandwagon, _____ _____ more _____ _____ _____ or _____ it.

10 _____ this _____, people tend _____ something _____ _____ other people _____ _____ _____.

11 Why do I _____ _____ _____ _____ pants and a bag _____ I _____ _____ a new coat?

12 Lisa buys a coat _____ she really loves. _____, she _____ _____ her pants do not _____ her new coat.

13 So, she buys new pants _____ perfectly _____ her new coat.

14 But she sees _____ _____ _____ her _____ _____ _____.

15 So, she _____ a new bag. _____ _____ _____ _____ spent _____ buying the new items _____ _____ her _____.

16 What _____ Lisa _____ _____ _____ immediately _____ _____ a new coat?

17 The "Diderot _____" may _____ _____. Denis Diderot, a French writer, _____ a new gown _____ a _____.

18 Soon _____ _____ the gift, he _____ _____ all of his _____ did not _____ _____ with his new gown. So, he ended up _____ _____ _____ _____.

19 The Diderot effect, _____, is the concept _____ _____ _____ _____ often _____ _____ more _____ _____.

20 Why do I buy things _____ _____ _____ _____ _____ _____?

21 Nathan _____ _____ _____ _____ and _____ a _____ of headphones.

22 He _____ the price and _____ _____ _____ they are $200. He thinks _____ the headphones are _____ _____.

23 The sales person _____ _____ and says, "You can get a 20 percent _____ _____ those headphones."

24 _____ _____ the discounted price _____ _____ not very _____, Nathan decides _____ _____ the headphones.

25 The situation _____ _____ is an _____ of the " _____ _____."

26 The price _____ first _____ our _____ _____ _____ _____ afterwards.

27 _____ _____, if we start with $200, then $160 will _____ _____ _____ _____ _____.

28 _____, as _____ _____ of the two prices _____ _____, the effect will _____ _____ _____.

29 _____ _____, the price _____ _____ acts as an " _____ " that _____ _____ _____ _____ about the price of an item.

30 _____ _____ Jeff and his friends, we tend _____ _____ things _____ seriously _____ _____ _____ _____ them.

31 _____ these effects _____ _____, many things _____ _____ _____.

32 _____ _____ _____ you _____ _____ _____ _____ something, _____ for a moment _____ _____ _____ _____ _____ it.

17 '디드로 효과'가 그것을 설명해 줄지도 모른다. 프랑스 작가인 Denis Diderot는 선물로 새 가운을 받았다.

18 그 선물을 받은 후에 곧 그는 그의 모든 가구가 새로운 가운과 어울리지 않는다는 것을 알아챘다. 그래서 그는 결국 대부분의 가구를 바꾸고 말았다.

19 그러므로 디드로 효과는 새로운 물품을 구입하는 것이 흔히 계획에 없던 더 많은 구매로 이어진다는 개념이다.

20 나는 왜 단지 할인 중이라는 이유로 물건을 구입하는 걸까?

21 Nathan은 진열된 상품을 구경하러 가서 헤드폰을 하나 본다.

22 그는 가격을 확인하고 그것이 200달러임을 알게 된다. 그는 그 헤드폰이 너무 비싸다고 생각한다.

23 점원이 그에게 다가와 "이 헤드폰에 20퍼센트 할인을 받을 수 있어요."라고 말한다.

24 비록 할인된 가격이 여전히 별로 저렴하지는 않지만 Nathan은 그 헤드폰을 사기로 결심한다.

25 위에 기술된 상황은 '앵커링 효과'의 한 예이다.

26 처음에 언급된 가격이 이후에 언급되는 가격에 대한 우리의 의견에 영향을 미친다.

27 예를 들어, 만약 우리가 200달러로 시작한다면, 비교해 볼 때 160달러는 저렴해 보일 것이다.

28 그뿐만 아니라, 두 가격의 차이가 커질수록 그 효과는 더욱 강력해질 것이다.

29 이와 같이 처음에 언급된 가격이 물건의 가격에 대한 우리의 생각을 고정하는 '닻'으로서 작동한다.

30 Jeff와 그의 친구들처럼, 우리는 우리가 왜 물건들을 사는지 진지하게 고려하지 않고 그것들을 구입하는 경향이 있다.

31 이러한 효과들이 보여 주듯이, 많은 것들이 우리의 구매에 영향을 미친다.

32 다음번에 여러분이 어떤 것을 구매하려고 결정할 때에는, 자신이 그것을 왜 사려는지 잠시 동안 생각해 보아라.

※ 다음 문장을 우리말로 쓰시오.

1 Have you ever wondered why you've bought things that you don't even want or need?
➡ _____

2 Let's consider what affects us when it comes to buying things.
➡ _____

3 Why do I want to buy what my friends bought?
➡ _____

4 Jeff goes to the shopping center and sees a pair of soccer shoes on display.
➡ _____

5 He recognizes the shoes at a glance because more than half of the boys on his soccer team wear them.
➡ _____

6 Although he already has many pairs of soccer shoes, he ends up buying another new pair.
➡ _____

7 We can use the "bandwagon effect" to explain Jeff's behavior.
➡ _____

8 A bandwagon is a wagon in a parade that encourages people to jump aboard and enjoy the music.
➡ _____

9 As more and more people get on the bandwagon, others are more likely to get on or follow it.
➡ _____

10 In this way, people tend to buy something just because other people have bought it.
➡ _____

11 Why do I buy a pair of pants and a bag after I have bought a new coat?
➡ _____

12 Lisa buys a coat that she really loves. Immediately, she realizes that her pants do not match her new coat.
➡ _____

13 So, she buys new pants that go perfectly with her new coat.
➡ _____

14 But she sees that none of her bags match her new clothes.
➡ _____

15 So, she buys a new bag. Most of her money is spent on buying the new items to complete her new look.
➡ _____

16 What made Lisa search for new items immediately after buying a new coat?
➡ _____

17 ▶ The "Diderot effect" may explain it. Denis Diderot, a French writer, received a new gown as a gift.

➡ _____

18 ▶ Soon after receiving the gift, he noticed that all of his furniture did not go well with his new gown. So, he ended up replacing most of it.

➡ _____

_____

19 ▶ The Diderot effect, therefore, is the concept that purchasing a new item often leads to more unplanned purchases.

➡ _____

20 ▶ Why do I buy things just because they are on sale?

➡ _____

21 ▶ Nathan goes window shopping and sees a pair of headphones.

➡ _____

22 ▶ He checks the price and finds out that they are $200. He thinks that the headphones are too expensive.

➡ _____

23 ▶ The sales person approaches him and says, "You can get a 20 percent discount on those headphones."

➡ _____

24 ▶ Even though the discounted price is still not very low, Nathan decides to buy the headphones.

➡ _____

25 ▶ The situation described above is an example of the "anchoring effect."

➡ _____

26 ▶ The price mentioned first affects our opinion of prices mentioned afterwards.

➡ _____

27 ▶ For example, if we start with $200, then $160 will seem cheap in comparison.

➡ _____

28 ▶ Furthermore, as the difference of the two prices becomes bigger, the effect will be more powerful.

➡ _____

29 ▶ As such, the price mentioned first acts as an "anchor" that fixes our thoughts about the price of an item.

➡ _____

30 ▶ Just like Jeff and his friends, we tend to buy things without seriously considering why we are buying them.

➡ _____

31 ▶ As these effects have shown, many things influence our purchases.

➡ _____

32 ▶ The next time you decide to buy something, think for a moment about why you are buying it.

➡ _____

※ 다음 괄호 안의 단어들을 우리말에 맞도록 바르게 배열하시오.

1 (you / have / wondered / ever / you've / why / things / bought / that / don't / you / want / even / need? / or)

➡ _____

_____

2 (consider / let's / affects / what / when / us / comes / it / buying / to / things.)

➡ _____

3 (do / why / want / I / buy / to / what / friends / my / thought?)

➡ _____

4 (goes / Jeff / the / to / center / shoppiing / and / a / sees / pair / soccer / of / on / shoes / display.)

➡ _____

_____

5 (recognizes / he / shoes / the / a / at / because / glance / more / half / than / the / of / boys / his / on / soccer / wear / team / them.)

➡ _____

_____

6 (he / although / has / already / many / of / pairs / shoes, / soccer / ends / he / buying / up / new / another / pair.)

➡ _____

7 (can / we / the / use / effect" / "bandwagon / to / Jeff's / explain / behavior.)

➡ _____

8 (bandwagon / a / is / wagon / a / in / parade / a / that / people / encourages / to / jump / and / aboard / the / enjoy / music.)

➡ _____

9 (more / as / and / people / more / on / get / bandwagon, / the / are / others / likely / more / get / to / or / on / it. / follow)

➡ _____

10 (this / in / way, / tend / people / buy / to / just / something / other / because / people / bought / have / it.)

➡ _____

11 (do / why / buy / I / pair / a / pants / of / and / bag / a / after / have / I / a / bought / coat? / new)

➡ _____

1 여러분은 원하거나 필요로 하지도 않는 것들을 자신이 왜 구입했는지 궁금해 한 적이 있는가?

2 물건들을 구입하는 것에 관하여 무엇이 우리에게 영향을 주는지 생각해 보자.

3 나는 왜 친구들이 산 것을 사고 싶은 걸까?

4 Jeff는 쇼핑센터에 가서 진열되어 있는 축구화 한 켤레를 보게 된다.

5 그의 축구팀에 있는 소년들의 반 이상이 그 축구화를 신기 때문에 그는 그 신발을 한눈에 알아챈다.

6 이미 그에게는 축구화가 많이 있지만 결국 그는 또 다른 새 축구화를 사 버리고 만다.

7 우리는 Jeff의 행동을 설명하기 위해 '밴드왜건 효과'를 이용할 수 있다.

8 밴드왜건(악대차)은 사람들이 올라타서 음악을 즐기게끔 부추기는 퍼레이드에 있는 사륜마차이다.

9 더 많은 사람들이 밴드왜건에 올라탈수록 다른 사람들이 더욱 그것에 올라타거나 그것을 따라가려 한다.

10 이런 식으로, 사람들은 단지 다른 사람들이 어떤 것을 샀다는 이유로 그것을 구매하는 경향이 있다.

11 나는 왜 새 코트를 구입한 후에 바지와 가방을 사는 걸까?

12 (buys / Lisa / coat / a / she / that / loves. / really // she / immediately, / that / realizes / her / do / pants / match / not / new / coat. / her)

➡ _____

_____

13 (she / so, / new / buys / that / pants / go / with / perfectly / her / coat. / new)

➡ _____

14 (she / but / that / sees / none / her / of / bags / her / match / clothes. / new)

➡ _____

15 (she / so, / a / buys / bag. / new // of / most / money / her / spent / is / buying / on / new / the / items / complete / to / new / her / look.)

➡ _____

_____

16 (made / what / search / Lisa / new / for / immediately / items / buying / after / new / a / coat?)

➡ _____

_____

17 ("Diderot / the / effect" / explain / may / it. // Diderot, / Denis / a / writer, / French / a / received / new / a / as / gown / gift.)

➡ _____

_____

18 (after / soon / the / receiving / gift, / noticed / he / all / that / his / of / did / furniture / not / well / go / his / with / gown. / new // so, / ended / he / up / most / replacing / it. / of)

➡ _____

_____

19 (Diderot / the / effect, / is / therefore, / concept / the / purchasing / that / new / a / often / item / to / leads / more / purchases. / unplanned)

➡ _____

_____

20 (do / why / buy / I / just / things / because / are / they / sale? / on)

➡ _____

12 Lisa는 정말 마음에 드는 코트를 산다. 그녀는 그녀의 바지가 새 코트와 어울리지 않는다는 것을 즉시 알아차린다.

13 그래서 그녀는 새 코트와 완벽하게 어울리는 새 바지를 구입한다.

14 하지만 그녀는 자신의 가방 중 어느 것도 새로운 옷들과 어울리지 않는다는 것을 알게 된다.

15 그래서 그녀는 새 가방을 산다. 그녀의 돈 대부분이 그녀의 새로운 모습을 완성하기 위하여 새로운 물품을 사는 데 쓰인다.

16 무엇이 Lisa로 하여금 새 코트를 산 후 즉시 새로운 물품을 찾게 했을까?

17 '디드로 효과'가 그것을 설명해 줄지도 모른다. 프랑스 작가인 Denis Diderot는 선물로 새 가운을 받았다.

18 그 선물을 받은 후에 곧 그는 그의 모든 가구가 새로운 가운과 어울리지 않는다는 것을 알아챘다. 그래서 그는 결국 대부분의 가구를 바꾸고 말았다.

19 그러므로 디드로 효과는 새로운 물품을 구입하는 것이 흔히 계획에 없던 더 많은 구매로 이어진다는 개념이다.

20 나는 왜 단지 할인 중이라는 이유로 물건을 구입하는 걸까?

21 (goes / Nathan / shopping / window / and / a / sees / of / pair / headphones.)

➡ _____

22 (checks / he / price / the / and / out / finds / they / that / $200. / are // thinks / he / that / headphones / the / too / are / expensive.)

➡ _____

_____

23 (sales / the / person / him / approaches / says, / and / can / "you / a / get / percent / 20 / on / discount / headphones." / those)

➡ _____

_____

24 (though / even / discounted / the / is / price / not / still / low, / very / decides / Nathan / buy / to / headphones. / the)

➡ _____

_____

25 (situation / the / above / described / an / is / of / example / the / effect." / "anchoring)

➡ _____

26 (price / the / first / mentioned / affects / opinion / our / prices / of / afterwards. / mentioned)

➡ _____

27 (example, / for / we / if / with / start / $200, / $160 / then / will / cheap / seem / comparison. / in)

➡ _____

_____

28 (as / furthermore, / the / of / difference / two / the / becomes / prices / bigger, / effect / the / will / more / be / powerful.)

➡ _____

_____

29 (such, / as / price / the / first / mentioned / acts / an / as / that / "anchor" / our / fixes / about / thoughts / the / of / price / item. / an)

➡ _____

_____

30 (like / just / and / Jeff / friends, / his / tend / we / buy / to / without / things / seriously / we / considering / why / buying / are / them.)

➡ _____

_____

31 (these / as / have / effects / shown, / things / many / our / influence / purchases.)

➡ _____

32 (next / the / you / time / to / decide / something, / buy / for / think / moment / a / about / you / why / buying / are / it.)

➡ _____

_____

21 Nathan은 진열된 상품을 구경하러 가서 헤드폰을 하나 본다.

22 그는 가격을 확인하고 그것이 200달러임을 알게 된다. 그는 그 헤드폰이 너무 비싸다고 생각한다.

23 점원이 그에게 다가와 "이 헤드폰에 20퍼센트 할인을 받을 수 있어요."라고 말한다.

24 비록 할인된 가격이 여전히 별로 저렴하지는 않지만 Nathan은 그 헤드폰을 사기로 결심한다.

25 위에 기술된 상황은 '앵커링 효과'의 한 예이다.

26 처음에 언급된 가격이 이후에 언급되는 가격에 대한 우리의 의견에 영향을 미친다.

27 예를 들어, 만약 우리가 200달러로 시작한다면, 비교해 볼 때 160달러는 저렴해 보일 것이다.

28 그뿐만 아니라, 두 가격의 차이가 커질수록 그 효과는 더욱 강력해질 것이다.

29 이와 같이 처음에 언급된 가격이 물건의 가격에 대한 우리의 생각을 고정하는 '닻'으로서 작동한다.

30 Jeff와 그의 친구들처럼, 우리는 우리가 왜 물건들을 사는지 진지하게 고려하지 않고 그것들을 구입하는 경향이 있다.

31 이러한 효과들이 보여 주듯이, 많은 것들이 우리의 구매에 영향을 미친다.

32 다음번에 여러분이 어떤 것을 구매하려고 결정할 때에는, 자신이 그것을 왜 사려는지 잠시 동안 생각해 보아라.

※ 다음 우리말을 영어로 쓰시오.

1 여러분은 원하거나 필요로 하지도 않는 것들을 자신이 왜 구입했는지 궁금해 한 적이 있는가?
➡ _____

2 물건들을 구입하는 것에 관하여 무엇이 우리에게 영향을 주는지 생각해 보자.
➡ _____

3 나는 왜 친구들이 산 것을 사고 싶은 걸까?
➡ _____

4 Jeff는 쇼핑센터에 가서 진열되어 있는 축구화 한 켤레를 보게 된다.
➡ _____

5 그의 축구팀에 있는 소년들의 반 이상이 그 축구화를 신기 때문에 그는 그 신발을 한눈에 알아챈다.
➡ _____
_____

6 이미 그에게는 축구화가 많이 있지만 결국 그는 또 다른 새 축구화를 사 버리고 만다.
➡ _____

7 우리는 Jeff의 행동을 설명하기 위해 '밴드왜건 효과'를 이용할 수 있다.
➡ _____

8 밴드왜건(악대차)은 사람들이 올라타서 음악을 즐기게끔 부추기는 퍼레이드에 있는 사륜마차이다.
➡ _____

9 더 많은 사람들이 밴드왜건에 올라탈수록 다른 사람들이 더욱 그것에 올라타거나 그것을 따라가려 한다.
➡ _____

10 이런 식으로, 사람들은 단지 다른 사람들이 어떤 것을 샀다는 이유로 그것을 구매하는 경향이 있다.
➡ _____

11 나는 왜 새 코트를 구입한 후에 바지와 가방을 사는 걸까?
➡ _____

12 Lisa는 정말 마음에 드는 코트를 산다. 그녀는 그녀의 바지가 새 코트와 어울리지 않는다는 것을 즉시 알아차린다.
➡ _____

13 그래서 그녀는 새 코트와 완벽하게 어울리는 새 바지를 구입한다.
➡ _____

14 하지만 그녀는 자신의 가방 중 어느 것도 새로운 옷들과 어울리지 않는다는 것을 알게 된다.
➡ _____

15 그래서 그녀는 새 가방을 산다. 그녀의 돈 대부분이 그녀의 새로운 모습을 완성하기 위하여 새로운 물품을 사는 데 쓰인다.
➡ _____
_____

16 무엇이 Lisa로 하여금 새 코트를 산 후 즉시 새로운 물품을 찾게 했을까?
➡ _____

17 ‘디드로 효과’가 그것을 설명해 줄지도 모른다. 프랑스 작가인 Denis Diderot는 선물로 새 가운을 받았다.

➡ _____

18 그 선물을 받은 후에 곧 그는 그의 모든 가구가 새로운 가운과 어울리지 않는다는 것을 알아챘다. 그래서 그는 결국 대부분의 가구를 바꾸고 말았다.

➡ _____

19 그러므로 디드로 효과는 새로운 물품을 구입하는 것이 흔히 계획에 없던 더 많은 구매로 이어진다는 개념이다.

➡ _____

20 나는 왜 단지 할인 중이라는 이유로 물건을 구입하는 걸까?

➡ _____

21 Nathan은 진열된 상품을 구경하러 가서 헤드폰을 하나 본다.

➡ _____

22 그는 가격을 확인하고 그것이 200달러임을 알게 된다. 그는 그 헤드폰이 너무 비싸다고 생각한다.

➡ _____

23 점원이 그에게 다가와 “이 헤드폰에 20퍼센트 할인을 받을 수 있어요.”라고 말한다.

➡ _____

24 비록 할인된 가격이 여전히 별로 저렴하지는 않지만 Nathan은 그 헤드폰을 사기로 결심한다.

➡ _____

25 위에 기술된 상황은 ‘앵커링 효과’의 한 예이다.

➡ _____

26 처음에 언급된 가격이 이후에 언급되는 가격에 대한 우리의 의견에 영향을 미친다.

➡ _____

27 예를 들어, 만약 우리가 200달러로 시작한다면, 비교해 볼 때 160달러는 저렴해 보일 것이다.

➡ _____

28 그뿐만 아니라, 두 가격의 차이가 커질수록 그 효과는 더욱 강력해질 것이다.

➡ _____

29 이와 같이 처음에 언급된 가격이 물건의 가격에 대한 우리의 생각을 고정하는 ‘닻’으로서 작동한다.

➡ _____

30 Jeff와 그의 친구들처럼, 우리는 우리가 왜 물건들을 사는지 진지하게 고려하지 않고 그것들을 구입하는 경향이 있다.

➡ _____

➡ _____

31 이러한 효과들이 보여 주듯이, 많은 것들이 우리의 구매에 영향을 미친다.

➡ _____

32 다음번에 여러분이 어떤 것을 구매하려고 결정할 때에는, 자신이 그것을 왜 사려는지 잠시 동안 생각해 보아라.

➡ _____

※ 다음 우리말과 일치하도록 빈칸에 알맞은 말을 쓰시오.

Language in Use

1. _____ is difficult _____ _____ the results _____ _____.
2. We _____ children _____ _____ _____ _____ _____.

1. 결과를 상세히 비교하는 것은 어렵다.
2. 우리는 아이들이 스스로 생각하도록 장려한다.

Grammar in Real Life B Look and Write

1. About _____ _____ the water _____ _____ _____ _____ _____ animals in the U.S.
2. _____ _____ _____ the world's food _____ _____ —1.3 _____ _____ every year.
3. In Somalia, _____ _____ _____ _____ the children _____ _____ _____.
4. _____ fourteen percent of all people _____ know _____ _____ _____ _____ _____ _____ education.

1. 그 물의 절반 가량이 미국에서 동물을 키우기 위해 사용된다.
2. 세계 식량의 삼분의 일, 즉 매년 13억 톤이 낭비된다.
3. 소말리아에서는 단지 10퍼센트의 아이들이 학교에 다닌다.
4. 전체 인구의 약 14퍼센트는 교육의 부족으로 읽는 법을 알지 못한다.

Think & Write C

1. I _____ _____ _____ about _____.
2. First, I asked 10 students _____ _____ _____ _____ _____ _____ _____.
3. Twenty percent of the students _____ _____ _____ every week and _____ _____ of the students _____ _____ _____ _____.
4. Second, I asked them _____ they _____ _____ _____ _____ _____.
5. _____ _____ _____ _____ is spent on clothes and _____ _____ of the allowance _____ _____ _____ _____.
6. Lastly, I asked them _____ _____ _____ that they _____ _____ _____ _____ _____.
7. _____ _____ _____ _____ _____ that they should get a higher allowance.

1. 저는 용돈에 관하여 설문 조사를 했습니다.
2. 우선, 저는 10명의 학생들에게 그들이 얼마나 자주 용돈을 받는지 물었습니다.
3. 20퍼센트의 학생들은 매주 용돈을 받고, 70퍼센트의 학생들은 매달 용돈을 받습니다.
4. 두 번째로, 저는 학생들에게 어디에 용돈의 대부분을 쓰는지 물었습니다.
5. 대부분의 용돈은 옷에 쓰이고, 용돈의 4분의 1은 간식에 쓰입니다.
6. 마지막으로, 저는 학생들에게 그들이 더 많은 용돈을 받아야 한다고 생각하는지 물었습니다.
7. 학생들의 90퍼센트는 그들이 더 많은 용돈을 받아야 한다고 생각합니다.

※ 다음 우리말을 영어로 쓰시오.

Language in Use

1. 결과를 상세히 비교하는 것은 어렵다.

➡ _____

2. 우리는 아이들이 스스로 생각하도록 장려한다.

➡ _____

Grammar in Real Life B Look and Write

1. 그 물의 절반 가량이 미국에서 동물을 키우기 위해 사용된다.

➡ _____

2. 세계 식량의 삼분의 일, 즉 매년 13억 톤이 낭비된다.

➡ _____

3. 소말리아에서는 단지 10퍼센트의 아이들이 학교에 다닌다.

➡ _____

4. 전체 인구의 약 14퍼센트는 교육의 부족으로 읽는 법을 알지 못한다.

➡ _____

Think & Write C

1. 저는 용돈에 관하여 설문 조사를 했습니다.

➡ _____

2. 우선, 저는 10명의 학생들에게 그들이 얼마나 자주 용돈을 받는지 물었습니다.

➡ _____

3. 20퍼센트의 학생들은 매주 용돈을 받고, 70퍼센트의 학생들은 매달 용돈을 받습니다.

➡ _____

_____

4. 두 번째로, 저는 학생들에게 어디에 용돈의 대부분을 쓰는지 물었습니다.

➡ _____

5. 대부분의 용돈은 옷에 쓰이고, 용돈의 4분의 1은 간식에 쓰입니다.

➡ _____

6. 마지막으로, 저는 학생들에게 그들이 더 많은 용돈을 받아야 한다고 생각하는지 물었습니다.

➡ _____

7. 학생들의 90퍼센트는 그들이 더 많은 용돈을 받아야 한다고 생각합니다.

➡ _____

※ 다음 영어를 우리말로 쓰시오.

01 surface _____

02 bend _____

03 connect _____

04 sunrise _____

05 contain _____

06 shortcut _____

07 crush _____

08 distance _____

09 changeable _____

10 attach _____

11 tough _____

12 eatable _____

13 achieve _____

14 eventually _____

15 detect _____

16 extend _____

17 unstable _____

18 bottom _____

19 layer _____

20 vast _____

21 persistent _____

22 instantly _____

23 apply _____

24 exist _____

25 gravity _____

26 lean _____

27 punch _____

28 infinite _____

29 lower _____

30 exploration _____

31 measure _____

32 theory _____

33 ongoing _____

34 incorrect _____

35 look back _____

36 figure out _____

37 according to~ _____

38 far away from _____

39 lie down _____

40 in theory _____

41 at the bottom of ~ _____

42 different from _____

43 in the blink of an eye _____

※ 다음 우리말을 영어로 쓰시오.

01 연구자, 조사자 _____

02 지름길 _____

03 몸을 숙이다, 굽히다 _____

04 계속 진행 중인 _____

05 승객, 탑승객 _____

06 부정확한, 사실이 아닌 _____

07 눌러 부수다, 찌부러뜨리다 _____

08 이론, 학설 _____

09 낮추다 _____

10 힘든, 어려운 _____

11 무한한 _____

12 적용하다, 응용하다 _____

13 끈질긴, 집요한, 지속적인 _____

14 맨 아랫부분, 바닥 _____

15 존재하다 _____

16 불안정한 _____

17 거대한, 광대한 _____

18 연결되다, 이어지다 _____

19 달성하다, 성취하다 _____

20 감지하다, 발견하다 _____

21 먹을 수 있는 _____

22 결국 _____

23 바뀔 수 있는, 변덕스러운 _____

24 탐사, 탐구 _____

25 중력 _____

26 붙이다 _____

27 ~이 들어 있다, 포함하다 _____

28 굽히다, 구부리다 _____

29 즉시 _____

30 층 _____

31 측정하다 _____

32 물리학 _____

33 거리 _____

34 축하하다 _____

35 맞추다 _____

36 눕다, 누워 있다 _____

37 ~의 속도로 _____

38 떠다니다 _____

39 ~에 따르면 _____

40 ~을 알아내다, 생각해 내다 _____

41 되돌아보다 _____

42 ~에서 멀리 떨어져 _____

43 ~의 아래에 _____

※ 다음 영영풀이에 알맞은 단어를 <보기>에서 골라 쓴 후, 우리말 뜻을 쓰시오.

1 _____ : extremely big: _____

2 _____ : to join or be joined with something else: _____

3 _____ : to fasten or join one thing to another: _____

4 _____ : the amount of space between two places: _____

5 _____ : not solid and firm and therefore not strong, safe, or likely to last: _____

6 _____ : to find out the size, length, or amount of something: _____

7 _____ : a professional cook, especially the most senior cook in a restaurant, hotel, etc.: _____

8 _____ : continuing to exist or develop, or happening at the present moment: _____

9 _____ : the time when the sun first appears in the sky in the morning: _____

10 _____ : a person who travels in a spacecraft into outer space: _____

11 _____ : to succeed in finishing something or reaching an aim, especially after a lot of work or effort: _____

12 _____ : to notice something that is partly hidden or not clear, or to discover something, especially using a special method: _____

13 _____ : the force that attracts objects towards one another, especially the force that makes things fall to the ground: _____

14 _____ : to do something special or enjoyable for an important event, occasion, holiday, etc.: _____

15 _____ : a person who is travelling in a car, bus, train, plane or ship and who is not driving it or working on it: _____

16 _____ : an extremely large, round mass of rock and metal, such as Earth, or of gas, such as Jupiter, that moves in a circular path around the sun or another star: _____

보기			
achieve	chef	sunrise	measure
celebrate	connect	passenger	vast
detect	unstable	gravity	ongoing
planet	distance	astronaut	attach

Step1

※ 다음 우리말과 일치하도록 빈칸에 알맞은 말을 쓰시오.

Listen & Talk 1 A

1. M: Welcome _____ _____ Earth, Irene. _____ was your favorite part about _____ in the space station?

   W: I _____ _____ a beautiful _____ 16 _____ _____. It was great.

   M: _____ _____ _____ _____ _____ the sunrise several times _____ _____ in space?

   W: Yes, it's _____ _____ we _____ _____ Earth every 90 minutes in the station.

   M: Wow, that's _____!

2. M: Irene, what was _____ _____ _____ _____ _____ in the space station?

   W: Hmm… . We _____ some vegetables and _____ them every day. They were pretty _____ _____ _____!

   M: Wow, _____ _____ _____ _____ _____ vegetables in the space station?

   W: Yes. _____ there's _____ _____ in space, we _____ _____ grow them in special bags. The bags _____ _____ _____ _____ _____.

   M: How interesting!

Listen & Talk 1 B

M: _____ _____ _____ _____ NASA is going to _____ a 3D printer _____ space?

W: They're _____ _____ _____ a 3D printer _____ _____ _____? Why?

M: _____ _____ _____ the 3D printer _____ _____ _____ _____ _____ food for astronauts.

W: Is it _____ _____ _____ food _____ a 3D printer?

M: Yes, it's possible. It can _____ _____ a fresh pizza _____ _____ _____ five minutes.

W: Really? I wonder _____ _____ _____ _____ _____.

해석

1. M: 지구에 돌아오신 것을 환영합니다, Irene 씨. 우주 정거장에서 보낸 시간 중 최고의 기억이 무엇인가요?
   W: 저는 하루에 16번씩 아름다운 일출을 볼 수 있었어요. 그것은 굉장했죠.
   M: 우주에서는 하루에 일출을 여러 번 보는 게 가능한가요?
   W: 네, 가능해요. 왜냐하면 우주 정거장이 지구 주위를 90분마다 돌았거든요.
   M: 와, 놀랍네요!

2. M: Irene 씨, 우주 정거장에서 드셨던 것 중 최고의 음식은 무엇이었나요?
   W: 음… . 우리는 채소를 키워서 매일 그걸 먹었어요. 그것은 매우 신선하고 맛있었어요!
   M: 와, 우주 정거장에서 채소를 키우는 것이 가능한가요?
   W: 네. 우주에는 중력이 없기 때문에, 우리는 그것을 특수한 봉지 안에서 키워야 했어요. 그 봉지는 뿌리가 자라는 데 도움을 줬어요.
   M: 참 흥미롭네요!

M: 나사(NASA)가 3D 프린터를 우주로 보낼 거라는 이야기 들어 봤니?
W: 그들이 3D 프린터를 우주로 보낸다고? 왜?
M: 우주 비행사들이 먹을 음식을 출력하는 데 3D 프린터가 쓰일 거라고 들었어.
W: 3D 프린터를 이용해 음식을 출력하는 게 가능해?
M: 응, 가능해. 그것은 신선한 피자를 5분도 안 되어서 출력해 낼 수 있어.
W: 정말? 그게 어떤 맛일지 궁금하다.

1. **M:** Look at these _____ pictures of the _____.

   W: Oh, they're beautiful. _____ _____ _____ _____ _____ Earth _____ space _____ _____ _____ _____.

   M: Actually, you can _____ _____ at the National Youth Space Center.

   W: Really?

   M: Yeah, you can use the VR glasses. I heard _____ you _____ _____ you are _____ _____ _____!

2. **W:** What _____ you _____?

   M: It's a documentary about life in space. Everything _____ so _____.

   W: Yes, _____ _____ there's _____ _____ in space.

   M: Right. _____ _____ _____ _____ _____ like an _____!

   W: Really? I don't. It _____ _____.

Listen & Talk 2 B

W: Look at this man, Jake. He _____ _____ space for one year.

M: It _____ _____ _____ _____ for him.

W: Right, but you know what's interesting? He grew 2 inches _____ _____ _____.

M: Really? How is that _____?

W: I'm _____ _____, but _____ _____ _____ _____ there's no _____ in space.

M: That's so cool. _____ _____ _____ _____ _____ space. That way, I could _____ _____.

W: _____ _____ _____ are other _____ _____ _____ _____ than _____ _____ _____.

1. **M:** 이 다채로운 색깔의 우주 사진들을 좀 봐.
   W: 오, 그것들은 아름다워. 내가 지구를 우주에서 직접 내 눈으로 볼 수 있으면 좋을 텐데.
   M: 사실 넌 국립 청소년 우주 센터에서 그걸 해 볼 수 있어.
   W: 정말?
   M: 응, 가상 현실(VR) 안경을 써 볼 수 있거든. 실제로 우주에 있는 것 같은 기분이 든다고 들었어!

2. **W:** 너는 무엇을 보고 있니?
   M: 우주에서의 삶에 관한 다큐멘터리야. 모든 것이 너무 달라 보여.
   W: 응, 왜냐하면 우주에는 중력이 없기 때문이지.
   M: 맞아. 나도 우주 비행사처럼 떠다닐 수 있다면 좋을 텐데!
   W: 정말이니? 나는 아니야. 그건 불편해 보여.

W: 이 남자 좀 봐, Jake. 그는 우주에서 1년 동안 살았어.
M: 그는 분명히 힘들었을 거야.
W: 맞아, 하지만 흥미로운 게 뭔 줄 아니? 그가 우주에 있는 동안 키가 2인치 자랐어.
M: 정말? 어떻게 그게 가능해?
W: 확실하진 않지만, 아마 우주에 중력이 없기 때문일 거야.
M: 정말 멋지다. 내가 우주에서 살 수 있으면 좋을 텐데. 그러면 난 키가 더 커질 수 있을 텐데.
W: 우주에 가는 것 말고 키가 더 커지는 다른 방법들이 있을 거라고 확신해.

Communication Step A

W: Hello, everyone, _____ _____ *All about Movies*! Today, we're going _____ _____ _____ the top three things from movies _____ _____ _____ _____ _____ .

M: Let's _____ _____ number three, the flying skateboard from *Back to the Future*.

W: It's a cool item. _____ _____ _____ _____ _____ a flying skateboard.

M: Actually, I read _____ _____ this is not _____ _____ .

W: Really? _____ _____ _____ _____ _____ on a skateboard?

M: Yes. Some companies _____ _____ physics _____ _____ flying skateboards.

Wrap Up

1. W: Mr. Scott, did you _____ your trip to space?

M: Yes, it was _____ _____ _____ of my life.

W: Can you tell us _____ _____ _____ _____ _____ _____ your trip?

M: I flew in space _____ _____ and saw our blue planet, Earth.

W: _____ _____ _____ _____ _____ in space _____ _____ ?

M: Yes, I _____ _____ to a special line, _____ it was _____ .

W: Sounds fantastic!

2. M: Hey, Cindy. I _____ _____ you went to the National Space Center last weekend. _____ was it?

W: It was great, Chris. I experienced _____ _____ and _____ _____ _____ .

M: Sounds fun. Did you meet _____ _____ in person?

W: Yes, and I _____ about their _____ stories.

M: Oh, I wish I could become an _____ like them and _____ _____ .

※ 다음 우리말에 맞도록 대화를 영어로 쓰시오.

Listen & Talk 1 A

1. M: _____
   _____
   W: _____
   M: _____
   W: _____
   M: _____

2. M: _____
   W: _____
   _____
   M: _____
   W: _____
   M: _____

Listen & Talk 1 B

M: _____
W: _____
M: _____
W: _____
M: _____
W: _____

 해석

1. M: 지구에 돌아오신 것을 환영합니다, Irene 씨. 우주 정거장에서 보낸 시간 중 최고의 기억이 무엇인가요?
   W: 저는 하루에 16번씩 아름다운 일출을 볼 수 있었어요. 그것은 굉장했죠.
   M: 우주에서는 하루에 일출을 여러 번 보는 게 가능한가요?
   W: 네, 가능해요. 왜냐하면 우주 정거장이 지구 주위를 90분마다 돌았거든요.
   M: 와, 놀랍네요!

2. M: Irene 씨, 우주 정거장에서 드셨던 것 중 최고의 음식은 무엇이었나요?
   W: 음… . 우리는 채소를 키워서 매일 그걸 먹었어요. 그것은 매우 신선하고 맛있었어요!
   M: 와, 우주 정거장에서 채소를 키우는 것이 가능한가요?
   W: 네. 우주에는 중력이 없기 때문에, 우리는 그것을 특수한 봉지 안에서 키워야 했어요. 그 봉지는 뿌리가 자라는 데 도움을 줬어요.
   M: 참 흥미롭네요!

M: 나사(NASA)가 3D 프린터를 우주로 보낼 거라는 이야기 들어 봤니?
W: 그들이 3D 프린터를 우주로 보낸다고? 왜?
M: 우주 비행사들이 먹을 음식을 출력하는 데 3D 프린터가 쓰일 거라고 들었어.
W: 3D 프린터를 이용해 음식을 출력하는 게 가능해?
M: 응, 가능해. 그것은 신선한 피자를 5분도 안 되어서 출력해 낼 수 있어.
W: 정말? 그게 어떤 맛일지 궁금하다.

Listen & Talk 2 A

1. M: _____

   W: _____

   M: _____

   W: _____

   M: _____

   _____

2. W: _____

   M: _____

   W: _____

   M: _____

   W: _____

Listen & Talk 2 B

W: _____

M: _____

W: _____

M: _____

W: _____

M: _____

W: _____

1. M: 이 다채로운 색깔의 우주 사진들을 좀 봐.
   W: 오, 그것들은 아름다워. 내가 지구를 우주에서 직접 내 눈으로 볼 수 있으면 좋을 텐데.
   M: 사실 넌 국립 청소년 우주 센터에서 그걸 해 볼 수 있어.
   W: 정말?
   M: 응, 가상 현실(VR) 안경을 써 볼 수 있거든. 실제로 우주에 있는 것 같은 기분이 든다고 들었어!

2. W: 너는 무엇을 보고 있니?
   M: 우주에서의 삶에 관한 다큐멘터리야. 모든 것이 너무 달라 보여.
   W: 응, 왜냐하면 우주에는 중력이 없기 때문이지.
   M: 맞아. 나도 우주 비행사처럼 떠다닐 수 있다면 좋을 텐데!
   W: 정말이니? 나는 아니야. 그건 불편해 보여.

W: 이 남자 좀 봐, Jake. 그는 우주에서 1년 동안 살았어.
M: 그는 분명히 힘들었을 거야.
W: 맞아, 하지만 흥미로운 게 뭔 줄 아니? 그가 우주에 있는 동안 키가 2인치 자랐어.
M: 정말? 어떻게 그게 가능해?
W: 확실하진 않지만, 아마 우주에 중력이 없기 때문일 거야.
M: 정말 멋지다. 내가 우주에서 살 수 있으면 좋을 텐데. 그러면 난 키가 더 커질 수 있을 텐데.
W: 우주에 가는 것 말고 키가 더 커지는 다른 방법들이 있을 거라고 확신해.

Communication Step A

W: _____

_____

M: _____

W: _____

M: _____

W: _____

M: _____

W: 안녕하세요, 여러분, '영화에 대한 모든 것(All about Movies)'에 오신 것을 환영합니다! 오늘 우리는 실제로 가능하기를 바라는 영화 속 물건들 중에서 상위 세 개에 관해 이야기해 보려고 합니다.

M: 우선 3위부터 시작하자면, '백 투 더 퓨처'에 나온, 날아다니는 스케이트보드입니다.

W: 멋진 물건이에요. 제가 날아다니는 스케이트보드를 가질 수 있다면 좋을 텐데요.

M: 사실, 전 그것이 전혀 불가능한 일은 아니라고 어딘가에서 읽었어요.

W: 정말요? 스케이트보드를 타고 날아다니는 것이 실제로 가능해요?

M: 네. 몇몇 회사들이 날아다니는 스케이트보드를 만들기 위해 물리학을 적용했어요.

Wrap Up

1. W: _____

M: _____

W: _____

M: _____

W: _____

M: _____

W: _____

2. M: _____

_____

W: _____

M: _____

W: _____

M: _____

1. W: Scott 씨, 우주로의 여행은 즐거우셨나요?

M: 네, 그것은 제 인생 최고의 경험이었어요.

W: 여행 중 어떤 부분이 최고였는지 말씀해 주실 수 있나요?

M: 혼자 우주를 날아서 우리의 푸른 행성인 지구를 보았어요.

W: 우주에서 혼자 나는 것이 가능한가요?

M: 네, 제 자신을 특수한 선에 연결해서 그건 안전했어요.

W: 환상적이네요!

2. M: 안녕, Cindy. 지난 주말에 네가 국립 우주 센터에 갔다고 들었어. 어땠어?

W: 굉장히 좋았어, Chris. 난 무중력 상태와 우주 비행사들의 우주 생활을 경험했어.

M: 재미있었겠다. 너는 직접 진짜 우주인을 만났어?

W: 응, 그리고 나는 그들의 모험 이야기를 들었어.

M: 오, 나는 그들처럼 우주인이 돼서 화성을 탐험하고 싶어.

※ 다음 우리말과 일치하도록 빈칸에 알맞은 것을 골라 쓰시오.

1 Sci Teen: Hi, science _____. Today, we're _____ to talk _____ space _____.
    A. travel   B. going   C. fans   D. about

2 _____ we all know, there is _____ faster than _____ in the _____.
    A. nothing   B. as   C. universe   D. light

3 So, if we _____ at the speed of light, we should be _____ to _____ to another planet in the _____ of an eye, right?
    A. blink   B. travel   C. get   D. able

4 Dr. Sci: That would be nice, but _____ is so _____ _____ it is not _____.
    A. possible   B. vast   C. space   D. that

5 In the movie, *Passengers*, a spaceship _____ to a different planet _____ at _____ the speed of _____.
    A. one-half   B. headed   C. light   D. travels

6 So it should _____ _____ _____ _____ very quickly, right?
    A. another   B. to   C. planet   D. get

7 But, the passengers sleep _____ 120 years because it is _____ to _____ that much time to _____ to a different planet.
    A. expected   B. get   C. for   D. take

8 Sci Teen: 120 years? Wow, that's a long time! Is there a _____ _____ to _____ _____ space?
    A. through   B. faster   C. travel   D. way

9 Dr. Sci: Well, _____ _____ to answer that question, I'd _____ you to _____ about this apple for a second.
    A. order   B. think   C. in   D. like

10 Imagine a worm is on this apple. It detects _____ _____ at the bottom and want to _____ from the top to the _____.
    A. sweet   B. bottom   C. something   D. move

11 For the _____, the apple's _____ is as _____ as our _____.
    A. universe   B. surface   C. worm   D. vast

12 Now the worm can _____ move _____ the outer layer _____ _____ a wormhole.
    A. or   B. down   C. either   D. around

13 Which do you _____ it will _____? Well, it would choose the wormhole _____ it is a _____.
    A. shortcut   B. choose   C. because   D. think

14 Sci Teen: Is _____ _____ _____ _____ in the universe?
    A. a   B. there   C. shortcut   D. such

15 Dr. Sci: According to some researchers, yes. Einstein _____ _____ that space and time are _____, and he called it _____.
    A. out   B. space-time   C. connected   D. figured

---

1 Sci Teen: 안녕하세요, 과학 팬 여러분. 오늘 우리는 우주여행에 대해 이야기할 것입니다.

2 우리가 모두 알다시피, 우주에서 빛보다 더 빠른 것은 없습니다.

3 그래서 만약 우리가 빛의 속도로 여행을 한다면, 우리는 다른 행성에 눈 깜박할 사이에 도달할 수 있어야 해요, 그렇죠?

4 Dr. Sci: 그렇다면 좋겠지만, 우주는 너무 광활해서 그건 불가능하답니다.

5 영화 〈Passengers〉에서 다른 행성으로 향하는 우주선이 빛의 속도의 절반으로 이동합니다.

6 그러면 그들은 다른 행성에 매우 빨리 도달해야겠지요, 그렇죠?

7 하지만 승객들은 120년 동안 잠을 자게 되는데, 왜냐하면 다른 행성에 도달하는 데 그만큼 많은 시간이 걸릴 것으로 예상되기 때문입니다.

8 Sci Teen: 120년이요? 우아, 그건 정말 긴 시간이네요! 우주를 여행하는 더 빠른 방법이 있나요?

9 Dr. Sci: 글쎄요, 그 질문에 답하기 위해서 여러분들이 이 사과에 대해 잠깐 생각해 보기 바랍니다.

10 한 마리 벌레가 이 사과 위에 있다고 상상해 보세요. 그것은 맨 아래에 있는 달콤한 무언가를 감지하고 맨 위에서 아래로 이동하기를 원합니다.

11 그 벌레에게 사과의 표면은 우리의 우주만큼이나 광대합니다.

12 이제 그 벌레는 바깥 표면의 껍질을 돌아서 이동하거나 벌레 구멍 아래로 이동할 수 있습니다.

13 그것이 어떤 것을 선택할 거라고 생각하십니까? 음, 그것은 벌레 구멍을 선택할 것인데 왜냐하면 그것이 지름길이기 때문입니다.

14 Sci Teen: 우주에 그런 지름길이 있나요?

15 Dr. Sci: 몇몇 연구자들에 따르면, 그렇습니다. 아인슈타인은 공간과 시간이 연결되어 있다는 것을 생각해 냈고, 그것을 시공간이라고 불렀습니다.

16 He thought that _____ could actually be _____. When it is bent, parts that are _____ _____ from each other are suddenly closer.

    A. bent   B. away   C. space-time   D. far

17 To _____ this, take a sheet of paper and make a small dot at the _____ of the paper and _____ at the _____ of the paper.

    A. top   B. understand   C. bottom   D. another

18 On a _____ _____ of paper, the dots are _____ _____ from one another.

    A. sheet   B. away   C. flat   D. far

19 Now, take the paper and _____ it with the dots _____ up. _____ a hole in the paper and the dots will be instantly _____.

    A. matched   B. connected   C. fold   D. punch

20 Like this, wormholes in space may _____ two _____, with a _____ _____ the two.

    A. connecting   B. contain   C. throat   D. mouths

21 Sci Teen: Just like a wormhole in the apple, right? If such wormholes _____ in space, we could _____ to _____ billions of light-years _____ quickly!

    A. existed   B. places   C. away   D. get

22 Dr. Sci: Yes, but it's too _____ to _____. Wormholes in _____ only.

    A. theory   B. early   C. exist   D. celebrate

23 Sci Teen: So _____ we need to _____ is _____ _____, right?

    A. find   B. all   C. one   D. do

24 Dr. Sci: _____ if we find one, there are many things to _____ before _____ going _____ one.

    A. through   B. even   C. consider   D. actually

25 A wormhole would be very _____. If a spaceship _____ into one, it might be _____ or _____ into pieces.

    A. unstable   B. crushed   C. flew   D. broken

26 Sci Teen: Ouch! That's not a _____ _____. So, are we _____?

    A. hopeless   B. picture   C. pretty

27 Is _____ in space through a wormhole _____ an idea that only _____ in _____?

    A. simply   B. traveling   C. exists   D. theory

28 Dr. Sci: I wouldn't say so. The debate about wormholes is still _____, but with _____ _____ and _____, I believe we will eventually find one and learn how to travel through it.

    A. exploration   B. ongoing   C. research   D. persistent

29 _____ _____ at our history. We've achieved so many things that _____ _____ at first.

    A. seemed   B. back   C. impossible   D. look

30 Who knows? _____ you can _____ the one to _____ the _____!

    A. maybe   B. answer   C. find   D. be

---

16 '그는 시공간이 실제로 구부러질 수 있다고 생각했습니다. 그것이 구부러질 때 서로 멀리 떨어져 있는 부분들이 갑자기 더 가까워질 수 있습니다.

17 이것을 이해하기 위해서, 종이를 한 장 갖고 와서 그 종이의 윗부분에 작은 점을 찍고 또 다른 점을 그 종이의 아랫부분에 찍어 보세요.

18 펼쳐 놓은 종이에서 그 점들은 서로 멀리 떨어져 있습니다.

19 이제 그 종이를 들고 점들이 맞춰지도록 그것을 접으세요. 종이에 구멍을 뚫으면 그 점이 즉시 연결될 것입니다.

20 이와 마찬가지로 우주의 웜홀은 두 개의 입과 그 둘을 연결하는 목구멍을 지니고 있을 겁니다.

21 Sci Teen: 사과에 있는 벌레 구멍처럼요, 그렇죠? 그런 웜홀이 우주에 존재한다면 우리는 수십억 광년 떨어져 있는 곳에 빠르게 도달할 수 있을 텐데요!

22 Dr. Sci: 그렇죠, 하지만 축하하기에는 너무 이릅니다. 웜홀은 이론상에서만 존재합니다.

23 Sci Teen: 그러면 우리가 해야 할 것이라고는 그것을 찾는 거네요, 그렇죠?

24 Dr. Sci: 우리가 그것을 찾는다고 하더라도 실제로 그걸 통과하여 가기 전에 고려해야 할 것들이 많이 있습니다.

25 웜홀은 매우 불안정할 것입니다. 만약 우주선이 그 안으로 날아가게 되면, 그것은 부서지거나 산산조각이 날 수도 있습니다.

26 Sci Teen: 어이쿠! 그건 좋은 광경이 아니네요. 그럼 우리는 가망이 없는 건가요?

27 우주에서 웜홀을 통하여 여행을 하는 것은 단지 이론상으로만 존재하는 아이디어인가요?

28 Dr. Sci: 그렇게 말하지는 않겠어요. 웜홀에 대한 논쟁은 여전히 진행 중이긴 하지만, 끊임없는 탐구와 연구로 우리가 결국 하나를 찾아 그것을 통해 여행하는 법을 배울 수 있을 거라고 믿습니다.

29 우리의 역사를 돌아보세요. 우리는 처음에는 불가능해 보였던 아주 많은 것들을 달성해 왔습니다.

30 누가 알겠어요? 아마도 여러분이 그 답을 찾아내는 그 사람이 될 수 있을지도요!

※ 다음 우리말과 일치하도록 빈칸에 알맞은 것을 골라 쓰시오.

1 Sci Teen: Hi, science fans. Today, we're _____ _____ _____ _____ _____ _____.

2 _____ _____ _____ _____ _____, there is _____ _____ _____ in the universe.

3 So, if we _____ _____ the speed of light, we should _____ _____ _____ _____ _____ _____ _____ another planet _____ _____ _____ _____ an eye, _____?

4 Dr. Sci: That would be nice, but space _____ _____ _____ _____ it is _____ _____.

5 In the movie, *Passengers*, a spaceship _____ _____ a different planet _____ at _____ the speed of light.

6 So it should _____ _____ _____ _____ very quickly, right?

7 But, the passengers sleep _____ _____ _____ because it _____ _____ _____ _____ that much time _____ _____ _____ a different planet.

8 Sci Teen: 120 years? Wow, that's a long time! Is there _____ _____ _____ _____ _____ space?

9 Dr. Sci: Well, _____ _____ _____ answer that question, I'd like _____ _____ _____ about this apple _____ _____ _____.

10 Imagine a worm is _____ _____ _____. It detects _____ _____ at the bottom and _____ _____ _____ _____ the top _____ the bottom.

11 For the worm, the apple's surface is _____ _____ _____ our universe.

12 Now the worm can _____ _____ _____ the outer layer _____ _____ a wormhole.

13 _____ _____ _____ _____ it will choose? Well, it would choose the wormhole _____ _____ _____ _____.

14 Sci Teen: Is there _____ _____ _____ in the universe?

15 Dr. Sci: _____ _____ some researchers, yes. Einstein _____ _____ that space and time _____ _____, and he called it _____.

---

1 Sci Teen: 안녕하세요, 과학 팬 여러분. 오늘 우리는 우주여행에 대해 이야기할 것입니다.

2 우리가 모두 알다시피, 우주에서 빛보다 더 빠른 것은 없습니다.

3 그래서 만약 우리가 빛의 속노로 여행을 한다면, 우리는 다른 행성에 눈 깜박할 사이에 도달할 수 있어야 해요, 그렇죠?

4 Dr. Sci: 그렇다면 좋겠지만, 우주는 너무 광활해서 그건 불가능하답니다.

5 영화 〈Passengers〉에서 다른 행성으로 향하는 우주선이 빛의 속도의 절반으로 이동합니다.

6 그러면 그들은 다른 행성에 매우 빨리 도달해야겠지요, 그렇죠?

7 하지만 승객들은 120년 동안 잠을 자게 되는데, 왜냐하면 다른 행성에 도달하는 데 그만큼 많은 시간이 걸릴 것으로 예상되기 때문입니다.

8 Sci Teen: 120년이요? 우아, 그건 정말 긴 시간이네요! 우주를 여행하는 더 빠른 방법이 있나요?

9 Dr. Sci: 글쎄요, 그 질문에 답하기 위해서 여러분들이 이 사과에 대해 잠깐 생각해 보기 바랍니다.

10 한 마리 벌레가 이 사과 위에 있다고 상상해 보세요. 그것은 맨 아래에 있는 달콤한 무언가를 감지하고 맨 위에서 아래로 이동하기를 원합니다.

11 그 벌레에게 사과의 표면은 우리의 우주만큼이나 광대합니다.

12 이제 그 벌레는 바깥 표면의 껍질을 돌아서 이동하거나 벌레 구멍 아래로 이동할 수 있습니다.

13 그것이 어떤 것을 선택할 거라고 생각하십니까? 음, 그것은 벌레 구멍을 선택할 것인데 왜냐하면 그것이 지름길이기 때문입니다.

14 Sci Teen: 우주에 그런 지름길이 있나요?

15 Dr. Sci: 몇몇 연구자들에 따르면, 그렇습니다. 아인슈타인은 공간과 시간이 연결되어 있다는 것을 생각해 냈고, 그것을 시공간이라고 불렀습니다.

16 He thought that _____ _____ _____ _____.
When it is bent, parts _____ _____ _____ _____ from
each other _____ _____ _____.

17 _____ _____ this, _____ a sheet of paper and _____
a small dot _____ _____ _____ _____ the paper and
_____ at the _____ of the paper.

18 _____ _____ _____ _____ of paper, the dots are
_____ _____ _____ one another.

19 Now, take the paper and _____ it _____ the dots _____
_____. _____ a hole in the paper and _____ _____
will _____ _____ _____.

20 Like this, wormholes in space may _____ _____ _____,
with a _____ _____ the two.

21 Sci Teen: _____ _____ a wormhole in the apple, right? If
such wormholes _____ in space, we could _____ _____
_____ billions of light-years _____ quickly!

22 Dr. Sci: Yes, but it's _____ _____ _____.
Wormholes _____ _____ _____ only.

23 Sci Teen: So _____ we need _____ _____ is _____
_____, right?

24 Dr. Sci: _____ _____ we find one, there are many things
_____ _____ before actually _____ _____ _____.

25 A wormhole _____ _____ very _____. If a spaceship
_____ _____ one, it might _____ _____ or _____
_____ _____.

26 Sci Teen: Ouch! That's not _____ _____ _____. So, are
we _____?

27 Is traveling in space _____ a wormhole _____ an idea
_____ only _____ in theory?

28 Dr. Sci: I _____ _____ so. The debate about wormholes
_____ still _____, but _____ _____ _____ and
_____, I believe we will eventually find _____ and _____
_____ _____ _____ _____ it.

29 _____ _____ _____ our history. We've achieved _____
_____ _____ _____ _____ _____ at first.

30 Who _____? Maybe you can be the one _____
_____ _____!

16 '그는 시공간이 실제로 구부러
질 수 있다고 생각했습니다. 그
것이 구부러질 때 서로 멀리 떨
어져 있는 부분들이 갑자기 더
가까워질 수 있습니다.

17 이것을 이해하기 위해서, 종이
를 한 장 갖고 와서 그 종이의
윗부분에 작은 점을 찍고 또 다
른 점을 그 종이의 아랫부분에
찍어 보세요.

18 펼쳐 놓은 종이에서 그 점들은
서로 멀리 떨어져 있습니다.

19 이제 그 종이를 들고 점들이 맞
춰지도록 그것을 접으세요. 종
이에 구멍을 뚫으면 그 점들이
즉시 연결될 것입니다.

20 이와 마찬가지로 우주의 웜홀은
두 개의 입과 그 둘을 연결하는
목구멍을 지니고 있을 겁니다.

21 Sci Teen: 사과에 있는 벌레 구
멍처럼요, 그렇죠? 그런 웜홀이
우주에 존재한다면 우리는 수십
억 광년 떨어져 있는 곳에 빠르
게 도달할 수 있을 텐데요!

22 Dr. Sci: 그렇죠, 하지만 축하하
기에는 너무 이릅니다. 웜홀은
이론상에서만 존재합니다.

23 Sci Teen: 그러면 우리가 해야
할 것이라고는 그것을 찾는 거
네요, 그렇죠?

24 Dr. Sci: 우리가 그것을 찾는다
고 하더라도 실제로 그걸 통과
하여 가기 전에 고려해야 할 것
들이 많이 있습니다.

25 웜홀은 매우 불안정할 것입니
다. 만약 우주선이 그 안으로 날
아가게 되면, 그것은 부서지거나
산산조각이 날 수도 있습니다.

26 Sci Teen: 어이쿠! 그건 좋은 광
경이 아니네요. 그럼 우리는 가
망이 없는 건가요?

27 우주에서 웜홀을 통하여 여행을
하는 것은 단지 이론상으로만
존재하는 아이디어인가요?

28 Dr. Sci: 그렇게 말하지는 않겠
어요. 웜홀에 대한 논쟁은 여전
히 진행 중이긴 하지만, 끊임없
는 탐구와 연구로 우리가 결국
하나를 찾아 그것을 통해 여행
하는 법을 배울 수 있을 거라고
믿습니다.

29 우리의 역사를 돌아보세요. 우
리는 처음에는 불가능해 보였던
아주 많은 것들을 달성해 왔습
니다.

30 누가 알겠어요? 아마도 여러분
이 그 답을 찾아내는 그 사람이
될 수 있을지도요!

※ 다음 문장을 우리말로 쓰시오.

1 Sci Teen: Hi, science fans. Today, we're going to talk about space travel.

➡ _____

2 As we all know, there is nothing faster than light in the universe.

➡ _____

3 So, if we travel at the speed of light, we should be able to get to another planet in the blink of an eye, right?

➡ _____

4 Dr. Sci: That would be nice, but space is so vast that it is not possible.

➡ _____

5 In the movie, *Passengers*, a spaceship headed to a different planet travels at one-half the speed of light.

➡ _____

6 So it should get to another planet very quickly, right?

➡ _____

7 But, the passengers sleep for 120 years because it is expected to take that much time to get to a different planet.

➡ _____

➡ _____

8 Sci Teen: 120 years? Wow, that's a long time! Is there a faster way to travel through space?

➡ _____

9 Dr. Sci: Well, in order to answer that question, I'd like you to think about this apple for a second.

➡ _____

10 Imagine a worm is on this apple. It detects something sweet at the bottom and wants to move from the top to the bottom.

➡ _____

➡ _____

11 For the worm, the apple's surface is as vast as our universe.

➡ _____

12 Now the worm can either move around the outer layer or down a wormhole.

➡ _____

13 Which do you think it will choose? Well, it would choose the wormhole because it is a shortcut.

➡ _____

➡ _____

14 Sci Teen: Is there such a shortcut in the universe?

➡ _____

15 Dr. Sci: According to some researchers, yes. Einstein figured out that space and time are connected, and he called it space-time.

➡ _____

➡ _____

16 He thought that space-time could actually be bent. When it is bent, parts that are far away from each other are suddenly closer.
➡ _____
_____

17 To understand this, take a sheet of paper and make a small dot at the top of the paper and another at the bottom of the paper.
➡ _____
_____

18 On a flat sheet of paper, the dots are far away from one another.
➡ _____

19 Now, take the paper and fold it with the dots matched up. Punch a hole in the paper and the dots will be instantly connected.
➡ _____

20 Like this, wormholes in space may contain two mouths, with a throat connecting the two.
➡ _____

21 Sci Teen: Just like a wormhole in the apple, right? If such wormholes existed in space, we could get to places billions of light-years away quickly!
➡ _____
_____

22 Dr. Sci: Yes, but it's too early to celebrate. Wormholes exist in theory only.
➡ _____

23 Sci Teen: So all we need to do is find one, right?
➡ _____

24 Dr. Sci: Even if we find one, there are many things to consider before actually going through one
➡ _____

25 A wormhole would be very unstable. If a spaceship flew into one, it might be crushed or broken into pieces.
➡ _____

26 Sci Teen: Ouch! That's not a pretty picture. So, are we hopeless?
➡ _____

27 Is traveling in space through a wormhole simply an idea that only exists in theory?
➡ _____

28 Dr. Sci: I wouldn't say so. The debate about wormholes is still ongoing, but with persistent exploration and research, I believe we will eventually find one and learn how to travel through it.
➡ _____
_____

29 Look back at our history. We've achieved so many things that seemed impossible at first.
➡ _____

30 Who knows? Maybe you can be the one to find the answer!
➡ _____

Step4

※ 다음 괄호 안의 단어들을 우리말에 맞도록 바르게 배열하시오.

1 (Sci Teen: / science / hi, / fans. // we're / today / to / going / about / talk / travel. / space)
➡ _____

2 (we / as / know, / all / is / there / faster / nothing / light / than / the / in / universe.)
➡ _____

3 (if / so, / travel / we / the / at / speed / light, / of / should / we / able / be / get / to / another / to / in / planet / blink / the / an / of / eye, / right?)
➡ _____

4 (Dr. Sci: / would / that / nice, / be / space / but / so / is / that / vast / is / it / possible. / not)
➡ _____

5 (the / in *Passengers*, / movie / spaceship / a / headed / a / to / planet / different / travels / at / the / one-half / of / speed / light.)
➡ _____

6 (it / so / get / should / another / to / planet / quickly, / very / right?)
➡ _____

7 (the / but, / sleep / passengers / for / years / 120 / because / is / it / to / expected / that / take / time / much / get / to / a / to / planet. / different)
➡ _____

8 (Sci Teen: / years? / 120 // that's / wow, / long / a / time! // there / is / faster / a / way / travel / to / space? / through)
➡ _____

9 (Dr. Sci: / in / well, / to / order / that / answer / question, / like / I'd / to / you / think / this / about / for / apple / second. / a)
➡ _____

10 (a / imagine / worm / on / is / apple. / this // detects / it / sweet / something / at / bottom / the / and / to / wants / from / move / top / the / the / to / bottom.)
➡ _____

11 (the / for / worm, / apple's / the / is / surface / vast / as / our / as / universe.)
➡ _____

12 (the / now / worm / can / move / either / the / around / outer / or / layer / a / down / wormhole.)
➡ _____

13 (do / which / think / you / will / it / choose? // it / well, / choose / would / wormhole / the / it / because / is / shortcut. / a)
➡ _____

14 (Sci Teen: / there / is / a / such / in / shortcut / universe? / the)
➡ _____

15 (Dr. Sci: / to / according / researchers, / some / yes. // figured / Einstein / out / that / and / space / time / connected, / are / he / and / called / space-time. / it)
➡ _____

1 Sci Teen: 안녕하세요, 과학 팬 여러분. 오늘 우리는 우주여행에 대해 이야기할 것입니다.

2 우리가 모두 알다시피, 우주에서 빛보다 더 빠른 것은 없습니다.

3 그래서 만약 우리가 빛의 속도로 여행을 한다면, 우리는 다른 행성에 눈 깜박할 사이에 도달할 수 있어야 해요, 그렇죠?

4 Dr. Sci: 그렇다면 좋겠지만, 우주는 너무 광활해서 그건 불가능하답니다.

5 영화 〈Passengers〉에서 다른 행성으로 향하는 우주선이 빛의 속도의 절반으로 이동합니다.

6 그러면 그들은 다른 행성에 매우 빨리 도달해야겠지요, 그렇죠?

7 하지만 승객들은 120년 동안 잠을 자게 되는데, 왜냐하면 다른 행성에 도달하는 데 그만큼 많은 시간이 걸릴 것으로 예상되기 때문입니다.

8 Sci Teen: 120년이요? 우아, 그건 정말 긴 시간이네요! 우주를 여행하는 더 빠른 방법이 있나요?

9 Dr. Sci: 글쎄요, 그 질문에 답하기 위해서 여러분들이 이 사과에 대해 잠깐 생각해 보기 바랍니다.

10 한 마리 벌레가 이 사과 위에 있다고 상상해 보세요. 그것은 맨 아래에 있는 달콤한 무언가를 감지하고 맨 위에서 아래로 이동하기를 원합니다.

11 그 벌레에게 사과의 표면은 우리의 우주만큼이나 광대합니다.

12 이제 그 벌레는 바깥 표면의 껍질을 돌아서 이동하거나 벌레 구멍 아래로 이동할 수 있습니다.

13 그것이 어떤 것을 선택할 거라고 생각하십니까? 음, 그것은 벌레 구멍을 선택할 것인데 왜냐하면 그것이 지름길이기 때문입니다.

14 Sci Teen: 우주에 그런 지름길이 있나요?

15 Dr. Sci: 몇몇 연구자들에 따르면, 그렇습니다. 아인슈타인은 공간과 시간이 연결되어 있다는 것을 생각해 냈고, 그것을 시공간이라고 불렀습니다.

16 (thought / he / space-time / that / actually / could / bent. / be // it / when / bent, / is / that / parts / far / are / from / away / other / each / suddenly / are / closer.)
➡ _____
_____

17 (understand / to / this, / a / take / of / sheet / paper / and / a / make / dot / small / at / top / the / the / of / paper / another / and / the / at / bottom / the / of / paper.)
➡ _____
_____

18 (a / on / sheet / flat / paper, / of / dots / the / far / are / from / away / another. / one)
➡ _____

19 (now, / the / take / and / paper / fold / with / it / dots / the / up. / matched // a / punch / hole / the / in / paper / and / dots / the / be / will / connected. / instantly)
➡ _____
_____

20 (this, like / in / wormholes / space / contain / may / mouths, / two / a / with / throat / the / connecting / two.)
➡ _____
_____

21 (Sci Teen: / like / just / wormhole / a / the / in / right? / apple, // such / if / existed / wormholes / space, / in / could / we / to / get / places / of / billions / away / light-years / quickly!)
➡ _____
_____

22 (Dr. Sci: / but / yes, / too / it's / to / early / celebrate. // exist / wormholes / theory / in / only.)
➡ _____
_____

23 (Sci Teen: / all / so / need / we / do / to / find / is / right? / one,)
➡ _____

24 (Dr. Sci: / if / even / find / we / one, / are / there / things / many / consider / to / actually / before / through / going / one.)
➡ _____

25 (wormhole / a / be / would / unstable. / very // a / if / flew / spaceship / one, / into / might / it / be / or / crushed / into / broken / pieces.)
➡ _____
_____

26 (Sci Teen: / ouch! // not / that's / pretty / a / picture. // are / so / hopeless? / we)
➡ _____

27 (traveling / is / space / in / a / through / simply / wormhole / idea / an / only / that / in / theory? / exists)
➡ _____

28 (Dr. Sci: / wouldn't / I / so. / say // debate / the / wormholes / about / is / ongoing, / still / with / but / exploration / persistent / and / I / research, / we / will / believe / eventually / one / find / and / how / learn / travel / to / it. / through)
➡ _____
_____

29 (back / look / our / at / history. // achieved / we've / many / so / that / things / seemed / at / impossible / first.)
➡ _____
_____

30 (knows? / who // you / maybe / be / can / one / the / find / to / answer! / the)
➡ _____

16 '그는 시공간이 실제로 구부러질 수 있다고 생각했습니다. 그것이 구부러질 때 서로 멀리 떨어져 있는 부분들이 갑자기 더 가까워질 수 있습니다.

17 이것을 이해하기 위해서, 종이를 한 장 갖고 와서 그 종이의 윗부분에 작은 점을 찍고 또 다른 점을 그 종이의 아랫부분에 찍어 보세요.

18 펼쳐 놓은 종이에서 그 점들은 서로 멀리 떨어져 있습니다.

19 이제 그 종이를 들고 점들이 맞춰지도록 그것을 접으세요. 종이에 구멍을 뚫으면 그 점들이 즉시 연결될 것입니다.

20 이와 마찬가지로 우주의 웜홀은 두 개의 입과 그 둘을 연결하는 목구멍을 지니고 있을 겁니다.

21 Sci Teen: 사과에 있는 벌레 구멍처럼요, 그렇죠? 그런 웜홀이 우주에 존재한다면 우리는 수십억 광년 떨어져 있는 곳에 빠르게 도달할 수 있을 텐데요!

22 Dr. Sci: 그렇죠, 하지만 축하하기에는 너무 이릅니다. 웜홀은 이론상에서만 존재합니다.

23 Sci Teen: 그러면 우리가 해야 할 것이라고는 그것을 찾는 거네요, 그렇죠?

24 Dr. Sci: 우리가 그것을 찾는다고 하더라도 실제로 그걸 통과하여 가기 전에 고려해야 할 것들이 많이 있습니다.

25 웜홀은 매우 불안정할 것입니다. 만약 우주선이 그 안으로 날아가게 되면, 그것은 부서지거나 산산조각이 날 수도 있습니다.

26 Sci Teen: 어이쿠! 그건 좋은 광경이 아니네요. 그럼 우리는 가망이 없는 건가요?

27 우주에서 웜홀을 통하여 여행을 하는 것은 단지 이론상으로만 존재하는 아이디어인가요?

28 Dr. Sci: 그렇게 말하지는 않겠어요. 웜홀에 대한 논쟁은 여전히 진행 중이긴 하지만, 끊임없는 탐구와 연구로 우리가 결국 하나를 찾아 그것을 통해 여행하는 법을 배울 수 있을 거라고 믿습니다.

29 우리의 역사를 돌아보세요. 우리는 처음에는 불가능해 보였던 아주 많은 것들을 달성해 왔습니다.

30 누가 알겠어요? 아마도 여러분이 그 답을 찾아내는 그 사람이 될 수 있을지도요!

※ 다음 우리말을 영어로 쓰시오.

1 Sci Teen: 안녕하세요, 과학 팬 여러분. 오늘 우리는 우주여행에 대해 이야기할 것입니다.

➡ _____

2 우리가 모두 알다시피, 우주에서 빛보다 더 빠른 것은 없습니다.

3 그래서 만약 우리가 빛의 속도로 여행을 한다면, 우리는 다른 행성에 눈 깜박할 사이에 도달할 수 있어야 해요, 그렇죠?

➡ _____

4 Dr. Sci: 그렇다면 좋겠지만, 우주는 너무 광활해서 그건 불가능하답니다.

➡ _____

5 영화 〈Passengers〉에서 다른 행성으로 향하는 우주선이 빛의 속도의 절반으로 이동합니다.

➡ _____

6 그러면 그들은 다른 행성에 매우 빨리 도달해야겠지요, 그렇죠?

➡ _____

7 하지만 승객들은 120년 동안 잠을 자게 되는데, 왜냐하면 다른 행성에 도달하는 데 그만큼 많은 시간이 걸릴 것으로 예상되기 때문입니다.

➡ _____

8 Sci Teen: 120년이요? 우아, 그건 정말 긴 시간이네요! 우주를 여행하는 더 빠른 방법이 있나요?

➡ _____

9 Dr. Sci: 글쎄요, 그 질문에 답하기 위해서 여러분들이 이 사과에 대해 잠깐 생각해 보기 바랍니다.

➡ _____

10 한 마리 벌레가 이 사과 위에 있다고 상상해 보세요. 그것은 맨 아래에 있는 달콤한 무언가를 감지하고 맨 위에서 아래로 이동하기를 원합니다.

➡ _____

11 그 벌레에게 사과의 표면은 우리의 우주만큼이나 광대합니다.

➡ _____

12 이제 그 벌레는 바깥 표면의 껍질을 돌아서 이동하거나 벌레 구멍 아래로 이동할 수 있습니다.

➡ _____

13 그것이 어떤 것을 선택할 거라고 생각하십니까? 음, 그것은 벌레 구멍을 선택할 것인데 왜냐하면 그것이 지름길이기 때문입니다.

➡ _____

14 Sci Teen: 우주에 그런 지름길이 있나요?

➡ _____

15 Dr. Sci: 몇몇 연구자들에 따르면, 그렇습니다. 아인슈타인은 공간과 시간이 연결되어 있다는 것을 생각해 냈고, 그것을 시공간이라고 불렀습니다.

➡ _____

16 그는 시공간이 실제로 구부러질 수 있다고 생각했습니다. 그것이 구부러질 때 서로 멀리 떨어져 있는 부분들이 갑자기 더 가까워질 수 있습니다.

➡ _____

17 이것을 이해하기 위해서, 종이를 한 장 갖고 와서 그 종이의 윗부분에 작은 점을 찍고 또 다른 점을 그 종이의 아랫부분에 찍어 보세요.

➡ _____
_____

18 펼쳐 놓은 종이에서 그 점들은 서로 멀리 떨어져 있습니다.

➡ _____

19 이제 그 종이를 들고 점들이 맞춰지도록 그것을 접으세요. 종이에 구멍을 뚫으면 그 점들이 즉시 연결될 것입니다.

➡ _____

20 이와 마찬가지로 우주의 웜홀은 두 개의 입과 그 둘을 연결하는 목구멍을 지니고 있을 겁니다.

➡ _____

21 Sci Teen: 사과에 있는 벌레 구멍처럼요, 그렇죠? 그런 웜홀이 우주에 존재한다면 우리는 수십억 광년 떨어져 있는 곳에 빠르게 도달할 수 있을 텐데요!

➡ _____
_____

22 Dr. Sci: 그렇죠, 하지만 축하하기에는 너무 이릅니다. 웜홀은 이론상에서만 존재합니다.

➡ _____

23 Sci Teen: 그러면 우리가 해야 할 것이라고는 그것을 찾는 거네요, 그렇죠?

➡ _____

24 Dr. Sci: 우리가 그것을 찾는다고 하더라도 실제로 그걸 통과하여 가기 전에 고려해야 할 것들이 많이 있습니다.

➡ _____

25 웜홀은 매우 불안정할 것입니다. 만약 우주선이 그 안으로 날아가게 되면, 그것은 부서지거나 산산조각이 날 수도 있습니다.

➡ _____
_____

26 Sci Teen: 어이쿠! 그건 좋은 광경이 아니네요. 그럼 우리는 가망이 없는 건가요?

➡ _____

27 우주에서 웜홀을 통하여 여행을 하는 것은 단지 이론상으로만 존재하는 아이디어인가요?

➡ _____

28 Dr. Sci: 그렇게 말하지는 않겠어요. 웜홀에 대한 논쟁은 여전히 진행 중이긴 하지만, 끊임없는 탐구와 연구로 우리가 결국 하나를 찾아 그것을 통해 여행하는 법을 배울 수 있을 거라고 믿습니다.

➡ _____
_____

29 우리의 역사를 돌아보세요. 우리는 처음에는 불가능해 보였던 아주 많은 것들을 달성해 왔습니다.

➡ _____

30 누가 알겠어요? 아마도 여러분이 그 답을 찾아내는 그 사람이 될 수 있을지도요!

➡ _____

※ 다음 우리말과 일치하도록 빈칸에 알맞은 말을 쓰시오.

After You Read A

1. _____ _____ _____ _____ _____ through space

2. ① _____ _____ an apple

3. A wormhole is a shortcut _____ _____ _____ _____ _____ from _____ _____ to _____ _____.

4. ② Wormholes _____ _____

5. Einstein thought _____ and _____ _____ _____ and _____ _____ _____ _____.

6. When it is bent, _____ _____ _____ _____ _____ each other can _____ _____.

7. Do wormholes _____ _____?

8. ③ _____ _____, wormholes _____.

9. Wormholes _____ _____ _____. A spaceship could _____ _____ or _____ _____ _____.

10. _____ I believe _____ _____ _____ and _____ we will find a wormhole!

Language in Use

1. Is the universe _____ _____ _____?

2. _____, the driver is _____ _____ _____ _____ _____ _____ after the accident.

Think & Write C

1. If I could make a planet _____ _____ _____ _____ in the future, I _____ _____ _____ _____ a planet _____ Atlas.

2. It would be a _____ _____ _____.

3. Its size would be _____ _____ _____ _____, but _____ _____ Earth.

4. _____ _____ of it _____ _____ _____ 30℃.

5. It would _____ _____ _____.

6. _____, if people _____ _____ it, they could _____ _____ animals _____ _____ _____.

1. 우주로 여행을 떠나는 더 빠른 방법
2. ① 사과에서 얻은 아이디어
3. 벌레 구멍은 벌레가 맨 위에서 아래로 이동하는 지름길이다.
4. ② 우주에서의 웜홀
5. 아인슈타인은 공간과 시간은 연결되어 있고 시공간은 구부러질 수 있다고 생각했다.
6. 그것이 구부러질 때, 서로 멀리 떨어져 있는 부분들이 더 가까워질 수 있다.
7. 웜홀이 실제로 존재할까?
8. ③ 이론상, 웜홀은 존재한다.
9. 웜홀은 불안정할 것이다. 우주선이 부서지거나 산산조각이 날 수도 있다.
10. 하지만 난 끊임없는 탐구와 연구로 우리가 결국 웜홀을 찾아낼 거라고 믿는다!

1. 우주는 유한할까 아니면 무한할까?
2. 운 좋게도, 그 운전자는 사고 이후에 안정적인 상태이다.

1. 만약 제가 미래에 우리가 살 행성을 만든다면, 나는 아틀라스라고 불리는 행성을 만들고 싶습니다.
2. 그것은 아름다운 푸른 행성일 것입니다.
3. 그것의 크기는 달보다 더 크지만 지구보다 더 작을 것입니다.
4. 그것의 온도는 약 섭씨 30도일 것입니다.
5. 그것은 아름다운 자연을 가지고 있을 것입니다.
6. 흥미롭게도, 만약 사람들이 그곳으로 간다면, 그들은 이 행성에서 동물들과 의사소통할 수 있을 것입니다.

※ **다음 우리말을 영어로 쓰시오.**

After You Read A

1. 우주로 여행을 떠나는 더 빠른 방법
➡ _____

2. ① 사과에서 얻은 아이디어
➡ _____

3. 벌레 구멍은 벌레가 맨 위에서 아래로 이동하는 지름길이다.
➡ _____

4. ② 우주에서의 웜홀
➡ _____

5. 아인슈타인은 공간과 시간은 연결되어 있고 시공간은 구부러질 수 있다고 생각했다.
➡ _____

6. 그것이 구부러질 때, 서로 멀리 떨어져 있는 부분들이 더 가까워질 수 있다.
➡ _____

7. 웜홀이 실제로 존재할까?
➡ _____

8. ③ 이론상, 웜홀은 존재한다.
➡ _____

9. 웜홀은 불안정할 것이다. 우주선이 부서지거나 산산조각이 날 수도 있다.
➡ _____

10. 하지만 난 끊임없는 탐구와 연구로 우리가 결국 웜홀을 찾아낼 거라고 믿는다!
➡ _____

Language in Use

1. 우주는 유한할까 아니면 무한할까?
➡ _____

2. 운 좋게도, 그 운전자는 사고 이후에 안정적인 상태이다.
➡ _____

Think & Write C

1. 만약 제가 미래에 우리가 살 행성을 만든다면, 나는 아틀라스라고 불리는 행성을 만들고 싶습니다.
➡ _____

2. 그것은 아름다운 푸른 행성일 것입니다.
➡ _____

3. 그것의 크기는 달보다 더 크지만 지구보다 더 작을 것입니다.
➡ _____

4. 그것의 온도는 약 섭씨 30도일 것입니다.
➡ _____

5. 그것은 아름다운 자연을 가지고 있을 것입니다.
➡ _____

6. 흥미롭게도, 만약 사람들이 그곳으로 간다면, 그들은 이 행성에서 동물들과 의사소통할 수 있을 것입니다.
➡ _____

MEMO

MEMO

2학기 전과정 plus

적중100

영어 기출 문제집

영어 기출 문제집

적중100

2학기

정답 및 해설

비상 | 김진완

중 3

적중100

Lesson **5**

Critical Minds

시험대비 실력평가 p.08

01 distrust 02 ④ 03 ① 04 ⑤

05 ⑤

06 (1) He had been wounded in the arm.

(2) I can't trust her anymore because she lied again.

(3) The temperature went up to forty today.

01 주어진 관계는 반의어 관계이다. trust: 신뢰하다, distrust: 불신하다

02 '해, 손상, 고통을 초래하는 사건'을 나타내는 말은 disaster(재난)이다.

03 trust는 명사로 '신뢰', 동사로 '신뢰하다'를 의미한다.

04 mine: 광산

05 보기에 주어진 judge는 '판단하다'를 의미한다. ⑤번은 '판사'를 뜻한다.

06 wound: 상처를 입히다, trust: 신뢰하다, temperature: 온도

서술형 시험대비 p.09

01 realize

02 (1) competitors (2) condition (3) confessed
(4) critical

03 (1) on the loose (2) think outside the box
(3) search for (4) catch a cold (5) got caught

04 (1) Don't you think the restaurant is extremely loud?

(2) Eating too much sugar is harmful for your teeth.

(3) He is almost the same height as my sister.

05 (1) She admitted that she had made mistakes.

(2) I had an argument with my boyfriend yesterday.

(3) Adults should pay an entrance fee, but children get in free.

01 형용사에 접미사 '-ize'를 붙여 동사를 만들 수 있다. realize: 실현하다, regularize: 합법화하다

02 competitor: 경쟁자, condition: 상태, confess: 고백하다, critical: 위독한

03 catch a cold: 감기에 걸리다, got caught -ing: ~하다가 걸리다, on the loose: 잡히지 않은, search for: ~을 찾다, think outside the box: 고정관념에서 벗어나다

04 extremely: 극도로, 극히, harmful: 해로운, height: 키

05 admit: 인정하다, argument: 논쟁, entrance fee: 입장료, adult: 어른

[교과서]

Conversation

핵심 Check p.10~11

1 (C) - (A) - (B) **2** makes you say so

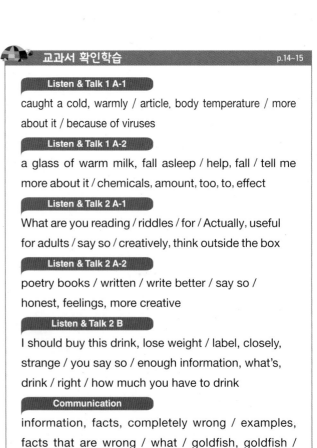

교과서 대화문 익히기

Check(√) True or False p.12

1 T 2 T 3 T 4 F

교과서 확인학습 p.14~15

Listen & Talk 1 A-1

caught a cold, warmly / article, body temperature / more about it / because of viruses

Listen & Talk 1 A-2

a glass of warm milk, fall asleep / help, fall / tell me more about it / chemicals, amount, too, to, effect

Listen & Talk 2 A-1

What are you reading / riddles / for / Actually, useful for adults / say so / creatively, think outside the box

Listen & Talk 2 A-2

poetry books / written / write better / say so / honest, feelings, more creative

Listen & Talk 2 B

I should buy this drink, lose weight / label, closely, strange, you say so / enough information, what's, drink / right / how much you have to drink

Communication

information, facts, completely wrong / examples, facts that are wrong / what / goldfish, goldfish /

recognize their owners / know that

interesting article, where it is / between, and / What color / guess / called / dangerous

---

시험대비 기본평가 p.16

01 ⓓ → make　　02 ⑤　　　　03 ⓓ → because of
04 (A) their low body temperature　(B) viruses

01 관계대명사의 선행사가 chemicals로 복수이므로 make가 적절하다.

02 우유 한 잔에 있는 특별한 성분의 양이 너무 적어서 효과가 없다.

03 뒤에 명사가 이어지므로 because of가 알맞다.

04 기사에 따르면 사람들은 체온이 낮아서가 아니라 바이러스 때문에 감기에 걸린다.

시험대비 실력평가 p.17~18

01 ⓔ → which　　　　　02 ⑤
03 She drinks a glass of warm milk.
04 They make people sleepy.
05 It's because the amount in a glass is too small to have any effect.
06 (C) → (A) → (D) → (B) → (E)　　　　07 ⑤
08 ⑤
09 We need to think outside the box to find the answers.
10 written　　11 ⑤　　　　12 children

01 관계대명사의 계속적 용법으로 which가 적절하다.

03 수지는 자기 전에 따뜻한 우유 한 잔을 마신다.

04 우유에 있는 화학물질이 사람들을 졸리게 만든다.

05 우유 한 잔에 들어 있는 화학물질의 양이 너무 적어 효과가 없다.

06 (C) 시집에 대한 설명 → (A) 확인 → (D) 자신의 의견 표현 → (B) 이유 질문 → (E) 이유 설명

07 사실을 알고 있는지 묻는 질문에 '무슨 말인지 알겠다.'라는 대답은 어색하다.

08 ⑤번을 제외한 나머지는 모두 이유를 묻는 표현이다.

10 어린이들에 의해 쓰여진 시로 과거분사 written이 알맞다.

11 ⑤번을 제외한 나머지는 모두 이유를 묻고 있다.

12 They는 아이들(children)을 가리킨다.

서술형 시험대비 p.19

01 Can you tell me more about it
02 She thinks (that) she caught a cold because she didn't dress warmly yesterday.
03 (A) Napoleon　(B) height　(C) the French measuring system　(D) the English one
04 Why do you say so?
05 They were written by children.
06 It is because they're really honest about their feelings and much more creative than adults.

02 여자는 어제 따뜻하게 옷을 입지 않았기 때문에 감기에 걸렸다고 생각한다.

03 나폴레옹은 정말 키가 작았을까? 우리는 나폴레옹의 키에 대해 잘못 알았다. 오해는 프랑스의 측정 체계와 영국의 측정 체계와의 차이에서 비롯되었다. 그는 실제로 약 168 cm였다.

05 시집에 있는 시들은 아이들에 의해 쓰여졌다.

06 어린이들은 감정에 매우 솔직하고 어른들보다 훨씬 더 창의적이기 때문에 Sue는 어른들보다 어린이들이 시를 더 잘 쓴다고 생각한다.

교과서
Grammar

핵심 Check p.20~21

1 (1) Living　(2) Listening
2 (1) that　(2) so that

시험대비 기본평가 p.22

01 ②
02 (1) Having　(2) Not knowing　(3) so that　(4) so that
03 ①
04 (1) Mom's face darkened looking at the report card.
　(2) We are going to the library so that we can borrow books.

01 'so that'은 '~하기 위해', '~하고자', '~하도록'의 의미로 '목적'이나 '의도'를 나타낸다.

02 (1) 접속사가 없으므로 '접속사+주어+동사'의 역할을 할 수 있는 분사구문 Having이 적절하다. (2) 분사구문의 부정은 분사

앞에 'not'이나 'never'를 쓴다. (3) '내 동생이 야생 동물들을 볼 수 있을지라도 동물원에 갔다'는 말은 어색하다. '목적'이나 '의도'를 나타내는 'so that'이 적절하다. (4) 'so that' 앞에 콤마(,)가 있고, '결과'의 부사절을 이끄는 '그래서, 그러므로'의 의미의 'so that'이 적절하다.

03 접속사 없이 '주어+동사'가 이어지고 있으므로 빈칸에는 '접속사+주어+동사'의 역할을 할 수 있는 분사구문이 되어야 한다.

04 (1) looking을 '접속사+주어+동사'의 역할을 하는 분사구문으로 하여 알맞게 배열한다. (2) 일반적으로 '주절+so that+주어+can/will(조동사)+동사원형 ~'의 형태로 쓰여, 'so that'은 '~하기 위해', '~하고자', '~하도록'의 의미로 '목적'이나 '의도'를 나타낸다.

시험대비 실력평가
p.23~25

01 ③   02 ③   03 ①

04 (1) that   (2) as   (3) order   (4) Neglecting
(5) processing   (6) Not knowing

05 ⑤   06 ③   07 ①   08 ⑤

09 Crossing   10 ②   11 ②

12 (1) he was   (2) she was   13 ④

14 (1) Don't throw trash in the sea in order that animals can live safely.

(2) Look for hidden ideas so that you can see what the writer really means.

(3) Swimming in the pond, she was wearing her swimming cap.

(4) It being fine, we went for a walk to the beach.

(5) Seen from high above, the cars looked tiny.

15 ⑤   16 ②, ③

17 They confessed that they made it up so that they could draw the readers' attention to the unsafe conditions at the zoo.

---

01 Aaron danced on the stage listening to the music.

02 The bird practiced flying hard so as to fly up high.

03 첫 번째 빈칸에는 접속사가 없으므로 '접속사+주어+동사'의 역할을 할 수 있는 reading이 적절하다. 두 번째 빈칸에는 '~하기 위해', '~하도록'이라는 의미의 '목적'이나 '의도'를 나타내는 'so that'의 so가 적절하다.

04 (1) '~하기 위해', '~하도록'이라는 의미의 '목적'을 나타내도록 that이 적절하다. (2) '목적'을 나타내는 'so that ~ can ...'은 주절과 종속절의 주어가 같은 경우, 'so as to부정사'로 바꿔 쓸 수 있다. (3) '목적'을 나타내는 'so that ~ can ...'은 'in order

---

that ~ can ...'으로 바꿔 쓸 수 있다.' (4) 접속사가 없으므로 '접속사+주어+동사'의 역할을 할 수 있는 분사구문으로 써야 한다. (5) 분사구문의 뜻을 명확히 하기 위해 접속사 When을 생략하지 않고 남겨둔 경우이다. (6) 분사구문의 부정은 분사 앞에 'not'이나 'never'를 쓴다.

05 '접속사+주어+동사'의 부사절을 분사구문으로 바꾸어 쓸 수 있다. 이때, 분사구문의 뜻을 명확히 하기 위해 접속사를 생략하지 않기도 한다.

06 (A) 'so that ~ can ...'은 주절과 종속절의 주어가 같은 경우 'so as to부정사'로 바꿔 쓸 수 있다. (B) 'so+형용사[부사]+that+주어+can ...(매우 ~해서 …할 수 있는)'은 '형용사+enough to ...(…할 정도로 충분히 ~한)'로 바꿔 쓸 수 있다.

07 접속사가 없으므로 분사구문 thinking으로 만들어야 한다. 분사구문이 문장의 중간에 삽입된 형태이다.

08 'so that ~ can ...'은 'in order that ~ can ...'으로 바꿔 쓸 수 있으며, 주절과 종속절의 주어가 같은 경우 '(in order[so as]) to부정사'로 바꿔 쓸 수 있다.

09 한 문장으로 쓰면 'When you cross the street, you should be careful.'이고, 분사구문으로 바꾸면 'When you cross'를 현재분사 Crossing으로 써야 한다.

10 일반적으로 '주절+so that+주어+can/will(조동사)+동사원형 ~'의 형태로 쓰여, '~하기 위해', '~하고자', '~하도록'의 의미로 '목적'이나 '의도'를 나타낸다.

11 주어진 문장과 ②번은 '양보'를 나타낸다. ① 이유, ③ 시간, ④ 동시동작, ⑤ 조건

12 부사절에서 주어가 주절의 주어와 같을 때 '주어+be동사'를 생략할 수 있으며 이것을 분사구문으로 고쳤을 때 being을 생략하고 접속사를 남겨둔 것과 같다.

13 'so+형용사[부사]+that+주어+can't'는 '너무 ~해서 …할 수 없다'라는 의미이며, 'too+형용사[부사]+to부정사'(…하기에 너무 ~한)로 바꿔 쓸 수 있다.

14 (1) for 뒤에 절이 오므로 for를 that으로 고쳐 'in order that'으로 쓰는 것이 적절하다. (2) 'so as to+부정사' 형태나 'so that+절'의 형태로 써야 하므로 as를 삭제해야 한다. (3) 수영을 하고 있는 '진행'의 의미이므로 Swum을 Swimming으로 고치는 것이 적절하다. (4) 'As it is fine, we went out.'을 분사구문을 이용해서 쓴 문장으로 주절의 주어와 부사절의 주어가 다르므로 독립분사구문으로 써야 한다. (5) Being이 생략된 분사구문으로 '보는' 것이 아니라 '보이는' 것이므로 Seeing을 Seen으로 고쳐야 한다.

15 'Though she had heard their names, Kathryn couldn't

---

recognize them.'을 분사구문으로 바꾼 것이므로 'Though she had heard' 대신에 'Having heard'로 쓰는 것이 적절하다.

16 ② I was stupid enough to believe him. ③ Come early so as to have plenty of time. 또는 Come early so that you can have plenty of time.

17 'so that'은 '~하기 위해', '~하고자', '~하도록'의 의미로 '목적'이나 '의도'를 나타낸다.

서술형 시험대비
p.26~27

01 (1) Catching a bad cold, my mom couldn't get to work.
(2) Finishing breakfast, I took a taxi to school.
(3) Mixing blue and yellow, you get green.
(4) Being nervous, she said it was a good experience.
(5) Not knowing what happened, I called my friend, Sam.
(6) If it being fine tomorrow, I will go hiking.

02 (1) Read the book carefully so that you can find hidden ideas.
(2) Sally bought a camera so that she could take great pictures.

03 (1) Not knowing the news was false, many people panicked.
(2) Leaving early, he was late for the meeting.
(3) He worked so hard that he finally became a lawyer.
(4) He got up early, so that he could catch the first bus.

04 (1) Exhausting → Exhausted
(2) Failing → Having failed

05 (1) so that she can
(2) in order to
(3) so as to

06 (1) It being
(2) Watching

07 (1) Turning to the left, you will find the house. / If you turn to the left, you will find the house.
(2) Being sick, she was absent from school. / Because[As, Since] she was sick, she was absent from school.
(3) Lisa bought some oranges so[in order] that her mother could make orange juice.

08 (1) Judy practices playing the piano in order that she can win the top prize.

(2) I got up early so that I could go jogging. 또는 I got up early so as to go jogging.
(3) Arriving late at the station, I saw the train leaving.

01 '접속사+주어+동사'로 이루어진 부사절의 주어가 주절의 주어와 일치할 때 접속사와 주어를 생략하고 동사를 분사(동사원형+-ing)로 만든다. (1) '이유', (2) '시간' (3) '조건' (4) '양보' (5) 분사구문의 부정은 분사 앞에 'not'이나 'never'를 쓴다. (6) 주절의 주어와 부사절의 주어가 다르므로 주어를 생략하면 안 된다.(독립분사구문)

02 so that은 '~하기 위해', '~하고자', '~하도록'의 의미로 '목적'이나 '의도'를 나타낸다. 일반적으로 '주절+so that+주어+can/will(조동사)+동사원형 ~'의 형태로 쓰인다.

03 (1), (2) 현재분사가 분사구문을 이끌도록 한다. 부정은 분사 앞에 'not'이나 'never'를 쓴다. (3) so와 that 사이에 수식어가 오면, '너무 ~해서 결국 …하다'라는 뜻이 된다. (4) 'so that'은 '결과'의 부사절을 이끌어 '그래서, 그러므로'의 의미를 갖는 접속사로 쓰이기도 하는데, 대개 앞에 쉼표(,)가 온다.

04 (1) '지친'의 뜻으로 '수동'의 의미가 되어야 하므로 Exhausting을 Exhausted로 고쳐 써야 한다. (2) 부사절의 시제가 주절보다 앞선 경우에는 완료분사구문(having+과거분사)으로 쓴다.

05 'so that ~ can …'은 'in order that ~ can …'으로 바꿔 쓸 수 있으며, 주절과 종속절의 주어가 같은 경우 '(in order[so as]) to부정사'로 바꿔 쓸 수 있다.

06 (1) 'Because it is rainy, ~'를 부사구문으로 고쳐 쓴다. 주절의 주어와 부사절의 주어가 다르므로 주어를 생략하면 안 된다.(독립분사구문) (2) 'While they are watching the rain, ~'을 부사구문으로 고쳐 쓴다.

07 (1), (2) '접속사+주어+동사'로 이루어진 부사절의 주어가 주절의 주어와 일치할 때 접속사와 주어를 생략하고 동사를 분사(동사원형+-ing)로 만들어서 분사구문으로 바꿔 쓴다. (3) so[in order] that은 '~하기 위해', '~하고자', '~하도록'의 의미로 '목적'이나 '의도'를 나타낸다. 일반적으로 '주절+so [in order] that+주어+can/will(조동사)+동사원형 ~'의 형태로 쓰인다.

08 (1), (2) 'so that ~ can …'은 'in order that ~ can …'으로 바꿔 쓸 수 있으며, 주절과 종속절의 주어가 같은 경우 '(in order[so as]) to부정사'로 바꿔 쓸 수 있다. (3) 내가 도착하는 능동의 의미이므로 현재분사를 쓰는 것이 적절하다.

확인문제   p.28

1 T   2 F   3 T   4 F

확인문제   p.29

1 T   2 F   3 T   4 F   5 T   6 F

확인문제   p.30

1 T   2 F   3 T   4 F   5 T   6 F

교과서 확인학습 A   p.31~33

01 Spot Fake News
02 interesting news   03 whether
04 what if, made up
05 in that, less informed, misled
06 Nevertheless, throughout history
07 such false information
08 thinking, the hidden motives
09 AWFUL   10 broke down
11 the other   12 hundreds of   13 on the loose
14 until further notice
15 described above
16 laughed out loud
17 got really worried
18 Not knowing, panicked   19 Some, others
20 make up such news
21 made it up so that, could
22 IN ARGUMENT
23 was shot, wounded
24 had an argument
25 led to, in the chest
26 in critical condition
27 after the shooting
28 are searching for, are warning
29 anything strange   30 backwards
31 why   32 so that, could, if
33 got caught stealing
34 admit, were harshly criticized   35 published
36 As, whether, or   37 How to spot
38 Source   39 reliable   40 trust
41 Check   42 new, old
43 Is, related to current
44 Beyond the Headlines

45 match the content   46 Supporting
47 related, similar

교과서 확인학습 B   p.34~36

1 Can You Spot Fake News?
2 Every day we watch, hear, or read interesting news.
3 However, have you ever seriously considered whether an article is really true?
4 Everyone likes an interesting news story but what if it is completely made up?
5 Fake news can be very harmful in that it can make people less informed or even misled.
6 Nevertheless, there have been various fake news reports throughout history.
7 Why have some people written such false information?
8 Let's look into some articles thinking about the hidden motives behind them.
9 AWFUL DISASTER
10 Last night, an angry group of rhinoceroses broke down the walls of the cage at the zoo and escaped.
11 They also broke down the walls of the other wild animals' cages.
12 These animals ran down the streets and injured hundreds of people.
13 Twelve of the animals are still on the loose.
14 Citizens should stay indoors until further notice.
15 Not a single act or incident described above has taken place.
16 At that time, those who read the article carefully laughed out loud.
17 Those who didn't read it to the end got really worried.
18 Not knowing the news was false, many people panicked.
19 Some tried to escape the city while others went into the parks with guns to hunt the animals.
20 So why did *The Herald* make up such news?
21 Later, they confessed that they made it up so that they could draw the readers' attention to the unsafe conditions at the zoo.
22 SLAV SHOOTS A FRIEND IN ARGUMENT
23 Mejk Swenekafew, a Slav worker at the Columbia Coal Mine, was shot and seriously wounded by

John Pecitello near the mining camp Thursday evening.

24 The two men had an argument during a meeting.

25 The argument led to a fight, and Pecitello shot Swenekafew twice, in the chest and leg.

26 He is now at the hospital in critical condition.

27 Pecitello ran away after the shooting.

28 The police are searching for him now and are warning citizens that he is extremely dangerous.

29 Is there anything strange about the article?

30 Read the Slav's name backwards; it spells, "we-fake-news."

31 Who wrote this and why?

32 *The Daily Telegram* published this fake article so that they could prove if *The Daily News*, their competitor, was stealing their articles.

33 *The Daily News* published the same article about "Swenekafew" the next day and thus got caught stealing.

34 The people at *The Daily News* had to admit their act and were harshly criticized by the public.

35 The two articles were special cases, but there are many "fake" news articles published every day.

36 As readers, we need to read critically and judge whether the news is real or fake.

37 How to spot fake news!

38 Consider the Source

39 Is it from a reliable source?

40 Can we trust the writer?

41 Check the Date

42 Is it a new or an old story?

43 Is it related to current events?

44 Read Beyond the Headlines

45 Does the headline match the content?

46 Find Supporting Sources

47 Do other related stories provide similar content?

시험대비 실력평가
p.37~41

01 ④	02 ③	03 ④
04 they → it	05 ②	06 ⑤	07 ②, ③, ⑤
08 ③	09 ①	10 ④

11 (A) shot (B) are (C) are

12 Swenekafew   13 ②

14 (A) in that (B) misled (C) such   15 ①, ④

16 ①   17 published 18 ④   19 ②

20 forward → backwards 21 ③, ⑤   22 ③

---

23 fake	24 ③, ⑤	25 some articles
26 ④	27 ⑤	

28 Those who didn't read it to the end got really worried.

29 made up it → made it up

---

01 ④ 앞에 나오는 내용과 상반되는 내용이 뒤에 이어지므로 However가 가장 적절하다. ① 게다가, 더욱이, ② 다시 말해서, ③ 그러므로

02 주어진 문장의 Nevertheless에 수복한다. 비록 ③빈 잎 문쟁의 내용이 사실이지만, 그럼에도 불구하고, 역사를 통틀어 다양한 가짜 뉴스 보도들이 존재해 왔다는 내용이므로 ③번이 적절하다.

03 가짜 뉴스는 사람들에게 정보를 '부족하게' 제공할 수 있다. well-informed: 사정에 정통한, 박식한, ① day after day: 매일, ③ damaging: 손해를 끼치는, 해로운

04 news는 단수로 취급하기 때문에, they를 it으로 고치는 것이 적절하다.

05 ⓐ on the loose 잡히지 않은, 탈주 중인, ⓑ until: ~까지(계속), by: ~까지는(완료)

06 ⑤ 그 중 열두 마리의 동물들이 아직 잡히지 않았다. on the loose 잡히지 않은, 탈주 중인

07 happen = occur = arise: (사고·일·문제 등이) 발생하다, 일어나다, be held = be hosted: 개최되다

08 ⓐ와 ②, ⑤: 이유, ①, ④: 양보, ③: 조건

09 ⓑ와 ①: (이야기 등을) 지어내다, 만들어 내다, ② (잃어버린 것) ~을 대신하다; ~에 대해 보상하다, ③ (~와) 화해하다, ④ (각 부분이) ~을 구성[형성]하다, ⑤ 화장하다, 분장하다

10 이 글은 '동물원의 안전하지 않은 상태에 대해 독자들의 주의를 끌기 위해 헤럴드사가 기사를 지어냈다는 것이므로, 주제로는 ④번 '독자들의 주의를 끌기 위한 거짓 뉴스'가 적절하다.

11 (A) '총상을 입었다'고 해야 하므로 shot이 적절하다. shoot-shot-shot: (총 등을) 쏘다, shut-shut-shut: (문 등을[이]) 닫다[닫히다], (눈을) 감다, (B) 'The police'는 복수 취급하므로 are가 적절하다. (C) 'The police'가 주어이므로 are가 적절하다.

12 'Swenekafew'를 가리킨다.

13 그가 왜 John Pecitello와 언쟁을 벌였는지는 알 수 없다. ① He worked at the Columbia Coal Mine. ③ He was shot on Thursday evening. ④ He was shot twice. ⑤ He is now at the hospital.

14 (A) '가짜 뉴스는 사람들을 잘못 이끌 수 있다는 점에서 매우 해로울 수 있다'고 해야 하므로 in that이 적절하다. in that: ~이

7

므로, ~라는 점에서, (B) 목적어인 people이 '잘못 이끌어질 수 있다'는 수동의 의미이므로, 과거분사 misled가 적절하다. (C) such+(a)+형용사+명사

15 ⓐ와 ①, ④: 경험 용법, ② 결과 용법, ③ 계속 용법, ⑤ 완료 용법

16 '매일 우리가 얼마나 많은 흥미로운 뉴스를 보거나 듣고, 읽는지'는 대답할 수 없다. ② Everyone likes an interesting news story. ③ Yes. ④ Yes. ⑤ Yes.

17 앞에 나온 명사 articles를 수식하도록 과거분사 published로 쓰는 것이 적절하다.

18 ⓑ와 ④: 현재의, the current year: 올해, ① 통용되는, ② (물·공기의) 흐름, 해류(명사), ③ 전류(명사), direct current: 직류, ⑤ 때의 흐름(course), 경향, 풍조(명사), swim against the current: 세상 풍조[천하대세]에 거스르다

19 가짜 뉴스 판별 방법 중의 하나인 'Read Beyond the Headlines(기사 제목 그 이상을 읽어라)'는 단순히 기사 제목만 읽고 뉴스의 내용을 짐작하여 판단하지 말고 그 기사의 내용까지 모두 읽으라는 의미이므로, ②번의 '제목으로 내용을 짐작하기'는 가짜 뉴스 판별 방법에 해당하지 않는다.

20 그 슬라브인의 이름을 '거꾸로' 읽어 보라고 하는 것이 적절하다. forward: 앞으로

21 ⓑ와 ③, ⑤: ~인지 아닌지, ①, ②, ④: (가정적 조건을 나타내어) (만약) ~이라면

22 ③ 그 다음 날 'Swenekafew'에 대한 동일한 기사를 발행한 것은 '데일리 뉴스 사'이다.

23 fake: 가짜의, 거짓된, genuine: 진짜의, 진품의

24 nevertheless: 그럼에도 불구하고(부사), even so, still, nonetheless 등과 바꿔 쓸 수 있다. ① despite ~: ~에도 불구하고(전치사), ② therefore: 그러므로(부사) ④ otherwise: (만약) 그렇지 않으면[않았다면](부사)

25 '몇 가지 뉴스 기사'를 가리킨다.

26 이 글은 '가짜 뉴스는 매우 해로울 수 있지만, 역사를 통틀어 다양한 가짜 뉴스 보도들이 존재해 왔다'는 내용의 글이므로, 제목으로는 ④번 '해로운 그러나 계속되는 가짜 뉴스 보도들'이 적절하다. continuous: 계속되는, 지속적인, ⑤ faithful: 충실한, from now on: 이제부터

27 '어떤 사람들은', '다른 사람들은'이라고 해야 하므로, Some, others가 적절하다. some: 처음 지칭하는 어떤 것[사람]들, others: 다른 것[사람]들, ① one: 2개 이상의 대상 중 불특정한 한 개를 처음으로 지칭할 때 사용하는 대명사, the other: 2개 중 나머지 한 개, ② the others: 앞에 지칭한 것들을 제외한 나머지 전부들, ③ another: 3개 이상의 대상에서 두 번째로 불특

정한 한 개를 지칭할 때 사용하는 대명사, ④ the first: 전자, the second: 후자

28 주격 관계대명사절 'who didn't read it to the end'가 선행사 those를 수식하도록 쓰는 것이 적절하다.

29 구동사의 목적어가 인칭대명사이므로 부사의 앞에 목적어를 쓰는 것이 적절하다

🦉 서술형 시험대비

01 (A) if   (B) harmful   (C) informed
02 Why have some people written such false information?
03 while we think about the hidden motives behind them
04 on the loose
05 has been taken place → has taken place
06 (A) No   (B) escape
07 in order that[so that], could[might]
08 such news
09 ②번 near from → near
10 (A) had an argument   (B) critical
11 Whether
12 *The Daily News* published the same article about "Swenekafew" the next day

01 (A) '만약 그것이 완전히 지어낸 것이라면 어떻게 할 것인가?'라고 해야 하므로 if가 적절하다. What if ~?: ~라면 어떻게 될까? (B) '가짜 뉴스는 사람들을 잘못 이끌 수 있다는 점에서 매우 해로울 수 있다'고 해야 하므로 harmful이 적절하다. harmless: 해가 없는, 무해한, (C) 목적어인 people이 '정보를 부족하게 제공받거나'라고 수동의 의미이므로, 과거분사 informed가 적절하다.

02 현재완료 시제의 의문문은 'Have+주어+p.p.'의 순서로 쓰는 것이 적절하다. such+(a)+형용사+명사

03 위 글의 밑줄 친 ⓑ는 동시동작을 나타내는 분사구문으로, '~하는 동안에'라는 의미의 접속사 while을 사용하여 부사절로 고치는 것이 적절하다.

04 on the loose: 잡히지 않은; 탈주 중인

05 take place는 '(사고·일·문제 등이) 발생하다, 일어나다'라는 뜻으로 수동태로 쓸 수 없다.

06 실제로는 어젯밤 동물들이 동물원에서 '도망치지' 않았기 때문에, 동물원에서 탈출한 동물들에 의해 '아무도' 다치지 않았다.

07 목적을 나타내는 부사적 용법의 to부정사는 복문으로 전환할 때 'in order that[so that]+주어+can[may]+동사원형'으로 고

8 정답 및 해설

치는 것이 적절하다.

08 '이러한 뉴스'를 가리킨다.

09 전치사 near 뒤에 바로 목적어를 쓰는 것이 적절하다. ① by+수동태의 행위자, ③ be shot in the ~: ~에 총을 맞다, ④ in critical condition: 위독한 상태로, ⑤ search for: ~를 찾다

10 Mejk Swenekafew는 John Pecitello와 회의 중에 '언쟁을 벌였고', Pecitello가 Swenekafew에게 총을 쐈다. Swenekafew는 지금 입원 중이고, 그의 상태는 '위독하다.'

11 if는 '~인지 아닌지'라는 의미의 명사절을 이끄는 접속사로 whether와 바꾸어 쓸 수 있으며, if가 이끄는 명사절이 동사 prove의 목적어이다.

12 '데일리 뉴스사가 그 다음 날 'Swenekafew'에 대한 동일한 기사를 발행한 것'을 가리킨다.

영역별 핵심문제   p.45~49

01 misunderstand   02 ②

03 (1) reliable   (2) riddle   (3) seriously   (4) shoot
     (5) source   04 ①   05 ⑤

06 (1) break down   (2) According to   (3) made up

07 (1) She described what happened last night.
     (2) This is one of the worst natural disasters.
     (3) A lion escaped from the zoo an hour ago.

08 (C) → (D) → (B) → (E) → (A)   09 ①

10 ⑤

11 It's because they help adults think more creatively.

12 We need to think outside the box.

13 ⑤   14 ⑤

15 (1) Linda was stupid enough to make a big mistake.
     (2) Bill is too poor to buy the house.

16 ①   17 ⑤

18 (1) Though[Although] the two articles were special cases
     (2) and[while] he smiled brightly
     (3) Because[As, Since] I was tired from the work

19 ②   20 ②   21 ⑤   22 ⑤

23 ③   24 ④

25 (A) the other   (B) further   (C) described

26 Twelve of the animals are still on the loose.

27 John Pecitello   28 ②   29 ④

30 ⓐ To draw the readers' attention to the unsafe conditions at the zoo.
     ⓑ To prove that *The Daily News* was stealing their articles.

01 접두사 'mis'는 '잘못된, 나쁜'을 의미한다. misunderstand: 오해하다, 잘못 이해하다

02 nevertheless: 그럼에도 불구하고

03 riddle: 수수께끼, seriously: 심하게, 진지하게, reliable: 믿을 만한, source: 출처, shoot: 쏘다

04 '갑자기 너무 걱정이 되어서 이성적일 수 없다고 느끼다'를 가리키는 말은 panic이다.

05 보기에 주어진 current는 '현재의'를 뜻한다. ⑤번은 '흐름, 해류'를 의미한다.

06 break down: 부수다, 무너뜨리다, according to: ~에 따르면, make up: 지어내다, 만들다

07 describe: 기술하다, disaster: 재난, escape: 탈출하다

08 (C) TV 뉴스를 보는 이유 질문 → (D) 이유 설명 → (B) TV가 가장 유용하다고 생각하는 이유 질문 → (E) 이유 설명 → (A) 반응 및 이해 표현

09 위 대화에서 Sandy는 '주의 깊은, 신중한' 성격임을 알 수 있다.

10 Sandy에 따르면 음료수가 무엇으로 만들어졌는지에 대한 정보가 없다.

11 John은 수수께끼 책들이 어른들이 좀 더 창의적으로 생각하도록 도와주기 때문에 유익하다고 생각한다.

12 수수께끼의 답을 찾기 위해 고정관념에서 벗어날 필요가 있다.

13 ⑤번을 제외한 나머지는 모두 자세한 설명을 요청하는 표현이다.

14 여자는 체온이 낮아서 감기에 걸렸다는 설명은 대화의 내용과 일치하지 않는다.

15 (1) 'so+형용사[부사]+that+주어+can ...'은 '형용사+enough to ...'로 바꿔 쓸 수 있다. (2) 'so+형용사[부사]+that+주어+can't ...'은 'too+형용사[부사]+to부정사'로 바꿔 쓸 수 있다.

16 'so that ~ can ...'은 'in order that ~ can ...'으로 바꿔 쓸 수 있다.

17 As she didn't hand out the report, she is responsible for the result.를 분사구문으로 쓴 것이므로 handing을 'having handed'로 고쳐야 한다.

18 (1) 내용상 '양보'가 적절하고, 주어가 다른 독립분사구문이므로 다른 주어를 써 주고, having been이 있으므로 한 시제 앞선 양보의 부사절로 쓴다. (2) 내용상 '동시동작'이나 '시간'의 부사절이 적절하다. (3) 내용상 '이유'의 부사절이 적절하다.

19 전치사 with는 '~한 채'의 뜻으로 부대 상황을 나타낸다.

20 앞에 나오는 내용과 상반되는 내용이 뒤에 이어지므로 Nevertheless가 가장 적절하다. ① 뿐만 아니라, 더욱이, ③ 똑같이, 비슷하게, ④ 즉[말하자면], ⑤ 따라서, 그러므로

21 ① every day = each day: 매일, ② whether = if: ~인지

아닌지, ③ what if는 회화에서 자주 쓰이는 줄임말로, 본래 표현은 'what would happen if'이며 '~한다면 어쩌지?'라는 뜻으로 사용된다. ④ in the sense that: ~라는 점에서, ⑤ motive: 동기, 이유, theme: 주제, 테마

22 look into: ~을 조사하다

23 문장 끝에서 '왜 어떤 사람들은 그러한 거짓 정보를 써 왔던 것일까? 그 뒤에 숨겨진 동기를 생각하면서 몇 가지 뉴스 기사를 살펴보자.'라고 했으므로, 뒤에 올 내용으로는 '그 뒤에 숨겨진 동기에 대해 생각할 수 있는 몇 가지 가짜 뉴스 기사'가 적절하다.

24 ⓐ와 ④: 부수다, ① 실패하다, 결렬되다, ②와 ⑤: (기계·차량이) 고장 나다, ③ 아주 나빠지다

25 (A) 뒤에 복수 명사가 이어지므로 the other가 적절하다. another+단수 명사, (B) '추후 안내가 있을 때까지'라고 해야 하므로 further가 적절하다. farther: (공간, 시간상으로) 더 멀리, further: 더 이상의, 추가의, (C) '위에 기술된 어떤 행동이나 사건도'라고 해야 하므로 described가 적절하다.

26 on the loose: 잡히지 않은, 탈주 중인

27 Mejk Swenekafew에게 총을 쏜 John Pecitello를 가리킨다.

28 주어진 문장의 The argument에 주목한다. ②번 앞 문장의 an argument를 받고 있으므로 ②번이 적절하다.

29 위 글은 '인터뷰'이다. ① (신문·잡지의) 글, 기사, ② 수필, ③ (책·연극·영화 등에 대한) 논평[비평], 감상문, ⑤ 요약, 개요

30 ⓐ: 동물원의 안전하지 않은 상태에 대해 독자들의 주의를 끌기 위해서. ⓑ: 데일리 뉴스 사가 그들의 기사를 훔치고 있다는 것을 증명하기 위해서

단원별 예상문제
p.50~53

01 ⑤
02 Can you give me more information about it?
03 ⑤ **04** ② **05** ④ **06** riddle
07 ⑤ **08** ⓐ → where it is **09** ⑤
10 ③
11 (1) As[Because, Since] I was driving my car, I couldn't reply to your text message.
  (2) While[When, As] I was walking down the street, I met my friend.
  (3) Although[Though] there was no work to do, he remained at his office until late.
12 playing the guitar **13** ④ **14** ②, ④
15 ②, ③, ⑤ **16** ⑤ **17** panicked
18 Because[As/Since] they didn't know the news was false **19** ④
20 ⑤

21 (A) *The Daily Telegram*
  (B) The people at *The Daily News*
22 the public harshly criticized the people at *The Daily News*

01 '알맞은 순서로 문자를 가지고 단어를 형성하다'를 가리키는 말은 spell이다.

03 수지가 잠을 잘 자기 위해 몇 잔의 우유를 마셔야 하는지는 대화를 통해 알 수 없다.

04 주어진 문장은 기사에 대한 구체적인 설명을 요청하므로 (B)에 들어가는 것이 적절하다.

05 왜 프랑스의 1인치가 영국과 달랐는지는 대화를 통해 알 수 없다.

06 '이해하기 힘든 질문으로 놀라운 답을 갖고 있고 게임으로 다른 사람에게 묻는 질문'을 가리키는 것은 riddle(수수께끼)이다.

07 think outside the box: 고정관념에서 벗어나다

08 간접의문문으로 '의문사+주어+동사'의 순서가 적절하다.

10 ③ She was too tired to think straight. 'so+형용사[부사]+that+주어+can't ...'는 '너무 ~해서 …할 수 없다'라는 의미이며, 'too+형용사[부사]+to부정사'(…하기에 너무~한)로 바꿔 쓸 수 있다.

11 (1), (2) 분사구문의 분사(동사원형+-ing)를 의미에 맞게 '접속사+주어+동사'로 이루어진 부사절로 만든다. (3) 분사구문의 주어가 주절의 주어와 일치하지 않으므로 부사절의 주어를 따로 써 주어야 한다.

12 '접속사+주어+동사'로 이루어진 부사절의 주어가 주절의 주어와 일치할 때 접속사와 주어를 생략하고 동사를 현재분사(동사원형+-ing)로 만든다.

13 Don't waste water in order to prevent water shortages.

14 ⓐ와 ②, ④: (신문·잡지 따위의) 기사, ①, ⑤: (종류가 같은 것의) 한 개, 한 가지(item), ③ 관사, a definite article: 정관사(the)

15 ⓑ와 ②, ③, ⑤: 현재분사, ①, ④: 동명사

16 이 글은 '가짜 뉴스는 매우 해로울 수 있지만, 역사를 통틀어 다양한 가짜 뉴스 보도들이 존재해 왔다'는 내용의 글이므로, 주제로는 ⑤번 '해로운 영향들에도 불구하고, 다양한 가짜 뉴스 보도들이 존재해 왔다'가 적절하다. ④ faithfully: (내용이 틀리지 않게) 충실히, 정확히

17 'panic'의 과거형은 끝에 '-ked'를 붙이는 것이 적절하다. 'paniced'로 쓰지 않도록 주의해야 한다. panic 겁에 질려 어쩔 줄 모르다

18 '이유'를 나타내는 부사절로 고치는 것이 적절하다.

19 헤럴드 사는 사람들에게 '겁주기 위하여' 이러한 뉴스를 만들어 낸 것이 아니라, '동물원의 안전하지 않은 상태에 대해 독자들의 주의를 끌기 위해' 그 기사를 지어냈다.

20 앞의 내용의 결과가 나오고 있으므로 thus가 가장 적절하다. ① 게다가, ② 그 대신에, 그렇지 않으면(둘째 대안을 소개할 때 씀), ③ 다른 한편으로는, 반면에, ④ 게다가, 더욱이

21 (A) 데일리 텔레그램 사, The Daily Telegram과 같이 특정 회사를 지칭할 때는 그 회사를 이루는 구성원 전체를 받아 they로 복수 취급하기도 한다. (B) 데일리 뉴스 사의 사람들을 가리킨다.

22 the public을 주어로 해서 능동태로 고치는 것이 적절하다.

서술형 실전문제
p.54~55

01 It says that Napoleon was actually fairly tall.

02 A French doctor wrote it down according to the French measuring system.

03 An inch in France was longer than an inch in England.

04 (1) Because[As, Since] Jenny won the first prize, she was so happy.
　(2) If you walk with Wing Walker, you burn more calories and get slimmer.
　(3) Using the hidden board technology, they strengthen leg muscles.
　(4) She studied very hard, passing the exam.

05 (1) in order that　(2) in[so] order[as] to
　(3) enough to　(4) too hot, to

06 that → whether[if]

07 what if it is completely made up?

08 (A) fake news　(B) fake news

09 the article

10 (in order/so as) to draw the readers' attention to the unsafe conditions at the zoo

11 (A) escape the city　(B) went into the parks

01 기사에 따르면 나폴레옹은 꽤 키가 컸다.

02 프랑스 의사가 나폴레옹의 키를 적었고 프랑스 측정 체계에 따라 적었다.

03 프랑스의 1인치는 영국의 1인치보다 더 길었다.

04 (1) 의미상 '이유'를 나타내는 분사구문이다. (2) 의미상 '조건'을 나타내는 분사구문이다. (3) 의미상 '이유'를 나타내는 분사구문으로 바꾼다. (4) 의미상 '연속상황'을 나타내는 분사구문으로 바꾼다.

05 (1), (2) 'so that ~ can ...'은 'in order that ~ can ...'으로 바꿔 쓸 수 있으며, 주절과 종속절의 주어가 같은 경우 '(in order[so as]) to부정사'로 바꿔 쓸 수 있다. (3), (4) 'so+형용사[부사]+that+주어+can ...'은 '형용사+enough to ...'로 바꿔 쓸 수 있으며, 'so+형용사[부사]+that+주어+can't ...'는 'too+형용사[부사]+to부정사'로 바꿔 쓸 수 있다. (4)번의 경우 주절과 종속절의 주어가 다르지만 일반인이 주어이므로 따로 밝혀 쓰지 않아도 된다.

06 '뉴스 기사가 정말로 긴실인지 신가하게 고려해 본 적이 있는가?'라고 해야 하므로, that을 whether로 고치는 것이 적절하다. that을 쓰면, '뉴스 기사가 정말로 진실이라는 것을 심각하게 고려해 본 적이 있는가?'라는 뜻이 되어 어색하다.

07 what if: ~라면 어떻게 될까?, make up 지어내다, 만들어 내다

08 '가짜 뉴스'때문에 사람들에게 정보가 부족하게 제공되거나 사람들이 잘못 이끌릴 수 있지만, 역사를 통틀어 다양한 '가짜 뉴스' 보도들이 존재해 왔다.

09 '그 기사'를 가리킨다.

10 so that+주어+can+동사원형 = (in order/so as) to+동사원형: ~하기 위하여(목적)

11 어떤 사람들은 '도시를 빠져나가려고 했고' 다른 사람들은 그 동물들을 사냥하기 위해 총을 들고 '공원으로 나갔다.'

창의사고력 서술형 문제
p.56

|모범답안|

01 (A) I drank a glass of warm milk
　(B) a glass of warm milk doesn't actually help me fall asleep
　(C) make people sleepy
　(D) amount

02 (A) the walking shoes, Wing Walker
　(B) burn more calories and get slimmer
　(C) the hidden board technology
　(D) scientifically proven
　(E) what materials

01 최근에 나는 잠을 잘 잘 수 없어서 잠들기 전에 따뜻한 우유를 한 잔 마셨다. 하지만 효과가 없었다. 나는 이에 대해 민수에게 이야기했다. 그는 한 잔의 따뜻한 우유가 실제로는 잠을 잘 자는 데 도움이 되지 않는다고 설명했다. 의사에 따르면 우유에는 사람들을 졸리게 만드는 특별한 화학물질이 있지만 우유 한 잔에 있는 양은 너무 적었다. 나는 잠을 잘 자기 위해 다른 방법을 찾아야겠다고 생각했다.

01 (D) → (C) → (A) → (B)

02 (1) awful   (2) chemicals   (3) chest   (4) citizen

03 (1) poems   (2) prove   (3) public   (4) published

    (5) recognize

04 ③   05 ④   06 ⑤

07 She reads the label of the drink closely.

08 It's because the label on the drink looks a bit
strange.

09 What's in the drink and how much one has to
drink to lose weight are not shown.   10 ②

11 ⑤

12 (1) Think critically and don't believe everything
    (that) they tell you.

    (2) Do not criticize or make fun of your
       classmates.

    (3) Is this your current address?

    (4) It's difficult to judge whether it's true or not.

13 (1) Sam saved some money so that he could buy
       a new backpack. 또는 Sam saved some
       money so as to buy a new backpack.

    (2) You must follow the rules in order for everyone
       to enjoy the experience. 또는 You must follow
       the rules in order that everyone may[can]
       enjoy the experience.

    (3) She saw Thomas entering[enter] the classroom.

    (4) Very embarrassed, she didn't tell us that news.

14 (1) Having no work to do, he goes fishing.

    (2) Susan spoke quietly so that other people
       couldn't hear her voice.

15 ③   16 ①, ③, ④

17 (1) 해석: Jinho는 외국인과 영어로 말할 수 있도록 영어를
       열심히 공부했다.
       차이: so that은 '~하기 위해', '~하고자', '~하도록'의
       의미로 '목적'이나 '의도'를 나타낸다. 일반적으로 '주절
       +so that+주어+can/will(조동사)+동사원형 ~'의 형태로
       쓰인다.

    (2) 해석: Jinho는 영어를 열심히 공부해서 외국인과 영어로
       말할 수 있었다.
       차이: so와 that 사이에 형용사나 부사가 오면, '너무 ~
       해서 결국 …하다'라는 뜻이 된다.

18 ①   19 an interesting news story

20 ③   21 ③   22 ④   23 ⑤

24 The two men had an argument during a meeting.

25 ③   26 ④

01 (D) 감기에 걸린 것 같다며 이유 설명 → (C) 기사 내용 설명
   → (A) 구체적인 설명 요청 → (B) 감기에 걸리는 이유에 대해

구체적인 설명

02 awful: 끔찍한, 지독한, chemical: 화학 물질, chest: 흉부, 가
   슴, citizen: 시민

03 public: 대중, recognize: 알아보다, publish: 출판하다,
   prove: 증명하다, poem: 시

04 mine은 명사로 '광산', 동사로 '채굴하다', 대명사로 '나의 것'을
   의미한다.

05 주어진 문장은 금붕어가 사실은 똑똑하다는 말 앞에 오는 것이 자
   연스러우므로 (D)가 적절하다.

06 위 대화를 통해 금붕어가 어떻게 주인을 알아보는지 알 수 없다.

07 Sandy는 음료의 라벨을 자세히 읽는다.

08 음료수의 라벨이 조금 이상해 보이기 때문에 Sandy는 David
   가 음료수를 사지 말아야 한다고 생각한다.

09 음료수에 무엇이 있는지 살을 빼기 위해 얼마나 마셔야 하는지
   볼 수 없다.

10 (A) useful: 유용한, useless: 무익한, (B) ordinarily: 평범
   하게, creatively: 창의적으로, (C) think outside the box:
   고정관념에서 벗어나다

11 위 대화를 통해 John의 상자 밖에 무엇이 있는지 알 수 없다.

12 critically: 비판적으로, criticize: 비판하다, current: 현재의,
   judge: 판단하다

13 (1) 'so that+절' 또는 'so as to부정사'가 되어야 한다. (2)
   'for everyone to enjoy'로 의미상의 주어를 쓰거나 'in order
   that+절'이 되어야 한다. (3) entered를 entering[enter]로 바
   꾸어 목적보어로 만든다. (4) 주어가 embarrassed되는 수동의
   관계이므로 being이 생략된 과거분사 embarrassed로 시작하
   는 문장으로 바꾼다.

14 (1) 분사구문을 이용하고 'no work to do'를 분사 Having의
   목적어로 이용한다. (2) 일반적으로 '주절+so that+주어+can/
   will(조동사)+동사원형 ~'의 형태로 so that은 '목적'이나 '의
   도'를 나타낸다.

15 Wear a swimming cap in order for the pool to be kept
   clean. 주절과 부사절의 주어가 다른 경우 서로 다른 주어를 나
   타내야 하는데 to부정사의 경우 'for+목적격'으로 쓴다.

16 ② Pass → Passing ⑤ Feeling not → Not feeling ⑥
   Meeting → Having met

17 'so that+주어+can …'과 'so+형용사[부사]+that+주어+can
   …'의 차이를 구별한다.

18 ⓑ와 ③: 계속 용법, ①: 결과 용법, ②, ④: 완료 용법, ⑤: 경험
   용법

19 '흥미로운 뉴스 기사'를 가리킨다.

20 ⓐ to the end: 끝까지, ⓑ draw one's attention to ~: ~에
   대해 …의 주의를 끌다

21 ③ 잠깐, 잠시(명사), ③을 제외한 나머지: [반대·비교·대조를 나타내어] 그런데, 한편(접속사)

22 주어진 문장의 such news에 주목한다. ④번 앞 단락에서 말한 '거짓 뉴스'를 가리키므로 ④번이 적절하다.

23 이 글은 '컬럼비아 광산 소속의 슬라브인 노동자 두 명이 언쟁을 벌이다가 한 명이 총상을 입어 심각하게 다쳤다'는 내용의 글이므로, 제목으로는 ⑤번 '슬라브인이 언쟁 중에 친구를 쏘다'가 적절하다. ④ criminal: 범인

24 had an argument: 언쟁을 벌였다

25 run away: 도망치다

26 경찰이 찾고 있는 것은 'Pecitello'이다.

Words of Wisdom

| 01 ④ | 02 ③ | 03 ② | 04 failure |
| 05 ② | 06 ① | 07 ⑤ | |

01 ④ novel(새로운)은 뒤에 ty를 붙여 novelty(새로움)를 만들 수 있다. ④ 이외의 보기에는 접미사 dom을 붙여 명사를 만들 수 있다. ① wise+-dom → wisdom 지혜 ② free+-dom → freedom 자유 ③ bore+-dom → boredom 지루함, 따분함 ⑤ fan+-dom → fandom 팬덤, 팬층

02 priceless: 대단히 귀중한, 값을 매길 수 없는 / 그는 주변 사람들이 편안함을 느끼게 만드는 귀중한 능력을 가진 사람이다. ① 가치가 없는, 하찮은 ② 가치 없는 ③ 귀중한 ④ 경제적인 ⑤ 비싼

03 (A) settle in: ~에 자리 잡다, 정착하다. 그는 몇 년 동안 여행을 한 후에, 뉴욕에 정착했다. (B) get stuck on: ~에 갇히다. 만약 네가 어려운 단어에 막히면, 도움을 청해라.

04 fail: 실패하다 failure: 실패 / 그의 새 영화는 완전한 실패였다.

05 ① character: 등장인물 / 그는 이 영화에서 가장 재미있는 등장인물이다. ② express: 표현하다 / 나는 나의 친구 지나에게 고마움을 표현하고 싶다. ③ reward: 보상 / 그들은 그가 열심히 일한 것에 대한 보상을 주었다. ④ situation: 상황, 환경 / 지금은 어려운 상황이고 나는 무엇을 해야 할지 모르겠다. ⑤ far-away: 멀리 떨어진 / 우리 할머니는 멀리 떨어진 산에서 사셨다.

06 hire: 고용하다 / 당신을 위해 특정한 일을 하도록 어떤 사람에게 일을 주거나 그에게 돈을 지불하다

07 make friends: 친구를 사귀다 / 나는 여름 캠프에서 많은 친구들을 사귀었다. make a wish: 소원을 빌다 / 그들은 유성이 떨어지는 것을 보면서 소원을 빌었다.

01 (b)ring back
02 (1) After a hard day's work   (2) explain myself
03 (t)ake care of
04 ran
05 (1) You have so much to learn throughout your life.
　(2) The price is supposed to go down this week.
　(3) All the students were puzzled by the question.

---

(4) This situation matters a lot.
(5) That's a philosophy I could live by.
06 with open arms

01 단어의 관계는 동의어이다. hire: 고용하다 employ: 고용하다 return: 돌려주다, 반납하다 bring back: 돌려주다

02 (1) after a hard day's work: 하루 종일 열심히 일하고 나서 (2) explain oneself: 자기 생각을 밝히다, 심중을 털어놓다

03 look after ~: ~을 살피다, 돌보다 take care of ~ : ~을 돌보다. 당신이 없을 때 아이들은 누가 돌볼 것인가요?

04 run out of: ~이 없어지다, 다 떨어지다 / 나는 그 시험을 끝내지 못했다. 나는 시간을 다 썼다. run: 달리다 / 나는 가능한 한 빨리 학교로 달려갔다.

05 (1) throughout one's life: 일생을 통해 (2) suppose: 추측하다, 추정하다 (3) puzzled: 당혹스러운, 어리둥절한 (4) matter: 중요하다 situation: 상황, 환경 (5) live by: (신조, 원칙 등)에 따라 살다

06 with open arms: 두 팔을 벌리고 / 이모는 나를 두 팔을 벌려 환영했다.

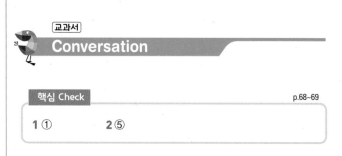

교과서
Conversation

1 ①   2 ⑤

교과서 대화문 익히기

1 T　2 F　3 F　4 T

5 F　6 T　7 T　8 T

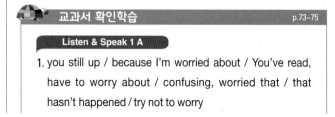

Listen & Speak 1 A

1. you still up / because I'm worried about / You've read, have to worry about / confusing, worried that / that hasn't happened / try not to worry

2. Nothing special / have to go to, can't find anyone / worry about / worried / supposed to be

Listen & Talk 1 B

worried / got a big part in / keep making mistakes / practice / making mistakes

Listen & Talk 2 A

1. lived forever / What would you do if / would / interesting

2. called / heard, come true / if you could make one wish / would make, stay, make all my wishes come true

Listen & Talk 2 B

one of, movies / what would you do if you could / prevent / would go to, meet

Communication Step A

How's / ran out / Don't worry about / character, What would you do if you were / find out if

Wrap Up

1. I've heard that / worried / I'm worried that, too difficult / Don't worry about, believe in yourself

2. watched / a man who was stuck on / tries, would, if you were him / alive / that's what the man did

---

시험대비 기본평가   p.76

01 ④   02 ①

01 'What would you do if you+과거시제 ~?'에 대한 대답으로 '나는 '~할 거야.'라는 의미로 'I would 동사원형 ~.' 형태의 가정법 과거를 사용하여 대답한다.

02 빈칸 다음의 남자가 'I'll try not to worry so much.(너무 걱정하지 않도록 해 볼게요.)'라고 말하는 것으로 보아 여자가 걱정하지 말라고 말하면서 상대방을 안심시켰을 것이다.

시험대비 실력평가   p.77~78

01 ②   02 ③   03 ①   04 ④
05 ②   06 ③   07 ③
08 I'll try not to worry so much. 09 ④   10 ⑤
11 ②

01 상대방을 안심시키는 표현으로는 'Don't worry about ~.'이라는 말을 쓸 수 있다. 위의 대화에서 마감이 이번 주말인데 아이디어가 다 떨어진 여자아이에게 남자가 안심시키는 것이 어울리므로 ②가 적절하다.

02 '마감이 이번 주말이다.'와 '아이디어가 다 떨어졌다.'는 역접의 접속사 'but(하지만)'이 들어가야 적절하다.

03 현재 사실과 반대되는 상황이나 일에 대해 가정하거나 현재 사실에 대한 후회나 아쉬움을 강조할 때, 가정법 과거를 쓴다. 즉, 현재 사실과 반대이므로 과거 시제를 쓴다. 조건절은 'if 주어+동사 과거형'으로, 주절은 '주어+would+동사원형 ~'을 쓴다. 이때 해석은 '~라면 …할 텐데.'라고 해석한다.

04 패션모델이라면 무엇을 할 것인지 묻는 말에, '나는 키가 클 수 있다.'라는 대답은 어울리지 않는다.

05 'What would you do if you+동사의 과거형 ~?'은 '네가 만약 ~한다면, 너는 무엇을 할 거니?'라는 의미의 가정법 과거로 현재 사실과 반대되는 것을 상상하여 말할 때 쓰인다. 그리고 책의 내용이 마법의 물을 마시고 영원히 살게 되게 된 한 가족에 대한 이야기이므로, 내용상 영원히 살게 되면 무엇을 할지 질문하는 것이 어울린다.

06 영원히 살게 된다면 여자아이는 전 세계의 다양한 도시에서 살고 싶다고 말했다.

07 주어진 문장은 '뭐가 걱정이니?'의 의미로 걱정에 대한 구체적인 내용을 묻고 있는 질문이다. 이에 대한 대답으로 'Some of the writers' names are confusing, so I'm worried that I might not remember them.(몇몇 작가들의 이름이 헷갈려서 그들을 기억하지 못할까봐 걱정이 돼요.)'이 어울리므로 ③이 적절하다.

08 to worry는 try의 목적어이다. to부정사를 부정하기 위해서 앞에 not을 쓴다. 'try to 동사원형'은 '~하기 위해 노력하다'라는 의미이므로, 'try not to 동사원형'은 '~하지 않기 위해 노력하다'로 해석할 수 있다.

09 빈칸에서 them은 the writers' names를 의미하는 것이고, 내용상 작가들의 이름이 헷갈려서 그 이름을 기억하지 못하는 것에 대한 걱정을 표현하는 것이 알맞으므로 ④가 적절하다.

10 주어진 문장에서 them은 mistakes를 가리키는 말이다. 더 연습을 하라고 말하면서, 실수하는 것에 대해 걱정하지 말고, 실수로부터 배울 수 있다고 말할 수 있으므로 ⑤가 어울린다.

11 아빠가 'Don't worry about making mistakes.(실수하는 것에 대해서는 걱정하지 마.)'라고 말하는 것으로 보아 Jane은 실수하는 것에 대해 걱정하고 있다.

서술형 시험대비   p.79

01 called   02 make
03 about   04 confusing
05 What would you do if you could live forever?
06 made → make

15

01 called는 과거분사로 '~라는 이름의, ~라고 불리는'의 의미로 앞에 있는 명사 a book을 수식하고 있다.

02 (A), (C), (D) make는 '~에게 …하게 하다'라는 의미를 가지는 사역동사로, 목적격보어로 동사원형을 쓴다. (B) make a wish: 소원을 빌다

03 'I'm worried about ~.'은 '나는 ~에 대해 걱정한다.'의 의미로 걱정을 나타낼 때 사용하는 표현이다.

04 감정을 나타내는 동사의 경우 현재분사는 '~하게 하는'의 뜻으로 감정을 유발하는 대상에 쓰인다. confuse: 혼란시키다, confusing: 혼란스러운

05 '만약 ~라면 어떻게 하겠니?'라고 실제가 아닌 상황이나 사실을 가정하여 물어볼 때는 가정법 과거를 이용하여 'What would you do if you+과거시제 ~?'로 표현한다. forever: 영원히

06 흥미로운 물건들을 모아서 박물관을 만들 거라는 의미로 collect와 make가 접속사 and에 의해 병렬로 연결되어 있다.

교과서
Grammar

핵심 Check   p.80~81

1 (1) It   (2) that
2 (1) finish   (2) broken   (3) to sing

시험대비 기본평가   p.82

01 ④   **02** ⑤
03 (1) repair   (2) stolen   (3) It   (4) who
04 (1) It was Minji that ate the pizza.
   (2) It is the school that Prince William went to.
   (3) Della was surprised that Jim had his leg broken.

01 'It ~ that …' 강조 구문은 'It is/was ~ that …'의 형태로, 강조하고자 하는 부분을 'It is/was'와 that 사이에 넣고, 나머지 부분을 that 뒤에 써서 주어, 목적어인 명사, 부사(구/절) 등을 강조한다. that이나 who가 들어가는 것이 적절하다.

02 의자가 고쳐지는 것(목적어가 목적격 보어의 동작을 당하는 대상)으로 수동의 의미이므로 과거분사를 써야 한다.

03 (1) 목적어가 목적격 보어의 동작을 하는 주체이므로 동사원형이 적절하다. (2) 돈이 도둑맞는 것(목적어가 목적격 보어의 동작을 당하는 대상)으로 수동의 의미이므로 과거분사가 적절하다. (3) 'It+is/was+강조어(구)+that …'의 형태로 특정 부분을 강조하여 나타낼 때 사용한다. That이 아닌 It이 적절하다. (4)

강조되는 어구가 사람일 때는 that 대신에 who를 쓸 수 있다.

04 (1) 'It ~ that …' 강조 구문은 'It is/was ~ that …'의 형태로, 강조하고자 하는 부분을 'It is/was'와 that 사이에 넣고, 나머지 부분을 that 뒤에 쓴다. '바로 민지'라고 주어를 강조하고 있으므로 Minji를 'It is/was'와 that 사이에 넣고 나머지를 that 뒤에 쓴다. (2) '바로 그 학교'라고 전치사 to의 목적어를 강조하고 있으므로 the school을 'It is/was'와 that 사이에 넣고 나머지를 that 뒤에 쓴다. (3) 다리가 부러졌다는 것으로 수동의 의미이므로 'have+목적어+과거분사'로 쓴다.

시험대비 실력평가   p.83~85

01 ③   **02** ②   **03** ①
04 (1) painted   (2) wash   (3) to bring   (4) who   (5) when
   (6) where
05 ④   **06** ②   **07** ③   **08** ⑤
09 ①   **10** ④   **11** ②
12 Mary had her table made by her brother.
13 ①   **14** buy, repaired   **15** ③
16 (1) The writer had his book printed at his own expense.
   (2) How can I get him to dress better?
   (3) I found out that it was the price that[which] frightened me.
   (4) It was when they are heated that metals expand.
   (5) It was at[in] the theater that I met Jack last weekend.   **17** ⑤

01 'It ~ that …' 강조 구문은 동사를 강조할 수 없다.

02 목적어가 목적격 보어의 동작을 하는 주체이므로 동사원형이 적절하다. How did you have him pose for this picture?

03 첫 번째 빈칸에는 'It ~ that …' 강조 구문으로 that이나 which가 적절하다. 두 번째 빈칸에는 목적어가 목적격 보어의 동작을 당하는 대상으로 수동의 의미이므로 과거분사 checked가 적절하다.

04 (1) 얼굴에 칠해지는 것이므로 과거분사가 적절하다. (2) 그가 설거지하는 것이므로 동사원형이 적절하다. (3) get 동사는 'get+목적어+to부정사'의 형태로 쓰인다. (4) 강조하는 것이 the princess로 사람이므로 who가 적절하다. (5) 강조하는 것이 시간을 나타내는 부사구 last night이므로 when이 적절하다. (6) 강조하는 것이 장소를 나타내는 부사구 'at the festival'이므로 where가 적절하다.

05 컴퓨터가 수리되는 것으로 목적어가 목적격 보어의 동작을 당하는 대상으로 수동의 의미이므로 과거분사 fixed가 적절하다.

06 (A)에는 'It ~ that ...' 강조 구문으로 that이 적절하고, (B) 과거의 일이므로 과거분사가 적절하다.

07 <보기>와 ③번은 강조 용법의 that이다. ① 지시대명사 [앞서 말한 명사의 반복을 피하기 위해] (~의) 그것. 코브라의 독은 방울뱀의 그것보다 더 치명적이다. ② 지시부사. [수량·정도를 나타내는 말을 한정하여] 그만큼, 그렇게, 그 정도로. 정말 그녀가 그렇게 젊다는 거냐? ③ 급소를 찌른 것은 바로 그 질문이었다. ④ 지시형용사. 그, 저; 또 다른. 우리는 그 일에 대하여 이렇게도 저렇게도 논의했다. ⑤ 접속사. [판단의 표준] ~이리니, ~하다니. 그런 짓을 하다니 미쳤나?

08 신발이 닦이는 것(목적어가 목적격 보어의 동작을 당하는 대상으로 수동의 의미)이므로 ⓔ의 clean은 과거분사 cleaned로 고치는 것이 적절하다.

09 'It ~ that ...' 강조 구문은 강조하고자 하는 부분을 'It is/was'와 that 사이에 넣고, 나머지 부분을 that 뒤에 쓴다.

10 get이 'get+목적어+과거분사'의 형태로 쓰여 have와 같은 의미를 갖는다.

11 'It ~ that ...' 강조 구문에서 강조하는 대상이 사람인 경우 that 대신에 who(주어)나 whom(목적어)을 쓸 수 있다.

12 탁자가 만들어지는 것(목적어가 목적격 보어의 동작을 당하는 대상으로 수동의 의미)이므로 make를 made로 고치는 것이 적절하다.

13 ①번은 'It: 가주어, that절: 진주어'이고 나머지는 모두 'It ~ that ...' 강조 구문으로 쓰였다.

14 '컴퓨터를 사도록 요청했다'는 말을 '컴퓨터를 사도록 시켰다'는 말로 쓸 수 있고, '컴퓨터를 고치도록 요청했다'는 말은 '컴퓨터가 고쳐지도록 했다'는 말로 쓸 수 있다. 보통 'have+사람+동사원형', 'have[get]+사물+과거분사'의 형태로 쓰인다.

15 ③번은 과거완료에 쓰인 과거분사이지만 <보기>와 나머지는 모두 'have+목적어+목적격보어'에서 수동의 의미로 쓰인 과거분사이다.

16 (1) 책이 인쇄되는 것이므로 과거분사가 적절하다. (2) get이 'get+목적어+to부정사'나 'get+목적어+과거분사'의 형태로 쓰여 have와 같은 의미를 가지므로 'dress'를 'to dress'로 고치는 것이 적절하다. (3) 강조하는 것이 'the price'이므로 who를 that이나 which로 고치는 것이 적절하다. (4) 강조하는 것이 'when they are heated'이므로 which를 that으로 고치는 것이 적절하다. (5) that 다음에 완전한 절이 나오므로 'the theater'를 강조하는 것이 아니라 'at[in] the theater'로 장소의 부사구를 강조하는 것으로 고치는 것이 적절하다.

17 강조하는 것이 '별똥별'이므로 'a shooting star'를 'It was'와 'that' 사이에 넣고 'Jenny saw at the park yesterday'를 that 뒤에 쓴다. 강조하는 것이 사물이므로 that 대신에 which를 쓸 수 있다.

---

01 (1) have the food prepared
  (2) got Harry to hand in his report
  (3) forced Nick to repair

02 (1) It was at the party that Romeo first met Juliet.
  (2) It was his notebook which I borrowed.
  (3) Jim was surprised that Della had her hair cut.
  (4) She needs to have the car washed.

03 (1) Tom made his son have his eyes checked.
  (2) He got his brother to do his homework for him.
  (3) It was pizza that[which] Jake ate at a cafe.
  (4) It is at[in] the restaurant that I'll have dinner with you this evening.
  (5) He read the letter more carefully again.

04 (1) had the dragon take
  (2) It was Steve Jobs who

05 (1) designed by Zaha Hadid
  (2) have them delivered to their homes

06 (1) It was Matthew who met Jake at the park last weekend.
  (2) Matthew did meet Jake at the park last weekend.
  (3) It was Jake who[whom] Matthew met at the park last weekend.
  (4) It was at the park where Matthew met Jake last weekend.
  (5) It was last weekend when Matthew met Jake at the park.

07 (1) It was last week that[when] they started a swimming class.
  (2) It was Mary and Mike that[who] danced hard to be a mascot.
  (3) It was the vase that[which] Robin broke yesterday.
  (4) Was it him that[who/whom] his sister taught how to play the guitar?

---

01 'have+목적어+목적격보어'의 형태로 목적어가 목적격 보어의 동작을 당하는 대상(주로 사물)이면 과거분사를 사용하고, 목적어가 목적격 보어의 동작을 하는 주체(주로 사람)면 동사원형을 사용한다. get이 'get+목적어+to부정사'나 'get+목적어+과거분사'의 형태로 쓰여 have와 같은 의미를 갖는다. (1) 'have+목적어+과거분사', (2) 'get+목적어+to부정사', (3) 'force+목적어+to부정사'를 쓰는 것이 적절하다.

02 (1) 장소(at the party)를 강조하는 'It ~ that ...' 강조 구문을 이용한다. (2) 사물(his notebook)을 강조하는 'It ~ that ...' 강조 구문을 이용한다. (3) 머리카락이 잘리는 것이므로 과거분사로 나

17

타낸다. (4) 차가 세차되는 것이므로 과거분사로 나타낸다.

03 (1) 눈이 검사하는 것이 아니라 검사를 받는 것이므로(목적어가 목적격 보어의 동작을 당하는 대상) 과거분사가 적절하다. (2) get이 'get+목적어+to부정사'나 'get+목적어+과거분사'의 형태로 쓰여 have와 같은 의미를 갖는다. 목적어가 목적격 보어의 동작을 하는 주체일 경우 to부정사를 쓴다. (3) 강조하는 것이 'pizza'이므로 who를 that이나 which로 고치는 것이 적절하다. (4) that 뒤에 완전한 절이 이어지므로 'the restaurant'을 강조하는 것이 아니라 'at the restaurant'으로 장소의 부사구를 강조하는 것으로 고치는 것이 적절하다. (5) 'It ~ that …' 강조 구문은 동사나 양태부사를 강조하는 데 쓰이지 않는다.

04 (1) 용이 공주를 태워 날고 있으므로(목적어가 목적격 보어의 동작을 하는 주체) 'have+목적어+동사원형'을 이용한다. (2) 주어 'Steve Jobs'를 강조하는 'It ~ that …' 강조 용법을 이용한다. 강조 대상이 사람이므로 who를 사용할 수 있다.

05 'have+목적어+목적격보어'의 형태로 목적어가 목적격 보어의 동작을 당하는 대상(주로 사물)이므로 과거분사를 사용 한다.

06 과거시제이므로 강조하고자 하는 부분을 It was와 that 사이에 넣고, 나머지 부분을 that 뒤에 쓴다. 이때 that을 사용하지 말라고 하였으므로, that 대신에 강조하고자 하는 것이 사람이면 who(주격/목적격) 또는 whom(목적격), 사물이면 which, 장소일 경우 where, 시간일 경우 when을 사용한다. 또한 'It is[was] ~ that …' 구문은 동사를 강조할 수 없으므로 동사는 동사의 원형 앞에 do/does/did를 사용하여 강조한다.

07 'It ~ that …' 강조 구문은 강조하고자 하는 부분을 'It is/was'와 that 사이에 넣고, 나머지 부분을 that 뒤에 쓴다. (4)번은 평서문으로 고친 후 강조 용법으로 쓰고 그것을 다시 의문문으로 바꾸면 쉽다.

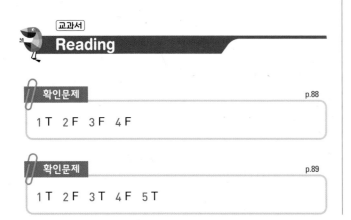

Reading

확인문제	p.88

1 T 2 F 3 F 4 F

확인문제	p.89

1 T 2 F 3 T 4 F 5 T

교과서 확인학습 A p.90~91

01 had two sons
02 passed away, called, to give them, last words of advice
03 Listen carefully, Live by, throughout your life
04 Build, every city, comfortably. Enjoy, Lastly, like
05 explain himself, passed away
06 his death, their share of, wealth, settled in
07 who had been following, no money left
08 was richer than ever
09 was puzzled about where, had gone wrong, to find out
10 welcomed, with open arms
11 sat down to chat, that had been on his mind
12 It was, that, in every city
13 always stay there, had, looked after
14 sleep comfortably, enjoy, had, designed, my meals prepared by
15 told, to spend like, what I wanted, worrying
16 look at me, empty-handed
17 not follow, father's wisdom
18 how did, get, rich
19 smiled, also followed, father's wisdom
20 it a bit differently
21 build, took it as having a place to stay
22 made friends, stayed at, those cities
23 comfortably, because, if I was sleeping, or
24 only when I was hungry, tasted great
25 like a rich man, continued
26 how to make money grow
27 on, that, bring me back, rather than on
28 it was, that, tried to explain
29 how foolish he had been
30 With, in mind

교과서 확인학습 B p.92~93

1 A rich and wise father had two sons, Puru and Puneet.
2 Before he passed away, he called his two sons to give them some last words of advice.
3 "Listen carefully, my dear sons. Live by these words throughout your life, and you will be happy," he said.
4 "Build a house in every city. Sleep comfortably. Enjoy your food. Lastly, spend money like a rich man... ."

5 Before he could explain himself, he passed away.

6 After his death, the two sons took their share of the father's wealth and settled in different cities.

7 Five years passed. Puru, who had been following his father's words carefully, had no money left.

8 But his brother was richer than ever.

9 Puru was puzzled about where he had gone wrong, so he visited Puneet to find out.

10 Puneet welcomed Puru with open arms.

11 That night, when the brothers sat down to chat after dinner, Puru asked the question that had been on his mind for days.

12 "It was our father's advice that I followed, but I am not happy. I built a house in every city.

13 But because I could not always stay there, I hired people and had the house looked after.

14 Father said we should sleep comfortably and enjoy our food, so I had my bed designed by experts and my meals prepared by a great chef.

15 He told us to spend like a rich man, so I bought what I wanted without worrying about money.

16 But look at me now! I am empty-handed.

17 Did you not follow our father's wisdom?

18 Tell me, brother, how did you get so rich?"

19 Puneet smiled and said, "My dear brother, I also followed our father's wisdom.

20 But I understood it a bit differently.

21 When he said 'build a house in every city,' I took it as having a place to stay all around the world.

22 So I made friends in every city and I stayed at their houses when I visited those cities.

23 Also, I slept comfortably each night because I would be tired after a hard day's work, and it did not matter if I was sleeping on a bed or on the hard floor.

24 I ate only when I was hungry, so even a simple meal tasted great."

25 "Spend money like a rich man?" continued Puneet.

26 "A rich man knows how to make money grow.

27 So, I tried to spend money on something that would bring me back more money rather than on luxurious things.

28 For me, it was this wisdom that our father tried to explain."

29 Now Puru realized how foolish he had been.

30 With this wisdom in mind, Puru started a new life.

---

01 ③　　　　02 death
03 They were Puru and Puneet.　　　　04 ⑤
05 He followed his father's advice.
06 ④　　　07 ④　　　08 ⑤　　　09 ③
10 ③
11 Because he ate only when he was hungry.
12 He stayed at his friends' houses when he visited cities all around the world.
13 ④　　　14 ③
15 He had no money left.　　16 ②
17 prepared　18 ⑤
19 He built a house in every city.
20 ③　　　21 ②　　　22 ②　　　23 ④
24 differently　25 ③

01 (A)에는 전치사 by가 들어간다. ① take part in: ~에 참여하다 ② consist of: ~으로 구성되다 ③ go by: (시간이) 흐르다 ④ be different from: ~와 다르다 ⑤ similar to: ~와 비슷한

02 '삶의 끝'은 '죽음(death)'을 의미한다.

03 두 아들의 이름은 Puru와 Puneet이라고 하였다.

04 부유하고 지혜로운 아버지는 죽어가고 있을 때 두 아들에게 마지막 충고의 말을 남겼다.

05 Puru는 아버지의 조언을 따랐지만 행복하지 않았다고 하였다.

06 위 글에 따르면 아버지의 조언은 '모든 도시에 집을 짓는 것, 편안하게 자는 것, 음식을 즐기는 것, 부자처럼 돈을 쓰라는 것'이므로 ④번이 아버지의 조언에 해당한다. take pleasure in: ~을 즐기다, 좋아하다

07 집은 돌보아지는 대상이므로 목적어와 수동의 관계에 있다. 따라서 과거분사 'looked after'라고 쓰는 것이 적절하다.

08 Puru는 돈 걱정을 하지 않고 원하는 것을 샀다.

09 부자들은 돈을 불리는 방법을 알고 있으므로 사치스러운 물건에 돈을 쓰는 것보다는 자신에게 더 많은 돈을 돌려줄 수 있는 것에 돈을 쓰려고 노력했다는 말이 들어가는 것이 적절하다.

10 '게다가, 또한'이라는 의미이므로 ③번이 가장 적절하다.

11 Puneet은 배고플 때만 먹었기 때문에 소박한 식사마저도 훌륭한 맛이 났다고 하였다.

12 Puneet은 전세계의 도시에서 친구를 사귀었고 그 도시들을 방문했을 때 그들의 집에 머물렀다고 하였다.

13 Puru가 당황한 이유는 자신에게는 남은 돈이 없었던 반면 그의 동생은 그 어느 때보다 더 부자가 되어 있었기 때문이었다. 따라서 ④번에 들어가는 것이 가장 적절하다.

14 Puru에게는 남은 돈이 없었지만 Puneet은 그 어느 때보다 더 부자가 되었다는 말에 그는 자신의 동생을 방문했다는 말로 끝나고 있으므로 ③번이 가장 적절하다. stop by: ~에 들르다

15 5년 후 Puru에게 남은 돈이 없었다.

16 밑줄 친 (A)는 재귀대명사의 재귀 용법으로, 주어와 목적어가 같을 때 쓰인다. 모두 재귀 용법으로 쓰였지만 ②번은 강조 용법으로 쓰인 재귀대명사이다.

17 사역동사 have의 목적격보어 자리로, 목적어 my meals와 수동의 관계에 있으므로 과거분사를 쓰는 것이 적절하다.

18 Puneet은 Puru를 두 팔 벌려 환영했다는 의미이므로 ⑤번이 가장 적절하다. reluctantly: 마지못해서

19 Puru는 모든 도시에 집을 지었다고 하였다.

20 Puru는 자신이 아버지의 조언을 따랐지만 빈털터리가 되었다고 말하며 동생 Puneet에게 어떻게 그렇게 부자가 되었느냐고 묻고 있으므로 이어질 내용으로는 ③번이 가장 적절하다.

21 on something과 병렬 관계로 연결이 이루어져야 하므로 ②번이 적절하다. spend+시간/돈+on A: A에 시간이나 돈을 쓰다

22 밑줄 친 내용으로 미루어 보아 두 형제의 아버지는 편안하게 잠자라는 말을 남겼음을 유추할 수 있다.

23 동생의 말을 들은 Puru는 그의 지혜를 마음에 새기고 새로운 삶을 시작했다고 하였다.

24 Puru와 달리 Puneet은 아버지의 지혜를 조금 다르게 이해했다고 하였다.

25 Puneet은 '모든 도시에 집을 지어라'라는 아버지의 말씀을 전 세계에 머물 수 있는 장소를 가지라는 말로 이해하여 모든 도시에서 친구를 사귀고 그 도시들을 방문할 때 그들의 집에 머물렀다고 하였다.

서술형 시험대비 p.98~99

01 It was because he wanted to give them some last words of advice.

02 He had been following his father's words carefully.

03 If you live by these words throughout your life, you will be happy.

04 Puru, Puneet

05 The two sons took their share of the father's wealth and settled in different cities.

06 knows how to make money grow

07 A simple meal tasted great to him because he ate only when he was hungry.

08 He tried to spend money on something that would bring him back more money rather than on luxurious things.

09 brother → father, poor → rich

10 It was because he worked hard all day.

11 He realized how foolish he had been.

12 Puru가 모든 도시에 지은 집에서

13 had the house looked after

14 Their father told them to spend like a rich man.

15 (A) Although   (B) unhappy   (C) broke

01 아버지는 죽기 전에 그의 두 아들을 부른 이유는 그들에게 마지막 충고의 말을 하기 위해서였다.

02 Puru는 아버지가 돌아가신 이후로 아버지의 말을 신중히 따랐다고 하였다.

03 '명령문, and …'는 '~해라. 그러면 …'이라는 의미이므로 명령문을 'If 조건절'로 바꾸고 and를 생략하여 같은 의미의 문장을 쓸 수 있다.

04 Puru와 달리 Puneet은 그 어느 때보다 더 부자가 되었다고 하였다.

05 아버지가 돌아가신 후, 두 아들은 아버지의 재산 중 자신들의 몫을 가지고 다른 도시에 정착했다.

06 사역동사 make는 목적격보어로 동사원형을 취하며, '의문사+to부정사'는 명사구 역할을 한다.

07 Puneet은 배고플 때만 먹었기 때문에 소박한 식사마저도 훌륭한 맛이 났다고 하였다.

08 Puneet는 사치스러운 물건에 돈을 쓰는 것보다는 자신에게 더 많은 돈을 돌려줄 수 있는 것에 돈을 쓰려고 노력했다.

09 글의 내용에 따르면 형제에게 조언의 말을 남긴 사람은 그들의 아버지이며, Puneet은 아버지의 말을 그의 형과 달리 해석하여 부자가 되었다.

10 Puneet이 잠자리를 가리지 않은 이유는 하루 종일 열심히 일했기 때문이었다.

11 Puru는 자신이 얼마나 어리석었는지를 깨달았다고 하였다.

12 Puru는 아버지의 조언대로 모든 도시에 집을 지었지만 그곳에 항상 머물 수 없었다는 의미이다.

13 집은 돌보아지는 대상이므로 사역동사 have의 목적격보어로 과거분사 looked after를 쓰는 것에 유의한다.

14 형제의 아버지는 그들에게 부자처럼 돈을 쓰라고 말하였다.

15 해석: Puru는 아버지의 조언을 따랐지만, 그는 불행한 삶을 살았고 무일푼이 되었다.

영역별 핵심문제 p.101~105

01 ①   02 deserted   03 ③   04 ④
05 ④   06 ②   07 ⑤
08 what would you do if you could time travel?
09 ②   10 character   11 ⑤   12 ②

13 ⑤　　　14 ④

15 at the cafe where Jane is reading

16 ⓐ, ⓓ, ⑨

17 Tom had Rene pick up his mom at the airport for him.

18 ①, ②　　　19 ①

20 have the writing contest held

21 ⑤　　　22 ①　　　23 luxurious

24 It did not matter if he was sleeping on a bed or on the hard floor.

25 It is because failure is also a good experience.

26 ③　　　27 (C)–(B)–(A)　　　28 ②

29 ④　　　30 ③

01 priceless: 대단히 귀중한, 값을 매길 수 없는

02 deserted island: 무인도 / 그는 10년 동안 혼자서 이 무인도에 살았다.

03 run out of: ~이 없어지다, 다 떨어지다 / 우리 종이가 다 떨어져 간다. 오늘 쓸 만큼은 충분히 있는 것 같습니까?

04 pass away: 세상을 떠나다, 돌아가시다

05 주어진 문장에서 it은 <시간 여행자의 아내>라는 영화이다. too는 '역시'이므로 여자가 그 영화를 가장 좋아하는 로맨스 영화 중 하나라고 말한 것에 대해 자신도 또한 아주 좋아했다는 말이 들어가야 알맞다.

06 review: 후기, 보고서

07 <시간 여행자의 아내>라는 영화에 대해서 가장 좋아하는 로맨스 영화 중 하나라고 언급하였지 어떤 종류의 영화를 좋아하는지에 대해서는 말하지 않았다.

08 '만약 ~라면 어떻게 하겠니?'라고 실제가 아닌 상황이나 사실을 가정하여 물어볼 때는 가정법 과거를 이용하여 'What would you do if you+과거시제 ~?'로 표현한다.

09 ⓐ How ⓑ ran, run out of: ~이 없어지다, 다 떨어지다 ⓒ were, 'What would you do if you+과거시제 ~?: 만약 ~라면 어떻게 하겠니?(실제가 아닌 상황이나 사실을 가정) ⓓ read ⓔ if, if: ~인지 아닌지

10 character: 등장인물 / 영화나 연극 혹은 이야기 속에 나오는 사람

11 ① 사람들의 생각을 읽을 수 있다. ② 마감이 다가오는데 아이디어가 다 떨어졌다. ③ 도와준다. ④ 이야기의 마감은 이번 주말이다. ⑤ 남자가 사람들의 마음을 읽을 수 있다면 좋아하는 여자아이가 나를 좋아하는지 알아보고 싶다고 말했다.

12 (B) 남자가 여자에게 <트리갭의 샘물>이라는 책을 읽어봤는지를 물어보자 (C) 읽어봤다고 대답하며 그 책의 내용에 대해 말한다. (A) 여자가 말한 책의 내용이 맞다고 대답하면서, 영원히

살게 된다면 무엇을 할지 질문을 하자 (D) 전 세계의 다양한 도시에서 살고 싶다고 대답한다.

13 'It ~ that ...' 강조 구문에서 강조하는 대상이 장소의 부사(구/절)일 경우, that 대신에 where로 바꿔 쓸 수 있다.

14 Dad had me return home as it was very late at night. 내가 돌아오는 '능동'의 의미이므로 동사원형으로 써야 한다.

15 The cafe is the place at which Jane is reading a comic book.을 'at the cafe'를 강조하며 쓰면 It is at the cafe where Jane is reading a comic book 이 된다.

16 ⓑ plant → planted ⓒ come → to come ⓔ when → that[where], steal → stolen ⓕ which → that[where]

17 Rene가 모셔오는(pick up) 것이므로 'have+목적어+동사원형'을 이용하여 영작한다.

18 ① I had my bed designed by experts and my meals prepared by a great chef. ② It was on the stage that BTS performed their first show.

19 'It ~ that ...' 강조 구문은 강조하고자 하는 부분을 'It is [was]'와 that 사이에 넣고, 나머지 부분을 that 뒤에 쓴다.

20 the writing contest가 개최되는(수동) 것이므로 'have+목적어+과거분사'를 이용한다.

21 사역동사 make는 동사원형을 목적격보어로 취한다. 따라서 grow라고 쓰는 것이 적절하다.

22 With this wisdom in mind: 이 지혜를 명심하고

23 특히 아주 비싼 것을 포함하여 매우 편안하거나 우아한 것은 '사치스러운, 호화스러운(luxurious)'이다.

24 Puneet은 하루 종일 열심히 일하고 나서 피곤해지곤 했기 때문에 침대에서 자든 딱딱한 바닥에서 자든 상관없었다고 하였다.

25 실패 역시 좋은 경험이기 때문에 글쓴이는 두려움 없이 무언가를 하려고 한다.

26 글쓴이는 나쁜 킥조차도 자신을 더 좋은 키커로 만들어 주었다는 것을 배웠다고 하였다.

27 (C) 아버지의 조언을 따라 모든 도시에 집을 지음. (B) 그곳에 항상 머물 수 없기 때문에 사람을 고용함. (A) 아버지의 또 다른 조언을 지켰지만 지금 빈털터리가 되었음을 말하며 Puneet이 어떻게 부자가 되었는지 물어봄.

28 동생 Puneet에게 어떻게 그렇게 부자가 되었는지를 묻는 말로 끝나고 있으므로 ②번이 가장 적절하다.

29 Puru는 모든 도시에 집을 지었다고 하였으므로 그의 집은 모든 도시에서 발견될 수 있었다고 말하는 것이 적절하다.

30 밑줄 친 ⓑ는 전치사 without의 목적어로 쓰인 동명사이다. 모두 동명사이지만 ③번은 진행 시제를 나타내는 현재분사이다.

01 ex   02 (r)eward

03 ③   04 ④   05 ③   06 would

07 ④   08 ①

09 would go to the Joseon Dynasty and meet King Sejong

10 in

11 Don't worry about something you can't change.

12 ④   13 ④   14 ②

15 (1) My dad has his car washed once a month.

    (2) Mom had a robot vacuum cleaner clean the floor.

    (3) Jane got Richard to guess her age when she first met him.

    (4) It was at[in] the restaurant that[where] Angelina had dinner with her friends.

    (5) It was a knife that[which] I forgot to bring to the cooking class.

16 that[who] had the table decorated   17 ②

18 Puneet was richer than Puru.   19 ⑤

20 He felt puzzled.   21 ③

22 our father's wisdom   23 ④   23 ②

---

01 특정 어근 앞에 'ex-'를 붙이면 '밖으로'라는 의미를 더한다. ex-+plain → explain 설명하다 ex-+hibit → exhibit 전시하다 ex-+press→ express 표현하다

02 '좋은 행동이나 업적 등의 대가로 주어지는 어떤 것'은 보상(reward)이다. 그들은 그가 열심히 일한 것에 대한 보상을 주었다.

03 (A) from head to toe: 머리에서 발끝까지 / 추워서 이불을 머리부터 발까지 담요를 뒤집어쓰고 잤다. (B) look after: ~을 살피다, 돌보다 / 하루 종일 3명의 아이들을 돌보는 것은 힘든 일이다.

04 lastly: 마지막으로, 끝으로 / 끝으로, 당신의 미래 계획에 대해 묻고 싶습니다.

05 ⓒ lives→lived, that은 주격 관계대명사이고, that 이하가 a family를 수식하고 있다. drank와 lived는 접속사 and로 연결되어 병렬 구문을 이루고 있다.

06 '만약 ~라면 어떻게 하겠니?'라고 실제가 아닌 상황이나 사실을 가정하여 물어볼 때는 가정법 과거를 이용하여 'What would you do if you+과거시제 ~?'로 표현한다. 대답으로는 '나는 `할 거야.'라는 의미로 'I would 동사원형 ~.'형태의 가정법 과거를 사용하여 대답한다.

07 현재 사실과 반대되는 상황이나 일에 대해 가정하거나 현재 사실에 대한 후회나 아쉬움을 강조할 때, 가정법 과거를 쓴다. 즉,

현재 사실과 반대이므로, 과거 시제를 쓴다. 조건절은 'if 주어+동사의 과거형'으로, 주절은 '주어+would+동사원형 ~'을 쓴다. 이때 해석은 '~라면 …할 텐데.' 라고 해석한다.

08 prevent: 예방하다 ② 표현하다 ③ 허락하다 ④ 얻다, 획득하다 ⑤ 전시하다

09 'What would you do if you+과거시제 ~?'에 대한 대답으로 '나는 `할 거야.'라는 의미로 'I would 동사원형 ~.'형태의 가정법 과거를 사용하여 대답한다.

10 believe in 사람: ~을[~의 능력을] 믿다

11 상대방을 안심시키는 표현으로는 'Don't worry about ~.(~에 대해 걱정하지 마.)'이라는 말을 쓸 수 있다. something과 you can't change 사이에 목적격 관계대명사 that이 생략되어 있다.

12 have+목적어+동사원형: 목적어가 ~하게 만들다

13 It was at the amusement park that Minsu rode the roller coaster.

14 첫 번째 문장에서는 저녁이 준비되는 것이므로 과거분사 prepared가 적절하다. 두 번째 문장에서는 'It ~ that ...' 강조 구문에서 강조하는 대상이 시간의 부사 yesterday이므로 that이나 when이 적절하다.

15 (1) 'have+목적어+목적격보어'의 형태로 목적어가 목적격보어의 동작을 당하는 대상(주로 사물)이면 과거분사를 사용한다. (2) 'have+목적어+목적격보어'의 형태로 목적어가 목적격보어의 동작을 하는 주체(주로 사람)면 동사원형을 사용한다. (3) get이 'get+목적어+to부정사'나 'get+목적어+과거분사'의 형태로 쓰여 have와 같은 의미를 갖는다. (4) that 뒤에 완전한 절이 나오므로 'at the restaurant'을 강조하는 것이 되어야 한다. which를 that이나 where로 써야 한다. (5) 강조하는 것이 'a knife'이므로 that이나 which로 써야 한다.

16 'It ~ that ...' 강조 구문에서 강조하는 대상이 the princess로 사람이므로 that이나 who를 쓰고, the table이 장식되는(수동) 것이므로 'have+목적어+과거분사'를 이용한다.

17 live on은 '~을 먹고 살다'라는 의미이다. live by: (신조, 원칙 등)에 따라 살다

18 5년 후 Puneet이 Puru보다 더 부자가 되어 있었다.

19 Puru는 아버지의 말을 신중히 따랐다고 하였으므로 ⑤번이 글의 내용과 일치한다. stick to: 굳게 고수하다

20 Puru는 자신과 달리 동생이 부자가 되었음을 알고 당황하였다.

21 주어진 문장은 ③번 앞 문장의 결과이므로 ③번에 들어가는 것이 가장 적절하다.

22 앞 문장의 '우리 아버지의 지혜'를 가리키는 말이다.

23 밑줄 친 (B)는 to부정사의 형용사적 용법으로, 앞선 명사 a place를 수식하고 있다. ① 부사적 용법 중 목적 ② 명사적 용법 중 목적격보어 ③ 명사적 용법 중 진주어 ④ 형용사적 용법 ⑤ 부사적 용법 중 감정의 원인

24 밑줄 친 (C)는 '이 지혜를 마음에 새기고'라는 의미이다. bear in mind: 명심하다, 마음에 새기다

서술형 실전문제   p.110~111

01 What would you do if you were him?

02 ③ easy → difficult

03 look

04 (1) Why don't you have the groceries delivered to your home?

(2) The students got their classroom painted.

(3) It was Matt that[who] had coffee at the office this morning.

05 They sat down to chat after dinner.

06 He took it as making many friends living in different places.

07 (1) built a house / made friends

(2) my bed designed by / tired, a hard day's work

(3) my meals prepared / I was hungry

08 He told us to spend money like a rich man

09 introduce

10 It means "Go and do things without fear because failure is also a good experience."

01 '만약 ~라면 어떻게 하겠니?'라고 실제가 아닌 상황이나 사실을 가정하여 물어볼 때는 가정법 과거를 이용하여 'What would you do if you+과거시제 ~?'로 표현한다.

02 'be worried (that) 주어+동사'는 '(주어)가 ~인 것이 걱정이다.'라는 의미로 걱정을 표현할 때 사용하는 표현이다. 글쓰기 대회의 주제가 나에게 너무 쉬울까봐 걱정이라는 말은 어색하다.

03 take care of = look after: ~을 돌보다

04 (1) 'have+목적어+목적격보어'의 형태로 목적어가 목적격보어의 동작을 당하는 대상(주로 사물)이면 과거분사를 사용한다. (2) get은 'get+목적어+과거분사'의 형태로 쓰여 have와 같은 의미를 갖는다. (3) 'It ~ that ...' 강조 구문에서 강조하고자 하는 것이 'Matt'로 사람이므로 which를 that이나 who로 고치는 것이 적절하다.

05 저녁 식사 후 두 형제는 이야기를 하려고 앉았다고 하였다.

06 Puneet은 모든 도시에 집을 지으라는 아버지의 조언을 여러 도

시에 살고 있는 많은 친구를 만들라는 말로 받아들였다.

07 모든 도시에 집을 지으라는 아버지의 유언에 Puru는 말 그대로 모든 도시에 집을 지었고, Puneet은 모든 도시에 친구들을 만들었다. 편안하게 잠을 자라는 아버지의 유언에 Puru는 전문가가 자신의 침대를 설계하게 하였고, Puneet은 하루 종일 열심히 일하고 나서 피곤해졌기 때문에 매일 밤 편안하히 잠을 잤다. 마지막으로 Puru는 훌륭한 요리사가 음식을 준비하게 하여 음식을 즐겼지만, Puneet은 배가 고플 때만 음식을 먹었다고 하였다.

08 tell은 목적격보어로 to부정사를 취하는 동사이다.

09 사역동사 let은 목적격보어로 동사원형을 취한다.

10 "Go for it!"은 "실패도 역시 좋은 경험이므로 두려움 없이 해라"라는 의미라고 하였다.

창의사고력 서술형 문제   p.112

|모범답안|

01 A: I would catch criminals and bring them to the police. / I would go to the food court and eat rare food.

02 (1) She had her ears checked.

(2) They had the Opera House in Sydney designed by Jørn Utzon.
They had Jørn Utzon design the Opera House in Sydney.

(3) Mom had me play a computer game after dinner.
Mom had a computer game played by me after dinner.

03 No Pain, No Gain! Without hard work, you can get nothing as a reward., I was a kicker in the school soccer team, even the bad kicks made me a better kicker at the end

02 'have+목적어+목적격보어'의 형태로 목적어가 목적격보어의 동작을 당하는 대상(주로 사물)이면 과거분사를 사용하고, 목적어가 목적격보어의 동작을 하는 주체(주로 사람)면 동사원형을 사용한다.

단원별 모의고사   p.113~116

01 ①   02 ④   03 take

04 (l)uxurious   05 ⑤

06 Don't worry about making mistakes.

07 What would you do if you had a magic carpet?

08 (A) that   (B) character   (C) if   (D) yourself

09 (1) Don't worry about it.　(2) Don't let it bother you.

10 ③　　　11 ①　　　12 take care　13 ⑤

14 ①, ③, ④, ⑥

15 (1) It was many bugs that[which] were in the bottle.

　(2) It was at the concert that[where] I saw her.

　(3) This morning I had my watch that I had bought last month repaired.

　(4) I'll help you so that you can have your homework finished before the movie starts.

16 have it returned　　　17 ③　　　18 ⑤

19 ④

20 He had his meals prepared by a great chef in order to enjoy his food.　21 ③

22 ②　　　23 ④

24 Because he wanted to find out where he had gone wrong.

25 They took their share of the father's wealth and settled in different cities.

26 ⑤

01 ①은 동의어, 나머지 보기들은 반의어 관계이다. ① puzzled: 당혹스러운, 어리둥절한 confused: 혼란스러운 ② hire: 고용하다 fire: 해고하다 ③ priceless: 대단히 귀중한, 값을 매길 수 없는 worthless: 가치 없는, 보잘 것 없는 ④ death: 죽음 life: 삶, 인생, 생명 ⑤ lastly: 마지막으로, 끝으로 firstly: 첫째로

02 believe in 사람: ~을[~의 능력을] 믿다

03 take ~ for a walk: ~를 산책하러 데리고 가다 / 나는 개를 산책하러 데리고 나갈 것이다. take care of: 돌보다 / 그는 스스로를 돌볼 만큼 나이가 들었다. take one's share: 자기 몫을 취하다, 차지하다 / 그는 단지 그의 몫을 차지하려고 했었다.

04 luxurious: 사치스러운, 호화로운 / 매우 편안하고 비용이 많이 드는

05 ⓐ worried ⓑ got ⓒ singing ⓓ making ⓔ learn

06 상대방을 안심시키는 표현으로는 'Don't worry about ~.(~에 대해 걱정하지 마.)'이라는 말을 쓸 수 있다. make a mistake: 실수하다

07 '만약 ~라면 어떻게 하겠니?'라고 실제가 아닌 상황이나 사실을 가정하여 물어볼 때는 가정법 과거를 이용하여 'What would you do if you+과거시제 ~?'로 표현한다.

08 (A) be worried (that) 주어+동사'는 '(주어)가 ~인 것이 걱정이다.'라는 의미로 걱정을 표현할 때 사용하는 표현이다. (B) character: 등장인물 (C) 실제로는 일어나기 어려운 상황을 가정하거나 상상하여 물을 때 'If you+동사의 과거형 ~, what

would you+동사원형 ~?'의 형태인 가정법 과거를 사용하여 현재 사실과 반대되는 것을 말할 수 있다. (D) 주어와 목적어가 같을 경우에 재귀대명사를 사용해야 하므로 yourself가 들어가야 적절하다

09 상대방을 안심시키는 표현으로는 'Don't worry about ~.'이라는 말을 쓸 수 있다. 이와 같은 표현으로는 'Don't let ~ bother you.(~에 대해 너무 신경 쓰지 마.)'가 있다.

10 부산으로 여행을 가야 하는데 Lucy에게 먹이를 줄 사람을 찾을 수 없다는 남자의 말에, 여자가 걱정하지 말라고 말하면서 개를 돌봐 준다고 말하는 것이 어울린다.

11 여행을 가지만 Lucy에게 먹이를 줄 사람을 아무도 찾을 수가 없다는 말이 어울리므로 '하지만'의 의미를 가지고 있는 접속사 but이 적절하다.

12 take care of: ~을 돌보다

13 suppose: 추측하다, 추정하다

14 ② How about having your pet cleaned from head to toe? ⑤ It was in the street that[where] I saw Jane this morning. ⑦ It was a cat that[which] went to save the princess.

15 (1) 'many bugs'를 강조하므로 where가 아니라 that이나 which를 써야 한다. (2) 접속사 없이 동사가 2개가 나온 형태이므로 'It ~ that ...' 강조 구문의 that이나 where를 넣어 주는 것이 적절하다. (3) 시계가 수리되는 것이므로 과거분사로 쓰는 것이 적절하다. (4) 숙제가 무엇인가를 끝내는 것이 아니라 끝내지는 것이므로 과거분사로 쓰는 것이 적절하다.

16 'have+목적어+목적격보어'의 형태로 목적어가 목적격보어의 동작을 당하는 대상(주로 사물)이면 과거분사를 사용한다.

17 It was at the park that[where] I met Tim last Sunday. that 뒤에 나오는 절이 완전하므로 'at the park'를 강조하는 문장으로 쓴다.

18 빈칸 (A)에는 관계대명사 what이 들어간다. ①, ③, ④ 명사절 접속사 that, ② 관계대명사 that, ⑤ 관계대명사 what

19 ④ 부자처럼 돈을 쓰라는 말에 '돈 걱정을 하지 않고' 돈을 썼다고 말하는 것이 자연스럽다. 따라서 without이라고 쓰는 것이 적절하다.

20 Puru는 음식을 즐기기 위해 훌륭한 요리사에 의해 자신의 식사가 준비되도록 하였다.

21 Puru가 전문가를 고용한 이유는 자신의 침대를 설계하기 위해서였다.

22 'explain oneself'는 '심중을 털어놓다'는 의미로, 아버지가 자

24 정답 및 해설

신이 전해준 조언의 말들이 실제로 어떤 의미가 있는지를 말해 준다는 의미이다.

23 아버지의 마지막 조언의 말은 두 아들들이 행복한 삶을 사는 데에 도움이 되는 말이었지만 두 형제는 대조되는 삶을 살았다.

24 Puru는 자신과 달리 동생이 부자가 되었음을 알고, 자신이 어디서 잘못했는지를 알아내기 위해 Puneet을 방문하였다.

25 아버지의 죽음 이후 두 형제는 아버지의 재산 중 자신들의 몫을 가지고 다른 도시에 정착하였다.

26 ⑤번의 he는 Puru를 가리키지만 나머지는 모두 A rich and wise father를 가리킨다.

Spend Wisely

01 ② 02 ① 03 When it comes to
04 ⑤ 05 ④ 06 ④ 07 ③

01 ②에서 en은 '안에'라는 'in'의 의미이다. en(= in)+close(닫다). 안에 넣고 닫다 → 둘러싸다, 동봉하다 ① en-+large → enlarge: 확대하다, 확장하다 ③ en-+able → enable: 가능케 하다 ④ en-+force → enforce: 집행하다, 강요하다 ⑤ en-+rich → enrich: 풍부하게 하다

02 replace: 바꾸다, 교체하다 / 우리는 이 양탄자를 곧 바꿔야 한다. ② 수리하다 ③ 제거하다 ④ 영향을 주다, 충격을 주다 ⑤ 지키다, 보호하다

03 when it comes to: ~에 관해서, ~에 대해 말하자면

04 consume: 소비하다, 소모하다 / 연료, 에너지, 혹은 시간을 특히 많은 양으로 쓰다, 또는 특히 어떤 것을 많이 먹고 마시다 ① 포함하다 ② 요구하다 ③ 유지하다 ④ 추정하다

05 <보기>는 동의어 관계이다. quality: 질, 품질, 특성, 자질 characteristic: 특질, 특징 ⓐ tight: 꽉 조이는 loose: 헐거운 ⓑ endanger: 위험에 빠뜨리다 save: 구하다 ⓒ effect: 결과, 효과 result: 결과, 성과 ⓓ replace: 바꾸다, 교체하다 substitute: 대신하다 ⓔ encourage: 부추기다, 조장하다 discourage: 낙담시키다

06 ① 그의 말은 위로하는 효과를 가지고 있었다. ② 아름다움의 개념을 정의하기는 어렵다. ③ 너의 의견은 많은 사람에게 영향을 줄 것이다. ④ allowance: 용돈 / 나는 부모님에게서 용돈을 받는다. ⑤ 그녀가 버스에 탔을 때, 그 버스는 거의 비어 있었다.

07 furthermore: 뿐만 아니라, 더욱이 / 그 셔츠는 예쁠 뿐만 아니라 싸다. ① 따라서, 그러므로 ② 그럼에도 불구하고 ④ 그러므로 ⑤ 똑같이, 비슷하게

01 com
02 (1) spending (2) next time (3) even though
(4) go window shopping
03 on
04 (1) with (2) In (3) for (4) at (5) As
05 (1) mention (2) compare (3) combine
(4) endangered

01 특정 어근 앞에 com-을 붙이면 '함께'라는 의미를 더한다. com-+parison → comparison: 비교 com-+promise → compromise: 타협(하다) com-+pose → compose: 구성하다

02 (1) record: 기록하다 spending: 지출, 소비 (2) the next time+주어+동사: 다음번에 ~할 때에 (3) even though: 비록 ~이지만 (4) go window shopping: 진열된 상품을 구경하고 다니다

03 on display: 진열된, 전시된 / 그림은 현재 뉴욕에 전시 중이다. on sale: 판매 중인 / 표는 매표소에서 판매하고 있다.

04 (1) go well with: ~와 잘 어울리다 / 나는 이 블라우스가 네가 입고 있는 치마와 잘 어울린다고 생각한다. (2) in comparison: 비교해 보면 / 그녀의 문제와 비교해 보면, 내 문제들은 사소해 보인다. (3) for a moment: 잠깐 / 너는 잠시 동안 숨을 참아야 한다. (4) at a glance: 한눈에, 즉시 / 나는 무슨 일이 일어났었는지 한눈에 알아챘다. (5) as such: 그렇게, 이와 같이 / 이와 같이 그는 인내력이 있는 인물이었다.

05 (1) mention: 언급하다, 말하다 / 내가 다음 달에 캐나다로 이사 간다고 말했니? (2) compare: 비교하다 / 너는 물건을 사기 전에 가격을 비교해야 한다. (3) combine: 결합하다 / 그는 일과 즐거움을 결합하고 싶어 한다. (4) endanger: 위험에 빠뜨리다 / 불은 숲 속에 있는 동물들을 위험에 빠뜨렸다.

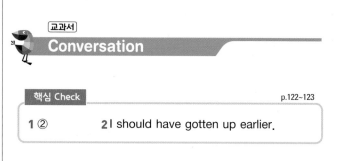

교과서
Conversation

핵심 Check p.122~123

1 ② 2 I should have gotten up earlier.

교과서 대화문 익히기

Check(√) True or False p.124

1 T 2 F 3 F 4 F

Check(√) True or False p.125

5 T 6 F 7 F 8 T

Listen & Talk 1 A

1. help / try on / How do you like / but, suits, have / one

2. to / I'm looking for / popular among, How do you like / green one is lighter than, one

Listen & Talk 1 B

bought, ago / looks, How do you like / convenient, anywhere, quality / How long, last / doesn't last / too bad / pretty happy

Listen & Talk 2 A

1. too uncomfortable / What's wrong with it / tight / you try it on before buying / so, should have tried, on

2. are going to watch / I've spent, allowance / get it / should have kept track of my spending

Listen & Talk 2 B

on sale / on sale, has just been released / is having / at full price / at, discount / should have checked the sales before

Communication Step A

heard that you bought / not happy, it / Why, What's / gets overheated, have read / for / won't give me back, I've used / calling, explaining / do

Wrap Up

1. I'd like to / How do you like this red one / that, one / striped, Its / take

2. online used store / let me see / is a little broken, said that / before / I just trusted, should have checked a bit more / should call, ask for a refund

---

시험대비 기본평가   p.130

01 ②   02 ⑤   03 ①

01 여자가 별들이 그려진 모자를 써 볼 수 있는지 질문하자 남자가 된다고 대답한다. 그리고 이어진 질문에 여자가 써 본 모자와 색깔에 대해서 말하고 있으므로, 상대방의 의견 혹은 만족 여부를 물을 때 사용하는 'How do you like ~?'을 이용한 ②번이 적절하다.

02 (C) 코트가 불편하다는 말에 (D) 상대방은 이유를 물어본다. (B) 너무 꽉 껴서 불편하다고 대답하다. (A) 사기 전에 입어 보지 않았냐고 질문하고 자신의 사이즈여서 그냥 사버렸다는 얘기를 하면서, 미리 입어 보지 않은 것에 후회를 나타낸다.

03 'should have p.p. ~.'는 어떤 일을 했어야 했다고, 또는 하지 말았어야 했다고 후회할 때 사용한다. try on: (옷 등을 시험 삼아) 입어 보다

01 'I love them. They are very comfortable.'은 '좋아요, 매우 편안해요.'의 의미로 빈칸에 어울리는 질문은 them에 해당하는 것에 대한 상대방의 만족이나 불만족을 물어보는 질문이 어울린다. 'How do you like ~?'는 '~는 어때?'의 의미이며, 'Are you satisfied[happy] with ~?', 'How is ~?', 'Are you enjoying ~?' 등으로 바꿔 쓸 수 있다.

02 (A) 코트가 불편하다는 말에, 여자가 왜 그런지 질문을 하는 말에 이어, 'What's wrong with it?(무슨 문제가 있니?)'이라고 했을 때 옷이 꽉 낀다고 말하는 것이 어울린다. (B) 'No. It was my size, so I just bought it.(아니. 내 사이즈여서 그냥 사 버렸어.)'이라고 대답하는 것으로 볼 때 옷을 살 때 안 입어봤는지 질문하는 것이 적절하다.

03 'should have p.p. ~.'는 어떤 일을 했어야 했다고, 후회할 때 사용한다. 'try it on'의 어순에 주의한다. try on: (옷 등을 시험 삼아) 입어 보다

04 온라인에서 산 아이스티가 만족스럽지 않다는 말에, 이유를 물어보니 너무 설탕이 많이 들어 있다고 대답한다. 빈칸에는 영양 분석을 확인했어야 했다고 말하는 것이 어울린다. nutrition fact: 영양 분석

05 일요일에 본 영화에 대해 만족을 묻는 말인 'How did you like it?'에 Yes나 No로 대답할 수 없다.

06 주어진 문장 'That's too bad.'는 '그것 참 안됐다.'라는 뜻으로 상대방의 실망에 대해 위로하는 표현이다. 정가를 주고 샀다는 남자아이의 말에 여자아이가 위로하는 것이 어울리므로 ④가 적절하다.

07 (A) release: 출시하다, 발매하다, it이 가리키는 것은 a new phone을 의미하는 것이므로 수동태가 들어가야 한다. just는 '방금'이라는 뜻으로 'have p.p.'인 현재완료 중에서 '완료'의 의미로 사용하였다. (B) 'should have p.p. ~'는 '~했어야 했는데(사실은 하지 않았다)'라는 뜻으로 과거 사실에 대한 유감을 나타내는 표현이다. 내용상 할인 판매를 확인했어야 했다는 내용이 들어가야 하므로 'should have p.p. ~'가 어울린다.

08 'How do you like ~?'는 '~는 어때?'라는 의미로 상대방에게 어떤 것에 대한 만족 또는 불만족을 묻는 표현이다.

09 Luke가 무엇을 위해 새 스피커를 사용할 것인지는 대화를 통해 알 수 없다. ① 새 스피커의 음질은 어떠한가? The sound quality is good. ③ Luke는 언제 새 스피커를 샀는가? He bought it a few weeks ago. ④ Luke는 새 스피커에 만족하는

27

가? He is pretty happy with it. ⑤ 배터리는 얼마나 지속되는 가? About 2 hours.

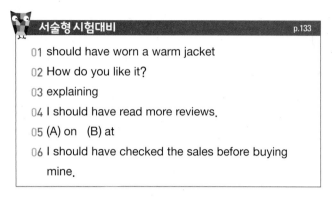

01 should have worn a warm jacket
02 How do you like it?
03 explaining
04 I should have read more reviews.
05 (A) on   (B) at
06 I should have checked the sales before buying mine.

01 'should have p.p. ~'는 '~했어야 했는데 (사실은 하지 않았다)'라는 뜻으로 과거 사실에 대한 유감을 나타내는 표현이다.

02 'Oh, I'm not happy with it.(아, 나는 별로 마음에 들지 않아.)'은 여자가 온라인으로 산 노트북에 대해 불만족을 표현하는 말이다. 그러므로 빈칸에는 어떤 것에 만족하거나 불만이 있는지 묻는 'How do you like it?'이 어울린다.

03 'How about ~?'은 '~하는 게 어때?'라는 뜻으로 상대방에게 권유할 때 사용하는 표현이고, about은 전치사이기 때문에 뒤에 명사나 동명사가 올 수 있다. explaining은 calling과 접속사 and로 연결되어 있다.

04 과거 사실에 대해 후회나 유감을 나타낼 때 '~했어야 했다'라는 의미로 'should have p.p. ~'를 쓴다. review: 후기

05 (A) on sale: 할인 중인 (B) at full price: 정가에, 제값에

06 대화의 흐름상 '사기 전에 할인 판매를 확인했어야 했다'라는 내용이 어울리므로, 'should have p.p. ~'를 이용해서 문장을 완성한다. 여기서 before는 전치사이므로 뒤에 동명사형이 온다.

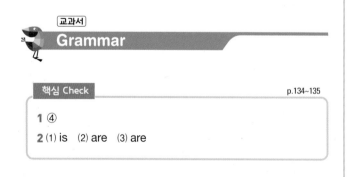

1 ④
2 (1) is   (2) are   (3) are

01 ④   02 ③   03 ①   04 ②
05 I love you as time goes by.

01 ④는 보어절을 이끄는 접속사 that이 적절하다.

02 부분을 나타내는 말은 뒤에 오는 명사의 수에 따라 그 수가 결정되는데, Half of 다음에 the money라고 단수 명사가 나오므로 ③번이 적절하다.

03 '~함에 따라'로 해석되는 '비례, 추이'를 나타내는 as가 적절하다.

04 ②번에는 부사절과 주절의 내용이 서로 상반되므로 양보의 접속사 Though[Although]가 적절하다. 나머지는 모두 as가 들어갈 수 있다. 각각 ① '시간' ③ '방식, 양태' ④ '비례, 추이' ⑤ '이유'를 나타낸다.

05 '비례, 추이(~함에 따라서, ~에 비례하여)'를 나타내는 as를 이용하여 영작한다.

01 ⑤   02 ②   03 ③   04 ⑤
05 ④   06 likes → like   07 ②   08 ①
09 ④   10 ③   11 ①   12 ⑤
13 ④   14 ②   15 ①
16 Strange as it may seem

01 ⑤는 '~으로, ~로서'라는 뜻으로 전치사로 쓰였다. 나머지는 모두 접속사 as로 사용되었다.

02 ②는 '~하기 때문에'라는 뜻이다. 나머지는 모두 '~함에 따라, ~할수록'이라는 비례의 의미를 나타낸다.

03 문맥상 '~하듯이, ~하는 것처럼'이라는 뜻의 접속사 As를 쓰는 것이 가장 적절하다.

04 '부분을 나타내는 명사+of' 다음에 명사가 올 때 동사의 수를 명사의 수에 일치시킨다. 모두 복수 명사가 이어지고 있으므로 복수 동사 were가 적절하다.

05 부분을 나타내는 말은 뒤에 오는 명사의 수에 따라 그 수가 결정되는데, 'About one third of' 다음에 all the students라고 복수 명사가 나오므로 wear가 적절하다.

06 '부분을 나타내는 말+단수 명사: 단수 동사', '부분을 나타내는 말+복수 명사: 복수 동사' the students로 복수 명사가 이어지고 있으므로 복수 동사 like가 적절하다.

07 (1) '비례, 추이'를 나타내는 접속사 (2) '이유'를 나타내는 접속사 (3) '~으로, ~처럼'의 뜻으로 쓰인 전치사

08 '비례, 추이(~함에 따라서, ~에 비례하여)'를 나타내는 접속사 as를 이용하는 것이 가장 적절하다.

09 'a number of+복수 명사+복수 동사' (많은= many), 'the number of+복수 명사+단수 동사' (~의 수). a great deal of = much

10 ① being 이하가 분사구문으로 쓰여서 as를 접속사로도 전치사로도 쓸 수 없다.(As → 삭제) ② as가 아니라 명사절을 이끄는 접속사가 필요하다.(as → that) ④ 내용상 know의 목적어 역할을 할 수 있는 '의문사+to부정사'가 적절하다. (as → what) ⑤ '부사구(In addition)'가 앞에 나온 문장으로, as는 접속사로도 전치사로도 쓸 수 없다.(as → 삭제)

11 부분을 나타내는 말이 있는 어구가 주어로 쓰일 때 뒤에 단수 명사가 나오면 단수 동사를 쓰고, 복수 명사가 나오면 복수 동사를 쓴다. ①은 is[was], 나머지는 모두 are[were]이다.

12 주어진 문장과 ⑤의 as는 '~함에 따라, ~할수록'이라는 뜻으로서 '비례, 추이'를 나타낸다. 나머지는 각각 ① 비록 ~할지라도, ~이지만(양보) ② ~ 때문에(이유) ③ ~하는 것처럼, ~하는 대로 (방식, 양태) ④ ~할 때(시간) 등이다.

13 서울에서 한국 음식을 먹어 봤고, 삼겹살을 먹어 봤으므로 '먹어 본 것 중의 하나'가 삼겹살이라고 쓸 수 있다. 'one of+복수 명사'가 주어일 경우 핵심이 되는 주어가 one이므로 동사는 단수로 쓴다.

14 ②는 '금반지를 껴도 원숭이는 원숭이다.'라는 뜻이다. 의미상 as를 양보의 접속사 though나 although 등으로 바꾸는 것이 적절하다.

15 주절의 동사가 과거시제인 경우 종속절의 시제는 과거나 과거완료가 나오지만 종속절이 불변의 진리, 격언, 현재의 습관, 과학적 사실 등을 나타내면 현재시제를 쓴다. 남편이 매일 아침 커피를 마시는 것은 '현재의 습관'이므로 현재시제로 나타낸다.

16 접속사 as가 '양보'의 의미로 쓰일 때는 '형용사/부사/무관사 명사'를 as 앞에 둔다.

서술형 시험대비 p.140~141

01 (1) Do as the Romans do when you are in Rome.
 (2) As the song became more popular, he was known to more people.
 (3) About half of the water is used to raise animals in the U.S.
 (4) About 14 percent of all people don't know how to read due to lack of education.

02 (1) I caught him just as he was leaving the building.
 (2) Brave as he was, he could not help weeping at the sight.
 (3) Each blind student was paired with a sighted student.
 (4) Jeff buys soccer shoes because more than half of the boys on his team wear them.

 (5) Most of the allowance is spent on clothes and one fourth of the allowance is spent on snacks.

03 (1) As you give more love, you will receive more love.
 (2) As you exercise harder, you become healthier.

04 is sitting

05 As you eat more

06 (1) like (2) are (3) knows (4) goes (5) decreases
 (6) ended

07 (1) About two thirds of the books Sophie wrote were read by Steve.
 (2) Some of the food that Mom made was thrown away by Mike.
 (3) One of Dominic's hobbies is basketball.

01 (1) ~하듯이, ~하는 대로(방식)의 접속사 as를 이용한다. (2) ~함에 따라서, ~에 비례하여(비례, 추이)의 접속사 as를 이용한다. (3), (4) 부분을 나타내는 말이 있는 어구가 주어로 쓰일 때 뒤에 단수 명사가 나오면 단수 동사를 쓰고, 복수 명사가 나오면 복수 동사를 쓴다.

02 (1) just though → just as (2) 문맥상 양보의 의미가 적절하므로 '형용사+as+주어+동사 ~'의 어순이 적절하다. (3) each 다음에는 단수 명사와 단수 동사가 이어진다. (4) 'half of' 다음에 'the boys on his team'라는 복수 명사가 나오므로 복수 동사 wear가 적절하다. (5) 'Most of'와 'one fourth of' 다음에 'the allowance'라는 단수 명사가 나오므로 단수 동사 is가 적절하다.

03 'the 비교급 …, the 비교급 ~' 구문을 '비례, 추이'를 나타내는 as를 이용하여 바꿔 쓸 수 있다.

04 'one of+복수 명사'가 주어일 경우 핵심이 되는 주어가 one이므로 동사는 단수로 쓴다.

05 '비례, 추이(~함에 따라서, ~에 비례하여)'의 부사절을 이끄는 as를 이용한다.

06 (1), (2) 부분을 나타내는 말 뒤에 오는 명사가 단수이면 단수 동사를 쓰고 복수이면 복수 동사를 쓴다. (3) 'none of+명사+동사'에서 명사가 단수일 경우, 동사의 수는 명사에 일치시켜 단수 동사로 쓴다. 명사가 복수일 경우에는 복수 동사나 단수 동사를 모두 쓸 수 있다. (4) 주절의 시제가 과거일지라도 종속절이 불변의 진리, 격언, 현재의 습관, 과학적 사실 등을 나타내면 현재시제를 쓴다. (5) the number of+단수[복수] 명사+단수 동사 (6) 역사적인 사실은 주절의 시제와 상관없이 과거시제를 쓴다.

07 부분을 나타내는 말은 뒤에 오는 명사의 수에 따라 그 수가 결정된다. (1) 'two thirds of the books'에서 'the books'로 복수이므로 were를 써야 한다. (2) 'Some of the food'에서 'the

food'로 단수이므로 was를 써야 한다. (3) 'one of' 다음에는 복수 명사가 나오며 핵심 주어가 one이므로 단수 동사로 받는다.

Reading

확인문제 p.142

1 T 2 F

확인문제 p.143

1 F 2 T 3 F

교과서 확인학습 A p.144~146

01 why you've bought things that
02 what affects us, buying
03 what my friends bought
04 goes, sees a pair of, on display
05 recognizes, because, half of the boys, wear
06 Although, many pairs of, ends up buying
07 bandwagon effect, to explain
08 that encourages, to jump aboard
09 more and more people, others are, likely to get on
10 to buy, just because, have bought it
11 buy a pair of, after, have bought
12 that, realizes that, match
13 that go, with
14 that none of her bags match
15 buys, Most of her money is, on, to complete
16 made, search for, after buying
17 explain it, received, as
18 after receiving, noticed that, furniture, go well, replacing most of it
19 therefore, that purchasing a new item, leads to, unplanned
20 they are on sale
21 goes window shopping, sees
22 checks, finds out that, that, too expensive
23 approaches him, discount on
24 Even though, is still, low, to buy
25 described above, anchoring effect
26 mentioned, affects, opinion of prices
27 For example, seem cheap in comparison
28 Furthermore, becomes bigger, be more powerful
29 As such, mentioned first, anchor, fixes our thoughts
30 Just like, to buy, considering why we are buying
31 As, have shown, influence
32 The next time, think, about why you are buying

교과서 확인학습 B p.146~147

1 Have you ever wondered why you've bought things that you don't even want or need?
2 Let's consider what affects us when it comes to buying things.
3 Why do I want to buy what my friends bought?
4 Jeff goes to the shopping center and sees a pair of soccer shoes on display.
5 He recognizes the shoes at a glance because more than half of the boys on his soccer team wear them.
6 Although he already has many pairs of soccer shoes, he ends up buying another new pair.
7 We can use the "bandwagon effect" to explain Jeff's behavior.
8 A bandwagon is a wagon in a parade that encourages people to jump aboard and enjoy the music.
9 As more and more people get on the bandwagon, others are more likely to get on or follow it.
10 In this way, people tend to buy something just because other people have bought it.
11 Why do I buy a pair of pants and a bag after I have bought a new coat?
12 Lisa buys a coat that she really loves. Immediately, she realizes that her pants do not match her new coat.
13 So, she buys new pants that go perfectly with her new coat.
14 But she sees that none of her bags match her new clothes.
15 So, she buys a new bag. Most of her money is spent on buying the new items to complete her new look.
16 What made Lisa search for new items immediately after buying a new coat?
17 The "Diderot effect" may explain it. Denis Diderot, a French writer, received a new gown as a gift.
18 Soon after receiving the gift, he noticed that all of his furniture did not go well with his new gown.

So, he ended up replacing most of it.

19 The Diderot effect, therefore, is the concept that purchasing a new item often leads to more unplanned purchases.

20 Why do I buy things just because they are on sale?

21 Nathan goes window shopping and sees a pair of headphones.

22 He checks the price and finds out that they are $200. He thinks that the headphones are too expensive.

23 The sales person approaches him and says, "You can get a 20 percent discount on those headphones."

24 Even though the discounted price is still not very low, Nathan decides to buy the headphones.

25 The situation described above is an example of the "anchoring effect."

26 "The price mentioned first affects our opinion of prices mentioned afterwards.

27 For example, if we start with $200, then $160 will seem cheap in comparison.

28 Furthermore, as the difference of the two prices becomes bigger, the effect will be more powerful.

29 As such, the price mentioned first acts as an "anchor" that fixes our thoughts about the price of an item.

30 Just like Jeff and his friends, we tend to buy things without seriously considering why we are buying them.

31 As these effects have shown, many things influence our purchases.

32 The next time you decide to buy something, think for a moment about why you are buying it.

시험대비 실력평가
p.148~151

01 ②   02 He goes to the shopping center.

03 behavior   04 ③   05 ④

06 ①, ④   07 ⑤

08 She bought a new bag.   09 ④   10 ③

11 ②   12 It is 200 dollars.

13 He says that Nathan can get a 20 percent discount on those headphones.

14 ③   15 ②

16 He sees a pair of soccer shoes on display.

17 ④

18 We can use the "bandwagon effect."

19 after I have bought a new coat

20 ⑤   21 his furniture   22 ③

23 ③   24 ②

25 They have shown that many things influence our purchases.

01 글의 내용은 다른 사람들이 어떤 것을 샀다는 이유로 그것을 구매하는 경향에 관한 것이므로 ②번이 가장 적절하다.

03 사람이나 동물이 하는 것은 '행동(behavior)'이다.

04 Jeff는 진열되어 있는 축구화 한 켤레를 보고 결국 사 버리고 말았다.

05 주어진 문장의 it은 Lisa로 하여금 새 코트를 산 후 즉시 새로운 물품을 찾게 하는 것을 가리킨다. 따라서 ④번에 들어가는 것이 가장 자연스럽다.

06 Lisa는 새 코트를 산 후 잇따라 바지와 가방을 샀다.

07 Lisa는 그녀의 새로운 모습을 완성하기 위하여 새로운 물품을 사는 데 돈의 대부분을 썼다고 하였다.

08 새로운 옷들을 산 후 Lisa는 새 가방을 샀다.

09 앵커링 효과는 처음에 언급된 가격이 이후에 언급되는 가격에 대한 우리의 의견에 영향을 미친다는 것이다. 처음에 언급된 가격이 물건의 가격에 대한 우리의 생각을 고정하는 닻으로서 작동하기 때문이다. 따라서 afterwards라고 쓰는 것이 적절하다.

10 예시를 들어 앞선 진술을 명확히 설명하고 있으므로 ③번이 가장 적절하다.

11 위 글은 "앵커링 효과"에 관한 글로, 단지 할인 중이라는 이유로 물건을 구입하는 이유에 관하여 설명하고 있다. 따라서 ②번이 가장 적절하다.

12 헤드폰의 가격에 대해 Nathan이 갖는 생각을 고정시키는 '닻' 역할을 하는 가격은 200달러이다.

13 점원은 Nathan에게 다가와 헤드폰에 20퍼센트 할인을 받을 수 있다고 말한다.

14 (C) Jeff는 쇼핑센터에서 축구팀에 있는 소년들의 반 이상이 신고 있는 축구화가 진열된 것을 봄 (A) 그에게 이미 축구화가 많이 있지만 결국 그것을 삼 (D) Jeff의 행동은 : '밴드왜건 효과'로 설명할 수 있는데, 밴드왜건에 사람들이 올라타서 음악을 즐기게 부추김 (B) 더 많은 사람들이 밴드왜건에 올라탈수록 다른 사람들도 그것을 따르려 함

15 when it comes to Ving: V에 대해서 말하자면

16 쇼핑센터에 간 Jeff는 진열되어 있는 축구화 한 켤레를 보게 된다고 하였다.

17 위 글은 원하거나 필요하지 않는 것들을 사는 이유에 대해 설명하는 글이다. 따라서 ④번 '우리가 돈을 쓰도록 만드는 것은 무엇인가?'가 가장 적절하다.

18 Jeff의 행동은 "밴드왜건 효과"로 설명할 수 있다.

19 위 글은 새 코트를 산 후 연이어 바지와 가방을 산 사례와 그 이유를 설명하는 내용이다.

20 빈칸 (B)에는 전치사 on이 들어간다. ① break down: 고장나다 ② stand for: 상징하다 ③ bring up: ~을 양육하다 ④ put off: ~을 미루다 ⑤ live on: ~을 먹고 살다

21 Diderot는 선물로 받은 새 가운과 자신의 모든 가구가 어울리지 않는 것을 알아채고 결국 대부분의 가구를 바꾸었다.

22 밑줄 친 (D)는 완전한 절을 이끄는 명사절 접속사이다. ③번은 불완전한 절을 이끄는 관계대명사이다.

23 approach는 타동사이므로 전치사 없이 목적어를 취한다. 따라서 'approaches him'이라고 쓰는 것이 적절하다.

24 글의 내용은 우리가 왜 물건들을 사는지 진지하게 고려하지 않고 구매한다는 것이다. 따라서 다음에 어떤 것을 구매하려고 결정할 때 자신이 그것을 왜 사려는지 잠시 동안 생각해 보라는 말이 들어가는 것이 적절하다.

25 이러한 효과들은 많은 것들이 우리의 구매에 영향을 미친다는 것을 보여주고 있다.

서술형 시험대비 p.152~153

01 what affects us when it comes to buying things

02 wear

03 a bandwagon

04 As more and more people get on the bandwagon, others are more likely to get on or follow it.

05 It's because other people have bought it.

06 She buys a coat (that she really loves).

07 She realizes (that) her pants do not match her new coat.

08 It was because he noticed that all of his furniture did not go well with his new gown.

09 planned → unplanned

10 He sees a pair of headphones.

11 He finds out that the headphones are 200 dollars.

12 anchor

13 The writer suggests that we should think for a moment about why we are buying it.

01 동사 consider의 목적어로 간접의문문을 쓰는 것에 유의한다. when it comes to Ving: V에 관하여

02 'half of+명사'는 명사에 수의 일치를 한다. 따라서 the boys에 맞추어 복수동사 wear를 쓴다.

03 퍼레이드에 있는 사륜마차인 밴드왜건을 가리키는 말이다.

04 더 많은 사람들이 밴드왜건에 올라탈수록 다른 사람들이 더욱 그것에 올라타거나 그것을 따라가려 한다.

05 '밴드왜건 효과'는 단지 다른 사람들이 어떤 것을 샀다는 이유로 그것을 구매하는 현상을 의미한다.

06 Lisa가 처음에 산 것은 코트이다.

07 새 코트를 산 후 Lisa는 그녀의 바지가 새 코트와 어울리지 않는다는 것을 즉시 알아차린다.

08 새 가운을 선물로 받은 Diderot는 그의 모든 가구가 새로운 가운과 어울리지 않는다는 것을 알아채고는 결국 대부분의 가구를 바꾸고야 말았다.

09 디드로 효과는 새로운 물품을 구입하는 것이 흔히 계획에 없던 더 많은 구매로 이어지는 개념이라고 하였다.

10 Nathan은 진열된 상품을 구경하러 가서 헤드폰을 하나 본다고 하였다.

11 헤드폰의 가격을 확인했을 때, Nathan은 가격이 200달러라는 것을 알게 된다.

12 배가 움직이지 않도록 물 속에 떨어뜨리는 것은 '닻(anchor)'이다.

13 글쓴이는 다음번에 우리가 어떤 것을 구매하려고 결정할 때, 자신이 그것을 왜 사려는지 잠시 동안 생각해 보라고 하였다.

영역별 핵심문제 p.155~159

01 ⑤   02 ①   03 encourages

04 More   05 ④

06 I should have kept track of my spending.

07 ⑤   08 ④   09 ④   10 like

11 (1) How do you like them?

   (2) Are you satisfied with them?   12 ②

13 ③   14 ②, ⑤   15 ⑤   16 ④

17 ①

18 (1) One third of the students are here.

   (2) Much of the house was ruined by the heavy rain.

   (3) Ten percent of the girls want to learn Spanish.

   (4) None of the furniture in our house is made of wood.

   (5) Last night she said that she takes a shower every day.

19 (1) as → though[although]

   (2) as → unless

(3) like → as
20 enjoys → enjoy   21 ⑤
22 ④번 → enjoy   23 no other → other
24 ②   25 ③
26 She buys (a pair of) new pants and a new bag.
27 He ended up replacing most of it.   28 ④
29 ⑤
30 Most of the allowance is spent on clothes.

01 affect: ~에 영향을 주다 influence: ~에 영향을 주다 / 어린 사람들은 그들의 동료 그룹에 의해 크게 영향을 받는 경향이 있다. ① 발명하다 ② 조절하다 ③ 향상시키다 ④ 발생하다 *tend to: ~하는 경향이 있다 *peer: 동료

02 저 재킷은 너의 치마와 완벽하게 어울린다. ① 어울리다 ② 소비하다 ③ 오래가다, (기능이) 지속되다 ④ 교체하다 ⑤ 맞추다, 조정하다

03 courage: 용기 encourage: 부추기다, 조장하다 / 새 선생님은 학생들이 창의적인 생각을 하도록 부추긴다.

04 more and more: 점점 더 많은 / 점점 더 많은 사람들이 인터넷을 이용하고 있다. more than half: 반 이상의 / 길은 30분 이상 동안 폐쇄되었다.

05 주어진 문장에서 it은 용돈을 의미한다. 용돈을 어떻게 다 써버렸는지에 대한 대답으로 'I'm not sure.(잘 모르겠어.)'가 어울리므로 ④가 적절하다.

06 과거 사실에 대해 후회나 유감을 나타낼 때 '~했어야 했다'는 의미로 'should have p.p. ~'를 쓴다. keep track of: ~을 기록하다 spending: 지출

07 (A) 'I heard that ~.'은 '~에 대해 들었다'의 뜻으로 알고 있거나 들은 것에 대해 말할 때 쓰는 표현이다. 접속사 that 뒤에는 절이 오며 'I've heard that ~'으로 바꿔 쓸 수 있다. (B) 'What's wrong?'은 상대방이 뭔가에 불만족하거나 실망하고 있는 것을 보고 그 원인을 물을 때 사용하는 표현이므로 빈칸에는 not happy가 어울린다. (C) 'should have p.p. ~.'는 어떤 일을 했어야 했다고 후회할 때 사용한다.

08 'How do you like ~?'는 '~는 어떠니?'라는 뜻으로 어떤 것에 대한 의견을 물을 때 쓰인다. 바꿔 쓸 수 있는 표현으로 'Are you satisfied[happy] with ~?', 'How is ~?', 'Are you enjoying ~?', 'Do you like ~?' 등이 있다.

09 캐릭터 티셔츠를 추천한 직원에게 여동생이 만화 캐릭터를 안 좋아한다고 얘기하면서 'Can I see the blue one?(파란 티셔츠 좀 볼 수 있을까요?)'이라고 물어본다.

10 (A) 'How do you like ~?'는 '~는 어떠니?'라는 뜻으로 어떤 것에 대한 의견을 물을 때 쓰인다. (B) like: 좋아하다

11 'How do you like ~?'는 상대방의 의견 혹은 만족 여부를 물

을 때 사용한다. 비슷한 표현인 'Are you satisfied[happy] with ~?'로 직접적으로 만족이나 불족족 여부를 물을 수 있다.

12 ⓐ 초록색 가방과 파란색 가방 중 무엇을 샀는가? (초록색 가방을 샀다.) ⓑ 초록색 가방과 파란색 가방 중 무엇이 더 가벼운가? (초록색 가방이 더 가볍다.) ⓒ 무슨 용도로 가방을 쓸 것인가? (하이킹할 때 사용할 것이다.) ⓓ 어떤 가방이 더 인기 있는가? (알 수 없다.)

13 각각 ①, ② '비례' ④ '시간' ⑤ '이유'이다. ③ as는 가정법의 if 대신 사용할 수 없다.

14 ① One of the highlights was seeing the Taj Mahal. ③ The number of employees was reduced from 40 to 25. ④ The rest of the money is used to run other government programs.

15 'Jane은 그가 건물을 나설 때 만났다.'는 내용으로서 so as는 어법상 어색하다. 'so as'를 'just as'로 바꾸는 것이 적절하다.

16 'a few of+복수 명사' 주어는 복수 동사로 받는다. Last weekend로 시제가 과거로 표시되어야 함에 주의한다.

17 주어진 문장과 ①의 접속사 As는 '~함에 따라'(비례)를 나타낸다. ② ~하는 동안(시간) ③ ~하는 대로(방식) ④ ~만큼(비교) ⑤ ~해서, ~ 때문에(이유)

18 (1), (3) 부분을 나타내는 말의 뒤에 단수 명사가 나오면 단수 동사를 쓰고 복수 명사가 나오면 복수 동사를 쓴다. (2) 'much of+단수 명사' 주어는 단수 동사로 받는다. (4) 'none of +명사+동사'에서는 명사가 단수일 경우 단수 동사를 쓰고 명사가 복수일 경우 복수 동사나 단수 동사를 모두 쓸 수 있다. (5) 주절의 시제가 과거일지라도 종속절이 불변의 진리, 격언, 현재의 습관, 과학적 사실 등을 나타내면 현재시제를 쓴다.

19 (1) 앞과 뒤의 절의 내용이 상반되므로 as가 아니라 though[although]가 적절하다. (2) 내용상 '정말로 춥지 않다면 창문을 열어 놓고 잠을 잔다.'고 하는 것이 자연스럽다. as를 unless로 고치는 것이 적절하다. (3) like는 전치사로 '~ 같은'이라는 뜻이고 as는 전치사로 '~로서'라는 뜻이다. 또한 'regard A as B'는 'A를 B로 여기다'라는 뜻이다.

20 부분을 나타내는 말은 뒤에 오는 명사의 수에 따라 그 수가 결정되는데, percent of 다음에 students라고 복수 명사가 나오므로 enjoy가 적절하다.

21 글의 내용은 '밴드왜건 효과'에 관한 것이므로 Jeff는 축구팀에 있는 소년들이 신는 축구화라는 이유로 결국 그 축구화를 사버리고 만다는 내용이 적절하다.

22 밴드왜건은 사람들이 올라타서 음악을 즐기게끔 부추기는 퍼레이드에 있는 사륜마차라는 의미이다. 따라서 to jump에 병렬 연결되도록 enjoy라고 쓰는 것이 적절하다.

23 다른 사람들이 어떤 것을 샀다는 이유로 그것을 구매하는 경향

이므로 부정어 no가 없어야 한다.

24 진열되어 있는 축구화 한 켤레를 본 Jeff는 그 신발을 한눈에 알아챘다고 하였다.

25 디드로 효과가 무엇인지를 설명한 후 한 문장으로 정리하여 진술하고 있으므로 결과를 이끄는 therefore가 적절하다.

26 Lisa는 새 코트를 산 후 새 바지와 새 가방을 샀다.

27 Diderot는 결국 대부분의 가구를 바꾸었다.

28 Lisa는 원래 마음에 드는 코트를 사려고 했지만 자신의 새로운 모습을 완성하기 위하여 계획에 없던 물건을 사고 있다.

29 이어지는 글의 내용으로 보아 용돈을 얼마나 자주 받는지 물어봤음을 알 수 있다.

30 대부분의 용돈은 옷에 쓰인다고 하였다.

단원별 예상문제 p.160~163

01 (1) (p)urchase (2) (t)ight 02 difference
03 ③
04 (a)ffect (c)ombine (c)oncept
   (1) concept (2) affects (3) combine
05 (D) → (B) → (C) → (A)
06 (A) ⓓ (B) ⓑ (C) ⓔ
07 suit 08 ② 09 for
10 ②
11 call the online shop and explain my problem
12 ① 13 ④ 14 was → were
15 As people eat more junk food, they may gain
   more weight.
16 ②
17 As you run more, you become stronger.
18 ③ 19 anchor, lower 20 ⑤
21 The price mentioned first affects our opinion of
   prices mentioned afterwards.
22 ⑤
23 They think (that) they should get a higher
   allowance. 24 ②

01 (1) 두 단어의 관계는 동의어 관계이다. immediately: 즉시, 바로 at once: 즉시 buy: 사다 purchase: 사다, 구입하다 (2) 두 단어의 관계는 반의어 관계이다. waste: 낭비하다, 소모하다 save: 낭비를 막다, 절약하다 loose: 헐거운, 느슨한 tight: 꽉 조이는, 딱 붙는

02 differ: 다르다 difference: 차이, 차이점 / 이 두 컴퓨터의 차이점이 무엇인가요?

03 (A) spend A on 동사ing: A를 ~하는 데 쓰다 / 우리는 예전보다 음식에 더 많은 돈을 쓰고 있는 중이다. (B) keep track of: ~을 기록하다 / 우리는 비용을 기록하는 시스템이 필요하다.

(C) lead to: ~로 이어지다 / 스트레스가 신체적인 병으로 이어질 수 있다는 것에는 의심의 여지가 없다.

04 (1) concept: 개념. 어떤 원리나 생각 / 우리는 지금 새로운 개념을 생각해 내야 할 필요가 있다. (2) affect: ~에 영향을 주다. 어떤 사람이나 사물에 영향을 미치다, 혹은 어떤 사람이나 사물에 변화를 야기하다 / 네가 하는 모든 선택은 너의 삶에 영향을 준다. (3) combine: 결합하다. 하나 하나의 혹은 집단으로 만들기 위해 합치다 / 그는 일과 즐거움을 결합하고 싶어 한다.

05 새로운 스피커인지 물어보는 질문에 (D) 맞다고 대답하면서 몇 주 전에 샀다고 말한다. (B) 새로운 스피커에 대한 의견을 물어본다. (C) 편리하고, 어디든지 가져가서 음악을 들을 수 있고, 음질도 좋다고 말한다. (A) 배터리는 얼마나 오래가는지 질문하자 2시간 정도라고 대답한다.

06 (A) '무엇을 도와드릴까요?'라고 묻는 질문에 별들이 그려진 모자를 써 볼 수 있는지 묻는 것이 어울린다. (B) 별들이 그려진 모자에 대해 의견을 물어보고, 디자인은 좋은데 색깔은 어울리지 않는다고 대답하는 것이 어울린다. (C) 같은 모양의 검은색이 있는지 질문을 하고 안쪽에서 가져다 드리겠다고 말하는 것이 어울린다.

07 suit: 어울리다 / 어떤 특정한 사람이나 상황, 경우에 알맞다

08 노트북이 마음에 들지 않는다는 여자의 말에 무슨 문제가 있는지 물어보고, 그 말에 소음이 심하고 과열이 된다고 대답을 해 주는 것이 어울린다.

09 ask for: 요청하다

10 일주일 동안 사용했기 때문에 온라인 가게는 환불을 해 주지 않을 거라고 말하는 것이 어울리므로 이유의 접속사 because가 알맞다.

11 온라인 가게에 전화해 문제를 설명하라고 충고하는 말에 '그렇게 해야 할 것 같다'라고 말하고 있으므로 'do that'은 '온라인 가게에 전화해 문제를 설명하는 것'을 가리킨다.

12 버스를 또 놓쳤다고 말하고 있으므로 빈칸에는 일찍 일어나지 않았던 것에 대해 유감을 표현하는 말이 들어가는 것이 적절하다. 'should have p.p. ~'는 '~했어야 했는데 (사실은 하지 않았다)'의 뜻으로 과거 사실에 대한 유감을 나타내는 표현이다.

13 ④번의 as는 전치사이고, 나머지는 모두 접속사이다.

14 부분을 나타내는 말은 뒤에 오는 명사의 수에 따라 그 수가 결정되는데, part of 다음에 the expenses라고 복수 명사가 나오므로 were가 적절하다.

15 '~함에 따라, ~할수록'이라는 비례의 의미를 갖는 접속사 as를 이용한다.

16 ②에는 부분을 나타내는 말(Some of)의 뒤에 단수 명사(the pie)가 나왔으므로 단수 동사 is가 적절하다. 나머지는 모두 are가 적절하다.

17 'the 비교급 …, the 비교급 ~' 구문을 '비례, 추이'를 나타내는 as를 이용하여 바꿔 쓸 수 있다.

18 (A) on sale: 할인 중인, for sale: 판매를 위한 (B) 종속절이 주절의 이유라기보다는 양보절을 이끄는 것이 더 적절하다. (C) "닻"은 우리의 생각을 고정하는 역할을 한다.

19 처음에 언급된 가격은 '닻'으로서 작용한다. 만약 나중에 언급된 가격이 처음의 가격보다 더 낮으면 당신은 그 상품이 싸다고 생각할 것이다.

20 Nathan은 헤드폰이 여전히 별로 서럼하시 잃다고 생각했지만 "앵커링 효과"에 영향을 받아 결국 헤드폰을 산다.

21 처음에 언급된 가격이 이후에 언급되는 가격에 대한 우리의 의견에 영향을 미친다고 하였다.

22 '~인지 아닌지'를 물어보았다는 표현이 적절하므로 that이 아니라 if나 whether를 써야 한다. 명사절 접속사 that은 확정적인 내용의 절을, if나 whether는 확정적이지 않은 내용의 절을 이끈다.

23 설문 조사에 참여한 10명의 학생 중 90퍼센트에 해당하는 9명의 학생들은 자신이 용돈을 더 많이 받아야 한다고 생각한다.

24 설문 조사를 받은 학생의 수는 10명이다.

서술형 실전문제 p.164~165

01 should have brought an umbrella
02 (1) Are you enjoying this dress?
　(2) Are you satisfied with this dress?
　(3) Are you happy with this dress?
03 I should have tried it on.
04 (1) was spent　(2) is　(3) died　(4) has
05 (1) Jason came up to me as I was speaking.
　(2) Young as he was, he was very wise.
　(3) As these effects have shown, many things influence our purchases.
　(4) One third of the world's food is wasted.
06 Because more than half of the boys on his soccer team wear them.
07 It is a wagon in a parade that encourages people to jump aboard and enjoy the music.
08 Because she wants to complete her new look.
09 The "Diderot effect" may explain it.
10 It is the concept that purchasing a new item often leads to more unplanned purchases.

01 'should have p.p. ~'는 '~했어야 했는데 (사실은 하지 않았다)'의 뜻으로 과거 사실에 대한 유감을 나타내는 표현이다.

02 어떤 것에 만족하거나 불만이 있는지 물어보는 표현으로 'How do you like ~?', 'Are you satisfied[happy] with ~?', 'Are you enjoying ~?' 등을 쓸 수 있다.

03 사기 전에 입어 보지 않았느냐는 질문에, 자신의 사이즈여서 그냥 사 버렸다고 말하고 있으므로 빈칸에는 입어 보지 않은 것에 대해 후회를 하는 말이 어울린다. try on: (옷 등을 시험 삼아) 입어 보다

04 (1) 부분을 나타내는 말 뒤에 오는 명사가 단수이면 단수 동사를 쓰고 복수이면 복수 동사를 쓴다. the money가 주어이므로 수동태로 써야 한에 주의한다. (2) 학문 이름은 단수 취급한다. (3) 역사적인 사실은 주절의 시제와 상관없이 과거시제를 쓴다. (4) the number of+단수(복수) 명사+단수 동사

05 (1) as가 '시간'을 나타내는 부사절을 이끌도록 쓴다. (2) 접속사 as가 '양보'의 의미로 쓰일 때는 '형용사/부사/무관사 명사를 as 앞에 둔다. (3) as가 '방식'을 나타내는 부사절을 이끌도록 쓴다. (4) 부분을 나타내는 말 뒤에 오는 명사가 단수이면 단수 동사를 쓰고 복수이면 복수 동사를 쓴다.

06 위 글의 내용에 따르면, Jeff가 축구화를 산 이유는 그의 축구팀에 있는 소년들의 반 이상이 그 축구화를 신기 때문에 그는 그 축구화를 산다.

07 밴드왜건(악대차)은 사람들이 올라타서 음악을 즐기게끔 부추기는 퍼레이드에 있는 사륜마차라고 하였다.

08 Lisa는 그녀의 새로운 모습을 완성하기 위하여 대부분의 돈을 쓴다고 하였다.

09 Lisa의 소비는 '디드로 효과'가 설명해 줄지도 모른다고 하였다.

10 디드로 효과는 새로운 물품을 구입하는 것이 흔히 계획에 없던 더 많은 구매로 이어진다는 개념이다

창의사고력 서술형 문제 p.166

|모범답안|

01 should have stayed at home / should have not gone to school
02 (1) I respected her more
　(2) I was so hungry
　(3) I need more money
　(4) he becomes more curious about the world
03 how often they get an allowance, Twenty, every week, seventy percent of the students get an allowance every month, spent on clothes, one fourth of the allowance, whether[if] they think that they should get a higher allowance, Ninety percent of the students think that they should get a higher allowance

01 어제 아픈데도 불구하고 학교 간 것에 대해 후회를 하는 말이 어울리므로, 학교를 가지 않았어야 했는데 간 것에 대해 후회하는 표현이 어울린다.

단원별 모의고사
p.167~170

01 go
02 (1) are likely to be   (2) comfortable
   (3) (s)oon, (a)fter   (4) at a glance
03 (1) When   (2) because   (3) Although
04 comparison   05 ③
06 How do you like this red one[T–shirt]?
07 I regret not checking the sales before buying
   mine.
   I wish I had checked the sales before buying
   mine.
08 ③
09 (A) should   (B) should   (C) won't   (D) should
10 ⑤
11 (A) used   (B) see   (C) broken   12 ④
13 ③
14 As we cut more trees to make land, more forests
   disappear on Earth.
15 One third of the power (that[which]) your body
   consumes comes from the food (that[which]) you
   eat.
16 ①, ②, ⑤   17 It is $160.
18 It is the price mentioned first.
19 ④   20 ③   21 ⑤
22 (B)–(A)–(C) 23 ②

01 go well with: ~와 잘 어울리다 / 어떤 신발이 이 옷에 가장 잘 어울리니? go window shopping: 진열된 상품을 구경하고 다니다 / 나는 다음 주말에 친구와 진열된 상품을 구경하고 다닐 것이다.

02 (1) be likely to: ~할 가능성이 있다, ~하기 쉽다 (2) comfortable: 편안한 tight: 꽉 조이는, 딱 붙는 (3) soon after: 직후 (4) at a glance: 한눈에, 즉시

03 (1) when it comes to: ~에 관해서, ~에 대해 말하자면 / 요리에 관해서라면, 그가 나보다 낫다. (2) just because: 단지 ~라는 이유로 / 단지 내가 불평을 안 하니까 사람들은 내가 만족하는 줄 안다. (3) although: 비록 ~이지만 / 비록 해가 비치고 있긴 했지만, 날이 별로 따뜻하지는 않았다.

04 compare: 비교하다 in comparison: 비교해 보면 / 이에 비해

서 부유하고 호화롭게 사는 사람들이 있다.

05 여자가 파란 줄무늬 티셔츠를 선택한 것으로 보아, 여동생이 만화 캐릭터를 별로 좋아하지 않는다는 것을 유추할 수 있다.

06 'How do you like ~?'는 상대방의 의견 혹은 만족 여부를 물을 때 사용한다.

07 과거 사실에 대해 후회나 유감을 나타낼 때 '~했어야 했다'라는 의미로 'should have p.p. ~'를 쓴다. 이때 조동사 should 뒤에는 과거의 일을 의미하므로 동사원형 대신 'have+p.p.'를 써야 한다. 이외에도 'I regret -ing.', 'I wish I had p.p. ~' 등으로 쓸 수 있다.

08 남자는 할인 판매를 확인하지 않았던 것에 대해 후회하고 있다.

09 (A) 과거 사실에 대해 후회나 유감을 나타낼 때 '~했어야 했다'는 의미로 'should have p.p. ~'를 쓴다. (B), (D) should: ~ 해야 한다 (C) '일주일 동안 사용해서 환불을 해 주지 않을 것이다'라는 내용으로 will not의 줄임말인 won't가 어울린다.

10 Riley는 일주일 동안 노트북을 사용해서 환불을 해주지 않을 것이라고 말한다.

11 (A) used: 중고의 (B) let은 '~에게 …하게 하다'라는 의미를 가지는 사역동사로, 목적격보어로 동사원형을 쓴다. (C) 바깥 부분이 부서진 것이므로 수동태인 'be broken'을 사용한다.

12 ⓓ must → should, 'should have p.p. ~.'는 어떤 일을 했어야 했다고 후회할 때 사용한다.

13 각 부분은, '~할수록', '~하는 대로', '~로서' 등으로 접속사와 전치사로 모두 쓸 수 있는 것은 as이다.

14 '~함에 따라, ~할수록'이라는 '비례'의 의미를 갖는 as를 이용하여 영작한다.

15 '부분을 나타내는 명사+of' 다음에 명사가 올 때 동사의 수를 명사의 수에 일치시킨다.

16 글의 내용으로 미루어 보아 Nathan은 헤드폰의 가격이 비싸다고 생각했음을 유추할 수 있다. *bargain: 헐값의

17 할인된 헤드폰의 가격은 160달러라고 하였다.

18 물건의 가격에 대한 우리의 생각을 고정하는 '닻'으로서 작용하는 것은 먼저 언급된 가격이다.

19 "앵커링 효과"는 나중에 언급된 가격이 먼저 언급된 가격을 더 비싸 보이게 만든다.

20 밴드왜건에 올라타 함께 음악을 즐긴다고 하였으므로 '그것에 올라타거나 그것을 따라가려고 한다'는 것이 가장 적절하다.

21 밴드왜건 효과는 다른 사람들이 어떤 것을 샀다는 이유로 그것을 구매하는 경향이므로, 친구들이 노트북을 샀기 때문에 자신도 노트북을 샀다고 말한 Ethan이 밴드왜건 효과의 영향을 받

았다고 말할 수 있다.

22 (B)의 it이 주어진 문장의 'Lisa가 새 코트를 산 후 즉시 새로운 물품을 찾은 것'을 가리킴 (A) the gift는 (B)에서 나온 새 가운임 (C) 새 가운이 자신의 모든 가구와 어울리지 않는다는 사실을 알아챈 결과로 대부분의 가구를 교체함.

23 해석: 디드로 효과에 따르면, 하나의 새로운 물건 때문에 예상치 못한 지출이 있을 수 있다.

Wonders of Space Travel

01 ④   02 ⑤   03 ③   04 ③
05 ⑤

01 ④의 접두사 in은 '안에'의 의미를 가지며 나머지 보기들은 '부정'을 나타낸다. ① infinite: 무한한 ② incorrect: 부정확한, 사실이 아닌 ③ insecure: 안전하지 못한 ④ insight: 통찰력 ⑤ inexpensive: 비싸지 않은, 저렴한

02 주어진 단어의 관계는 동의어 관계이다. vast: 거대한, 광대한, huge: 막대한, 거대한 ⓐ achieve: 달성하다, 성취하다, accomplish: 이루다, 성취하다 ⓑ persistent: 끈질긴, 집요한, 지속적인, occasional: 이따금씩, 가끔씩 ⓒ tough: 힘든, 어려운, easy: 쉬운, 수월한 ⓓ bottom: 맨 아랫부분, 바닥, top: 꼭대기, 정상 ⓔ attach: 붙이다, stick: 붙이다

03 ③ stick: 찌르다 ① 웜홀은 두 개의 다른 우주를 연결할 수 있다. ② 왜 공룡이 멸종되었는지에 관한 많은 이론들이 있다. ③ 그들은 물 주머니에 튜브를 찌르고 마신다. ④ 모든 승객은 안전벨트를 매야 한다. ⑤ 지구는 태양에서 3번째로 가까운 행성이다.

04 (A) different from: ~와 다른 / 우주에서의 생활이 지구에서의 생활과 어떻게 다른가? (B) in theory: 이론상으로는, 원칙상으로는 / 이론상으로는 웜홀이 존재한다. (C) figure out: ~을 알아내다, 생각해 내다 / 아인슈타인은 우주와 시간에 대해 무엇을 생각해 내었는가?

05 ① detect: 감지하다, 발견하다 / 딱정벌레는 그들의 길을 별로 발견한다. ② connect: 연결되다, 이어지다 / SNS의 요점은 다른 사람들과 연결하는 것이다. ③ bend: 굽히다, 구부리다 / 너의 근육을 늘리기 위해 등을 굽혀야 한다. ④ punch: 구멍을 뚫다 / 이 벨트가 너무 커서 나는 여분의 구멍을 뚫을 것이다. ⑤ contain: ~이 들어 있다, 포함하다 / 즉석 면류는 많은 소금을 포함하고 있다.

01 able
02 (1) surface (2) layer (3) bottom (4) dots
03 (1) According to (2) (f)ar (a)way (f)rom

(3) float around (4) in the blink of an eye
(5) look back on   04 if
05 (1) eatable (2) incorrect (3) impossible
(4) changeable

01 동사 뒤에 –able을 붙이면 '~할 수 있는'이라는 의미의 형용사가 된다. eatable: 먹을 수 있는 / 그 음식은 먹을 수 있지만 좋지는 않다. changeable: 바뀔 수 있는, 변덕스러운 / 그 규칙들은 아주 바뀔 수 있다.

02 (1) surface: 표면 / 너는 태양의 표면에서 작은 검은 점을 볼 수 있다. (2) layer: 층 / 엄마는 양파의 바깥쪽 층을 제거했다. (3) bottom: 맨 아랫부분, 바다 / 그들의 부리 덕분에, 돌고래들은 바다의 맨 아랫부분에서 물고기를 사냥할 수 있다. (4) dot: 점 / 나의 새로운 치마는 파란색에 하얀 점들이 있다.

03 (1) according to ~: ~에 따르면 (2) far away from: ~에서 멀리 떨어져 (3) float around: 떠다니다 (4) in the blink of an eye: 눈 깜박할 사이에 (5) look back on: ~을 되돌아보다

04 even if는 '~이지만, 비록 ~일지라도'라는 뜻이며, 상반된 내용의 두 문장을 연결하는 접속사로 양보의 부사절을 이끈다. 단순 조건절에서 접속사 if는 '만일 ~라면'의 의미로 조건절을 이끈다. • 훈민정음이 많은 책에 언급되어 있을지라도, 어느 누구도 그것이 정말 어디에 있는지 알지 못했다. • 그가 돌아오기 전에 그 음식을 먹으면, 그는 화가 날 거야.

05 (1) eatable: 먹을 수 있는 / 그 음식점의 음식은 먹을 수가 없다. (2) incorrect: 부정확한, 사실이 아닌 / 이렇게 많은 부정확한 대답들로는 테스트에 통과할 수 없다. (3) impossible: 불가능한 / 물 없이 사는 것은 불가능하다. (4) changeable: 바뀔 수 있는, 변덕스러운 / 런던의 날씨는 매우 변덕스럽다.

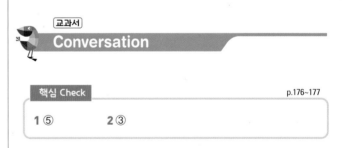

교과서
Conversation

핵심 Check   p.176~177

1 ⑤   2 ③

교과서 대화문 익히기

Check(√) True or False   p.178

1 T   2 F   3 T   4 T

probable[likely] ~?'로 바꿔 쓸 수 있다. 하지만 that 다음에는 주어와 동사인 절의 형태가 나와야 한다.

03 빈칸에는 우주에서는 하루에 일출을 여러 번 보는 게 가능한지 묻는 질문에 대답을 해야 하므로 'Yes. It's possible because we moved around Earth every 90 minutes in the station.(네, 가능해요. 왜냐하면 우주 정거장이 지구 주위를 90분마다 돌았거든요.)'이 어울린다.

교과서 확인학습
p.181~183

Listen & Talk 1 A

1. to, What, being / could see, times a day / Is it possible to see, a day / possible because / amazing

2. the best food you ate / grew, ate, fresh and tasty / is it possible to grow / Since, had to, helped the roots to

Listen & Talk 1 B

Have you heard that, send / into space / I've heard that, will be used to print out / possible to print out / in less than / what it would taste like

Listen & Talk 2 A

1. I wish I could see, from, with my own eyes / do that / that, in space

2. seems, different / it's because, no gravity / I wish I could, astronaut / looks uncomfortable

Listen & Talk 2 B

lived in / must have been tough / while in space / possible / it's because, gravity / I wish I could live in, become taller / I'm sure there, ways to become taller

Communication Step A

to talk about, that we wish were real / start with / I wish I could have / somewhere that / Is it actually possible to fly / have applied

Wrap Up

1. enjoy, the best experience, what was the best part, by myself, Is it possible to fly, by yourself, attached myself

2. heard that, How / zero gravity / real astronauts / adventure / astronaut, explore Mars

시험대비 기본평가
p.184

01 ②   02 ③   03 ⑤

01 어떤 일이 이루어지기를 바라는 같은 표현으로 '~ would be a dream come true.', 'How I wish I could ~!', 'It would be great if I could ~.' 등이 있다.

02 'Is it possible to 동사원형 ~?'은 '~하는 것이 가능할까?'라는 뜻으로 상대방에게 가능성을 물을 때 사용한다. 'Is it

시험대비 실력평가
p.185~186

01 ③   02 ①, ③   03 ④
04 Is it possible to wash their body in space
05 from   06 ⑤   07 ①   08 ④
09 ②   10 saw
11 Is it possible to fly in space by yourself?

01 국립 청소년 우주 센터에서 가상 현실 안경을 써 봄으로써 실제로 우주에 있는 것 같은 기분이 들게 할 수 있다고 말하고 있으므로 빈칸에는 지구를 우주에서 직접 자신의 눈으로 보는 것을 바라는 말이 들어가는 것이 적절하다.

02 ① 국립 청소년 우주 센터는 어디에 있는가? ② 여자는 무엇을 하기를 원하는가? (지구를 우주에서 직접 자신의 눈으로 보기를 원한다.) ③ 그들은 언제 국립 청소년 우주 센터에 갈 것인가? ④ 그들은 무엇을 보고 있는 중인가? (우주 사진들을 보고 있다.) ⑤ 어디서 여자는 우주에 있는 것 같은 기분을 느낄 수 있는가? (국립 청소년 우주 센터)

03 많은 돈을 벌면 무엇을 하기를 원하는지 소망을 물어보는 말에 많은 돈을 버는 것이 가능하지 않다고 말하는 것은 어색하다.

04 어떤 일이 실제로 가능한지 묻는 표현으로 'Is it possible to ~?'를 쓸 수 있다.

05 different from: ~와 다른

06 우주 비행사처럼 떠다니는 것에 대해 소망을 표현하는 남자의 말에 여자는 그렇지 않다고 말한 것과 떠다니는 모습이 편안해 보인다는 말은 어울리지 않는다.

07 'must have+과거분사'는 과거 사실에 대한 강한 추측을 나타내는 표현으로 '~이었음에 틀림이 없다'라는 의미를 가진다.

08 '키가 더 커지기 위해 우주에 가기를 바라는 남자에게 우주에 가는 것 말고 키가 더 커지는 방법들이 있다고 말하는 것이 어울린다.

09 남자가 얼마나 더 키가 크고 싶어하는지에 대해서는 언급되어 있지 않다.

10 flew와 saw는 문장의 동사로 접속사 and로 연결되어 있다.

11 'Is it possible to+동사원형 ~?'은 '~하는 것이 가능한가요?'라

는 의미로 가능 여부를 물을 때 사용하는 표현이다. by oneself: 혼자서

서술형 시험대비 p.187

01 what was the best food you ate in the space station
02 (p)ossible
03 grow / to grow
04 vegetables
05 I wish I could see Earth from space with my own eyes.
06 to print
07 Is it possible to print out food using a 3D printer?

01 the best food와 you ate 사이에 목적격 관계대명사 which나 that이 생략되어 있으므로, you ate in the space station이 the best food를 수식하고 있다.

02 'Is it possible to 동사원형 ~?'은 '~하는 것이 가능한가요?'의 의미로 상대방에게 가능성을 묻는 표현이다.

03 'help+목적어+목적격보어'는 '…에게 ~하도록 도움을 주다'이며, 목적격보어에는 동사원형이나 to부정사가 올 수 있다.

04 우주 정거장에서 채소를 키우는 것이 가능한지 묻는 질문에, 중력이 없기 때문에 그것을 특수한 봉지 안에서 키워야 한다고 말하고 있으므로 them은 vegetables(채소)를 의미한다.

05 'I wish I could ~.'는 '내가 ~할 수 있으면 좋겠다.'의 뜻으로 현재 사실과 반대되거나 현재 이룰 수 없는 소망을 말할 때 사용한다.

06 be used to 동사원형: ~하기 위해 사용되다

07 어떤 일이 실제로 가능한지 묻는 표현으로 'Is it possible to ~?'을 쓸 수 있다. print out: (프린터로) 출력하다

교과서

Grammar

핵심 Check p.188~189

1 If I were you, I would start looking for another job.
2 (1) turned (2) crying

시험대비 기본평가 p.190

01 (1) has → had (2) can → could
   (3) know → knew (4) will → would
02 ③   03 ④
04 (1) with her legs crossed
   (2) with the cool wind blowing

01 문제에서 모든 문장이 가정법 문장이라고 했으며, 모든 문장의 구조는 '가정법 과거' 형태이므로, 부사절의 동사를 과거로, 주절의 조동사도 과거형으로 고치는 것이 적절하다.

02 with+명사(구)+분사: ~이 …한 채로, ~이 …하면서

03 주절에 조동사의 과거형이 나왔으므로, 가정법 문장이다. 문장의 구성상 be동사의 과거형이 필요한데, 일반적으로 가정법 과거에서 be동사의 과거형은 were를 쓴다.

04 'with+명사(구)+분사'는 '~이 …한 채로, ~이 …하면서'라는 뜻으로 동시 동작이나 부가적인 상황을 생생하게 표현할 때 사용한다. 이때 명사와 분사가 능동 관계이면 현재 분사를, 수동 관계이면 과거 분사를 쓴다. (1) 다리가 교차시키는 것이 아니라 교차되는 것이므로 수동의 과거분사가 적절하다. (2) 바람이 부는 것이므로 능동의 현재분사가 적절하다.

시험대비 실력평가 p.191~193

01 ④   02 ②   03 ①   04 ⑤
05 ③
06 (1) won (2) had (3) finished (4) flying   07 ③
08 ②   09 ①   10 ④   11 ②
12 ⑤   13 ④   14 ③
15 (1) with her umbrella folded
   (2) with a book in her hand
   (3) with her hair blowing
16 (1) If I could travel into the past, I would bring back all the latest technology.
   (2) If your coach were here, he would be proud of you.
   (3) Andy slept with the door closed.

01 가정법 문장이라면 will을 would로, 직설법 문장이라면 studied를 studies로 쓰는 것이 적절하다.

02 'with+명사+분사'에서 명사와의 관계가 능동이면 현재분사를, 수동이면 과거분사를 쓴다.

03 주절에 조동사의 과거형인 might가 나와 있고 내용상 가정법으로 보아야 하므로 fly를 flew로 고치는 것이 적절하다.

04 'with+명사+분사'에서 명사와의 관계가 수동이므로 turning이 아니라 turned가 나와야 한다.

40 정답 및 해설

05 ①번과 ④번은 직설법 전환이 잘못된 이상한 문장이며, ②번은 가정법 과거가 아닌 가정법 과거완료를 전환한 것이고, ⑤번은 가정법 전환이 잘못된 이상한 문장이다.

06 (1), (2) 주절에 조동사의 과거형이 나왔으므로, 가정법 문장이다. (3) 명사와의 관계가 수동이므로 finished가 나와야 한다. (4) 명사와의 관계가 능동이므로 flying이 나와야 한다.

07 가정법 과거 시제의 문장으로 쓴다. 'If Sam didn't wake up early'로 종속절을 쓰고, 주절에 조동사의 과거형 could not을 쓰는 것에 유의한다.

08 'with+명사+분사'의 어순으로 셔츠가 밖으로 드러난 것으로 능동이므로 현재분사가 적절하다.

09 'with+명사+분사'에서 명사와의 관계가 능동이면 현재분사를, 수동이면 과거분사를 쓴다.

10 가정법 과거의 문장들이다. If절에는 동사의 과거형을, 주절에는 조동사의 과거형을 쓰는 것이 적절하다. Were it not for computers = If there were no computers = Without computers = But for computers

11 옳은 문장은 ⓒ, ⓔ 2개이다. ⓐ am → were[was], ⓑ can → could, ⓓ have → had ⓕ closing → closed ⓖ folding → folded ⓔ는 분사 자리에 형용사가 온 경우이다.

12 가정법 과거 문장은 현재시제의 직설법으로 바꿔 쓸 수 있다. 가정법은 반대로 가정하는 것이므로 부정하는 것이 서로 바뀌는 것에 주의한다.

13 'with+명사(구)' 다음에는 분사, 형용사, 부사, 전치사구' 등이 올 수 있으며, 분사의 경우 명사와의 관계가 능동이면 현재분사를, 수동이면 과거분사를 쓴다. 'with the alarm ringing'이 적절하다.

14 '~가 없다면'이라는 가정법 표현은 'If there were no ~'로 나타낸다. If there were no corn = If it were not for corn = Were it not for corn = Without corn = But for corn

15 'with+명사(구)' 다음에는 분사, 형용사, 부사, 전치사구' 등이 올 수 있으며, 분사의 경우 명사와의 관계가 능동이면 현재분사를, 수동이면 과거분사를 쓴다.

16 가정법 과거는 'If+주어+were/동사의 과거형 ~, 주어+조동사의 과거형(would/should/could/might)+동사원형 …'의 형태이므로 (1)에서는 can을 could로 고치는 것이 적절하고 (2)에서는 will을 would로 고치는 것이 적절하다. (3) 'with+명사(구)+분사'에서 명사와의 관계가 능동이면 현재분사를, 수동이면 과거분사를 쓰므로 'closing'을 'closed'로 고치는 것이 적절하다.

01 If I went to space, I would take a selfie.
02 Chris looked at the stars through a telescope with one eye closed.
03 (1) If it were not for (2) Were it not for
   (3) If there were not (4) But for (5) As there is
04 in his hand
05 came
06 turned on
07 could live, would live
08 (1) If we lived on the moon, we would weigh less.
   (2) If we had more time, we could help you.
   (3) Lower your head to the ground with your arms stretched.
   (4) Alice was standing with tears running down her cheeks.
09 can → could, will → would, calling → called
10 (1) If I were[was] an architect, I could build my own house.
   (2) If Mom had an apple, she would make me apple pie.
   (3) If it rained, we would not go on a picnic.
   (4) If she had had enough time, she could have spent time with us.
11 (1) is → were[was] (2) can → could
   (3) with her closed eyes → with her eyes closed
   (4) played → playing

01 가정법 과거 시제의 문장으로 쓴다. 'If I went to space'로 종속절을 쓰고 주절에 조동사의 과거형 would를 쓰는 것에 유의한다.

02 'with+명사(구)+분사'에서 명사와의 관계가 능동이면 현재분사를, 수동이면 과거분사를 쓴다. 눈이 감기는 것이므로 수동의 과거분사가 적절하다.

03 '게으르지만 않다면, 그는 좋은 사람일 텐데.'라는 뜻이다. 가정법 과거의 경우, 'Without = If it were not for = Were it not for = If there were no(not) = But for'이다.

04 'with+명사(구)' 다음에는 분사, 형용사, 부사, 전치사구' 등이 올 수 있으며, 여기서는 전치사구 'in his hand'가 적절하다.

05 주절에 '주어+could'가 나오므로 가정법 과거의 문장이며, 'If+주어+동사의 과거형/were ~, 주어+조동사의 과거형(would/should/could/might)+동사원형 …'의 형태이다.

06 'with+명사(구)+분사'에서 2 단어로 써야 하고, 명사와의 관계가 수동이므로 'turned on'이 적절하다.

07 가정법 과거는 현재 사실과 반대되는 가정을 나타낼 때 사용하므

41

로 직설법 문장을 가정법으로 나타낼 수 있다.

08 (1), (2) '가정법 과거를 이용한다. (3), (4) 'with+명사(구)+분사'에서 명사와의 관계가 능동이면 현재분사를, 수동이면 과거분사를 쓴다.

09 가정법 과거는 'If절에 동사의 과거형이나 were, 주절에 조동사의 과거형+동사원형 …'의 형태로 나타내며, Zetopia로 불리는 것이므로 과거분사 called가 되어야 한다.

10 직설법 현재 문장을 가정법 과거 문장으로 바꿀 때, 종속절에는 동사의 과거형을, 주절에는 '조동사의 과거형+동사원형'을 쓰는 것에 유의한다. (4)번은 가정법 과거완료로 과거의 사실을 반대로 가정하거나 실현 가능성이 없는 일에 대해서 가정할 때 쓰며, 'If+주어+had+p.p. ~, 주어+조동사의 과거형(would/should/could/might)+have+p.p. ~'의 형태로 쓴다.

11 (1) 주절에 would가 있는 가정법 과거 문장이다. is를 was나 were로 고치는 것이 적절하다. (2) 가정법 과거 문장이므로 can을 could로 고치는 것이 적절하다. (3) 감긴 눈으로 냄새를 맡는 것이 아니므로 'with+명사(구)+분사'의 어순으로 쓴다. (4) 'with+명사(구)+분사'에서 명사와의 관계가 능동이므로 현재분사를 쓴다.

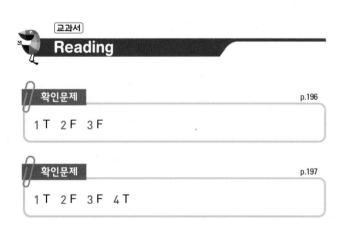

교과서 Reading

확인문제   p.196

1 T   2 F   3 F

확인문제   p.197

1 T   2 F   3 F   4 T

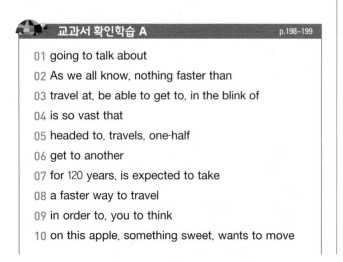

교과서 확인학습 A   p.198~199

01 going to talk about

02 As we all know, nothing faster than

03 travel at, be able to get to, in the blink of

04 is so vast that

05 headed to, travels, one-half

06 get to another

07 for 120 years, is expected to take

08 a faster way to travel

09 in order to, you to think

10 on this apple, something sweet, wants to move

11 as vast as

12 either move around, or down

13 Which do you think, because it is a shortcut

14 such a shortcut

15 figured out, are connected, space-time

16 space-time could actually be bent, that are far away, are

17 To understand, take, make, at the top of, another, bottom

18 On a flat sheet, far away

19 fold, with, matched up, Punch, the dots, be, connected

20 contain two mouths, connecting

21 Just like, existed, get to places, away

22 too early to celebrate, exist

23 all, to do, find one

24 Even if, to consider, going through one.

25 would be, unstable, flew into, be crushed, broken

26 a pretty picture, hopeless

27 through, that, exists

28 wouldn't say, is, ongoing, with persistent exploration, research, one, learn how to travel

29 Look back at, so many things that

30 knows, to find the answer

교과서 확인학습 B   p.200~201

1 Sci Teen: Hi, science fans. Today, we're going to talk about space travel.

2 As we all know, there is nothing faster than light in the universe.

3 So, if we travel at the speed of light, we should be able to get to another planet in the blink of an eye, right?

4 Dr. Sci: That would be nice, but space is so vast that it is not possible.

5 In the movie, *Passengers*, a spaceship headed to a different planet travels at one-half the speed of light.

6 So it should get to another planet very quickly, right?

7 But, the passengers sleep for 120 years because it is expected to take that much time to get to a different planet.

8 Sci Teen: 120 years? Wow, that's a long time! Is there a faster way to travel through space?

9 Dr. Sci: Well, in order to answer that question, I'd like you to think about this apple for a second.

10 Imagine a worm is on this apple. It detects something sweet at the bottom and wants to move from the top to the bottom.

11 For the worm, the apple's surface is as vast as our universe.

12 Now the worm can either move around the outer layer or down a wormhole.

13 Which do you think it will choose? Well, it would choose the wormhole because it is a shortcut.

14 Sci Teen: Is there such a shortcut in the universe?

15 Dr. Sci: According to some researchers, yes. Einstein figured out that space and time are connected, and he called it space-time.

16 He thought that space—time could actually be bent. When it is bent, parts that are far away from each other are suddenly closer.

17 To understand this, take a sheet of paper and make a small dot at the top of the paper and another at the bottom of the paper.

18 On a flat sheet of paper, the dots are far away from one another.

19 Now, take the paper and fold it with the dots matched up. Punch a hole in the paper and the dots will be instantly connected.

20 Like this, wormholes in space may contain two mouths, with a throat connecting the two.

21 Sci Teen: Just like a wormhole in the apple, right? If such wormholes existed in space, we could get to places billions of light-years away quickly!

22 Dr. Sci: Yes, but it's too early to celebrate. Wormholes exist in theory only.

23 Sci Teen: So all we need to do is find one, right?

24 Dr. Sci: Even if we find one, there are many things to consider before actually going through one

25 A wormhole would be very unstable. If a spaceship flew into one, it might be crushed or broken into pieces.

26 Sci Teen: Ouch! That's not a pretty picture. So, are we hopeless?

27 Is traveling in space through a wormhole simply an idea that only exists in theory?

28 Dr. Sci: I wouldn't say so. The debate about wormholes is still ongoing, but with persistent exploration and research, I believe we will eventually find one and learn how to travel through it.

29 Look back at our history. We've achieved so many things that seemed impossible at first.

30 Who knows? Maybe you can be the one to find the answer!

01 ③　　　　02 ②

03 They're going to talk about space travel.

04 ⑤　　　　05 ④

06 It is as vast as our universe.　　　　07 ③

08 ⑤　　　　09 a wormhole

10 We've achieved so many things that seemed impossible at first.

11 if we travel at the speed of light　　12 ②

13 (C)—(B)—(A)　　　　14 ④

15 On the apple, it detects something sweet at the bottom.

16 ③　　　　17 ⑤

18 The dots on the paper will be instantly connected.

19 ②　　　　20 ⑤　　　　21 impossible

01 영화 <Passengers>에서 다른 행성으로 향하는 우주선이 빛의 속도 절반으로 이동함에도 120년이나 걸릴 것으로 예상한다고 하였다. 따라서 우주가 매우 광활하다고 할 수 있다.

02 앞 문장에서 말한 '눈 깜박할 사이에 다른 행성에 도달할 수 있어야 한다'는 것을 가리키는 말이다.

03 오늘 우주여행에 대해 이야기할 것이라고 하였다

04 이어지는 글의 내용으로 보아 우주를 여행하는 더 빠른 방법이 있는지를 묻는 말이 가장 적절하다.

05 모두 벌레를 가리키는 말이지만 ④는 벌레구멍을 가리키는 말이다.

06 벌레에게 사과의 표면은 우리의 우주만큼이나 광대하다고 하였다.

07 주어진 문장의 this가 가리키는 것은 시공간이 구부러질 때 서로 멀리 떨어져 있는 부분들이 갑자기 더 가까워질 수 있다는 것이다. 따라서 ③번에 들어가는 것이 적절하다.

08 아인슈타인은 시간과 공간이 연결되어 있다는 것을 생각해 냈다고 하였다.

09 '웜홀'을 가리키는 말이다.

10 역사를 돌아보면 우리는 처음에는 불가능해 보였던 아주 많은 것들을 달성해 왔다고 하였다.

11 '빛의 속도'는 'the speed of light'이다. If는 조건절을 이끄는 부사절 접속사로 '~라면'이라고 해석된다.

12 과학 팬들에게 인사를 하며 대화를 시작하고 있다. 따라서 ②번이 글의 내용과 일치한다..

13 (C) 영화 <Passengers>에서 다른 행성으로 향하는 우주선이 빛의 속도의 절반으로 이동함 (B) 그렇게 이동하면 다른 행성에

매우 빨리 도달해야겠지만 (A) 다른 행성에 도달하는 데 120년이 걸릴 것으로 예상되어 승객들이 120년 동안 잠을 잠.

14 밑줄 친 (A)는 to부정사의 형용사적 용법으로 쓰였다. ① 명사적 용법 중 진주어 ② 부사적 용법 중 목적 ③ 부사적 용법 중 감정의 원인 ④ 형용사적 용법 ⑤ 명사적 용법 중 목적격 보어

15 사과 위에서 벌레는 맨 아래에 있는 달콤한 무언가를 감지한다고 하였다.

16 위 글은 우주에 지름길로서 존재하는 웜홀에 대한 설명이므로 ③번이 가장 적절하다.

17 펼쳐 놓은 종이에서 그 점들은 서로 멀리 떨어져 있지만 그 종이를 들고 점들이 맞춰지도록 접고, 종이에 구멍을 뚫으면 그 점들이 즉시 연결된다는 의미이다. 따라서 hold가 아닌 fold라고 쓰는 것이 자연스럽다.

18 종이에 구멍을 뚫으면 그 점들이 즉시 연결될 것이라고 하였다.

19 unstable, insecure: 불안정한, exclusive: 배타적인

20 핵심 주어는 The debate이므로 단수 취급하여 is라고 쓰는 것이 적절하다.

21 역사를 되돌아보면 처음에는 불가능해 보였던 아주 많은 것들을 달성해 왔다고 하였다.

---

03 해석: 우주는 너무 광활해서 우리가 빛의 속도로 여행을 한다 해도 다른 행성에 눈 깜빡할 사이에 도달할 수 없다.

04 지름길이라고 하였으므로. 바깥 표면의 껍질을 돌아서 이동하는 것이 아닌 구멍 아래로 이동하는 것이 적절하다.

05 would like는 to부정사를 목적격 보어로 취하여 'would like+목적어+to부정사' 형태로 쓰인다.

06 앞 문장 'When it is bent, parts that are far away from each other are suddenly closer.'를 가리키는 말이다.

07 종이에 점들을 찍은 후 종이를 들고 점들이 맞춰지도록 그것을 접어야 한다.

08 아인슈타인은 시간과 공간이 연결되어 있고 시공간이 구부러질 수 있다고 생각했다. 이것이 구부러질 때 서로 멀리 떨어져 있는 부분들이 갑자기 더 가까워지는데, 이렇게 두 개의 입과 그 둘을 연결하는 목구멍을 지니고 있을 것이라고 추정하는 것이 우주의 웜홀이다.

09 웜홀은 이론상에서만 존재하기 때문에 축하하기에는 너무 이르다고 말한 것이다.

10 우리가 결국 웜홀 하나를 찾으면 그것을 통해 여행하는 법을 배울 수 있을 것이라고 믿는다고 하였다.

11 만약 우주선이 웜홀 안으로 날아가게 되면, 우주선이 부서지거나 산산조각이 날 수도 있다고 하였다.

12 웜홀에 대한 논쟁은 여전히 진행 중이라고 하였다.

서술형 시험대비 p.206~207

01 It travels at one-half the speed of light.
02 Because it is expected to take that much time to get to a different planet.
03 get to another planet in the blink of an eye
04 wormhole
05 I'd like you to think about this apple for a second.
06 시공간이 구부러질 때 서로 멀리 떨어져 있는 부분들이 갑자기 더 가까워질 수 있는 것
07 We need to take the paper and fold it with the dots matched up.
08 Wormholes, connected, bent, bent, closer
09 It is because wormholes exist in theory only.
10 We will learn how to travel through it.
11 It might be crushed or broken into pieces.
12 No, it's still ongoing.

01 영화 <Passengers>에 나오는 우주선은 빛의 속도의 절반으로 이동한다고 하였다.

02 영화 <Passengers>에서 승객들이 120년 동안 잠을 자게 되는 이유는 다른 행성에 도달하는 데 그만큼 많은 시간이 걸릴 것으로 예상되기 때문이다.

영역별 핵심문제 p.209~213

01 ④　　02 movable　　03 exploration
04 ④　　05 (A) from (B) from
06 ③　　07 ②　　08 gravity
09 I wish I could float around like an astronaut!
10 impossible　11 ②　　12 ③　　13 ③
14 ④　　15 ②
16 with a throat connecting
17 didn't lie, would not be
18 (1) crossed　(2) blowing　(3) closed　(4) following (5) closed
19 became, could enjoy　20 ④　　21 ①
22 ②　　23 ④
24 Light is the fastest thing in the universe.
25 Sci Teen thinks if we travel at the speed of light, we should be able to get to another planet in the blink of an eye.
26 ③　　27 ③　　28 ③　　29 ②
30 ④, ⑤
31 They could communicate with animals on the planet 'Atlas'.

01 correct의 반의어는 incorrect이다.

02 동사 뒤에 –able을 붙이면 '~할 수 있는'이라는 의미의 형용사가 된다. movable: 움직일 수 있는

03 explore: 탐험하다, exploration: 탐사, 탐구 / 우주 탐사는 나에게 흥미로워 보인다.

04 (A) too ~ to+동사원형: 너무 ~해서 …할 수 없다 / 이 퍼즐은 너무 복잡해서 조립할 수 없다. (B) such+(부정관사)+형용사+명사: 그렇게 ~한 / 나는 그렇게 신나는 게임을 본 적이 없다.

05 (A) different from: ~와 다른 / 그들은 여러 면에서 서로 아주 다르다. (B) far away from: ~에서 멀리 떨어져 / 우리 집은 여기서 멀리 떨어져 있지 않다.

06 (B) 우주 정거장에서 보낸 시간 중 최고의 기억이 무엇인지 물어보는 질문에 (C) 하루에 16번 일출을 볼 수 있었다고 대답한다. (D) 하루에 일출을 여러 번 보는 것이 가능한지 물어보는 질문에 (A) 그렇다고 대답하면서 우주 정거장이 지구 주위를 90분마다 돌기 때문이라고 이유를 설명하고 있다.

07 주어진 문장은 '모든 것이 너무 달라 보인다.'라는 뜻으로, 이어지는 말로 'Yes, it's because there's no gravity in space. (응, 왜냐하면 우주에는 중력이 없기 때문이지.)'가 어울리므로 ②가 적절하다.

08 gravity: 중력 / 물체를 서로 당기는 힘으로, 특히 사물을 땅으로 떨어지게 하는 힘

09 어떤 일이 이루어지기를 바라는 표현으로 'I wish I could ~.'를 쓸 수 있다. 이는 가능성이 낮거나 이루어지기 힘든 일에 대해 '할 수 있으면 좋겠다'라는 바람의 의미로 쓰인다. float around: 떠다니다 astronaut: 우주 비행사

10 스케이트보드를 타고 날아다니는 것이 실제로 가능하다고 말하고 있으므로 전혀 불가능한 일이 아니라고 말하는 것이 어울린다. impossible: 불가능한

11 apply: 적용하다, 응용하다

12 남자가 아니라 여자가 날아다니는 스케이트보드를 가지기를 원한다.

13 ③번의 if는 간접의문문에 쓰였지만 나머지는 모두 가정법의 조건절을 이끌고 있다.

14 'with+명사(구)+분사'에서 명사와의 관계가 수동이므로 과거분사를 써야 한다. crossing을 crossed로 고쳐야 한다.

15 가정법 과거는 'If+주어+were/동사의 과거형 ~, 주어+조동사의 과거형+동사원형 …'의 형태로 나타낸다.

16 'with+명사(구)+분사'에서 명사와의 관계가 능동이면 현재분사를, 수동이면 과거분사를 쓴다.

17 가정법 과거에는 조건절에 동사의 과거형이 나오고 주절에는 '조동사의 과거형(would/should/could/might)+동사원형'이 나온다.

18 'with+명사(구)+분사'에서 명사와의 관계가 능동이면 현재분사를, 수동이면 과거분사를 쓴다. (1), (3), (5) 명사와의 관계가 수동이므로 각각 과거분사 crossed, closed, closed를 써야 한다. (2), (4) 명사와의 관계가 능동이므로 각각 현재분사 blowing, following을 써야 한다.

19 가정법 과거는 'If+주어+were/동사의 과거형 ~, 주어+조동사의 과거형(would/should/could/might)+동사원형 …'의 형태이다.

20 'with+명사(구)+분사'는 부대상황을 나타내며, 목적어와 능동의 관계일 경우 현재분사를 쓴다.

21 ① Jean and Tom are listening to music with their eyes closed.

22 지름길이기 때문에 웜홀을 선택한다는 의미이다. 따라서 ②번이 적절하다.

23 영작하면 'Which do you think it will choose?'이므로 think이다. 생각동사 think는 간접의문문의 의문사를 문두에 배치하는 것에 유의한다.

24 우주에서 가장 빠른 것은 빛이다.

25 Sci Teen은 우리가 빛의 속도로 여행을 한다면, 우리는 다른 행성에 눈 깜박할 사이에 도달할 수 있다고 생각한다.

26 영화에서 승객들은 다른 행성에 도달하는 120년 동안 잠을 잔다고 하였다.

27 'ongoing'은 진행 중이라는 의미이다. 따라서 ③번이 가장 적절하다. ① 다가오는 ② 유망한 ⑤ 근원적인

28 Dr. Sci는 끊임없는 탐구와 연구로 결국 웜홀 하나를 찾아 그것을 통해 여행하는 법을 배울 수 있을 것이라고 믿는다고 말하며, 여러분이 그 답을 찾아내는 사람이 될 수 있을지도 모른다고 말하고 있다. encouraging: 격려하는, 용기를 북돋아주는

29 행성 위에서 사는 것이므로 'a planet to live on'이라고 쓰는 것이 어법상 적절하다. ① to부정사의 의미상 주어로 'for+목적격'을 쓴다.

30 행성의 위치와 그곳에 갈 방법은 위 글에 나와 있지 않다.

31 사람들은 행성 '아틀라스'에서 동물들과 의사소통을 할 수 있을 것이라고 하였다.

단원별 예상문제 p.214~217

01 changeable

02 (1) tough (2) ongoing (3) unstable (4) persistent

03 ① 04 ① 05 ① 06 ③

07 out 08 ② 09 ② 10 ①

11 ⑤ 12 (C) → (A) → (B) → (D) 13 ③

14 (1) has → had, can → could
   (2) extending → extended

15 (1) If Carrie passed the exam, she would be a lawyer. / As Carrie doesn't pass the exam, she won't be a lawyer.

(2) If we traveled at the speed of light, we could go to Mars in 13 minutes. / Since we don't travel at the speed of light, we can't go to Mars in 13 minutes.

(3) Take the paper and fold it with the dots matched up.

16 ④　　　17 ⑤　　　18 (B)–(A)–(C) 19 ④

20 theory　　21 ③　　　22 ②

23 It is Atlas.

---

01 unstable: 불안정한, changeable: 변덕스러운 / 정치 상황이 여전히 매우 불안정하다.

02 (1) tough: 힘든, 어려운 / 부산으로 이사 가는 것은 어려운 결정이었다. (2) ongoing: 계속 진행 중인 / 계속 진행 중인 이 이슈에 대해 어떻게 생각하니? (3) unstable: 불안정한 / 나는 저 의자가 불안정해 보인다. (4) persistent: 끈질긴, 집요한, 지속적인 / 나는 지속적인 두통과 목 통증이 있다.

03 achieve: 달성하다, 성취하다 / 특히 많은 작업이나 노력 후에 일을 끝내거나 목적을 달성하는 데 성공하다

04 apply: 적용하다, 응용하다 / 그 규칙은 아이들에게는 적용되지 않는다.

05 우주에 중력이 없기 때문에 채소를 특수한 봉지 안에서 키워야 한다고 하고 있으므로 이유의 접속사 since가 들어가는 것이 적절하다.

06 어떤 일이 실제로 가능한지 묻는 표현으로 'Is it possible to ~?'를 쓸 수 있다. 같은 표현으로 'Are we able to ~?', 'Can we actually ~?', 'Is there a possibility that 주어+동사 ~?', 'Would it be possible ~?' 등이 있다. ③의 should는 '~해야 한다'의 의미이므로 어울리지 않는다.

07 print out: (프린터로) 출력하다

08 어떤 일이 실제로 가능한지 묻는 표현으로 'Is it possible to ~?'를 쓸 수 있다.

09 ⓐ that, 'Have you heard that 주어+동사 ~?'는 '~를 들어 본 적 있니?'의 의미로 알고 있는지 묻는 표현이다. ⓑ into, send A into B: A를 B로 보내다 ⓒ to print, be used to 동사원형: ~하기 위해 사용되다 ⓓ possible, 신선한 피자를 5분도 안 돼서 출력해 낼 수 있다고 말하고 있으므로 3D프린터를 이용해 음식을 만드는 것은 가능하다. ⓔ what

10 'Actually, you can do that at the National Youth Space

Center.'에서 do that이 'see Earth from space with your own eyes'를 의미하므로 ①이 적절하다.

11 직접 자신의 눈으로 우주에서 지구를 볼 수 있기를 희망하는 여자에게 국립 청소년 우주 센터에서 가상 현실 안경을 쓰면 실제로 우주에 있는 것 같은 기분이 든다고 얘기하고 있다.

12 무엇을 보고 있는지 물어보는 질문에 (C) 우주에서의 삶에 관한 다큐멘터리를 보고 있다고 대답하면서 모든 것이 달라 보인다고 말한다. (A) 우주에 중력이 없기 때문에 달라 보인다고 얘기해 준다. (B) 자신도 우주 비행사처럼 떠다니는 것을 바란다고 말하자 (D) 상대방은 자신은 아니라고 대답하면서 불편해 보인다고 말한다.

13 ① If I were the principal of my school, I would let students have PE class every day. ② If there were no cold air and warm air, a wind could not be made. ④ Were it not for water, no living things could survive. ⑤ But for your advice, I would ruin my reputation.

14 (1) 가정법 과거에서 종속절에는 동사의 과거형을 쓴다. (2) 'with+명사(구)+분사'에서 명사와의 관계가 능동이면 현재분사를, 수동이면 과거분사를 쓴다. 다리가 무엇을 뻗도록 하는 것이 아니라 뻗게 되는 것이므로 수동의 과거분사가 적절하다.

15 (1), (2) 가정법 과거 문장은 현재시제의 직설법으로 바꿔 쓸 수 있다. (3) 'with+명사(구)+분사'는 부대상황을 나타내며, 목적어와 수동의 관계일 경우 과거분사를 쓴다.

16 If there were no ~ = If it were not for ~ = Were it not for ~ = But for ~ = Without ~

17 이어지는 설명으로 보아 우주에 지름길이 존재하는지를 묻는 말이 들어가는 것이 자연스럽다.

18 (B)의 this는 '시공간이 구부러질 때 서로 멀리 떨어져 있는 부분들이 갑자기 더 가까워질 수 있다'는 앞 문장을 받음 (A) the dots는 (B)에서 찍은 점들을 가리킴 (C) 멀리 있던 점들이 구멍을 뚫으면 즉시 연결됨

19 밑줄 친 ⓐ는 완전한 절을 이끄는 명사절 접속사이다. ④번은 불완전한 절을 이끄는 관계대명사 that이다.

20 어떠한 학문의 바탕이 되는 규칙을 정식으로 진술하는 것은 '이론(theory)'이다.

21 웜홀이 다른 행성으로 안전하게 이동하는 것을 가능하게 한다는 말은 나와 있지 않다.

22 행성 위에서 사는 것이므로 'on'이 가장 적절하다.

23 글쓴이가 만들기를 원하는 행성의 이름은 아틀라스이다.

01 (1) I wish I could take a space trip.
  (2) Taking a space trip would be a dream come true.
  (3) It would be great if I could take a space trip.

02 (1) I wish I could open my (own) restaurant.
  (2) I also wish (that) I could appear on a cooking show.

03 Is it possible to lie down / their sleeping bag to

04 (1) As Mary doesn't hear the news, she isn't happy.
  (2) My father doesn't know the fact, so he lets me go there.
  (3) If the man could speak English, I would employ him.
  (4) Were the weather fine, Jini would go on a picnic.
  (5) Without television, half the pleasure of our daily lives could be lost.

05 (1) Mr. Jones is sitting on a chair with his legs crossed.
  (2) Bella laughed out loud with her finger pointing at me.
  (3) It was a beautiful morning, with little wind blowing.

06 matched

07 He figured out that space and time are connected.

08 A throat connects them.

09 light

10 (B) headed   (C) travels   (D) expected

01 어떤 일이 이루어지기를 바라는 표현으로 'I wish I could ~.'를 쓸 수 있다. 이는 가능성이 낮거나 이루어지기 힘든 일에 대해 '할 수 있으면 좋겠다'라는 바람의 의미로 쓰인다. 같은 표현으로 '~ would be a dream come true.', 'How I wish I could ~!', 'It would be great if I could ~.' 등이 있다.

02 어떤 일이 이루어지기를 바라는 표현으로 'I wish I could ~.'를 쓸 수 있다. 이는 가능성이 낮거나 이루어지기 힘든 일에 대해 '할 수 있으면 좋겠다'라는 바람의 의미로 쓰인다. appear: 나타나다, 등장하다

03 어떤 일이 실제로 가능한지 묻는 표현으로 'Is it possible to ~?'를 쓸 수 있다. lie down: 눕다, 누워 있다

04 (1)~(3) 가정법 과거 문장은 현재시제의 직설법으로 바꿔 쓸 수 있다. (4) 가정법으로 고친 후, if를 생략하고 were를 문두에 쓰고 도치시킨다. (5) if there were no = if it were not for =

were it not for = without = but for

05 'with+명사(구)+분사'는 부대상황을 나타내며, 목적어와 능동의 관계일 경우 현재분사를, 목적어와 수동의 관계일 경우 과거분사를 쓴다. (1) 다리가 교차되는 것이므로 과거분사crossed를 쓴다. (2) 손가락이 나를 가리키는 것이므로 현재분사 pointing을 쓴다. (3) 바람이 부는 것이므로 현재분사 blowing을 쓴다.

06 'with+명사+분사' 형태로 부대 상황을 나타낸다. 분사의 의미상 주어인 the dots가 분사와 수동의 관계이므로 과거분사인 matched를 쓰는 것이 적절하다.

07 아인슈타인은 공간과 시간이 연결되어 있다는 것을 생각해 냈다고 하였다.

08 우주의 웜홀은 두 개의 입과 그 둘을 연결하는 목구멍을 지니고 있을 것이라고 하였다.

09 뒤에서 빛의 속도로 이동하면 다른 행성에 눈 깜박할 사이에 도달할 수 있다고 말하고 있으므로 '우주에서 빛보다 더 빠른 것은 없다'로 말하는 것이 적절하다.

10 (B) 다른 행성으로 향한다는 의미로 head는 타동사이므로 과거분사로 쓴다. (B) 주어가 a spaceship이며 빛의 속도의 절반으로 이동한다는 의미이므로 단수동사 travels를 쓴다. (D) 다른 행성에 도달하는 데 그만큼 많은 시간이 걸릴 것으로 예상된다는 의미이므로 수동태를 쓴다.

|모범답안|

01 (1) I wish I could sing better.
  (2) I wish I could play soccer better.
  (3) I wish I were a famous writer.

02 (1) If Earth had no air, the sky would always be black.
  (2) (a) If there were no gravity, the air would go away to space.
    (b) If it were not for gravity, the air would go away to space.
    (c) Were it not for gravity, the air would go away to space.
    (d) But for gravity, the air would go away to space.
    (e) Without gravity, the air would go away to space.

03 Minas / pink / bigger than the moon, but smaller than Earth / 20℃ / cotton candy mountains / feel time pass slowly on this planet

01 어떤 일이 이루어지기를 바라는 표현으로 'I wish I could[were] ~.'를 쓸 수 있다.

02 if there were no = if it were not for = were it not for = without = but for임을 숙지하는 것이 좋다.

01 ②, ⑤   02 ③

03 (1) extend   (2) attach   (3) crushed   (4) exists

04 (1) billions of   (2) (c)elebrate   (3) (d)etect
    (4) (e)ventually

05 (A) comfortable   (B) impossible

06 distance   07 ⑤   08 ③

09 I wish I could live in space.   10 ④

11 I wish I could become an astronaut like them and explore Mars.

12 ⓐ, ⓒ, ⓓ   13 ③   14 ④   15 ②

16 (1) They jogged with their dog following them.
   (2) Drake walked for a long time with his eyes fixed upon the floor.
   (3) The prince entered the hall with the people cheering.

17 (1) If I were[was] an astronaut, I would walk in space.
   (2) If it stopped raining, we could play baseball.
   (3) I wish I could bring my mom back to life.
   (4) Balance on your arms with your knees resting on the upper arms.
   (5) My teacher worked all day with the door closed.

18 with a throat connecting the two

19 ③

20 The worm can either move around the outer layer or down a wormhole.   21 ⑤

22 ④   23 ②

24 We will do that with persistent exploration and research.

25 We could get to places billions of light-years away quickly.

01 ① in theory: 이론상으로는, 원칙상으로는 / 이론상 그 산을 오르는 데는 이틀 밖에 안 걸리지만 실제로는 그건 불가능하다. ② print out: (프린터로) 출력하다 / 너의 보고서를 출력해 줄래? ③ in the blink of an eye: 눈 깜짝할 사이에 / 그것은 눈 깜짝할 사이에 사라져 버렸다. ④ in order to 동사원형: ~하기 위하여 / 나는 내가 그 시험에 통과할 수 있도록 열심히 공부했다. ⑤ lie down: 눕다, 누워 있다 / 여기 누워서 좀 쉬어라.

02 ① im-+partial → impartial 공정한 ② im-+patient → impatient 안달하는 ③ un-+usual → unusual 보통이 아닌, 평소와 다른 ④ in-+credible → incredible 믿을 수 없는, 믿

기 힘든 ⑤ in-+sensitive → insensitive 둔감한, 몰이해한

03 (1) extend: (팔, 다리를) 뻗다 / 바닥에 누워서 다리를 뻗어라. (2) attach: 붙이다 / 너는 이 양식에 너의 사진을 붙여야 한다. (3) crush: 눌러 부수다, 찌부러뜨리다 / 이 차들은 그 사고에서 찌부러졌다. (4) exist: 존재하다 / 너는 생명체가 다른 행성들에 존재한다는 것을 믿니?

04 (1) billions: 수십억의 (2) celebrate: 축하하다 (3) detect: 감지하다, 발견하다 (4) eventually: 결국

05 (A) comfortable: 편안한, 우주에 중력을 만드는 것이 가능하다면, 우주 여행이 더 편해질 것이다. (B) impossible: 불가능한, 과학자들이 기술을 개발하고 있는 중이라고 말했으므로, 우주에 중력을 만드는 것이 전혀 불가능 일이 아니라고 하는 것이 적절하다.

06 distance: 거리 / 두 장소 사이의 공간의 총계

07 우주에 살면 키가 더 커질 수 있다는 말에 여자가 우주에 가는 것 말고 키가 더 커지는 다른 방법이 있을 거라고 확신하다고 말하는 것이 어울린다.

08 (A) while 뒤에 주어와 be동사가 생략되어 있다. while: ~하는 동안 (B) 'It's because'는 '~하기 때문이다'라는 의미로 이유를 말할 때 사용한다.

09 'I wish I could ~.'는 소망이나 바람을 나타낼 때 사용하는 표현으로 '내가 ~할 수 있다면 좋을 텐데.'라는 뜻이다.

10 주어진 문장은 직접 진짜 우주인을 만났는지 물어보는 질문으로 대답으로는 'Yes, and I heard about their adventure stories.(응, 그리고 나는 그들의 모험 이야기를 들었어.)'가 어울리므로 ④가 적절하다.

12 ⓐ Cindy는 국립 우주 센터에서 무엇을 했는가? (무중력 상태와 우주 비행사들의 우주 생활을 경험했다.) ⓑ Cindy가 우주 비행사가 되는 것은 가능한가? ⓒ Cindy가 언제 국립 우주 센터에 갔는가? (지난 주말에) ⓓ Cindy는 우주인을 만났는가? (만났다.)

13 ③ 내가 마법의 램프를 갖고 있기 때문에, 행복과 건강을 빌 수 있다. ①, ②, ④, ⑤ 내가 마법의 램프를 갖고 있다면, 행복과 건강을 빌 수 있을 텐데. (내가 마법의 램프를 갖고 있지 않기 때문에, 행복과 건강을 빌 수 없다.)

14 'with+명사(구)+분사'는 부대상황을 나타내며, 목적어와 능동의 관계일 경우 현재분사를, 목적어와 수동의 관계일 경우 과거분사를 쓴다.

15 ②번의 if는 간접의문문으로 명사절을 이끄는 접속사이며, 나머지는 모두 가정법의 조건절을 이끄는 종속접속사이다.

16 'with+명사(구)+분사'는 부대상황을 나타내며, 목적어와 능동의 관계일 경우 현재분사를, 목적어와 수동의 관계일 경우 과거분사를 쓴다. (1) 개가 따라오는 것이므로 능동의 현재분사 following을 써야 한다. (2) 눈이 고정되는 것이므로 수동의 과거분사 fixed를 써야 한다. (3) 사람들이 갈채를 보내는 것이므로 능동의 현재분사 cheering을 써야 한다.

17 (1), (2) '만약 ~라면 …할 텐데'라는 뜻으로, 현재 사실을 반대로 가정하거나 실현 가능성이 없는 일에 대해서 가정할 때 사용하는 가정법과거로 'If+주어+were/동사의 과거형 ~, 주어+조동사의 과거형(would/should/could/might)+동사원형 …'의 형태로 쓴다. (3) 'I wish I could ~.'는 현재는 이룰 수 없는 어떤 소망에 대해 말할 때 사용된다. (4) 'with+명사(구)+분사'는 부대상황을 나타내며, 목적어와 능동의 관계이므로 현재분사를 써야 하는 것에 유의한다. (5) 'with+명사(구)+분사'는 부대상황을 나타내며, 목적어와 수동의 관계이므로 과거분사를 써야 하는 것에 유의한다.

18 두 점을 맞춰지도록 종이를 접고 종이에 구멍을 뚫으면 그 점들이 즉시 연결되듯, 웜홀 역시 두 개의 입과 그 둘을 연결하는 목구멍을 지니고 있다는 의미이다. 'with+목적어+분사'에서 목적어와 분사의 관계가 능동이므로 현재분사를 쓰는 것에 유의한다.

19 주어진 문장의 the dots는 종이 윗부분과 아랫부분에 찍은 각각의 점을 가리키는 말이다. 또한 펼쳐진 종이에서는 이 점들이 서로 멀리 떨어져 있지만 이것을 들어서 점들이 맞춰지도록 접고 종이에 구멍을 뚫으면 점들이 즉시 연결이 된다는 흐름이 자연스럽다.

20 벌레는 바깥 표면의 껍질을 돌아서 이동하거나 벌레 구멍 아래로 이동할 수 있다고 하였다.

21 아인슈타인이 시공간이 연결되어 있는 것을 어떻게 발견하게 되었는지는 위 글을 읽고 답할 수 없다.

22 웜홀은 매우 불안정할 것이므로 실제로 그것을 통과하여 가기 전에 고려해야 할 것들이 많이 있다고 하였다.

23 위 글은 웜홀을 통한 우주여행에 관한 글이므로 ②번이 가장 적절하다.

24 Dr. Sci는 끊임없는 탐구와 연구로 우리가 결국 웜홀을 찾아 그것을 통해 여행하는 법을 배울 수 있을 것이라고 믿는다고 하였다.

25 웜홀이 존재한다면 우리는 수십억 광년 떨어져 있는 곳에 빠르게 도달할 수 있을 것이라고 하였다.

교과서 파헤치기

Lesson 5

01 진지하게, 심각하게   02 인정하다, 자백하다
03 비판적으로   04 끔찍한, 지독한   05 극도로, 극히
06 가짜의, 거짓의   07 고백하다, 인정하다
08 위험한, 위독한   09 해로운, 유해한   10 시민
11 잘못 이끌다, 오해하게 하다   12 키, 신장
13 강하게 하다, 더 튼튼하게 하다   14 성인, 어른
15 논쟁, 언쟁   16 발행하다, 출판하다, 게재하다
17 알아보다   18 사건   19 비난하다
20 입증하다, 증명하다   21 현재의, 지금의
22 참사, 재난   23 달아나다, 탈출하다, 벗어나다
24 판단하다   25 기술하다
26 그럼에도 불구하고 27 믿을 만한, 신뢰할 만한
28 상처를 입히다   29 근육
30 (사실임을) 입증하다, 뒷받침하다   31 광산; 채굴하다
32 측정하다, 재다 33 출처, 자료   34 가슴, 흉부
35 ~와 연관되다   36 조사하다, 들여다보다
37 지어내다, 만들어 내다
38 ~을 부수다, ~을 무너뜨리다   39 ~에 따르면
40 ~의 관심을 …로 끌다
41 고정관념에서 벗어나다   42 ~에게 유용하다
43 잡히지 않은, 탈주 중인

01 admit   02 muscle   03 nevertheless
04 competitor   05 seriously   06 adult
07 mislead   08 mine   09 criticize
10 prove   11 critically   12 disaster
13 escape   14 public   15 strengthen
16 fake   17 confess   18 extremely
19 harmful   20 incident   21 argument
22 reliable   23 awful   24 citizen
25 judge   26 measure   27 current
28 publish   29 critical   30 recognize
31 source   32 describe   33 support
34 wound   35 look into   36 search for
37 be related to   38 draw one's attention to
39 fall asleep   40 break down   41 according to
42 be useful for   43 make up

1 shoot, (총 등을) 쏘다   2 fake, 거짓의   3 citizen, 시민
4 disaster, 참사, 재난   5 describe, 기술하다
6 panic, 겁에 질려 어쩔 줄 모르다   7 chest, 가슴, 흉부
8 spell, 철자를 말하다, 쓰다   9 criticize, 비난하다
10 source, 출처, 자료   11 wound, 상처를 입히다
12 incident, 사건   13 publish, 발행하다, 출판하다
14 trust, 신뢰하다   15 prove, 입증하다
16 argument, 논쟁, 언쟁

Listen & Talk 1 A-1

caught a cold, because, dress warmly / article, cold, body temperature, low / more about it / because of viruses

Listen & Talk 1 A-2

a glass of warm milk, fall asleep / help, fall asleep / tell me more about it / chemicals, make, sleepy, amount, too, to, effect

Listen & Talk 2 A-1

What are you reading / riddles / for / Actually, useful for adults / say so / help, think, creatively, think outside the box to find

Listen & Talk 2 A-2

poetry books / written by / write better pomes / say so / honest, feelings, more creative than adults

Listen & Talk 2 B

I should buy this drink, help, lose weight / Let me read, label, closely, strange / you say so / enough information, what's, drink / right / how much you have to drink to lose weight

Communication

pieces of information, facts, completely wrong / there were, examples, facts that are wrong / what / goldfish, goldfish, actually smart / tell, more / recognize their owners / know that

Wrap Up 2

interesting article, where it is / between, and, right / What color, it is / guess / called, tell moe more / because, dangerous

Listen & Talk 1 A-1

W: I think I caught a cold because I didn't dress warmly yesterday.

M: Well, I've read an article saying that you don't catch a cold because your body temperature is low.

W: Really? Can you tell me more about it?

M: The article said that people catch colds because of viruses.

Listen & Talk 1 A-2

W: I usually drink a glass of warm milk before I go to bed, but it doesn't help me fall asleep.

M: I saw a show on TV, and a doctor said that a glass of warm milk doesn't actually help you fall asleep.

W: Oh, it doesn't? Can you tell me more about it?

M: Milk has special chemicals that make people sleepy. But the amount in a glass is too small to have any effect.

Listen & Talk 2 A-1

W: What are you reading, John?

M: I'm reading a book of riddles.

W: Riddles? Aren't they for children?

M: Actually, no. Books of riddles are really useful for adults.

W: Really? Why do you say so?

M: They help us think more creatively. We need to think outside the box to find the answers.

Listen & Talk 2 A-2

M: Are these all poetry books?

W: Yeah. These are all poems written by children.

M: By children?

W: Yeah. I think children write better poems than adults.

M: Why do you say so?

W: They're really honest about their feelings and much more creative than adults.

Listen & Talk 2 B

M: Hey, Sandy. Do you think I should buy this drink? It is said that it can help me lose weight.

W: Let me read the label more closely. Hmm, it looks a bit strange to me, David.

M: Why do you say so?

W: There isn't enough information about what's in the drink.

M: Oh, you're right.

W: Also, it doesn't tell you how much you have to drink to lose weight.

Communication

W: There are so many pieces of information we call "facts" that are completely wrong.

M: Why do you say so?

W: I read a book, and there were a lot of examples of these facts that are wrong.

M: Like what?

W: Well, most people think goldfish are not smart. But, goldfish are actually smart.

M: Really? Can you tell me more about that?

W: They can recognize their owners.

M: Oh, I didn't know that

Wrap Up 2

W: I read an interesting article about the Black Sea. Do you know where it is?

M: Yes. It's between Eastern Europe and Western Asia, right?

W: Right. What color do you think it is?

M: Well, black, I guess.

W: No, it isn't. It's blue.

M: Really? Then why is it called the Black Sea? Can you tell me more about it?

W: People call it the Black Sea because it is very dangerous.

본문 TEST Step 1   p.09~11

01 Spot Fake News

02 watch, hear, interesting news

03 seriously considered whether, article

04 what if, made up

05 harmful, less informed, misled

06 Nevertheless, various, throughout history

07 written such false information

08 thinking, hidden motives behind

09 AWFUL DISATER

10 broke down, cage, escaped

11 broke down, other, cages

12 ran dawn, injured hundreds

13 still on the loose

14 stay, until further notice

15 incident described, taken place

16 article, laughed out loud

17 Those, got really worried

18 Not knowing, false, panicked

19 Some, escape, others, hunt

20 make up such news

21 confessed, up, attention, unsafe

22 SLAV SHOOTS, IN ARGUMENT

23 shot, wounded, near, mining

24 had, argument during

25 led, shot, twice, chest

26 in critical condition

27 ran away after, shooting

28 searching, warning citizens, dangerous

29 there anything strange, article

30 Read, backwards, spells

31 Who wrote, why

32 so that, competitor, stealing

33 published, article, caught stealing

34 admit, harshly criticized, public

35 special cases, articles published

36 critically, judge whether, fake　　37 How to spot

38 Consider, Source

39 from, reliable source

40 Can, trust, writer　　　　　41 Check, Date

42 new, old story

43 Is, related to current

44 Beyond the Headlines

45 headline match, content

46 Supporting Sources

47 related, provide similar content

---

23 was shot, seriously wounded by

24 had an argument during

25 led to, twice, in the chest

26 in critical condition

27 ran away after the shooting

28 are searching for, are warning, extremely dangerous

29 anything strange, article　　　30 backwards

31 wrote, why

32 pubilshed, so that, could, if, their articles

33 got caught stealing

34 had to admit, were harshly criticized

35 special cases, published

36 As, critically, judge whether, or　　37 How to spot

38 Consider, Source

39 reliable source　　　　　40 trust, writer

41 Check　　　　　　　42 new, old story

43 Is, related to current

44 Beyond the Headlines

45 match the content

46 Supporting Sources

47 related, similar content

---

01 Spot Fake News

02 interesting news

03 have, considered whether

04 what if, completely made up

05 harmful in that, less informed, misled

06 Nevertheless, various fake, throughout history

07 written such false information

08 Let's look into, thinking, the hidden motives behind

09 AWFUL

10 broke down, escaped

11 broke down, the other

12 ran down, injured hundreds of　13 on the loose

14 Citizens, until further notice

15 described above, taken place

16 laughed out loud

17 got really worried

18 Not knowing, false, panicked

19 Some, to escape, others, to hunt

20 make up such news

21 made it up so that, could, readers' attention to

22 SHOOTS, IN ARGUMENT

---

1 당신은 가짜 뉴스임을 알아챌 수 있는가?

2 매일 우리는 흥미로운 뉴스를 보고, 듣고, 읽는다.

3 그러나 당신은 뉴스 기사가 정말로 진실인지 심각하게 고려해 본 적이 있는가?

4 모든 사람이 흥미로운 뉴스 기사를 좋아하지만, 만약 그것이 완전히 지어낸 것이라면 어떻게 할 것인가?

5 가짜 뉴스는 사람들에게 정보를 부족하게 제공하거나 사람들을 잘못 이끌 수 있다는 점에서 매우 해로울 수 있다.

6 그럼에도 불구하고, 역사를 통틀어 다양한 가짜 뉴스 보도들이 존재해 왔다.

7 왜 어떤 사람들은 그러한 거짓 정보를 써 왔던 것일까?

8 그 뒤에 숨겨진 동기를 생각하면서 몇 가지 뉴스 기사를 살펴보자.

9 끔찍한 참사

10 어젯밤, 화가 난 코뿔소 떼가 동물원 우리의 벽을 부수고 도망쳤다.

11 그들은 또한 다른 야생 동물 우리의 벽도 부수었다.

12 이 동물들은 거리를 뛰어다니며 수백 명의 사람들에게 부상을 입혔다.

13 그중 열두 마리의 동물들이 아직 잡히지 않았다.

14 시민들은 추후 안내가 있을 때까지 집 안에 머물러야 한다.

15 위에 기술된 어떤 행동이나 사건도 일어나지 않았다.

16 그 당시 이 기사를 주의 깊게 읽었던 사람들은 크게 웃었다.

17 그것을 끝까지 읽지 않은 사람들은 정말로 걱정하였다.

18 그 기사가 거짓이라는 것을 알지 못했기 때문에 많은 사람이 겁에 질려 어쩔 줄 몰랐다.

19 어떤 사람들은 도시를 빠져나가려고 했고 다른 사람들은 그 동물들을 사냥하기 위해 총을 들고 공원으로 나갔다.

20 그렇다면 왜 헤럴드 사는 이러한 뉴스를 만들어 냈을까?

21 나중에 그들은 동물원의 안전하지 않은 상태에 대해 독자들의 주의를 끌기 위해 그 기사를 지어냈다고 고백했다.

22 슬라브인이 언쟁 중에 친구에게 총을 쏘다

23 목요일 저녁 채굴 야영지 근처에서, 컬럼비아 광산 소속의 슬라브인 노동자 Mejk Swenekafew가 John Pecitello에 의해 총상을 입어 심각하게 다쳤다.

24 그 두 사람은 회의 중에 언쟁을 벌였다.

25 언쟁이 싸움으로 번졌고, Pecitello가 Swenekafew의 가슴과 다리에 두 번 총을 쏘았다.

26 현재 그는 위독한 상태로 입원 중이다.

27 Pecitello는 총격 이후 도주했다.

28 경찰이 지금 그를 찾고 있으며, 그가 극히 위험하다고 시민들에게 경고하고 있다.

29 이 기사에 뭔가 이상한 점이 있는가?

30 그 슬라브인의 이름을 거꾸로 읽어 보아라. 그것의 철자는 " 우리는 뉴스를 조작한다."가 된다.

31 누가 이것을 썼고 왜 그랬을까?

32 데일리 텔레그램 사는 그들의 경쟁자인 데일리 뉴스 사가 그들의 기사를 훔치는지를 증명하기 위해서 이 거짓 기사를 발행했다.

33 데일리 뉴스 사는 그 다음 날 'Swenekafew'에 대한 동일한 기사를 발행했고 그래서 훔친 것이 발각되었다.

34 데일리 뉴스 사의 사람들은 그들의 행동을 인정해야만 했고 대중들로부터 혹독한 비난을 받았다.

35 이 두 기사는 특별한 경우였지만, 매일 발행되는 '가짜' 뉴스 기사는 많이 있다.

36 독자로서, 우리는 비판적으로 읽고 그 뉴스가 진짜인지 가짜인지 판단할 필요가 있다.

37 가짜 뉴스 판별 방법!

38 출처를 고려하라

39 그것은 믿을 만한 출처에서 온 것인가?

40 우리는 그 필자를 신뢰할 수 있는가?

41 날짜를 확인하라

42 그것은 새로운 이야기인가 혹은 오래된 이야기인가?

43 그것은 현재의 사건들과 관련된 것인가?

44 기사 제목 그 이상을 읽어라

45 기사 제목이 기사 내용과 일치하는가?

46 뒷받침하는 자료를 찾아라

47 다른 관련된 이야기도 비슷한 내용을 제공하는가?

1 Can You Spot Fake News?

2 Every day we watch, hear, or read interesting news.

3 However, have you ever seriously considered whether an article is really true?

4 Everyone likes an interesting news story but what if it is completely made up?

5 Fake news can be very harmful in that it can make people less informed or even misled.

6 Nevertheless, there have been various fake news reports throughout history.

7 Why have some people written such false information?

8 Let's look into some articles thinking about the hidden motives behind them.

9 AWFUL DISASTER

10 Last night, an angry group of rhinoceroses broke down the walls of the cage at the zoo and escaped.

11 They also broke down the walls of the other wild animals' cages.

12 These animals ran down the streets and injured hundreds of people.

13 Twelve of the animals are still on the loose.

14 Citizens should stay indoors until further notice.

15 Not a single act or incident described above has taken place.

16 At that time, those who read the article carefully laughed out loud.

17 Those who didn't read it to the end got really worried.

18 Not knowing the news was false, many people panicked.

19 Some tried to escape the city while others went into the parks with guns to hunt the animals.

20 So why did *The Herald* make up such news?

21 Later, they confessed that they made it up so that they could draw the readers' attention to the unsafe conditions at the zoo.

22 SLAV SHOOTS A FRIEND IN ARGUMENT

23 Mejk Swenekafew, a Slav worker at the Columbia Coal Mine, was shot and seriously wounded by John Pecitello near the mining camp Thursday evening.

24 The two men had an argument during a meeting.

25 The argument led to a fight, and Pecitello shot Swenekafew twice, in the chest and leg.

26 He is now at the hospital in critical condition.

27 Pecitello ran away after the shooting.

28 The police are searching for him now and are warning citizens that he is extremely dangerous.

29 Is there anything strange about the article?

30 Read the Slav's name backwards; it spells, "we-fake-news."

31 Who wrote this and why?

32 *The Daily Telegram* published this fake article so that they could prove if *The Daily News*, their competitor, was stealing their articles.

33 *The Daily News* published the same article about "Swenekafew" the next day and thus got caught stealing.

34 The people at *The Daily News* had to admit their act and were harshly criticized by the public.

35 The two articles were special cases, but there are many "fake" news articles published every day.

36 As readers, we need to read critically and judge whether the news is real or fake.

37 How to spot fake news!

38 Consider the Source

39 Is it from a reliable source?

40 Can we trust the writer?

41 Check the Date

42 Is it a new or an old story?

43 Is it related to current events?

44 Read Beyond the Headlines

45 Does the headline match the content?

46 Find Supporting Sources

47 Do other related stories provide similar content?

Wrap Up 3

1. title says, going to have a longer vacation

2. should check, if it is true

3. Why, say so

4. uses a shocking title, its content may tell

5. should read beyond

Read & Think After You Read B

1. write, Awful Disaster

2. draw the readers' attention, unsafe conditions

3. Actually, were very upset to find, false. How about, motive

4. wanted to prove that, was stealing their articles

Read & Think After You Read C

1. Among, think is the most important

2. finding supporting sources is, because, if, information is correct

---

Wrap Up 3

1. A: Wow! The news title says "Longer Vacation for Students." Hey, we're going to have a longer vacation!

2. B: Wait! We should check first if it is true.

3. A: Why do you say so?

4. B: Some news uses a shocking title but its content may tell a different story.

5. A: Oh, I see. I should read beyond the news title.

Read & Think After You Read B

1. Reporter: Why did *The Herald* write the "Awful Disaster" story, Mr. Right?

2. Mr. Right: They just wanted to draw the readers' attention to the unsafe conditions at the zoo.

3. Reporter: Actually, readers were very upset to find that it was false. How about "Slav Shoots a Friend in Argument?" What was the motive?

4. Mr. Right: *The Daily Telegram* wanted to prove that *The Daily News* was stealing their articles.

Read & Think After You Read C

1. A: Among the four tips, which do you think is the most important, and why?

2. B: I think finding supporting sources is the most important because I can check if the information is correct.

---

7 chef, 요리사   8 deadline, 기한, 마감 일자

9 dragon, 용   10 reward, 보상   11 exhibit, 전시하다

12 expert, 전문가   13 explain, 설명하다

14 failure, 실패   15 wisdom, 지혜, 현명함   16 castle, 성

단어 TEST Step 1   p.26

01 영원히	02 추측하다, 추정하다	
03 혼란스러운, 헷갈리는		04 설계하다
05 전시하다	06 자유	07 비싼, 돈이 많이 드는
08 쌍둥이의	09 대단히 귀중한, 값을 매길 수 없는	
10 편안하게	11 스타덤, 스타의 반열	
12 죽음	13 당혹스러운, 어리둥절한	
14 지혜, 현명함	15 전문가	16 중요하다
17 선장	18 좌우명	19 실패
20 표현하다	21 어리석은, 바보 같은	
22 사치스러운, 호화로운		23 난장이
24 고용하다	25 숲, 삼림, 산림	26 용
27 마지막으로, 끝으로		28 기한, 마감 일자
29 마술의, 마력이 있는		30 멀리 떨어진
31 보상	32 상황, 환경	33 성
34 등장인물	35 채우다	36 돌려주다
37 투옥시키다	38 세상을 떠나다, 돌아가시다	
39 ~이 없어지다, ~이 다 떨어지다		40 ~에 갇히다
41 이루어지다, 실현되다		
42 (신조, 원칙 등)에 따라 살다		
43 ~을 살피다, ~을 돌보다		

단어 TEST Step 2   p.27

01 motto	02 chat	03 exhibit
04 death	05 stardom	06 luxurious
07 express	08 deadline	09 freedom
10 captain	11 hire	12 dragon
13 situation	14 magical	15 comfortably
16 forever	17 dwarf	18 foolish
19 failure	20 confusing	21 priceless
22 expensive	23 puzzled	24 reward
25 far-away	26 castle	27 forest
28 expert	29 suppose	30 lastly
31 twin	32 wisdom	33 explain
34 design	35 bring back	36 live by
37 lock up	38 pass away	39 run out of
40 settle in	41 look after	42 go wrong
43 come true		

단어 TEST Step 3   p.28

1 express, 표현하다   2 luxurious, 사치스러운, 호화로운

3 priceless, 대단히 귀중한, 값을 매길 수 없는

4 captain, 선장   5 character, 등장인물   6 hire, 고용하다

대화문 TEST Step 1   p.29~31

Listen & Talk 1 A

1 you still up / because I'm worried about / You've read, have to worry about / confusing, worried that, might not remember/ Don't worry, that hasn't happened / try not to worry

2 Nothing special / have to go to, can't find anyone to feed / worry about, take care of / worried / for a walk, supposed to be

Listen & Talk 1 B

worried, matter / got a big part in / heard, singing / keep making mistakes, worried / a little, practice / making mistakes

Listen & Talk 2 A

1 have, read / magical water, lived forever / What would you do if, forever / would, different cities / interesting

2 called / heard, come true / if you could make one wish / would make, stay, forever, make all my wishes come true / smart

Listen & Talk 2 B

writing a review / one of, movies / what would you do if you could / would travel, prevent, How about / would go to, meet, big fan of

Communication Step A

How's, going / ran out / Don't worry about / character, What would you do if you were / find out if, likes

Wrap Up

1 I've heard that, writing contest / already / worried, wrong / I'm worried that, too difficult / Don't worry about, believe in yourself

2 watched, haven't / a man who was stuck on, deserted island / tries, would, if you were him / alive, build, hunt / that's what the man did

대화문 TEST Step 2   p.32~34

Listen & Talk 1 A

1 W: James, why are you still up? It's 11 o'clock!

M: I can't sleep because I'm worried about the Bookworm Competition tomorrow.

W: You've read all of the books on the list. What do

you have to worry about?

M: Some of the writers' names are confusing, so I'm worried that I might not remember them.

W: Don't worry about something that hasn't happened yet. You'll do fine.

M: Thanks. I'll try not to worry so much.

2 M: Sujin, what are you doing this weekend?

W: Nothing special, why?

M: I have to go to Busan for a family trip tomorrow but I can't find anyone to feed my dog, Lucy.

W: Don't worry about Lucy. I'll take care of her.

M: Oh, thank you so much. I was so worried.

W: I'll take her for a walk in the park, too. The weather's supposed to be nice tomorrow.

Listen & Talk 1 B

M: Jane, you look worried. What's the matter?

W: I got a big part in the school musical.

M: I heard you singing. You sound great!

W: It's just that I keep making mistakes. I'm so worried.

M: Oh, you just need a little more practice. Don't worry about making mistakes. You can actually learn from them.

W: Thanks, Dad. I hope I do a good job.

M: You'll do great.

Listen & Talk 2 A

1 M: Caroline, have you read the book, *Tuck Everlasting*?

W: Yeah, it is about a family that drank magical water and lived forever, right?

M: Right. What would you do if you could live forever?

W: Well, I would live in different cities all around the world.

M: Really? I would collect interesting items and make a museum.

W: Cool.

2 W: Jason, what are you reading?

M: I'm reading a book called *Three Wishes*.

W: Oh, I've heard about it. A genie makes a boy's wishes come true, right?

M: Yeah. What would you do if you could make one wish?

W: I would make the genies stay with me forever. Then, I could make all my wishes come true.

M: That's smart!

Listen & Talk 2 B

W: What are you doing, Jinho?

M: I'm writing a review of the movie, *The Time Traveler's Wife*.

W: I saw that movie, too. It's one of my favorite romantic movies.

M: I loved it, too. Emily, what would you do if you could time travel?

W: I would travel to the 1940s and prevent World War II. How about you?

M: I would go to the Joseon Dynasty and meet King Sejong. I'm a big fan of him.

Communication Step A

M: How's your online story going, Amy?

W: Not well. The deadline is this weekend but I ran out of ideas.

M: Don't worry about it. I can help you.

W: That would be great. My main character has special powers. What would you do if you were able to read people's minds?

M: Well, I would find out if the girl I like likes me.

W: That's a good idea. Thanks.

Wrap Up

1 M: I've heard that you're going to be in the writing contest next week.

W: Yeah, it's already next week.

M: You look worried. What's wrong?

W: I'm worried that the topic would be too difficult for me.

M: Don't worry about something you can't change. Just believe in yourself.

W: Thanks. I'll try.

2 M: Lisa, have you watched the movie, Cast Away?

W: No, I haven't. What is it about?

M: It's about a man who was stuck on a deserted island for 4 years.

W: It sounds interesting.

M: Yeah, the man tries everything to stay alive. What would you do if you were him?

W: To stay alive? Well, I would build a tree house and hunt for food.

M: Yeah, me too. And that's what the man did in the movie.

본문 TEST Step 1   p.35~36

01 rich, wise, had, sons

02 passed away, words, advice

03 Live by, throughout, life

04 Build, comfortably, Lastly, like
05 explain himself, passed away
06 death, share, wealth, settled
07 passed, following, words, left
08 richer than ever
09 puzzled, wrong, find out
10 welcomed, with open arms
11 down, chat, been, mind
12 It, that, built, every
13 stay, had, looked after
14 comfortably, had, designed, prepared
15 spend like, what, worrying
16 look at, empty-handed
17 not follow, father's wisdom
18 how did, get, rich
19 smiled, also followed, wisdom
20 a bit differently
21 build, took, as, stay
22 made friends, stayed at
23 comfortably, tired, work, floor
24 only when, hungry, tasted
25 Spend, like, rich, continued
26 how to make, grow
27 bring, back, rather, luxurious
28 it, that, tried, explain
29 how foolish, had been
30 With, in mind, life

13 always stay there, hired, had, looked after
14 sleep comfortably, enjoy, had, designed, my meals prepared by
15 told, to spend like, what I wanted, worrying
16 look at me, empty-handed
17 not follow, father's wisdom
18 how did, get, rich
19 smiled, also followed, father's wisdom
20 it a bit differently
21 build, took it as having a place to stay
22 made friends, stayed at, those cities
23 comfortably, because, if I was sleeping, or, hard floor
24 only when I was hungry, tasted great
25 like a rich man, continued
26 how to make money grow
27 on, that, bring me back, rather than on luxurious things
28 it was, that, tried to explain
29 how foolish he had been
30 With, in mind

01 rich, wise, had two sons
02 passed away, called, to give them, last words of advice
03 Listen carefully, Live by, throughout your life
04 Build, every city, comfortably. Enjoy, Lastly, spend, like
05 explain himself, passed away
06 his death, their share of, wealth, settled in different cities
07 passed, who had been following, no money left
08 was richer than ever
09 was puzzled about where, had gone wrong, to find out
10 welcomed, with open arms
11 sat down to chat, that had been on his mind for days
12 It was, that, in every city

1 부유하고 지혜로운 아버지에게 두 아들, Puru와 Puneet이 있었다.
2 아버지는 돌아가시기 전에, 마지막 충고의 말을 하기 위해 그의 두 아들을 불렀다.
3 "주의 깊게 듣거라, 사랑하는 아들들아. 너희의 일생 동안 이 말대로 살면, 행복해질 것이다." 그는 말했다.
4 "모든 도시에 집을 지어라. 편하게 자거라. 음식을 즐기거라. 마지막으로, 돈을 부자처럼 쓰거라…."
5 아버지는 그 말을 설명하기도 전에 돌아가셨다.
6 그의 죽음 후에, 두 아들은 아버지의 재산 중 자신들의 몫을 가지고 다른 도시에 정착했다.
7 5년이 지났다. 아버지의 말을 신중히 따라온 Puru는 남은 돈이 없었다.
8 그러나 그의 동생은 그 어느 때보다 더 부자가 되었다.
9 Puru는 그가 어디서부터 잘못했는지 어리둥절했고, 그래서 그는 (그것을) 알아내기 위해 Puneet을 방문했다.
10 Puneet은 Puru를 두 팔 벌려 환영했다.
11 그날 밤, 형제가 저녁식사 후 이야기를 하려고 앉았을 때, Puru는 며칠간 자신의 마음에 있었던 그 질문을 했다.
12 "내가 따른 건 바로 우리 아버지의 조언이었지만, 나는 행복하지 않아. 나는 모든 도시에 집을 지었어.
13 그러나 나는 그곳에 항상 머물 수 없었으므로 사람들을 고용하여 집을 돌보게 했지.

14 아버지께서 우리는 편하게 자고 음식을 즐겨야 한다고 말씀하셔서 나는 내 침대를 전문가들에 의해 설계되게 했고, 내 식사는 훌륭한 요리사에 의해 준비되도록 했단다.

15 아버지는 우리에게 부자처럼 돈을 쓰라고 하셨으므로, 나는 돈 걱정을 하지 않고 내가 원하는 것을 샀지.

16 그렇지만 지금 나를 봐! 나는 빈털터리야.

17 너는 우리 아버지의 지혜를 따르지 않았니?

18 나에게 말해 보렴, 동생아, 너는 어떻게 그렇게 부유해졌니?"

19 Puneet은 웃으며 말했다, "친애하는 형님, 저 또한 우리 아버지의 지혜를 따랐습니다.

20 하지만 저는 조금 다르게 이해했지요.

21 아버지가 '모든 도시에 집을 지어라'라고 말하셨을 때, 저는 그것을 전 세계에 머물 수 있는 장소를 가지는 것으로 여겼지요.

22 그래서 저는 모든 도시에서 친구를 사귀었고 그 도시들을 방문했을 때 그들의 집에 머물렀어요.

23 또한, 저는 하루 종일 열심히 일하고 나서 피곤해지곤 했기 때문에 침대에서 자든 딱딱한 바닥에서 자든 상관없이 매일 밤 편안하게 잠을 잤지요.

24 저는 배고플 때만 먹었기 때문에 간단한 식사마저도 훌륭한 맛이 났습니다."

25 "부자처럼 돈을 쓰라고요?" Puneet은 계속했다.

26 "부자는 돈을 불리는 방법을 알고 있어요.

27 그래서 저는 사치스러운 물건에 돈을 쓰는 것보다는 저에게 더 많은 돈을 돌려줄 수 있는 것에 돈을 쓰려고 노력했지요.

28 저에게는 이게 우리의 아버지가 설명하려고 하셨던 바로 그 지혜입니다."

29 이제 Puru는 그가 얼마나 어리석었는지를 깨달았다.

30 이 지혜를 마음에 새기고, Puru는 새로운 삶을 시작했다.

본문 TEST Step 4 · Step 5 p.41~44

1 A rich and wise father had two sons, Puru and Puneet.

2 Before he passed away, he called his two sons to give them some last words of advice.

3 "Listen carefully, my dear sons. Live by these words throughout your life, and you will be happy," he said.

4 "Build a house in every city. Sleep comfortably. Enjoy your food. Lastly, spend money like a rich man... ."

5 Before he could explain himself, he passed away.

6 After his death, the two sons took their share of the father's wealth and settled in different cities.

7 Five years passed. Puru, who had been following his father's words carefully, had no money left.

8 But his brother was richer than ever.

9 Puru was puzzled about where he had gone wrong, so he visited Puneet to find out.

10 Puneet welcomed Puru with open arms.

11 That night, when the brothers sat down to chat after dinner, Puru asked the question that had been on his mind for days.

12 "It was our father's advice that I followed, but I am not happy. I built a house in every city.

13 But because I could not always stay there, I hired people and had the house looked after.

14 Father said we should sleep comfortably and enjoy our food, so I had my bed designed by experts and my meals prepared by a great chef.

15 He told us to spend like a rich man, so I bought what I wanted without worrying about money.

16 But look at me now! I am empty-handed.

17 Did you not follow our father's wisdom?

18 Tell me, brother, how did you get so rich?"

19 Puneet smiled and said, "My dear brother, I also followed our father's wisdom.

20 But I understood it a bit differently.

21 When he said 'build a house in every city,' I took it as having a place to stay all around the world.

22 So I made friends in every city and I stayed at their houses when I visited those cities.

23 Also, I slept comfortably each night because I would be tired after a hard day's work, and it did not matter if I was sleeping on a bed or on the hard floor.

24 I ate only when I was hungry, so even a simple meal tasted great."

25 "Spend money like a rich man?" continued Puneet.

26 "A rich man knows how to make money grow.

27 So, I tried to spend money on something that would bring me back more money rather than on luxurious things.

28 For me, it was this wisdom that our father tried to explain."

29 Now Puru realized how foolish he had been.

30 With this wisdom in mind, Puru started a new life.

Language in Use

1. freedom of speech, expression
2. explain the rules, before we start playing at

Grammar in Real Life B Look and Write

1. need to have, fixed
2. Why don't, have your hair cut
3. How about having
4. decorated with flowers, Look for

Think & Write C

1. Let, introduce
2. for
3. means, without fear, good experience
4. made, my motto when I was a kicker
5. From, even, made, a better kicker at the end
6. It, that changed my life

Language in Use

1. Everyone has freedom of speech and expression.
2. Can you explain the rules of the game before we start playing at?

Grammar in Real Life B Look and Write

1. Do you need to have the computer fixed? Call the Computer Doctor.
2. Why don't you have your hair cut at Susie's Hair Studio?
3. How about having your pet cleaned from head to toe? Come to Happy Pet.
4. Do you want to have your party room decorated with flowers? Look for Mary's Flowers.

Think & Write C

1. Let me introduce my motto.
2. It is "Go for it!"
3. It means "Go and do things without fear because failure is also a good experience."
4. I made it my motto when I was a kicker in the school soccer team.
5. From the motto, I learned that even the bad kicks made me a better kicker at the end.
6. It is this motto that changed my life!

Lesson 7

01 편리한, 간편한   02 오래가다, (기능이) 지속되다
03 어울리다   04 경쟁하다   05 용돈
06 구매하다, 구입하다   07 출시하다, 발매하다
08 ~에 영향을 주다   09 사라지다   10 행동, 행위
11 결합하다   12 바꾸다, 교체하다   13 언급하다, 말하다
14 ~에 탑승하고, ~에 타서   15 할인; 할인하다
16 부추기다, 조장하다   17 효과
18 비교하다   19 환불   20 지출
21 개념   22 위험에 빠뜨리다   23 완성하다
24 고정하다   25 줄무늬가 있는   26 차이, 차이점
27 즉시, 바로   28 꽉 조이는, 딱 붙는   29 ~에 영향을 주다
30 부족, 결핍   31 닻; 닻을 내리다   32 10억
33 지나치게 뜨거운, 과열된   34 소비하다, 소모하다
35 진열된, 전시된   36 비교해 보면   37 ~와 잘 어울리다
38 단지 ~라는 이유로   39 ~을 기록하다
40 ~에 관해서, ~에 대해 말하자면
41 ~할 가능성이 있다, ~하기 쉽다   42 반 이상의
43 한눈에, 즉시

01 allowance   02 combine   03 immediately
04 effect   05 convenient   06 deal
07 billion   08 complete   09 affect
10 mention   11 consume   12 anchor
13 behavior   14 miss   15 difference
16 compare   17 encourage   18 compete
19 endanger   20 concept   21 striped
22 refund   23 release   24 influence
25 lack   26 disappear   27 discount
28 match   29 purchase   30 raise
31 replace   32 spending   33 tight
34 waste   35 on display   36 at a glance
37 in comparison   38 keep track of   39 as such
40 just because   41 go well with
42 when it comes to   43 be likely to

1 immediately, 즉시, 바로   2 concept, 개념
3 disappear, 사라지다   4 purchase, 구입하다, 구매하다
5 release, 출시하다   6 suit, 어울리다
7 tight, 꽉 조이는, 딱 붙는   8 combine, 결합하다
9 waste, 낭비하다, 소모하다

10 convenient, 편리한, 간편한

11 encourage, 부추기다, 조장하다

12 allowance, 용돈 13 consume, 소비하다, 소모하다

14 endanger, 위험에 빠뜨리다 15 lack, 부족, 결핍

16 affect, ~에 영향을 주다

대화문 TEST Step 1

p.50~52

Listen & Talk 1 A

1 help, with / try on, with / How do you like / but, suits, have / one / take

2 Welcome to / I'm looking for / popular among, How do you like / green one is lighter than, one, lighter one / choice

Listen & Talk 1 B

bought, few weeks ago / looks, How do you like / convenient, anywhere, quality, too / How long, last / About, doesn't last / too bad / pretty happy, anyway

Listen & Talk 2 A

1 too uncomfortable / What's wrong with it / tight / you try it on before buying / so, bought, should have tried, on

2 are going to watch / to join / love to, I've spent, allowance / get it, ago / should have kept track of my spending

Listen & Talk 2 B

like mine / on sale / on sale, has just been released / is having, sale / at full price / selling, at, discount / should have checked the sales before

Communication Step A

heard that you bought, How, like / not happy, it / Why, What's / gets overheated, have read, reviews / ask for / won't give me back, I've used / calling, explaining / do

Wrap Up

1 I'd like to / How do you like this red one, among / that, one / striped, Its / take

2 package / bought, online used store, ago / let me see / is a little broken, said that / before / I just trusted, should have checked a bit more / should call, ask for a refund

대화문 TEST Step 2

p.53~55

Listen & Talk 1 A

1 M: Hi, can I help you with anything?

W: Yes, can I try on that cap with stars over there?

M: Sure. How do you like it?

W: The design is nice, but I don't think the color suits me. Do you have it in black?

M: Yes. I'll get one from the back. (*pause*) Here it is.

W: Great. I'll take it.

2 M: Good morning. Welcome to Kelly's Sporting Goods Store.

W: Hi, I'm looking for a backpack for hiking.

M: These two are popular among hikers. How do you like them?

W: The green one is lighter than the blue one. I'll take the lighter one.

M: Great choice.

Listen & Talk 1 B

W: Hi, Luke. Is that a new speaker?

M: Yes, I bought it a few weeks ago.

W: It looks cool. How do you like it?

M: It's convenient. I can take it anywhere and listen to music. The sound quality is good, too.

W: Great. How long does the battery last?

M: About 2 hours. The battery doesn't last long.

W: That's too bad.

M: Yeah, but I'm pretty happy with it, anyway

Listen & Talk 2 A

1 M: Oh, this coat is too uncomfortable.

W: Why? What's wrong with it?

M: It's too tight.

W: Didn't you try it on before buying it?

M: No. It was my size, so I just bought it. I should have tried it on.

2 W: Hey, Eric. Camilla and I are going to watch a movie. Do you want to join us?

M: I'd love to, but I can't. I've spent all of my allowance for this week.

W: Didn't you just get it a few days ago? How did you spend it all?

M: I'm not sure. I should have kept track of my spending.

Listen & Talk 2 B

M: Did you get a new phone, Jamie? It's just like mine.

W: Yeah, I got it last weekend on sale.

M: It was on sale? But it has just been released, hasn't it?

W: Right, but the store on Green Street is having a year-end sale.

M: Oh, I bought mine at full price!

W: Really? That's too bad. They're selling them at a 40 percent discount.

M: I should have checked the sales before buying mine.

Communication Step A

M: Hi, Riley. I heard that you bought a laptop online. How do you like it?

W: Oh, I'm not happy with it.

M: Why ? What's wrong?

W: It makes too much noise and gets overheated. I should have read more reviews.

M: Oh, then you should ask for your money back.

W: The online store won't give me back my money because I've used it for a week.

M: How about calling the online shop and explaining your problem?

W: Yeah, I think I should do that.

Wrap Up

1 M: Good morning. May I help you?

W: I'd like to buy a T-shirt for my sister. She's eleven years old.

M: How do you like this red one? This character is quite popular among children.

W: Well, she doesn't like animation characters that much. Can I see the blue one?

M: You mean this blue striped T-shirt? Its design is simple and cool.

W: Yes, I think my sister will like it. I'll take it.

2 W: Jake, here's a package for you.

M: It's my helmet. I bought it at an online used store a few days ago.

W: Oh, open it and let me see it.

M: Okay. (pause) Oh, this outer part is a little broken. The seller said that it's perfectly fine though.

W: Didn't you check the pictures of the helmet before you bought it?

M: No, I just trusted the seller. I should have checked a bit more.

W: You should call the seller and ask for a refund.

01 wondered why, bought, even

02 what affects, comes, buying

03 what my friends bought

04 goes, pair, on display

05 recognizes, because, half, wear

06 Although, ends up, another

07 effect, to explain, behavior

08 parade, encourages, jump aboard

09 others, likely get, follow

10 way, tend, just, bought

11 buy, pair, after, bought

12 that, Immediately, realizes, match

13 buys, go perfectly with

14 sees, none, match, clothes

15 Most, on, items, complete

16 made, search, after buying

17 explain, received, as, gift

18 noticed, furniture, go, replacing

19 therefore, purchasing, leads, unplanned

20 just because, on sale

21 goes window, sees, pair

22 checks, finds out, expensive

23 sales, approaches, discount on

24 though, discounted, still, low

25 described above, example, effect

26 mentioned, affects, opinion, prices

27 seem cheap in comparison

28 Furthermore, becomes bigger, powerful

29 As such, fixes, thoughts

30 like, things, considering, buying

31 As, shown, influence, purchases

32 time, think, about, buying

01 why you've bought things that

02 what affects us, comes to buying

03 what my friends bought

04 goes, sees a pair of, on display

05 recognizes, because, half of the boys, wear

06 Although, many pairs of, ends up buying another

07 bandwagon effect, to explain, behavior

08 that encourages, to jump aboard

09 more and more people, others are, likely to get on, follow

10 In, way, to buy, just because, have bought it

11 buy a pair of, after, have bought

12 that, Immediately, realizes that, match

13 that go, with

14 that none of her bags match, new clothes

15 buys, Most of her money is, on, to complete, new look

61

16 made, search for new items, after buying

17 effect, explain it, received, as, gift

18 after receiving, noticed that, furniture, go well, replacing most of it

19 therefore, that purchasing a new item, leads to, unplanned purchases

20 just because they are on sale

21 goes window shopping, sees, pair

22 checks, finds out that, that, too expensive

23 approaches him, discount on

24 Even though, is still, low, to buy

25 described above, example, anchoring effect

26 mentioned, affects, opinion of prices mentioned

27 For example, seem cheap in comparison

28 Furthermore, the difference, becomes bigger, be more powerful

29 As such, mentioned first, anchor, fixes our thoughts

30 Just like, to buy, without, considering why we are buying

31 As, have shown, influence our purchases

32 The next time, decide to buy, think, about why you are buying

---

본문 TEST Step 3 p.61~62

1 여러분은 원하거나 필요로 하지도 않는 것을 자신이 왜 구입했는지 궁금해 한 적이 있는가?

2 물건들을 구입하는 것에 관하여 무엇이 우리에게 영향을 주는지 생각해 보자.

3 나는 왜 친구들이 산 것을 사고 싶은 걸까?

4 Jeff는 쇼핑센터에 가서 진열되어 있는 축구화 한 켤레를 보게 된다.

5 그의 축구팀에 있는 소년들의 반 이상이 그 축구화를 신기 때문에 그는 그 신발을 한눈에 알아챈다.

6 이미 그에게는 축구화가 많이 있지만 결국 그는 또 다른 새 축구화를 사 버리고 만다.

7 우리는 Jeff의 행동을 설명하기 위해 '밴드왜건 효과'를 이용할 수 있다.

8 밴드왜건(악대차)은 사람들이 올라타서 음악을 즐기게끔 부추기는 퍼레이드에 있는 사륜마차이다.

9 더 많은 사람들이 밴드왜건에 올라탈수록 다른 사람들이 더욱 그것에 올라타거나 그것을 따르려 한다.

10 이런 식으로, 사람들은 단지 다른 사람들이 어떤 것을 샀다는 이유로 그것을 구매하는 경향이 있다.

11 나는 왜 새 코트를 구입한 후에 바지와 가방을 사는 걸까?

12 Lisa는 정말 마음에 드는 코트를 산다. 그녀는 그녀의 바지가

새 코트와 어울리지 않는다는 것을 즉시 알아차린다.

13 그래서 그녀는 새 코트와 완벽하게 어울리는 새 바지를 구입한다.

14 하지만 그녀는 자신의 가방 중 어느 것도 새로운 옷들과 어울리지 않는다는 것을 알게 된다.

15 그래서 그녀는 새 가방을 산다. 그녀의 돈 대부분이 그녀의 새로운 모습을 완성하기 위하여 새로운 물품을 사는 데 쓰인다.

16 무엇이 Lisa로 하여금 새 코트를 산 후 즉시 새로운 물품을 찾게 했을까?

17 '디드로 효과'가 그것을 설명해 줄지도 모른다. 프랑스 작가인 Denis Diderot는 선물로 새 가운을 받았다.

18 그 선물을 받은 후에 곧 그는 그의 모든 가구가 새로운 가운과 어울리지 않는다는 것을 알아챘다. 그래서 그는 결국 대부분의 가구를 바꾸고 말았다.

19 그러므로 디드로 효과는 새로운 물품을 구입하는 것이 흔히 계획에 없던 더 많은 구매로 이어진다는 개념이다.

20 나는 왜 단지 할인 중이라는 이유로 물건을 구입하는 걸까?

21 Nathan은 진열된 상품을 구경하러 가서 헤드폰을 하나 본다.

22 그는 가격을 확인하고 그것이 200달러임을 알게 된다. 그는 그 헤드폰이 너무 비싸다고 생각한다.

23 점원이 그에게 다가와 "이 헤드폰에 20퍼센트 할인을 받을 수 있어요."라고 말한다.

24 비록 할인된 가격이 여전히 별로 저렴하지는 않지만 Nathan은 그 헤드폰을 사기로 결심한다.

25 위에 기술된 상황은 '앵커링 효과'의 한 예이다.

26 처음에 언급된 가격이 이후에 언급되는 가격에 대한 우리의 의견에 영향을 미친다.

27 예를 들어, 만약 우리가 200달러로 시작한다면, 비교해 볼 때 160달러는 저렴해 보일 것이다.

28 그뿐만 아니라, 두 가격의 차이가 커질수록 그 효과는 더욱 강력해질 것이다.

29 이와 같이 처음에 언급된 가격이 물건의 가격에 대한 우리의 생각을 고정하는 '닻'으로서 작동한다.

30 Jeff와 그의 친구들처럼, 우리는 우리가 왜 물건들을 사는지 진지하게 고려하지 않고 그것들을 구입하는 경향이 있다.

31 이러한 효과들이 보여 주듯이, 많은 것들이 우리의 구매에 영향을 미친다.

32 다음번에 여러분이 어떤 것을 구매하려고 결정할 때에는, 자신이 그것을 왜 사려는지 잠시 동안 생각해 보아라.

본문 TEST Step 4 · Step 5 p.63~67

1 Have you ever wondered why you've bought things that you don't even want or need?

2 Let's consider what affects us when it comes to buying things.

3 Why do I want to buy what my friends bought?

---

4 Jeff goes to the shopping center and sees a pair of soccer shoes on display.

5 He recognizes the shoes at a glance because more than half of the boys on his soccer team wear them.

6 Although he already has many pairs of soccer shoes, he ends up buying another new pair.

7 We can use the "bandwagon effect" to explain Jeff's behavior.

8 A bandwagon is a wagon in a parade that encourages people to jump aboard and enjoy the music.

9 As more and more people get on the bandwagon, others are more likely to get on or follow it.

10 In this way, people tend to buy something just because other people have bought it.

11 Why do I buy a pair of pants and a bag after I have bought a new coat?

12 Lisa buys a coat that she really loves. Immediately, she realizes that her pants do not match her new coat.

13 So, she buys new pants that go perfectly with her new coat.

14 But she sees that none of her bags match her new clothes.

15 So, she buys a new bag. Most of her money is spent on buying the new items to complete her new look.

16 What made Lisa search for new items immediately after buying a new coat?

17 The "Diderot effect" may explain it. Denis Diderot, a French writer, received a new gown as a gift.

18 Soon after receiving the gift, he noticed that all of his furniture did not go well with his new gown. So, he ended up replacing most of it.

19 The Diderot effect, therefore, is the concept that purchasing a new item often leads to more unplanned purchases.

20 Why do I buy things just because they are on sale?

21 Nathan goes window shopping and sees a pair of headphones.

22 He checks the price and finds out that they are $200. He thinks that the headphones are too expensive.

23 The sales person approaches him and says, "You can get a 20 percent discount on those headphones."

24 Even though the discounted price is still not very

low, Nathan decides to buy the headphones.

25 The situation described above is an example of the "anchoring effect."

26 The price mentioned first affects our opinion of prices mentioned afterwards.

27 For example, if we start with $200, then $160 will seem cheap in comparison.

28 Furthermore, as the difference of the two prices becomes bigger, the effect will be more powerful.

29 As such, the price mentioned first acts as an "anchor" that fixes our thoughts about the price of an item.

30 Just like Jeff and his friends, we tend to buy things without seriously considering why we are buying them.

31 As these effects have shown, many things influence our purchases.

32 The next time you decide to buy something, think for a moment about why you are buying it.

구석구석지문 TEST Step 1 p.68

Language in Use

1. It, to compare, in detail
2. encourage, to think for themselves

Grammar in Real Life B Look and Write

1. half of, is used to raise
2. One third of, is wasted, billion tons
3. only ten percent of, go to school
4. About, don't, how to read due to lack of

Think & Write C

1. did a survey, allowance
2. how often they get an allowance
3. get an allowance, seventy percent, get an allowance every month
4. what, spend most of their allowance on
5. Most of the allowance, one fourth, is spent on snacks
6. whether they think, should get a higher allowance
7. Ninety percent of the students think

구석구석지문 TEST Step 2 p.69

Language in Use

1. It is difficult to compare the results in detail.
2. We encourage children to think for themselves.

Grammar in Real Life B Look and Write

1. About half of the water is used to raise animals in the U.S.

2. One third of the world's food is wasted—1.3 billion tons every year.

3. In Somalia, only ten percent of the children go to school.

4. About fourteen percent of all people don't know how to read due to lack of education.

Think & Write C

1. I did a survey about allowance.

2. First, I asked 10 students how often they get an allowance.

3. Twenty percent of the students get an allowance every week and seventy percent of the students get an allowance every month.

4. Second, I asked them what they spend most of their allowance on.

5. Most of the allowance is spent on clothes and one fourth of the allowance is spent on snacks.

6. Lastly, I asked them whether they think that they should get a higher allowance.

7. Ninety percent of the students think that they should get a higher allowance.

Lesson 8

단어 TEST Step 1   p.70

01 표면	02 굽히다, 구부리다	03 연결되다, 이어지다
04 일출	05 ~이 들어 있다, 포함하다	
06 지름길	07 눌러 부수다, 찌부러뜨리다	
08 거리	09 바뀔 수 있는, 변덕스러운	
10 붙이다	11 힘든, 어려운	12 먹을 수 있는
13 달성하다, 성취하다		14 결국
15 감지하다, 발견하다		16 (팔, 다리를) 뻗다
17 불안정한	18 맨 아랫부분, 바닥	19 층
20 거대한, 광대한	21 끈질긴, 집요한, 지속적인	
22 즉시	23 적용하다, 응용하다	
24 존재하다	25 중력	26 몸을 숙이다, 굽히다
27 구멍을 뚫다	28 무한한	29 낮추다
30 탐사, 탐구	31 측정하다	32 이론, 학설
33 계속 진행 중인	34 부정확한, 사실이 아닌	
35 되돌아보다	36 ~을 알아내다, 생각해 내다	
37 ~에 따르면	38 ~에서 멀리 떨어져	
39 눕다, 누워 있다	40 이론상으로는, 원칙상으로는	
41 ~의 아래에	42 ~와 다른	43 눈 깜박할 사이에

단어 TEST Step 2   p.71

01 researcher	02 shortcut	03 lean
04 ongoing	05 passenger	06 incorrect
07 crush	08 theory	09 lower
10 tough	11 infinite	12 apply
13 persistent	14 bottom	15 exist
16 unstable	17 vast	18 connect
19 achieve	20 detect	21 eatable
22 eventually	23 changeable	24 exploration
25 gravity	26 attach	27 contain
28 bend	29 instantly	30 layer
31 measure	32 physics	33 distance
34 celebrate	35 match up	36 lie down
37 at the speed of ~		38 float around
39 according to~	40 figure out	41 look back
42 far away from	43 at the bottom of ~	

단어 TEST Step 3   p.72

1 vast, 거대한, 광대한   2 connect, 연결되다, 이어지다

3 attach, 붙이다   4 distance, 거리   5 unstable, 불안정한

6 measure, 측정하다   7 chef, 요리사

8 ongoing, 계속 진행 중인　9 sunrise, 일출

10 astronaut, 우주 비행사　11 achieve, 달성하다, 성취하다

12 detect, 감지하다, 발견하다　13 gravity, 중력

14 celebrate, 축하하다　15 passenger, 승객, 탑승객

16 planet, 행성

Listen & Talk 1 A

1 back to, What, being / could see, sunrise, times a day / Is it possible to see, a day / possible because, moved around / amazing

2 the best food you ate / grew, ate, fresh and tasty / is it possible to grow / Since, no gravity, had to, helped the roots to grow

Listen & Talk 1 B

Have you heard that, send, into / going to send, into space / I've heard that, will be used to print out / possible to print out, using / print out, in less than / what it would taste like

Listen & Talk 2 A

1 colorful, universe / I wish I could see, from, with my own eyes / do that / that, feel like, actually in space

2 are, watching / seems, different / it's because, no gravity / I wish I could float around, astronaut / looks uncomfortable

Listen & Talk 2 B

lived in / must have been tough / while in space / possible / not sure, maybe it's because, gravity / I wish I could live in, become taller / I'm sure there, ways to become taller, going to space

Communication Step A

welcome to, to talk about, that we wish were real / start with / I wish I could have / somewhere that, entirely impossible / Is it actually possible to fly / have applied, to create

Wrap Up

1 enjoy / the best experience / what was the best part during / by myself / Is possible to fly, by yourself / attached myself, so, safe

2 heard that, How / zero gravity, astronauts' space life / real astronauts / heard, adventure / astronaut, explore Mars

Listen & Talk 1 A

1 M: Welcome back to Earth, Irene. What was your favorite part about being in the space station?

W: I could see a beautiful sunrise 16 times a day. It was great.

M: Is it possible to see the sunrise several times a day in space?

W: Yes, it's possible because we moved around Earth every 90 minutes in the station.

M: Wow, that's amazing!

2 M: Irene, what was the best food you ate in the space station?

W: Hmm.… We grew some vegetables and ate them every day. They were pretty fresh and tasty!

M: Wow, is it possible to grow vegetables in the space station?

W: Yes. Since there's no gravity in space, we had to grow them in special bags. The bags helped the roots to grow.

M: How interesting!

Listen & Talk 1 B

M: Have you heard that NASA is going to send a 3D printer into space?

W: They're going to send a 3D printer into space? Why?

M: I've heard that the 3D printer will be used to print out food for astronauts.

W: Is it possible to print out food using a 3D printer?

M: Yes, it's possible. It can print out a fresh pizza in less than five minutes.

W: Really? I wonder what it would taste like.

Listen & Talk 2 A

1 M: Look at these colorful pictures of the universe.

W: Oh, they're beautiful. I wish I could see Earth from space with my own eyes.

M: Actually, you can do that at the National Youth Space Center.

W: Really?

M: Yeah, you can use the VR glasses. I heard that you feel like you are actually in space!

2 W: What are you watching?

M: It's a documentary about life in space. Everything seems so different.

W: Yes, it's because there's no gravity in space.

M: Right. I wish I could float around like an astronaut!

W: Really? I don't. It looks uncomfortable.

Listen & Talk 2 B

W: Look at this man, Jake. He lived in space for one year.

M: It must have been tough for him.

W: Right, but you know what's interesting? He grew 2 inches while in space.

M: Really? How is that possible?

W: I'm not sure, but maybe it's because there's no gravity in space.

M: That's so cool. I wish I could live in space. That way, I could become taller.

W: I'm sure there are other ways to become taller than going to space.

Communication Step A

W: Hello, everyone, welcome to *All about Movies*! Today, we're going to talk aboutthe top three things from movies that we wish were real.

M: Let's start with number three, the flying skateboard from *Back to the Future*.

W: It's a cool item. I wish I could have a flying skateboard.

M: Actually, I read somewhere that this is not entirely impossible.

W: Really? Is it actually possible to fly on a skateboard?

M: Yes. Some companies have applied physics to create flying skateboards.

Wrap Up

1 W: Mr. Scott, did you enjoy your trip to space?

M: Yes, it was the best experience of my life.

W: Can you tell us what was the best part during your trip?

M: I flew in space by myself and saw our blue planet, Earth.

W: Is it possible to fly inspace by yourself?

M: Yes, I attached myself to a special line, so it was safe.

W: Sounds fantastic!

2 M: Hey, Cindy. I heard that you went to the National Space Center last weekend. How was it?

W: It was great, Chris. I experienced zero gravity and astronauts' space life.

M: Sounds fun. Did you meet real astronauts in person?

W: Yes, and I heard about their adventure stories.

M: Oh, I wish I could become an astronaut like them and explore Mars.

본문 TEST Step 1   p.79~80

01 fans, going, about, travel
02 As, nothing, light, universe
03 travel, able, get, blink
04 space, vast that, possible
05 headed, travels, one-half, light
06 get to another planet
07 for, expected, take, get
08 faster way, travel though
09 in order, like, think
10 something sweet, move, bottom
11 worm, surface, vast, universe
12 either, around, or down
13 think, choose, because, shortcut
14 there such a shortcut
15 figured out, connected, space-time
16 space-time, bent, far away
17 understand, top, another, bottom
18 flat sheet, far away
19 fold, matched, Punch, connected
20 contain, mouths, throat connecting
21 existed, get, places, away
22 early, celebrate, exist, theory
23 all, do, find one
24 Even, consider, actually, through
25 unstable, flew, crushed, broken
26 pretty picture, hopeless
27 traveling, simply, exists, theory
28 ongoing, persistent exploration, research
29 Look back, seemed impossible
30 Maybe, be, find, answer

본문 TEST Step 2   p.81~82

01 going to talk about space travel
02 As we all know, nothing faster than light
03 travel at, be able to get to, in the blink of, right
04 is so vast that, not possible
05 headed to, travels, one-half
06 get to another planet
07 for 120 years, is expected to take, to get to
08 a faster way to travel through
09 in order to, you to think, for a second
10 on this apple, something sweet, wants to move from, to
11 as vast as
12 either move around, or down

13 Which do you think, because it is a shortcut

14 such a shortcut

15 According to, figured out, are connected, space-time

16 space-time could actually be bent, that are far away, are suddenly closer

17 To understand, take, make, at the top of, another, bottom

18 On a flat sheet, far away from

19 fold, with, matched up, Punch, the dots, be instantly connected

20 contain two mouths, throat connecting

21 Just like, existed, get to places, away

22 too early to celebrate, exist in theory

23 all, to do, find one

24 Even if, to consider, going through one

25 would be, unstable, flew into, be crushed, broken into pieces

26 a pretty picture, hopeless

27 through, simply, that, exists

28 wouldn't say, is, ongoing, with persistent exploration, research, one, learn how to travel through

29 Look back at, so many things that seemed impossible

30 knows, to find the answer

1 Sci Teen: 안녕하세요, 과학 팬 여러분. 오늘 우리는 우주여행에 대해 이야기할 것입니다.

2 우리가 모두 알다시피, 우주에서 빛보다 더 빠른 것은 없습니다.

3 그래서 만약 우리가 빛의 속도로 여행을 한다면, 우리는 다른 행성에 눈 깜박할 사이에 도달할 수 있어야 해요, 그렇죠?

4 Dr. Sci: 그렇다면 좋겠지만, 우주는 너무 광활해서 그건 불가능하답니다.

5 영화 〈Passengers〉에서 다른 행성으로 향하는 우주선이 빛의 속도의 절반으로 이동합니다.

6 그러면 그들은 다른 행성에 매우 빨리 도달해야겠지요, 그렇죠?

7 하지만 승객들은 120년 동안 잠을 자게 되는데, 왜냐하면 다른 행성에 도달하는 데 그만큼 많은 시간이 걸릴 것으로 예상되기 때문입니다.

8 Sci Teen: 120년이요? 우아, 그건 정말 긴 시간이네요! 우주를 여행하는 더 빠른 방법이 있나요?

9 Dr. Sci: 글쎄요, 그 질문에 답하기 위해서 여러분들이 이 사과에 대해 잠깐 생각해 보기 바랍니다.

10 한 마리 벌레가 이 사과 위에 있다고 상상해 보세요. 그것은 맨

아래에 있는 달콤한 무언가를 감지하고 맨 위에서 아래로 이동하기를 원합니다.

11 그 벌레에게 사과의 표면은 우리의 우주만큼이나 광대합니다.

12 이제 그 벌레는 바깥 표면의 껍질을 돌아서 이동하거나 벌레 구멍 아래로 이동할 수 있습니다.

13 그것이 어떤 것을 선택할 거라고 생각하십니까? 음, 그것은 벌레 구멍을 선택할 것인데 왜냐하면 그것이 지름길이기 때문입니다.

14 Sci Teen: 우주에 그런 지름길이 있나요?

15 Dr. Sci: 몇몇 연구자들에 따르면, 그렇습니다. 아인슈타인은 공간과 시간이 연결되어 있다는 것을 생각해 냈고, 그것을 시공간이라고 불렀습니다.

16 '그는 시공간이 실제로 구부러질 수 있다고 생각했습니다. 그것이 구부러질 때 서로 멀리 떨어져 있는 부분들이 갑자기 더 가까워질 수 있습니다.

17 이것을 이해하기 위해서, 종이를 한 장 갖고 와서 그 종이의 윗부분에 작은 점을 찍고 또 다른 점을 그 종이의 아랫부분에 찍어 보세요.

18 펼쳐 놓은 종이에서 그 점들은 서로 멀리 떨어져 있습니다.

19 이제 그 종이를 들고 점들이 맞춰지도록 그것을 접으세요. 종이에 구멍을 뚫으면 그 점들이 즉시 연결될 것입니다.

20 이와 마찬가지로 우주의 웜홀은 두 개의 입과 그 둘을 연결하는 목구멍을 지니고 있을 겁니다.

21 Sci Teen: 사과에 있는 벌레 구멍처럼요, 그렇죠? 그런 웜홀이 우주에 존재한다면 우리는 수십억 광년 떨어져 있는 곳에 빠르게 도달할 수 있을 텐데요!

22 Dr. Sci: 그렇죠, 하지만 축하하기에는 너무 이릅니다. 웜홀은 이론상에서만 존재합니다.

23 Sci Teen: 그러면 우리가 해야 할 것이라고는 그것을 찾는 거네요, 그렇죠?

24 Dr. Sci: 우리가 그것을 찾는다고 하더라도 실제로 그걸 통과하여 가기 전에 고려해야 할 것들이 많이 있습니다.

25 웜홀은 매우 불안정할 것입니다. 만약 우주선이 그 안으로 날아가게 되면, 그것은 부서지거나 산산조각이 날 수도 있습니다.

26 Sci Teen: 어이쿠! 그건 좋은 광경이 아니네요. 그럼 우리는 가망이 없는 건가요?

27 우주에서 웜홀을 통하여 여행을 하는 것은 단지 이론상으로만 존재하는 아이디어인가요?

28 Dr. Sci: 그렇게 말하지는 않겠어요. 웜홀에 대한 논쟁은 여전히 진행 중이긴 하지만, 끊임없는 탐구와 연구로 우리가 결국 하나를 찾아 그것을 통해 여행하는 법을 배울 수 있을 거라고 믿습니다.

29 우리의 역사를 돌아보세요. 우리는 처음에는 불가능해 보였던 아주 많은 것들을 달성해 왔습니다.

30 누가 알겠어요? 아마도 여러분이 그 답을 찾아내는 그 사람이 될 수 있을지도요!

1 Sci Teen: Hi, science fans. Today, we're going to talk about space travel.

2 As we all know, there is nothing faster than light in the universe.

3 So, if we travel at the speed of light, we should be able to get to another planet in the blink of an eye, right?

4 Dr. Sci: That would be nice, but space is so vast that it is not possible.

5 In the movie, *Passengers*, a spaceship headed to a different planet travels at one-half the speed of light.

6 So it should get to another planet very quickly, right?

7 But, the passengers sleep for 120 years because it is expected to take that much time to get to a different planet.

8 Sci Teen: 120 years? Wow, that's a long time! Is there a faster way to travel through space?

9 Dr. Sci: Well, in order to answer that question, I'd like you to think about this apple for a second.

10 Imagine a worm is on this apple. It detects something sweet at the bottom and wants to move from the top to the bottom.

11 For the worm, the apple's surface is as vast as our universe.

12 Now the worm can either move around the outer layer or down a wormhole.

13 Which do you think it will choose? Well, it would choose the wormhole because it is a shortcut.

14 Sci Teen: Is there such a shortcut in the universe?

15 Dr. Sci: According to some researchers, yes. Einstein figured out that space and time are connected, and he called it space-time.

16 He thought that space—time could actually be bent. When it is bent, parts that are far away from each other are suddenly closer.

17 To understand this, take a sheet of paper and make a small dot at the top of the paper and another at the bottom of the paper.

18 On a flat sheet of paper, the dots are far away from one another.

19 Now, take the paper and fold it with the dots matched up. Punch a hole in the paper and the dots will be instantly connected.

20 Like this, wormholes in space may contain two mouths, with a throat connecting the two.

21 Sci Teen: Just like a wormhole in the apple, right? If such wormholes existed in space, we could get to places billions of light-years away quickly!

22 Dr. Sci: Yes, but it's too early to celebrate. Wormholes exist in theory only.

23 Sci Teen: So all we need to do is find one , right?

24 Dr. Sci: Even if we find one, there are many things to consider before actually going through one.

25 A wormhole would be very unstable . If a spaceship flew into one, it might be crushed or broken into pieces.

26 Sci Teen: Ouch! That's not a pretty picture. So, are we hopeless?

27 Is traveling in space through a wormhole simply an idea that only exists in theory?

28 Dr. Sci: I wouldn't say so. The debate about wormholes is still ongoing, but with persistent exploration and research, I believe we will eventually find one and learn how to travel through it.

29 Look back at our history. We've achieved so many things that seemed impossible at first.

30 Who knows? Maybe you can be the one to find the answer!

After You Read A

1. A faster way to travel

2. Idea from

3. for a worm to move, the top, the bottom

4. in space

5. space, time are connected, space-time can be bent

6. parts far away from, become closer

7. really exist

8. In theory, exist

9. would be unstable, be crushed, broken into pieces

10. Still, with persistent exploration, research

Language in Use

1. finite or infinite

2. Luckily, is in a stable condition

Think & Write C

1. for us to live on, would like to make, called

2. beautiful green planet

3. bigger than the moon, smaller than

4. The temperature, would be about

5. have beautiful nature

6. Interestingly, moved to, communicate with, on this planet

After You Read A

1. A faster way to travel through space

2. ① Idea from an apple

3. A wormhole is a shortcut for a worm to move from the top to the bottom.

4. ② Wormholes in space

5. Einstein thought space and time are connected and space-time can be bent.

6. When it is bent, parts far away from each other can become closer.

7. Do wormholes really exist?

8. ③ In theory, wormholes exist.

9. Wormholes would be unstable. A spaceship could be crushed or broken into pieces.

10. Still I believe with persistent exploration and research we will find a wormhole!

Language in Use

1. Is the universe finite or infinite?

2. Luckily, the driver is is in a stable condition after the accident.

Think & Write C

1. If I could make a planet for us to live on in the future, I would like to make a planet called Atlas.

2. It would be a beautiful green planet.

3. Its size would be bigger than the moon, but smaller than Earth.

4. The temperature of it would be about 30.

5. It would have beautiful nature.

6. Interestingly, if people moved to it, they could communicate with animals on this planet.

MEMO

MEMO

MEMO

2학기 전과정

적중100 plus

영어 기출 문제집

정답 및 해설

비상 | 김진완

적중 1○○ + 특별부록

Plan B

우리학교
최신기출

비상 · 김진완 교과서를 배우는

학교 시험문제 분석 · 모음 · 해설집

전국단위 학교 시험문제 수집 및 분석
출제 빈도가 높은 문제 위주로 선별
문제 풀이에 필요한 상세한 해설

중3-2
영어

비상 · 김진완

적중 **100** + 특별부록

Plan B

우리학교
최신기출

중3-2
영어

비상 · 김진완

◎ 선택형 문항의 답안은 컴퓨터용 수정 싸인펜을 사용하여 OMR 답안지에 바르게 표기하시오.
◎ 서술형 문제는 답을 답안지에 반드시 검정 볼펜으로 쓰시오.
◎ 총 26문항 100점 만점입니다. 문항별 배점은 각 문항에 표시되어 있습니다.

[경북 ○○중]

01 다음 문장의 빈칸 (A), (B)에 들어갈 것으로 가장 적절한 것은? (4점)

• Talking (A)_____ the phone with her friend, Sumi is cooking dinner.
• According (B)_____ research, people feel sad on rainy days.

	(A)	(B)
①	for	at
②	to	to
③	on	on
④	to	of
⑤	on	to

[부산 ○○중]

02 다음 'real'이라는 단어에 어떤 접미사를 조합하니 2가지의 뜻을 지닌 동사가 된다면, 빈칸의 접미사는? (3점)

r e a l + ? ? ? = 깨닫다 실현하다

① dom ② ize ③ ion
④ ous ⑤ ful

[서울 서초구 ○○중]

03 다음 대화의 흐름을 고려할 때, 다음 중 화자 B가 말할 내용으로 어법상 올바르지 <u>않은</u> 것은? (4점)

A: Wow. Mike woke up so early! Why so?
B: Well, _____.

① he usually gets up early to catch the first subway

② he got up early today so that he might catch the first subway

③ he got up early in order that he caught the first subway

④ he usually gets up early so that he may catch the first subway

⑤ he got up early today so as to catch the first subway

[경기 ○○중]

04 다음 대화의 내용과 일치하는 것은? (4점)

Sumi: I read an article saying that Napoleon was actually fairly tall.
John: Oh, really? Can you tell me more about it?
Sumi: According to the article, a French doctor wrote down Napoleon's height according to the French measuring system, not the English one.
John: What was the difference?
Sumi: At that time, an inch in France was longer than an inch in England. So, Napoleon was actually about 168cm tall, which was not that short in those times.

① Napoleon was really short in those times.

② John wants to know more about Napoleon's life.

③ The French measuring system was not correct at that time.

④ An inch in France was longer than an inch in England at that time.

⑤ A French doctor wrote down Napoleon's height according to the English measuring system.

[5~6] 다음 대화를 읽고 물음에 답하시오.

> Jin: There are so many pieces of information we call "facts" ⓐthat are completely wrong.
> Lisa: Can you tell me more about it?
> Jin: I read a book, and there were a lot of examples of ⓑthese kinds of facts.
> Lisa: Like what?
> Jin: Well, most people think goldfish are not smart. But, goldfish are smart in fact.
> Lisa: Really?
> Jin: Yeah, they can recognize their owners.
> Lisa: Oh, I didn't know that.

05 위 대화의 밑줄 친 ⓐ의 쓰임과 같은 것은? (4점)

① That is what I want to get.
② I didn't know that you were sick.
③ The girl that sang a song was my sister.
④ I heard the news that he had had a car accident.
⑤ It was at this shop that I wanted to buy a watch.

06 위 대화의 밑줄 친 ⓑ가 의미하는 것은? (5점)

① facts that are always true
② facts that are about goldfish
③ facts that have many examples
④ facts that aren't actually true
⑤ facts that are believed to be true

07 다음 빈칸 (A)에 어울리는 표현이 아닌 것은? (3점)

> Jenny: I think Clara got a boyfriend during the vacation.
> Jimin: (A) _____
> Jenny: She's got a new ring on her left hand.

① What do you think?
② Why do you say so?
③ Why do you think so?
④ Do you have any reason?
⑤ What makcs you think so?

[8~9] 다음 대화를 읽고 물음에 답하시오.

> A: I read an article saying that Napoleon was actually fairly tall.
> B: Oh, really? Can you tell me more about it?
> A: According to the article, a French doctor wrote down Napoleon's height according to the French measuring system, not the English one.
> B: What was the difference?
> A: At that time, an inch in France was longer than an inch in England. So, Napoleon was actually about 168cm tall, which was not that short in those times.

08 위 대화의 밑줄 친 부분의 의도로 알맞은 것은? (2점)

① 이의 제기하기
② 자세한 설명 요청하기
③ 상대방의 의견 묻기
④ 선호에 대해 묻기
⑤ 의견에 대한 이유 묻기

09 위 대화의 내용으로 알 수 없는 것은? (4점)

① 나폴레옹의 실제 키는 168cm 정도였다.
② 어떤 프랑스 의사가 나폴레옹의 키를 적었다.
③ 나폴레옹의 키는 프랑스식 측정법으로 기록되었다.
④ 당시 프랑스 사람들이 영국 사람들보다 키가 더 컸다.
⑤ 당시 프랑스에서의 1인치는 영국의 1인치보다 더 길었다.

10 Choose the best answer for the blank. (3점)

> A: There are so many pieces of information we call "facts" that are completely wrong.
> B: Why do you say so?
> A: I read a book, and there were a lot of examples of these "facts" that are wrong.
> B: Like what?
> A: Well, most people think that goldfish are not smart. But, goldfish are actually smart.
> B: Really? _____
> A: They can recognize their owners.
> B: Oh, I didn't know that.

① How do you know that?
② Can you give me some?
③ Why did you tell me about that?
④ Can you tell her more about that?
⑤ Can you explain it in more detail?

11 다음 〈보기〉와 같은 방식으로 문장을 바꿔 쓸 때, 어법상 <u>어색</u>한 것은? (정답 2개) (4점)

> 보기
> • When I arrived home late at night, I saw some fruits and ate them.
> → Arriving home late at night, I saw some fruits and ate them.

① As he felt so excited, he jumped high.
  → Feeling so excited, he jumped high.
② Because she was sick, she was absent from school.
  → Being sick, she was absent from school.
③ As she broke her arm, she is absent from school.
  → Breaking her arm, she is absent from school.

④ After she went inside the room, she turned the lights on.
  → Going inside the room, she turned the lights on.
⑤ Since the bakery was closed, I couldn't buy breakfast for the next day.
  → Being closed, I couldn't buy breakfast for the next day.

12 다음 글에서 문법상 <u>어색한</u> 것은 몇 개인가? (4점)

> I usually get up at 7 a.m. Today, I woke up at 8 a.m.! Without breakfast, I took a taxi to school. Strangely, I couldn't see anyone to enter the classroom.
> Not knowing what happened, I called my friend, Sam. He said everyone was at Seoul Land. Right! Today was a field trip day! Felt so embarrassed, I took a taxi again. Luckily, I met all of my classmates who had arrived at Seoul Land.

① 1개　② 2개　③ 3개　④ 4개　⑤ 5개

13 다음 주어진 우리말의 밑줄 친 부분을 영어로 바르게 옮긴 것을 <u>모두</u> 고른 것은? (5점)

> • 나는 <u>바깥 풍경을 보기 위해</u> 보통 창가 옆에 앉는 것을 좋아한다.
> → I usually like to sit by the window _____.

> ⓐ too see the view outside
> ⓑ in order to see the view outside
> ⓒ enough to see the view outside
> ⓓ so that I can see the view outside
> ⓔ in order that I can see the view outside
> ⓕ to see the view outside

① ⓐ, ⓑ, ⓓ
② ⓑ, ⓓ, ⓔ
③ ⓒ, ⓔ, ⓕ
④ ⓐ, ⓑ, ⓓ, ⓔ
⑤ ⓑ, ⓓ, ⓔ, ⓕ

[14~15] 다음 글을 읽고 물음에 답하시오.

Every day we watch, hear, or read interesting news. However, have you ever seriously considered whether an article is really true? Everyone likes an interesting news story but (A)_____ it is completely made up?
ⓐFake news can be very harmful that it can make people less informed or even misled. Nevertheless, ⓑthere have been various fake news reports throughout history. ⓒWhy have some people written such false information? ⓓLet's look into some articles as we think about the hidden motives behind them.

14 위 글의 빈칸 (A)에 적절한 것은? (3점)

① if   ② as   ③ as if
④ though   ⑤ what if

15 위 글의 밑줄 친 ⓐ~ⓓ 중에서 어법상 어색한 것만 고른 것은? (4점)

① ⓐ, ⓑ   ② ⓐ   ③ ⓑ, ⓒ
④ ⓒ   ⑤ ⓓ

[16~17] 다음 글을 읽고 물음에 답하시오.

SLAV SHOOTS A FRIEND IN ARGUMENT
Mejk Swenekafew, a Slav worker at the Columbia Coal Mine, was shot and seriously ⓐwound by John Pecitello near the mining camp Thursday evening.
The two men ⓑhad an argue during a meeting. The argument ⓒled to a fight, and Pecitello shot Swenekafew twice, in the chest and leg. He is now at the hospital ⓓin critically condition. Pecitello ran away after the shooting. The police ⓔis searching at him now and are warning citizens that he is extremely dangerous.

Is there anything strange about the article? Read the Slav's name backwards; it spells "we-fake-news." Who wrote this and why?
The Daily Telegram published this fake article so that they could prove if *The Daily News*, their competitor, was stealing their articles. *The Daily News* published the same article about "Swenekafew" the next day and thus got caught stealing. The people at *The Daily News* had to admit their act and were harshly criticized by the public.

16 위 글의 ⓐ~ⓔ 중 낱말의 쓰임이 적절한 것은? (4점)

① ⓐ   ② ⓑ   ③ ⓒ   ④ ⓓ   ⑤ ⓔ

17 위 글에 대한 질문에 알맞게 답한 것은? (5점)

① Q: Why is Swenekafew at the hospital?
   A: Because he was injured by a group of animals.
② Q: How many times did Pecitello shoot Swenekafew?
   A: He shot Swenekafew three times.
③ Q: Why did *The Daily Telegram* write the fake news?
   A: Because they wanted to make people laugh.
④ Q: What did *The Daily News* publish the next day?
   A: They published the same article the next day.
⑤ Q: How did the public react to *The Daily News* after they came to know the truth?
   A: The public tried to encourage *The Daily News*.

[18~21] 다음 글을 읽고 질문에 답하시오.

Everyone likes an interesting news story but _____ _____ _____ is _____ _____? (만약 그것이 완전히 지어낸 것이라면 어떻게 할 것인가?) Fake news can be very harmful in that it can make people less informed or even misled. Nevertheless, there have been various fake news reports throughout history. Why have some people written such false information? Let's look into some articles thinking about the hidden motives behind them.

AWFUL DISASTER

(A) Last night, an angry group of rhinoceroses broke down the walls of the cage at the zoo and escaped. (B) These animals ran down the streets and injured hundreds of people. Twelve of the animals are still on the loose. (C) Citizens should stay indoors until further notice. (D)
*Not a single act or incident described above has taken place. (E)

At that time, those who read the article carefully laughed out loud. Those who didn't read it to the end got really worried. Not knowing the news was false, many people panicked. Some tried to escape the city while others went into the parks with guns to hunt the animals. So why did *The Herald* make up such news? Later, they confessed that they made it up so that they could draw the readers' attention to the unsafe conditions at the zoo.

18 위 글의 빈칸에 들어갈 말을 아래 조건에 유의하여 영작하시오.
(5점)

> 조건
> 1. 문맥과 우리말 뜻에 맞게 작성할 것.
> 2. completely, it, make up을 활용하되 필요할 경우 어형 변형 가능.

→ _____ _____ _____ is _____ _____ _____?

19 위 글의 흐름으로 보아 주어진 문장이 들어가기에 적절한 곳은?
(3점)

> They also broke down the walls of the other wild animals' cages.

① (A) ② (B) ③ (C) ④ (D) ⑤ (E)

20 위 글의 AWFUL DISASTER에 대한 내용으로 일치하지 <u>않는</u> 것은?
(4점)

① The Herald의 기사 제목이다.
② 언급된 사건은 하나도 일어나지 않았다.
③ 기사의 첫 경고 문장을 놓친 사람들은 걱정했다.
④ 많은 사람들이 기사 내용이 가짜라는 것을 몰랐기 때문에 겁에 질렸다.
⑤ 어떤 사람들은 총을 들고 동물들을 사냥하러 갔다.

21 Why did The Herald make up the news? (4점)

① To publish another magazine about the zoo.
② To make people panicked for the medical test.
③ To make a lot of money by drawing the readers' attention.
④ To draw the readers' attention to dangerous wild animals.
⑤ To draw the readers' attention to the unsafe conditions at the zoo.

[22~23] 다음 글을 읽고 물음에 답하시오.

As readers, we need to read ⓐcritically and judge ⓑwhether the news is real or fake.

How to ⓒspot fake news!

1. Consider the Source
   Is it from a reliable source?
   Can we trust the writer?
2. Check the Date
   Is it a new or an old story?
   Is it related to ⓓcurrent events?
3. Read Beyond the Headlines
   Does the headline match the content?
4. Find Supporting Sources
   Do other ⓔrelated stories provide similar content?

22 위 글의 밑줄 친 ⓐ~ⓔ 중 우리말 해석이 어색한 것은? (정답 2개) (3점)

① ⓐ 비판적으로   ② ⓑ ~에 상관없이
③ ⓒ 장소   ④ ⓓ 현재의
⑤ ⓔ 연관된

23 위 글의 내용을 기반으로 가짜 뉴스를 가장 올바르게 판별하는 사람은? (4점)

① 승희: 새로운 뉴스를 접하면 다른 여러 언론사 기사를 비교해서 읽어.
② 영웅: 난 사실과는 별개로 흥미롭고 자극적인 뉴스를 공유하는 걸 좋아해.
③ 지민: SNS에 자주 언급되고 공유되는 기사들은 그만큼 믿을 만하기 때문이야.
④ 수호: 나는 시간을 아끼기 위해 하교 후에 오늘의 뉴스를 헤드라인만 모아서 훑어봐.
⑤ 유라: 나의 동아리 친구들은 아주 똑똑하기 때문에 그들이 들려주는 뉴스는 믿을 수 있어.

[24~25] 다음 글을 읽고 물음에 답하시오.

Walk and You'll Get Slim and Strong!
Our new walking shoes, Wing Walker, have various strong points. Walking with Wing Walker, you burn more calories and get slimmer. They also strengthen leg muscles because they use the hidden board technology. Upgrade your walking experience with Wing Walker!

24 위 글의 종류로 가장 적절한 것은? (4점)

① advertisement   ② novel   ③ essay
④ poetry   ⑤ diary

25 위 글에 대한 다음 물음의 답으로 가장 적절한 것은? (4점)

> Question: What are the strong points of the product, new walking shoes?
> Answer: When people walk with Wing Walker, they _____.

① use the hidden board technology
② burn more calories and get slimmer
③ consume less calories and get slim
④ can strength their new walking shoes
⑤ may not upgrade their walking experience

26 다음 글에 이어질 내용으로 가장 알맞은 것은? (4점)

> Every day we watch, hear, or read interesting news. However, have you ever seriously considered if an article is really true? Everyone likes an interesting news story but what if it is completely made up? There have been various fake news reports throughout history. Why have some people written such false information? Let's look into some articles thinking about the hidden motives behind them.

① 가짜 뉴스의 배경
② 가짜 뉴스의 위험성
③ 가짜 뉴스의 숨겨진 동기
④ 가짜 뉴스의 역사와 피해 정도
⑤ 가짜 뉴스와 진짜 뉴스의 비교

◎ 선택형 문항의 답안은 컴퓨터용 수정 싸인펜을 사용하여 OMR 답안지에 바르게 표기하시오.
◎ 서술형 문제는 답을 답안지에 반드시 검정 볼펜으로 쓰시오.
◎ 총 24문항 100점 만점입니다. 문항별 배점은 각 문항에 표시되어 있습니다.

[경북 ㅇㅇ중]

01 다음 영영풀이가 어색한 것은? (4점)

① disaster: a strong disagreement in talking or discussing something
② panic: to suddenly feel so worried that you cannot be reasonable
③ mislead: to cause someone to believe something that is not true
④ spot: to see or notice someone or something
⑤ fake: not real but made to seem real

[충북 ㅇㅇ중]

02 다음 중 빈칸에 공통으로 들어갈 알맞은 단어는? (3점)

• I think you _____ the meaning of the word.
• You _____ what I'm saying.
• Sometimes people _____ each other.

① mistake   ② misunderstand
③ mislead   ④ miscount
⑤ misbehave

[경북 ㅇㅇ중]

03 다음 대화의 빈칸에 들어갈 표현으로 적절한 것은? (3점)

Woman: Are these all poetry books?
Man: Yeah. These are all poems written by children.
Woman: By children?

Man: Yeah. I think children write better poems than adults.
Woman: _____
Man: They're really honest about their feelings and much more creative than adults.

① What's the matter?
② Why the long face?
③ Why do you say so?
④ Why are you upset?
⑤ What's the difference?

[경기 ㅇㅇ중]

04 다음 대화의 빈칸에 들어갈 남자의 응답으로 가장 적절한 것은? (4점)

W: I think I caught a cold because I didn't dress warmly yesterday.
M: Well, I've read an article saying that you don't catch a cold because your body temperature is low.
W: Really? Can you tell me more about it?
M: The article said that _____.

① taking a walk is good for our health
② people catch colds because of viruses
③ we should be careful not to catch a cold
④ the thermometer is getting more expensive
⑤ we have to check the weather report every day

[경북 ㅇㅇ중]

05 다음 대화의 빈칸에 들어갈 어휘로 가장 적절한 것은? (4점)

A: The weather can _____ people's feelings.
B: Can you tell me more about it?

① guess   ② spend   ③ watch
④ affect   ⑤ improve

06 다음 대화의 빈칸에 적절한 표현은? (4점)

Man: There are so many pieces of information we call "facts" that are completely wrong.

Woman: Why do you think so?

Man: I read a book, and there were a lot of examples of these "facts" _____.

Woman: Like what?

Man: Well, most people think goldfish are not smart. But, goldfish are actually smart.

Woman: Really? Can you tell me more about that?

Man: They can recognize their owners.

Woman: Oh, I didn't know that.

① that are right
② that are wrong
③ that are not easy
④ that are complete
⑤ that are not useful

07 Choose the incorrect answer for the blank. (4점)

A: Hey, do you think I should buy this drink? It's said that it can help me lose weight.

B: Let me read the label more closely. Hmm, it looks a bit strange to me, David.

A: _____

B: There isn't enough information about what's in the drink.

A: Oh, you're right.

B: Also, it doesn't tell you how much you have to drink to lose weight.

① Why do you think so?
② What makes you say so?
③ What makes you think so?
④ Why makes you think that?
⑤ Why do you hold that view?

[8~9] 다음 대화를 읽고 물음에 답하시오.

W: I read an article saying that Napoleon was actually fairly tall.

M: Oh, really? ⓐ_____

W: According to the article, a French doctor wrote down Napoleon's height according to the French measuring system, not the English one.

M: What was the difference?

W: At that time, an inch in France was longer than an inch in England. So, Napoleon was actually about 168cm tall, which was not that short in those times.

08 위 대화에서 빈칸 ⓐ에 들어갈 알맞은 문장은? (4점)

① Did you know that?
② What do you think?
③ Why do you say that?
④ What makes you think so?
⑤ Can you tell me more about it?

09 위 대화를 읽고 아래 신문 기사 내용에서 흐름상 어색한 것은? (4점)

DAILY NEWS   May 7th, 2020

ⓐWas Napoleon Really Short?

ⓑWe have been wrong about Napoleon's height. ⓒThe misunderstanding came from the difference between the French measuring system and the English one. ⓓAn inch in France was shorter than an inch in America. ⓔHe was actually about 168 cm tall!

① ⓐ   ② ⓑ   ③ ⓒ   ④ ⓓ   ⑤ ⓔ

10 다음 대화의 내용과 맞지 <u>않는</u> 것은?　　(4점)

> Yujin: I think I caught a cold because I didn't dress warmly yesterday.
>
> Sangho: Well, I've read an article saying that you don't catch a cold because your body temperature is low.
>
> Yujin: Really? Can you tell me more about it?
>
> Sangho: The article said that people catch colds because of viruses.

① Perhaps Yujin had a cold.

② Yujin didn't dress warmly yesterday.

③ Sangho says a different opinion from Yujin's.

④ Sangho says viruses are active when it's cold.

⑤ Sangho read an article about the cause of a cold.

11 다음 중 같은 의미가 되는 문장으로 알맞게 바꾼 것은?　(5점)

① We were so late that we missed the train.
= We were late in order to miss the train.

② The insect is so small that I can't see it with my eyes.
= The insect is too small for me not to see it with my eyes.

③ She worked hard so that everything could be ready in time.
= She worked too hard for everything to be ready in time.

④ The music was so loud that I could hear it from far away.
= The music was loud enough for me to hear from far away.

⑤ There has been a great increase in car production, so that the quality of the air is very poor.
= There has been a great increase in car production, in order that the quality of the air is very poor.

12 다음 중 분사구문으로 잘못 바꾼 것은?　　(5점)

① Because Jack had no classes, he played with his friends all day. → Having no classes, Jack played with his friends all day.

② While I was watching a soccer game, I ate a pizza at my friend's house. → Watching a soccer game, I ate a pizza at my friend's house.

③ Because I didn't feel hungry, I didn't eat the fruit on the table. → Feeling not hungry, I didn't eat the fruit on the table.

④ When I waited for a bus, I met my English teacher. → Waiting for a bus, I met my English teacher.

⑤ Because I am tired of staying home, I'm planning to go to the festival. → Being tired of staying home, I'm planning to go to the festival.

13 다음 밑줄 친 부분을 분사구문을 사용하여 바꿔 쓰시오.　(3점)

> · <u>Because I felt hungry</u>, I ate some food I had brought from home.

→ _____, I ate some food I had brought from home.

[14~16] 다음 글을 읽고 물음에 답하시오.

Last night, an angry group of rhinoceroses broke down the walls of the cage at the zoo and escaped. They also broke down the walls of the other wild animals' cages. These animals ran down the streets and injured hundreds of people. Twelve of the animals are still on the loose. Citizens should stay indoors until further notice.

At that time, those who read the article carefully laughed out loud. Those who didn't read it to the end got really worried. (A)_____ _____, many people panicked. Some tried to escape the city while others went into the parks with guns to hunt the animals.

So why did *the Herald* make up such news? Later, they confessed that they made it up so that they could draw the readers' attention to the unsafe conditions at the zoo.

14 위 글의 빈칸 (A)에 들어갈 가장 적절한 것은? (4점)

① Knowing the news was false

② Knowing the news wasn't false

③ Not knowing the news was false

④ Knowing not the news was false

⑤ Not knowing the news wasn't false

15 위 글을 읽고 대답할 수 없는 질문은? (5점)

① Why can fake news be harmful?

② How many people were injured?

③ What happened at the zoo last night?

④ How many animals are still on the loose?

⑤ What happened to those who did not know the news was false?

16 위 글의 내용과 <u>다른</u> 것은? (4점)

① 화가 난 코뿔소 떼가 동물원 우리의 벽을 부수고 도망친 것은 어젯밤이었다.

② 코뿔소들은 다른 야생 동물 우리의 벽도 부수었다.

③ 시민들은 추후 안내가 있을 때까지 집 안에 머물러야 한다.

④ 많은 사람들이 겁에 질린 것은 그 기사가 거짓이라는 것을 몰랐기 때문이다.

⑤ 그 당시 이 기사를 주의 깊게 읽었던 사람들은 미소를 지었다.

[17~18] 다음 글을 읽고 물음에 답하시오.

Is there anything strange about the article? Read the Slav's name, Swenekafew, backwards; it spells, "(A)_____. Who ⓐwrote this and why?

The Daily Telegram published this fake article so that they ⓑcould prove if *The Daily News*, their competitor, was stealing their articles. *The Daily News* published the same article about "Swenekafew" the next day and thus ⓒgot caught stealing. The people at *The Daily News* ⓓhad to admit their act and were harshly ⓔcriticizing by the public.

17 위 글의 ⓐ~ⓔ 중 어법상 <u>어색한</u> 것은? (4점)

① ⓐ　　② ⓑ　　③ ⓒ　　④ ⓓ　　⑤ ⓔ

18 위 글의 빈칸 (A)에 들어갈 문장은? (5점)

① we catch stealing the same article

② we publish this fake article

③ we fake news

④ we make news

⑤ we prove the fact

[19~21] 다음 글을 읽고 물음에 답하시오.

Can You Spot Fake News?
Every day we watch, hear, or read interesting news. (A) However, have you ever seriously considered ⓐwhether an article is really true? (B) Everyone likes an interesting news story but what if it is completely made up? (C) Fake news can be very harmful in that it can make people ⓑless informed or even misled. (D) Why have some people written such false information? (E) Let's look into some articles thinking about the hidden motives behind ⓒthem.

AWFUL DISASTER
Last night, an angry group of rhinoceroses broke down the walls of the cage at the zoo and escaped. They also broke down the walls of the other wild animals' cages. These animals ran down the streets and injured hundreds of people. Twelve of the animals are still on the loose. Citizens should stay indoors until further notice.
(Not a single act or incident ⓓdescribed above has taken place.)

At that time, those who read the article carefully laughed out loud. Those who didn't read it to the end got really worried. Not knowing the news was false, many people panicked. Some tried to escape the city while ⓔothers went into the parks with guns to hunt the animals.
So why did *The Herald* make up such news? Later, ⓕthey confessed that they made it up ⓖso that they could draw the readers' attention to the unsafe conditions at the zoo.

19 위 글의 흐름으로 보아, 주어진 문장이 들어가기에 가장 알맞은 곳은? (4점)

> Nevertheless, there have been various fake news reports throughout history.

① (A)　② (B)　③ (C)　④ (D)　⑤ (E)

20 위 글의 내용과 일치하는 것은? (4점)

① No one in this city believed the article at all.
② The article said that all the animals were caught in the end.
③ The Herald made up the fake story in order to sell more newspapers.
④ Fake news can be very harmful because it can make people more informed.
⑤ The people who read the article carefully came to know that the article was not true.

21 위 글의 ⓐ~ⓖ에 대한 Julia의 영어 노트입니다. 필기 내용 중 알맞은 것을 있는 대로 고른 것은? (5점)

Can You Spot Fake News?
ⓐ 접속사로서 이 문장에서 'have considered'의 목적어가 되는 명사절을 이끈다.
ⓑ 'informed'는 'less'를 'misled'는 'even'을 꾸며주는 과거분사들이다.
ⓒ 앞에 있는 'some people'을 가리키는 인칭대명사이다.
ⓓ 앞에 있는 명사를 꾸며주는 과거분사구이다.
ⓔ 의미상 'the other'로 바꿔 쓸 수 있다.
ⓕ *The Herald*를 가리킨다.
ⓖ 'in order to draw'라는 표현으로 바꿀 수 있다.

① ⓐ, ⓓ, ⓖ
② ⓐ, ⓓ, ⓕ, ⓖ
③ ⓑ, ⓒ, ⓓ, ⓔ
④ ⓑ, ⓒ, ⓔ, ⓕ
⑤ ⓐ, ⓒ, ⓓ, ⓔ, ⓕ, ⓖ

[22~24] Read the below and answer the questions.

(article 1) AWFUL DISASTER
Last night, an angry group of rhinoceroses broke down the walls of the cage at the zoo and escaped. They also broke down the walls of the other wild animals' cages. These animals ran down the streets and injured hundreds of people. Twelve of the animals are still ⓐon the loose. Citizens should stay indoors ⓑuntil further notice.
 **Not a single act or incident described above has ⓒtaken place.*

At that time, those who read the article carefully ⓓlaughed out loud. Those who didn't read it to the end got really worried. Not knowing the news was false, many people panicked. Some tried to escape the city while others went into the parks with guns to hunt the animals.
So why did *The Herald* make up such news? Later, they confessed that they made it up so that they could draw the readers' attention to the unsafe conditions at the zoo.

(article 2) SLAV SHOOTS A FRIEND IN ARGUMENT
The two men had an argument during a meeting. The argument led to a fight, and Pecitello shot Swenekafew twice, in the chest and leg. He is now at the hospital ⓔin critical condition. Pecitello ran away after the shooting. The police are searching for him now and are warning citizens that he is extremely dangerous.

The Daily Telegram published this fake article so that they could prove if *The Daily News*, their competitor, was stealing their articles. *The Daily News* published the same article about "Swenekafew" the next day and thus got caught stealing. The people at *The Daily News* had to admit their act and were harshly criticized by the public.

22 위 글의 내용과 일치하는 것은? (5점)

① 기사 2의 총격 사건은 실제 사건에 기반하여 쓰였다.
② 기사 1은 야생 동물의 위험성에 대한 독자의 관심을 끌기 위해 쓰였다.
③ The Daily Telegram 사는 거짓 기사를 보도하여 대중에게 비난받았다.
④ 기사 1을 끝까지 읽은 사람들은 도시를 탈출하거나 탈출한 동물을 잡으러 나갔다.
⑤ The Herald 사와 The Daily Telegram 사는 특정한 목적을 위해 가짜 뉴스를 보도하였다.

23 위 글의 밑줄 친 ⓐ~ⓔ의 의미가 바르게 연결되지 않은 것은? (4점)

① ⓐ - 잡히지 않은
② ⓑ - 추후 안내가 있을 때까지
③ ⓒ - 발생했다
④ ⓓ - 크게 웃었다
⑤ ⓔ - 중요한 상태로

24 위 글을 읽고 독자로서 우리가 가져야 하는 자세에 대한 짧은 글을 완성하시오. (주어진 철자로 시작하여 쓰시오.) (5점)

As readers, we need to read c_____ and judge whether the news is real or fake. To spot fake news, we should read beyond the h_____ and find s_____ sources.

→ _____, _____, _____

3학년 영어 2학기 중간고사(6과) 1회

문항수 : 선택형(24문항) 서술형(2문항)

반		점수	
이름			

20 . . .

◎ 선택형 문항의 답안은 컴퓨터용 수정 싸인펜을 사용하여 OMR 답안지에 바르게 표기하시오.

◎ 서술형 문제는 답을 답안지에 반드시 검정 볼펜으로 쓰시오.

◎ 총 26문항 100점 만점입니다. 문항별 배점은 각 문항에 표시되어 있습니다.

[서울 종로구 ○○중]

01 다음 중 밑줄 친 단어의 뜻이 가장 올바른 것은? (4점)

① The island mainly exports sugar and fruit. 수입하다

② The company plans to extend its business. 확장하다

③ They will exhibit their new designs at the gallery. 설명하다

④ Let me explain how I felt about the situation. 표현하다

⑤ Many teenagers think expressing themselves is difficult. 전시하다

[서울 서초구 ○○중]

02 다음 밑줄 친 단어들의 의미를 영어로 풀이한 것 중 옳은 것은? (5점)

① confusing: easy to understand because it is well organized or explained

② run out of: to use up a supply of something

③ matter: to be unimportant to you because it has no effect on you or on a particular situation

④ luxurious: extremely comfortable, elegant, or enjoyable, especially in a way that doesn't involve great expense

⑤ priceless: extremely unimportant or useless

[경기 ○○중]

03 다음 빈칸에 들어갈 수 있는 말 중 의미가 <u>다른</u> 것은? (5점)

> Dad: Jane, you look worried. What's the matter?
>
> Jane: I got a big part in the school musical.
>
> Dad: I heard you singing. You sound great!
>
> Jane: It's just that I keep making mistakes. I'm so worried.
>
> Dad: Oh, you just need a little more practice. _____ You can actually learn from them.
>
> Jane: Thanks, Dad. I hope I do a good job.
>
> Dad: You'll do great.

① Don't keep making mistakes.

② Don't sweat over making mistakes.

③ Don't worry about making mistakes.

④ Don't let making mistakes bother you.

⑤ Don't think twice about making mistakes.

[경북 ○○중]

04 다음 중 짝지어진 대화가 <u>어색한</u> 것은? (3점)

① A: What would you do if you could time travel?

B: Time travel will bring about disaster.

② A: Seunghi, what are you doing this weekend?

B: Nothing special, why?

③ A: What would you do if you could live forever?

B: I would live in different cities all around the world.

④ A: Jason, what are you reading?

B: I'm reading a book called Three Wishes.

⑤ A: Yeonhee, you looked worried. What's up?

B: I got a big part in the school musical.

[5~6] Read the dialogue and answer the questions.

A: Caroline, have you read the book, *Tuck Everlasting*?
B: Yeah, it is about a family that drank magical water and lived forever, right?
A: Right. (A)What would you _____ _____ you _____ live forever?
B: Well, I would travel and live in different cities all around the world.
A: Really? I would collect interesting items and make a museum.
B: Cool.

05 Choose the correct one. (4점)

① Caroline would live in different countries.

② The book 'Tuck Everlasting' is about travelling.

③ Caroline's friend asks her about an interesting museum.

④ Caroline and her family members drank the magical water.

⑤ Caroline would collect interesting things and make a museum.

06 Complete the sentence (A). (4점)

→ What would you _____ _____ you _____ live forever?

07 다음 대화에서 ⓐ~ⓓ를 흐름에 맞게 배열한 것은? (4점)

M: Sujin, what are you doing this weekend?
ⓐ Never mind, Lucy. I'll take care of her.
ⓑ Oh, thank you so much. I was so worried.
ⓒ I have to go to Busan for a family trip tomorrow but I can't find anyone to feed my dog, Lucy.
ⓓ Nothing special, why?
W: I'll take her for a walk in the park, too. The weather's supposed to be nice tomorrow.

① ⓐ→ⓑ→ⓒ→ⓓ   ② ⓒ→ⓑ→ⓐ→ⓓ
③ ⓒ→ⓓ→ⓑ→ⓐ   ④ ⓓ→ⓐ→ⓑ→ⓒ
⑤ ⓓ→ⓒ→ⓐ→ⓑ

08 다음 대화의 빈칸에 들어갈 말로 가장 적절한 것은? (3점)

W: James, why are you still up? It's 11 o'clock!
M: I can't sleep because I'm worried about the Bookworm Competition tomorrow.
W: You've read all of the books on the list. What do you have to worry about?
M: Some of the writer's names are confusing, so I'm worried that I might not remember them.
W: _____ You'll do fine.
M: Thanks, Nayeon. I'll try not to worry so much.

① Don't trust anyone except your family.

② Don't worry about something that hasn't happened yet.

③ The deadline is this weekend. You need to hurry.

④ I can take care of your castle this Friday afternoon.

⑤ Whatever happens, I will not forget your help.

09 다음 대화의 순서를 바르게 연결한 것으로 가장 적절한 것은?

(4점)

> (A) What is it about?
> (B) What are you reading?
> (C) Sounds touching. What would you do if you found out you had a twin sister?
> (D) I am reading a book called Twin Sisters.
> (E) I would invite her to my house and show her pictures all night.
> (F) It's about twin sisters who find out about each other.

① (A)-(F)-(C)-(E)-(B)-(D)
② (A)-(F)-(C)-(E)-(D)-(B)
③ (F)-(C)-(E)-(B)-(D)-(A)
④ (B)-(D)-(A)-(F)-(E)-(C)
⑤ (B)-(D)-(A)-(F)-(C)-(E)

10 다음 중 어법상 맞는 문장을 모두 고른 것은? (5점)

> ⒜ It is Tim that he works very hard!
> ⒝ It was certain which I lost my phone.
> ⒞ It was Judy whom won the race then.
> ⒟ I had my brother make a model plane.
> ⒠ Having met me before, Kate found me easily.
> ⒡ It was the Kim's Market that Sujin saw Tim.
> ⒢ It was this morning that I met Yura at the shop.
> ⒣ We have to wear a mask in order to keep us from COVID-19.

① ⒜, ⒝, ⒠, ⒢
② ⒝, ⒞, ⒟, ⒢
③ ⒝, ⒟, ⒠, ⒣
④ ⒟, ⒠, ⒢, ⒣
⑤ ⒟, ⒠, ⒡, ⒣

11 다음 밑줄 친 부분의 쓰임이 나머지와 <u>다른</u> 하나는? (3점)

① It was certain <u>that</u> Minho cried a lot.
② It was a phone <u>that</u> I lost yesterday.
③ It was the princess <u>that</u> killed the dragon.
④ It was for an hour <u>that</u> she walked today.
⑤ It was that boy <u>that</u> missed the school bus.

12 다음 문장의 빈칸에 들어갈 말로 가장 적절한 것은? (4점)

> • Jim was surprised that Jenny had her bicycle _____.

① done
② saved
③ fixed
④ planted
⑤ updated

13 다음 문장에서 밑줄 친 that과 쓰임이 같은 것은? (3점)

> • It was the violin <u>that</u> Nauen played in the school festival.

① It is amazing <u>that</u> you can keep cool in a crisis.
② It is important <u>that</u> we should respect each other.
③ It was because of her sweet voice <u>that</u> I fell in love with her.
④ Nana had the belief <u>that</u> she would become an idol.
⑤ Suhee was so kind <u>that</u> she showed me the way to the post office.

[14~19] 다음 글을 읽고 물음에 답하시오.

That night, when the brothers sat down to chat after dinner, Puru asked the question that had been on his mind for days.

"It was our father's advice that I followed, but I am not happy. I built a house in every city. But because I could not always stay there, I hired people and had the house (A)[look after]. Father said we should sleep comfortably and enjoy our food, so I had my bed (B)[design] by experts and my meals (C)[prepare] by a great chef. He told us to spend like a rich man, so I bought what I wanted without worrying about money. But look at me now! I am (D)_____. Did you not follow our father's wisdom? Tell me, brother, how did you get so rich?"

ⓐPuneet smiled and said, "My dear brother, I also followed our father's wisdom. ⓑBut I understood it a bit differently. ⓒWhen he said 'build a house in every city,' I took it as having a place to stay at their houses when I visited those cities. ⓓAlso, I slept comfortably each night because I would be tired after a hard day's work. ⓔAnd it mattered if I was sleeping on a bed or on the hard floor. I ate only when I was hungry, so even a simple meal tasted great." "Spend money like a rich man?" continued Puneet. "A rich man knows (E)_____.

So, I tried to spend money on something that would bring me back more money rather than on luxurious things. For me, (F)우리 아버지가 설명하려고 하셨던 것은 바로 이 지혜였다."

Now Puru realized (G)_____. With this wisdom in mind, Puru started a new life.

14 위 글의 괄호 (A), (B), (C) 안의 동사 유형으로 가장 적절한 형태는? (5점)

	(A)	(B)	(C)
①	looks after	designs	prepares
②	looking after	designing	preparing
③	to look after	to design	to prepare
④	look after	design	prepare
⑤	looked after	designed	prepared

15 위 글의 빈칸 (D)에 들어갈 어휘로 가장 적절한 것은? (3점)

① empty hand　　② empty hands
③ empty-handed　　④ an empty hand
⑤ with empty hands

16 위 글의 문맥상 빈칸 (E)에 들어갈 구문으로 가장 적절한 것은? (4점)

① when to visit there
② how to make a friend
③ how to make money grow
④ what to do to make money
⑤ where to go to make money

17 위 글의 밑줄 친 (F)를 영문으로 적절하게 옮긴 것은? (3점)

① it was our father that tried to explain this wisdom
② it was this wisdom that our father tried to explain
③ it is this wisdom that our father tries to explain
④ it is our father that tries to explain this wisdom
⑤ our father tried to explain this wisdom

18 위 글의 빈칸 (G)에 들어갈 것으로 가장 적절한 것은? (5점)

① how foolish he had been

② how foolish he has been

③ how diligent he had been

④ how smart he had been

⑤ how smart he has been

19 위 글의 밑줄 친 ⓐ~ⓔ에서 어색한 것을 고르시오. (3점)

① ⓐ ② ⓑ ③ ⓒ ④ ⓓ ⑤ ⓔ

20 Which question can be answered after reading the passage below? (3점)

> Puneet smiled and said, "My dear brother, I also followed our father's wisdom. But I understood it a bit differently. When he said 'build a house in every city,' I took it as having a place to stay all around the world. So I made friends in every city and I stayed at their houses when I visited those cities.
> Also, I slept comfortably each night because I would be tired after a hard day's work, and it did not matter if I was sleeping on a bed or on the hard floor. I ate only when I was hungry, so even a simple meal tasted great."

① How many friends did Puneet make?

② What is the name of Puneet's brother?

③ When did Puneet sleep at his own house?

④ Why did Puneet only have a simple meal?

⑤ How did Puneet understand his father's words differently?

[21~22] 다음 글을 읽고 물음에 답하시오.

> A rich and wise father had two sons, Puru and Puneet. Before ⓐhe passed away, he called his two sons to give them some last words of advice. "Listen carefully, my dear sons. Live by these words throughout your life, and you will be happy," ⓑhe said. "Build a house in every city. Sleep comfortably. Enjoy your food. Lastly, spend money like a rich man …." Before ⓒhe could explain himself, he passed away.
> After ⓓhis death, the two sons took their share of the father's wealth and settled in different cities. Five years passed. Puru, who had been following his father's words carefully, had no money left. But ⓔhis brother was richer than ever. Puru was puzzled about where he had gone wrong, so he visited Puneet to find out.

21 위 글의 밑줄 친 ⓐ~ⓔ 중 가리키는 대상이 다른 하나는? (3점)

① ⓐ ② ⓑ ③ ⓒ ④ ⓓ ⑤ ⓔ

22 위 글을 읽고, 다음 질문에 답할 수 없는 것은? (4점)

① Why did Puneet become rich after he followed his father's will?

② What did the two sons do after their father died?

③ What advice did the father give his two sons?

④ Who become richer after five years?

⑤ Why did the father call his two sons?

[23~26] 다음 글을 읽고 물음에 답하시오.

(A) Puneet welcomed Puru with open arms. That night, when the brothers sat down to chat after dinner, Puru asked the question that had been on this mind for days.

(B) "It was our father's advice that I followed. but I am not happy. I built a house in every city. But because I could not always stay there. I hired people and had the house ⓐlooked after. Father said we should sleep comfortably and enjoy our food, so I had my bed ⓑdesigned by experts and my meals ⓒprepared by a great chef. He told us ⓓspent like a rich man, so I bought what I wanted without worrying about money. But look at me now! I am empty-handed. Did you not follow our father's wisdom? Tell me, brother, how did you get so rich?"

(C) Punnet smiled and said, "My dear brother, I also followed our father's wisdom. But I understood it a bit differently. When he said 'build a house in every city,' I took it as having a place to stay all around the world. So I made friends in every city and I stayed at their houses when I visited those cities. Also, I slept comfortably each night because I would be ⓔtired after a hard day's work, and it did not matter if I was sleeping on a bed or on the hard floor. I ate only when I was hungry, so even a simple meal tasted great."

(D) "A rich man knows how to make money grow. So I tired to spend money on something that would bring me back more money rather than on luxurious things. For me, Ⓐ이게 우리의 아버지가 설명하려고 했던 바로 그 지혜입니다.

(E) Now Puru realized how foolish he had been. With this wisdom in mind, Puru started a new life.

23 위 글의 흐름상 〈보기〉가 들어갈 가장 적합한 곳은? (4점)

보기

"Spend money like a rich man?" continued Puneet.

① (A) ② (B) ③ (C) ④ (D) ⑤ (E)

24 위 글의 ⓐ~ⓔ 중 어법상 <u>어색한</u> 것은? (3점)

① ⓐ ② ⓑ ③ ⓒ ④ ⓓ ⑤ ⓔ

25 위 글의 내용과 일치하는 것은? (4점)

① Puru는 모든 도시에서 친구를 사귀었다.
② Puneet은 Puru를 환영했다.
③ Puru는 Puneet보다 부유해졌다.
④ Puneet은 아버지의 지혜를 따르지 않았다.
⑤ Puru는 돈 걱정을 하면서 원하는 것을 사지 못했다.

26 위 글의 밑줄 친 Ⓐ의 우리말과 뜻이 같도록 〈보기〉에 주어진 단어를 사용하여 〈조건〉에 맞게 문장을 완성하시오. (5점)

보기

tried to, our father, explain, this wisdom

조건

• 〈보기〉에 주어진 단어들을 모두 사용할 것.
• It ~ that 강조 구문으로 쓸 것.
• 과거시제로 쓸 것.
• 필요시 단어 추가 가능.

→ For me, _____.

3학년 영어 2학기 중간고사(6과) 2회

문항수 : 선택형(26문항) 서술형(2문항)   20 . . .

◎ 선택형 문항의 답안은 컴퓨터용 수정 싸인펜을 사용하여 OMR 답안지에 바르게 표기하시오.
◎ 서술형 문제는 답을 답안지에 반드시 검정 볼펜으로 쓰시오.
◎ 총 28문항 100점 만점입니다. 문항별 배점은 각 문항에 표시되어 있습니다.

[서울 구로구 ○○중]

01 다음 문장의 빈칸에 들어갈 수 <u>없는</u> 것은?   (4점)

> • Everyone has _____ of speech and expression.
> • Something that is _____ makes it difficult for people to know exactly what is happening or what to do.
> • A(n) _____ is a person who is very skilled at doing something or who knows a lot about a particular subject.
> • To _____ means to start to feel comfortable in a new home.

① expert   ② exhibit   ③ freedom
④ settle in   ⑤ confusing

[서울 종로구 ○○중]

02 다음 중 단어와 영영풀이가 올바르게 짝지어진 것은?   (3점)

① death: at the end

② lastly: the end of life

③ chat: to talk with someone in a casual way

④ expert: a skilled and trained cook who works in a hotel or restaurant

⑤ chef: a person who has special skill or knowledge related to a particular subject

[경기 ○○중]

03 다음 대화의 빈칸에 들어갈 말을 〈보기〉에서 골라 순서대로 알맞게 나열한 것은?   (4점)

> Emily: What are you doing, Jinho?
> Jinho: I'm writing a review of the movie, *The Time Traveler's Wife*.
> Emily: I saw that movie, too. _____
> _____
> Jinho: I'm glad that we have the same taste in movies.
> Emily: Yeah, I couldn't agree more.
> Jinho: _____
> Emily: I would travel to the 1940s and prevent World War Ⅱ. How about you?
> Jinho: I would go to the Joseon Dynasty and meet King Sejong. _____
> _____

> **보기**
> ⓐ I'm a big fan of him.
> ⓑ It's one of my favorite romantic movies.
> ⓒ What would you do if you could time travel?
> ⓓ Let's say that you could read any books you want.
> ⓔ I can imagine how hard it is to write a review of the movie.

① ⓑ, ⓒ, ⓐ   ② ⓑ, ⓓ, ⓔ   ③ ⓒ, ⓓ, ⓐ
④ ⓓ, ⓒ, ⓑ   ⑤ ⓓ, ⓔ, ⓐ

[부산 ○○중]

04 다음 대화에서 어법상 <u>어색한</u> 문장은?   (3점)

> A: ⓐRomeo first met Juliet in the garden.
> B: No, ⓑit was at the party that Romeo first met Juliet. Also, ⓒit was several hours later that he went to the garden.
> C: No, ⓓit was Juliet that went to the garden.
> A: Really? I thought ⓔit was first met that Romeo and Juliet in the garden.

① ⓐ   ② ⓑ   ③ ⓒ   ④ ⓓ   ⑤ ⓔ

05 다음 괄호 안의 주어진 단어를 우리말과 뜻이 같도록 〈조건〉에 맞게 문장을 완성하시오. (4점)

> M: Jane, (A)너 걱정돼 보이는구나. (worried, see, you, like, look) What's the matter?
> W: I got a big part in the school musical. It's just that I keep making mistakes. I'm so worried.
> M: Oh, you just need a little more practice. (B)실수하는 거 걱정하지 마. (what, worry, don't, making, about, mistakes, it)

조건
> • 괄호 안의 단어를 바르게 배열하여 문장을 완성할 것.
> • 괄호 안의 필요 없는 단어는 제외할 것.

→ (A) _____

(B) _____

06 다음 대화를 바르게 이해한 사람은? (4점)

> Jinsu: What are you doing this weekend?
> Sujin: Nothing special, why?
> Jinsu: I have to go to Busan for a family trip tomorrow, but I can't find anyone to feed my dog, Lucy.
> Sujin: Don't worry about Lucy. I'll take care of her.
> Jinsu: Oh, thank you so much. I was so worried.
> Sujin: I'll take her for a walk in the park, too. The weather's supposed to be nice tomorrow.

① 재은: Lucy will take care of herself this weekend.
② 지수: Sujin has made special plans for this weekend.
③ 은주: Jinsu and Lucy have to go to Busan this weekend.
④ 서완: Sujin expects that it won't be sunny tomorrow.
⑤ 시온: Sujin will go to the park with Jinsu's dog this weekend.

07 다음 대화의 빈칸 (A) 안에 들어갈 알맞은 것은? (3점)

> W: What are you doing, Jinho?
> M: I'm writing a review of the movie, *The Time Traveler's Wife*.
> W: I saw that movie, too. It's one of my favorite romantic movies.
> M: I loved it, too. Emily, (A)_____ you could time travel?
> W: I would travel to the 1940s and prevent World War II. How about you?
> M: I would go to the Joseon Dynasty and meet King Sejong. I'm a big fan of him.

① what did you do that
② what do you mean that
③ what were some things that
④ what would you do if
⑤ what will you do for me if

08 다음 대화를 읽고 답할 수 있는 것은? (3점)

> Tim: How's your online story going, Amy?
> Amy: Not well. The deadline is this weekend but I ran out of ideas.
> Tim: Don't worry about it. I can help you.
> Amy: That would be great. My main character has special powers. What would you do if you were able to read people's minds?
> Tim: Well, I would find out if the girl I like likes me.
> Amy: That's a good idea. Thanks.

① What problem does Amy have?

② When can Tim read Amy's online story?

③ What is the title of Amy's online story?

④ What does Tim want to know for his girl friend?

⑤ Who is the main character in the online story?

09 What can you say to James to comfort him? Choose the best answer. (4점)

> James is still up at 11:30 p.m. He can't sleep because he's feeling nervous about the Bookworm Competition tomorrow. He read all of the books on the list but some of the writers' names are confusing, so he's really worried that he might forget them.

① Let's go.

② Don't dwell on it.

③ Don't bother me.

④ Aren't you feeling worried?

⑤ Please stop making mistakes.

10 다음 중 어법상 어색한 문장은? (3점)

① It is Jack that grows potatoes in the garden.

② It was at the park that Jenny saw a shooting star.

③ It was yesterday that I played tennis with Mike.

④ It was on the bus that Mina got her wallet stolen.

⑤ It was studied that Tom math in the library yesterday.

11 다음 〈보기〉와 기능이 같고 어법상 올바른 것은? (4점)

> 보기
> • It was this wisdom that our father tried to explain.

① It was chicken soup which I made for Jane.

② It was necessary that she attended the meeting.

③ It was last Saturday where we won the gold medal.

④ It was in front of the bank when he lost his phone.

⑤ It was my mother whom turned the TV on after dinner.

12 다음 빈칸에 들어갈 말을 바르게 짝지은 것은? (4점)

> (A) Why don't you have your furniture _____?
> (B) The teacher had the students _____ their homework.

	(A)	(B)
①	recycled	finished
②	recycled	finish
③	recycle	finishing
④	recycle	finish
⑤	recycling	finished

[13~16] 다음 글을 읽고 물음에 답하시오.

A rich and wise father had two sons, Puru and Puneet. Before he died, he called his two sons to give them some last words of advice.

"Listen carefully, my dear sons. Live (A)_____ these words throughout your life, and you will be happy," he said.

"Build a house in every city. Sleep comfortably. Enjoy your food. Lastly, spend money (B)_____ a rich man… ." Before he could explain himself, he passed (C)_____.

After his death, the two sons took their share of the father's wealth and settled in different cities. Five years passed. Puru, who had been following his father's words carefully, had no money left. But his brother was richer (D)_____. Puru was puzzled about where he had gone wrong, so he visited Puneet to find out. Puneet welcomed Puru ⓐwith open arms.

13 위 글의 빈칸 (A)~(C)에 들어갈 것으로 가장 적절한 것은? (4점)

	(A)	(B)	(C)
①	by	alike	away
②	by	like	away
③	on	like	way
④	on	alike	out
⑤	with	like	out

14 위 글의 빈칸 (D)에 들어갈 것으로 적절한 것은? (3점)

① before then   ② worse than ever

③ than ever   ④ before

⑤ former days

15 위 글을 읽고 다음 물음의 답으로 가장 적절한 것은? (4점)

Question: What was Puru puzzled about?
Answer: _____

① No, he didn't.

② Yes, he puzzled about that matter.

③ He followed his father's words carefully.

④ He was puzzled about where he had gone wrong.

⑤ He took his share and settled in different cities.

16 위 글의 밑줄 친 ⓐ의 뜻으로 적절한 것은? (3점)

① 두 팔을 벌리고   ② 두 손을 들고

③ 두 손 모아   ④ 두 팔을 내리고

⑤ 두 팔을 잡고

[17~20] 다음 글을 읽고 질문에 답하시오.

Puru asked, "Did you not follow our father's wisdom? Tell me, brother, how did you get so rich?"

Puneet smiled and said, "ⓐMy dear brother, I also followed our father's wisdom. But I understood it a bit differently. When ⓑhe said 'build a house in every city,' I took it as having a place to stay all around the world. So I made friends in every city and I stayed at their houses when I visited those cities. Also, I slept comfortably each night because I would be tired after a hard day's work, and it did not matter if I was sleeping on a bed or on the hard floor. I ate only when I was hungry, so even a simple meal tasted great."

"Spend money like a rich man?" continued Puneet.

"A rich man knows how to make money grow. So, I tried to spend money on something that would bring me back more money rather than on luxurious things. For me, it was this wisdom that our father tried to explain." Now ⓒPuru realized how foolish ⓓhe had been. With this wisdom in mind, ⓔhe started a new life.

17 위 글의 내용과 일치하는 것은? (3점)

① Puneet은 아버지의 지혜를 Puru와는 조금 다르게 이해했다.
② Puneet은 세계 곳곳을 다니며 부서진 집을 고쳤다.
③ Puru는 Puneet의 이야기를 듣고 그를 비난했다.
④ Puneet은 피곤할 때 주로 바닥에서 잠이 들었다.
⑤ Puru는 Puneet의 집에서 함께 살기로 결심했다.

18 위 글의 밑줄 친 this wisdom이 의미하는 바로 가장 적절한 것은? (4점)

① To buy a lot of houses around the world
② To sleep well anywhere and anytime
③ To make friends, work hard, and spend money on something that will bring more money
④ To always feel hungry and prepare food with a famous chef in the country
⑤ To buy as many luxurious things as possible

19 위 글의 밑줄 친 ⓐ~ⓔ 중 지칭하는 대상이 나머지 넷과 <u>다른</u> 것은? (2점)

① ⓐ   ② ⓑ   ③ ⓒ   ④ ⓓ   ⑤ ⓔ

20 위 글의 내용을 다음과 같이 요약하고자 한다. 빈칸 (A), (B)에 들어갈 말로 가장 적절한 것은? (4점)

> Puneet understood has father's wisdom in a (A)_____ way. He stayed at their houses when he visited those cities by making friends in every city. He slept comfortably after a hard day's work. He ate only when he was hungry. He made money (B)_____ like a rich man who spends money on the things to bring him back more money.

	(A)	(B)
①	serious	fly
②	different	grow
③	surprising	call
④	boring	leave
⑤	foolish	escape

[부산 ○○중]

[21~23] 다음 글을 읽고 질문에 답하시오.

Puneet welcomed Puru with open arms. (A) That night, when the brothers sat down to chat after dinner, Puru asked the question ⓐthat had been on his mind for days. (B)
(가)"I followed our father's advice, but I am not happy. (C) I built a house in every city. (D) Father said we ⓑshould sleep comfortably and enjoy our food, so I had my bed designed by experts and ⓒmy meals to prepare by a great chef. (E) He told us ⓓto spend like a rich man, so I bought what I wanted ⓔwithout worrying about money. But look at me now! I am empty-handed."

21 위 글의 밑줄 친 (가) 부분을 It ~ that 강조구문을 사용하여 바꿔 쓰시오. (5점)

→ _____ _____ _____ father's _____
_____ _____ _____.

22 위 글의 흐름으로 보아, 주어진 문장이 들어가기에 가장 적절한 곳은? (3점)

> But because I could not always stay there, I hired people and had the house looked after.

① (A)   ② (B)   ③ (C)   ④ (D)   ⑤ (E)

23 위 글의 밑줄 친 ⓐ~ⓔ 중 어법상 <u>어색한</u> 것은? (4점)

① ⓐ   ② ⓑ   ③ ⓒ   ④ ⓓ   ⑤ ⓔ

[24~28] 다음 글을 읽고 물음에 답하시오.

That night, when the brothers sat down to chat after dinner, ⓐPuru asked the question that he had been on his mind for days.

"It was our father's advice that I followed. Ⓐ＿＿＿＿＿ I am not happy. I built a house in every city. Ⓑ＿＿＿＿＿ because I could not always stay there, ⓑI hired people and had the house look after. Father said we should sleep comfortably and enjoy our food, so I had my bed designed by experts and ⓒI had a great chef prepare my meals. He told us to spend like a rich man, so I bought what I wanted without worrying about money. Ⓒ＿＿＿＿＿ look at me now! I am empty-handed. Did you not follow our father's wisdom? Tell me, brother, how did you get so rich?"

Puneet smiled and said, "My dear brother, I also followed our father's wisdom. Ⓓ＿＿＿＿＿ ⓓI understood it a bit different. When he said 'build a house in every city,' I took it as having a place to stay all around the world. So I made friends in every city and ⓔI stayed at their houses which I visited those cities. Ⓔ＿＿＿＿＿, I slept comfortably each night because I would be tired after a hard day's work, and it did not matter if I was sleeping on a bed or on the hard floor. I ate only when I was hungry, so even a simple meal tasted great."

"Spend money like a rich man?" continued Puneet.

"A rich man knows (가)＿＿＿＿＿＿＿＿＿＿＿. So, I tried to spend money on something that would bring me back more money rather than on luxurious things. For me, it was this wisdom that our father tried to explain."

Now Puru realized how foolish he had been. With this wisdom in mind, Puru started a new life.

24 위 글을 읽고 답할 수 있는 것을 모두 고르면? (정답 2개) (4점)

① How did Puru get rich?
② Where did Puneet build a house?
③ What did Puneet ask Puru after dinner?
④ What did Puru do to spend money like a rich man?
⑤ Why did a simple meal taste great to Puneet?

25 위 글의 ⓐ~ⓔ 중 어법상 맞는 것은? (3점)

① ⓐ   ② ⓑ   ③ ⓒ   ④ ⓓ   ⑤ ⓔ

26 위 글의 빈칸 (가)에 들어갈 가장 적당한 말은? (4점)

① when to eat
② where to sleep
③ what to do for his father
④ how to waste his wealth
⑤ how to make money grow

27 위 글을 읽고 알 수 있는 것은? (4점)

① Puru didn't follow his father's advice.
② Puneet misunderstood his father's words.
③ Puru realized he had to travel all around world.
④ Puru's father advised his sons to live comfortably.
⑤ The father's wisdom shows the value of wise advice in life.

28 위 글의 빈칸 Ⓐ~Ⓔ 중 들어갈 말이 다른 것은? (3점)

① Ⓐ   ② Ⓑ   ③ Ⓒ   ④ Ⓓ   ⑤ Ⓔ

◎ 선택형 문항의 답안은 컴퓨터용 수정 싸인펜을 사용하여 OMR 답안지에 바르게 표기하시오.

◎ 서술형 문제는 답을 답안지에 반드시 검정 볼펜으로 쓰시오.

◎ 총 28문항 100점 만점입니다. 문항별 배점은 각 문항에 표시되어 있습니다.

[경북 ○○중]

01 다음 문장의 빈칸에 들어갈 어휘로 가장 적절한 것은? (3점)

> • It is difficult to _____ the result in detail.

① compare ② wonder ③ move

④ compete ⑤ return

[서울 서초구 ○○중]

02 다음 밑줄 친 단어들의 의미를 영어로 풀이한 것 중 옳지 <u>않은</u> 것은? (4점)

① <u>be likely to</u>: to be expected to happen or to be probably

② <u>bandwagon</u>: an activity, or movement that has become successful and popular and attracts many new people

③ <u>think outside the box</u>: to explore creative ideas that are not limited or controlled by rules or tradition

④ <u>injure</u>: to hurt or cause physical harm to a person or animal

⑤ <u>keep track of</u>: to make uncertain that you know what is happening or has happened to someone or something

[경북 ○○중]

03 다음 대화의 빈칸에 적절한 것은? (3점)

> Sumi: I heard you bought VR glasses. _____ _____
>
> Jemin: I am very happy. Because the style and color are very cool. Furthermore, the price is pretty economic.

① How do you like it?

② How do you like them?

③ What's the price of VR glasses?

④ How often do you use VR glasses?

⑤ What's the problem of VR glasses?

[경북 ○○중]

04 다음 중 짝지어진 대화가 <u>어색한</u> 것은? (3점)

① A: What's wrong with you?
   B: I regret that I didn't tell her the truth.

② A: I don't have an umbrella today.
   B: Me, neither. We have checked the weather forecast.

③ A: Are you happy with your new shoes?
   B: Yes. I'm satisfied with them.

④ A: I wish I could travel abroad alone.
   B: So do I.

⑤ A: How do you like this scarf?
   B: The design is nice, but I don't think the color suits me.

[경북 ○○중]

05 다음 대화의 빈칸에 적절한 것은? (4점)

> Jeff: What's the problem with you?
> Nasa: I'd like to buy a new headphone, but I don't have enough money. _____

① I must have lost my headphone.

② I must have saved my allowance.

③ I should have saved my allowance.

④ I shouldn't have saved my allowance.

⑤ I could save my allowance, and I did.

06 다음 대화의 내용과 일치하지 <u>않는</u> 것은? (3점)

M: Hi, Riley. I heard that you bought a laptop online. How do you like it?

W: Oh, I'm not happy with it.

M: Why? What's wrong?

W: It makes too much noise and gets overheated.

M: Oh, then you should ask for your money back.

W: The online store won't give me back my money because I've used it for a week.

M: How about calling the online shop and explaining your problem?

W: Yeah, I think I should do that.

① Riley bought a laptop online.

② Riley is not satisfied with her laptop.

③ Riley's laptop is silent when it gets overheated.

④ Riley has used the laptop for a week.

⑤ Riley guesses that the online store will not give her money back.

08 Choose the unnatural dialogue. (3점)

① A: What's wrong with your coat? It looks uncomfortable.

　B: I went to the dress shop late, so I didn't check the size and just bought it.

② A: How do you like BTS' new song "*Dynamite*"?

　B: I'm enjoying it. I like the disco feel.

③ A: Luke, are you satisfied with your new speakers?

　B: Yes, it's really convenient. I take it anywhere and the sound quality isn't good.

④ A: How long does the battery last?

　B: Just one hour. It doesn't last long.

⑤ A: Are you enjoying the weather these days?

　B: It's a bit cold these days but I'm really enjoying it.

07 다음 대화를 순서대로 바르게 배열한 것은? (4점)

(A) Oh, that's too bad.

(B) That's a good idea.

(C) Clara, are you okay?

(D) Hey, we ride our bikes to school. Why don't you join us? You can save money and work out, too.

(E) Yeah, I missed the school bus again. I should have gotten up earlier. I spend too much money on bus fares.

① (A)-(E)-(C)-(D)-(B)　② (C)-(D)-(B)-(E)-(A)

③ (C)-(E)-(A)-(D)-(B)　④ (D)-(E)-(A)-(C)-(B)

⑤ (D)-(B)-(E)-(A)-(C)

09 다음 대화의 빈칸 ⓐ가 괄호 안의 뜻이 되도록 빈칸을 채워 대화를 완성하시오. (5점)

A: A store on Green Street is having a year-end sale.

B: Oh. You said you wanted to get a new phone. Let's go there.

A: I know..., but I bought mine already at full price!

B: Really? That's too bad. They're selling them at a 40% discount.

A: Yeah. ⓐI _____ not _____ _____ sales _____ _____ mine. (내 것을 사기 전에 할인을 확인하지 않은 것을 후회해.)

→ I _____ not _____ _____ sales _____ _____ mine.

10 다음 대화의 빈칸 ⓐ에 후회하는 표현을 사용하여 대화를 완성하시오. (keep, my를 활용할 것.) (5점)

A: Hey, Eric. Camilla and I are going to watch a movie. Do you want to join us?
B: I'd love to, but I can't. I've spent all of my allowance for this week.
A: Didn't you just get it a few days ago? How did you spend it all?
B: I'm not sure. ⓐI should _____ _____ _____ _____ _____ _____.

→ I should _____ _____ _____ _____ _____ _____.

12 다음 문장의 빈칸에 들어갈 수 <u>없는</u> 것은? (3점)

> • _____ have their own computers.

① None of the members
② A number of teachers
③ One third of the people
④ Every student in the course
⑤ Most of the students in the class

13 다음 중 어법상 올바른 문장을 <u>모두</u> 고른 것은? (2개) (4점)

① Two hours seems enough to take a walk.
② The number of the students decrease day by day.
③ Two thirds of the students is here.
④ A number of students likes online classes.
⑤ The rest of the people are working on another project.

11 다음 주어진 우리말 문장을 영작한 것으로 적절한 것은? (3점)

> • 사람들은 나이가 들수록 더 쇠약해진다.

① As people become older, they get weaker.
② As people become older, as they get weaker.
③ As people become weaker, they become older.
④ So people become older, as they get weaker.
⑤ So people become weaker, as they become older.

14 다음 중 빈칸에 들어갈 be동사의 형태가 <u>다른</u> 하나는? (4점)

① None of this money _____ ours.
② More than half of the report _____ already completed.
③ One-third of the population of this town _____ from Europe.
④ It says that the number of imported cars _____ increasing every year.
⑤ Forty percent of the student council members _____ in the meeting room.

[15~21] 다음 글을 읽고 물음에 답하시오.

Why do I buy a pair of pants and a bag after I have bought a new coat?

Lisa buys a coat that she really loves. Immediately, she realizes that her pants do not match her new coat. ⓐ_____, she buys new pants that go perfectly ⓑ_____ her new coat. But she sees that none of her bags match her new clothes. So, she buys a new bag. Most of her money is spent ⓒ_____ buying the new items to complete her new look.

What made Lisa search for new items immediately after buying a new coat? The "Diderot effect" may explain it. Denis Diderot, a French writer, received a new gown as a gift. Soon after receiving the gift, he noticed that all of his furniture did not go well with his new gown. ⓓ_____, he ended up replacing most of it.

Why do I buy things just because they are on sale?

Nathan goes window shopping and sees a pair of headphones. He checks the price and finds out that they are $200. He thinks that the headphones are too expensive. The sales person approaches him and says, "You can get a 20 percent discount ⓔ_____ those headphones." Even though the ⓕ[discount / to discount / discounted] price is still not very low, Nathan decides to buy the headphones.

The situation ⓖ[describe / to describe / described] above is an example of the "anchoring effect." Ⓐ The price mentioned first affects our opinion of prices mentioned afterwards. ⒷFor example, if we start with $200, then $160 will seem cheap in comparison. ⒸFurthermore, as the difference of the two prices becomes bigger, the effect will be more powerful. ⒹAs such, the price mentioned first acts as an "anchor" that fixes our thoughts about the price of an item. ⒺJust like Lisa and Nathan, we tend to buy things with seriously considering why we are buying them. As these effects have shown, many things influence our purchases. The next time you decide to buy something, think for a moment about why you are buying it.

15 위 글의 빈칸 ⓐ와 ⓓ에 공통으로 들어갈 말로 적절한 것은?
(3점)

① So   ② As   ③ When
④ Even if   ⑤ Though

16 위 글의 빈칸 ⓑ, ⓒ, ⓔ에 들어갈 말로 적절한 것은? (4점)

	ⓑ	ⓒ	ⓔ
①	with	on	on
②	with	on	with
③	on	with	away
④	on	on	out
⑤	with	on	out

17 위 글의 밑줄 친 Ⓐ~Ⓔ 중에서, 어법상 어색한 것은? (3점)

① Ⓐ   ② Ⓑ   ③ Ⓒ   ④ Ⓓ   ⑤ Ⓔ

18 위 글을 읽고, 다음 주어진 물음에 대한 답으로 가장 적절한 것은? (4점)

> • What kind of concept is the "Diderot effect?"

① It is the concept that approaching a good item often leads to more necessary purchases.

② It is the concept that approaching a new item often leads to more unplanned purchases.

③ It is the concept that purchasing a good item often leads to more planned purchases.

④ It is the concept that purchasing a new item often leads to more unplanned purchases.

⑤ It is the concept that purchasing a new item leads to more planned purchases.

19 위 글의 내용과 일치하지 <u>않는</u> 것은? (4점)

① Nathan이 구입한 헤드폰 가격은 낮은 편이 아니다.

② 물건을 구매할 때, 그것을 왜 사는지 잠시 동안 생각해야 한다고 글쓴이는 제안한다.

③ Lisa는 대부분의 돈을 새로운 모습을 완성하기 위한 물품을 사는 데 쓴다.

④ 물건을 살 때, 처음에 언급된 물건의 가격은 두 번째 물건의 가격에 영향을 주지 않는다.

⑤ '디드로 효과'에서 '디드로'는 프랑스 작가의 이름에서 유래한 것이다.

20 위 글의 내용으로 보아 알 수 <u>없는</u> 것은? (4점)

① The "Diderot effect" may explain Lisa's spending.

② After receiving a new gown, Diderot replaced his furniture.

③ Lisa realizes that her pants don't match her new coat.

④ The "anchoring effect" comes from the difference of the prices.

⑤ When the price of an item is higher than before, people buy more.

21 위 글의 괄호 ⓕ, ⓖ에 들어갈 동사의 형태로 가장 적절한 것은? (3점)

	ⓕ	ⓖ
①	discounted	to describe
②	discounted	described
③	discount	to describe
④	to discount	described
⑤	to discount	describe

[22~24] 다음 글을 읽고 물음에 답하시오.

> **Why We Buy What We Buy**
> Have you ever wondered why you've bought things that you don't even want or need? Let's consider what Ⓐ＿＿＿＿＿ us when it comes to buying things. Why do I want to buy what my friends bought?
> (A) Jeff goes to the shopping center and sees a pair of soccer shoes on display. (B) Jeff recognizes the shoes at a glance because more than half of the boys on his soccer team wear them. (C) We can use the "bandwagon effect" to explain Jeff's behavior. (D) A bandwagon is a wagon in a parade that encourages people to jump aboard and enjoy the music. (E) When more people get on the bandwagon, others are more likely to get on or follow it. In this way, people tend to buy something just because other people Ⓑ＿＿＿＿＿ it.

22 위 글의 빈칸 Ⓐ와 Ⓑ에 들어갈 말로 적절한 것은? (4점)

	Ⓐ	Ⓑ
①	affects	had bought
②	affect	have bought
③	affected	bought
④	affects	have bought
⑤	affect	bought

23 위 글의 (A)~(E) 중에서, 다음 문장이 들어갈 곳으로 적절한 것은? (3점)

> Although Jeff already has many pairs of soccer shoes, he ends up buying another new pair.

① (A) ② (B) ③ (C) ④ (D) ⑤ (E)

24 위 글의 내용과 <u>다른</u> 것은?　　　　　(4점)

① 위 글은 물건의 구매에 관한 글이다.

② Jeff는 쇼핑센터에 가서 전시된 축구화를 보게 된다.

③ Jeff의 축구팀에 있는 소년들의 반이 축구화를 신는다.

④ 밴드왜건은 퍼레이드에 있는 사륜마차이고 사람들이 음악을 즐기도록 부추긴다.

⑤ 사람들은 다른 사람들이 어떤 것을 사면 그것을 구매하는 경향이 있다.

[서울 종로구 ○○중]

25 다음 글의 제목으로 가장 알맞은 것은?　　(3점)

> Have you ever wondered why you've bought things that you don't even want or need? We tend to buy things without seriously considering why we are buying them. We need to consider what affects us when it comes to buying things. The next time you decide to buy something, think for a moment about why you are buying it.

① Buy Things Considerately

② Saving Is Getting

③ The Joy of Shopping

④ The Effects of Shopping

⑤ How to Find a Reasonable Price

[경북 ○○중]

26 다음 글 바로 앞에 나왔을 내용은?　　　(3점)

> Just like Jeff and his friends, we tend to buy things without seriously considering why we are buying them. As these effects have shown, many things influence our purchases. The next time you decide to buy something, think for a moment about why you are buying it.

① Some cases of buying things without serious consideration

② Things to watch out when you pay for something

③ Some tips for buying good things on sale

④ The effects of overspending on the economy

⑤ How to buy things online

[서울 서초구 ○○중]

[27~28] 다음 글을 읽고 물음에 답하시오.

> Nathan goes window shopping and sees a pair of headphones. He checks the price and finds out that they are $200. (A) He thinks that the headphones are too expensive. (B) The sales person approaches ⓐ[him / to him] and says, "You can get a 20 percent discount on them." (C) The situation described above is an example of the "anchoring effect." (D) The price mentioned first ⓑ[affects / affecting] our opinion of prices mentioned afterwards. For example, if we start with $200, then $160 will seem cheap in comparison. (E) Furthermore, as the difference of the two prices becomes ⓒ[smaller / bigger], the effect will be more powerful. As such, the price mentioned ⓓ[earlier / later] acts as an "anchor" that fixes our thoughts about the price of an item.

27 위 글의 (A)~(E) 중 주어진 문장이 들어갈 문맥상 알맞은 곳은?　　　　　(3점)

> Even though their price is still not very low, he decides to buy the item.

① (A)　② (B)　③ (C)　④ (D)　⑤ (E)

28 괄호 ⓐ~ⓓ에 들어갈 어법상 또는 문맥상 적절한 단어들로만 바르게 연결한 것은?　　　(4점)

	ⓐ	ⓑ	ⓒ	ⓓ
①	him	affects	smaller	later
②	to him	affects	bigger	later
③	to him	affecting	bigger	earlier
④	him	affects	bigger	earr
⑤	him	affecting	smaller	earlier

Lesson 7 Spend Wisely　**31**

◎ 선택형 문항의 답안은 컴퓨터용 수정 싸인펜을 사용하여 OMR 답안지에 바르게 표기하시오.

◎ 서술형 문제는 답을 답안지에 반드시 검정 볼펜으로 쓰시오.

◎ 총 29문항 100점 만점입니다. 문항별 배점은 각 문항에 표시되어 있습니다.

[부산 ○○중]

01 다음 우리말 뜻에 맞도록 빈칸에 알맞은 단어를 고른 것은? (3점)

> • It is difficult to _____ the results in detail.
> • 결과를 상세하게 비교하는 것은 어렵다.

① combine ② compete ③ compose
④ compare ⑤ compromise

[부산 ○○중]

02 다음 우리말 뜻에 맞도록 빈칸에 알맞은 단어를 고른 것은? (3점)

> • We _____ children to think for themselves.
> • 우리는 아이들이 스스로 생각하도록 격려한다.

① enjoy ② endanger ③ enlarge
④ enhance ⑤ encourage

[전북 ○○중]

03 다음 대화의 내용이 자연스럽게 이어지도록 문장을 순서대로 배열한 것은? (4점)

> M: Did you get a new phone, Jamie? It's just like mine.
> (A) Right, but the store on Green Street is having a year-end sale.
> (B) Really? That's too bad. They're selling them at a 40 percent discount.
> (C) Yeah, I got it last weekend on sale.
> (D) Oh, I bought mine at full price!
> (E) It was on sale? But it has just been released, hasn't it?
> M: I should have checked the sales before buying mine.

① (A)-(B)-(C)-(D)-(E) ② (B)-(A)-(C)-(E)-(D)
③ (C)-(E)-(A)-(D)-(B) ④ (D)-(C)-(E)-(B)-(A)
⑤ (E)-(D)-(C)-(B)-(A)

[경북 ○○중]

04 다음 대화의 밑줄 친 ⓐ~ⓔ 중 문맥상 낱말의 쓰임이 적절하지 않은 것은? (4점)

> A: I heard that you bought VR glasses. How do you like them?
> B: I'm not happy with them. They ⓐdon't work with my smartphone. I ⓑshouldn't have checked the information more carefully.
> A: Oh, then you should ask for your money back.
> B: I've used them for a week, so I'm ⓒnot sure if the store will give me back my money.
> A: But I think you ⓓshould call the store and explain your problem.
> B: Okay. I ⓔwill try that.

① ⓐ ② ⓑ ③ ⓒ ④ ⓓ ⑤ ⓔ

[전북 ○○중]

05 다음 중 어법상 바르지 않은 것은? (3점)

① Every rule has its exception.

② A number of people are gathering to see the boy band.

③ Only 10 percent of the people agree with the new rule.

④ Each member in the group have a nickname.

⑤ The number of students in our class is twenty.

06 다음 대화의 빈칸 (A)에 들어갈 알맞은 문장은? (3점)

> M: Hi, can I help you with anything?
> W: Yes, can I try on that cap with stars over there?
> M: Sure. (A)_____
> W: The design is nice, but I don't think the color suits me. Do you have it in black?
> M: Yes. I'll get one from the back. (*pause*) Here it is.
> W: Great. I'll take it.

① How much is it?

② How do you like it?

③ How did you make that cap?

④ How are the caps these days?

⑤ How could you see that stars?

07 다음 대화를 순서에 맞게 배열한 것은? (4점)

> (A) M: Good morning. May I help you?
> (B) W: Well, she doesn't like animation characters that much. Can I see the blue one?
> (C) M: How do you like this yellow one? This character is quite popular among children.
> (D) W: I'd like to buy a T-shirt for my sister. She's twelve years old.
> (E) M: You mean this blue striped T-shirt? Its design is simple and cool.
> (F) W: Yes, I think my sister will like it. I'll take it.

① (A)-(B)-(C)-(D)-(E)-(F)

② (A)-(B)-(C)-(F)-(E)-(D)

③ (A)-(D)-(C)-(B)-(E)-(F)

④ (A)-(D)-(C)-(F)-(E)-(B)

⑤ (A)-(F)-(E)-(B)-(C)-(D)

08 다음 대화의 밑줄 친 부분이 의도하는 바로 알맞은 것은? (3점)

> W: Hey, Eric. Camilla and I are going to watch a movie. Do you want to join us?
> M: I'd love to, but I can't. I've spent all of my allowance for this week.
> W: Didn't you just get it a few days ago? How did you spend it all?
> M: I'm not sure. <u>I should have kept track of my spending.</u>

① 알고 있는 내용 표현하기

② 후회하는 일 말하기

③ 어떤 것에 만족하거나 불만이 있는지 묻기

④ 어떤 일이 실제로 가능한지 묻기

⑤ 이루어지기를 바라는 일 표현하기

09 다음 대화의 빈칸 (A)~(E) 중 주어진 문장이 들어가기에 가장 적절한 곳은? (3점)

> W: Daniel, here's a package for you.
> M: (A) It's my helmet. I bought it at an online used store a few days ago.
> W: Oh, open it and let me see it.
> M: (B) Okay. Oh, this outer part is a little broken. The seller said that it's perfectly fine though.
> W: (C) Didn't you check the pictures of the helmet before you bought it?
> M: (D) I should have checked a bit more.
> W: (E) You should call the seller and ask for a refund.

> No, I just trusted the seller.

① (A) ② (B) ③ (C) ④ (D) ⑤ (E)

10 다음 문장의 문법상 <u>어색한</u> 부분을 찾아 바르게 고치시오. (4점)

> • Most of the time is spent on the bus during the last trip.

_____ → _____

11 다음 대화의 내용과 일치하는 것은? (3점)

> Ally: Hi, Josh. Is that a new speaker?
> Josh: Yes, I bought it a few weeks ago.
> Ally: It looks cool. How do you like it?
> Josh: It's convenient. I can take it anywhere and listen to music. The sound quality is good, too.
> Ally: Great. How long does the battery last?
> Josh: About 2 hours. The battery doesn't last long.
> Ally: That's too bad.
> Josh: Yeah, but I'm pretty happy with it, anyway.

① Josh는 어제 새로운 스피커를 구매했다.
② Josh는 스피커의 외관이 멋있다고 생각한다.
③ Josh는 스피커를 사용하기가 불편하다고 느낀다.
④ Josh는 스피커의 음질에 만족한다.
⑤ Josh의 스피커는 배터리 지속 시간이 길다.

12 다음 주어진 단어를 이용하여 뜻에 맞게 문장을 완성하시오. (4점)

> • 밤이 더 어두워질수록 별들은 더 밝아진다.
> → _____, the stars become brighter. (become, as)

> 조건
> • 주어진 2개의 단어를 모두 포함할 것. (필요한 경우 형태를 변형할 것.)

> → _____

13 다음 중 우리말의 영작이 어색한 것은? (3점)

① 모든 그림이 하루 만에 다 팔렸다.
　→ All of the paintings were sold in a day.
② 나는 이번 주 용돈을 다 써버렸다.
　→ I've spent all of my allowance for this week.
③ 결과를 상세히 비교하는 것은 어렵다.
　→ It is difficult to compare the results in detail.
④ 돈의 절반이 어려운 사람들에게 기부되었다.
　→ Half of the money was donated to people in need.
⑤ 우리는 아이들이 스스로 생각하도록 격려한다.
　→ We discourage children to think for themselves.

14 다음 대화의 빈칸 (A)에 들어갈 말로 가장 적절하지 않은 것은? (3점)

> A: Hi, can I help you?
> B: Yes. Can I try on that cap?
> A: Sure. (A)_____
> B: The design is nice, but I don't think the color suits me. Do you have it in black?
> A: Yes, I'll get one from the back.

① How is it?
② How are you?
③ Do you like it?
④ How do you like it?
⑤ Are you satisfied with it?

15 다음 대화의 빈칸 (A)에 들어갈 말로 가장 적절한 것은? (3점)

> A: Oh, this coat is too uncomfortable.
> B: Why? What's wrong with it?
> A: It's too tight.
> B: Didn't you try it on before buying it?
> A: No, it was my size, so I just bought it. (A)_____.

① I must have tried it on.
② I might be tried it on.
③ I should have tried it on.
④ I could have tried it on.
⑤ I wish I could try it on.

Why do I want to buy ⓐ<u>what</u> my friends bought? Have you ever wondered why you've bought things that you don't even want or need? Let's consider what affects us when it comes to buying things.

Jeff goes to the shopping center and sees a pair of soccer shoes on display. He recognizes the shoes at a glance because more than half of the boys on his soccer team wear them. Although he already has many pairs of soccer shoes, he ends up buying another new pair.

We can use the "bandwagon effect" to explain Jeff's behavior. A bandwagon is a wagon in a parade that encourages people to jump aboard and enjoy the music. As more and more people get on the bandwagon, others are more likely to get on or follow it. In this way, people tend to buy something just because other people have bought it.

16 위 글의 ⓐwhat과 쓰임이 <u>다른</u> 것은? (3점)

① This is <u>what</u> Tom told me yesterday.

② <u>What</u> I like is a watermelon.

③ Sally gave me <u>what</u> she had found.

④ Tell me <u>what</u> it is.

⑤ He knows <u>what</u> you saw in the room.

17 위 글에 나온 "Bandwagon Effect"의 예시로 알맞은 것은? (4점)

① 석진이는 홈쇼핑을 보다가 '매진 임박'이라는 문구를 보고, 다른 사람들이 모두 그 물건을 사니까 나도 사야 한다는 생각에 충동적으로 구매 버튼을 눌렀다.

② 태형이는 초록색 액자를 선물 받아 거실에 두었는데 집의 인테리어와 어울리지 않아서 보라색 에어컨을 새로 샀다.

③ 윤기는 가전 매장 옆을 지나가다 '오늘만 반값!'이라는 광고 문구를 보고 계획에도 없던 대형 TV를 사게 되었다.

④ 지민이는 새로 산 핸드폰의 디자인에 맞추어 머리색을 바꾸고 신발과 옷까지 사게 되었다.

⑤ 남준이는 석진이와 함께 홈쇼핑을 보고 있었지만, 사고 싶은 마음을 꾹 참고 그 돈을 아껴 저축을 했다.

Lisa buys a coat that she really loves. Immediately, she realizes that her pants do not match her new coat. (A) So, she buys new pants that go perfectly with her new coat. But she sees that none of her bags match her new clothes. (B) So, she buys a new bag. Most of her money is spent on buying the new items to complete her new look.

What made Lisa search for new items immediately after buying a new coat? The "Diderot effect" may explain it. Denis Diderot, a French writer, received a new gown as a gift. (C) Soon after receiving the gift, he noticed that all of his furniture did not go well with his new gown. (D) The Diderot effect, therefore, is the concept that purchasing a new item often leads to more unplanned purchases. (E)

18 위 글의 (A)~(E) 중, 다음 문장이 들어가기에 알맞은 곳은? (4점)

So, he ended up replacing most of it.

① (A)　② (B)　③ (C)　④ (D)　⑤ (E)

19 위 글에 언급되지 <u>않은</u> 것은? (3점)

① Lisa가 산 것

② Lisa가 물건을 산 이유

③ Diderot의 국적

④ Diderot의 성별

⑤ Diderot가 바꾼 가구의 종류

[20~21] 다음 글을 읽고 물음에 답하시오.

Jeff goes to the shopping center and sees a pair of soccer shoes (A)_____ display. He recognizes the shoes (B)_____ a glance because more than half of the boys on his soccer team wear them. Although he already has many pairs of soccer shoes, he ends up buying another new pair. We can use the "bandwagon effect" to explain Jeff's behavior. A bandwagon is a wagon in a parade that encourages people to jump aboard and enjoy the music. As more and more people (C)_____ the bandwagon, others are more likely to (C)_____ or follow it. In this way, people tend to buy something just because other people have bought it.

20 위 글의 빈칸 (A), (B)에 들어갈 말로 가장 적절한 것은? (3점)

(A)	(B)
① at	for
② in	of
③ on	at
④ on	of
⑤ for	on

21 위 글의 빈칸 (C)에 공통으로 들어갈 말로 가장 적절한 것은?
(3점)

① get on   ② get off   ③ put on

④ put off   ⑤ put out

[22~24] 다음 글을 읽고 물음에 답하시오.

Nathan goes window shopping and sees a pair of headphones. He checks the price and finds out that they are $200. He thinks that the headphones are too expensive. The sales person approaches him and says, "You can get a 20 percent discount on those headphones." Even though the (A)_____ price is still not very low, Nathan decides to buy the headphones.

The situation (B)_____ above is an example of the "(가)_____ effect." The price mentioned first affects our opinion of prices mentioned afterwards. For example, if we start with $200, then $160 will seem cheap in comparison. Furthermore, as the difference of the two prices becomes bigger, the effect will be more powerful. As such, the price mentioned first (C)_____ as an "anchor" that fixes our thoughts about the price of an item.

22 위 글의 빈칸 (A), (B), (C)에 들어갈 알맞은 단어로 짝지어진 것은? (3점)

	(A)	(B)	(C)
①	discount	describing	acted
②	discounting	described	acting
③	discounted	described	acts
④	discounting	describes	acts
⑤	discounted	describing	acted

23 위 글의 내용과 일치하는 것은? (4점)

① Nathan은 할인 전 가격이 비싸지 않다고 생각했다.

② 점원은 헤드폰 가격을 할인해서 $200로 깎아주었다.

③ 처음에 언급된 가격이 나중에 언급된 가격에 대한 우리의 의견에 영향을 미친다.

④ 두 가격의 차이가 커질수록 효과는 작아진다.

⑤ Nathan은 찾던 헤드폰이 없어서 가게를 나왔다.

24 위 글에 나오는 단어를 이용하여, 빈칸 (가)에 들어갈 말을 한 단어로 쓰시오. (4점)

→ _____

[부산 ○○중]

Why do I want to buy what my friends bought?

Jeff goes to the shopping center and ⓐsee a pair of soccer shoes on display. He recognizes the shoes at a glance because more than half of the boys on his soccer team ⓑwears them. Although he already has many pairs of soccer shoes, he ends up ⓒbuy another new pair.
We can use the "bandwagon effect" to explain Jeff's behavior. A bandwagon is a wagon in a parade ⓓthat encourages people to jump aboard and enjoy the music. (A)<u>더 많은 사람들이 밴드왜건에 올라탈수록 다른 사람들이 더욱 그것에 올라타거나 그것을 따라가려 한다.</u> In this way, people tend to buy something just because other people ⓔbuys it.

25 위 글을 읽고 답할 수 없는 질문은? (4점)

① Where does Jeff go?
② What kind of wagon is a bandwagon?
③ What does Jeff see at the shopping center?
④ What is the best selling soccer shoes these days?
⑤ Why does Jeff buy a pair of soccer shoes on display?

26 위 글의 밑줄 친 ⓐ~ⓔ 중 어법상 알맞은 것은? (3점)

① ⓐ   ② ⓑ   ③ ⓒ   ④ ⓓ   ⑤ ⓔ

27 위 글의 밑줄 친 (A)의 우리말을 문맥을 고려하여 <조건>에 맞게 영작하시오. (6점)

> 조건
> 1. 다음 단어들을 활용할 것. (more / like / be / follow / to / as)
> 2. like, be는 문맥과 맥락에 맞는 알맞은 형태로 활용하여 바꿔 쓰시오.

_____ more and more people get on the bandwagon, others _____ _____ _____ _____ get on or _____ it.

[경북 ○○중]

Amy buys a coat that she really loves. Immediately, she realizes that her skirts do not match her new coat. (A) So, she buys new skirts that go perfectly with her new coat. (B) So, she buys a new bag. (C) Most of her money is spent on buying the new items to complete her new look.

What made Amy search for new items immediately after buying a new coat? (D) The "Diderot effect" may explain it. (E) Denis Diderot, a French writer, received a new gown as a gift. Soon after receiving the gift, he noticed that all of his furniture did not go well with his new gown. So, he ended up replacing most of it. The Diderot effect, _____, is the concept that purchasing a new item often leads to more unplanned purchases.

28 위 글의 빈칸 (A)~(E) 중 주어진 문장이 들어가기에 가장 적절한 곳은? (3점)

> But she sees that none of her bags match her new clothes.

① (A)   ② (B)   ③ (C)   ④ (D)   ⑤ (E)

29 위 글의 빈칸에 들어갈 말로 가장 적절한 것은? (3점)

① however   ② moreover
③ therefore   ④ furthermore
⑤ nevertheless

◎ 선택형 문항의 답안은 컴퓨터용 수정 싸인펜을 사용하여 OMR 답안지에 바르게 표기하시오.

◎ 서술형 문제는 답을 답안지에 반드시 검정 볼펜으로 쓰시오.

◎ 총 27문항 100점 만점입니다. 문항별 배점은 각 문항에 표시되어 있습니다.

① ⓐ: change   ② ⓑ: continuing

③ ⓒ: shorter   ④ ⓓ: fail

⑤ ⓔ: able

[경북 ○○중]

01 다음 대화의 빈칸에 공통으로 들어갈 말로 적절한 것은? (3점)

> A: Make a _____ before you blow out the candles.
> B: I _____ I could enter the same high school as my best friend.

① win   ② want   ③ wish

④ pray   ⑤ bless

[서울 서초구 ○○중]

02 다음 〈B〉는 〈A〉의 ⓐ~ⓔ에 대한 영영풀이이다. ⓐ~ⓔ에 들어갈 말로 적절한 것은? (5점)

> **<A>**
>
> Dr. Sci: Even if we find a wormhole, there are many things to consider before actually going through one. A wormhole would be very ⓐunstable. The debate about wormholes is still ⓑongoing, but with ⓒpersistent exploration and research, I believe we will eventually find one and learn how to travel through it. Look back at our history. We've ⓓachieved so many things that seemed ⓔimpossible at first. Who knows? Maybe you can be the one to find the answer!

> **<B>**
>
> (A) <u>unstable</u>: not solid or firm and therefore not likely to ⓐ_____
> (B) <u>ongoing</u>: ⓑ_____ to develop
> (C) <u>persistent</u>: continuing to exist or happen, especially for ⓒ_____ than is usual
> (D) <u>achieve</u>: to ⓓ_____ in finishing something or reaching an aim
> (E) <u>impossible</u>: ⓔ_____ to happen

[서울 종로구 ○○중]

03 다음 문장을 가정법을 사용하여 의미가 통하도록 다시 쓰시오. (4점)

> • As Joe lies, we cannot trust him.

→ _____

[경북 ○○중]

04 다음 중 어법상 올바른 문장의 개수는? (4점)

> • Mina counted the stars with her finger pointing at each of them.
> • If we traveled at the speed of light, we could go to Mars in 13 minutes.
> • If John was a doctor, he can save his people at the war.
> • Jenny was standing with her arms folded.
> • Lower your head to the ground with your arms stretched.
> • If I could travel into the future, I would bring back all the latest technology.

① 2개   ② 3개   ③ 4개   ④ 5개   ⑤ all

[서울 종로구 ○○중]

05 다음 문장을 가정법을 사용하여 의미가 통하도록 다시 쓰시오. (4점)

> • As he doesn't have a key, he can't open the door.

→ _____

06 다음 중에서 밑줄 친 부분의 쓰임이 <u>어색한</u> 것은? (4점)

① She rode a bike <u>with her hair blowing</u>.

② Sit <u>with your legs extended and lean forward</u>.

③ The old lady was sleeping <u>with the TV turned on</u>.

④ She counted the stars <u>with her finger pointed at each of them</u>.

⑤ Lower your head to the ground <u>with your arms stretched</u>.

07 다음 주어진 우리말을 영어로 바르게 옮긴 것은? (4점)

> • 만약 내가 우주선을 만든다면, 나는 화성에 갈 텐데.

① If I make a spaceship, I go to the Mars.

② If I make a spaceship, I would go to the Mars.

③ If I made a spaceship, I will go to the Mars.

④ If I made a spaceship, I would go to the Mars.

⑤ If I have made a spaceship, I would go to the Mars.

08 주어진 의미에 따라 쓰인 문장의 밑줄 친 <u>어색한</u> 부분을 고친 것으로 어법상 바른 것은? (4점)

① 내가 선생님이라면, 학생들에게 숙제를 내주지 않을 텐데. If I <u>did</u> a teacher, I wouldn't give homework to students. → are

② 그가 숙제를 더 일찍 한다면, 축구를 할 수 있을 텐데. If he <u>had done</u> his homework earlier, he could play soccer. → done

③ 내가 Ann의 주소를 안다면, 그녀에게 카드를 보낼 텐데. If I <u>knows</u> Ann's address, I might send her a card. → were known

④ Lisa가 돈이 있다면, 새 컴퓨터를 살 텐데. If Lisa <u>have</u> money, she might buy a new computer. → have had

⑤ Mike가 키가 더 크다면, 롤러코스터를 탈 수 있을 텐데. If Mike <u>is</u> taller, he could ride the roller coaster. → were

09 밑줄 친 ⓐ~ⓔ 중 어법상 옳지 <u>않은</u> 것은? (4점)

> Sci Teen: Ouch! That's not a pretty picture. So, are we hopeless? Is traveling in space through a wormhole simply an idea that only ⓐ<u>exists</u> in theory?
>
> Dr Sci: I wouldn't say so. The debate about wormholes ⓑ<u>is</u> still ongoing, but with persistent exploration and research, I believe ⓒ<u>that</u> we will eventually find one and learn how to travel through it. Look back at our history. We've achieved so many things ⓓ<u>that</u> seemed impossible at first. Who knows? Maybe you can be the one to ⓔ<u>be found</u> the answer!

① ⓐ   ② ⓑ   ③ ⓒ   ④ ⓓ   ⑤ ⓔ

10 밑줄 친 ⓐ~ⓔ 중 가리키는 것이 <u>다른</u> 하나는? (3점)

> Imagine ⓐ<u>a worm</u> is on this apple. ⓑ<u>It</u> detects something sweet at the bottom and wants to move from the top to the bottom. For the worm, the apple's surface is as vast as our universe. Now ⓒ<u>it</u> can either move around the outer layer or down a wormhole. Which do you think ⓓ<u>it</u> will choose? Well, it would choose the wormhole because ⓔ<u>it</u> is a shortcut.

① ⓐ   ② ⓑ   ③ ⓒ   ④ ⓓ   ⑤ ⓔ

[11~14] 다음 글을 읽고 물음에 답하시오.

Sci Teen: Is there a faster way to travel through space?

Dr. Sci: Well, in order to answer that question, I'd like you (가)think about this apple for a second. Imagine a worm is on this apple. It ⓐdetects something sweet at the bottom and wants to move from the top to the bottom. For the worm, the apple's ⓑsurface is as ⓒvast as our universe. Now the worm can either move around the outer layer (나)nor down a wormhole. Which do you think it will choose? Well, it would choose the wormhole because it is a ⓓshortcut.

Si Teen: Is there such a shortcut in the universe?

Dr. Sci: Yes. Some ⓔresearchers think there is. Einstein figured out that space and time (다)was connected, and he called it space-time. He thought that space-time could actually be bent. When it is bent, parts that are far away from each other (라)were suddenly closer. To understand this, take a sheet of paper. (A) Then make a small dot at the top of the paper and another at the bottom of the paper. (B) On a flat sheet of paper, the dots are far away from one another. (C) Now, take the paper and fold it with the dots matched up. (D) Like this, wormholes in space may contain two mouths, with a throat (마)connected the two. (E)

Sci Teen: Just like a wormhole in the apple, right?

Dr. Sci: Yes, but wormholes exist in theory only.

11 위 글의 ⓐ~ⓔ의 영영풀이로 적절하지 않은 것은? (4점)

① ⓐ: to notice something that is partly hidden or not clear

② ⓑ: the inner part or layer of something

③ ⓒ: extremely large

④ ⓓ: a quicker route that leads from one place to another

⑤ ⓔ: someone whose job is to study a subject carefully

12 위 글의 (가)~(마)를 어법에 맞게 고친 것으로 바르지 않은 것은? (4점)

① (가)think → to think

② (나)nor → or

③ (다)was → are

④ (라)were → is

⑤ (마)connected → connecting

13 위 글의 (A)~(E) 중 〈보기〉의 문장이 들어가기에 흐름상 가장 적절한 것은? (3점)

> **보기**
> Punch a hole in the paper and the dots will be instantly connected.

① (A) ② (B) ③ (C) ④ (D) ⑤ (E)

14 위 글에 대한 참(T), 거짓(F)을 나타낸 것 중 바른 것은? (5점)

① A worm would pick the wormhole because it is a shortcut. (F)

② Einstein found out that space and time cannot be connected. (T)

③ Einstein thought that space-time could actually be crushed. (T)

④ According to Einstein, when space-time is bent, parts that are far away from each other can become slowly closer. (T)

⑤ Wormholes have actually been found in space. (F)

[15~20] 다음 글을 읽고 물음에 답하시오.

Wormholes: Fact or Theory?

Sci Teen

Hi, science fans. Today, we're going to talk about space travel. ⒶAs we all know, there is nothing faster than light in the universe. ⒷSo, if we travel at the speed of light, we should can get to another planet in the blink of an eye, right?

Dr. Sci

ⒸThat would be nice, but space is so vast that it is not possible. ⒹIn the movie, Passengers, a spaceship headed to a different planet travels at one-half the speed of light. ⒺSo it should get to another planet very quickly, right? But, the passengers sleep for 120 years because it is expected to take that much time to get to a different planet.

Sci Teen

120 years? Wow, that's a long time! Is there a faster way to travel through space?

Dr. Sci

Well, in order to answer that question, I'd like you to think about this apple for a second. Imagine a worm is on this apple. It detects something sweet at the bottom and wants to move from the top to the bottom. For the worm, the apple's surface is as vast as our universe. Now the worm can Ⓕ_____ move around the outer layer Ⓖ_____ down a wormhole. Which do you think it will choose? Well, it would choose the wormhole because it is a shortcut.

Sci Teen

Is there such a shortcut in the universe?

Dr. Sci

ⓐ_____ some researchers, yes. Einstein figured out that space and time are connected, and he called it space-time.

ⓑWhen it is bent, parts that are far away from each other are suddenly closer.
ⓒEinstein thought that space-time could actually be bent.
ⓓTo understand this, take a sheet of paper and make a small dot at the top of the paper and another at the bottom of the paper.
ⓔOn a flat sheet of paper, the dots are far away from one another.
Now, take the paper and fold it with the dots Ⓕ [match / matching / matched] up. Punch a hole in the paper and the dots will be Ⓖ[instant / instantly] connected.

15 위 글의 밑줄 친 Ⓐ~Ⓔ 중에서 어법상 어색한 것은? (3점)

① Ⓐ ② Ⓑ ③ Ⓒ ④ Ⓓ ⑤ Ⓔ

16 위 글의 밑줄 친 Ⓕ, Ⓖ에 들어갈 어휘가 순서대로 적절하게 된 것은? (4점)

① both – and ② either – or

③ between – and ④ neither – nor

⑤ some – others

17 위 글의 빈칸 ⓐ에 들어갈 말로 적절한 것은? (3점)

① Because of ② Owing to

③ According to ④ Instead of

⑤ In place of

18 위 글의 밑줄 친 문장 ⓑ~ⓔ를 글의 흐름에 맞게 적절하게 연결한 것은? (4점)

① ⓑ-ⓒ-ⓓ-ⓔ ② ⓒ-ⓓ-ⓑ-ⓔ

③ ⓓ-ⓔ-ⓑ-ⓒ ④ ⓑ-ⓓ-ⓔ-ⓒ

⑤ ⓒ-ⓑ-ⓓ-ⓔ

19 위 글의 괄호 ⓕ, ⓖ에 들어갈 말로 적절한 것은? (4점)

	ⓕ	ⓖ
①	match	instant
②	match	instantly
③	matched	instant
④	matched	instantly
⑤	matching	instant

20 위 글의 내용과 <u>다른</u> 것은? (4점)

① 펼쳐 놓은 종이에서 점들은 서로 멀리 떨어져 있다.

② 몇몇 연구자들에 따르면, 우주에는 지름길이 있다.

③ 아인슈타인은 공간과 시간이 연결되어 있다는 것을 생각해 냈다.

④ 아인슈타인은 시공간이 실제로 구부러질 수 있다고 생각했다.

⑤ 시공간이 구부러질 때 서로 멀리 떨어져 있는 부분들은 아주 천천히 가까워진다.

[경북 ○○중]

[21~23] 다음 글을 읽고 물음에 답하시오.

Sci Teen: Hi, science fans. Today, we're going to talk about space travel. As we all know, <u>빛은 우주에서 가장 빠르다</u>. So, if we travel at the speed of light, we should be able to get to another planet in the blink of an eye, right?

Dr Sci: That would be nice, but space is so (A)[narrow / wide] that it is not possible. In the movie, Passengers, a spaceship (B)[crashed to / left for] a different planet travels at one-half the speed of light. So it should get to another planet very quickly, right? But, the passengers sleep for 120 years (C)[although / since] it is expected to take that much time to get to a different planet.

21 위 글의 밑줄 친 우리말을 영어로 옮긴 것 중 <u>어색한</u> 것은? (4점)

① light is the fastest in the universe

② nothing is faster than light in the universe

③ light is as fast as any other thing in the universe

④ light is faster than any other thing in the universe

⑤ light is faster than all the other things in the universe

22 위 글의 괄호 (A), (B), (C) 안에서 어법에 맞는 표현으로 적절한 것은? (5점)

	(A)	(B)	(C)
①	narrow	crashed to	although
②	narrow	left for	since
③	wide	left for	since
④	wide	crashed to	since
⑤	wide	left for	although

23 위 글을 읽고 답할 수 있는 질문이 <u>아닌</u> 것은? (4점)

① What are they going to talk about today?

② What is the fastest thing in the universe?

③ How fast is the spaceship heading for another planet in the movie, Passengers?

④ Why do the passengers in the movie, Passengers, sleep so long?

⑤ What technology was used for the interstellar space travel?

*interstellar: 별과 별 사이의

[24~26] 다음 글을 읽고 물음에 답하시오.

Sci Teen: Is there such a shortcut in the universe?

Dr Sci: According to some researchers, yes. Einstein figured out that space and time ⓐare connected, and he called it space-time. He thought that space-time ⓑcould actually be bent. When it is bent, parts that are far away from each other are suddenly closer.

(A) Punch a hole in the paper and the dots ⓒwill be instantly connected. Like this, wormholes in space may contain two mouths, ⓓwith a throat connected the two.

(B) On a flat sheet of paper, the dots are far away from one another. Now, take the paper and fold it with the dots ⓔmatched up.

(C) To understand this, take a sheet of paper and make a small dot at the top of the paper and another at the bottom of the paper.

24 위 글의 밑줄 친 ⓐ~ⓔ 중 어법상 옳지 <u>않은</u> 것은? (4점)

① ⓐ ② ⓑ ③ ⓒ ④ ⓓ ⑤ ⓔ

25 위 글의 흐름상 (A)~(C)를 자연스럽게 배열한 것은? (4점)

① (A)-(B)-(C) ② (B)-(A)-(C)
③ (B)-(C)-(A) ④ (C)-(A)-(B)
⑤ (C)-(B)-(A)

26 위 글의 내용과 일치하지 <u>않는</u> 것은? (3점)

① wormhole은 일종의 우주 지름길이다.
② Einstein은 시간과 공간이 연결되어 있다고 생각했다.
③ Einstein이 생각해 낸 시공간은 구부러질 수 있다.
④ 시공간이 구부러질 때, 서로에게서 멀리 떨어진 부분은 천천히 더 가까워진다.
⑤ 우주의 wormhole은 두 개의 입과 그 둘을 연결하는 목구멍으로 구성되어 있을 것이다.

27 다음 글을 읽고, 아래 질문에 답할 수 <u>없는</u> 것은? (4점)

Sci Teen: Just like a wormhole in the apple, right? If such wormholes existed in space, we could get to places billions of light-years away quickly!

Dr Sci: Yes, but it's too early to celebrate. Wormholes exist in theory only.

Sci Teen: So all we need to do is find one, right?

Dr Sci: That's right. Even if we find one, there are many things to consider before actually going through one. A wormhole would be very unstable. If a spaceship flew into one, it might be crushed or broken into pieces.

① What could we do if wormholes existed in space?
② What makes a wormhole in space?
③ What should we do to prove a wormhole's existence?
④ What would happen if a spaceship flew into a wormhole?
⑤ Do wormholes really exist in our space?

◎ 선택형 문항의 답안은 컴퓨터용 수정 싸인펜을 사용하여 OMR 답안지에 바르게 표기하시오.

◎ 서술형 문제는 답을 답안지에 반드시 검정 볼펜으로 쓰시오.

◎ 총 27문항 100점 만점입니다. 문항별 배점은 각 문항에 표시되어 있습니다.

[부산 ○○중]

01 다음 문장의 빈칸에 알맞은 말은?   (3점)

> • Luckily, the driver is in a _____ condition after the accident.

① changeable
② impossible
③ persistent
④ unstable
⑤ stable

[전북 ○○중]

02 다음 중 단어와 그 영영 풀이가 바르게 짝지어진 것은?   (4점)

① detect: to have something inside or include something as a part

② surface: to press something very hard so that it is broken

③ exist: to notice something that is partly hidden or not clear

④ passenger: a person who is traveling in a vehicle but is not operating it

⑤ universe: a vehicle used for travel in space

[경북 ○○중]

03 다음 빈칸에 들어갈 어휘로 가장 적절한 것은?   (3점)

> It is possible for astronauts to wash in space. Astronauts use waterless soap, and wipe their body with a wet towel. It seems interesting. Life in space is so different from _____ on Earth.

① it
② that
③ one
④ this
⑤ what

[전북 ○○중]

04 Why does Jake wish to live in space?   (3점)

> W: Look at this man, Jake. He lived in space for one year.
> M: It must have been tough for him.
> W: Right, but you know what's interesting? He grew 2 inches while in space.
> M: Really? How is that possible?
> W: I'm not sure, but maybe it's because there's no gravity in space.
> M: That's so cool. I wish I could live in space. That way, I could become taller.
> W: I'm sure there are other ways to become taller than going to space.

① to make money
② to become taller
③ to experience gravity
④ to find a way to survive
⑤ to travel around the space

[경북 ○○중]

05 다음 우리말을 가정법 문장으로 영작한 것으로 가장 적절한 것은?   (4점)

> • 만약 수미가 우주인이라면, 그녀는 침낭을 벽에 붙일 수 있을 텐데.

① If Sumi is an astronaut, she would attach the sleeping bag to the wall.

② If Sumi was an astronaut, she can attach a sleeping bag to a wall.

③ If Sumi were an astronaut, she should attach a sleeping bag to a wall.

④ If Sumi were an astronaut, she will attach a sleeping bag to the wall.

⑤ If Sumi were an astronaut, she could attach a sleeping bag to a wall.

[6~7] 다음 대화를 읽고 물음에 답하시오.

M: Have you heard that NASA is going to send a 3D printer into space?

W: They're going to send a 3D printer into space? Why?

M: I've heard that the 3D printer will be used to print out food for astronauts.

W: Is it possible to print out food using a 3D printer?

M: Yes, it's possible. It can print out a fresh pizza in less than five minutes.

W: Really? I wonder what it would taste like.

06 위 대화의 밑줄 친 부분과 바꾸어 쓸 수 없는 것은? (3점)

① Would you like to print out food

② Can we actually print out food

③ Are we able to print out food

④ Is it possible that we can print out food

⑤ Is there a possibility that we could print out food

07 위 대화를 아래처럼 신문 기사로 바꿀 때, 대화의 내용과 일치하지 않는 것은? (4점)

ⓐNASA is going to send ⓑa 3D printer into space. Then, ⓒastronauts can print out ⓓfood using this machine. Surprisingly, it takes less than five minutes to print out ⓔall kinds of food.

① ⓐ ② ⓑ ③ ⓒ ④ ⓓ ⑤ ⓔ

08 다음 대화의 밑줄 친 부분의 뜻에 가장 가까운 것은? (4점)

W: Hello, everyone, welcome to *All about Movies*! Today, we're going to talk about the top three things from movies that we wish were real.

M: Let's start with number three, the flying skateboard from *Back to the Future*.

W: It's a cool item. I wish I could have a flying skateboard.

M: Actually, I read somewhere that this is not entirely impossible.

W: Really? Is it actually possible to fly on a skateboard?

M: Yes. Some companies have applied physics to create flying skateboards.

① A flying skateboard is likely to be possible.

② It is unlikely that skateboards can fly.

③ It is impossible for skateboards to fly.

④ A flying skateboard is out of the question.

⑤ It is not possible to have a flying skateboard.

09 Which of the following is FALSE from the dialogue? (4점)

M: Welcome back to Earth, Irene. What was your favorite part about being in the space station?

W: I could see a beautiful sunrise 16 times a day. It was great.

M: Is it possible to see the sunrise several times a day in space?

W: Yes, it's possible because we moved around Earth every 90 minutes in the station.

M: Wow, that's amazing!

① Irene saw the sunset six times a day.

② Irene was in a space station.

③ Irene went around Earth every ninety minutes.

④ Irene watched the sunrise 16 times a day.

⑤ Irene's favorite part about the trip was seeing the sunrise sixteen times a day.

10 다음 우리말과 같은 뜻이 되도록 빈칸에 알맞은 말을 쓰시오.

(6점)

(1) 텔레비전이 켜진 채로 공부하는 것은 안 좋다.

→ It is not good to study _____ _____

_____ _____ _____.

(2) 그 여자는 다리를 꼰 채 의자에 앉아 있었다.

→ The woman was sitting on the chair

_____ _____ _____ _____.

11 다음 주어진 단어를 이용하여 우리말과 같은 뜻이 되도록 문장을 쓰시오.

(5점)

> • 내가 만약 부유해진다면, 해외로 여행을 갈 텐데. (become / travel / abroad / rich)

조건

> • 주어진 4개의 단어를 모두 포함할 것. (필요한 경우 형태를 변형할 것.)

→ _____

12 다음 빈칸에 들어갈 말로 가장 적절한 것은?

(3점)

> Astronaut Philip Hansu finally returned to Earth. Surprisingly, he grew 2 inches taller _____ in space. It is because there is no gravity in space.

① for   ② after   ③ while

④ before   ⑤ through

13 다음 (A), (B), (C)에 들어갈 말로 바르게 짝지어진 것은? (4점)

> • If I (A)[am / were] an astronaut, I would walk in space.
> • If I went to space, I (B)[would take / would have taken] a selfie.
> • If we (C)[traveled / have traveled] at the speed of light, we could go to Mars in 13 minutes.

	(A)	(B)	(C)
①	am	would take	traveled
②	am	would have taken	have traveled
③	were	would take	traveled
④	were	would have taken	have traveled
⑤	were	would take	have traveled

14 다음 빈칸에 들어갈 내용으로 가장 적절한 것은? (3점)

> Ted: Have you heard that NASA is going to send a 3D printer into space?
> Amy: They're going to send a 3D printer into space? Why?
> Ted: I've heard the 3D printer will be used to print out food for astronauts.
> Amy: _____
> Ted: Yes. It can print out a fresh pizza in less than five minutes.
> Amy: Really? I wonder what it would taste like.

① How will the 3D printer be used in space?

② What is NASA going to send with a 3D printer?

③ Do you think it is possible to eat pizza in space?

④ How long does it take to print out a fresh pizza?

⑤ Is it possible to print out food using a 3D printer?

[15~19] 다음 글을 읽고 물음에 답하시오.

Sci Teen: Is there such a shortcut in the universe?

Dr. Sci: (A)According to some researchers, yes. Einstein figured out space and time are connected, and he called it space-time. He thought space-time could actually be bent. When it is bent, parts that are (B)far away from each other are suddenly closer. To understand this, take (C)a sheet of paper and make a small dot at the top of the paper and another at the bottom of the paper. On a flat sheet of paper, the dots are far away from one another. Now, take the paper and fold it with the dots (가)match up. Punch a hole in the paper and the dots will be instantly connected. Like this, wormholes in space may contain two mouths, with a throat (나)connect the two.

Sci Teen: Just like a wormhole in the apple, right? If such wormholes existed in space, we could get to places (D)billions of light-years away quickly!

Dr. Sci: Yes, but it's too early to celebrate. Wormholes exist in theory only.

Sci Teen: So all we need to do is find _____, right?

Dr. Sci: (E)Even if we find _____, there are many things to consider before actually going through _____. A wormhole would be very unstable. If a spaceship flew into a wormhole, it might be crushed or broken into pieces.

Sci Teen: Ouch! ⓐThat's not a pretty picture. So, are we hopeless? Is traveling in space through a wormhole simply an idea that only exists in theory?

Dr. Sci: I wouldn't say so. ⓑThe debate about wormholes is still ongoing. But there is persistent exploration and research. ⓒI believe we will eventually find a wormhole and learn how to travel through it. ⓓThe wormhole is so unstable that it is useless to find it. Look back at our history. ⓔWe've achieved so many things that seemed impossible at first. Who knows? Maybe you can be the one to find the answer!

15 위 글의 빈칸에 공통으로 들어갈 단어로 가장 적절한 것은?
(3점)

① one　　　② all　　　③ what
④ which　　⑤ this

16 위 글의 밑줄 친 ⓐ~ⓔ 중에서 전체 흐름과 관련이 없는 것은?
(4점)

① ⓐ　　② ⓑ　　③ ⓒ　　④ ⓓ　　⑤ ⓔ

17 위 글의 밑줄 친 (A)~(E)의 의미가 어색한 것은?
(3점)

① (A) ~에 따르면
② (B) ~로부터 멀리 떨어진
③ (C) 한 장의
④ (D) 수백억의
⑤ (E) 비록 ~일지라도

18 위 글의 (가)와 (나)에 주어진 동사의 형태로 가장 적절한 것은?
(4점)

	(가)	(나)
①	matched up	connecting
②	to match up	connected
③	matching up	connecting
④	match up	to connect
⑤	matched up	connected

19 위 글의 내용과 일치하지 않는 것은? (4점)

① Einstein figured out that space and time are connected.

② Dr. Sci thought that there isn't a shortcut in the universe.

③ Einstein was the scientist that used the word 'space-time'.

④ Dr. Sci thinks wormholes may exist in space and someone will find a wormhole.

⑤ To explain wormholes in space, Dr. Sci tells Sci Teen to punch a hole in the paper.

[전북 ○○중]

[20~21] 다음 글을 읽고 물음에 답하시오.

> Sci Teen: Hi, science fans. Today, we're going to talk about space travel. As we all know, ⓐthere is nothing faster than light in the universe. So, if we travel at the speed of light, we should be able to get to another planet in the blink of an eye, right?
>
> Dr Sci: That would be nice, but space is so vast that it is not possible. In the movie, *Passengers*, a spaceship headed to a different planet travels at one-half the speed of light. So it should get to another planet very quickly, right? But, the passengers sleep for 120 years because it is expected to take that much time to get to a different planet.

20 위 글의 밑줄 친 ⓐ와 의미가 같은 것은? (3점)

① Light is faster than the universe.

② Light is the fastest in the universe.

③ The universe is the faster than light.

④ Light is not faster than anything in the universe.

⑤ There is something slower than light in the universe.

21 위 글을 읽고 답할 수 없는 질문은? (4점)

① What is Sci Teen going to talk about?

② How many passengers are there in the movie?

③ What is the title of the movie mentioned above?

④ How fast does the spaceship travel in the movie?

⑤ Is it possible to reach another planet very quickly?

[전북 ○○중]

[22~23] 다음 글을 읽고 물음에 답하시오.

> Sci Teen: Well, in order to answer that question, I'd like you to think about this apple for a second. Imagine a worm is on this apple. ⓐIt detects something sweet at the bottom and wants to move from the top to the bottom. For the worm, the apple's surface is as vast as our universe. Now ⓑit can (A)_____ move around the outer layer (B)_____ down a wormhole. Which do you think ⓒit will choose? Well, ⓓit would choose the wormhole because ⓔit is a shortcut.

22 위 글의 빈칸 (A), (B)가 '둘 중 하나'라는 의미가 되도록 바르게 짝지어진 것은? (4점)

	(A)	(B)
①	either	or
②	both	and
③	neither	nor
④	both	or
⑤	either	and

23 위 글의 밑줄 친 ⓐ~ⓔ가 가리키는 것이 다른 하나는? (3점)

① ⓐ　② ⓑ　③ ⓒ　④ ⓓ　⑤ ⓔ

[24~25] 다음 글을 읽고 물음에 답하시오.

Sci Teen: (A)_____

Dr Sci: ⓐAccording to some researchers, yes. Einstein ⓑfigured out that space and time are connected, and he called it space-time. He thought that space-time could actually be bent. When it is bent, parts that are ⓒfar away from each other are suddenly closer. To understand this, take a sheet of paper and make a small dot ⓓat the top of the paper and another at the bottom of the paper. On a flat sheet of paper, the dots are far away from ⓔone another. Now, take the paper and fold it with the dots matched up. Punch a hole in the paper and the dots will be instantly connected. Like this, wormholes in space may contain two mouths, with a throat connecting the two.

24 위 글의 밑줄 친 ⓐ~ⓔ의 뜻이 잘못 짝지어진 것은? (3점)

① ⓐ: ~에 따르면
② ⓑ: 알아냈다
③ ⓒ: ~로부터 멀리 떨어진
④ ⓓ: ~의 윗부분에
⑤ ⓔ: 또 다른 하나

25 위 글의 흐름으로 보아 빈칸 (A)에 알맞은 것은? (4점)

① Is there a shortcut in the universe?
② Why does space-time exist in space?
③ What do wormholes in space contain?
④ Why is it impossible to travel in space?
⑤ Are there many dots matched up in the universe?

26 다음 글을 읽고 요약할 때, 빈칸에 들어갈 단어를 글에서 찾아 쓰시오. (5점)

Dr Sci: Even if we find one, there are many things to consider before actually going through one. A wormhole would be very unstable. If a spaceship flew into one, it might be crushed or broken into pieces.

Sci Teen: Ouch! That's not a pretty picture. So, are we hopeless? Is traveling in space through a wormhole simply an idea that only exists in theory?

Dr Sci: I wouldn't say so. The debate about wormholes is still ongoing, but with persistent exploration and research, I believe we will eventually find one and learn how to travel through it. Look back at our history. We've achieved so many things that seemed impossible at first. Who knows? Maybe you can be the one to find the answer!

↓

If we were to find a real wormhole, using it would be difficult because of its (A)_____ conditions. However, Dr. Sci says that still there is (B)_____ that we will learn how to travel through it.

(A): _____ (B): _____

27 다음 대화의 빈칸에 들어갈 표현으로 어색한 것은? (3점)

Sumi: Wish upon the bright moon. Then your dreams will come true!
Hansu: I wish _____.

① I could take a space trip
② I would be a famous star
③ I could drive a robotic car
④ I would fail the final exam
⑤ I would travel abroad alone

정답 및 해설

Lesson 5 (중간) 1회

01 ⑤	02 ②	03 ③	04 ④	05 ③	06 ④	07 ①	08 ②
09 ④	10 ⑤	11 ③,⑤		12 ②	13 ⑤	14 ⑤	15 ②
16 ③	17 ④	18 what if it is completely made up?			19 ②		
20 ③	21 ⑤	22 ②,③		23 ①	24 ①	25 ②	26 ③

01 (A) on the phone: 전화로 (B) according to: ~에 따르면[의하면]

02 몇몇 명사나 형용사에 접미사 '-ize'를 붙여서 동사로 만들 수 있다.

03 ③번은 'he got up early in order that he might catch the first subway'로 쓰는 것이 적절하다.

04 'At that time, an inch in France was longer than an inch in England.'라고 했다.

05 ⓐ와 ③: 관계대명사 ① 지시대명사 ②, ④ 접속사 ⑤ It ~ that 강조 용법

06 앞에서 언급된 '실제로는 진실이 아닌 사실들'을 가리킨다.

07 모두 '이유'를 묻는 표현으로 쓸 수 있으나 ①번은 '무슨 생각을 하니?'로 다른 의미이다.

08 'Can you tell me more about ~?'은 '~에 대해 더 말해 줄 수 있니?'라는 의미로 상대방에게 자세한 설명을 요청할 때 사용하는 표현이다.

09 '당시 프랑스 사람들이 영국 사람들보다 키가 더 컸다.'라는 언급은 없다.

10 'Can you tell me more about ~?', 'Can you explain ~ in more detail?' 등으로 상대방에게 자세한 설명을 요청할 수 있다.

11 ③ Breaking → Having broken ⑤ Being closed → The bakery being closed

12 to enter → entering[enter], Felt → Feeling

13 '~하기 위해'는 'to부정사', 'in order to부정사', 'so that 주어 can ~', 'in order that 주어 can ~' 등으로 나타낸다.

14 what if는 '~라면 어떻게 될까'라는 의미이다.

15 that → in that. in that: ~이므로, ~라는 점에서

16 ⓐ wound → wounded ⓑ argue → argument
ⓓ critically → critical
ⓔ is searching at → are searching for

17 '*The Daily News* published the same article about "Swenekafew" the next day and thus got caught stealing.'이라고 했다.

18 what if는 '~라면 어떻게 될까'라는 의미이며 '지어낸' 것이므로 '수동태'로 쓴다.

19 주어진 문장의 They가 (B) 앞의 'an angry group of rhinoceroses'를 가리키므로 (B)가 적절하다.

20 'Those who didn't read it to the end got really worried.'라고 했다.

21 'Later, they confessed that they made it up so that they could draw the readers' attention to the unsafe conditions at the zoo.'라고 했다.

22 whether: ~인지 아닌지, spot: 발견하다, 찾아내다

23 'Do other related stories provide similar content?'라고 했다.

24 위 글은 Wing Walker라는 신발을 광고하는 글이다.

25 'Walking with Wing Walker, you burn more calories and get slimmer.'라고 했다.

26 마지막 문장에서 'Let's look into some articles thinking about the hidden motives behind them.'이라고 했으므로 ③번이 적절하다.

Lesson 5 (중간) 2회

01 ①	02 ②	03 ③	04 ②	05 ④	06 ②	07 ④	08 ⑤
09 ④	10 ④	11 ④	12 ③	13 Feeling hungry		14 ③	
15 ①	16 ⑤	17 ⑤	18 ③	19 ④	20 ⑤	21 ②	22 ⑤
23 ⑤	24 critically / headlines / supporting						

01 disaster: an event causing great harm, damage, or suffering ①번은 argument에 대한 풀이다.

02 misunderstand: 잘못 이해하다, 오해하다

03 이유를 묻는 ③번이 적절하다.

04 'Can you tell me more about it?'으로 상대방이 한 말에 대해 추가적인 설명을 요청하고 있으므로 감기에 대해 추가 설명하는 ②번이 적절하다.

05 affect: 영향을 미치다

06 뒤에 잘못된 사실의 예가 나오므로 ②번이 적절하다.

07 모두 '이유'를 묻는 표현이지만 ④번은 Why를 What으로 고쳐야 적절한 표현이 된다.

08 뒤에서 자세히 설명해 주고 있으므로 'Can you tell me more about it?'으로 상대방에게 자세한 설명을 요청할 때 사용하는 표현이 적절하다.

09 ⓓ는 'An inch in France was longer than an inch in England.'로 고치는 것이 적절하다.

10 상호가 '추울 때 바이러스가 활동적이다'라고 언급한 내용은 없다.

11 ① '기차를 놓치려고 늦었다'는 이상한 의미로 잘못 바꿨음. ② not to see it → to see ③ '너무 열심히 일해서 모든 것이 제시간에 준비되지 않았다'라는 이상한 의미로 잘못 바꿨음. ⑤ '공기의 질이 매우 나쁘도록'이라는 이상한 의미로 잘못 바꿨음.

12 분사구문의 부정은 not이나 never를 분사 앞에 쓴다.

13 분사구문은 '접속사+주어+동사'를 '동사+ing' 형태로 바꾸는 것이므로 'Because I felt'를 'Feeling'으로 바꿔 쓴다.

14 앞에서 'Those who didn't read it to the end got really worried.'라고 했으므로 ③번이 적절하다.

15 왜 가짜 뉴스가 해로울 수 있는지는 대답할 수 없다.

16 'those who read the article carefully laughed out loud'라고 했다.

17 비난을 받는 것이므로 과거분사 criticized가 적절하다.

18 Swenekafew를 거꾸로 쓰면 we fake news이다.

19 Nevertheless로 볼 때 앞의 내용과 상반되는 내용이 와야 하므로 (D)가 적절하다.

20 'those who read the article carefully laughed out loud'라고 했으므로 ⑤번이 일치함을 알 수 있다.

21 ⓑ 'less'는 'informed'를 'even'은 'misled'를 꾸며주며 'informed'와 'misled'는 make의 목적격보어이다. ⓒ them은 앞에 있는 'some articles'를 가리키는 인칭대명사이다. ⓔ 'the other'는 둘 중에서 '나머지 하나'를 가리킨다.

22 'Later, they confessed that they made it up so that they could draw the readers' attention to the unsafe conditions at the zoo.'라고 했고, '*The Daily Telegram* published this fake article so that they could prove if *The Daily News*, their competitor, was stealing their articles.'라고 했다.

23 in critical condition: 위독한 상태로

24 독자로서 우리는 비판적으로 읽을 필요가 있으며 뉴스가 사실인지 거짓인지 판단할 필요가 있다. 가짜 뉴스를 판별하기 위해 우리는 기사 제목 그 이상을 읽고 뒷받침하는 자료를 찾아야 한다.

Lesson 6 (중간)   1회

01 ②	**02** ②	**03** ①	**04** ①	**05** ①	**06** do if, could	**07** ⑤
08 ②	**09** ⑤	**10** ④	**11** ①	**12** ③	**13** ③	**14** ⑤	**15** ③
16 ③	**17** ②	**18** ①	**19** ⑤	**20** ⑤	**21** ⑤	**22** ①	**23** ④
24 ④	**25** ②					

26 it was this wisdom that our father tried to explain

01 ① 수출하다 ③ 전시하다 ④ 설명하다 ⑤ 표현하다

02 ① difficult to understand because it isn't well organized

or explained ③ matter: to be important to you because it has much effect on you or on a particular situation ④ doesn't involve → involves ⑤ extremely important or useful

03 모두 '실수하는 것에 대해서 걱정하지 마'라는 의미인데 ①번은 '계속 실수하지 마.'라는 뜻으로 어울리지 않는다.

04 가정법으로 물었으므로 가정법으로 대답하는 것이 적절하다. will → would

05 'Well, I would travel and live in different cities all around the world.'라고 했다.

06 전 세계의 다른 도시들로 여행 가서 살아보겠다는 답으로 보아 '영원히 산다면 무엇을 할지' 물어보는 것이 적절하다.

07 주말에 무엇을 할지 묻자 ⓓ 특별한 일은 없다며 이유를 묻고 → ⓒ 내일 부산에 가야 하는데 개에게 먹이를 줄 사람을 못 찾겠다고 하자 → ⓐ 자기가 개를 돌봐 주겠다고 하고 → ⓑ 고맙다며 너무 걱정했었다고 말하는 순서가 적절하다.

08 이어지는 'You'll do fine.'으로 보아 ②번이 적절하다.

09 (B) 무엇을 읽고 있는지 묻자 (D) Twin Sisters라는 책을 읽고 있다고 답하고 (A) 무엇에 관한 것인지 묻자 (F) 서로에 대해 알게 되는 쌍둥이 자매에 관한 것이라고 답하고 (C) 쌍둥이 자매가 있는 것을 알게 되면 무엇을 할지 묻자 (E) 집으로 초대해서 밤새 사진을 보여주겠다는 순서가 적절하다.

10 Ⓐ he 삭제 Ⓑ which → that Ⓒ whom → who Ⓕ the Kim's Market → at the Kim's Market

11 모두 'It ~ that 강조 구문'에서 강조하고자 하는 어구를 It is[was]와 that 사이에 두어 강조하고 있는데 ①번은 'certain'을 강조하는 형태가 되어 어색하다.

12 'have+목적어+과거분사'의 형태로 '목적어가 ~되게 하다'라는 의미이다. '자전거를 고치게 했다'라는 의미가 자연스럽다.

13 주어진 문장과 ③: It ~ that 강조 구문 ①, ②, ④, ⑤: 접속사

14 (A) 집이 돌보아지는 것이므로 looked after (B) 침대가 설계되는 것이므로 designed (C) 식사가 준비되는 것이므로 prepared가 적절하다.

15 am의 보어로 형용사화 된 empty-handed가 적절하다.

16 뒤에서 '더 많은 돈을 돌려줄 수 있는 것에 돈을 쓰려고 노력했다'라고 했으므로 ③번이 적절하다.

17 '바로 이 지혜였다'로 '이 지혜'를 강조하고 있으므로 'this wisdom'을 강조하는 형태인 ②번이 적절하다. 현재시제가 아닌 과거시제임에 유의한다.

18 'realized'가 과거형이므로 그동안 어리석었던 것은 과거완료로 나타내는 것이 적절하다.

19 ⓔ는 하루 종일 열심히 일하고 나서 피곤해지곤 했으므로 '침대에서 자든 딱딱한 바닥에서 자든 중요하지 않았다.'라는 문맥이 적절

하므로 And it did not matter로 고쳐야 한다.

20 'But I understood it a bit differently.'라고 한 후, 어떻게 다르게 이해했는지 이어서 설명하고 있다.

21 ⓔ의 his는 Puru를 가리키지만 나머지는 모두 father를 가리킨다.

22 왜 Puneet이 아버지의 유언을 따른 뒤 부자가 되었는지에 대한 언급은 나와 있지 않다.

23 (D) 다음부터 <보기>의 질문에 대한 답이 나오므로 (D)가 적절하다.

24 told의 목적격보어로 to부정사가 적절하다.

25 'Puneet welcomed Puru with open arms.'라고 했다.

26 우리말에서 '바로 이 지혜였다'로 '이 지혜'를 강조하고 있으므로 'this wisdom'을 강조하는 형태로 써야 한다. 'It ~ that 강조 구문'에서 강조하고자 하는 어구를 It is[was]와 that 사이에 두고, 나머지 부분은 that 뒤로 보낸다.

Lesson 6 (중간)

> **01** ② **02** ③ **03** ① **04** ⑤
> **05** (A) You look worried.
>   (B) Don't worry about making mistakes.
> **06** ⑤ **07** ④ **08** ① **09** ② **10** ⑤ **11** ① **12** ② **13** ②
> **14** ③ **15** ④ **16** ① **17** ① **18** ③ **19** ② **20** ②
> **21** It was our father's advice that I followed **22** ④ **23** ③
> **24** ④, ⑤ **25** ③ **26** ⑤ **27** ⑤ **28** ⑤

01 순서대로 • freedom • confusing • expert • settle in이 들어간다.

02 ① lastly ② death ④ chef ⑤ expert

03 뒤에서 '같은 취향'을 갖고 있다고 한 것으로 보아 첫 빈칸에는 ⓑ, '1940년대로 가서 제2차 세계 대전을 막고 싶다'는 대답으로 보아 ⓒ, 조선 시대로 가서 세종대왕을 만나겠다는 말로 보아 ⓐ가 적절하다.

04 'It ~ that 강조 구문'에서 강조하고자 하는 어구를 It is[was]와 that 사이에 두고, 나머지 부분은 that 뒤로 보낸다. ⓔ의 경우 'first met'이 강조되는 어구에 해당되는데 'It ~ that 강조 구문'에서 동사는 강조할 수 없다.

05 (A) look+형용사(worried): ~해(걱정돼) 보이다
   (B) worry about: ~에 대해 걱정하다

06 'I'll take her for a walk in the park, too.'라고 했다.

07 '1940년대로 가서 제2차 세계 대전을 막고 싶다'는 대답으로 보아 ④번이 적절하다.

08 'Not well. The deadline is this weekend but I ran out of

ideas.'라고 했다.

09 걱정하고 있는 James에게 '너무 깊이 생각하지 마'라는 위로의 말이 적절하다.

10 'It ~ that 강조 구문'에서 동사는 강조할 수 없다.

11 <보기>와 ①: It ~ that 강조 구문 ② 진주어 - 가주어 구문으로 attended를 attend로 고쳐야 한다. ③ where를 that 또는 when 으로 고쳐야 한다. ④ when을 that 또는 where로 고쳐야 한다. ⑤ whom을 who로 고쳐야 한다.

12 (A) 'have+목적어+과거분사'의 형태로 '목적어가 ~되게 하다' 라는 의미이다.
   (B) 사역동사로 쓰여 'have+목적어+동사 원형'의 형태가 적절하다.

13 (A) live by: (신조, 원칙 등)에 따라 살다
   (B) like: ~처럼
   (C) pass away: 세상을 떠나다, 돌아가시다

14 비교급 richer에 대응하는 than이 있는 ③번이 적절하다.

15 'Puru was puzzled about where he had gone wrong'이라고 했다.

16 with open arms: 두 팔을 벌리고

17 'I also followed our father's wisdom. But I understood it a bit differently.'라고 했다.

18 앞에서 설명한 것을 종합하면 ③번이 적절하다.

19 ⓑ의 he는 아버지를 가리키고 나머지는 Puru를 가리킨다.

20 (A) 'But I understood it a bit differently.'라고 했다.
   (B) 'A rich man knows how to make money grow. So, I tried to spend money on something that would bring me back more money rather than on luxurious things.'라고 했다.

21 'It ~ that 강조 구문'에서 강조하고자 하는 어구를 It is[was]와 that 사이에 두고, 나머지 부분은 that 뒤로 보낸다.

22 주어진 문장의 there가 (D) 앞의 'a house in every city'를 가리키므로 (D)가 적절하다.

23 'have+목적어+과거분사'의 형태로 '목적어가 ~되게 하다'라는 의미이다. to prepare를 prepared로 고치는 것이 적절하다.

24 'I bought what I wanted without worrying about money.'라고 했고 'I ate only when I was hungry, so even a simple meal tasted great.'라고 했다.

25 ⓐ he → 삭제
   ⓑ look → looked
   ⓓ different → differently
   ⓔ which → when

26 뒤에서 '더 많은 돈을 돌려줄 수 있는 것에 돈을 쓰려고 노력했다'라고 했으므로 ⑤번이 적절하다.

Lesson 7 (기말)

---

01 ① **02** ⑤ **03** ② **04** ② **05** ③ **06** ③ **07** ③ **08** ③

09 I regret not checking the sales before buying mine.

10 I should have kept track of my spending. **11** ① **12** ④

13 ①, ⑤ **14** ⑤ **15** ① **16** ① **17** ⑤ **18** ④ **19** ④

20 ⑤ **21** ② **22** ④ **23** ③ **24** ③ **25** ① **26** ② **27** ③

28 ④

---

01 의미상 compare(비교하다)가 적절하다.
② wonder: 궁금해하다 ④ compete: 경쟁하다

02 keep track of: ~을 기록하다, 끊임없이 ~의 정보를 얻어내다
uncertain을 certain으로 바꿔야 한다.

03 구매한 VR glasses에 대해 평가하고 있으므로 ②번이 적절하다.
glasses로 복수이므로 them으로 받는 것에 주의한다.

04 우산을 안 가져왔다는 말에, 자기도 그렇다며 날씨를 확인했다고
하는 것은 어색하다.

05 'should have p.p.'는 '~했어야 했는데 (못했다)'라는 후회의 의
미이다.

06 'It makes too much noise and gets overheated.'라고 했다.

07 (C) 괜찮은지 묻자 (E) 학교 버스를 또 놓쳤다며 일찍 일어났어야
했다고 하자 (A) 안 됐다고 위로하고 (D) 자전거로 함께 통학하자
고 하자 (B) 좋은 생각이라고 하는 순서가 적절하다.

08 만족하는지 묻자 그렇다고 한 후, 음질이 좋지 않다고 하는 것은 어
색하다.

09 regret+동명사: ~한 것을 후회하다. 동명사의 부정은 앞에 not을
붙인다.

10 I should have p.p. ~."는 어떤 일을 했어야 했다고, 또는 하지 말
았어야 했다고 후회할 때 사용한다. keep track of: ~을 기록하다

11 접속사 as가 '비례'를 나타내어 '~함에 따라, ~하면 할수록'이라
는 의미로 쓰였다.

12 동사가 have이므로 단수 주어가 쓰인 ④번은 쓸 수 없다. Every
는 단수로 받는다.

13 ② the number of+복수 명사: 단수 취급 ③ 부분을 나타내는 말
(분수) of+복수 명사: 복수 취급, 부분을 나타내는 말 of+단수 명
사: 단수 취급 ④ a number of+복수 명사: 복수 취급

14 ⑤번에는 are가 들어가야 하고(부분을 나타내는 말 of+복수 명
사: 복수 취급) 나머지에는 모두 is가 들어가야 한다.(① None
of+단수 명사: 단수 취급 ②, ③ 부분을 나타내는 말 of+단수 명
사: 단수 취급 ④ the number of+복수 명사: 단수 취급)

15 결과에 해당하는 내용을 이끌고 있으므로 So가 적절하다.

16 ⓑ go with: ~와 어울리다
ⓒ spend on -ing: ~에 (돈을) 쓰다
ⓔ a discount on: ~에 대한 할인

17 ⓔ에서 with를 without으로 고치는 것이 적절하다.

18 Lisa가 새 코트를 산 후 즉시 새 코트와 어울리는 새 바지와 가방을
사게 됐으며, '디드로 효과'가 그것을 설명해 줄지도 모른다고 했
으므로 ④번이 적절하다.

19 'As such, the price mentioned first acts as an "anchor"
that fixes our thoughts about the price of an item.'이라고
했다.

20 물건의 가격이 전보다 비싸면 사람들이 그것들을 산다는 내용은 나
와 있지 않다.

21 ⓕ '할인된 가격'이므로 discounted
ⓖ '기술된 상황'이므로 described가 적절하다.

22 Ⓐ what이 주어이므로 affects가 적절하다.
Ⓑ '다른 사람들이 어떤 것을 샀다'는 현재완료로 나타내는 것이
적절하다.

23 (C) 다음에 나오는 'Jeff's behavior'가 주어진 문장의 내용을
가리키므로 (C)가 적절하다.

24 'more than half of the boys on his soccer team wear
them'이라고 했다.

25 왜 구매를 하는지 생각해 보고 결정하라는 내용의 글이다.

26 첫 문장에서 'Just like Jeff and his friends, we tend to buy
things without seriously considering why we are buying
them.'이라고 했으므로 ①번이 적절하다.

27 주어진 문장의 'their price is still not very low'가 (C) 앞의
'get a 20 percent discount'를 말하므로 (C)가 적절하다.

28 ⓐ approaches는 타동사이므로 전치사 없이 him
ⓑ 동사가 필요한 자리이므로 affects
ⓒ 영향이 강력하려면 가격차가 더 커야 하므로 bigger
ⓓ '닻' 역할을 하는 것은 앞에서 말한 가격이므로 earlier가 적절
하다.

Lesson 7 (기말) 2회

---

01 ④ **02** ⑤ **03** ③ **04** ② **05** ④ **06** ② **07** ③ **08** ②

09 ④ **10** is → was **11** ④

12 As the night becomes darker **13** ⑤ **14** ② **15** ③

16 ④ **17** ① **18** ④ **19** ⑤ **20** ③ **21** ① **22** ③ **23** ③

24 anchoring **25** ④ **26** ④

27 As / are more likely to / follow **28** ② **29** ③

---

01 compare: 비교하다

02 encourage: 격려하다

03 새 전화기를 샀는지 묻자 (C) 지난주에 할인할 때 샀다고 답하자 (E) 막 출시되었는데 할인 중이었는지 묻고 (A) 맞다며 연말 할인 판매를 했다고 하자 (D) 자기는 정가를 주고 샀다고 하고 (B) 참 안됐다고 하는 순서가 적절하다.

04 ⓑ는 후회를 나타내는 'should have checked'가 적절하다.

05 Each 다음에는 단수 명사가 오고 동사는 단수로 받는다.

06 W가 'The design is nice, but I don't think the color suits me.'라고 답했으므로 ②번이 적절하다.

07 (A) 인사를 하고 (D) 12살짜리 여동생에게 티셔츠를 사 주고 싶다고 하자 (C) 노란색 티셔츠가 어떤지 묻고 (B) 만화 캐릭터를 좋아하지 않는다며 파란색 티셔츠 볼 수 있는지 묻고 (E) 파란색 줄무늬 티셔츠를 말하는지 묻자 (F) 그걸 사겠다는 순서가 적절하다.

08 'should have p.p. ~'로 '후회하는 일'을 말할 수 있다.

09 (D) 뒤에서 '좀 더 확인을 했어야 했어.'라고 후회하고 있으므로 (D)가 적절하다.

10 'during the last trip'이 과거를 나타내므로 is를 was로 쓰는 것이 적절하다.

11 'The sound quality is good'이라고 했다.

12 as: ~할수록

13 discourage를 encourage(격려하다)로 바꾸는 것이 적절하다.

14 'How are you?'는 인사말이고 나머지는 만족하는지 묻는 표현이다.

15 후회하는 표현인 ③번이 적절하다.

16 ④번은 의문대명사이고 나머지는 모두 관계대명사이다.

17 밴드왜건 효과(Bandwagon Effect)는 남이 사니까 나도 사게 되는 편승 효과를 말하며 충동구매를 유발하는 마케팅으로 활용되고 있다.

18 주어진 문장의 So로 (D) 앞의 내용의 결과가 나오므로 (D)가 적절하다.

19 Diderot가 바꾼 가구의 종류는 언급되지 않았다.

20 (A) on display: 진열된, 전시된 (B) at a glance: 한눈에, 즉시

21 get on: ~을 타다

22 (A) discounted(할인된), (B) described(묘사된), (C) acts가 적절하다.

23 'The price mentioned first affects our opinion of prices mentioned afterwards.'라고 했다.

24 'the price mentioned first acts as an "anchor" that fixes our thoughts about the price of an item'이라고 했으므로 anchoring이 적절하다.

25 요즘 가장 잘 팔리는 축구화가 무엇인지는 알 수 없다.

26 ⓐ sees ⓑ wear ⓒ buying ⓔ buy가 적절하다.

27 as: ~할수록, be likely to: ~하기 쉽다, ~할 가능성이 있다

28 (B) 다음의 So로 주어진 문장의 결과가 나오므로 (B)가 적절하다.

29 결과를 나타내는 therefore가 적절하다.

Lesson 8 (기말) 〔1회〕

01 ③	**02** ②	**03** If Joe didn't lie, we could trust him.
04 ④	**05** If he had a key, he could open the door.	**06** ④

07 ④ **08** ⑤ **09** ⑤ **10** ⑤ **11** ② **12** ④ **13** ④ **14** ⑤
15 ② **16** ② **17** ③ **18** ⑤ **19** ④ **20** ⑤ **21** ③ **22** ③
23 ⑤ **24** ④ **25** ⑤ **26** ④ **27** ②

01 make a wish: 소원을 빌다. 'I wish I could ~.'를 이용해 바람이나 소원에 대해 말한다.

02 ⓐ last ⓒ longer ⓓ succeed ⓔ unable이 적절하다.

03 현재의 사실과 반대되는 일이나 실현 가능성이 희박한 현재의 일을 가정해서 말할 때 가정법과거로 'If+주어+동사의 과거형 ~, 주어+would/should/could/might+동사원형 ~'을 써서 나타낸다.

04 순서대로 • 맞음 • 맞음 • can → could • 맞음 • 맞음 • 맞음

05 가정법과거는 'If+주어+동사의 과거형 ~, 주어+would/should/could/might+동사원형 ~'으로 나타낸다.

06 'with+명사+분사'는 명사와 분사가 능동 관계이면 현재분사를, 수동 관계이면 과거분사를 쓴다. pointed → pointing

07 가정법과거는 'If+주어+동사의 과거형 ~, 주어+would/should/could/might+동사원형 ~'으로 나타낸다.

08 ① are → were
② done → did
③ were known → knew
④ have had → had

09 해답을 '찾아내는' 것이므로 'to find'가 되어야 한다.

10 ⓔ는 'the wormhole'을 가리키지만 나머지는 'a worm'을 가리킨다.

11 surface: the outer or top layer of something

12 parts가 주어이므로 are가 되어야 한다.

13 (D) 다음의 this가 주어진 문장의 내용을 가리키므로 (D)가 적절하다.

14 'but wormholes exist in theory only'라고 했다.

15 조동사 두 개를 겹쳐서 쓸 수 없으므로 'should can'을 'should be able to'로 고쳐야 한다.

16 '두 가지 중의 하나'이므로 'either ~ or'가 적절하다.

17 according to: ~에 따르면

18 ⓑ의 it이 ⓒ의 'space-time'을 가리키므로 ⓒ 다음에 ⓑ가 오

고, ⓓ의 this가 ⓑ의 내용을 가리키므로 ⓑ 다음에 ⓓ가 이어지고 ⓔ의 'the dots'가 ⓓ에서 만든 dots이므로 ⓓ 다음에 ⓔ가 오는 것이 적절하다.

19 ⓕ 점들이 맞춰지는 것으로 수동의 의미이므로 matched ⓖ connected를 수식하는 부사 instantly가 적절하다.

20 'When it is bent, parts that are far away from each other are suddenly closer.'라고 했다.

21 ③번은 '빛은 우주에서 다른 어떤 것만큼 빠르다'라는 의미로 최상급의 표현이 아니다.

22 (A) 우주는 '넓다'
(B) leave for: ~로 떠나다
(C) 이유를 나타내는 내용이 이어지므로 since가 적절하다.

23 별과 별 사이의 우주 여행에 사용됐던 기술이 무엇인지는 알 수 없다.

24 그 두 개의 입을 '연결하는' 목구멍이므로 connecting이 적절하다.

25 (C)의 this가 'When it is bent, parts that are far away from each other are suddenly closer.'를 가리키므로 먼저 오고 (B)의 'the dots'가 (C)에서 만든 dots이므로 (C) 다음에 오고 (A)가 마지막에 오는 순서가 적절하다.

26 'When it is bent, parts that are far away from each other are suddenly closer.'라고 했다.

27 무엇이 사과의 웜홀을 만드는지는 알 수 없다.

Lesson 8 (기말)

```
01 ⑤  02 ④  03 ②  04 ②  05 ⑤  06 ①  07 ⑤  08 ①
09 ①
10 (1) with the TV[television] turned on
   (2) with her legs crossed
11 If I became rich, I would travel abroad.    12 ③  13 ③
14 ⑤  15 ①  16 ④  17 ④  18 ①  19 ②  20 ②  21 ②
22 ①  23 ⑤  24 ⑤  25 ①  26 (A) unstable (B) hope
27 ④
```

01 stable: 안정된

02 각각 ① contain ② crush ③ detect ⑤ spaceship이다.

03 지시대명사 that이 적절하다.

04 'That way, I could become taller.'라고 했다.

05 가정법 과거는 'If+주어+동사의 과거형 ~, 주어+조동사의 과거형+동사원형 …'의 형태로 쓰며, If절에는 주어의 인칭이나 수에 관계없이 be동사는 were를 쓴다. 구어에서는 주어가 1, 3인칭 단수일 때 were 대신 was를 쓰기도 한다. '~할 수 있을 텐데'는

could를 쓴다.

06 ①번은 '음식을 프린트하고 싶은지' 묻고 있지만 나머지는 모두 가능성을 묻고 있다.

07 'It can print out a fresh pizza in less than five minutes.'라고 했다.

08 'not+전체를 나타내는 말'은 부분 부정이다.

09 일몰(sunset)에 대한 언급은 나와 있지 않다.

10 'with+명사+분사'는 동시에 일어나는 상황이나 부가적인 상황을 묘사할 때 쓰며 '~한 상태로'라는 의미를 나타낸다. 여기서 의미상 주어인 명사와 분사의 관계가 능동이면 현재분사를, 수동이면 과거분사를 쓴다.

11 가정법과거는 'If+주어+동사의 과거형 ~, 주어+would/should /could/might+동사원형 …'의 형태로 쓴다.

12 while: ~(하는) 동안

13 (A) 가정법과거의 If절에는 주어의 인칭이나 수에 관계없이 be동사는 were를 쓴다. 단, 1, 3인칭 단수에는 was를 쓰기도 한다.
(B), (C) 가정법과거는 'If+주어+동사의 과거형 ~, 주어+would /should/could/might+동사원형 …'의 형태로 쓴다.

14 뒤에서 'Yes. It can print out a fresh pizza in less than five minutes.'로 답하므로 가능성을 묻는 ⑤번이 적절하다.

15 'a wormhole' 대신 쓸 수 있는 one이 적절하다.

16 웜홀을 통해 우주를 여행할 수도 있을 것이라는 말 중에 웜홀을 발견하는 것은 쓸 데 없다는 ⓓ는 어색하다.

17 billion: 십억

18 (가) 점들이 맞춰지는 것이므로 matched up (나) 둘을 연결하는 것이므로 connecting이 적절하다.

19 Dr. Sci는 wormholes가 존재할 것이라고 믿고 있다.

20 'there is nothing+비교급 than ~ = 부정 주어+비교급 than ~'은 최상급의 의미이다.

21 그 영화에 얼마나 많은 승객이 있는지는 알 수 없다.

22 'either A or B'는 'A 또는 B 둘 중의 하나'라는 뜻이다.

23 ⓔ는 the wormhole을 가리키지만 나머지는 the worm을 가리킨다.

24 one another: 서로

25 According to some researchers, yes.'라고 답하고 웜홀을 설명했다.

26 (A) 'A wormhole would be very unstable.', (B) 'I believe we will eventually find one and learn how to travel through it.'이라고 했다.

27 소원을 비는 내용으로 ④번은 적절하지 않다.

적중10〇 + 특별부록

Plan B

우리학교
최신기출

비상 · 김진완 교과서를 배우는

학교 시험문제 분석 · 모음 · 해설집

전국단위 학교 시험문제 수집 및 분석
출제 빈도가 높은 문제 위주로 선별
문제 풀이에 필요한 상세한 해설

중3-2
영어

비상 · 김진완

값 6,000원